"*Schifferes picks up where Dr. Spock leaves off.* His discussions offer the reader around 2,400 medical subjects from *Abasia* to *Zymurgy*. . . . Latest with the mostest on hospitals, modern medicine, health and disease."

—*New Orleans Times-Picayune*

▶ "This book *can be well recommended to physicians for their patients* not alone because its distinguished board of advisory editors guarantees accuracy but also because it provides information for the layman without crossing the border lines into alleged self-treatment."

—*New York Medicine*

▶ "With numerous drawings in the text, this sensible and comprehensive manual is *lively reading as well.*"

—*Saturday Review*

▶ "A book to be kept close at hand for quick reference . . . fascinating to browse in . . . *a complete guide to health and medical care for the whole family . . .*"

—*Minnesota Medicine*

▶ "*An excellent medical dictionary* for public libraries and home bookstores. It is *encyclopedic in scope,* weighted with cross references and rich in drawings."

—*Library Journal*

The Family Medical Encyclopedia was originally published by Little, Brown and Company.

Advisory Editorial Board

Schifferes'
FAMILY MEDICAL
ENCYCLOPEDIA

JUSTUS J. SCHIFFERES, Ph.D.

Illustrated by
LOUISE BUSH, Ph.D.

A Health Education Council Book

PUBLISHED BY POCKET BOOKS NEW YORK

SCHIFFERES' FAMILY MEDICAL ENCYCLOPEDIA

Little, Brown edition published March, 1959

POCKET BOOK edition published November, 1959

28th printing........August, 1972

This POCKET BOOK edition includes every word
contained in the original, higher-priced edition. It is printed
from brand-new plates made from completely reset, clear, easy-to-read
type. POCKET BOOK editions are published by POCKET BOOKS, a division
of Simon & Schuster, Inc., 630 Fifth Avenue, New York, N.Y. 10020.
Trademarks registered in the United States and other countries.

L

To the memory of my friend, Van

E. A. Van Steenwyk, 1905–1962

Preface

HOW TO USE THIS BOOK FOR FIRST AID IN EMERGENCIES

For first-aid treatment of emergencies, look up in the alphabetical order of words the word which describes the emergency, for example: asphyxia, bleeding, bruises, burns, carbon monoxide, fainting, fractures, frostbite, headache, insects, poison, poison ivy, sunstroke, or unconsciousness.

Also, if necessary, look up the part of the body affected, for example: ears, eyes, joints, nose, skin, stomach, teeth, or throat. See Emergency! First-Aid Index on page xvii.

This book is not primarily a first-aid text; but it will tell you what to do—and what not to do—about common medical and household emergencies. The first step in first aid is to call a doctor.

WHAT YOU WILL FIND IN THIS BOOK

The far wider purpose of this book is to provide easily understood, common-sense information whose mastery will render medical and life emergencies less likely to happen. More than that, it aims to create attitudes toward health, disease, and specific disease conditions which will lead toward healthier living generally and permit a person to overcome the obstacles of disease. The psychological as well as the physical aspects of health are considered.

Approximately 2,500 medical topics of general interest and importance are described or defined herein. Taken altogether, they provide a brief but comprehensive summary of modern medical knowledge, at the level at which the average person is interested.

In one sense this book is an ABC of up-to-date medical and scientific knowledge, set down in simple, nontechnical language. Every effort has been made to keep it realistic and practical by avoiding theory and dealing with questions that are most commonly asked.

This book is no substitute for a doctor. It is opposed to self-diagnosis and self-treatment of disease, for these are among the best ways of making a bad situation worse. There are many places in this text where the need for prompt and competent medical attention is set down as imperative. On the other hand, it is frankly noted when you do not have to hurry off to the doctor.

This book is designed to help your doctor help you—by getting you to him when you should go and by answering questions that you don't quite get around to asking him. There are a great many medical terms that the average person does not understand—even when they have been explained orally. This book provides a convenient reference work in which these words can be looked up and their meanings and implications comprehended.

Resort to this book should often replace doubt, uneasiness, and ignorance about a medical subject with certainty, satisfaction, and knowledge. It must be recognized, however, that medical knowledge itself is not complete; there are great and important gaps in knowledge. Indeed, many diseases remain devastating because crucial facts concerning their cause or cure are still obscure and unknown. Cancer and the common cold are representative examples.

HOW TO GET ALL THE INFORMATION YOU WANT OUT OF THIS BOOK

The alphabetical, encyclopedic arrangement of material in this book offers a number of advantages. It allows for quick answers to many questions pursued simply by looking up the name of a disease (e.g. diabetes, cerebral palsy), a symptom (e.g. headache, dizziness), a drug (e.g. chloroform, sulfa), or a body part (e.g. liver, eyes). Furthermore, it allows for a simple system of *cross references* which can be followed through to supply fairly full information on desired subjects.

This is how the cross-reference system works. Whenever a word or phrase is set in SMALL CAPITAL LETTERS, LIKE THIS, it means that the word or phrase is further described and discussed elsewhere in the book; that is, it can be looked up in its own alphabetical listing and will add to the information sought on the subject originally consulted. The cross references are selective; a word is set in SMALL CAPITALS for cross reference only when it has something significant to contribute to the original subject. For example:

Abscess—an accumulation of PUS, formed from infected, broken-down tissue . . . treated by draining off the pus, as in lancing a boil, and getting rid of the underlying INFECTION.

The words PUS and INFECTION are set in SMALL CAPITALS in the entry on abscess. This means that PUS can be looked up under *P* and INFECTION under *I*. By looking up these words, you will get a fuller understanding of the nature of an abscess.

This is a book to be kept on hand for ready reference; it is also a book to browse in. By looking up the medical subjects in which you are particularly interested, you will be led into a wide range of topics.

WHY THIS BOOK EMPHASIZES HEALTH OF ADULTS

This book places emphasis on adult health. The sequence of topics on diet, digestive system, fat, vitamins, etc., for example, should prove particularly rewarding in the development of a healthy regimen of living. Some economic aspects of medical and hospital care are also covered in such entries as health insurance and Blue Cross. This book picks up where

Dr. Spock's famous POCKET BOOKS volume, *Baby and Child Care,* leaves off.

While this book does not claim to be unique, it has several important points of originality. First, it has all been freshly written "from scratch" to give the widest possible range of authoritative and up-to-the-minute information in the briefest space. It is a new work which has not appeared in print before. Second, the approach to every major topic—and to a certain extent to every entry—has been taken from the practical point of view, which asks, "Why is the reader interested in looking up this subject? What are the questions about it he really has in his mind?" Third, the selection of entries and subject headings has been made with full recognition that the average reader is often more familiar with the popular and even the slang expressions for many medical subjects than he is with the authentic medical terminology. This book, therefore, has not hesitated to include slang and popular terms, with cross references to the formal and correct terms. Thus, for example, you will find extensive entries under such headings as shots, hangover, piles, and female troubles; and mention of such terms as bad blood, clap, wet dreams, and test-tube babies.

It may also be worth pointing out that never before has so comprehensive a medical encyclopedia and dictionary been generally available to the public at so low a price as this one. If the information included herein keeps even a few people from toppling over the brink of health folly, it will have been worth the effort of compiling it. If it helps many to take sensible steps toward escaping the needless ravages of disease and ignorance, it will have amply served its purpose. For all error in this work, I must assume responsibility.

I am grateful to the members of the editorial board for their encouragement and advice; and particularly to Dr. Austin Smith for reading the galleys of the entire book. I want to thank Mr. E. A. Van Steenwyck and Mr. Alfred Golden for initiating the opportunity to prepare this book.

I wish to give acknowledgment to John Wiley & Sons, Inc., for their gracious permission to reproduce in this edition several of the illustrations from one of my previous books, *Healthier Living*.

Finally, I want to express my appreciation to Freeman Lewis and Lawrence Hughes, of Pocket Books, for their unfailing encouragement and wise advice in helping me to bring this task to completion.

—JUSTUS J. SCHIFFERES

Livingston, N.J.
January 1, 1959

Contents

Emergency! First-Aid Index

For immediate treatment of some common but unexpected household and medical emergencies, look up the appropriate words below and turn to the pages indicated. If the emergencies requiring attention are not covered here, you will find them under their alphabetical listing in the body of this book. Remember—the first rule of first aid is to call a doctor.

Schifferes'
Family Medical
Encyclopedia

O blessed health! thou art above all gold and treasure, the poor man's riches, the rich man's bliss.

—ROBERT BURTON
The Anatomy of Melancholy, 1621

Health is a state of complete physical, mental and social well-being and not merely the absence of disease or infirmity.

—WORLD HEALTH ORGANIZATION
(WHO), 1946

A

Any word printed in SMALL CAPITALS *can be looked up under its own alphabetical listing for further information.*

Abasia—inability to walk, although legs may still retain their muscular power.

Abdomen—a body cavity bounded above by the DIAPHRAGM and below by the PELVIS. Some

THE ABDOMEN

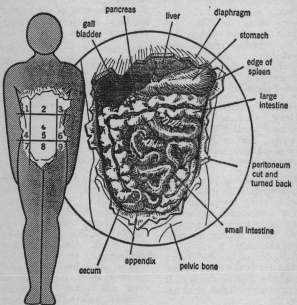

The 9 regions of the abdomen: 1. right hypochondriac, 2. epigastric, 3. left hypochondriac, 4. right lumbar, 5. umbilical, 6. left lumbar, 7. right inguinal or iliac, 8. hypogastric or pubic, 9. left inguinal or iliac.

people use the word abdomen to include the pelvis. The abdomen is lined by a sheet of tissue (membrane) called the PERITONEUM.

Inside the abdomen are the STOMACH, LIVER, PANCREAS, INTESTINES, SPLEEN, and other internal organs.

The abdomen is arbitrarily divided into nine regions. The middle region, centered in the "belly button" (umbilicus), is called the *umbilical* region. Immediately above it is the *epigastric* region, in which the stomach lies. Immediately below the umbilical region is the hypogastric, or *pubic*, region. On either side of the pubic region are the left and right *inguinal* regions.

Abdominal—pertaining to the abdomen, such as *abdominal pain*, usually called *"bellyache."* Abdominal pain or distress has many possible causes. (See APPENDICITIS; STOMACH ACHE.)

Abduction—moving part of the body away from its middle line (median axis); the position resulting from such movement. When you raise your arm, you are abducting it from the midline of the body.

Abduction of the foot means the twisting of the foot outward around the axis of the leg. It occurs in some forms of CLUBFOOT.

Abductor—a muscle that draws or pulls a body part away from its midline, or axis. The muscle that pulls the other way, back

toward the midline, is an *adductor*.

Aberration—anything ABNORMAL. We speak, for example, of aberrations in growth (gigantism or dwarfism), and mental aberrations, which are slight mental or emotional derangements. (See MENTAL ILLNESS.)

Abirritant—anything that relieves irritation, soothes.

Ablation—removal, by amputation or otherwise, of any part of the body, or of any harmful or abnormal growth.

Abnormal—not normal, irregular, often unhealthful, outside the range of the normal (which is quite wide). The concept of abnormal has meaning only when it permits a valid comparison with normal practices, conditions, formations, conduct, habits, and the like. What is normal for one person may be abnormal for another.

Abortion—the detachment and expulsion from the pregnant womb of the product of conception—fertilized ovum, embryo, or fetus—before it has become viable, that is, before the 28th week. Abortion occurs spontaneously in many instances, and it also can be artificially induced. Induced abortions are either therapeutic abortions, undertaken on proper medical indications "to save the life and health of the mother," or criminal abortions, commonly known as "illegal operations."

A criminal abortion is a

threat to the life and health of the woman who undergoes it. Whether self-induced or furtively performed by money-hungry racketeers, these operations leave a trail of infection, bleeding, subsequent sterility, and death.

Spontaneous abortions, often called *miscarriages*, are accidents of nature. Women who lose their potential babies repeatedly in the early months of pregnancy are said to suffer from *habitual abortion*. The principal sign of a "threatened abortion" is bleeding from the vagina, with or without cramps.

The causes of spontaneous abortion are imperfectly known and are certainly multiple. Some can be traced to disease, deficiency, or accident to the mother. Rarely, however, are they caused by falls, blows, or other physical violence. In perhaps 4 out of 5 spontaneous abortions, the defect is in the embryo. These miscarriages sometimes are nature's way of correcting a mistake that might result in an abnormal, deformed child.

It is estimated that 1 in every 4 or 5 pregnancies terminates in abortion.

Abrasion—rubbing or scraping off of skin or mucous membrane, as on a knee "skinned" by falling.

Abreaction—a psychological term meaning to relive past, forgotten (repressed) experience by talking or acting it out, and thus work off its damaging

pressure on the UNCONSCIOUS MIND. (See PSYCHOANALYSIS.)

Abscess—an accumulation of PUS, formed from infected, broken-down tissue, within a more or less walled-off space. A boil is an abscess on the surface of the skin. Abscesses occur in many parts of the body, for example, at the roots of the teeth, in the ear, liver, and bones (osteomyelitis). Abscesses are treated by draining off the pus, as in lancing a boil, and getting rid of the underlying INFECTION.

Abstinence—the act of completely giving up something, such as alcoholic liquors, narcotics, certain foods, sexual intercourse.

Acacia—gum arabic; a demulcent.

Accidents can happen any time, anywhere. First aid in accidents is often crucial to life and limb. In the United States, every year now about 10,000,000 people are injured in accidents, 100,000 killed.

Faced with an accident victim, keep cool. Go yourself or send someone else immediately to call for professional help. Call a doctor, an ambulance, or the police department.

Look first to the three "B's" —breathing, bleeding, and broken bones.

If the victim is not breathing, give ARTIFICIAL RESPIRATION (which see for directions).

If he is bleeding (see BLEEDING), stop it with pressure.

Look carefully for broken bones. FRACTURES (which see) must be put in splints before the patient is moved.

Handle the victim gently at all times. *Don't* move him, or let him move. *Don't* pull at him or try to get him to sit up or stand up. *Don't* give an unconscious patient anything to drink.

Keep the victim quiet, warm, and as comfortable as possible to minimize shock. Loosen tight clothing, especially the collar and belt.

Cover BURNS and wounds as soon as possible with sterile gauze.

If the victim vomits, turn his head to one side so vomit will not go into his lungs.

Remove victims of gas poisoning (CARBON MONOXIDE) to fresh air.

See also EAR TROUBLE, EYE TROUBLE, POISON, UNCONSCIOUSNESS in text and EMERGENCY! FIRST-AID INDEX on pages xvii-xviii.

Accommodation—adjustment. It most commonly refers to the ability of the eye to adjust to vision at different distances by changing the curvature of its crystalline lens. (See EYES and EYE TROUBLE.)

Accouchement—confinement for delivery; childbirth.

Acetabulum—the cup-shaped cavity in the hip bone into which the rounded head of the thigh bone fits to form a ball-and-socket JOINT.

Acetanilid—a painkilling drug

that lowers fever and relieves pain; sometimes used in treating rheumatism and neuralgia; inadvisable in the presence of heart disease.

Acetylcholine—a chemical substance, manufactured in the body. Among other actions, it aids the transmission of NERVE impulses and relaxes the CAPILLARIES.

Achilles Tendon—the tendon that binds muscles in the calf of the leg to the heel bone (calcaneus). This tendon is named after the Greek hero, Achilles, whose mother held him by the heel when she dipped him in the River Styx to make him invulnerable to weapons. There is also an Achilles BURSA. (See illustration for MUSCLES.)

Achlorhydria—lack of hydrochloric acid in the stomach, where it should normally be as part of the gastric secretions.

Achylia—lack of hydrochloric acid and rennin in gastric juice; a cause of STOMACH TROUBLE.

Acid—a chemical substance that, in solution, releases hydrogen ions. Acids taste sour, turn blue litmus red, unite with bases to form salts, and in general have chemical properties opposed to those of *alkalis*. Many thousands of acids are known to chemistry; hundreds of them are useful to medicine and scores of them are present in the human body.

Some common acids are:

Acetylsalicylic acid, which is aspirin;

Ascorbic acid, which is vitamin C;

Boric acid, used as an antiseptic on skin and mucous membranes;

Acetic acid, the acid of vinegar, which can be concentrated into a poisonous caustic (glacial acetic acid) that removes warts;

Hydrochloric acid, which is secreted by the stomach and is a normal part of the gastric juice;

Nicotinic acid, also called niacin, the pellagra-preventive factor in the vitamin B complex;

Folic acid, a widely distributed vitamin with special influence on the blood-forming system;

AMINO ACIDS, a group of organic compounds, containing nitrogen, that are the essential building blocks of protein. Some amino acids are essential to human nutrition.

Acidosis—a tendency toward a higher acid reaction in the blood stream and usually a lower alkaline reaction. The body's alkaline reserve is depleted. This condition occurs in advanced diabetes or under other circumstances, such as prolonged diarrhea, in which the body loses sodium bicarbonate. Retention of carbon dioxide in the blood, as occurs in drowning, when the lungs are underventilated, also induces acidosis. Patients with severe acidosis may gasp for breath, go into a coma, even

die. This is because the carbon-dioxide content of the blood importantly regulates the breathing process. Mild "acidity" is nothing to worry about and does not require any special diet.

Acid Stomach—a condition in which the stomach produces too much acid, or certain foods, fermenting in the stomach, leave too large an acid residue. The commonly reported symptoms are heartburn, belching, and pain in the upper abdomen. True stomach acidity is far less common than generally believed. The reported symptoms are more likely to be an allergic reaction to some food component other than acid, or the warning signals of a more serious ailment of the digestive tract. A persistent acid stomach should be carefully investigated by a physician. The control of symptoms with *antacid* powders or tablets on the part of the patient may mask a more dangerous underlying condition.

Acne—a SKIN disorder. See SEBORRHEA. Eruption of pimples and blackheads has no connection whatsoever with MASTURBATION or other sex experience.

Acrocyanosis—cold and blue hands and feet.

Acromegaly results from overfunction of the pituitary gland. It is marked by great enlargement of the bones and soft parts of the hands, feet, and face. If this ENDOCRINE disorder begins early in life, it produces completely giant stature.

ACTH — adrenocorticotrophic hormone. Manufactured in the pituitary gland, it stimulates the adrenal gland to release the hormone CORTISONE. ACTH has proved useful in the treatment of arthritis and many other disease conditions. See ENDOCRINES.

Actinomycosis—a FUNGUS infection of men and cattle, sometimes called *lumpy jaw* or *wooden tongue.*

Acute—severe, usually crucial, often dangerous.

"Acute Abdomen" describes extreme pain, distress, or disorder inside the abdomen, often but not always requiring early surgery.

Acute Illness—a sudden, severe, or dangerous illness in which relatively rapid changes are occurring. For example, FEVER may rise sharply. In acute INFECTIONS the germs (MICROBES) causing the disease are probably multiplying rapidly. Infectious illnesses are usually acute in their earlier stages. We speak of acute POLIO, acute APPENDICITIS, and the like. PNEUMONIA is always acute. CANCER, on the other hand, is rarely if ever called acute. It is insidious and CHRONIC.

When a person has passed through the acute stage of an illness, we usually say that he is "out of danger" or has "passed the crisis." After recovery from the acute stage comes the CONVALESCENT stage, which may be

relatively brief or long. Long-term illnesses are called CHRONIC.

Adams-Stokes Disease (or syndrome)— repeated FAINTING (unconsciousness), sometimes with convulsions; a condition frequently associated with some kinds of HEART DISEASE.

Addison's Disease—"bronze skin" disease, named after British physician Thomas Addison (1803-1860). It results from underactivity of the adrenal (ENDOCRINE) glands, and is often caused by tuberculosis of the adrenal glands. Before adrenal hormones were isolated to treat it, the disease was almost always fatal.

Adenitis—inflammation of a gland, usually a LYMPH gland.

Adenoids—clusters of lymph tissue high in the back of the throat, where the nasal passages enter it. Children often have enlarged adenoids, which may block the nasal passageways, causing mouth breathing and encouraging colds, sinus infections, and ear infections. Removal of the adenoids is sometimes indicated, usually along with tonsils. (See illustration for THROAT.)

Adhesions—the sticking together of body tissues not normally joined. Distressing adhesions sometimes follow surgery. As a result of inflammation, a lung may adhere to its outer (pleural) lining.

Adrenalin—epinephrine; the

"emergency hormone" produced by one part of the adrenal (ENDOCRINE) glands.

Adrenals—ENDOCRINE GLANDS that secrete adrenalin and other hormones.

Aerophagia—air swallowing, sometimes hysterical. It causes belching.

Aerosol—a solution atomized into a fine mist, either a drug for inhalation or a bactericide for spraying in a room. See NOSE.

Afterbirth—placenta and membranes expelled from the womb a few minutes after the birth of a child. (See CHILDBIRTH.)

Agammaglobulinemia—lack of necessary gamma GLOBULIN in the blood.

Agar—an extract of seaweed often used as a culture medium on which to grow bacteria in the laboratory. *Agar-agar* is a LAXATIVE.

Agranulocytosis—a rare but often (perhaps 75%) fatal disease in which the bone-marrow is affected and the manufacture of essential white BLOOD CELLS severely diminished—from a normal 7500 per cubic millimeter to as few as 1000 or even less. The disease symptoms usually come on suddenly; they are high fever; ulcerations in the mouth, throat and gut; great weakness and prostration. Treatment is difficult and prolonged; it includes guarding the patient against all manner of infections from which a normal

complement of white blood cells would otherwise protect him. ANTIBIOTICS are generously used.

While the exact cause of agranulocytosis is not known, it apparently includes a special sensitivity (allergy) to certain drugs and poisons, notably amidopyrine and some other coal-tar derivatives. Sulfa drugs have occasionally been indicted. This disease has many names, including *granulocytopenia, malignant leukopenia* or *neutropenia,* and *agranulocytic angina.*

Ague—fever, or chills and fever. It is an old word commonly associated with the chills and fever sensations produced by MALARIA. Metallic fumes, poisons, can produce similar symptoms; for example, *brass-founders ague.*

Ailurophobia—morbid fear of cats.

Airsickness results from a combination of lack of oxygen (ALTITUDE SICKNESS) and unaccustomed rapid motion *(motion sickness)* that occurs also in travel by train, car and boat. Airsickness can usually be prevented or minimized by taking Dramamine, or similar drugs, half an hour before flying and by scheduling flights in pressurized cabin planes. See EARS for further information on motion sickness.

Albumin—the common and important PROTEIN substance

found in almost all animal, including human, tissues. It is soluble in water and coagulates when heated. Its exact chemical composition has not been determined, though it is known to contain carbon, hydrogen, nitrogen, oxygen, and sulfur. The white of an egg is chiefly albumin. *Serum albumin* is a main protein constituent of blood plasma, the fluid part of the blood. One place that albumin should not appear is in the urine. If it does, the condition is known as ALBUMINURIA, and frequently betokens disease.

Albuminuria—the presence of ALBUMIN or other protein substances, such as serum globulin, in the urine. Albumin can be detected when a sample of urine is heated. Albuminuria is frequently, but not always, a sign of disease. Harmless albuminuria often occurs temporarily in pregnancy, in adolescence, and after strenuous exercise or eating certain foods. A "touch of albumin in the urine" was once recommended by Sir William Osler for frightening men over forty into serious consideration of healthier ways of living.

A normal kidney does not usually permit albumin to pass into the urine. Hence albuminuria is frequently a sign of kidney disease, especially if pus and blood also appear in the urine. Among other diseases and disorders to which albuminuria may point are HEART DISEASE, GOUT, GOITER, LIVER TROUBLE, BRAIN DAMAGE, and nutritional deficiencies.

Alcohol—see ALCOHOLISM.

ALCOHOLISM

Alcoholism means poisoning with alcohol; it may be acute or chronic. Acute alcoholism is drunkenness, the temporary result of overindulgence in alcoholic beverages. Chronic alcoholism is a sickness, the outcome of prolonged and repeated use of alcohol to compensate for deep-seated personality problems.

Acute alcoholism, or intoxication, depends on the amount of alcohol—ordinary ethyl alcohol—imbibed and absorbed through the stomach and intestinal tract. Individuals differ in their tolerance. The degree of intoxication can be estimated from the amount of alcohol in the blood stream; this is the basis of "drunkometer" tests. When the blood alcohol reaches a concentration of 0.3 to 0.4%, the drinker is unconscious, "out cold." He may require medical treatment. (See HANGOVER.)

Contrary to popular opinion, alcohol is a *depressant* drug, not a stimulant. It chiefly affects the nerve cells of the brain, to which the blood stream carries it fairly quickly from the stomach. By depressing the higher nerve centers, it releases inhibitions and gives a temporary sense of well-being that has been valued for centuries. As the amount of alcohol reaching the brain increases, the unpleasant, depressive, anesthetic effects of the drug appear.

Alcohol, even in small amounts, impairs judgment and coordination, although the drinker usually fools himself into thinking he is more efficient physically and psychologically. This has been proved in many psychological and performance tests. It is the basis for the emphatic rule: *If you drink, don't drive.*

Because it causes the blood vessels to expand, alcohol is sometimes prescribed for patients with some forms of HEART DISEASE. Elderly patients suffering from chronic diseases may also be permitted or encouraged to use alcohol medicinally to spur appetite and ease minor pains and aches.

The best-informed medical opinion now holds that the temperate, moderate, occasional use of alcoholic beverages has little, if any, residual effect on health.

Chronic alcoholism afflicts perhaps 3 million people, mostly males, in the United States. Of these, something over 2 million are heavy drinkers, excessive drinkers, or inebriates, who harm themselves physically, psychologically, and socially by their drinking. The residue are chronic alcoholics—problem drinkers, compulsive drinkers, literal slaves to drink.

The continued, excessive use of alcohol brings physical and mental deterioration and ultimately death. Excessive drinkers shorten their lives; their resistance to disease, notably pneumonia, is decreased; their nervous and digestive systems are impaired; they are subject to alcoholic psychoses, such as DELIRIUM TREMENS (DT's). Since they eat poorly, chronic alcoholics often suffer from nutritional deficiencies, especially lack of vitamin B, which exaggerates their nervous difficulties.

Why do some people become chronic alcoholics, crossing the line from social drinking to problem drinking? There is no final answer, but psychiatric studies offer some powerful hints. Regardless of his life circumstances, the psychiatrists say, the alcoholic feels basically insecure. He suffers from painful, deep-seated, unconscious inner conflicts, from which he needs release more pressingly than other people. The origins of these neurotic conflicts may go back to childhood. They often embrace feelings of long-repressed anger against parents who betrayed, rejected, or frustrated him as a child. Alcohol temporarily releases this dreadful inner feeling of guilt, frustration, and insecurity, so the alcoholic resorts to it more and more. He is fleeing from himself.

How can chronic alcoholism be treated and overcome? Most alcoholics need psychiatric help to overcome the intensity of their inner conflicts. Few get it. The aversion treatment, combined with psychotherapy, is often helpful. The patient takes a drug like *antabuse,* which makes him exceedingly sensitive to alcohol. He becomes ill and vomits whenever he takes a drink. This reaction enforces sobriety for many months while the patient is in the process of acquiring an improved attitude toward his inner problems.

Alcoholics Anonymous (AA), an organization of ex-alcoholics started in the United States in 1935, has done great service in saving chronic alcoholics. They estimate that 50 to 75% of those who join their ranks and make a real effort to free themselves from compulsive drinking succeed in doing so. The cured alcoholic can never take another drink if he wants to stay cured.

Aldosterone—a new steroid hormone from the adrenal cortex, first isolated in 1952. It maintains life in animals whose adrenal glands have been removed. It helps regulate the body's electrolyte balance.

Alienist—PSYCHIATRIST; an old word for an expert called to court to testify to the sanity of the accused or other witnesses.

Alimentary—related to food, feeding, diet, nourishment or DIGESTION. The *alimentary canal* is the food tube or gastro-intestinal tract of the living organism, from mouth to anus.

Alkali—the opposite of ACID; a chemically *basic* substance (base) that turns red litmus blue. Among the alkalis are potassium (potash), sodium, and ammonia. Mixed with fatty acids, alkalis form soluble *soaps.*

Alkalosis—an excess of alkali in the fluids and tissues of the body; usually too much bicarbonate in the blood. It is the opposite of ACIDOSIS. It may occur as a result of taking too much sodium bicarbonate ("bicarb") for stomach ailments, or after prolonged vomiting.

Allergen—see ALLERGY.

ALLERGY

The allergic (that is, oversensitive) person reacts to something in his environment to which most people would not react at all. The offending substance or circumstance is called an *allergen.* The most common allergens include pollen, food, drugs, bacteria, and house dust. However, some people have allergic reactions to cold, heat, or light, and even to emotional stress. (See ANTIGEN.)

The parts of the body in which allergic reactions most often show up are the skin, bronchial tree, nose, and digestive system. The common allergic disorders are hives (urticaria), eczema, hay fever, drug rashes, bronchial asthma, and food allergy. Some allergies are apparently hereditary; others are acquired. No one knows exactly why oversensitivity occurs. Even minute quantities of an allergen can set off a violent reaction.

How can allergies be managed? The way to prevent allergy is to identify the offending allergen and then avoid it. This is not always easy. *Patch tests* on the skin are often used for this purpose. Tiny amounts of many suspected allergens are placed on the skin, which then often reacts by forming a blister or wheal. Skin tests, however, do not always identify offending foods.

Since the substance histamine often accumulates in the presence of allergies, ANTIHISTAMINE drugs sometimes relieve symptoms. Certain allergies, notably the pollen allergies, like hay fever, can often be treated by desensitization. In this process the offending substance is injected in increasing doses over a period of weeks.

Bronchial asthma is the most serious allergic disease, being the one most often fatal. The bronchial tubes are narrowed by spasmodic contractions, and they secrete an excess of MUCUS Hence breathing becomes difficult. The victim wheezes and coughs, and feels as if his chest were caught in a vise. An asthmatic attack may last for minutes, hours, or days. The spasm of the bronchial muscles can usually be relieved by ADRENALIN. Every effort must be made to identify the offending allergen, for long-continued asthma can produce serious changes in the lungs.

Hay fever is the most common allergic disorder, afflicting perhaps 3,000,000 people in the United States. Sensitivity to ragweed pollen is the most frequent cause; in such cases it is a seasonal disease, reaching its peak in late fall. The symptoms are those of a bad head cold, notably an itchy, running nose and much sneezing. When these symptoms are year-round, the condition is called *vasomotor rhinitis*, and the allergen is likely to be something other than pollen—for example, house dust, animal dander, cosmetics, or food.

Hives (urticaria) is an allergic skin reaction in which pale raised welts, or wheals, appear along with intense itching. They may be small or "giant hives." See HIVES; ITCHING.

Eczema is another skin ailment often attributed to allergy—particularly food allergy in infants. The skin bears rough, red patches that itch and hang on for a long time.

Drug allergy, or idiosyncrasy, produces reactions, sometimes violent, to medications ordinarily safe. Allergy to penicillin and aspirin is not uncommon.

Food allergies often upset the gastrointestinal tract, produce skin symptoms and headaches. It may be difficult to find the offending food. It can sometimes be done by an elimination diet, in which groups of foods are omitted from the diet according to plan until the allergic food(s) are discovered. Often, but not necessarily, the allergen turns out to be a protein found in milk, eggs, wheat, chocolate, seafood, nuts, or onions. When the allergen is found, foods containing it must thenceforth be avoided. Children often outgrow their early food allergies.

Alopecia—*baldness.* See HAIR.

Altitude Sickness—a condition that occurs at high altitudes, as on mountain tops *("mountain sickness")* or in airplanes *("blackout").* In any case it is owing to lack of OXYGEN in the blood and brain *(anoxia).* The higher above sea-level one goes, the less oxygen there is in the atmosphere.

The symptoms of altitude sickness are those associated with lack or shortage of oxygen: dizziness, headache, loss of mental acuity; sometimes vomiting, difficulty in seeing and hearing; and, at high altitudes, nosebleed, slight fever, weakness of limbs, prostration and eventually unconsciousness.

The treatment for altitude sickness is oxygen, inhaled from an oxygen supply (tank). People who habitually reside in high altitudes get used to the diminished supply of oxygen because they develop an in-

crease in red blood cells to carry oxygen. This compensates for the atmospheric defect. People climbing mountains, however, are likely to be made ill by the experience. People differ in the heights that make them ill.

"Pressurized cabins" are used in commercial airplanes to keep a near-ground-level saturation of oxygen in the cabins. See AIRSICKNESS.

Alum—acts as an astringent, styptic (as in styptic pencils for shaving cuts) and hemostatic to stop superficial surface BLEEDING. Since alum is somewhat injurious to teeth, it should not be used as a gargle or mouthwash and should not be taken internally.

Aluminum Hydroxide Gel (and aluminum phosphate gel)—excellent ANTACIDS, often prescribed for stomach ulcers. See STOMACH TROUBLE.

Alveolitis—usually inflammation

of tooth sockets and gums; sometimes another word for pyorrhea alveolaris. See TEETH.

Alveolus—(pl., alveoli); air sac of the LUNGS; also socket of TEETH.

Amblyopia—dim or poor vision, not the result of disease of the structure of the EYE itself. It often results from disease of the BRAIN or optic nerve; poisoning by chemicals, drugs (notably quinine), nicotine (tobacco), alcohol (especially wood, or methyl, alcohol); UREMIA and violent injuries. See EYE and EYE TROUBLE.

Ameba—a tiny one-celled animal.

Amebiasis—infection with troublesome species of ameba which take up lodging in the bowels and sometimes produce amebic dysentery.

Amenorrhea—absence or stoppage of MENSTRUATION, a "missed period." This may be due to PREGNANCY or disease, especially HORMONE imbalance, or other reasons. Excessive fatigue, worry, and so forth can cause temporary amenorrhea. See FEMALE TROUBLES.

Amino Acid—any one of some 30 or more chemical compounds, containing nitrogen, that are the building blocks of PROTEIN. When meat and other protein foods are eaten, they are broken down into amino acids, which the body stores and uses to build and rebuild its own flesh. About 10 of the amino acids are considered essential to life and must be supplied in food (or as medicine). Some of the amino acids are asparagine, cystine, glycine, glutamic acid, histidine, and tryptophan.

Aminophylline—a drug sometimes used in the treatment of HEART DISEASE and ASTHMA.

Ammonia—a chemical that contains nitrogen and hydrogen (NH_3). It has a pungent, characteristic odor. Aromatic spirits of ammonia are sometimes used as "smelling salts."

Amnesia—loss of memory, forgetfulness of past experience.

Amphetamine—a drug that stimulates the central nervous system. Inhaled, it constricts blood vessels and shrinks nasal mucosa. This is a common ingredient in so-called "pep pills"; one brand name for it is *benzedrine*. This drug should be used only under strict medical supervision. In many cases its stimulating effect is undesirable.

Ampule—a sealed glass tube containing a measured amount of sterile medication, usually to be given by injection ("SHOTS").

Amyl Nitrite—causes blood vessels to dilate promptly. It is given by inhalation; a vial is broken in a handkerchief and sniffed up. It relieves pains of angina pectoris, asthma and convulsions. It is chemically related to *nitroglycerine*, which has similar uses.

Amyotrophic Lateral Sclerosis —"GEHRIG'S DISEASE."

Analgesic—pain-killer.

Anasarca—"dropsy" or ASCITES; accumulation of fluid in tissues.

Anatomy—the science, or branch of knowledge, that deals with the parts and structure of human and animal bodies. Anatomy discloses what is present; PHYSIOLOGY tells how it works (function); PATHOLOGY explains why it isn't working (disease).

Modern medical science stems from a detailed knowledge of human anatomy. The Belgian surgeon, Vesalius, whose great illustrated work, "The Anatomy of the Human Body" (*"De Humani Corporis Fabrica"*) was published in 1543, is the father of modern anatomy.

Gross anatomy deals with body parts visible to the naked eye; for example, the bones. *Microscopic anatomy*, also called *histology*, treats with the smaller structures that can be seen only through a microscope; for example, the tiny canals that traverse the bones. *Morbid anatomy* is *pathology*. *Comparative anatomy* provides comparison between the structures of different animals, and men, and offers the basis for the reconstruction of human and animal figures from fossils and remnants; for example, the construct of extinct animals like dinosaurs.

Androgen—MALE SEX HORMONE.

Anemia—a BLOOD disease, sometimes called "thin blood." There are a great many types of anemia, but the most common are *iron-deficiency anemias* and *pernicious anemia*. Some anemias result from the destruction of too many red blood cells (hemolytic anemias) or the loss of too many red blood cells through direct or hidden bleeding (hemorrhagic anemias). However, the more common forms of anemia are caused by failure of the blood-forming system, located in the bone marrow, to manufacture enough or the right kind of red BLOOD CELLS. This failure may be the result of a lack of adequate amounts of iron or other essentials in the diet.

What are the symptoms of anemia? Pallor—pale skin and mucous membranes—loss of appetite, low energy, easy fatigue, shortness of breath, palpitation of the heart, and general weakness are usually observed. In pernicious anemia, in which the nerves in the spinal cord may be affected, the gradual onset of the disease may also be marked by numbness, tingling, and needles-and-pins sensations in the arms and legs. The tongue may be sore and smooth.

Iron-deficiency anemias occur because the relatively small amount of iron needed for manufacture of HEMOGLOBIN is missing. This is the essential element in the red blood cell and is responsible for the transport of oxygen from the lungs to other body cells.

Some people become anemic because their systems cannot absorb or assimilate the iron they take in. Mostly, however, the failure lies in the diet. There are many borderline anemias, because the average diet, especially in young women, is too low in iron. Preventing and treating this type of anemia depend on getting more iron into the body. In severe anemias, doctors may prescribe iron compounds (for example, ferrous sulfate). However, foods rich in iron should be eaten regularly. Among these are liver, lean meat, molasses, egg yolk, green vegetables, and nuts.

Pernicious anemia is a nutritional-deficiency disease, but the missing element is not iron. In this condition the stomach, from which the normal amount of hydrochloric acid is usually missing, fails to secrete a certain "intrinsic factor"—a chemical substance needed to produce mature red blood cells. This missing substance can be supplied by liver. The treatment of pernicious anemia, therefore, has depended on injections of liver extracts. Folic acid and vitamin B_{12}, normally found in liver, have also relieved the symptoms of pernicious anemia.

Anesthesia—loss of sensation; in particular, the temporary loss of the feeling of pain effected by *anesthetic* drugs. Anesthetics may be either *general* or *local*. The first general anesthetic introduced into medical practice was ether. The discovery of its usefulness, back in the 1840's, is credited both to W. T. G. Morton, a Boston dentist, and Crawford Long, a Georgia physician. This was a great discovery, for by abolishing pain, anesthesia vastly extended the range of surgery.

General anesthesia is commonly administered to patients about to undergo surgery. They usually breathe in a mixture of air and anesthetic gases or fumes, notably ether, chloroform, nitrous oxide ("laughing gas"), cyclopropane, and others. After a few whiffs, they are unconscious, their muscles relax, and they are insensible to pain. However, some general anesthetics can also be given by injection, rectum, or mouth.

The administering of anesthesia is so important—and sometimes so complicated—that a specially trained member of the operating-room team, the anesthetist, usually looks after this matter exclusively. The patient must be carefully watched and the depth of the anesthesia carefully regulated. Anesthetists are fully entitled to fees or other payment for their very special services.

Local anesthesia deadens or prevents pain in a limited part of the body and does not render the patient unconscious. In effect, it temporarily blocks or deadens the nerve endings or nerve pathways that carry pain sensations. Local anesthetics are usually injected. Typical local anesthetics are novocain, procaine, nupercaine, and cocaine hydrochloride. Skill must be used in injecting the anesthetic agent so that just the right nerves are blocked.

Spinal anesthesia, calling for injections beneath the membranes, of the spinal canal, is sometimes used for surgery.

Dentists inject local anesthetics around face nerves to reduce or eliminate the pain of tooth extractions and other dental operations. Parts of the face feel numb for some time thereafter.

A special field for anesthetic agents is in easing the pains of childbirth. (See CHILD-BIRTH.)

Aneurysm—the bulging out of the walls of an artery or vein. Sometimes the weakened and ballooned-out part ruptures, spilling out blood. Aneurysm occurs most frequently in the aorta, the large blood vessel leading from the heart. Syphilis is a common but not exclusive cause of aneurysm of the aorta.

Angina—any repeated, suffocating pain; or the disease that causes it. *Angina pectoris*—pain in the chest, breast pang—is a form of *heart disease*. See HEART DISEASE.

Angioneurotic Edema—swelling of the skin, mucous membranes, or sometimes of internal organs; may be associated with HIVES (*urticaria*), angry red spots, or purpura. The causes include ALLERGY and NEUROSIS.

Animal Bites—wash wounds freely with water. If possible, hold under running tap for sev-

eral minutes. Apply sterile gauze compress, and see a doctor immediately. Obtain name and address of owner of animal, so it may be held in quarantine.

Ankle—the JOINT between the leg bones (tibia and fibula) and the ankle bone (talus, astragalus) of the foot. It is subject to twists, wrenches, *sprains*, strains, and FRACTURES. For management of a *sprained ankle*, see JOINTS. A break in the fibula on the outer side of the ankle is called a *Pott's fracture*. See FRACTURES; BONES; FOOT and FOOT TROUBLE.

Ankylosis—a stiff joint, resulting from disease or deliberate operation to immobilize the joint.

Anopheles—the kind of mosquitoes that carry MALARIA. At least 75 species of this genus of mosquito transmit malaria. Some carry other disease parasites.

Anorexia—no appetite for food.

Anoxemia—too little oxygen in the blood.

Anoxia—lack of oxygen.

Antabuse—brand name for tetraethylthiuram disulfide, a chemical which has the peculiar property of making those who take it violently sick when followed by alcohol. The drug is used in the aversion treatment of ALCOHOLISM.

Antacid—a substance, usually a drug, that counteracts stomach acidity; for example, sodium bicarbonate ("bicarb") or milk. See ACID STOMACH. The overuse of antacids as self-prescribed drugs can be dangerous, inciting ALKALOSIS.

Antagonist—anything that acts against something else; for example, a muscle that opposes the action of another muscle, its agonist. Certain drugs, hormones, and enzymes are antagonistic to one another.

Antemortem—before death.

Antenatal—occurring before birth.

Antepartum—occurring before childbirth (parturition).

Anterior—anything situated in front or ahead of anything else; for instance, the face is anterior to the back of the head. The opposite position is POSTERIOR.

Anthelmintic—any drug that destroys or chases worms from the body; a vermifuge.

Anthrax—a disease of animals and men, caused by the anthrax bacillus. In man it often causes difficult-to-heal ulcers and carbuncles on the face and hands; more rarely, but more dangerously, in the lungs, brain and intestines. The control of the disease is a public health and veterinary problem, making sure that meat, hides, bristles or other parts of infected animals do not come in contact with human beings. Anthrax is also called—indicating its origin —*woolsorter's* and *ragsorter's* disease.

Antibiotics—a whole group of drugs that kill or stop the growth of harmful bacteria (MICROBES) in the body. A sufficient quantity of the drug must reach the germs if it is to do any good. There are hundreds of different antibiotics—so many, in fact, that a dictionary of antibiotics has been published. Different antibiotics act against different invading microbes. Those that are effective against a great number of microbes are called *broad-spectrum antibiotics*.

Penicillin was the first practical antibiotic. Discovered by Alexander Fleming in 1929 but first produced in useful quantities during World War II, penicillin is derived from cultures of certain species of molds belonging to the penicillium family.

Most antibiotics are derived from cultures of molds or bacteria. For some, however, the chemical structure is known, and they can be produced synthetically. Among the well-known antibiotics are penicillin, streptomycin, aureomycin, terramycin, chloramphenicol, and achromycin. They are not effective against virus diseases.

Penicillin has proved especially useful in treating pneumonia, syphilis, gonorrhea, and many other bacterial infections. It can be given by mouth or injection. (See DRUGS, "SHOTS.")

Antibody—an obscure but important substance produced in and by the living body that protects against specific disease infections. For example: there are three types of POLIO virus and three types of antibody that can be invoked in the body —either by polio vaccine or by polio virus infection—to protect against the multiplication of the virus and subsequent damage to the nervous system by the virus. Every antibody has its ANTIGEN.

The antigen is the chemical substance, or disease MICROBE, or anything else, that prompts the body to manufacture antibodies to beat off the effects of the antigen. Antibodies are known by, and measured by, their effect, in the body or in test tubes, on the antigens that invoke them. Thus, polio antibodies stop polio viruses from multiplying.

Once the body learns how to form antibodies against specific disease germs, it rarely, if ever, forgets how. That is why most people rarely contract an infectious disease more than once— if the infecting microbe is the kind that teaches the body how to manufacture antibodies.

Second attacks of polio, shingles, mumps and measles, for example, are exceedingly rare; the first attack "tools up" the body for antibody formation. On the other hand, second and subsequent attacks of the common cold and venereal diseases are common because the original infection does not invoke adequate antibody formation for future defense.

Antibodies are chemically and biologically related to white blood cells and are probably produced partly in the blood-forming (reticulo-endothelial) system. *Circulating antibodies* are those antibodies which appear in the blood stream, whence they can be deposited in any part of the body. They can often be detected and measured in samples of blood and serum.

Antidote—anything that counteracts a poison.

Antigen—anything that incites the formation of ANTIBODIES and reacts with them, inside or outside the living body, in some detectable way.

For example, the famous Wassermann reaction, for the detection of syphilis, depends upon the presence in a chemical testing solution of an antigen with which syphilitic blood serum will react. The antigen in this case is, strangely enough, *beef-heart*, prepared in special ways. This test-tube antibody-antigen reaction is called a complement fixation test, or reaction.

Again, the polio virus is the antigen that invokes (and reacts with) polio antibodies either inside the body or in the test tube.

Pollen antigens are extracted from the pollen of plants; they are specific proteins. People sensitive to these pollens react to the antigens. An extensive reaction is the disease state called ALLERGY, expressed in such terms as HAY FEVER, asthma, rose fever and the like.

Antihistamine—anything, usually a drug, that counteracts the effect of histamine in the body. Antihistaminic drugs are commonly used in treating ALLERGY and other diseases; they often have a slightly sedative or hypnotic effect, acting as "sleeping pills." The evidence that they prevent common colds is not convincing. HISTAMINE is a complex chemical substance found in all animal and vegetable tissues.

Antiseptics—agents that inhibit the growth of disease-producing micro-organisms. They are usually used in or on the human body and are not quite so strong as DISINFECTANTS, which see. Common and useful household antiseptics (for external application) include tincture of iodine, boric acid, hydrogen peroxide, rubbing alcohol (isopropyl and ethyl alcohol), and various organic mercurials, such as mercurochrome.

Antitoxin—a substance in the blood serum which specifically fights a particular poison, or toxin, that invades a body; for example, DIPHTHERIA antitoxin. When produced by or injected into the human body, it neutralizes the specific, choking poison produced by infection with the diphtheria bacillus.

Antitoxins for treatment of human disease are principally produced by immunizing animals (horses, monkeys, rabbits) against the disease; then collecting the antitoxin substance from their blood serum and

purifying it before injection into human beings. Among the conditions for which protective antitoxins are available are: DIPHTHERIA, tetanus (LOCKJAW), BOTULISM, snake bite, GAS GANGRENE, and SCARLET FEVER.

Antrum—a hollow space, a "little cave" or cavity, especially in a bone. The bones of the skull, above the nose, have many an antrum, connected by canals (*sinuses*).

Anuria—patient can't void his URINE.

Anus—the far end of the gastrointestinal tract, food-tube or gut, from which the waste-products of DIGESTION (feces) are finally discharged. The anus is the outside terminus of the rectum. It is held tightly shut, except during the act of defecation, by a strong but sensitive ring of muscles, the *anal sphincters*. Because of the multiple innervation of the anus—many nerves supply the skin and muscles located at this site —the anus is quite sensitive to injury or trauma from within or without the body; for example, a hard stool or anal surgery. (See illustrations for DIGESTIVE SYSTEM.)

Anxiety—not quite the same thing as worry, though the two terms are often confused. Anxiety is a form of fear. It expresses itself as an uneasiness of mind, often accompanied by such physical symptoms as sweating, fast heartbeat, rapid breathing, higher blood pressure, and trembling. Normal worry and fear occur when there is a real threat in the world outside us. Anxiety is a reaction against one's own unconscious impulses, the repressed fears that linger in the unconscious mind. In a sense, the anxious person worries when he has nothing really to worry about. He often masks this by seeking a degree of security or perfection unattainable in the real world. See PSYCHOANALYSIS, MENTAL ILLNESS, NEUROSIS.

Aorta—the large curved BLOOD VESSEL, the prime artery, that carries blood directly from the HEART (left ventricle) for distribution through lesser blood vessels to all parts of the body. Rupture (tearing) of the aorta is almost invariably fatal; it occurs when the great blood vessel has been weakened by degenerative (for example, aneurysm) or infectious disease.

SYPHILIS was once the most common cause of inflammation of the aorta (aortitis) and its subsequent rupture. (See illustrations for HEART.)

Aortitis—inflammation of the AORTA, often due to SYPHILIS.

Aperient—a mild LAXATIVE or cathartic.

Aphasia—loss of speech and other power of communication, caused either by organic damage to the BRAIN or MENTAL ILLNESS.

Aphrodisiac—anything that stimulates sexual desire or appetite.

Aphthae—white spots in the mouth, accompanying THRUSH (stomatitis).

Apoplexy—a STROKE resulting from a damaged blood vessel in the brain and marked by unconsciousness usually followed by paralysis.

APPENDICITIS

Appendicitis is the inflammation of the useless worm-shaped (vermiform) appendix, a small pocket, or projection, 1 to 6 inches long, that protrudes from the part of the large bowel called the *cecum*. The name, diagnosis and condition—appendicitis—was first called to the attention of surgeons in 1886, by Reginald Fitz, of Boston. This was the time when abdominal surgical operations were being made materially safer by the discoveries of Pasteur and Lister.

Appendicitis rapidly became a popular surgical diagnosis and the basis for many life-saving surgical operations. The diagnosis itself is a difficult one. Pain in the right side, one of the common symptoms of appendicitis, may have many other causes. The appendix runs close to the bladder and rectum, which may be at fault. Also, the pain from a diseased appendix, which causes trouble out of all proportion to its size and functional importance, may be reflected in other parts of the body; for example, the back or the shoulder-blades.

Other symptoms suggestive of appendicitis are rigidity and tenderness at McBurney's point—halfway between the navel and the crest of the hip-bone—accompanied by nausea, vomiting and sometimes sweating and dizziness. A high white BLOOD CELL count is usually obtained, indicating INFECTION.

For the person who has a "pain in his belly" that might possibly suggest appendicitis (whose attacks often come on suddenly), these are the paramount rules:

1. Eat nothing! Take nothing by mouth (except perhaps small sips of water).

2. Above all, *don't take a laxative!*

3. If pain persists more than an hour, call a doctor.

4. Lie down and rest quietly in the meantime.

The great risk in appendicitis is perforation or rupture of the appendix, flooding the intestines with infectious microbes and causing an inflammation of the entire bowel cavity and its linings *(peritonitis)*.

The basic treatment for appendicitis is surgery—*appendectomy,* removal of the diseased appendix. The operation has been performed so many times and is so well standardized that almost any surgeon can perform it easily and with safety. The patient is usually out of bed in a few days and home in a few more. At one time appendectomies were almost always hurry-up surgical emer-

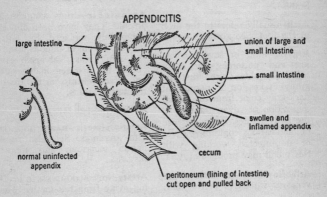

APPENDICITIS

large intestine

union of large and small intestine

small intestine

swollen and inflamed appendix

normal uninfected appendix

cecum

peritoneum (lining of intestine) cut open and pulled back

gencies, demanding prompt operation before the inflamed appendix burst.

Since the coming of the SULFA DRUGS, and later, the ANTI-BIOTICS, the emergency character of appendicitis has been greatly diminished—and also the death rate from the condition. All these drugs keep the appendiceal infection under control and from spreading to other parts of the bowel or body. In many cases, now, it has become possible to treat, control and even prevent attacks of appendicitis by judicious use of medication. Surgery, if necessary, is also much safer, since the antibiotics control and almost eliminate the risk of secondary infection (peritonitis).

The disease, appendicitis, is most common in the late teens and middle age; though it also occurs among children and in old people. Up through the middle 1930's it was one of the principal causes of death in the United States. Since that time, when sulfa drugs first came in, the disease has been steadily diminishing in importance, and is much less common today.

Since early adequate treatment is almost always life-saving, medical help should be obtained immediately upon the slightest suspicion (one hour's notice) that appendicitis is lurking in the intestine. (See illustrations for ABDOMEN; DIGESTIVE SYSTEM.)

Appetite—see DIET.

Arachnoidism—poisoning by spider bite (usually the red widow spider in the United States).

Arch—usually refers to the arch of the foot. See FOOT TROUBLE.

Argyria—mild or severe coloring and poisoning by *silver salts*. The skin (often first the gums) takes on a permanent dark-gray color from the actual deposition of silver granules in the body tissues. Prolonged use of medications containing silver or unprotected working with this metal may produce argyria.

Ariboflavinosis—too little of the VITAMIN riboflavin in the diet; may be revealed by skin cracks at the corners of mouth or eyes.

Arrythmia—out of time; *cardiac arrythmia,* off-beat HEART.

Arsenicals—drugs containing arsenic. They have been almost completely replaced by antibiotics. The most famous arsenical drug was "salvarsan" or "606," the first reasonably safe and effective drug for the treatment of SYPHILIS.

Arteriole—small ARTERY.

Arteriosclerosis—HARDENING OF THE ARTERIES. See also HIGH BLOOD PRESSURE and HEART DISEASE.

Artery—any BLOOD VESSEL leading away from the HEART. The first and largest is the AORTA. Larger arteries branch off into smaller arteries, making what is called an "arterial tree"; these, in turn, into arterioles and then into still smaller capillaries, which finally connect with venules, through which the blood returns to the heart by way of the veins. (See illustrations for HEART.)

Arthralgia—JOINT pains; see ARTHRITIS.

ARTHRITIS

Arthritis—literally, inflammation of a joint—is one of a number of diseases and disorders commonly called RHEUMATISM. Arthritis arises from many causes, some well identified, some still obscure, and it is treated in many different ways.

Arthritis has been classified as follows: (1) arthritis caused by infection, (2) arthritis resulting from RHEUMATIC FEVER; (3) rheumatoid arthritis; (4) degenerative arthritis; (5) arthritis due to joint injuries; (6) arthritis caused by GOUT; and (7) arthritis originating from the nervous system. Rheumatoid arthritis and arthritis caused by rheumatic fever are classified as COLLAGEN DISEASES.

Rheumatoid arthritis and degenerative arthritis are the two most common types; millions of men and women are afflicted with them. But good medical treatment, begun early and continued faithfully, can often do much to alleviate the pain, crippling, and disability.

What is rheumatoid arthritis? We know now that it is a disease not of the joints alone but of the whole bodily system—in particular, the connective tissue. This tissue reacts sensitively to substances in the body; sometimes to invading bacteria and their products, sometimes to secretions of the ENDOCRINE GLANDS, sometimes to nervous or emotional stimulation, sometimes to all of them and still other factors. Worry makes it worse. This may be why the depressing effect of cold, damp days also makes the joint pains seem worse. However, exposure to cold and damp, unhygienic surroundings, and frequent infections of the upper respiratory tract may induce or predispose to the disease in otherwise susceptible people.

Some of the other names by which rheumatoid arthritis is called indicate its varied character. These names are *chronic infectious arthritis, arthritis deformans, proliferative arthritis,* and *atrophic arthritis.* Poorly or ineffectually treated, this condition can become chronic, hanging on for years. It may follow infections of various kinds. It can become so severe that it creates bodily deformities, usually of the hands, or puts its victims in a wheel chair or hospital bed. It may bring about peculiar changes— proliferating growths visible in X-ray pictures—at the ends of the bones where they come together to form joints.

Rheumatoid arthritis may appear suddenly or gradually. Fatigue, loss of weight, and poor appetite can be early signs. Sometimes it comes on suddenly with an acute fever and pain, swelling, and disability in many joints. Any joint can be involved, including those of the spine, but the hands and feet are most commonly affected. In the early stages vague and fleeting pains and stiffness of many joints may be noticed on rising in the morning and at the end of the day. By the time joints appear swollen the condition is usually well advanced. See JOINTS.

Rheumatoid arthritis often starts with weakness and pain in the hands. The palms (and the soles of the feet if they are involved) feel cold and clammy. The joints where the fingers join the hand become swollen and gnarled, so that all the fingers slant away to the outside, giving the whole hand a distorted flipperlike appearance. Unused muscles surrounding painful and swollen joints may waste away (atrophy) so that the patient or part of him becomes thin and weak.

The pain associated with rheumatoid arthritis sometimes hangs on almost unbearably, although the disease sometimes disappears spontaneously. In particular, it usually disappears during pregnancy and upon the appearance of jaundice.

Who gets rheumatoid arthritis? Anyone can get it, but women appear to be afflicted about three times as often as men. Children, too, can be affected, suffering from a condition called *Still's disease*. In general, rheumatoid arthritis strikes at earlier ages than other types of arthritis. It is more common in cool than in warm climates.

The toll of rheumatoid arthritis in the U.S. is terrific. It is estimated that 7½ million Americans are chronic sufferers from the disease and that 150,000 a year are invalided by it. That means that it is about ten times as common as tuberculosis or diabetes, seven times as frequent as cancer, twice as prevalent as heart disease!

What can be done for rheumatoid arthritis? A wide variety of treatment is available. The earlier it is begun, the better the outlook. Sometimes progress is extremely slow; but patients should do their best not to become discouraged. A treatment that has failed with one may help somebody else.

Spectacular new drugs in the treatment of rheumatoid arthritis are CORTISONE, ACTH, and others like them. Taken by mouth or injected into particularly painful joints, they have brought relief to thousands. However, cortisone and similar drugs are not the last and only word in treatment. Their dosage must be carefully controlled to avoid unpleasant side-effects. They do not alter the underlying changes that have taken place in the joints. But they do bring early relief from pain and permit muscle movements that were previously difficult or impossible.

Other drugs used in treating rheumatoid arthritis include SALICYLATES (aspirin), iodides, sulfur, vaccines, serums, and non-specific proteins. Gold salts are sometimes tried, but they must be used most cautiously, since gold is not tolerated by all patients and may damage the kidneys. Pain-killing drugs and drugs that permit rest and sleep are often prescribed. CURARE-like drugs are used to relieve pain by relaxing muscle spasms. X-RAY treatments help some patients, especially those who have back pains and have developed a poker-stiff spine. These patients benefit by sleeping on beds with hard mattresses.

There is no specific diet for the cure of arthritis. A good general diet, with adequate quantities of protein, carbohydrates, fat, vitamins, and minerals, should be taken to insure adequate nutrition.

Rest is indicated when the disease is active and pain severe. However, when these difficulties subside, motion of the joints, though not beyond the fatigue point, is in order. Guided physical therapy, including both active and passive movements, can be very helpful to the arthritic, both physically and psychologically. Casts, braces, and footrests may make patients more comfortable.

Application of heat is a time-honored treatment for painful joints. This may be given in many ways—with hot-water bottles, hot baths, hot wet packs, infra-red lamps, and heat cradles.

Orthopedic surgery may play an important role in treating rheumatoid arthritis. The orthopedist may prescribe many methods of keeping the patient with the active disease more comfortable and free from contractures and deformities. After the disease has "burned itself out," the orthopedic surgeon can operate to correct deformities and restore greater usefulness.

What is degenerative arthritis? This is a chronic joint disease of older people, rarely occurring before the age of 40. It is the result of the stress of everyday use and the normal aging of joint tissue. Weight-bearing, minor injuries, and anything else that adds to "wear and tear" on the joints contribute to this disease. Overweight and long hours of standing or physical labor may be factors. Changes inside the joint can often be revealed by X-ray examinations. These show deposits of calcium, overgrowth of the ends of the bones, worn-down and out-of-shape bone ends, and sometimes, in the joint capsule, broken-off loose bodies called "joint mice." Other names for degenerative arthritis, reflecting these changes, are *osteoarthritis* and *hypertrophic arthritis*.

Probably 80% of all people who reach their 50th birthday have some degenerative changes in their joints; but only 5 to 10% have any trouble from them. With one exception—fingers—the joints most commonly involved are the weight-bearing ones: knees, ankles, hips, and spinal vertebrae. The early symptoms are usually mild stiffness and aching in or around the affected joint. This is relieved by using the joint.

Peculiar to women, an early sign of the disease is a knobby swelling of the joints at the tips of the fingers, a condition called *Heberden's nodes*. This is annoying but rarely painful.

What can be done for degenerative arthritis? Changes in the bone or cartilage cannot be reversed. But except for some hip involvements, this disease is neither crippling nor deforming, and symptoms can usually be relieved.

Excessive use of the involved joints can be damaging. They should not be exercised continually in the false belief that this prevents loss of motion in the joint. Weight reduction is important in overweight arthritics. Physical therapy can be valuable. All forms of heat are beneficial, especially hot wet packs. Gentle massage may relieve pain and reduce swelling. A firm mattress, bedboard, and regular bed rest often help patients with upper- or lower-back pain and stiffness.

SALICYLATES in sufficient dosage are the drugs usually given to relieve pain. Injections of hydrocortisone directly into the joint capsule also relieve pain and soreness. Surgery is rarely indicated. However, in some patients with severe hip involvements, a replacement of the worn-out ball-and-socket joint with a metal or plastic model (PROSTHESIS) may be worth trying.

Arthritis owing to infection and other factors: Some forms of arthritis are definitely associated with infections, notably the hemolytic streptococcal infection associated with RHEUMATIC FEVER; GONORRHEA, SYPHILIS, TUBERCULOSIS, and UNDULANT FEVER (brucellosis). As these infections have been brought under control with sulfas, antibiotics, and other drugs, the incidence of arthritis caused by them has declined.

There is one form of arthritis associated with the skin disease psoriasis; this demands treatment of the skin disease.

Women at the menopause are sometimes afflicted with a form of arthritis.

Anxiety and emotional distress can produce arthritic and rheumatic pains—and they usually make them worse. A definitely psychogenic form of arthritis is sometimes seen; it disappears when underlying psychological tensions and fears are cleared up. (See BACKACHE.)

Artificial Respiration—any means of restoring the breathing cycle when it has been lost, as in ASPHYXIA from drowning or bulbar POLIO, or as a result of poisoning, electrical shock, or other disease or accident. When indicated, it should be pursued consistently—for hours if necessary—12 to 15 times a minute. It can be done by machine—resuscitator or pulmotor—or by hand. See right for description of Schafer "prone-pressure" method. In this method the operator sits astride the back of the person being resuscitated, who is face down. (See illustrations on pages 28 and 29.)

Another method of artificial respiration, now recommended by several official bodies, is the Holger-Nielsen "back-pressure-arm-lift" method. In this procedure, the operator takes a position kneeling above the head of the patient, who is lying face down. He compresses the lungs by leaning forward and pressing down with the palms of his hands on the patient's back. As the operator rocks back to the erect kneeling position, he grasps the patient's arms just above the elbows and draws the arms toward him; finally he releases the arms and returns them folded back again to the ground. This cycle of operations is repeated steadily 12 to 15 times a minute until the patient breathes again or is pronounced dead by a physician.

Artificial respiration for amateurs (Schafer method):

1. Lay the victim face down, the head turned slightly to the side.

2. Pull the tongue forward. See that the mouth is not clogged. Clear it out with your finger if necessary.

3. Cover the victim with a coat or blanket. At any rate, keep him warm.

4. Straddle the patient; your buttocks against his.

5. Put your hands, fingers *(Continued on page 30)*

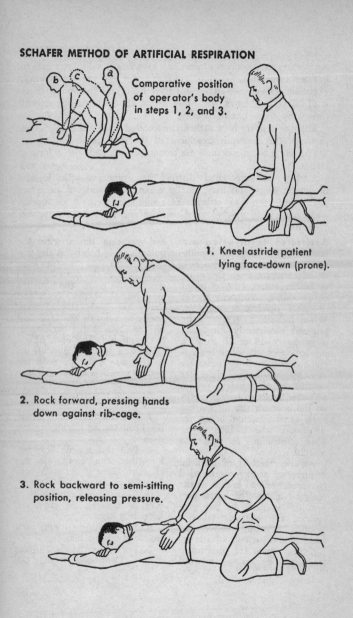

SCHAFER METHOD OF ARTIFICIAL RESPIRATION

Comparative position of operator's body in steps 1, 2, and 3.

1. Kneel astride patient lying face-down (prone).

2. Rock forward, pressing hands down against rib-cage.

3. Rock backward to semi-sitting position, releasing pressure.

HOLGER-NIELSEN METHOD OF ARTIFICIAL RESPIRATION

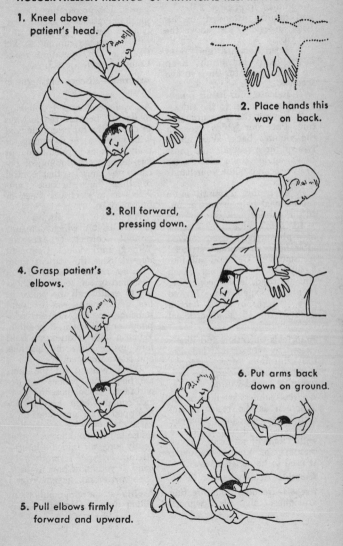

1. Kneel above patient's head.

2. Place hands this way on back.

3. Roll forward, pressing down.

4. Grasp patient's elbows.

5. Pull elbows firmly forward and upward.

6. Put arms back down on ground.

(Continued from page 27)
and thumbs extended, on his back and sides, just above the last rib.

6. Lean forward and press down gently but firmly. Keep up the pressure for three to five seconds.

7. Release your hands *quickly*. Slide them off to the sides.

8. Repeat the pressure gesture. Put your hands back on the victim's back. Wait about two or three seconds and press down again; then, after three to five seconds, slide your hands off again.

9. Keep this up until more professional help arrives or until the patient revives.

10. *Don't give up*. Victims of asphyxia have been revived after *hours* of manual artificial resuscitation. Get yourself into a rhythm of breathing. When you are tired, let someone else, if present, spell you. Try to give the asphyxiated victim from 12 to 15 good artificial breaths a minute.

Ascariasis—infection and illness caused by WORMS that lodge in the intestine; for example, *Ascaris lumbricoides*, the eel-worm or round-worm.

Ascites—painless swelling of the abdomen as the result of accumulation of fluid therein. Ascites is frequently associated with HEART FAILURE, LIVER TROUBLE or KIDNEY TROUBLE. It used to be called DROPSY.

Ascorbic Acid—VITAMIN C.

Asepsis—freedom from infecting MICROBES; that is, without germs. The preparation for surgical operations is *aseptic*, excluding germs as far as possible rather than attempting to kill them in the operating room. Compare with ANTISEPTIC.

Aspermia—absence of sperm in SEMEN.

Asphyxia—suffocation, "choking to death," because the airways to and in the lungs are clogged with water, as in drowning; or body fluids, as in pneumonia; or gas, as in gas poisoning; or because the muscles that control breathing have become paralyzed, as in electrical shock or bulbar polio.

Asphyxia is always an EMERGENCY which demands prompt, correct treatment. Wrong and violent treatment may damage the patient more than no treatment at all. If you ever find or see someone choking to death, call the police or fire department; run or send someone to the nearest telephone or policeman, if possible. When a baby is CHOKING, hold him upside down by his legs and shake him gently.

While waiting for the first-aid help from police, fire department, ambulance, or first-aid squad—which are usually equipped with any one of a variety of effective mechanical resuscitators (pulmotors) that gently force air into the lungs—attempt *artificial respiration* by hand, if you know how to do it. (See ARTIFICIAL RESPIRATION.)

Aspirin—still a remarkable pain-killing drug, safely and widely used for the relief of headache, rheumatic aches and pains,—for which, incidentally, there are few, if any, better drugs—,the discomfort of head colds, and the reduction of FEVER. It is one of the safest and most widely used of common drugs. The usual dose is 5 grains (the ordinary size aspirin tablet) or 10 grains (2 tablets), repeated every two to four hours as needed. More than 2 tablets at a time will do no extra good.

In its chemical composition aspirin is related to the wintergreen family of drugs and herbs; it is the king of the lot. Do not pay needlessly high prices for aspirin compounded with a few other drugs under some fancy name. The correct chemical name for aspirin is *acetylsalicylic acid*. It is a *salicylate*.

Cautions about aspirin: Some people are decidedly allergic to this drug and react very violently even to traces of it. Don't take aspirin tablets if you have never taken them before and don't know whether or not you may be sensitive to this drug.

Excessive doses of aspirin may cause aspirin poisoning and stomach irritation. While it is safe enough to take aspirin, without a doctor's prescription, for occasional aches and pains, don't go on masking pains by continuing to dose yourself with aspirin or any other pain-killer. Visit a doctor and find out what is really wrong. If mild headache, joint aches or fever persist for more than 12 to 24

hours, especially after you have taken about half a dozen aspirin tablets at intervals, see a doctor.

Children's aspirin comes in 1¼ grain tablets. Do not give children aspirin without first consulting a doctor. *Candy-flavored children's aspirin can be dangerous.* If not kept out of reach, some children will mistake it for candy and eat enough to make themselves deathly sick. Few actually die of aspirin poisoning; but this is a harrowing experience which no wise parent would want to go through—especially if it were the result of his own carelessness.

Asthenia—weakness, exhaustion, fatigue. *Neurocirculatory asthenia* is a psychosomatic illness ("soldier's heart"). See MENTAL ILLNESS.

Asthma—wheezing breathing. See ALLERGY.

Astigmatism—a common EYE TROUBLE. Vision is distorted because of irregularities in the shape of the cornea or crystalline lens of the EYE. See EYE TROUBLE.

Atabrine—a QUININE substitute; a drug for MALARIA.

Ataraxic—new name for new class of so-called "tranquilizing" drugs. They calm excitement. Ataraxics should not be taken without prescription and without medical supervision. Their repeated use may often mask more serious underlying conditions for which proper treatment, if delayed, will be more difficult and expensive.

Atelectasis—collapse of the LUNG; failure of the lungs to expand completely at birth.

Atherosclerosis—a form of HARDENING OF THE ARTERIES in which the inner lining (intima) is chiefly involved as a result of fat deposits in it. This condition is the forerunner of several kinds of HEART DISEASE, which see.

Athlete's Foot—advertising copywriter's name for ringworm of the feet, or *dermatophytosis*, meaning a FUNGUS infection on the skin. See FOOT TROUBLE for cause and treatment.

ATOMIC ENERGY

Atomic energy is produced when atoms break up. Among other things that happen under these circumstances is that *gamma rays* are emitted from the site of the breakup. Gamma rays are electromagnetic waves, much like X RAYS, but of shorter wave length. Very powerful gamma rays and X rays can penetrate several feet of lead. When atomic energy is kept under control, it is readily possible to protect against its hazards. When it is uncontrolled and reaches critically high levels, it may produce acute or delayed RADIATION SICKNESS, which see.

Human beings on the planet Earth are being constantly bombarded by atomic energy from "natural sources," such as cosmic rays and naturally occurring radium and other radioactive substances in the Earth's crust. It is estimated that this amounts to about 3 ROENTGENS (the standard measure of radiation) in 30 years.

Radiation hazards. In 1956 the National Academy of Sciences published a study on atomic radiation hazards. The study committees sought, among other things, to decide what amount of radiation the male and female SEX ORGANS could safely take without undue risk of producing GENE changes that might be harmful to future generations. They arrived at the tentative conclusion that exposure to man-made radiation, such as diagnostic and therapeutic X rays, should not exceed 10 roentgens during the first 30 years of life, counting from the date of CONCEPTION.

They said, however: "This is a reasonable quota [for a population], not a harmless one. It should most emphatically *not* be assumed that any exposure less than ten roentgens is, so to speak, all right. The idea is to stay as far under the quota as possible. As geneticists we say, 'Keep the dose as low as you can.'"

The National Academy of Sciences report also estimated that the amount of man-made radiation resulting from A-bomb and H-bomb tests continued indefinitely at the 1950-55 rate would add ⅒ a roentgen in 30 years of exposure to the other radiation sources to which human beings are exposed.

The report further recommended that every effort should be made "to reduce the radiation exposure from X rays to the lowest limit consistent with medical necessity."

"Proper safeguards always [should] be taken to minimize the radiation dose to the reproductive cells," the report emphasized.

In 1958 the United Nations Scientific Committee on Effects of Atomic Radiation issued a similar report.

Use of X rays necessary. "Medical necessity" requires that X rays be used to save life and limb and protect against ravages of disease. In fact, over 50 million diagnostic X-ray films or fluoroscopic examinations for medical purposes are now made annually in the United States. Dentists take twice as many—over 100 million X-ray pictures of teeth a year. The important thing is that all X-raying be done with the highest possible safety standards and that as little radiation as possible reach sex organs.

Needless, and to be deplored, is the use of atomic energy by shoe clerks in stores that employ fluoroscopes for fitting shoes.

Atony—lack of "tone" or strength; usually refers to smooth MUSCLE tissues of bladder, uterus, and bowels.

Atrophy—wasting away of flesh, tissue, cell or organ. A "withered arm" represents an atrophy of muscles. The causes of atrophy are numerous; it may be a normal or abnormal body process. Normally, for example, tonsils atrophy with increasing age.

Atropine—a drug obtained from the *belladonna* plant, or made synthetically. It paralyzes NERVE endings in the parasympathetic nervous system. Hence it has uses to widen the pupils of the eye (an "eye drop" or mydriatic), to relax spasms in the bronchi of the lungs, to quicken the heart beat, to suppress acid secretions of the stomach and to induce bowel movements *(peristalsis)*.

Audiometer—an electronic machine for measuring with considerable accuracy the amount and acuteness of hearing a person has in one or both EARS. The machine often seems to "squeak and squeal" when it is being used for testing hearing; it is supposed to sound that way.

Aura—the warning sensation that an attack of something is coming on; often experienced by patients with repeated attacks of *migraine, epilepsy* and *asthma*. It is the warning signal, the calm before the storm, during which effective preventive treatment should be sought and tried. The premonitory sensations may be dreams (intellectual aura), feelings of prickling of the skin, sinking feeling in the pit of the stomach, chest pains, apparent lightning flashes before the eyes, and many other indefinable subjective sensations.

Aureomycin—a gold-colored ANTIBIOTIC.

Auricle—usually an upper chamber of the HEART, atrium; sometimes means the outer EAR. (See illustrations for HEART.)

Auricular Fibrillation—a form of HEART DISEASE in which the upper chambers of the heart are beating very fast (flutter) and out of time. Proper medication can usually arrest this flutter promptly.

Auscultation means listening for body sounds that indicate health or disease; notably, heart sounds, lung sounds and the like. When the physician applies his STETHOSCOPE to the skin of the body, he is listening for sounds that will help him make a correct DIAGNOSIS.

Autoclave—an apparatus found in doctor's offices and hospitals for sterilizing instruments, dressings and so forth. It effectively destroys MICROBES by applying steam (heat) under pressure. See ASEPSIS.

Autoeroticism—MASTURBATION.

Autogenous—self-made. The term is usually applied to *autogenous vaccines* which are made from MICROBES taken from the patient himself. Such vaccines often, but not invariably, bring relief from the debilitating effects of chronic, low-grade infections, expressed as repeated colds, sinusitis and other upper respiratory infections.

Autointoxication — self-poisoning. UREMIA may represent a form of autointoxication, but CONSTIPATION NEVER!

Autonomic—self-governing, as the *autonomic nervous system*. See NERVES.

Autopsy—postmortem, necropsy; examination of a body after death to determine, among other things, the exact cause of death. Scientific medicine requires for its progress that autopsies be frequently performed following death, especially from unexplained or suspicious causes (in which case they are usually required by law to rule out any suspicion of foul play).

When a patient dies in a hospital, permission of the next of kin is usually asked, and generally granted, for the performance of an autopsy. If religious scruples possibly permit, the next of kin should always grant permission for an autopsy if it is requested. This request is sometimes made through the funeral director (mortician).

The body is not mutilated by a properly performed autopsy and has the same appearance in a coffin as a non-autopsied body. It is in the highest spirit of science, humanity and religion for a grieving relative nevertheless to permit an autopsy to be made on the deceased. This is one of the most direct gifts that the dead can still make to the living. Autopsies are performed upon almost all famous people after death.

Many people will their bodies (and its various parts, such as eyes to "eye banks") for the sake of those who are still alive. When the dust returns to the dust that made it, not only does the spirit live on —but part of the body also lives on for immediate human good.

Avitaminosis—mild or severe disease state caused by lack of VITAMINS, which see.

Axilla—armpit.

B

Any word printed in SMALL CAPITALS *can be looked up under its own alphabetical listing for further information.*

Baby—see INFANT.

Bacillus—a germ. Specifically, a rod-shaped BACTERIUM. There are a great many different kinds of bacilli; for example there is the tubercle bacillus, which is the cause of tuberculosis.

Bacitracin—an ANTIBIOTIC derived from BACTERIA (specifically, *Bacillus subtilis*) which had infected a wound in a man named Tracy.

BACKACHE

Backache, pain in the back, is one of the commonest complaints doctors have to deal with, but an accurate diagnosis of what causes the backache is one of the most difficult in medicine.

Some say that at least half the cases are wholly or partly psychological in origin. The pain is real enough, but it is primarily caused by deep-seated mental stress or hidden emotional conflict projected on the back. Such backaches are described as *functional, psychosomatic,* or *psychogenic.* Treatment requires some correction of the underlying psychic factor.

Poor POSTURE, sometimes aggravated by standing or sitting in a peculiar position all day at work, is one of the commonest causes of backache and one of the easiest to correct. Improper footwear, especially too high heels, may be partly responsible. *Straining* the back by sudden twisting, jerking, lifting too heavy weights, or lifting the wrong way may also bring on backache. Poor *sleeping habits* and a hollow, lumpy, slanting, *too soft mattress* may also be factors.

Organic diseases that cause backache are many. Among the indirect causes are KIDNEY TROUBLE (middle-back pain), FEMALE TROUBLES (low-back pain), GALLSTONES, and STOMACH TROUBLE (high-back pain). Infectious diseases, such as pneumonia, influenza, malaria, and smallpox, are almost always accompanied by back pain.

RHEUMATISM and ARTHRITIS, which see, are the most frequent direct organic causes of backache. Others include *pulled ligaments* or muscles, especially in the region of the SACROILIAC joints, CURVATURE OF THE SPINE, *slipped* or *ruptured* DISKS (the little cushions that lie between the vertebrae), and BONE DISEASES.

Since the kinds and causes of backache are so numerous, there are no simple home remedies (except application of heat for immediate relief of *some kinds* of back pain). The back sufferer should put himself under the care of a competent physician and follow his advice. Depending on the diagnosis, effective treatment may range anywhere from changing shoes or mattress and losing weight to surgical operations and specially prescribed corsets, belts, or braces.

Prevention of backache in its most common forms can be partly achieved by developing good posture, good sleeping habits, and a good level of general health; by avoiding overweight, strain, and accident (learn how to lift properly!); by dodging communicable diseases or getting prompt treatment for them; and by cultivating a high level of mental health.

Bacteremia—bacteria in the blood stream.

Bacteria—GERMS; MICROBES, which see. There are many different kinds of bacteria, and they are classified in many ways. Not all are disease-producing (pathogenic); some, indeed, such as those that normally inhabit the lower intestinal tract, are almost essential. Nevertheless, the discovery that bacteria cause disease was one of the greatest of all advances in medical science. Chief credit for the germ theory of disease goes to the French chemist, Louis Pasteur, and the German country doctor, Robert Koch. Their lifesaving work was done in the last third of the 19th century.

Bacteria are tiny one-celled plants, without green coloring

matter (chlorophyll), that can be seen only under a compound microscope that magnifies them from 600 to 1200 times. Bacteria come in many different sizes but in three principal shapes: (1) *rod-* or *pencil-*shaped, the bacilli, which produce diseases like tuberculosis and leprosy; (2) *spherical* or *dot-*shaped, the cocci; and (3) *spiral* or *comma-*shaped, such as the corkscrew *spirochete* of syphilis or the cholera vibrio.

The cocci come in pairs *(diplococci)*, strings or chains *(streptococci)*, or clusters, like grapes *(staphylococci)*. Typical diplococci are the gonococcus, cause of gonorrhea, and the pneumococcus, cause of pneumonia. Streptococci are responsible for "strep" infections, such as the sore throat that is often a forerunner of rheumatic fever. Staphylococci are often present in boils.

Bactericide—anything that kills bacteria; an antiseptic. Some chemicals or circumstances, however, simply stop the growth and reproduction of bacteria; they are called *bacteriostatics*.

Bacteriology—the science that deals with bacteria. However, since far more tiny, microscopically visible *micro-organisms* than those classed as bacteria are now known to affect the welfare and diseases of humans and animals, the name of this science has been expanded to *microbiology*.

Bacteriophage—or "phage," a very tiny, ultramicroscopic, agent that attacks and kills BACTERIA. It is usually a bacterial virus, too small to be seen under an ordinary microscope, that invades the bacterial cell; but it may be an enzyme. The bacterial virus is a parasite on the host cell.

Bad Blood—SYPHILIS.

BAL—abbreviation for *B*ritish *A*nti-*L*ewisite, a chemical substance developed during World War II as an antidote against arsenical war gases. Injected into the muscle, it is very valuable in treating many kinds of poisoning with arsenic and heavy metals.

Balanitis—inflammation of head of the penis, usually associated with a tight foreskin. See SEX ORGANS, MALE.

Baldness—loss or absence of HAIR *(alopecia)*. There is no scientifically demonstrated cure for the common, garden variety of baldness that afflicts a certain number of men and women. Baldness is usually an inherited characteristic. No hair tonic or "treatments" will restore hair in the man whose heredity has destined him for baldness, usually of a particular pattern. Hair cells are not "starved" by lack of circulation in the scalp. When heavy or complete loss of hair follows an acute, debilitating disease, it usually grows back. Baldness may also be associated with some chronic illnesses; for example, AVITA-

MINOSIS and hypothyroidism (see ENDOCRINES).

Bandages—pieces of cloth applied to different parts of the body to cover wounds, burns, or other injuries, or to support an injured member (e.g., arm sling). Practically speaking, there are two chief kinds of bandages: (1) rolled, sterile gauze bandages of varying widths (½ to 4"), and (2) triangular bandages, usually of heavier material, which can be ingeniously folded and tied to be applied to almost any body part.

For application of such bandages to the head, eye, hand, foot, chest, back, elbow, knee, hip, and fingers, see the simple directional illustrations on page 39.

Bandages should be tied firmly but not too tightly—they should not impair blood circulation. Practice makes perfect in learning to apply them. Most bandages are not applied directly to the wound or injury but are used to hold in place sterile gauze pads or compresses (folded layers of gauze). Very often it is more convenient to hold the sterile gauze pad in place with adhesive tape strips.

Banti's Disease—enlarged SPLEEN, with anemia, low white-blood-cell count, followed by hardening (cirrhosis) of the liver, jaundice, and accumulation of fluids in the abdomen (ASCITES).

Barbiturates—NARCOTIC drugs; chemical compounds of many varieties and names (such as phenobarbital) that are commonly used as *sleeping pills*. Under medical supervision, they are safe to use even over comparatively long periods. Self-medication with barbiturates is dangerous, for it is possible to become addicted to them.

Chronic barbiturate poisoning produces dullness of memory, speech difficulties, hallucinations, and possibly blood damage. Large doses of barbiturates, commonly described as *"an overdose of sleeping pills,"* may have even more damaging effects and end in death. All sensations are dulled, the sleep produced verges into stupor, the skin becomes cold and clammy, breathing becomes shallow, circulation weak.

A person poisoned by sleeping pills should be promptly taken to a hospital, where he will get brain stimulants, such as caffeine and amphetamine, oxygen, and other supportive treatment.

Barbiturates can be treacherous. The person addicted to them may take larger and larger doses while becoming stupefied and not realizing what he is doing.

Barium—a chemical element, one of the alkaline earths. *Barium sulfate* is a tasteless white powder that has a particular use in medical diagnosis because it is impervious to the passage of X rays. When a doctor wants to get an X-ray pic-

BANDAGES

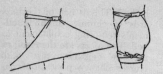

1. Bandage for the hip.

2. Bandage for the elbow or knee.

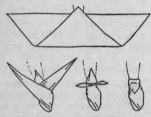

3. Bandage for the hand or foot.

4. Bandage for the fingers.

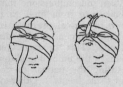

5. Bandage for the eye.

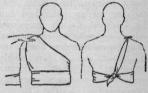

6. Bandage for the chest or back.

7. Bandage for the head.

ture of the stomach and other parts of the gastrointestinal canal, he gives the patient barium sulfate dissolved in milk (sometimes a chocolate milk shake). The course of this barium meal passing through the digestive tract shows up plainly on the X-ray pictures.

Bartholinitis—inflammation of BARTHOLIN'S GLANDS.

Bartholin's Glands—two small lubricating glands at the vestibule of the vagina. See SEX ORGANS, FEMALE.

Basal Metabolism—the amount of energy required by the body at rest. It represents the minimum amount of energy that the body must expend to keep up all its normal functions, such as digestion of food, circulation of the blood, and maintenance of body temperature. Basal metabolism of an individual can be fairly accurately measured with a suitable apparatus, called a calorimeter. The basal-metabolic rate is surprisingly constant in adults. Certain endocrine disorders, notably overactivity of the thyroid gland, can send it way up. Basal metabolism is higher in children than adults, lower in older people.

BCG—abbreviation for a widely used antituberculosis vaccine orginally prepared from the Bacillus Calmette-Guérin.

Bedbugs—see INSECTS.

Bedsore—an ulcer of the skin resulting from prolonged stay in bed. This is one of the hazards of chronic, disabling ailments requiring confinement to bed. The ulcers are the result of pressure against the skin. Nurses change position of patients in bed partly to prevent bedsores.

Belladonna—literally, "beautiful lady," a medicinal extract of the leaves and root of the plant called "deadly nightshade." The name derives from the fact that a few drops of belladonna in the eyes cause the pupils to dilate. The active principle in belladonna is the drug *atropine*.

Bends—an occupational disease of "sand hogs," deep-sea divers, and anyone else who works in an atmosphere of compressed air. Other names for it are caisson disease, diver's paralysis, and compressed-air illness. When decompression, that is, the return from high air pressure to normal pressure, is too rapid, nitrogen bubbles form in tissues. This produces terrific pain in the limbs and abdomen, causing the patient to double up ("the bends"). Other symptoms are "staggers" (vertigo), "chokes" (asphyxia), itch, and unconsciousness.

Benign—harmless, not malignant. Usually refers to tumors for which the outlook for recovery is favorable.

Benzedrine—a brand name for AMPHETAMINE. Benzedrine sulfate is the active ingredient in many so-called "pep pills."

Benzoin—a balsam tree resin.

The compound tincture (which includes 10% benzoin) is often given by steam inhalation for upper respiratory infections.

Benzyl Benzoate—a soapy solution for external application to the skin to drive off ITCH-mites and body-LICE. Very effective.

Beriberi—a deficiency disease due to lack of vitamin B_1 (thiamine) and characterized by inflammatory changes in the nerves (polyneuritis). The disease is common in the Far East among populations that subsist on polished white rice. A similar condition is noted among chronic alcoholics. Severe beriberi can be a completely exhausting illness. Its symptoms include weakness, paralysis, staggering gait, muscular wasting, nerve pains, anemia, and edema.

Biceps—any two-headed muscle, but usually the strong muscle of the upper arm which, when flexed, is taken as an index of muscular strength. (See illustrations for JOINTS; MUSCLES.)

Bile—a complex fluid manufactured in the liver, stored and concentrated in the gall bladder, and poured into the intestines, where it acts principally as a fat solvent in the normal process of digestion. Brown to yellow in color, it is exceedingly bitter to taste. Bile backing up in the blood stream produces the condition called JAUNDICE. Bile salts from animal sources (for example, ox bile) are sometimes used to stimulate a sluggish liver.

Biliousness—a condition of general discomfort, popularly attributed to an excess of bile in the system. The bile probably has very little to do with the discomfort. The term is a hangover from the days when a man's character was supposed to be determined by the composition of his primary body fluids, such as bile and blood. (See LIVER TROUBLE.)

Bilirubin—a fraction of hemoglobin; a red pigment found in bile, gallstones, and jaundiced skin. Its presence in the urine usually indicates liver disease.

Biologicals—a class of drugs made from living organisms and their by-products. Typical examples are polio *vaccine*, made from live polio virus killed in the process of manufacture; *insulin* for diabetes, derived from the pancreas of meat animals; diphtheria *antitoxin*, obtained by injecting animals (usually horses) with diphtheria toxin; and *blood plasma*, obtained by removing blood cells from human blood.

In contrast to biologicals are drugs manufactured as sheer chemical compounds; for example, sulfa drugs, barbiturates. See CHEMOTHERAPY.

Biopsy—careful removal of small bits of living tissue from the body for further study and examination, usually under the microscope. Biopsy is an important technique of diagnosis in suspected cancer and in some blood diseases (where a bit of bone marrow is punched out of the breastbone).

Birth—see CHILDBIRTH.

Birth Injury—some serious damage to the infant in the process of being born. Limbs may be broken or damaged, but more important is the brain damage that may occur. Brain injury at birth may produce such conditions as CEREBRAL PALSY, mental defectiveness, and possibly EPILEPSY. Paralysis of the arm (Erb's palsy) is the result of birth injury.

Birthmarks—parts of the SKIN that fail to develop normally during life before birth. They are often bizarre in shape and sometimes contain an excess of blood vessels. There is no truth whatsoever in the ancient superstition that an infant can be birthmarked as the result of a weird or shocking experience suffered by its mother during pregnancy.

Many birthmarks, but not all, can be removed by competent physicians. Practically all birthmarks can be concealed by harmless cosmetics.

Blackheads—dried and discolored plugs of skin oil (sebum) lodged in the pores, usually on the nose and other parts of the face. Blackheads, along with pimples, are a particular affliction of adolescence, being a part of the unpleasant picture of ACNE. They seem to come along with the increased activity of the endocrine glands at puberty. Blackheads should not be carelessly fingered and squeezed. After careful washing of the face with hot water and soap, the core of the blackhead may be gently expressed by pressing on the skin *away from* rather than toward the blackhead. See SEBORRHEA.

Bladder—the part of the URINARY SYSTEM that stores and releases URINE. (See illustrations for SEX ORGANS, MALE and FEMALE.)

Bladder Trouble is usually indicated by difficulties or abnormalities in passing URINE—especially frequency, urgency, and pain. Infection and inflammation of the bladder (cystitis) is generally associated with infection in other parts of the URINARY SYSTEM. It may come from the kidneys or from the outside, by way of the urethra. Long-continued bladder infections are almost invariably associated with obstruction somewhere along the line to urine flow. This urinary stasis may be the result of pregnancy, an enlarged prostate, a narrowed ureter, kidney stones, malformations of the kidney, or other kinds of KIDNEY TROUBLE. Once the blockage is corrected, which may require surgery, the bladder infection can usually be cleared up quickly with antibiotics.

Sometimes the bladder becomes paralyzed as a result of injury to or disease of the spinal cord. The nerve pathways that carry the impulses making bladder control possible are thus interrupted. Constant dribbling of urine (incontinence) is the unpleasant consequence.

Blastomycosis—a systemic FUNGUS infection.

Bleb—a blister of the skin.

Bleeder's Disease—*hemophilia;* a peculiar hereditary disease affecting males only but transmitted to them through their mothers as a sex-linked characteristic. The bleeder's blood lacks elements necessary for normal clotting; hence slight cuts or even a tooth extraction may result in excessive blood loss. Several royal families have been subject to hemophilia for many generations.

Bleeding—hemorrhage; abnormal flow of BLOOD from any part of the body. (Menstrual bleeding, however, is normal although abnormal bleeding from the vagina can occur. See MENSTRUATION and FEMALE TROUBLES.)

Bleeding is obviously caused by cuts and wounds. Control of bleeding is an important part of operative surgery.

Bleeding from any body opening—mouth, lungs, nipples, anus, ears, nose—is a danger signal and demands prompt medical investigation. External and internal bleeding frequently occur as the result of disease, which must be properly diagnosed and treated to correct the source of the bleeding.

First aid for external bleeding: Most bleeding can be stopped by simple direct pressure continued on the bleeding area until the blood stops. This pressure is preferably applied by a sterile gauze bandage (pressure bandage), padded as thickly as necessary to soak up the blood. In an emergency pressure may be exerted directly with the fingers or the whole hand. Elevating the bleeding part also helps. An antiseptic, such as iodine, may be applied to the area after bleeding stops.

When spurts of bright red blood indicate that a major artery has been severed, and control of bleeding is difficult, it may be necessary to apply a *tourniquet* to a limb. This is a piece of cloth or tubing tied together and twisted with a stick just tightly enough to stop the bleeding. The tourniquet *must be released* every 20 minutes or gangrene will result.

Blindness may be total or partial, temporary or permanent. There are about 260,000 "legally" or "industrially" blind persons in the United States. A legally blind person is one so blind as to be unable to perform any work for which eyesight is essential. The principal causes of blindness are infectious and degenerative diseases of the eye and accidents to the eyes. (See EYE TROUBLES.) Great strides have been made in preventing blindness, but perhaps half the cases are still preventable. The National Society for the Prevention of Blindness (1790 Broadway, New York, N.Y.), a voluntary health agency founded in 1908, has done yeoman service in encouraging the elimination of once-common causes of blindness—for example, Fourth of July fireworks accidents and "babies' sore eyes" (gonorrheal infection). Eye safety in industry is constantly stressed.

Blisters—limited collections of fluid under the skin. They may arise from disease, such as fever blisters of the lips; from burns; from the deliberate application of counterirritants, like mustard plaster and Spanish fly, to the skin; from contact with poison ivy or irritating chemicals; and from pressure on and chafing of the skin, very frequently the skin of the feet.

A water blister involves only the upper layers of the skin and is filled with lymph fluid. In a blood blister the lower layers of the skin are broken, and blood from the capillaries mixes with the lymph.

Painful blisters are relieved by puncturing them with a sterile needle, passed through a flame. The skin should first be treated with iodine or alcohol and the puncture made at the edge of the blister. Broken, or unbroken, it is best to cover the pressure blister with an adhesive bandage.

The unbroken skin over a blister is its best protection from infection. Hence it is best to leave a blister alone. If it breaks, the loose skin should be cut off with a manicure scissors sterilized by boiling for ten minutes. If the blistered area becomes red and inflamed, see a doctor.

Blood—the red fluid that circulates through the body by way of the blood vessels. It is a very complex substance, and more is constantly being learned about it. It is the flowing part of the circulatory system, which may be called the transportation system of the body.

The adult human body contains between 5 and 6 quarts of blood, weighing about 7 to 8 pounds and accounting for about 5% of the body weight. If about one-third of the blood is lost, death usually occurs (unless the blood is replaced). A pint of blood, however, can be readily spared at proper intervals. Blood in the arteries is bright red in color; blood in the veins is much darker, sometimes a brownish red.

Blood consists of many elements, liquid and solid. These include red and white BLOOD CELLS (which see), blood *platelets*, and blood *plasma*. The plasma is the liquid part of the blood, something over 90% water. In it are dissolved essential elements that have to be carried from one place to another. These include, for example, organic constituents, such as blood sugar (glucose) and urea; inorganic elements, such as sodium and calcium; gases, such as oxygen and carbon dioxide; and secretions from the endocrine glands (hormones), antibodies, enzymes, and plasma proteins.

The plasma proteins make up about 7 to 8% of the plasma. By electrical methods developed during and after World War II, these proteins can be broken down into various fractions. Best known is the fraction called *gamma globulin,* which contains *antibodies* against several diseases, notably measles and polio.

Among the many specific functions of the blood are the following: It transfers oxygen and carbon dioxide between the lungs and the body cells. It carries from the digestive system the nutriments that cells need and gets rid of their waste products via the kidneys and other organs of excretion. It conveys hormones. It helps regulate body temperature. It provides substances that fight off infection.

Blood Bank—a depository for human blood to be used in blood transfusions. Most large hospitals have a blood bank, in which blood of all types is stored, under refrigeration, for immediate use. Any patient who withdraws blood must see that an equal amount is deposited. Friends or relatives must give blood for him or he may be charged for blood taken from a paid donor. Community blood banks have been established in some localities.

Blood Cells are of three kinds:

red blood cells (erythrocytes), white blood cells (leukocytes and lymphocytes), and blood platelets.

Red blood cells are approximately round, disk-shaped with high edges. They measure approximately 1/3,000 of an inch in diameter. The healthy male has about 5 million red blood cells per cubic millimeter of blood. A healthy woman has about 10% fewer.

Hemoglobin is the key element in the red blood cell. It is a complex protein that requires *iron* for its formation. Oxygen picked up in the lungs during the circulation of the blood combines loosely with hemoglobin. Then, in every part of the body where it is needed for cell metabolism, oxygen is released by the hemoglobin, which picks up carbon dioxide on the return journey to the heart and lungs.

Red blood cells are destroyed and replaced at a rate of about 1% a day. These cells are formed in the bone marrow, particularly in the spine and hip bones, the ribs and breastbone. They are destroyed largely in the *spleen.*

White blood cells are about 1½ to 2 times as large as red blood cells, which outnumber them by at least 500 to 1. The average number of white blood cells in the healthy adult is around 7,000 per cubic millimeter. In the presence of infection this number may go as high as 40,000. A great increase in the white blood count is almost always a sign of infection.

White blood cells play the role of scavenger. Most of them engulf and devour bacteria and other particles of foreign matter in the blood stream. Hence they prevent and fight infection and aid in wound repair. Pus is made up largely of dead white blood cells.

The names of various different kinds of white blood cells are long and complicated: for example, polymorphonuclear eosinophil. Because they devour bacteria, they are also called phagocytes. White blood cells are made in the bone marrow, the lymph nodes, and other places in the body.

Blood platelets are about 1/3 as large as red blood cells. They are concerned with BLOOD CLOTTING, which see.

Blood Clotting—the body's defense against bleeding. It is an exceedingly complicated biochemical process. Among the substances that must be present at the site of the clot are *thrombin,* derived from blood platelets; *fibrinogen,* formed largely in the liver; and *calcium,* usually present in the blood stream. The clot itself is *fibrin,* a network of crystals or needles in which red blood cells come to lodge.

Blood tends to clot not only when a blood vessel is cut open but also when the blood flow is slowed down by thickening of the arterial walls (atherosclerosis). Such clots may form an EMBOLUS or a THROMBUS with serious results. See HEART DISEASE.

Blood Count is an important facet of diagnosis, for blood changes often occur in disease. In the hospital or doctor's office a small sample of blood is taken by pricking the finger or ear lobe. A tiny, diluted sample is then dropped on a glass slide, diamond-ruled into very small squares. Under the microscope the red and white blood cells on each square can be counted. The percentages and proportions of the various different kinds of white blood cells per cubic millimeter of blood often have particular significance.

BLOOD DISEASES

There are a great many diseases popularly called blood diseases when, strictly speaking, they are not. In particular, *syphilis* is called a blood disease (or sometimes "bad blood"), when it is really a generalized infection with a specific spirochete. In *blood-poisoning (septicemia),* also a generalized infection, the tissues reached by the blood, rather than the blood itself, react to the results of bacterial invasion. Even the diseases affecting the formed elements of the blood (*anemia,* for example) are more properly considered as diseases of the blood-forming or blood-destroying organs.

Since blood reaches all parts of the body, it mirrors and reflects disease anywhere in the body and must, by its very nature, carry along in it some of the evidence and results of this disease process. A long series of words ending in "emia" nicely reflects this fact; for example, UREMIA (urea in the blood) is the result of kidney trouble; *glycemia* (sugar in the blood) arises from the digestive system; *bacteremia* means bacteria in the blood.

ANEMIA signifies a decrease in the number of circulating red blood cells. It may be due to blood loss (open or hidden bleeding) or increased blood destruction (in the spleen), to faulty nutrition (e.g. lack of iron in the diet), poisons that depress the activity of the bone marrow, or other causes. (See ANEMIA.)

Polycythemia means an increase in the number of circulating red blood cells or in the iron content of these cells. Sometimes this is a compensation for high altitudes or other conditions that decrease the normal oxygen supply. True polycythemia, however, is the result of abnormal production of red blood cells by the bone marrow. In this condition the blood often becomes heavier and stickier than normal, flows more slowly, clots too readily. The patient's face looks constantly flushed and slightly blue. Treatment includes irradiation of the bone marrow, bleeding, and the use of some drugs.

Leukemia, sometimes called cancer of the blood, is a disease, usually fatal, characterized by a great overgrowth of the tissues that form white blood cells. This overgrowth may occur in the lymph tissue or the bone marrow. The disease may progress slowly (chronic) or rapidly (acute). A great increase in the number of white blood cells is usually found, and there is also an increase in the undeveloped, immature forms of white blood cells. Some hopeful progress has been made in delaying the course of the disease with certain chemical substances. (See CANCER.)

Leukopenia means a decrease in the number of circulating white blood cells. Among its causes are chemical poisoning (agranulocytosis), sometimes from drugs; chronic tuberculosis; pernicious anemia; measles; and a variety of other infectious diseases.

Hemophilia is BLEEDER'S DISEASE, which see.

Purpura describes a variety of conditions in which spontaneous bleeding occurs beneath the skin, from mucous membranes, or into the joints. Small hemorrhages are called *petechiae*. Purpura occurs in many acute diseases, for example, scarlet fever and diphtheria; in scurvy (bleeding gums due to lack of vitamin C), anemia, and leukemia; and as the result of a decrease in the number of blood platelets.

Bone marrow, which makes blood, may be injured by heavy metal poisoning and some drugs, overdoses of X-ray, and tumors.

Blood Groups—blood types; classifications of blood according to certain clumping substances (agglutinins) in them. Everybody belongs to one blood group or another. There are many groupings, but the most important is the O, A, B, AB one. Next in practical importance is the RH FACTOR group.

The reason for blood grouping, or blood typing, lies in blood TRANSFUSION. If the donor's blood does not match the recipient's blood, serious and perhaps fatal reactions can occur. Specifically, the serum of an unmatched blood will cause the red blood cells of the other person to clump together (agglutinate). (Blood serum is blood plasma minus the clotting factor, fibrinogen.)

Before a blood transfusion is given, the blood of both recipient and donor must be typed and matched.

There are two principal clumping factors in human blood, now commonly designated as A and B. If a person has A factor in his red blood cells, he belongs to group A; B factor, group B; both factors, group AB; neither factor, group O. Since the red cells of group O blood are free from any agglutinating factors, group O blood can in an emergency be given to anyone. This is the most common blood group in the American population.

Blood Pressure—the force exerted by the blood beating against the artery walls. It is a rhythmic, variable pressure. It is highest at the instant when the left ventricle of the heart contracts, the moment when the heart is said to be in *systole.* It is lowest at the time the heart is at rest, or in *diastole.* Hence everyone has two measurable blood pressures, systolic and diastolic. The diastolic pressure is always lower than the systolic, but it is more significant, for it represents the lowest constant pressure on the arteries.

Blood pressure is measured by a blood-pressure apparatus, called a sphygmomanometer, which includes an inflatable cuff wound around the arm and a device for measuring the blood pressure in terms of the height in millimeters of a column of mercury. The average normal systolic blood pressure at the age of 20 is about 120; the diastolic, about 80. However, there is a wide range of normal pressures for different people, and the same person may have different pressures under different circumstances. Excitement, for example, shoots the pressure up. Blood pressure usually increases with age and increase in body weight.

Persistent HIGH BLOOD PRESSURE (which see), called hypertension, may have serious consequences. Low blood pressure, called hypotension, is normal for many people. With others it may result from malnutrition or extended bed rest and exhibit itself only in faintness or weakness. Following extreme blood loss and certain injuries producing SHOCK, blood pressure may fall to dangerously or fatally low levels.

Blood pressure depends on many factors, including the strength of the heartbeat, volume and thickness of the blood, elasticity of the arteries, and resistance to blood flow offered by the capillaries, the smallest blood vessels.

Blood Test—any laboratory test performed with a blood sample. Such tests are made to detect many different diseases—for example, typhoid fever, undulant fever, and syphilis. In popular understanding, however, a blood test means a test for SYPHILIS.

Such tests are required by most states before a marriage license can be issued. Actually, these tests are more properly called *serologic tests,* because only the blood serum is used. They are complicated laboratory tests, depending on the presence of antibodies in the blood serum.

Most of these blood tests are named after the men who worked them out. Best known is the Wassermann test; others include Kahn, Kline, Hinton, and Eagle flocculation tests. The outcome of these laboratory tests is usually reported as "negative," meaning no syphilis; "doubtful," in which case the test will have to be repeated; or "positive," indicating presence of the disease. A four-plus (4 +) reading merely means a completely positive laboratory reaction; it does not indicate the clinical severity of the syphilitic infection.

In the presence of certain other diseases, false positives sometimes occur. Hence all positive tests should be repeated. With the effective modern treatment now available, blood tests should be taken by anyone who fears he may have contracted syphilis.

The term "blood test" is also used to indicate BLOOD GROUP typings done in court cases of disputed paternity. Since blood type is an hereditary characteristic, blood-group studies can definitely rule out a specific man as the father of a particular child; but they cannot tell who the father is.

Blood Vessels—tubes of varying sizes that carry blood throughout the body to and from the heart; namely, arteries, arterioles, veins, venules, and capillaries. (See illustrations for RESPIRATORY SYSTEM; HEART DISEASE.)

BLUE CROSS

"Blue Cross" means protection against HOSPITAL charges or, the other way around, freedom from fear of excessive, catastrophic hospital bills. Blue Cross is the acknowledged symbol for more than 80 Blue Cross group hospitalization plans in the United States, 5 in Canada, and 1 in Puerto Rico. It is the most widely accepted form of HEALTH INSURANCE in the United States.

The idea of such voluntary community protection against the risk of ruinous hospital bills took root in the 1930's. By 1958, well over 50,000,000 Americans were protected against hospital expenses, wholly or in large part, under Blue Cross contracts. Over 60% of the income from patients in America's hospitals now comes from Blue Cross.

Blue Cross, which pays hospital bills, should not be confused with BLUE SHIELD, which pays doctors' bills. However, the two of them often work together.

Blue Cross was the unique, pioneering American movement to bring hospital service within the financial means of millions of men and women and their families who might otherwise have to go without it. In the present era of medical progress and longer life, there is no way of escaping increased hospital costs for individuals and communities. More people go to hospitals and more can be done for them there. The rates which Blue Cross subscribers pay for their protection must of course reflect this progress.

Different from commercial insurance. Blue Cross differs from hospital insurance written by commercial insurance companies in that it involves the hospitals themselves. Blue Cross plans are backed by the capital assets and physical facilities of the hospitals which are members of the plan. For this reason Blue Cross plans are able to render and guarantee hospital service to their subscribers regardless of cash indemnity payments. Under some conditions and circumstances cash payments are made by Blue Cross plans; but the essence of the idea is the *"service* contract." Blue Cross guarantees its subscribers and their dependents hospital *service* if, as, and when they need it.

This need is quite frequent on the American scene. Approximately 1 in every 8 Americans goes to a hospital in any given year. And, not so strangely, a very high percentage of those who go that year also go the next year and the next. They are the chronically and repetitively ill patients. Furthermore, the older people in America's aging population need about 2½ times as much hospital service as younger people.

Blue Cross does not cancel its subscribers' contracts because of repeated illness or old age. It has the social responsibility for these people that goes along with *nonprofit* character. In this important respect it is a social movement and not to be compared directly with commercial hospital insurance. Generally speaking, a community with a vigorous, active Blue Cross plan enjoys more efficient hospital service all around—and devotes a smaller percentage of its taxes to hospital and welfare expenses.

The origin of Blue Cross. Blue Cross plans, as they now operate, had their origin in Dallas, Texas, in 1929. A group of school teachers there made an arrangement with Baylor University Hospital to prepay $3 apiece each semester, and in exchange the hospital agreed to provide up to 21 days of hospital care for any of them who needed it. As the news spread, other teachers and other hospitals asked to participate in such a plan. It soon became evident, however, that a large number of the hospitals in any community would have to be included in the group hospitalization plan if it was to work out successfully.

Within a few years groups of hospitals in Sacramento, California, Essex County (Newark), New Jersey, St. Paul, Minnesota (where the Blue Cross symbol originated), and Durham, North Carolina, had established plans for delivering hospital service as needed to prepaid subscribers. The largest of the present Blue Cross plans, that which operates in New York City, was established in 1935.

Most large cities—Chicago, Philadelphia, Pittsburgh, Cleveland, and Detroit, for example—soon set up Blue Cross plans; and many statewide plans, as in New Jersey, Massachusetts, Wisconsin, and others, came into operation. Of the more than 80 Blue Cross plans operating in the United States today, over 10% have more than 1,000,000 subscribers. In ten American cities, over half the population is enrolled in Blue Cross.

An important feature of Blue Cross coverage is that it protects not only the enrolled subscriber; it also protects his dependents. *Indeed, about 60% of the people covered by Blue Cross are dependents.*

Most Blue Cross subscribers and their dependents receive hospital care in their own communities. However, through an Inter-Plan Service Benefit Bank and other arrangements, Blue Cross takes care of its subscribers away from home, giving them the same benefits they would get if they were hospitalized in their home territories. The plans also own a national insurance company, Health Service, Inc., organized in the state of Illinois, through which hospital service benefits for national employers and unions can conveniently be provided. Many union contracts with employers specify Blue Cross coverage for workers.

What Blue Cross subscribers get. The basic idea of all Blue Cross plans is the same; but rates and coverage differ somewhat among them. In general, the individual rates for semiprivate (usually four to a room) hospital accommodations have varied from $12 to $24 a year; the family rates (including unmarried children under 18) from $24 to $60 a year. Rates are rising, however, reflecting rapidly increasing hospital costs.

Practically all Blue Cross plans provide full benefits (in semiprivate accommodations) for 21 to 30 days a year. In some, this figure goes as high as 120 days. The care includes bed, board, general nursing care, ordinary drugs, use of operating rooms and equipment, some laboratory tests, and occasionally payment toward X-ray service. In some plans subscribers get a certain number of "discount" ("half-price") days after the initial full coverage is used up. No two plans are exactly alike; but as nonprofit community service organizations, all Blue Cross plans seek to extend as much protection as is financially possible to their subscribers and dependents.

About 95% of the total national enrollment in Blue Cross plans is through employed groups. People join where they work. This has many advantages of economy, efficiency, and maintenance of a fair selection of risks. Groups as small as five are usually accepted; and, of course, they run into many thousands. Payment is usually made as a payroll deduction. However, in probably 100,000 Blue Cross groups there are volunteer group leaders, something like shop stewards, who make collections and look after the interest of the group.

Most Blue Cross plans feel it necessary, as part of their public service outlook, to extend enrollment opportunities beyond employed groups. Many will sign up individual subscribers at somewhat higher rates. Some require a medical questionnaire. However, there is usually no age limit after enrollment. In some places—small towns and villages—community enrollment plans taking in at least 50% of the population have been tried and worked out. Co-operation is also being extended to farm organizations to increase the number of farmers who are protected against hospital charges.

Hospitalization is only one, albeit a major, cost of illness. The growth of Blue Cross plans soon raised hopes that a similar means of meeting doctors' bills could be worked out. It was not long in coming—under the name of Blue Shield plans. These plans require the interest and co-operation of local medical societies. There are now nearly 80 Blue Shield plans, 60 of which work together with Blue Cross. See BLUE SHIELD.

Who controls Blue Cross? Each of the Blue Cross plans is autonomous and governs its own affairs. Each is a public-service organization governed by its own Board of Trustees (or Directors). These trustees are representative of the entire community—including industry, labor, business, civic organizations, subscribers (consumers), the medical profession, and the hospitals themselves. Their policy decisions are based on the community ideal for which Blue Cross stands—namely, the widest delivery of the highest standard of hospital care under conditions and at rates the community can afford. The local trustees of Blue Cross plans, who have made an enviable record for community service, develop plans which are fair both to the hospitals and the public.

Standards for Blue Cross plans were formulated as early as 1933 by the American Hospital Association, and these recommendations have been revised, extended, and encouraged ever since by the Blue Cross Commission of the Association. This Commission has no legal authority over the separate plans, but it generally has their support and allegiance.

The crucial points in the standards for Blue Cross plans are these:

1. Their trustees must be truly representative of the communities served.

2. They must be strictly nonprofit.

3. They must assure free choice of hospitals and physicians.

4. They must have sound financial policies, adequate (though not large) reserves, and good records.

It has long been an arguable academic question whether Blue Cross plans are actually insurance companies or simply corporations engaged in the distribution of hospital services. In most states they are under the supervision of state departments of insurance, although a few still operate as membership corporations. The insurance supervision has generally been an advantage.

There is a growing competition for subscribers between commercial insurance companies and Blue Cross plans. The essential difference between them is that Blue Cross plans usually pay service benefits directly to the hospitals in terms of the patients' needs, whereas commercial insurance usually provides fixed cash indemnity payments regardless of hospital charges. Furthermore, as a public service organization, Blue Cross has been more generous in assuming risks.

BLUE SHIELD

"Blue Shield" is the name and symbol for over 75 local HEALTH INSURANCE plans in the United States, Canada, and Puerto Rico, which offer protection against the burden of surgical and medical expenses. They operate on a prepayment basis. In return for premiums paid in advance, the Blue Shield plans pay all or part of specified surgical and medical expenses when they occur. Payments are made directly to doctors in accordance with an established fee schedule.

Blue Shield should not be confused with BLUE CROSS, which stands for prepayment plans that pay *hospital* bills. However, there is usually a close working relationship between Blue Cross and Blue Shield.

The use of the Blue Shield symbol by any local plan means that it conforms to standards established by the national Blue Shield Medical Care Plans.

The common denominator of Blue Shield plans is medical sponsorship. Blue Shield is "the doctors' plan." All plans have the official approval of the state and county medical societies in the areas where they operate. An approximately 2 to 1 majority representation on the governing boards of local Blue Shield plans (and on the national Blue Shield Commission itself) is held by doctors of medicine (M.D.'s). Participation of physicians in the operation of Blue Shield plans is very high. More than 122,000 physicians participate. This is nearly 90% of all physicians in private practice in areas served by the plans.

Blue Shield plans are all nonprofit organizations; their trustees serve without compensation; and their surpluses, if any, are utilized for further extension in the community of the services that they provide.

The popularity of Blue Shield plans is indicated by the rapidity with which they have grown since 1939, when the California Physicians Service undertook the first of the plans that have since blossomed into Blue Shield. By 1957 the total enrollment in Blue Shield plans was over 38,000,000 people—covering more than one-fifth of the population of the United States. The plans are now paying out between $400,000,000 and $500,000,000 a year for surgical and medical expenses.

The origin of Blue Shield. The idea of prepayment for medical and surgical care, if, as, and when needed, is an ancient one. Even in the United States it far antedates the California Physicians Service. Medical services were long ago delivered on a contract basis to lumberjacks and miners in remote camps in the Pacific Northwest.

The California plan of 1939 was based on recommendations formulated several years earlier by a national Committee on the Cost of Medical Care. It offered a comprehensive service at a low rate ($1.70 a month) to members of employed groups *with incomes under $3,000 a year.* Doctors were paid on a unit basis, the unit being $2.50 for an office visit, and other services in multiples of this unit.

The demand for services far exceeded expectations; and the plan might have failed dismally if the doctors who sponsored the plan had not been willing to accept devalued unit payments until the stability of the plan, with some changes in the rules, could be assured. The Michigan Medical Service, organized by the Michigan State Medical Society in 1940, was another pioneer in prepayment plans. It had gained 500,000 members in less than two years of operation; but experience here, too, showed that rates and benefits had to be based on realistic experience and usage. No plan can endure that must pay out more money than it takes in.

In 1943 the American Medical Association set up a Council on Medical Service to assist in the development of plans which were arising on local initiative all over the country. In 1946, with AMA help, Associated Medical Care Plans was incorporated in Illinois as a nonprofit association; and in 1950 the name was changed to Blue Shield Medical Care Plans, since this symbol had come into common use.

Each Blue Shield plan is an independent local organization. Membership in the national association simply means that the local plan has voluntarily accepted the minimum standards for operation established by the association.

What are service benefits? The most distinctive feature of Blue Shield coverage of medical expenses is that most of the plans (at least two-thirds) provide *service* benefits as well as cash indemnities for the payment of doctor bills. A service benefit means that the physician who renders medical service to a patient is willing to accept the payment made to him by the Blue Shield plan, according to an agreed-on schedule of fees, as payment in full. He does not bill the patient.

However, this full service benefit is rendered only to patients whose own or family incomes are below an agreed ceiling level. These income ceilings vary from place to place; generally speaking service benefits are limited to individuals with incomes under $3,000 or families under $4,500. In a few localities the income ceiling is as high as $6,500 for a family.

When the Blue Shield subscriber's income is higher than the ceiling level, the fee paid to the physician by the plan is only part of the total charge. It may be considered a "cash indemnity" payment against the usual professional fee. Most of the time it appears as a substantial credit on the doctor's bill.

What services does Blue Shield provide? These vary according to local plans and contracts. Most plans write a number of contracts with different provisions. The United Medical Service of New York—New York's Blue Shield—writes three basic contracts; for example: a *surgical plan,* which covers operations and other SURGERY in the hospital, office, or home; maternity care; electroshock therapy and radiation therapy for malignancy; a *surgical-medical plan,* which covers all the benefits of the surgical plan plus the doctor's visits for medical care in the hospital and one specialist's consultation per hospital admission; and a *general medical plan,* which covers all the benefits of the surgical-medical plan plus medical care at home or in the doctor's office and specialists' consultations. To these basic contracts other and increased coverages can be added in the direction of larger consultation allowances, payments for diagnostic services of pathologists and radiologists, and payments to the anesthetist.

The very least that any Blue Shield plan provides is a schedule of surgical benefits—and usually some benefits for medical service to hospitalized patients. From there up, the benefits can be of all varieties; but they will be reflected in the rates paid for the contracts. The more comprehensive the available services, the higher the rates. Most contracts place some limitation, expressed in time, dollars, or otherwise, on the total services and indemnities which they will provide.

How to join Blue Shield plans. Enrollment in Blue Shield plans is principally through employed groups. Membership fees are collected as payroll deductions. Most Blue Shield plans accept very small employed groups (as few as 4 employees, for example) and make provisions for direct enrollments at slightly higher fees for unemployed, self-employed, and retired people. Most important is that fact that wives (or husbands) and children of the employee can also be protected under Blue Shield.

Boils—more or less painful but limited infections, beginning in hair follicles and usually caused by staphylococcus germs. A simple boil, or *furuncle,* has a single core and may be no more than a pimple. More serious are a mass of boils, close together and with several cores, called a *carbuncle.*

Boils generally occur where the skin and hair roots are chafed or irritated, as on the back of the neck, in the armpits, and on the buttocks of rowers and riders. People with diabetes and kidney disease are especially subject to repeated attacks of boils. "Bad blood" does not cause them.

Boils should not be indiscriminately pinched or squeezed —especially those on the face or in the ear. The walled-off infection may thus be induced to spread dangerously.

Small simple boils can be treated by protecting them from irritation with a small adhesive-tape and gauze bandage until the boil comes to a head in about a week, breaks, and evacuates its small core of pus. The bandage should be continued until healing is complete. A boil can be brought to a head more quickly by applying hot cloths and a continuous wet dressing. A solution of magnesium sulfate (epsom salts), one tablespoon to a cup of water, or common table salt may be used to wet the bandage.

Large or painful boils should

SKELETON IN ACTION

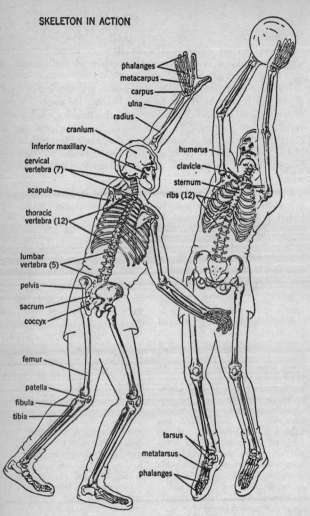

phalanges
metacarpus
carpus
ulna
radius
cranium
inferior maxillary
cervical vertebra (7)
scapula
thoracic vertebra (12)
lumbar vertebra (5)
pelvis
sacrum
coccyx
femur
patella
fibula
tibia
humerus
clavicle
sternum
ribs (12)
tarsus
metatarsus
phalanges

The bones of the human body—its skeletal framework or system—are shown here in three-quarter-front and three-quarter-back views.

not be tampered with. See a physician. He may have to lance the boil to let out pus. He may also administer an antibiotic, probably penicillin. For repeated boils autogenous vaccine (made from the victim's own skin germs) may prove of value.

Bolus—a mass of chewed food ready to be swallowed. Also, a rounded mass of medicine larger than a pill.

Bones are the scaffolding on which the rest of the body hangs. Together with cartilage, joints, and muscles, they make up the *musculoskeletal system*. The system is held together, giving shape to the body, by bands of fibrous tissue called *ligaments* and *tendons*.

There are approximately 206 bones, nearly 700 muscles, and about 250 joints in the human body. Except for tooth enamel, bone is the hardest tissue in the body. The densest part of a bone is on the outside; the inner portion is more spongy (cancellous). Most of the mineral substance of the body, notably calcium and phosphorus, is deposited in the bones and gives them their hardness. Bones are living tissue. Even the hardest is traversed by microscopically small channels (*Haversian canals*), through which blood, lymph fluid, and nerves enter the bone. Bones have an outer lining, called the *periosteum*, which contains many blood vessels, nerves, and lymphatic spaces.

In the hollow interior of the bones is found *bone marrow*, which is the principal *blood-forming* organ.

Bones are classified as *long* (e.g. femur), *short* (e.g. wrist bones), *flat* (e.g. skull bones), and *irregular* (e.g. spinal vertebrae). Most bones are laid down in softer connective tissue, *cartilage*, before they accumulate minerals and become harder. Adults' bones are more brittle than children's.

Bones are subject to damage by breaking (FRACTURE) and by BONE DISEASES, which see.

(See illustration for JOINTS.)

A BLOCK OF BONE

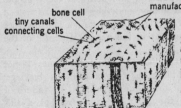

hard bone substance
manufactured by cells

bone cell
tiny canals
connecting cells

canal with blood vessels and nerves

This block of bone, cut out from a long bone of the body and greatly magnified in the illustration, shows the internal structure of bones. They are living tissue—with blood vessels and nerves.

BONE DISEASES

Bone diseases and deformities include acute and chronic infections, congenital deformities, traumatic deformities as the result of accident, bone changes as a result of nutritional deficiencies or endocrine disorders, and a variety of benign and malignant tumors.

Osteomyelitis means inflammation of the bone and its central cavity. It most commonly affects the femur (hip bone) and the tibia (shin bone). It is predominantly a disease of childhood. The acute disease is attended by high fever, severe pain, increased white-blood-cell count, swelling of the limb, and sometimes delirium. The infecting germ is usually *staphylococcus aureus,* which is particularly susceptible to penicillin. Early penicillin treatment usually makes unnecessary the surgery and long invalidism formerly associated with osteomyelitis.

Osteitis is a general term for bone inflammations. Overactivity of the parathyroid glands produces one form (osteitis fibrosa, or von Recklinghausen's disease), in which bones become thickened and softened. In another form (osteitis deformans, or Paget's disease), cause unknown, the long bones become curved and the skull bones thickened.

Syphilis and *tuberculosis* can damage the bones. Untreated syphilitic infection can destroy the ends of the bones, where they meet in joints, and seriously impair locomotion (Charcot's joints). Tuberculosis of the bone may cause crumbling and softening (caries). This sometimes occurs in the vertebrae, causing curvature of the spine (Pott's disease).

Brittle bones, which tend to break on slight violence, are usually the result of hereditary influences if the condition occurs early in life. It usually disappears at puberty. The bones of older people become increasingly brittle generally, and they must take special care to avoid bone-breaking falls. Their bones do not knit together as well, either. Particularly serious in the aged is fracture of the head or neck of the femur.

Rickets, a disease of early childhood in which the bones do not harden as they should, produces such deformities as bowlegs, pigeon breast, and beading of the ribs. It is caused by failure of absorption of calcium from the gastrointestinal tract, and this arises from *deficiency of vitamin D in the diet.* Rickets can readily be prevented by giving young children adequate amounts of vitamin D as cod-liver oil or synthetic (irradiated) vitamin D and exposure to sunshine.

Osteomalacia, an adult form of rickets, is a softening of the bones caused by lack of vitamin D.

Congenital malformations of the bones include various forms of clubfoot and dislocations of the hip and other joints. In congenital dislocation of the hip, the head of the femur lies outside a poorly formed socket (acetabulum). If this is on one side, the victim walks with a limp; if on both sides, with a waddling gait.

Cancer (carcinoma) originating in the breast, prostate gland, kidney, or stomach frequently migrates to the bones. Primary bone cancer, *sarcoma,* may destroy bone tissue rapidly, causing easy breaking, or produce great growths of new bone.

FRACTURES, which see, sometimes result in bone deformities. CURVATURE OF THE SPINE is sometimes the result of bone diseases, but has other causes.

Boric Acid—a mild antiseptic and astringent drug for external application only. Dissolve crystals in water. Boron poisoning has sometimes been reported but the danger of boric acid dusting powder has probably been overstressed.

Botulism—a severe, often fatal, form of food poisoning caused by poison given off by the microbe *Clostridium botulinus* (bacillus botulinus). This organism grows in improperly canned or preserved food. The early symptoms are vomiting, abdominal pain, and difficulty in seeing, followed later by double vision, drooping of the eyelids, and other symptoms indicating that the poison has gotten to the central nervous system. The botulinus toxin is one of the most powerful poisons known.

Bovine—pertaining to or derived from cows; for example, bovine tuberculosis.

Bowels—intestines; see DIGESTION, DIGESTIVE SYSTEM, CONSTIPATION.

Bradycardia—an abnormally slow heartbeat. The pulse rate is 60 or lower.

BRAIN

The human brain, well protected by the thick bones of the skull, is the controlling organ of the human body; it enables man to think, reason, plan, feel, in ways that distinguish him from the lower animals. Injury by disease or accident to parts of the brain deprives a person of his intellectual and emotional capacities. The brain and the spinal cord comprise the *central nervous system.* (See NERVES AND THE NERVOUS SYSTEM.)

The brain is a mass of nerve cells (gray matter) and nerve fibers (white matter). In the adult it weighs about 3½ to 4 pounds, the male brain being slightly heavier than the female. The brain grows rapidly up to the fifth year of life, generally ceases to grow at about the age of 20, and with advancing years actually loses weight. Although scientific study has revealed much about the brain, there is still a great deal unknown about how it functions. The brain is the seat of the mind; it perceives, remembers, integrates, and creates, at both conscious and unconscious levels. Yet the relationship between brain and mind—between nerve cells and intelligence—is not clearly mapped out and leaves much that is unsolved and mysterious.

The principal divisions of the brain are the cerebrum, the cerebellum, the pons, and the brain stem, including the medulla oblongata.

The *cerebrum,* or forebrain, often regarded as the brain proper, is by far the largest part of the brain. It fills most of the upper portion of the skull. It is divided into two hemispheres. Its outer shell, or cerebral cortex, about ⅛ inch thick, is a solid mass of gray matter, made up of associative neurons; it is presumed that this is the site of the highest intellectual functions.

Buried deep within the cerebral hemispheres are basal nuclei (or ganglia), nerve masses concerned with motor function; also the *thalamus* and the *hypothalamus,* which are primitive parts of the brain. The thalamus is the main relay station for sensory impulses directed to the cerebral cortex. The hypothalamus includes centers that regulate in part some of the body's most primitive needs; for example, body temperature, sleep, water balance, digestion and utilization of food.

The *cerebellum,* or hindbrain, lies in the lower back part of the skull. It is concerned with regulating equilibrium and with coordinating muscular movements. An athlete needs a good cerebellum. Injury to it may produce a staggering gait, trembling muscles (palsy), and slurred speech.

The *pons* is a bundle of nerve fibers that bridges various parts of the brain.

The *brain stem,* including the medulla oblongata, is the extension and upper terminal of the spinal cord, and is found at the base of the skull cavity. The twelve cranial NERVES originate in

THE HUMAN BRAIN

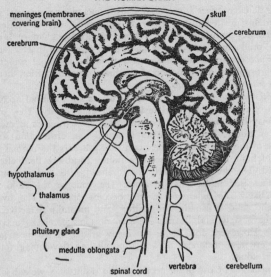

A midsection of the human brain and the upper part of the spinal cord.

or near it. The medulla serves as an organ of communication between the spinal cord and the brain. In it are found centers that govern many of the most important functions of life; for example, breathing, heartbeat, and swallowing.

A switchover of nerves takes place in the brain stem. Here the nerves originating in or coming from the left side of the body switch over to the right side of the brain—and vice versa. In general, therefore, an injury to the right side of the skull and brain will show its effects, such as paralysis, on the left side of the body.

The brain contains hollow areas, called ventricles, in which cerebrospinal fluid is produced. It is further protected by three layers of coverings, the MENINGES.

BRAIN DAMAGE

Brain damage arises from many causes, including congenital malformations; birth injuries; *water on the brain;* violence producing
concussion, contusion, or laceration; circulatory changes in the
brain, producing *"softening of the brain";* infections that engender
brain abscess and *brain fever,* as well as the manifold symptoms
of neurosyphilis; inflammation of the brain covering (MENINGITIS);
brain tumors; and poisons, like lead.

Water on the brain, or hydrocephalus, is an abnormal accumulation of cerebrospinal fluid inside the cranial cavity. The condition may be congenital or acquired from such diseases as meningitis or tumor. The mechanism is usually an obstruction somewhere in the ventricles of the brain that prevents the normal outflow of fluid. Sometimes there is a failure to absorb fluid already
formed. The skull, particularly the forehead, often enlarges under
this increased intracranial pressure. The younger the child, the
more likely the enlargement will become marked. The hydrocephalic child is usually dull, listless, and mentally defective. He
may have sight and hearing defects, develop paralysis, and die
young. However, since there are many grades of hydrocephalus,
there are also instances of a hydrocephalic's developing into a
normal adult.

Concussion of the brain occurs as the result of a violent jar or
shock to the head, blow to the head, or severe shake to the body.
It may be considered a bruise of the brain arising from shaking or
vibrating it. A concussion is less severe than a *contusion,* in which
there is generally a skull fracture and bleeding into the brain, or
a *laceration,* the outcome of gunshot injury or skull fracture with
displacement of bone, in which the brain is actually torn, tissue
destroyed, and bleeding severe.

Symptoms of concussion of the brain are dizziness, loss of
consciousness, nausea, shallow and rapid breathing, cold and
clammy skin, and a fall in blood pressure. There are many degrees of concussion, from mild to fatal. In a mild concussion the
symptoms may be limited to dizziness and headache for an hour
or two, with no further complications. In severe cases unconsciousness may persist for weeks; the patient lies somnolent and can
be awakened only with difficulty. The treatment is rest in bed and
good nursing. Loss of memory for events, and even loss of personal identity, sometimes follows concussion. Convalescence may

be slow and stormy. However, the outlook for complete recovery is usually good.

"*Softening of the brain*" is a term used in both a scientific and popular sense. In the scientific sense, it is one of the many changes that can occur in the circulation of blood to the brain. It is a *slow apoplexy*, or STROKE, and exhibits many of the same symptoms, but coming on more slowly. There is an actual softening in some areas of brain tissue as a result of the blood supply's being cut off by gradual blocking or plugging of blood vessels. A chronic inflammation may also induce softening. Popularly, the phrase "softening of the brain" describes the cause of mental deterioration in anyone, but especially an elderly victim of neurosyphilis, chronic alcoholism, or the psychoses of old age. But such psychoses are usually associated with damage to the blood vessels of the brain.

Prolonged or even temporary loss of blood supply and its oxygen to the brain can have exceedingly serious consequences. The mild and not-so-serious cases are those of *fainting* and of "*blacking out*," which sometimes momentarily afflicts airplane pilots making power dives.

The really damaging circulatory change in the brain is a *cerebral hemorrhage*—bleeding caused by the breaking of a blood vessel in the brain. It is usually one of the smaller blood vessels in the branches of the middle cerebral artery that breaks. This vessel is under especially high pressure. Hence high blood pressure generally and accompanying arteriosclerosis may evoke cerebral hemorrhage. The condition that follows is *stroke*, with a resultant paralysis in the areas of the body governed by the specific areas of the brain affected by the hemorrhage. Plugging of the blood vessels produces the same results as breaking. All together these events are described as "intracranial lesions of vascular origin," and they are the third principal cause of death in the U.S.

Neurosyphilis is a form of late syphilis, arising 10 to 15 or even more years after the initial infection of *untreated* syphilis. In this disease the spirochete attacks the brain (and the spinal cord). Without treatment, the patient may suffer a wide range of mental and physical deterioration, including general paralysis of the insane (paresis) and tabes dorsalis (shooting pains and wasting muscles). The attack on neurosyphilis lies in early treatment of syphilis with penicillin and other suitable drugs. Neurosyphilis responds to penicillin. It is no longer the ghastly disease it seemed in the 19th century.

Brain fever is a popular term that describes an infection of the brain (ENCEPHALITIS) or its coverings (MENINGITIS). It is also used to indicate a state of extreme mental fatigue ("brain fag"), which may be classed as a mild MENTAL ILLNESS. The patient with brain fever may sometimes go into a delirious state, but he is more commonly listless and lethargic. If the brain fever results from an infection that responds to modern antibiotic and other drugs, it can be cleared up rather quickly. But if it is a virus infection, which it often is, little good can be expected from most antibiotic drugs. In these cases brain fever may be synonymous with *sleeping sickness.*

Brain abscess is just what the name implies: infection, inflammation, and pus in the brain. The early symptoms may be vague, but sooner or later violent headaches, vomiting, high fever, and often visual disturbances intervene. The great danger in brain abscesses arises from the fact that in the closed cavity of the skull there is little opportunity for pus to drain off. These abscesses are usually the extension of suppurative processes in nearby areas, especially the bones of the skull. They are usually secondary to infections in the middle ear (the "running ear"), the mastoid bone, or the frontal sinuses. Brain abscesses can often be cleared up by antibiotic drugs. In extreme cases, it may be necessary to open the skull (trephine) and drain the abscess. This treatment usually succeeds.

Brain tumor is a growth of new and unwanted tissue in the brain. Depending on its location and size, it may produce a wide variety of symptoms, first vague and later definite. Among the general symptoms are headache, dizziness, uncontrolled vomiting, and tenderness of the head on pressure. As the tumor enlarges, it continues to build up pressure inside the skull. Changes in the appearance of the retina of the eye, blindness, and mental symptoms may come on. There may be a progressive loss of function in parts of the body or in the special senses.

There was a time when brain tumors, malignant or not, seemed almost hopeless. Progress in neurosurgery has eliminated this sense of hopelessness, and competent brain surgeons now save the lives of many who would formerly have been doomed. Success of the surgery often depends on careful preoperative diagnosis and a careful search for the exact location of the tumor before the operation. Ingenious ways of taking X-ray pictures of the inside of the skull to locate the tumor have been devised (encephalography, ventriculography). In addition, the information gained from an analysis of brain waves (electroencephalography) can be immensely helpful. The earlier the tumor is diagnosed and located, the better the chances for successful surgery. Not every patient is saved, but the percentage of success is constantly growing.

Research in brain damage. There is a great deal of research yet to be done in assigning adequate causes for brain damage and finding explanations for brain malfunctioning without visible or organic reasons. The Brain Research Foundation to investigate such problems has been organized in the U.S.

(For further discussion of brain and central-nervous-system disorders, see EPILEPSY, MIGRAINE, CEREBRAL PALSY, STROKE, and MENTAL ILLNESS.)

Breasts—mammary glands. See PREGNANCY, CHILDBIRTH, MASTITIS.

Breathing—See LUNGS.

Bright's Disease—a common form of KIDNEY TROUBLE, which see.

Bromides—salts of the element *bromine*, they are sedative and hypnotic drugs used to quiet the nerves. They are often self-prescribed for hangovers. Bromides depress the central nervous system and dull the brain. Hence they induce sleep. Under medical supervision bromides have a useful place in treating sleeplessness, hysteria, CONVULSIONS, and EPILEPSY. They are likely, however, to produce a skin rash.

Taken recklessly, bromides can become habit-forming. Long-continued indulgence may produce *bromide poisoning* (bromism); symptoms include impairment of memory, the "blues" (depression), disorientation, delirium, headache, fetid breath, weakness, acne, and loss of sexual powers. The symptoms disappear after the drug is withdrawn.

Bronchi—the branches of the windpipe (trachea) going into the LUNGS. The smaller branches are called *bronchioles*. Taken all together they form the *bronchial tree*. (See illustration for RESPIRATORY SYSTEM.)

Bronchiectasis—a coughing sickness, much like and sometimes the outcome of chronic *bronchitis*. Repeated attacks of coughing stretch and dilate the bronchial tubes, often leaving pockets where pus can form. These ballooned-out spots may exist in one or many parts of both lungs.

When the disease is far advanced, the patient may cough and spit up great quantities of foul-smelling mucus and sputum—as much as a quart a day. His breath is therefore offensive. Paroxysms of coughing may tear the lining of the bronchial tubes, so that blood appears in the sputum.

Approximately two-thirds of the people who get bronchiectasis acquire it before they are 20, frequently as a complication of whooping cough or measles. The disease can, however, appear in a severe form in later life.

Bronchiectasis can sometimes be ameliorated by drugs that clear up chronic infections in the lungs. *Postural drainage* of the lungs, with the patient lying head down several times a day, may be required to drain pus out of the lungs. In many cases surgical removal of the severely involved portions of the lung offers the only hope of cure.

Bronchitis—inflammation of the bronchial tubes. It usually occurs as a complication following a COMMON COLD or other infection of the respiratory tract. It can also result from breathing in irritating gases, fumes, or dusts, and from exposure to cold.

Acute bronchitis usually begins with frequent bouts of coughing, more severe at night, that bring on chest pains. Other symptoms are fever (generally low) and difficult breathing (dyspnea). A thick, purulent fluid is often raised from the lungs by coughing, although dry cough also occurs.

Chronic bronchitis, a long-continued form of the disease that tends to recur, sometimes develops when acute attacks have not been adequately managed. A clean, temperate atmosphere may help this condition. Young children run the greatest risk of bronchitis.

Treatment of bronchitis includes cough medicines that increase the flow of mucus and make it easier to raise sputum, inhalation of steam, and in some cases, ANTIHISTAMINE drugs.

Bronchopneumonia—a form of *pneumonia* beginning in the bronchial tubes. The disease is often secondary to colds and other respiratory-tract infections. It is a common primary infection in infants and aged or weakened individuals. See PNEUMONIA.

Bronchoscope—an instrument for looking into the larger BRONCHI and occasionally for removing something from them. The expert who uses it is called a *bronchoscopist.*

Brucellosis—UNDULANT FEVER, which see.

Bruise, or contusion, is the result of a blow or fall that breaks the skin capillaries, usually without breaking the skin. Blood oozes into the tissues, making the bruise at first red and swollen. Later, as the blood clots, the bruise becomes discolored, "black and blue." A black eye is a bruise. Treat a bruise by applying cold cloths or an ice bag for 20 to 25 minutes.

Bubo—a swollen LYMPH GLAND in the groin or, more rarely, in the armpit. The cause is a specific infection, notably LYMPHO-GRANULOMA VENEREUM, SYPHILIS, GONORRHEA, and PLAGUE. The swollen, infected gland often breaks through the skin, forming an open abscess or running sore most difficult to heal.

Buerger's Disease—THROMBO-ANGIITIS obliterans.

"Bug," as popularly used in such phrases as "I'm sick. I've got the bug," means a GERM, MICROBE, or micro-organism causing disease. The actual microbe may be a bacterium or a virus; the "bug" is most commonly associated with viruses causing the COMMON COLD or stomach flu.

Bunion—swelling at the ball of the big toe or on other parts of the foot; a common form of FOOT TROUBLE, which see.

Burns result from the application of too much heat to the skin. Scalds are caused by hot liquids or vapors. Burns are classified by extent, whether limited or extensive, and by degree. Any extensive burn, covering a large area of body surface, is serious, regardless of the degree. Shock and infection dangerously accompany large or deep burns. *First-degree* burns show redness of the unbroken skin; *second-degree*, skin blisters and some breaking of the

skin; *third-degree*, destruction of the skin and underlying tissues; *fourth-degree*, more or less charring and blackening.

A serious burn demands *immediate* medical attention. Great progress has been made in recent years in saving the lives of severely burned people and restoring them to usefulness.

First-aid treatment of extensive burns should be kept as simple as possible. The victim should be kept warm and quiet, lying down with head slightly lowered. No meddling with the burned area should be attempted. A doctor should be summoned immediately and all treatment left to him.

Minor burns. Exclude air by applying petroleum ointment (white vaseline), a standard burn ointment, or even, if necessary, a vegetable shortening from the kitchen. Do not apply iodine or other antiseptics to burns; it makes matters worse.

All burns are potentially serious, and it is difficult to classify a "minor burn." Even if the burned area is very small, the burn itself may be deep and medical attention advisable.

Bursa—a small sac of heavy fluid placed between muscle and tendon or between bone, muscle, and tendon to reduce friction and facilitate their movements. Bursae are named for their locations; for example, the prepatellar bursa is in the front of the kneecap, the Achilles bursa is in the heel.

Bursitis—inflammation, often chronic and painful, of a BURSA. Acute bursitis can be considered and treated as an *abscess*. Chronic bursitis is usually caused by excess movement or pressure on the bursa; a typical example is "housemaid's knee." Surgical removal of the bursa (bursectomy) is sometimes indicated. It can be considered a form of RHEUMATISM, which see.

C

Any word printed in SMALL CAPITALS *can be looked up under its own alphabetical listing for further information.*

Cachexia—extreme weight loss and weakness as the result of serious disease.

Caduceus—a common symbol of medicine; usually one or two snakes entwined around a straight wand or staff, sometimes surmounted by a pair of wings. It represents the ancient god of healing, Mercury.

Caesarean Section—delivery of an infant through an incision in the abdominal wall and the uterus. Julius Caesar is supposed to have been delivered in this manner, though this has never been proved. Less than 1% of all deliveries are Caesarean. This method is indicated when other methods of delivery, especially normal, spontaneous delivery, may fail. The decision to do a Caesarean section demands the very best obstetric judgment. It should never be considered an elective operation. If a woman has once been delivered by Caesarean section, it is most usual that subsequent deliveries must be made in the same way.

Caffeine—a stimulating drug present in coffee, tea, cocoa, chocolate, and some cola drinks. It stimulates the heart, nervous system, and kidneys.

Calamine—zinc-oxide lotion or powder, pink, used as a soothing application on the skin.

Calcaneus—heel bone.

Calcification—deposit of calcium (lime salts) in body tissues, hardening them.

Calcium—a primary element, an earthy metal, sometimes called *lime*. It is present in nearly all body tissues, but concentrated in the bones and teeth. Essential to blood clotting, muscle tone and other metabolic processes.

Calculus—a stone formed in the body; GALLSTONE or KIDNEY STONE.

Calf—the fleshy bunch of muscle (gastrocnemius muscles) at the back of the lower leg. Ballet dancers often have bulging calves.

Callus—hardened, thickened skin, a common FOOT TROUBLE. Also, the substance exuded by the ends of a broken bone in the process of reuniting.

Calomel—a drug containing mercury; once commonly used in treating SYPHILIS. It is also a purge.

Calorie—a unit of heat. The large calorie is the amount of heat needed to raise one kilogram of water one degree Centigrade. The calorie is commonly used as the measure of energy (heat) yielded by different *foods. Counting calories* means watching the amount of food intake, usually to reduce caloric intake and thus reduce weight.

CANCER

Cancer is a frightening word, but fear of cancer often outruns the facts. One should have *respect* for the risk of getting cancer, but *panic* is unwarranted.

Can cancer be cured or is it always fatal? Cancer can be cured. It is not universally fatal. About ¼ to ⅓ of all cancer patients are now being cured. Again as many could be cured if adequate treatment was begun *in time.* Delay in seeking treatment makes cancer fatal to a great number of people who could otherwise be saved. The curability of cancer—in the present state of knowledge—is highlighted in the following table set forth by the former medical and scientific director of the American Cancer Society:

Site of cancer	Present cures in	Cures are possible in	Site of cancer	Present cures in	Cures are possible in
Skin	85%	95%	Larynx	40%	65%
Uterus	30%	70%	Mouth	35%	65%
Rectum	25%	70%	Stomach	5%	60%
Breast	35%	70%	Lung	5%	50%

Cancer does kill about one-quarter million people in the U.S. annually; however, it strikes around another half a million—of whom better than half could be saved.

Who gets cancer? Mostly adults in middle and late life. However, about 4,000 children and young people under 21 are stricken every year.

What is cancer? Actually cancer is not one but many diseases. Under the microscope hundreds of different varieties of cancer cells can be identified. Cancer is therefore a *group* of diseases characterized by abnormal, uncontrolled, "lawless" growth of body cells. Plants and animals are also subject to cancerous growths.

Cells are the fundamental units of all living matter. In the normal process of growth and repair, cells grow and take their places in the economy of the body according to what may be called the "rules of nature." Cell growth and development is an extremely complicated process whose central secrets have not yet been fathomed.

Sometimes, for reasons still unknown, a cell or group of cells breaks the ordinary rules of nature. They behave in a disorderly way; they grow wildly. There is no place for them in the normal structure and function of the body. Like weeds in a garden, they crowd out normal, useful cells and steal their food supply. When enough of these wild cells cluster together, they can sometimes be felt as a lump. Unless the growth of these abnormal cancer cells can be checked by some means (usually outside intervention), they oust so many normal cells that the body can no longer function and the victim dies. For example, when cancer cells invade the stomach, they crowd out the specialized stomach cells necessary for digesting food. Hence the patient eventually partially starves to death.

Cancer cells can start in any part of the body, but some sites are more favored. Unfortunately these cells rarely remain where they originate. Clusters or clumps of cancer cells break off and travel in the blood stream to other parts of the body—from the breast to the armpits, for example. This spread of cancer cells is called *metastasis*.

Cancer cells are definitely different from ordinary cells, and these differences can be observed in tiny sections of tissue examined under a microscope. Identifying cancer cells is an important part of the job of the pathologist.

Many names have been given to the different cancer cells identified. Most end in the suffix "oma." Thus, for example, carcinoma is cancer of the epithelial tissues (skin, glands, membranes); sarcoma, of connective tissue (bone, muscle); melanoma, of the pigment cells of skin. Leukemia, so-called cancer of the blood, reflects a disturbance in the blood-forming organs, which manufacture so many white blood cells that the essential red blood cells are crowded out.

Not all new growths are *"malignant,"* as cancerous growths are described. Many, if not most, new growths are *benign*. They do not spread wildly; they can be safely removed. Since benign tumors are so common, the presence of a lump should not awake wild, unrealistic fear. It should simply send you *promptly* to a physician. *Tumor* is another word for new growth or swelling.

Where does cancer usually strike? Nearly half the cases begin somewhere in the alimentary canal, most commonly the stomach. The reproductive system appears to be the next most vulnerable site (mainly the uterus in women and the prostate gland in men); about one fifth of the cases begin in these sites. The breast is the third most common area, accounting for about 10% of the cases. Next come the blood-forming organs, where leukemia originates. The rest of the cases occur in the respiratory system, mainly the lung; in the urinary system, mainly the bladder; in the brain and spinal cord; and on the skin and elsewhere.

There are significant differences between men and women in the most important sites of cancer attack. For example, fatal cancer of the breast is 90 times more frequent in women; fatal respiratory (lung) cancer is 4 times more frequent in men.

What causes cancer? Nobody yet knows. However, many contributing and predisposing factors have been sorted out. One of the best-known is prolonged irritation by chemical, physical, or thermal (heat) exposures. It has been abundantly demonstrated that coal tars are carcinogenic (cancer-invoking) agents. However, there are many other potential carcinogens in the environment, including solar rays, X rays, and radioactive substances. For example, prolonged exposure to sun and wind seems to predispose to skin cancer; certainly skin cancer is more common among outdoor workers, like ranchers and sailors, than among housewives.

Research has wiped out many cancer superstitions, giving assurance that there are many things that *don't* cause cancer. Dismiss the notions that cancer is caused by any specific kind of food or beverage, by blows or violence, by bacteria, or by such far-fetched circumstances as kissing, cooking in aluminum pots, or contact with animals.

Cancer is neither contagious nor communicable. You cannot "catch" cancer from cancer patients.

Many lines of research into possible causes are now under way. In essence they must deal with the factors that cause cells to grow and break down (cell metabolism). Among the factors being investigated are the chemical composition of cells; cell nutrition;

the effects of viruses, hormones, and enzymes on the cell; and the problem of heredity.

Does smoking cause cancer? There has been much popular and scientific speculation on this question and many statistical studies to show that cigarette smoking appears to be a factor in lung cancer. However, this evidence has not been generally accepted as proving a real cause-and-effect relationship between smoking and cancer. For the average person, the personal decision to smoke or not to smoke must be made in the light of more evidence than has yet been adduced. See TOBACCO.

Is cancer inherited? This is an extremely complex question. With inbred strains of mice, elaborate patterns of the hereditary influences in cancer have been worked out. However, it cannot be assumed arbitrarily that what applies to inbred mice necessarily applies to man. There are no such pure, inbred strains of the human species. It is possible that a tendency to develop cancer can be inherited by human beings. However, it does not now appear that heredity is the critical or most important factor in human cancer. Dr. Clarence Cook Little, an outstanding authority in cancer research, has summed up the situation: "The role which heredity plays is so complex, so well concealed, and so difficult of evaluation that it is both unnecessary and unwise for individuals to consider it a personal problem."

How is cancer treated? Cancer is treated by three basic and approved methods: surgery, X ray, and radium. Of course, other methods of treatment are constantly being tested by research teams, and many become the subject of popular reports. However, legitimate scientific experiment should be distinguished from the false claims of cancer quacks, who advertise and promise cures. Among the newer methods of cancer treatment that have proved partially beneficial in the hands of legitimate investigators are chemosurgery, a combination of chemistry and surgery applied to skin and other cancers; administration of female sex hormones for cancer of the prostate gland; and the use of such chemical substances as nitrogen mustards in treating leukemia. Progress in drug therapy is being made, but there is as yet no spectacular achievement for general use.

Surgery, X ray, and radium are used alone or in any combination, depending on the particular case. The aim of surgery is to remove all cancer cells. Modern surgery has made it possible to invade deeper and deeper recesses of the body to cut out cancerous tissue. Lung surgery affords a remarkable example.

X ray, radium, and more recently, radioactive isotopes yielded in atomic-energy research, are all forms of irradiation treatment. Radium may be implanted in the body in very small quantities. High-voltage X ray may penetrate even where radium cannot reach; millions of volts are produced by some of the newer machines. Radioactive isotopes, such as radioactive iodine for certain types of thyroid-gland cancer, may be administered as drugs. Irradiation treatment depends on the fact that many types of cancer cells are more radiosensitive than normal cells; they are destroyed while nearby normal cells are not severely injured. However, great caution is required in administering irradiation treatment.

How can I escape cancer? You cannot escape the undesirable growth of cancer cells in your body, but you have many ways of escaping damage or death from them. Make sure that, if cancer strikes, you discover it early and get early treatment. Cancer can be diagnosed only by a physician, using several methods of diagnosis. Your problem is simply to make sure that you get to the doctor in time for him to make an early diagnosis.

The periodic physical examination—if not exclusively relied on—has much to recommend it as a means of discovering cancer early. For women from approximately 30 to 50 this may mean a gynecological examination twice a year. For both men and women from 40 on, the periodic examination may well include a chest X ray.

Monthly self-examination of the breasts in front of a mirror is to be recommended to women over 35. These are the findings that should send her promptly to her doctor: painless lump in either breast, best felt with fingers held flat and pressed against the breast; change in shape of either breast; one breast higher than the other; nipple retracted or discharging; skin dimpled or pulled in; glands in the armpit enlarged.

What are the warning signs of cancer? An intelligent person should be equipped with a high "index of suspicion" against early cancer. This does not mean, however, a constant fear of cancer (cancerophobia, as it is sometimes called). He should be aware of the following warning signs, or little danger signals, that may, but not necessarily do, betoken cancer:

1. A sore that does not heal, particularly about the mouth, tongue, or lips.

2. A painless lump or thickening, in the breast or elsewhere.
3. Bloody discharge from any body opening.
4. Any change in color or size of a mole or wart.
5. Persistent indigestion or difficulty in swallowing.
6. Persistent hoarseness or cough.
7. Any change in normal bowel habits.

(Pain is not a signal of early cancer; when it occurs, the condition may be well along.)

If these danger signals are heeded and a physician promptly consulted, chances of untimely death from cancer are greatly cut down. Most of the time the person who follows up these signals will happily leave his doctor's office with the assurance that he does not have cancer.

Canker Sore—a small ulcer in the mouth or on the lips. Unless it is a symptom of more serious underlying infection or other disease, it usually disappears without any specific treatment.

Cannabis—marihuana. See NARCOTICS.

Cantharides—Spanish fly; a drug made from ground-up Spanish fly, also known as blister bug. It is sometimes applied to the skin as a counterirritant. Taken internally, it is a powerful poison, irritating especially to the sex and urinary organs. It should not be taken to stimulate waning sexual powers, that is, as an aphrodisiac; it is too dangerous.

Capillaries—the smallest blood vessels, at the far end of the *circulatory system,* which link the arterioles and the venules.

Carbohydrates—one of the chief classes of foodstuffs, embracing starches, sugars, and other so-called "energy foods." A carbo-hydrate is an organic chemical compound containing carbon, hydrogen, and oxygen. The hydrogen and oxygen are in the same proportion as in water (H_2O), that is, two parts of hydrogen to one part of oxygen.

Carbon—a basic element found in diamonds, coal, carbohydrates, and thousands of other compounds.

Carbon Dioxide—a gas (CO_2) normally formed by the tissues of the human body in burning carbon. It is present in the blood stream and exhaled in the lungs. It helps to regulate the breathing process. Harmless in reasonable concentrations, it is the gas that gives the fizz to carbonated water.

Carbon Monoxide—a highly poisonous gas (CO), colorless and odorless, formed by the incomplete burning (combustion) of carbon. *Carbon-monoxide poisoning* is a special hazard of industrial civilization, as carbon monoxide is contained in *manufactured gas* used for cooking and heating (but not in natural gas), forms whenever manufactured or natural gas is burned, is commonly present in coal mines, and is a regular by-product of combustion engines (automobile exhaust). Protection lies in adequate ventilation; that is, keeping carbon monoxide from accumulating where it may be breathed into the lungs in sufficient concentration to cause damage. Small amounts are not particularly harmful.

Carbon monoxide has an even stronger affinity than oxygen for the hemoglobin of the red blood cells. Breathed into the lungs, it displaces the oxygen by firmly attaching itself to the hemoglobin. The symptoms of carbon-monoxide poisoning, therefore, are the symptoms of insidious ASPHYXIATION: rapid and difficult breathing, a warning headache and constriction of the scalp, mental confusion, weakness and incoordination (especially of the legs), cherry-red skin, unconsciousness, and death—unless rescue comes in time.

First aid: Get the victim into fresh air. Apply artificial respiration if breathing has stopped or comes in gasps. Call the police department for an oxygen inhalator. Rub the limbs toward the heart. Keep the patient quiet for a long time.

Carbuncle—a large BOIL, which see.

Carcinoma—CANCER; specifically a form of cancer that arises in epithelial tissues of skin, glands, and membranes. There are many kinds of carcinoma; some yield readily to proper treatment; others may spread (metastasize) dangerously.

Cardiac—referring to the *heart;* as a *cardiac patient, cardiac condition,* or *cardiac drug.*

Cardiologist—heart specialist.

Cardiospasm—annoying spasms or contractures of certain muscles of the STOMACH (cardiac sphincter). The food tube (esophagus) is also usually involved.

Caries—bone decay. *Dental caries* means tooth decay. See TEETH.

Carotid—the chief artery of the neck. Just above its division into two main branches is situated the *carotid sinus* and the *carotid* gland, which has a very rich nerve supply. Overactivity or overstimulation of this nerve center can cause FAINTING, dizziness, and convulsions.

Car Sickness—see MOTION SICKNESS, also EAR TROUBLE. Young children often get car sick because they cannot see out of the windows of the moving vehicle.

Cartilage—gristle, the hard but plastic connective tissue that is not quite bone (for example, cartilage of the ribs) but is, in the unborn and growing child, the forerunner and model of bone before calcium is deposited in it. (See illustration for JOINTS.)

Cascara Sagrada—a LAXATIVE derived from the bark of a tree.

Castor Oil—a powerful cathartic, derived from the seed of the castor bean (*Ricinus communis*).

Castration of the male means removal of the testicles (and sometimes removal of the penis also). This may occur, rarely, as a result of accident or by deliberate surgical intent, as, for example, in treatment of cancer of the testes. When castration occurs before puberty, the secondary sex characteristics of the male do not develop; the castrate is called a *eunuch*.

Castration of the female means removal of both ovaries. It can also mean destruction of the ovaries' power to function by extensive irradiation (non-surgical castration).

Fear of castration or injury to the sex organs is a deep-seated unconscious fear in many people. It symbolizes fear of loss of self or of injury to the body anywhere. When young children become aware of the anatomy of the opposite sex, little girls may secretly fear that they have lost a sex organ, little boys that their organs will be taken away from them. This may be the origin of the so-called "castration complex."

Catalepsy—a strange state of muscular rigidity in which the patient does not move from whatever position he has been placed in.

Catalyst—any substance that speeds up or slows down a chemical reaction without itself being changed at the end of the reaction. ENZYMES, for example, are catalysts that promote the chemical digestion of food.

Cataract—clouding of the crystalline lens of the eye. See EYE TROUBLE.

Catarrh—a very old word for inflammatory discharge from a mucous membrane. It now generally refers to a running nose and other symptoms of a COMMON COLD.

Cathartic—a medicine that induces bowel movements; a laxative. Cathartics should not be self-prescribed or used indiscriminately. See CONSTIPATION.

Catheter—a hollow tube of metal, rubber, or plastic for draining fluids from the body; most commonly, for draining urine from the bladder, through the urethra.

Caul—sometimes a child is born with part of the membrane of the bag of waters (in which he lived in the womb) over his head and face. This membrane, or caul, is superstitiously considered a sign of good luck.

Causalgia—a burning-pain sensation.

Caustic—something that strongly irritates, burns, corrodes, or destroys living tissue, such as *caustic soda* or *zinc chloride*.

Cautery—an instrument or chemical substance (caustic) that destroys tissue. It is applied, however, to help the patient, such as in sealing a persistently bleeding vessel. In the old days of medicine a cautery was a hot iron. Today an electric current at the tip of a metal instrument is commonly employed (electrocautery).

Celiac Disease—a disease of infants and children in which they fail to obtain adequate nourishment because food is not properly assimilated from their intestinal tracts. Infants with this disease are usually cranky, have bulging abdomens, excrete pale and bulky stools. The disease usually responds to changes in diet; for example, reduction of fat and sugar, or addition of bananas.

CELLS

Cells are the fundamental units of all living things—human, animal, plant, microbe. There are one-cell creatures, for example, the ameba; and many-celled creatures, for example, man. The human body is a congregation of an estimated 26 trillion cells that all started with a single fertilized egg cell.

Most cells are so small that they can be seen only when greatly magnified; the cells of the human body vary in size from about 1/10,000 to 1/1,000 of an inch.

A cell is essentially a mass of protoplasm—a jellylike living substance—circumscribed by a cell wall and containing a nucleus. The nucleus is, crudely, the heart and reproductive system of the cell. New cells are formed by division of old ones, a process called *mitosis*. A group of cells form a *tissue*, like muscle tissue.

Each cell has its own life span. It is born (by the process of cell division), lives, feeds itself and gets rid of waste products (the process called *metabolism*), grows, reproduces itself by division or degenerates, dies, and is replaced. Cells respond to stimuli from the environment outside their walls. They also function, that is, perform the special task designed for them in the total economy of the living body. Thus, for example, muscle cells stretch and contract, nerve cells carry signals, endocrine-gland cells manufacture hormones.

Cells can be damaged and killed by direct injury, by poison from chemical substances or bacterial invasion, and by lack of foodstuff or oxygen. Anything that cuts off the blood supply to a part of the body kills and damages cells. A disease process is in essence damage or deformity of cells, which can no longer perform their functions. Many injured cells can replace themselves or be replaced by other tissue; a broken bone, for example, heals by replacement of cells. Unfortunately nerve cells do not regenerate.

There are many different kinds of cells in the human body, but they can generally be classified as follows:

1. *Epithelial cells,* which are found in the skin, membranes, and glands. Their function is to protect surfaces and pour out secretions. (See illustration for SKIN.)

2. *Connective tissue cells,* found in bones, cartilage, ligaments, and tendons, make up the supporting tissues of the body. Scar tissue is a replacement of other tissue with connective tissue cells. (See illustrations for BONES.)

3. *Muscle cells,* which have the power to expand and contract, are of three kinds: (a) *striped (striated) muscle cells,* found in the voluntary muscles of the body; (b) *smooth muscle cells,* which appear in the walls of blood vessels, the alimentary canal, and other body tubes and organs that operate by involuntary control; and (c) *cardiac muscle cells,* found only in the heart.

4. NERVE *cells,* found in the brain, spinal cord, ganglia, and all other nerves. (See illustrations for NERVES AND THE NERVOUS SYSTEM.)

5. BLOOD CELLS (which see), red and white, found in the blood stream and the blood-forming organs (bone marrow).

6. *Sex or germ cells,* which are the *egg cells* (ova) formed in the female ovary and the *sperm* cells generated in the male testes. (See illustration for SPERM.)

Cellulitis—inflammation of soft tissue; commonly refers to pelvic tissues. See FEMALE TROUBLES.

Cerebellum—the lower, smaller part of the BRAIN at the base of the skull; the hindbrain.

Cerebral Hemorrhage—bleeding in the brain, resulting in STROKE or apoplexy. See BRAIN DAMAGE.

CEREBRAL PALSY

Cerebral palsy describes a diverse group of childhood disabilities—primarily a lack of muscular control—arising from BRAIN DAMAGE before, during, or soon after birth. The term itself is fairly new and there is not complete agreement on how far it extends. It may be taken to include all diseases of the nervous system manifested by paralytic symptoms in infancy and childhood. Somewhat analogous conditions occur in later life, for example, PARKINSON'S DISEASE or shaking palsy. The term cerebral palsy was introduced by Dr. W. M. Phelps, of Baltimore, who did much to explore the problems of the kinds of patients described by his term.

Cerebral palsy is certainly not a single disease and it has a wide variety of manifestations. The two principal types are *athetoid*, which means without voluntary control of affected muscles; and *spastic*, in which the muscles tighten up and become rigid. Some patients have tremors, others show incoordination of movement (ataxia). The unhappy practical outcome of these neurological disabilities is that the youngster often cannot move his feet and arms properly, cannot feed and dress himself, cannot speak distinctly, makes facial grimaces and jerky purposeless movements.

With the increased professional and public interest in cerebral palsy, and the application of "team" management to specific cases, the outlook for the cerebral palsied child is better than it ever was. Further fundamental research in brain function and damage may yield new information to assist in the management of the cerebral palsied. But the fact must be faced that the child with cerebral palsy often has multiple handicaps. It is estimated that about half of these children are mentally retarded, half suffer from eye and vision defects, half or better from speech defects, a quarter from hearing impairment, and a third from convulsions.

These handicaps are present in varying degrees of severity. In some cases cerebral palsied children are mistakenly classified as mentally retarded; if given suitable educational opportunity, they will be able to learn.

The incidence of cerebral palsy is estimated at about 1 in every 170 live births, and the number of cerebral palsied in the United States at any time is calculated to lie between 500,000 and 600,000.

What can be done for cerebral palsy? There are no quick, shortcut, or "miracle" cures. Nevertheless proper treatment may produce considerable improvement in what may look at the outset to be a hopeless case. The first step in treatment is a detailed and complete diagnostic examination, including assessment of intellectual capacities, with repeated check-ups on specific points as needed to note progress. The outlook for the patient and the kind of treatment needed can thus be ascertained.

The first objective of treatment is to make the child as physically independent as possible in performing normal activities of daily living. The basic treatment is muscle re-education, brought about through muscular relaxation, repeated practice of voluntary muscle control, and the development of proper movement patterns. This program of physical therapy may be aided by muscle-relaxing drugs, orthopedic surgery (particularly tendon transplants and lengthening), and application of braces and splints. At the same time the intellectual development and social and emotional adjustment of the child must be attended to. Speech therapy is often called for, but neurosurgery does not yet have much to offer.

In spite of all efforts, there remains a residuum of pitiful patients who cannot be helped. The question then arises whether the child should be placed in an institution. There is no hard and fast rule. If the child can still benefit by contact with his parents, he should probably be kept at home. If there is no bond of attachment between the child and parents, or if the presence of the child threatens to break up the home, he should probably be placed in an institution.

The prevention of cerebral palsy depends upon better understanding of its causes. Direct injuries (traumas) to the brain in the process of birth were once thought to be the principal cause of cerebral palsy. It is now known that a great many other causative factors are involved; for example, toxemia of pregnancy and maternal infection before birth; premature birth; asphyxia during the birth process, sometimes related to anesthetics used; infectious disease (meningitis and encephalitis) soon after birth.

There are a number of national agencies concerned with the problems of the cerebral palsied child, notably the United Cerebral Palsy Associations, Inc., in New York City, and the National Society for Crippled Children and Adults, Inc., in Chicago.

Cerebrum—the large, main, upper, "thinking" part of the BRAIN, which see. It is divided into two hemispheres.

Cerumen—earwax.

Cervical—pertaining to the neck, as cervical vertebrae, or to any other cervix.

Cervicitis—inflammation of the neck of the womb (uterine cervix). See FEMALE TROUBLES.

Cervix—a neck or narrow part; most commonly, the neck of the womb (cervix uteri). See SEX ORGANS, FEMALE.

Chalazion—stye; see EYE TROUBLE.

Chancre—the first open sign of SYPHILIS, which see. It is a small, painless sore or ulcer that appears on the penis or in the vagina (or elsewhere), at the site where the infecting spirochete of syphilis entered the body.

Chancroid—a venereal disease, *soft chancre,* caused by a specific germ (*Hemophilus ducreyi*). It begins as a small pustule and advances rapidly and painfully to large discharging ulcers on the external sex organs and in the groin. The disease is most common in tropical and subtropical countries among sexually promiscuous individuals of lower economic classes.

Change of Life—see MENOPAUSE.

Charley Horse—the painful result of overstretching or overstraining (pulling) a muscle, particularly a thigh muscle. Tissues inside may actually be torn, resulting in pain, swelling, bleeding, and black-and-blue discoloration. Treatment is begun by placing the limb at rest, elevating it, applying cold compresses or an ice bag. Later stages of treatment are application of heat, gentle massage, tight bandaging, and gradual return to use of the muscles.

Cheilitis—inflammation of lips and sometimes corners of the mouth. It can be caused by sunburn, lipstick, chemical irritants, avitaminosis. See SKIN TROUBLE.

Cheilosis—fissures and scales on lips and at the corners of the mouth; often associated with too little riboflavin, a VITAMIN, in the diet.

Chemotherapy—treatment of disease with chemical substances; such drugs are called chemotherapeutic agents. The great trick in chemotherapy is to develop a drug that will cure or alleviate the disease without harming the patient. Successful chemotherapy is a comparatively new—20th century—development, but modern medicine relies heavily on it. Sulfa drugs, antibiotics, pain-killers, synthetic hormones and vitamins, isoniazid, and thousands of other compounds, made in the laboratory, are the gifts of chemistry to medicine. They have proved particularly effective in destroying infective bacteria. In contrast to chemotherapeutic agents are BIOLOGICALS, made from living organisms (e.g. VACCINES). See DRUGS.

Cheyne-Stokes Respiration—a peculiar kind of breathing usually observed with unconscious patients. They seem to stop breathing altogether for 5 to 40 seconds; then start up again with gradually increasing intensity until they get out of breath (dyspnea); stop breathing once more and repeat the performance.

Chicken Pox—varicella; a common childhood disease caused by a specific virus. It is usually a mild disease whose symptoms are a slight fever, some mild discomfort, and a skin eruption (exanthem), usually beginning on the body, face, or scalp. Little raised pimples come out on the skin, a few at a time. Some of these turn into small blisters, which break in a few hours, leaving a dry crust. The disease runs its course in about a week.

Chicken pox is one of the most contagious diseases, especially in the early stages of the eruption. The incubation period is two to three weeks. Probably 70% of the people in the U.S. have had chicken pox by the time they are 15 years old. With rare exceptions, one attack confers immunity.

Chiggers—the developing larvae of the harvest mite, or red bug, lodged on or under the skin, usually in a hair follicle. Their bites produce wheals and in-tense itching. This mite inhabits tall grass and areas overgrown with weeds and brush. Not the same as JIGGERS.

Chilblain—an inflamed condition of the skin of toes, fingers, or ears as a result of exposure to cold and damp weather. Itching, pain, redness, and swelling, followed by blisters, usually accompany chilblain. Proper protection against cold weather—wool socks, mittens, and earmuffs—is a requirement for people subject to recurrent chilblain, which can be serious.

CHILDBIRTH

Childbirth is the normal termination of PREGNANCY. In the United States today it is a very safe procedure and can be made relatively painless. Only 1 in 1,500 or 2,000 women does not come through childbirth safely. The risks of modern childbirth have been greatly minimized by better prenatal care, which often prevents complications from arising; better obstetrical practices; new drugs; and the fact that most women can now afford to, and actually do, have their babies in a hospital instead of at home.

In 1920, half the American babies were born at home. Today close to 90% are born in well-equipped hospitals, where the facilities for overcoming most obstetrical emergencies are available. It is interesting to see that the *fall* in maternal and infant deaths has paralleled the *rise* of Blue Cross and other insurance coverage for the hospitalization expenses of having a baby.

All childbirth is a natural and normal process, whether one pain-relieving technique or another is used. Of the techniques of "natural childbirth," credited to Dr. Grantly Dick Read, the most important thing that can be said is "It's nice work if you can get it." If it works, it's fine; but it doesn't work for everyone. The natural pains of childbirth may still have to be relieved by measures beyond preliminary education about childbirth and exercises to strengthen the abdominal muscles that help to expel the infant from the womb.

NORMAL SPONTANEOUS DELIVERY I

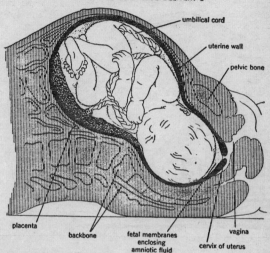

At term, as the first stage of labor begins. *This illustration shows the position of the fetus in the uterus at the beginning of labor. The cervix has not begun to dilate (open up).*

Needless fear of childbirth has been bred into many young women by their families and associates—and blithely accepted by their husbands. A classic cartoon shows a young husband and his wife, who is ready for delivery, entering the admitting office of a hospital. The caption reads, "Honey, are you sure you want to go through with this?" Some women (and men) fear childbirth because they have heard their mothers and other female relatives complain of it. Others fear childbirth because it is associated with what Alan Guttmacher calls "the larger, terrifying fear of sex." Childbirth is no picnic, but abnormal, neurotic fear undoubtedly tightens up the muscles employed in childbirth and makes it seem more difficult. There is no escaping some violence and some pain in childbirth.

The contracting uterus is a powerful muscle, and being forced

NORMAL SPONTANEOUS DELIVERY II

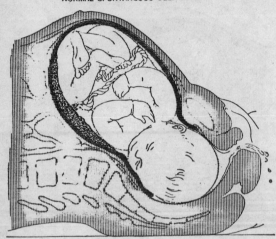

At the end of the first and the beginning of the second stage of labor. *The rupture of the membranes ("bag of waters") usually occurs at the end of the first stage of labor. The cervix of the uterus is now completely dilated.*

through the birth canal can hardly be a pleasant experience for the infant. To what extent *birth trauma* is a factor in subsequent psychological development (and a causative factor in later MENTAL ILLNESS) is highly debatable.

Some women rate their doctors by the amount of pain they suffer in childbirth. This is nonsensical. The attending physician must consider the total welfare of both mother and baby.

Labor is well-named. It is hard work. The mother sweats, sometimes losing several pints of fluid. A normal fatigue usually follows labor. Women accustomed to hard physical labor every day may be less affected by childbirth.

Labor is normally divided into three stages. The *first stage* extends from the beginning of labor pains to the time of full dilation (opening) of the mouth and neck of the womb. It is the longest stage, lasting perhaps 10 to 16 hours. The *second stage*

NORMAL SPONTANEOUS DELIVERY III

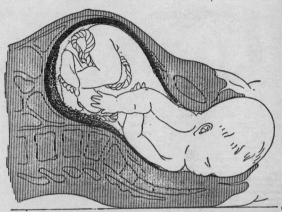

The second stage of labor, when the child is actually born. *The infant's head is impelled into the birth canal (vagina), now greatly enlarged, by the force of uterine contractions. The top of the infant's head appears here at the vaginal orifice.*

extends from the time of the dilation of the cervix until the actual birth of the baby. It may take anywhere up to two hours. The *third stage* extends from the birth of the baby to the expulsion of the afterbirth (placenta). It may be completed in two or three, but usually five to ten, minutes.

The length of labor varies in different women and in the same women in different pregnancies. Sometimes it may be over in less time than it takes for a taxicab to get to a hospital. On the average, though averages mean little, a woman bearing her first child will be in labor for about 18 hours; if she has already had a child, about 12 hours. The management of prolonged labors requires the best kind of judgment by the doctor; he must know whether or not to interfere; if so, when; and when, how. If labor is unexpectedly prolonged, the wise doctor and family will insist on immediate consultation with the best available specialist in obstetrics.

NORMAL SPONTANEOUS DELIVERY IV

The moment of birth, the end of the second stage of labor. *The physician gently grasps the head of the infant and prepares to help the rest of his body into the world.*

If a difficult labor is anticipated, this expert consultation should be obtained beforehand, during the later months of pregnancy.

Labor pains usually begin in the small of the back and progress to the abdomen. True labor pains are always associated with contractions of the uterus. Between pains (contractions) there is usually no discomfort. The first contractions may come on every quarter or half hour and last a quarter to half a minute. The pains gradually begin to last longer, and become more frequent, more intense, and at more regular intervals. As soon as they become *regular* it is time to call the doctor and, on his advice, be off to the hospital. False labor pains (*"false alarms"*) often occur, frequently about a month before the baby is born. The diagnosis here is a problem for the doctor. False labor pains are usually irregular.

Painless childbirth has been a goal of obstetrics since the middle of the 19th century, shortly after the discovery of ether as a surgical anesthetic. In 1853 Queen Victoria accepted obstetric anesthesia during the birth of her seventh child—and women everywhere have since demanded painless childbirth. The queen got intermittent doses of chloroform, just enough at each labor pang to ease the pain but not enough to make her unconscious.

A great variety of anesthetic agents are now available for obstetric anesthesia and analgesia (pain-killing without loss of consciousness). They must, however, be used with discretion so as not to harm the baby or make delivery more difficult. *"Twilight sleep"* is produced by infusing the rectum with an oil-ether or other anesthetic solution. Among the newer methods are nerve-blocking injections of local anesthetics in the pelvic region; for example, caudal anesthesia, in which injections are made at the tail end of the spinal canal.

Education for childbirth is another direction of effort to reduce labor pains. These are the techniques that have been given the name *"natural childbirth."* Their aim is to reduce false fears about childbirth and thus greatly diminish the pains associated with it. In many cases it may help to reduce pains, but it rarely eliminates them. HYPNOTISM has also been tried.

Delivery (childbirth). Most women are admitted to the hospital while still in the first stage of labor. The woman is immediately put to bed and prepared by nurses for an aseptic delivery. Pubic hair is shaved, an enema usually given. Members of the hospital house-staff of physicians may look in and perhaps examine the patient rectally. Her pains are timed by an attendant. If necessary, one or more narcotic drugs may be injected to help relieve pain or discomfort. This is the screaming stage.

When examination reveals that the cervix is fully dilated—it has a temporary diameter of about 4 inches—the mother-soon-to-be is taken into the delivery room, usually on a wheel table, and placed on the delivery table. It has elevated leg rests, or stirrups, on two corners.

The woman lies on her back, her feet elevated by the leg rests. Her body is draped with sheets.

About this time the bag of waters breaks, and amniotic fluid pours out of the vagina. This sometimes happens early in the first stage of labor, causing a so-called *"dry labor."* In other cases, the doctor has to puncture a thick membrane.

The rhythmic contractions of the uterus continue, exerting a powerful force squeezing the child out into the world. The contractions or pains cannot be voluntarily controlled by the mother. She can, however, "bear down" by using abdominal muscles to help along the contractions. Or she can relax and let the uterus work.

At length, in about 95 out of 100 cases, the top of the baby's head appears at the vaginal orifice. It recedes somewhat as the

NORMAL SPONTANEOUS DELIVERY V

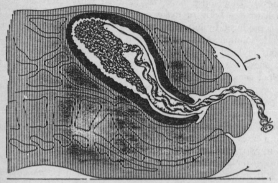

The third stage of labor. *The child has already been born and the umbilical cord cut and tied. In the third stage of labor the placenta, loosened from the uterine wall, is expelled from the uterus along with the remains of the fetal membranes. Note that there is already a thickening of the uterine walls as the uterus begins to shrink and return to its normal, nonpregnant, size and shape.*

contraction that brought it down subsides. With each new contraction, the baby's head comes out farther and farther—and finally does not recede between pains.

At this point the doctor grasps the child under the chin. He turns the head gently to one side and then the other as he releases the shoulder. The rest of the child can be easily lifted out of the birth canal. He is still attached to his mother by the umbilical cord.

While waiting for the third stage of labor to be concluded (delivery of the afterbirth), the doctor immediately swabs out the baby's mouth and waits for the first cry. Most infants cry lustily as soon as they are born (a few, even, just before). If regular breathing is not quickly established, the doctor may hold the baby upside down, give him a few gentle slaps on the buttock, or if necessary, apply a tiny oxygen mask. Breathing air is the first of the many new experiences that await the baby. Rapid changes occur in his lungs and heart while he is getting used to it.

After a final surge of blood from the placenta, the umbilical cord is tied off, about three inches above the navel, and cut. The cord stump is covered with a sterile dressing and placed over the abdomen. Infection must be avoided.

Drops of silver nitrate or other acceptable antiseptic (e.g. penicillin) are immediately put into the baby's eyes to protect against possible gonorrheal infection and blindness. The baby is cleaned off as much as necessary, wrapped in a blanket, weighed, footprinted, encircled with an identification bracelet (so that babies can't possibly get mixed up), placed in a warm crib.

When the afterbirth is expelled, the physician examines it to be sure that it is all out. Immediately after the child has been expelled, the uterus begins to contract. In so doing it squeezes off the blood vessels that were broken when the placenta was torn off. To speed this process and prevent needless bleeding, the doctor may give drugs (ergot and pituitrin), which are called *oxytocics*. Only ¼ to ½ pint of blood is usually lost. If more, it can be promptly replaced by transfusion from the BLOOD BANK.

Complications of childbirth. These do occur, but most of them are prevented by adequate prenatal care (see PREGNANCY). Approximately 95% of all babies present themselves to the world head first and go through the normal spontaneous delivery just described. In about 4% the buttocks show first (breech presentation). In the other 1% a shoulder, leg, or arm may first present. All these presentations can be handled by appropriate obstetric maneuvers ("turning the baby"), or more common today, by CAESAREAN SECTION.

Hardly one birth in 20 today requires *instrumental delivery;* that is, the application of high, mid-, or low FORCEPS to extract the child. Doctors do not try to hasten normal delivery with forceps—"meddlesome obstetrics." *Birth injuries* are thus kept to a minimum.

These should not be confused with the strangely misshapen head an occasional baby is born with. This occurs because the baby's head bones are not firmly knit together (a natural safety factor in childbirth). They can slip over each other as the head goes down the narrow passage of the birth canal and between the pelvic bones. Many mothers and fathers are temporarily shocked because they think their baby has been born with a pointed head.

This temporary freakish shape returns to normal in a few weeks.

Episiotomy and repair, a surgical incision to widen the opening from the vagina and prevent lacerations, is sometimes performed.

The *placenta* may make some trouble. It may separate prematurely, it may block the opening of the cervix (placenta previa), or fragments may be retained after childbirth and cause bleeding (postpartum hemorrhage).

Bleeding after childbirth, which can be serious, results also when the uterus fails to contract tightly. This uterine inertia, or lack of muscle tone, may be owing to the fact the uterus was stretched too much, as by twins or an excess amount of amniotic fluid (hydramnios). It may also result from prolonged labor, from having had many children (multiparity), or from ANESTHESIA. Treatment of this type of uterine bleeding includes blood transfusion, giving ergot and other oxytocic drugs, packing the uterus, surgery, and sometimes, in extreme cases, removal of the uterus (hysterectomy).

Infections. The old bugaboo of childbearing, infection known as "childbed fever," puerperal septicemia, or blood poisoning, has been almost completely eliminated by aseptic (germ-free) obstetrical practice and sulfa and antibiotic drugs. Doctors' hands no longer carry infection to mothers, as Ignaz Semmelweis and Oliver Wendell Holmes properly charged in the 1840's.

Following delivery the new mother usually sleeps. Doctors now make every effort to get the mother back on her feet as soon as possible after childbirth—anywhere from the first day on. A week to ten days convalescence in the hospital is usually enough—if there are no complications. Many women are anxious to leave earlier. The maternity ward is usually the gayest one in the hospital. A gradually increasing schedule of activity and social life is desirable. Visitors with colds or other communicable infections should not be welcomed. It takes about six weeks for the mother's body to return to the shape it was in before pregnancy.

See PREGNANCY; FEMALE TROUBLES.

Chill—a sudden feeling of being cold, accompanied by shivering and chattering of the teeth. People with high fever as a result of infection often *feel* cold; hence, *chills and fever.* Poisoning by metal fumes produces chills; so do certain stages of malaria. To "take a chill" means essentially to catch a cold. Exposure to chilling may be a predisposing factor that brings on a cold or other respiratory infection.

Chiropodist—foot specialist, who treats minor ailments of the feet. See FOOT TROUBLE.

Chiropractor—a member of a group, licensed under some state laws, to practice a system of healing unacceptable to the tenets of organized medicine. Chiropractic assumes that disease is due to malfunctioning of the nervous system and that cure or relief can be obtained by manipulations largely directed toward the spinal column.

Chloral Hydrate—a powerful but dangerous sleep-producing drug; the common ingredient in "knock-out drops" and "Mickey Finns."

Chloramphenicol—the ANTIBIOTIC drug derived from the organism *Streptomyces venezuelae* or manufactured synthetically.

Chlorination—the process of treating water supplies with chlorine compounds to render them reasonably free from harmful bacteria. Sanitary engineers now have tests for so-called "free residual chlorine" in treated water supplies. If the water still contains one part of chlorine per million parts of water thirty minutes after treatment, it can be considered safe to drink.

Chlorine—a basic chemical element; it is a yellowish-green, suffocating, poisonous gas. However, in chemical combination with other elements, notably sodium, it is essential to the

human body. *Sodium chloride* is common table salt; the chloride in it goes to form hydrochloric acid, found in the gastric juice. Even low concentrations of chlorine and certain of its compounds are actively germicidal.

Chloroform—a powerful *anesthetic* drug that can be very conveniently given by inhalation. In small doses by mouth it is an effective pain-killer and antispasmodic drug; applied to the skin it is a counterirritant sometimes used as a liniment in treating rheumatism. Chloroform has gone out of favor since the discovery that even small doses of it may seriously damage the liver. The strong etherlike odor of this heavy, volatile, colorless liquid was once the common source of a characteristic "hospital smell."

Chlorophyll—the green coloring matter in plants by which they accomplish photosynthesis. It has some value as a *deodorant*.

Chlorpromazine—one of the first of the effective tranquilizing drugs (ATARAXICS) used in treatment of MENTAL ILLNESS and HEART DISEASE. Thorazine is one brand name for chlorpromazine.

Choking—ASPHYXIA. Treat by artificial respiration; see ASPHYXIA treatment. When babies and small children are choking, and even seem to be turning blue, they often have a peanut, marble or other small object lodged in their throats, clogging the airway. This can often be taken out with a deft finger. If not, hold the child upside down and *shake him gently* in an effort to dislodge the object from the throat. Call for doctor, ambulance, police, fire department or first-aid squad immediately. In gas poisoning, see that the victim is promptly removed to fresh air—indoors or outside.

Cholecystectomy—surgical removal of the GALL BLADDER.

Cholecystitis—inflammation of the GALL BLADDER.

Cholera—an acute communicable disease, caused by the comma-shaped cholera vibrio. In mild cases diarrhea may be the chief or only symptom. In severe cases, often fatal, extreme diarrhea ("rice-water stools") is accompanied by great dehydration, with thirst, vomiting, pain and cramps in the abdomen, prostration, and unconsciousness.

Asiatic cholera, or *Indian cholera,* has long been an epidemic scourge of the Far East. It is absent from the Western hemisphere (except when introduced from foreign countries). The primary source of infection is in the *bowel discharges* of infected cholera victims and in convalescent or healthy carriers of the cholera germ. The disease is spread through contact with these discharges, which are carried by *water* and *raw food* and by *flies.*

Far-reaching sanitary and public-health measures—water

purification, fly control, and the like—must be taken to wipe out or prevent epidemic cholera.

Cholesterol—a fatlike substance found in all animal fats and oils, and in many other tissues of the human body. According to some theories not yet completely proved or accepted, cholesterol is the villain that brings about HIGH BLOOD PRESSURE, HARDENING OF THE ARTERIES, and many other disease conditions. It is usually found in gallstones.

Chorditis—inflammation of a cord—vocal or spermatic. See THROAT or SEX ORGANS, MALE.

Chorea—St. Vitus dance; twitching, jerky, uncontrolled movements of the arms and legs, often accompanied by other nervous symptoms. *Sydenham's chorea,* appearing in children and adolescents, is a symptom and aftermath of RHEUMATIC FEVER, which see. HUNTINGTON'S CHOREA is one of the few hereditary diseases that first appear in adult life; its symptoms include speech difficulties, twitching movements, mental deterioration.

Chorioretinitis—an EYE disease; specifically inflammation of choroid coat of the eye and the retina.

Choroid—skinlike; but usually refers to the pigmented coat or layer of the eyeball between the sclera and the retina. See EYES.

Choroiditis—inflammation of the CHOROID. See EYE TROUBLE.

Chromosomes—colored bodies, thread- or rod-like in shape, visible under a microscope when a "mother cell" divides into two "daughter cells." *Genes*, which control heredity, are located in or on the chromosomes. See HEREDITY.

Chronic—long-continued, persistent, prolonged, repeated. A *chronic illness* is one that lasts for a long time; it is the opposite of an *acute illness*, which runs a comparatively short course. However, some acute illnesses may become chronic; for example, arthritis, bronchitis. The care of patients with chronic illness, many of them in the older age brackets, is one of the great medical and economic problems of this day.

Cicatrix—scar tissue, the new flesh that forms when a wound heals.

Cigarettes—see TOBACCO.

Cinchona—the tree, native to South America, from whose bark QUININE is derived.

Circulation of the BLOOD. See HEART.

Circumcision—cutting away the foreskin or any part of it. This is an ancient surgical procedure; it is performed as a ritual among Jews, Mohammedans, and some other peoples. It has hygienic values, preventing cheesy secretions of the foreskin (smegma) from accumulating and irritating the head of the penis. The operation does not increase or decrease sexual satisfaction. Circumcision should not be confused with *castration*, which means removal of the testicles.

Cirrhosis—hardening of an organ as the result of inflammation or other disease process. *Cirrhosis of the liver* and destruction of its important functioning cells, for which a leathery connective tissue is substituted, may be brought about gradually by chronic infection, particularly syphilis and malaria; by any obstruction to the outflow of its bile, for example, gallstones; by chronic alcohol poisoning; and by other causes. Alcoholism is far from being the only cause. See LIVER TROUBLE.

Clap—GONORRHEA.

Claudication—lameness. There is a peculiar form of *intermittent claudication* associated with disease of the arteries. The patient has no pain while resting but suffers intense pain in the legs and goes lame when he starts to walk.

Claustrophobia—abnormal fear of being shut up in a closed space; the *opposite* of *agoraphobia*, the dread of being left alone in wide open spaces.

Clavicle—the collar bone. (See illustrations for BONES; JOINTS.)

Cleft Palate—an opening or fissure in the roof of the mouth; it is usually accompanied by *harelip*, a notch in the center of the upper lip, giving it the appearance of a rabbit's lip.

Both cleft palate and harelip are *congenital malformations,* discovered at birth. Their cause is unknown. They represent failures of nature to complete the full development of an unborn child. Normally the completion of the roof of the mouth and the joining of the upper lip take place by growth of tissues from both sides toward the middle line. The cleft, or failure to close, may be minor or extreme. The treatment is surgery, at as early an age as the surgeon deems it wise to operate.

Climacteric—MENOPAUSE, change of life.

Climate has a significant influence on health and disease, but the details of these effects are far from being worked out. There are, for example, a host of tropical diseases that are rarely seen in temperate latitudes. Conversely, there are many diseases, notably upper-respiratory infections and their consequences, that are much less significant in warmer climates. Change of climate is sometimes recommended to patients suffering from rheumatism, rheumatic fever, chronic bronchitis, or certain other diseases; but this medical prescription is by no means as common as it used to be. It has been quite clearly demonstrated, for example, that change of climate has no definite beneficial effect on tuberculosis. The effect of *weather changes*—for example, barometric pressure, temperature, relative humidity—on the course of disease and the maintenance of health has been studied carefully without as yet yielding any definite answers.

Clinic comes from the Greek word meaning *bed.* Today a clinic means a place where a group of doctors practice medicine together and frequently teach medicine. In some places a clinic signifies the outpatient department of a hospital, where free or low-cost medical service is available to qualified clients if they have time to sit around and wait for it. Doctors contribute their services.

Clinical signifies bedside medicine, the actual practice and knowledge of medicine gained from observing and treating real, live patients. In contrast stand experimental, laboratory, and academic medicine.

Clinician is a doctor whose judgment has been sharpened by long experience with patients.

Clitoris—the erectile FEMALE SEX ORGAN analogous to the male *penis;* it is situated in the forward fold of the labia of the vagina. See SEX ORGANS, FEMALE.

Clot—the mass that forms when blood clots. See BLOOD CLOTTING and HEART DISEASE.

Clubfoot—talipes; a deformity of the foot, which is so twisted at the ankle that it no longer rests properly on the ground.

There are many varieties of clubfoot, described by the particular direction of the twist. For example, the toes may be twisted up so that the person can walk only on his heel (talipes calcaneus), or the heel may be pulled up so that he can walk only on his toes (talipes equinus). Again, the sole may be turned inward so that the person walks on the outer edge of the foot (talipes varus), or the sole may be twisted outward so that he walks on the inner border (talipes valgus).

Clubfoot is usually a *congenital malformation*, discovered at birth; such cases may be considered the result of faulty development or irregular position of the unborn infant in the womb, but never the result of prenatal fright of the mother. Clubfoot deformities may also occur in later life, as the result of *poliomyelitis* (infantile paralysis), muscular spasms, or scar tissue and contractures caused by burns and inflammations.

Clubfoot in early infancy can often be corrected by application of splints and bandages, massage and gentle but frequent manipulation of the foot to twist it back into its correct position. Severe or neglected cases and those arising in later life usually require extensive *orthopedic surgery* and *physical therapy*.

Coagulate—to clot, as blood; to curdle, as milk solids becoming cheese.

Coal Tar Ointment—an antiseptic and irritant substance sometimes useful in the treatment of certain SKIN troubles. Long-continued use is dangerous.

Cocaine—a NARCOTIC drug obtained from coca leaves. It is dangerously habit-forming. Addicts call it "snow." Cocaine salts are used very effectively as *local anesthetics*.

Coccidioidomycosis—a lung disease resulting from inhaling spores of a specific fungus *(coccidioides)*, sometimes called *valley fever*. In its early stages it may be mistaken for tuberculosis. In later stages the fungus involves the skin and other organs.

Coccus—any spherical berry-shaped microbe; for example, strepto*coccus*.

Coccyx—tail bone; the last bone(s) at the lower end of the spine. (See illustrations for BONES; SPINE.)

Cochlea—a part of the inner ear, a spiral passage resembling a snail shell. (See illustration for EARS.)

Cocoa—a beverage that contains *theobromine;* a drug and chemical similar to the CAFFEINE found in COFFEE and tea, but not quite so stimulating to the nerves.

Codeine—a NARCOTIC drug, derived from opium and related to morphine. It is less powerful than morphine and carries much less danger of addiction. It is often prescribed for abdominal pain and cramps and in *cough* medicines.

Cod-Liver Oil—rich but distasteful source of VITAMINS A and D.

Coffee contains CAFFEINE (about 1½ grains per cup), a stimulant to heart, nerves, and kidneys. Millions of people drink 2 to 6 cups of coffee a day without harm and with a good personal knowledge of their tolerance for it. Other people avoid it because it keeps them awake at night, makes them jittery, or gives them a headache. Physicians restrict coffee in patients who may be harmed by the nerve stimulation it provides. *Children*, who are normally very active, do not need this stimulation. Strong coffee is an antidote for drugs that depress the nervous system; for example, alcohol and BARBITURATES. In *decaffeinated coffee*, about 97% of the caffeine has been removed.

Cup for cup, coffee and *tea* contain about the same amount of caffeine. Tea leaves contain about twice as much caffeine (2 to 4%) as coffee beans (1 to 2%), but well-brewed coffee is usually made about twice as strong as well-steeped tea.

Coitus—sexual intercourse. *Coitus interruptus* means withdrawal of the penis just before ejaculation. It is a very unsatisfactory and uncertain method of preventing conception.

"Cold"—see COMMON COLD.

Cold Sores—a mild virus infection; needs no treatment. See HERPES.

Colic—a severe, cramping, griping pain in or referred to the abdomen; in popular terms a stomach ache or bellyache, although the stomach is not usually primarily responsible for the pain. Colic also means the severe pain sometimes associated with the presence or passage of GALLSTONES or KIDNEY STONES.

The origins of colic or bowel pain are numerous. The most obvious is overeating or eating foods that do not agree with you. But colic is also a symptom of appendicitis, bowel obstruction, mental or emotional distress, and lead poisoning (lead colic, painter's colic). If colicky pains last more than an hour, or return repeatedly, see a doctor.

Colic in infants is a fairly common condition, though one that leads to much upset of the child's and the household's routine. The common symptom is irritable crying far into the night. The food he gets is not to be considered the sole cause of the infant's colic; changing formulas rarely helps. The colicky reaction is a part of the whole picture of his development and the total care and attention he is getting. Most babies outgrow colic by the time they are three months old. If colic is persistent or severe, parents should consult a physician.

Until the doctor sees the baby, these things may help: Turn the baby on his stomach. Hold him face down across your knees. Put a well-padded (with towel) hot-water bag or bottle under his stomach. Rub his back and the back of his neck. Rock him gently in your arms or over your shoulder; "cuddle-coo" him. In rare instances a warm enema may be justified and give relief.

If your doctor has prescribed a pain-relieving medicine, give it to the baby as indicated. Do not give other medicine (e.g. paregoric) without medical advice.

Colitis—sore bowels. Sometimes it means actual inflammation and visible changes in the bowel, which can be seen by the doctor through an electrically lighted metal instrument — sigmoidoscope — introduced through the anus.

Bowel inflammation can result from infection with a specific germ, though it is very difficult to pick out the offending one. In such cases, the patient may develop an acute or chronic form of *ulcerative colitis*, which produces severe diarrhea (up to 20 stools a day), small ulcers that sometimes bleed, great abdominal pain, weakness, emaciation, and anemia. This can be a stubborn and recurrent disease, sometimes fatal. *Ulcerative colitis*, a serious disease, should not be confused with the far more common causes of sore bowels.

Irritation of the bowel is often the result of true food poisoning; of food sensitivity or allergy, which must be carefully ferreted out; of too much roughage, like bran, in the diet; and of abuse of laxatives (the "laxative habit"). See CONSTIPATION. Overdoses of some of the new antibiotic drugs may also upset the bowels.

Mucous colitis, once a very fashionable disease, is not a true colitis. The bowel feels sore, sensitive, and irritable, but it is not infected or inflamed. It is prone, however, to produce and shed large quantities of mucus in response to various kinds of distressing stimuli. The mucus is not harmful. Since spasm or cramp in the bowels is the most frequent symptom, this condition is more properly called *mucous colic*. Judicious prescription by a physician of spasm-relieving drugs will help many patients. Repeated flushing of the colon with enemas, medicated or not, is not likely to bring any long-lasting relief, although it may not do any harm.

The underlying cause of persistent mucous colic is usually psychological. Distress and anger are foisted on the colon. The trouble, however, is not in the bowels but in the patient herself and her reactions to the life situations in which she finds herself. (The condition is far more common in women than men.)

COLLAGEN DISEASES

Collagen diseases are those involving the connective tissues of the body. Collagen itself is the principal substance in these tissues. It is an ALBUMINlike protein, which, when boiled, turns into gelatin or glue. Collagens are found in the skin, blood vessels, bones, tendons, cartilages, and other connective tissues. They are the part of the elastic tissue that gives it strength and the ability to support other tissues.

The idea of collagen diseases is comparatively new, dating only from about 1950. Two common and four rare diseases are now commonly grouped together as collagen diseases. They are RHEUMATIC FEVER, rheumatoid ARTHRITIS (there are many other kinds of arthritis), periarteritis nodosa, lupus erythematosus, scleroderma, and dermatomyositis.

In *rheumatic fever* and *rheumatoid arthritis* the chief sites of involvement are the joints, heart, serous membranes lining body cavities, and subcutaneous tissue just under the skin. The changes that occur in the collagen fractions of these tissues produce a great variety of symptoms. Among them are pain in the joints, weakness, fatigue, weight loss, lack of appetite, and fever. These symptoms are common in the other collagen diseases, except scleroderma.

Periarteritis nodosa is the rare disease in which collagen changes occur in the small blood vessels, arteries, and arterioles. This disease appears most commonly in men between 20 and 40. Only about 500 cases have ever been reported.

Lupus erythematosus is the rare collagen disease that may involve the heart, kidneys, spleen, and serous membranes of body cavities. It occurs chiefly in females from 15 to 40. It is a chronic, progressive, usually fatal disorder. A butterfly-shaped inflammation over the nose is a common symptom.

Scleroderma means hardening of the skin. In this rare collagen disease, which principally afflicts women between 30 and 50 and which comes on insidiously, patches of skin become swollen and then gradually harden. The skin loses its color, may become mottled, and tightens up to give a hidebound appearance. While scarring and hardening of the skin is the principal manifestation of this disease, other tissues may also be affected, notably the heart, intestinal tract, and tissues under the top layers of skin.

Dermatomyositis is a serious, common, and frequently fatal collagen disorder in which skin, subcutaneous tissue, and muscles are involved in inflammation, degeneration, and wasting away. Symptoms depend on what organs and muscles are involved, which may include eyes, throat, diaphragm, and rib muscles. Hence difficulties in vision, breathing, and swallowing may appear. Weight loss and weakness are also common. This condition afflicts both males and females from about 10 to 50 years of age.

What is the treatment for collagen diseases? The research that led to the grouping of these diseases has also brought hope of improved treatment. Very significant is the fact that all of them respond, at least temporarily, to CORTISONE and ACTH. But this is not the sole method of treating these diseases. Aspirinlike drugs, salicylates, are frequently given to relieve pain. In rheumatic fever a program of preventing future infection of the upper respiratory tract with hemolytic streptococci is indicated.

Colon—the large bowel or intestine, extending from the cecum to the rectum. See DIGESTIVE SYSTEM. An *irritable colon*, presenting symptoms of tenderness, pain, and gas, is very frequently the outcome of a misguided "laxative habit." See CONSTIPATION.

Color Blindness is the inability, more or less, to discriminate between colors, most commonly a failure to sort out reds and greens. Millions of people are color-blind without knowing it. Color blindness is perhaps ten times as common in males as in females. It is an *hereditary defect* in the structure of the eye, and nothing yet known can remedy it. A color-blind boy always gets his defective gene (for color) from his mother. (See EYE TROUBLE.)

Colostomy—a surgical operation in which the colon is brought out to form a permanent opening in the wall of the abdomen. A *colostomy bag* is worn over the opening to receive bowel movements. Colostomy is indicated when the lower end of the bowel (rectum) must be removed, usually because of cancer.

Colostrum—the milky fluid that issues from the breasts a few days before or after childbirth. It is different from regular breast milk.

Coma—unconsciousness from which a patient can be aroused only with great effort and with proper medical treatment, if at all. Coma is an end result of many possible complex causes; notably head injuries, poisoning, APOPLEXY, BRAIN tumors, ALCOHOL, NARCOTICS, UREMIA, DIABETES (diabetic coma).

Comedo—BLACKHEAD.

COMMON COLD

Common cold is certainly the most common infection that afflicts and annoys mankind. It has been estimated that colds outnumber other diseases 25 to 1. A variety of different names are used to describe the common cold and reflect its particular site: for example, coryza, catarrh, upper-respiratory infection, rhinitis, and nasopharyngitis.

Colds are costly; in the U.S. it is estimated that up to 90,000,000 working days and $3 billion in wages are lost to productive work because of the common cold. Industrial employees lose an average of from 1 to 3 days a year from colds. Colds are responsible for about one-quarter of all absences from school.

Who gets colds? Practically anyone. Susceptibility is universal. Only inhabitants of small, isolated communities seem to escape—and even they don't when an infected individual enters the community. Few people in any clime are completely free from colds. In the U.S. almost everyone has a cold a year; about half the people have at least two colds. An additional quarter have three or more colds. During the "cold season," the months of October and November, there have been times, according to Gallup surveys, when 1 out of every 7 people had a cold.

Children under five seem somewhat more likely to contract colds than adults or older children.

A brief period—about a month—of relative immunity to the common cold is conferred by an attack of the disease.

What causes colds? The specific infecting agent is a virus—or a number of them. New work on viruses is beginning to identify certain groups of viruses with the onset of the common cold, but there is no common agreement yet on these findings. If filterable viruses alone were the cause of colds, they might all be short and mild. Secondary infection with bacteria, larger germs, is often superimposed on tissues softened up by the viruses. This usually prolongs the cold for two to three weeks and is responsible for the thick, yellow nasal discharge. Colds that begin as sore throats may have bacteria as the primary invaders.

The symptoms of the common cold represent attempts of the invaded tissues to get rid of the invaders. The stuffy nose is suffused with extra blood; its air passages are partly shut off with extra mucus released to wash out the invaders. Sneezing and coughing are attempts to dislodge irritations in the respiratory tract. A most eloquent description of the well-known symptoms of the common cold was given by Charles Dickens: "I am at this moment deaf in the ears, hoarse in the throat, red in the nose, green in the gills, damp in the eyes, twitchy in the joints and fractious in temper from a most intolerant and oppressive cold."

A dry, scratchy, irritated feeling in the nose or the back of the throat is usually the first sign that a cold is coming. From this point it may be a half day to three days before the cold really blooms. (This is to say, the incubation period is from 12 to 72 hours.)

A slight elevation of temperature, chilly sensations, and a general feeling of fatigue may also mark the first day or two of a cold.

How do you catch a cold? From someone who has a cold. The usual method of transmission is by droplet infection. The cold victim sneezes, coughs, and talks; in so doing he scatters cold virus, in droplets of mucus, into the air around him. These droplets are inhaled at close range and may engender a cold in the next fellow.

But colds are also indirectly transmitted by handkerchiefs, eating utensils, and other articles recently soiled by discharges from the cold victim. The virus picked from the throat can be conveyed on the hands. This is one of the strong arguments for hand washing as a disease-preventive measure.

Colds are most catching in the early stages, usually the first day. By the third or fourth day, it is unlikely that the virus will be transferred; it is almost certain that it will not be after the first week.

Many factors beyond the presence of the virus are involved in catching a cold. Environment and resistance of the host are concerned. Overfatigue, malnutrition, and other illness may have weakened the body's powers to resist the virus and bacterial invasion.

Weather plays a part. Getting chilled in cold, damp weather; sudden changing from dry, warm interiors to cold wet outdoor weather (the normal living process for most sedentary workers); getting wet feet; and frequenting crowded rooms where other people already have colds—all these circumstances seem to help the process of catching cold. Cold weather does not seem to induce colds. It is the change in weather, from warm to sudden cold, that does it.

How should colds be treated? With respect. There is no specific remedy against the viruses of the common cold, although there are many SULFA DRUGS and ANTIBIOTICS to control secondary bacterial invaders. Aspirin may make the patient more comfortable and bring down the temperature. Nose drops and other inhaled medications that shrink the membranes of the nose may be used to relieve obstruction to the air passages. Most time-honored treatments are worthless. Little help can be expected from forcing (or restricting) fluids or fruit juices or from cathartics, antiseptic gargles, hot or cold compresses, mustard plasters, exercise ("sweating out a cold"), or inhaled vapors. Hot gargles and hot baths followed by rest in bed without chilling may help.

The sovereign remedy for the common cold is rest in bed during the early stages. This enables the body to mobilize its resources to throw off the infection. Unfortunately, too many people refuse this remedy; indeed they take the opposite course of fighting the cold, sometimes with disastrous results. Bed rest also has the advantage of reducing exposure of others to your cold.

Use of disposable paper tissues during the course of a cold is recommended. Much-used cloth handkerchiefs may reinfect.

An old adage had it that the treatment of a cold was two weeks and two dozen linen handkerchiefs, and that treated or untreated, the cold would run the same course. Actually, most people recover in 5 to 10 days. If a cold hangs on for more than two weeks, treatment for secondary invaders is probably indicated.

The early symptoms of the common cold are much like those of INFLUENZA and many childhood diseases. Certain symptoms in the course of a cold, however, are danger signals that demand prompt, definite medical attention because they may betoken PNEUMONIA. These signals are chills and fever, rapidly rising temperature, difficult breathing, pain in the chest or side. Call or recall your doctor if these symptoms appear.

How can colds be prevented? There is no guarantee that this can be done, but the following suggestions may be helpful:

Keep away from people who have colds, especially if they insist on coughing, sneezing, or talking in your face.

Mind the weather. Dress properly for it—neither too warmly nor too lightly. Children have to be watched in this respect. Keep your feet dry.

Avoid, if possible, overheated rooms, sitting in drafts, and becoming needlessly chilled.

Get adequate rest and sleep. Do not become overfatigued. Maintain adequate nutrition with a well-balanced diet.

Put little faith in highly touted and advertised methods of cold prevention. Scientific evidence has discredited most of the fads that have periodically swept the country. You will not prevent colds by overdosing yourself with vitamins, exposing yourself to ultraviolet light, hardening yourself up by taking cold baths or sleeping in cold rooms, ingesting antihistamine drugs or other medications, or getting "cold shots." (For some victims of repeated colds, it may be worth-while to try a vaccine made up with their own bacteria and viruses—so-called autogenous vaccines.)

Complex—complicated, not simple. *Complex* is also a psychological term signifying a group of thoughts and feelings, partly conscious, partly unconscious, strongly linked by their emotional connection. The term *complex* was popularized by Adler, a disciple of Freud. It is most commonly used in such phrases as *"inferiority complex"* and *"superiority complex,"* which describe more or less rigid and consistent patterns of reaction and behavior.

Compress—folded cloth or cloth pads applied to any part of the body to stop bleeding, apply heat or cold or moisture (wet compress) or medication.

Conception—fertilization of the ovum by the sperm, the very beginning of PREGNANCY. This event takes place in the uterine tubes and does not occur for many hours after deposit of sperm in the vagina—sometimes as long as 72 hours. See SEX ORGANS, FEMALE; MENSTRUATION; STERILITY; OVULATION; CONTRACEPTION; RHYTHM METHOD.

Concussion of the brain is a bruise of the brain, the result of a blow, fall, or other violence to the head. The skull may or may not be fractured. The symptoms vary, depending on the severity and extent of the injury. In mild cases they may be no more than slight dizziness or giddiness and headache that passes off in an hour or two. In somewhat more serious cases nausea and vomiting, a weak pulse, and slow breathing also occur. In very serious cases the outstanding symptom is unconsciousness (coma), sometimes lasting for weeks. The outlook for recovery is usually good, though often slow. During convalescence, the patient may be extremely irritable and suffer memory lapses (amnesia).

Condom—correct name for the rubber sheath ("safe") sometimes worn over the penis during sexual intercourse.

Condyloma—a wartlike growth near the external SEX ORGANS or the anus.

Congenital deformities or diseases are those existing at birth. In general, congenital conditions are those *acquired* during intrauterine life, such as congenital syphilis, and not those, like color blindness and hemophilia, that are *inherited* and passed on in the germ plasm.

Congestion—accumulation of blood in any part of the body or excess mucous secretion (phlegm) in the lungs.

Conjunctiva—the delicate mucous membrane that lines the eyelids and covers the front of the eyeball.

Conjunctivitis—inflammation of the *conjunctiva*. See EYE TROUBLE.

Connective-Tissue Diseases, involving skin, blood vessels, muscles, bones, tendons, cartilage, and other connective tissues, are called COLLAGEN DISEASES.

CONSTIPATION

Constipation is the retention of feces, or inability to have a bowel movement, for any reason. But to most people it means failure to move their bowels when they think they should and therefore is a fine thing to worry about. Constipation is a symptom and not a disease. When it appears suddenly and acutely, as a change from previous bowel habits, it may indicate a dangerous disorder in the gastrointestinal tract—for example, cancer. Such a warning signal should serve as prompt stimulus to visit a physician and receive treatment for the underlying cause. But constipation that has been hanging on for years is a horse of a different color.

Is chronic constipation a serious threat to health? No. It is usually a delusion or an expression of an emotional conflict or a self-induced ailment. Often it is caused by the very remedy, a laxative, that the victim has himself prescribed for his imaginary ailment. It is hard for many people who hug the delusion of constipation as an appropriate physical reason for the insecurities that assail them to give up this small but comforting delusion. Perhaps they should not try.

The ill effects of constipation are exaggerated. Any number of vague symptoms—weariness, headache, bad taste in the mouth, and the like—are falsely attributed to it. The core of this false belief is the notion that an accumulation of waste products in the lower reaches of the bowel will somehow produce self-poisoning. This condition even has a name—autointoxication. Nonsense! Intestinal wastes (feces) have an unpleasant odor, but they are not very toxic. The body knows how to handle them. Very little but water is absorbed through the final segments of the intestinal tract.

How often is it necessary to move one's bowels? There is no set rule. Individuals differ. A change in type and quantity of diet changes the pattern. One bowel movement a day is a common pattern, but it is not the only one. Many people are accustomed to two movements a day, others to one every two or three days. There is no law that says a man must have a bowel movement every day. Actually, the sense of guilt that many people feel at missing or skipping a daily bowel movement stems back to their very early childhood experience when they were being toilet-trained. Some constipated individuals are really withholding their feces in unconscious resentment against the toilet-training rigors that they were forced into in childhood.

How can constipation be overcome? The first step is to stop worrying about it. The bowels function very well if left alone. So far as constipation can or needs to be overcome, a good hygienic way of living will do it. This means attention to one's attitude toward living, adequate diet (with a normal amount of roughage), and sufficient fluid intake, mild exercise, and an effort to establish a regular pattern of evacuation in the course of daily living. When the bowels are ready to be evacuated, they signal this readiness. The signal should be heeded, not neglected. Physicians find legitimate occasions for prescribing laxatives of various types. However, patients should not treat themselves needlessly with laxatives. Don't get the laxative habit.

Consumption—TUBERCULOSIS of the lungs; phthisis. "Galloping consumption" is rapidly advancing tuberculosis.

Contact Dermatitis—a SKIN disorder; for example, poison ivy.

Contact Lenses—small lenses, made of glass or plastic, that fit directly over the cornea of the eye and under the eyelids. They must be carefully fitted to the exact shape of the cornea. They are invisible when worn in the eye. Many improvements in the manufacture and fitting of contact lenses have been made since they were first introduced, about 1910. A suction cup is no longer needed to insert and remove the lenses. However, they usually become uncomfortable after a few hours' wear, although some people can wear them for six to eight hours at a stretch. Contact lenses are unbreakable, but expensive. Your eye specialist should be consulted to advise you whether contact lenses are suitable and practical for you.

Contraception—prevention of conception; that is, birth control. It should not be confused with *abortion,* something entirely different. There is no ideal method of contraception known. All the methods now in use have some objection. The search continues for a method that will be *at the same time* 100% effective in preventing pregnancy, temporary in this desired effect, completely harmless physically and psychologically, simple to use (and teach the use of), inexpensive, easily available when needed, and esthetically and psychologically acceptable.

Contracture—shortening of muscles or their attachments either in response to use normal physiological or electrical stimulation or as a result of disease or injury. The growth of scar tissue may produce a contracture, with some deformity. *Dupuytren's contracture* is a shortening of the fascia of the palm of the hand that causes a claw-like deformity of the fingers.

Contraindication—any good reason for not giving a particular drug or applying a particular treatment. Every drug has its *indications* for use, when it may be helpful, and its contraindications, when it is more likely to do harm than good. Good doctors are always mindful of contraindications; quacks and laymen are usually ignorant or conveniently forgetful of them.

Contusion—a BRUISE.

Convalescence—the period of recovery from an acute disease or surgical operation when the danger is past but full health and strength are not yet restored. Convalescence can be tedious, but it must not be rushed. Rest *and* activity up to the limited point of fatigue are both indicated, along with good food, cheerful company, and a forward-looking attitude toward life.

Convulsions—also known as "fits" or seizures, they are uncontrollable muscular contractions, usually alternated with relaxation of the muscles. They cause irregular movements of the body and limbs and are generally accompanied by unconsciousness. Almost any condition that can cause COMA can also cause convulsions.

Convulsions are the result of brain irritation. The causes are numerous and tend to differ at various ages. Convulsions in newborn infants are usually the result of brain *injury* during birth. In older infants they may be the result of TETANY associated with lack of vitamin D and disturbed calcium metabolism. In young children they are commonly seen at the sudden onset of diseases producing high FEVER. These convulsions are frightening but not in themselves serious. An alcohol rub or a hot bath may quickly relieve this type of convulsion.

Any BRAIN disease, disorder, or injury can cause convulsions; for example, meningitis, brain tumor, or skull fracture. These can occur at any age.

EPILEPSY, which see, is the usual cause of repeated convulsive attacks, but the causes of epilepsy are still uncertain. It is only in so-called *grand mal,* or major attacks, that the person has fits and loses consciousness.

Any convulsion deserves prompt medical attention and investigation of its underlying causes.

What to do if confronted by a person in convulsion: Do not attempt to restrain his movements any more than is necessary to keep him from hurting himself or falling against hard objects. If possible, lay him on his back and loosen his clothing. Put a cloth pad or small stick wrapped in cloth between his teeth to keep him from biting or injuring his tongue or mouth.

"Cootie"—World War I term for body lice. See INSECTS.

Copulation—sexual intercourse.

Corium—the lower layer of the SKIN.

Corn or clavus, probably the commonest FOOT TROUBLE, which see.

Cornea—the transparent front membrane of the EYES.

Coronary usually refers to the "little crown" of blood vessels (arteries) that supply the nourishment of the HEART *muscle.* (See illustrations for HEART.)

Coronary Occlusion—anything that stops the flow of blood through the CORONARY arteries of the heart; a form of HEART

DISEASE that is often described as a heart attack.

Coronary Thrombosis—a heart attack; a blood clot in the coronary arteries causing CORONARY OCCLUSION. See HEART DISEASE.

Corpuscle—an old word for cell, usually red or white blood cell; now stands for any small round mass or body.

Corpus Luteum—literally, yellow body; a yellow mass that appears in the place from which an ovum has been discharged from the ovary. The corpus luteum acts as a temporary ENDOCRINE gland, produces a luteinzing hormone. (See illustrations for ENDOCRINE GLANDS.)

Cortex—the outer shell, substance, or layers of an internal organ; equivalent to the bark of a tree or the rind of fruit. Cortex particularly refers to the *adrenal cortex,* of the adrenal gland; the *cerebral cortex,* of the brain; and the *renal cortex,* of the kidney.

Cortin—a hormone secreted by the adrenal (ENDOCRINE) glands.

Cortisone—a hormone normally produced in the cortex of the adrenal gland. It is now manufactured as a drug and is useful in treating and alleviating scores of disease conditions, notably rheumatoid ARTHRITIS, other COLLAGEN *diseases,* certain eye and skin ailments. Overdosage can be damaging. Many drugs that have effects like cortisone's have been developed since cortisone was discovered in 1949.

Coryza—running nose, indicating an acute head cold. See COMMON COLD.

Cosmetics, besides adding momentarily to your appearance, may damage your SKIN for a long time. Cosmetics offered for sale in the United States are usually pure and safe under conditions of use noted on the package or label *(always read the label or package enclosure)*. Cosmetics sold in interstate commerce must abide by the Federal Food, Drug and Cosmetic laws. But no law can protect you against safe and commonly used ingredients of cosmetics to which you personally are especially sensitive or allergic. Contact dermatitis, evident in ITCHING, SKIN rashes, and skin blotches, also ASTHMA and other symptoms of ALLERGY may result from some cosmetics in some people. Remember that other members of your family, or your close friends, may turn out to be allergic to your cosmetics.

Cough—a sign that something is wrong in the THROAT or LUNGS. It means that the respiratory system is not working properly, that parts of it are being irritated by some foreign object(s)—for example, smoke or bacteria—or abnormal fluids.

Coughing is the body's normal reaction for getting unwanted substances out of the throat and lungs—just as sneezing is the normal reaction for blowing irritants out of the nose. When you find yourself coughing frequently or excessively, the important thing is to find out what is causing the coughing, not just to get rid of it. Consult a physician. The long-continued or indiscriminate use of cough medicines, purchased without a doctor's prescription, can be dangerous.

Cowpox—the virus disease of cattle, *vaccinia*, which transmitted to man by VACCINATION (which see) protects against SMALLPOX.

Crabs—pubic *lice* that infest the coarse pubic hairs or sometimes the hairs in other parts of the body: armpits, eyebrows, mustache. They itch but do not spread other disease. Treatment is with larkspur ointment, old-fashioned "blue ointment," and other specialized ointments, rubbed thoroughly into the infested parts (except eyebrows, from which lice and nits should be removed with a tweezers).

Cramps—painful muscular contractions that may affect almost any voluntary or involuntary muscle. The term is most frequently applied to painful MENSTRUATION (see FEMALE TROUBLES), abdominal pain or COLIC ("bellyache"), swimmer's cramp, periodic pains in arms or legs (CLAUDICATION), and various occupational paralyses (e.g. writer's cramp).

Leg cramps are usually the result of the temporary failure of some muscles, particularly muscles of the calf, to get adequate oxygen. The condition may appear during violent running, after sitting in a cramped position, or even during sleep. Briskly rubbing the leg, applying hot or cold compresses, or just kicking the leg in a direction that will stretch the affected muscle usually relieves the cramp.

Swimmer's cramp comes on as a result of great exertion and undue cold. Spasm of the arteries as well as the muscles often occurs. To avoid this condition, don't swim beyond the point of fatigue, don't swim in too cold water, don't swim too long, and don't go into the water too soon after eating.

Cramps in the abdomen, or colic, are caused by a great variety of things: for example, too much eating or drinking, food poisoning, food allergy, lead poisoning, *colitis,* appendicitis, bowel obstruction, and emotional distress. Treatment and prevention depend on the cause. If the pain lasts more than an hour or recurs, see a doctor. *Don't take or give a laxative;* don't take food or drink (beyond a few sips of cool water).

Heat cramps are the result of excessive sweating, in which the body loses both salt and water. This condition can be prevented by taking salt tablets along with drinking water.

Occupational paralyses like writer's cramp are often expressions of *neuroses,* whose basic cause is emotional conflict. The writer can't write, the musician can't play, the watchmaker can't work, not so much because the necessary muscles are damaged as because his whole personality rebels against using them. He can usually use exactly the same muscles, without cramp or spasm, to do other things that he wants to do. There are instances, however, when continued use of one set of muscles produces a true muscular fatigue which makes further effort impossible.

Cranium—the skull containing the brain. (See illustrations for BONES.)

Cretin—a dwarfed, misshapen, mentally retarded child or adult who got that way because of deficient thyroid secretion in intrauterine life and during early infancy. Usually his mother lacked sufficient iodine in her diet. *Cretinism* is most common in Switzerland. The condition can often be very successfully treated by administration of thyroid extract. Cretinism was once common in the Great Lakes region of the United States. It has been practically eliminated by the use of diets adequate in iodine (iodized salt). (See ENDOCRINES.)

Cross-Eye is the result of imbalance of the external muscles that control movement of the eyeball. This is one form of *strabismus,* or *squint.* (See EYE TROUBLE.)

Croup—a childhood disease, commonest at the ages of two and three, made evident by harsh, hoarse, croaking—croupy —cough and labored breathing. The voice box (larynx) is usually swollen or inflamed or tightened up or covered with a "false membrane" that partially blocks the entrance of air.

Spasmodic croup usually comes on suddenly at night and is not accompanied by fever. The emergency treatment for this is *warm, moist air.* One way or another the child should be placed in a well-steamed atmosphere. He can, for example, be taken into a bathroom steamed up by turning on the hot water in the tub or shower.

Any kind of croup or laryngitis in children warrants prompt attention. There is a more serious form of croup accompanied by fever, very difficult breathing, and a real chest cold. *Diphtheria* affecting the voice box also produces croup, with increasing hoarseness, cough, labored breathing, and fever. However, a child inoculated against diphtheria is practically never in danger from *diphtheritic croup.*

Crypt—tiny erosion or pocket found on the mucous membranes of, for example, the tongue, the gall bladder and the rectum. Tonsils and teeth can also have crypts, somewhat larger.

Cryptitis—inflammation of a CRYPT; often refers to rectal irritation and inflammation.

Cryptorchid—describes failure of testicle(s) to descend normally into the scrotum. See SEX ORGANS, MALE.

Curare, originally a South American arrow poison, has been introduced into medical practice, in nonpoisonous doses, to relax muscles. It is used in *anesthesia* and in treating spastic paralysis, muscular rigidity, lockjaw, and other diseases. Curare paralyzes to greater or less degree the end plates of motor nerves.

Curettage—the business of using a spoon-shaped surgical instrument, called a *curet,* to scrape out the contents of a body cavity; for example, the uterine cavity.

Curvature of the Spine may be abnormally forward *(lordosis),* backward *(kyphosis),* or to one side *(scoliosis).*

Lordosis, or swayback, presents an exaggerated forward curve in the small of the back. A person may be born that way or acquire the condition through poor posture or metabolic disease.

Kyphosis, or hunchback, is most frequently the result of BONE DISEASE, specifically rickets or tuberculosis of the spine. Lesser degrees of humpback may originate in poor posture and inadequate nutrition.

Scoliosis may be due to congenital deformities, loss of muscle control as a result of muscle paralysis (as in infantile paralysis), bone or muscle changes arising from abnormal metabolism, or habitually bad posture. Corrective exercises may sometimes help, especially in scoliosis of postural origin.

Cushing's Syndrome—either a disease of the pituitary (ENDOCRINE) gland or a particular kind of BRAIN tumor. Harvey Cushing was a great American brain surgeon.

Cutaneous—relating to the SKIN.

Cuticle—in popular terms, a hangnail; that is, a little bit of skin split off and hanging loosely at the base or side of a finger nail. Hangnails should be carefully snipped off with a manicure scissors, not roughly pulled off, lest they become infected.

Cutis—the true SKIN.

Cyanosis—blue appearance of the skin, especially on the face and extremities, indicating a lack of sufficient oxygen in the arterial blood.

Cyclopropane—an ANESTHETIC gas.

Cyst—a membranous sac enclosing a thin or heavy fluid; a hollow tumor. There are many kinds of cysts. Quite common are *cysts of the ovary* (see FEMALE TROUBLES).

Cystitis—inflammation of the bladder (see BLADDER TROUBLE).

Cystoscope—an instrument for examining the inside of the bladder. It has a metal tube that is inserted through the URETHRA and a small electric light at the tip.

D

Any word printed in SMALL CAPITALS *can be looked up under its own alphabetical listing for further information.*

Dandruff consists of little scales of skin formed on the scalp. It sometimes signifies a chronic scalp disorder, marked by itching, falling out of the hair, and lusterless hair. Ordinary dandruff can be removed from the scalp by washing or shampooing the hair thoroughly with any good soap or detergent. If dandruff is persistent or annoying, consult a physician—not a barber or beauty-parlor operator. It will save you money in the end.

DEAFNESS

Some people are born deaf; others become deaf later on from infections, accidents, degenerative diseases, aging, and possibly hereditary tendencies. Total deafness is rare; partial deafness is common. Loss of hearing may be temporary or permanent, static or progressive. In many adults the impairment is so gradual that 25 to 50% of hearing is lost before the individual realizes his difficulty and does something about it.

Since inability to hear clearly cuts a person off from many of the good things in life, it is not to be wondered that extremely deaf people often become seclusive, suspicious, and despondent. Nevertheless there are many ways of relieving the trials of deafness, many occupations in which it may be an advantage. History, past and current, reveals many distinguished individuals whose life achievement has not been stopped by deafness; for example, Beethoven, Martin Luther, Bernard Baruch.

Modern progress in medicine, surgery—and electronics—offers more hope than ever before for preventing deafness, conserving hearing, and rehabilitating the hard of hearing.

Preventing deafness is linked to the manifold causes of deafness. See EAR TROUBLE.

What causes deafness? The list is long, and it must first be recognized that deafness is of varying degrees. Chronic *infection* of various parts of the EAR is undoubtedly close to the top. Many childhood diseases (measles, scarlet fever, meningitis, for example) as well as most nose and throat infections (colds, tonsillitis, sore throat, sinusitis) may be directly or indirectly responsible. Most damaging, usually, are infections that attack the auditory (hearing) nerve and produce "nerve deafness."

Probably the commonest cause, however, is one of the easiest to diagnose and cure: accumulation of *wax in the ears!* Foreign bodies in the ear, blows to the head, ruptured eardrum, and explosive noises may also cause deafness.

Hysterical deafness sometimes occurs; it is related to other forms of hysteria and mental illness and requires psychiatric treatment. *Occupational deafness* is not uncommon in noisy trades and industries, such as boilermaking, drop forging, and sawmill tending. It usually comes on after a few years in the trade and results from overstimulation of the hearing mechanism. Precautions (e.g. ear plugs) should be taken before deafness ensues.

In middle life the great risk of deafness is from formation of spongy bone in the middle and inner ear, the condition known as *otosclerosis* or *progressive deafness*. The cause is unknown: hereditary tendency may play a role; women are afflicted more frequently than men. For fuller discussion, see EAR TROUBLES.

What to do about deafness. Deafness is a symptom. It should prompt immediate attention from a physician, who may refer the patient to an ear specialist (otologist). He can determine the extent and cause of the deafness and undertake either its cure or relief, if this is possible. Diagnostic tests, including those performed with the *audiometer* (which measures hearing), may be required.

A peculiar pride has long kept people from admitting that they were hard of hearing or taking any steps to remedy this condition. This is nonsense. There is much evidence that this foolish pride is breaking down—partly because so much more can now be done for the deaf. Besides medical and surgical treatment (the fenestration operation for selected cases of otosclerosis, for example), the recapture of hearing loss by means of suitable and reasonably priced electronic *hearing aids* has made rapid strides. As they have become smaller and more efficient, their use has expanded. In general, today, a hearing aid does not make a person any more conspicuous than eyeglasses. Indeed, the newest hearing aids are built into spectacle frames.

Hearing aids are of two general types: air conduction and bone conduction. An ear specialist, not a salesman, should be consulted in selecting the type most likely to benefit a particular individual. Some experience in using a hearing aid is necessary before its full value can be appreciated. Hearing aids, however, cannot be fitted with the precision of eyeglasses, and a person's own reaction to a particular aid must determine how helpful it can be to him.

In total deafness, skill in lip reading may have to be developed. Several national organizations are devoted to the problems of the deaf and hard of hearing, and there are a few special schools for the deaf.

Decalcification—the disappearance of calcium (lime salts) from the BONES or teeth, weakening them.

Decompensation—heart failure. See HEART DISEASE.

Decompression—removal of pressure. A *decompression chamber* gradually lowers the high air pressure under which "sand hogs" labor under water; it keeps them from getting the BENDS. Pressures built up in the *skull* by bleeding and other causes are sometimes relieved by taking out a flap of skull or boring a hole into it. This is one of the most ancient surgical procedures.

Decubitus—BEDSORE; skin ulcer.

Defecate—move the bowels, discharge feces.

Deglutition—swallowing.

Dehydration—the condition that results when an excessive or abnormal amount of water is removed from the body. It may result from extreme perspiration, repeated vomiting, urination, or diarrhea. Dehydration is accompanied by *thirst*.

Delirium—a state of restlessness, excitement, and wild talk, usually brief, that sometimes follows a high fever, head injury, or disease. The delirious patient usually rambles incoherently in his speech and sees or hears things that are not there.

Delirium Tremens—the DT's or "the horrors"; the severe mental and physical disturbance that afflicts the chronic alcoholic who has gone on one too many drinking sprees. It is the result of alcohol acting as a direct poison on the brain cells. Attacks last 3 to 5 days, and 10% end fatally. Prompt treatment, including administration of vitamin B, can shorten the attack and prevent death. The victim of delirium tremens is markedly anxious, restless, suspicious, and usually talkative. He suffers frightening hallucinations; for example, he sees snakes and "pink elephants," feels that bugs and mice are crawling over him.

Deltoid—the triangular muscle that covers the shoulder and stretches down the upper part of the arm. (See illustration for MUSCLES.)

Delusion—a false belief or irrational idea that a mentally ill or emotionally deranged person clings to despite all logical proof or evidence to the contrary. For example, a patient with *delusions of persecution* cannot be shaken from his false belief that secret enemies are constantly plotting to destroy him. The person with *delusions of grandeur*, though dressed in rags, may be convinced that he is Napoleon or the new Messiah.

Dementia—loss of the mind, mental deterioration. The condition may be temporary or permanent, slight or extreme. It is a symptom and end result of damage to the brain or affliction of the mind. The damage may be caused by drugs, infections, bleeding, or emotional disturbances. *Dementia praecox* is a synonym for SCHIZOPHRENIA (which see), a form of MENTAL ILLNESS that overcomes comparatively young people. *Senile dementia* signifies the loss of mental capacity sometimes seen in old age.

Demulcents—substances that soothe or allay irritation, particularly of the alimentary canal. Among them are glycerin, licorice, gum tragacanth, acacia, and Irish moss.

Dengue—also called break-bone fever; an acute, infectious disease common in the tropics and subtropics. Caused by a virus, it is transmitted by the bites of certain mosquitoes. The symptoms include rapid high fever, pain in the joints and bones, and skin eruption.

Depression—"the blues," hanging on; a very melancholy and downcast *mood;* MELANCHOLIA. When extreme and prolonged, especially if suicidal tendencies appear, depression must be considered a form of MENTAL ILLNESS. If actively and appropriately treated, depressions can usually be lifted in a comparatively short time.

Dermatitis—inflammation of the skin from any cause, e.g. sunlight, allergy, drugs, poison ivy (contact dermatitis), cold, industrial chemicals, cosmetics, X ray. See SKIN DISEASES.

Dermatologist—skin specialist.

Dermatomycosis—FUNGUS disease of the skin; athlete's foot is a typical example.

Dermatomyositis—a serious COL-LAGEN DISEASE affecting muscles.

Dermatophytosis— ATHLETE'S FOOT, ringworm; a superficial fungus infection of feet or hands.

Dermis—the lower layer of the SKIN.

Dermographia—a strangely sensitive skin condition in which writing on the skin (as with a finger nail) remains evident for some time in the form of elevated reddish marks (welts).

Desensitization usually refers to a process of greatly reducing an individual's sensitivity to some substance to which he is annoyingly or dangerously allergic. "Hay-fever shots" offer a common example. Over a period of weeks or months the patient gets gradually increasing doses of the pollens he is sensitive to. His body learns to handle this allergen and not to react violently to it, as in a hay-fever attack.

DIABETES

Diabetes is probably the pleasantest of all chronic diseases. It is not painful, disfiguring, depressing, contagious, or otherwise devastating—if recognized and kept under control. There are an estimated 2 million diabetics in the U.S., but only half know they have the disease. People still die of diabetes—more exactly, of its uncontrolled complications—but it is no longer considered the pitiful, progressively fatal disease that it was deemed for centuries. Progress in the control of diabetes has been astonishingly rapid since 1922, the year that insulin became available for treating diabetes. In 1957 another great stride forward was made with the introduction of a drug—tolbutamide—which taken by mouth successfully controls diabetic symptoms in selected adults.

What is diabetes? Diabetes mellitus is a disease state in which the body is unable to manage its food intake properly. It is classified as a disease of nutrition or metabolism or a deficiency disease. In diabetes, the body is unable to burn up its intake of sugars, starches, and other carbohydrates because one element necessary to that normal combustion is missing in adequate amount. That missing spark is insulin, a hormone normally produced in sufficient quantities in the islet cells ("islands of Langerhans") of the pancreas. When the carbohydrate metabolism is upset, other metabolic changes also occur.

Under these circumstances blood sugar accumulates in the blood stream. The kidneys are very sensitive to too much sugar (glucose) in the blood. When the sugar-laden blood passes through the kidneys, they are quick to filter it out along with enough fluid to dissolve it in the urine. This results in an outflow of considerable quantities of sweet urine. It also explains why untreated diabetics are almost always thirsty. A description of diabetes made in the first century A.D. was: "a melting of the flesh, which flows away in the urine." Untreated diabetics are usually emaciated.

What are the symptoms of diabetes? The commonest symptoms are unusual thirst, frequent urination, loss of weight despite increased appetite and food intake, weakness and drowsiness, and often itching and boils. The onset of the disease is usually slow and insidious, though sometimes it is not discovered until the patient has sunk into a diabetic coma.

Diagnosis of diabetes is made by detecting abnormal amounts of sugar in the urine and blood. The diabetic has more than twice as much sugar in his blood, after fasting, as a nondiabetic.

Who gets diabetes? Mainly middle-aged, overweight individuals whose parents also had diabetes. Heredity and obesity appear to be significant factors. Women are afflicted more often than men. Elliott Joslin estimated that over two thirds of the cases appear after age 45. Children also get diabetes; there are probably 50,000 diabetic children, under the age of 15, in the U.S. This is a gain, not a loss, since juvenile diabetes was almost always quickly fatal until the advent of insulin. Today the average life span of diabetics is about three-quarters the life span of the rest of the population; with the best treatment, a diabetic can live out a normal life span.

Can diabetes be cured? No, but it can be almost completely controlled. This is a condition that the medical profession well understands; hence self-treatment or treatment by quack or cult is particularly deplorable. The core of diabetic treatment is a careful regimen of diet, exercise, personal hygiene, and insulin, if and as needed. The diabetic diet usually restricts but does not eliminate carbohydrates. The dietary intake is balanced with insulin injections, if needed. The insulin is extracted from the pancreas of meat animals. The discovery of the crucial steps necessary to isolate insulin was made by Banting and Best in 1921. Until then most diabetics had been condemned to a "starvation diet." Improvements in insulin products have since been made. With long-acting insulin, a diabetic may require but one injection a day. The diabetic must stick to his diabetic regimen; he must know how to say no to amounts of food not on his diet.

What are the complications of diabetes? Very few, if the diabetic takes care of himself. Before insulin, diabetic acidosis and coma were common occurrences and causes of death. Now a diabetic can get too much insulin by injection and suffer from insulin shock (or hyperinsulinism). This can be quickly overcome by ingestion or injection of carbohydrates. Diabetics do not tolerate infections well; hence infections should be avoided, if possible, or treated promptly. The diabetic must watch out for his feet. He must be careful that they are not injured by careless cutting of toenails, corns, or calluses, by badly fitting shoes or stockings, or by fungus infections. Cleanliness is of high importance. Gangrene, especially of the toes and feet, remains a prime risk.

Are there other forms of diabetes besides diabetes mellitus? Yes, *diabetes insipidus,* sometimes called the "thirsty disease," results from disorder in the posterior lobe of the pituitary gland. An untreated patient may consume and void as much as ten gallons of water a day.

Diagnosis—the doctor's best judgment of what is specifically wrong with a patient. This is the heart of the art of medicine. *Differential diagnosis* is the effort to determine exactly which of several possible diseases is afflicting a patient. Diagnosis is the doctor's job; self-diagnosis should be strictly avoided. Treatment depends on diagnosis.

A doctor makes a diagnosis by hearing and evaluating a patient's history, making a physical examination (which can't be done over the telephone or by mail!), observing a sequence of symptoms and signs of disease, and interpreting the findings of laboratory tests and examinations. Many laboratory tests—examinations of blood and urine, for example—aid in diagnosis, but the doctor, not the test, makes the diagnosis.

Many patients are mystified by the tools and methods of modern medical diagnosis, especially when they are sent to a hospital or clinic for a complete check-up. In effect, all diagnostic instruments simply extend the range of the five senses, by means of which physicians have from time immemorial examined their patients. X-ray pictures enable the doctor to see what is going on (and has happened) inside the body. "Scopes" of various sorts, such as the cystoscope or ophthalmoscope, also extend the range of sight. The ophthalmoscope permits the doctor to see into the interior of the eyeball, the cystoscope into the bladder. The stethoscope magnifies the sounds of the heart. The electrocardiograph records the electrical reactions of the heart; the electroencephalograph detects even fainter electrical phenomena in the brain.

Because of the complexity of disease processes, a doctor cannot always make a positive diagnosis. Even a specialist called in consultation may have to make a *tentative diagnosis* and await future developments to confirm or change his judgment.

Diaper Rash—a SKIN ailment found on buttocks and genitals of infants and some incontinent adults, which, if persistent, demands skilled medical atten-

tion and not just talcum powder.

Diaphragm—the sheet of muscle that separates the chest cavity from the abdominal cavity. Moving up and down, it supplies most of the muscle power used in breathing. (See illustrations for ABDOMEN; HEART; RESPIRATORY SYSTEM; URINARY SYSTEM.)

A *vaginal diaphragm* is a fitted rubber or plastic cap that covers the mouth of the womb.

Diarrhea—loose bowels; frequent or excessive bowel movements. It is a *symptom* of some disorder, trivial or severe, in the body and the bowels. The causes are numerous; for example, overeating, food poisoning, infection (notably CHOLERA, DYSENTERY), abuse of cathartic drugs, emotional stress (COLITIS, which see), and even change of weather or pure fatigue. Accurate medical diagnosis of the underlying cause is usually essential. Diseases producing diarrhea are more common in hot weather and in tropical climates.

Relief of the simple diarrhea that follows dietary indiscretion or extreme fatigue can often be obtained by refraining from food for twenty-four to forty-eight hours. Hot water and tea at frequent intervals are permissible. When looseness has ceased for twelve hours, a cautious trial may be made of such bland foods as well-cooked rice, apple sauce, junket, custard, and strained infant foods. The diet must be carefully watched to avoid irritating foods for several days or even weeks after a diarrheic attack.

An effective drug for control of diarrhea is KAOLIN, a fine clay.

Diarrhea in infants can be especially serious. It usually indicates an intestinal infection. Medical advice should be promptly sought, especially if the stools are watery, contain blood or pus, are accompanied by fever, vomiting, or a generally sick appearance. Epidemic diarrhea of the newborn and so-called "summer complaint" were once serious killers of young infants. Sanitation has brought them under control.

Diastole—the resting stage of the heart between beats (systole). *Diastolic* BLOOD PRESSURE is the pressure recorded at this in-between time.

Diathermy—the use of high-frequency electric current to apply heat to deep-lying tissues of the body. The heat is produced by resistance of the tissues to the high-frequency oscillations, which range from 1,000,000 to 100,000,000 per second. By concentrating the heat in a small electrode, *surgical diathermy* can be used to coagulate and cauterize tissues.

DIET

Diet—food intake—may be considered under these two general headings: (1) the nutritionally adequate, or balanced, diet, which maintains and promotes health and vigor, and (2) special diets prescribed for treatment or prevention of disease states—for example, the low-calorie diet prescribed for obesity.

A nutritionally adequate, or balanced, diet contains necessary amounts of the six essentials of human nutrition: proteins, carbohydrates, fats, vitamins, minerals, and water. An immense amount of scientific research has gone into the subject of human nutrition. For practical purposes this has been summed up in a single table, *Recommended Daily Dietary Allowances,* published by the Food and Nutrition Board of the (U.S.) National Research Council. As this table shows, food needs differ with age, sex, height, weight (and pregnancy).

Occupation and amount of physical activity may also change dietary needs; the heavy laborer needs more calories than the sedentary student.

A good variety of common foods will supply adequate quantities of all nutritional essentials. A normal person, whose appetite is unprejudiced by previous conditioning or stubborn belief in false food fads, will select a good mixed diet for himself without con-

RECOMMENDED DAILY DIETARY ALLOWANCES,[1] REVISED 1958
FOOD AND NUTRITION BOARD, NATIONAL RESEARCH COUNCIL
DESIGNED FOR THE MAINTENANCE OF GOOD NUTRITION OF HEALTHY PERSONS IN THE U.S.A.
(Allowances are intended for persons normally active in a temperate climate)

	Age Years	Weight kg. (lb.)	Height cm. (in.)	Calories	Protein gm.	Calcium gm.	Iron mg.	Vitamin A I.U.	Thiamine mg.	Riboflavin mg.	Niacin[2] mg. equiv.	Ascorbic Acid mg.	Vitamin D I.U.
Men......	25	70 (154)	175 (69)	3200[3]	70	0.8	10	5000	1.6	1.8	21	75	
	45	70 (154)	175 (69)	3000	70	0.8	10	5000	1.5	1.8	20	75	
	65	70 (154)	175 (69)	2550	70	0.8	10	5000	1.3	1.8	18	75	
Women...	25	58 (128)	163 (64)	2300	58	0.8	12	5000	1.2	1.5	17	70	
	45	58 (128)	163 (64)	2200	58	0.8	12	5000	1.1	1.5	17	70	
	65	58 (128)	163 (64)	1800	58	0.8	12	5000	1.0	1.5	17	70	
	Pregnant (second half)			++ 300	+20	1.5	15	6000	1.3	2.0	++ 3	100	400
	Lactating (850 ml. daily)			++ 1000	+40	2.0	15	8000	1.7	2.5	++ 2	150	400
Infants[4]	0-1/12				←								
	2/12-6/12	6 (13)	60 (24)	kg.x120	←	0.6	5	1500	0.4	0.5	6	30	400
	7/12-12/12	9 (20)	70 (28)	kg.x100	←	0.8	7	1500	0.5	0.8	7	30	400
Children..	1-3	12 (27)	87 (34)	1300	40	1.0	7	2000	0.7	1.0	8	35	400
	4-6	18 (40)	109 (43)	1700	50	1.0	8	2500	0.9	1.3	11	50	400
	7-9	27 (59)	129 (51)	2100	60	1.0	10	3500	1.1	1.5	14	60	400
	10-12	36 (79)	144 (57)	2500	70	1.2	12	4500	1.3	1.8	17	75	400
Boys.....	13-15	49 (108)	163 (64)	3100	85	1.4	15	5000	1.6	2.1	21	90	400
	16-19	63 (139)	175 (69)	3600	100	1.4	15	5000	1.8	2.5	25	100	400
Girls....	13-15	49 (108)	160 (63)	2600	80	1.3	15	5000	1.3	2.0	17	80	400
	16-19	54 (120)	162 (64)	2400	75	1.3	15	5000	1.2	1.9	16	80	400

[1] The allowance levels are intended to cover individual variations among most normal persons as they live in the United States under usual environmental stresses. The recommended allowances can be attained with a variety of common foods, providing other nutrients for which human requirements have been less well defined.

[2] Niacin equivalents include dietary sources of the preformed vitamin and the precursor, tryptophan. 60 milligrams tryptophan equals 1 milligram niacin.

[3] Calorie allowances apply to individuals usually engaged in moderate physical activity. For office workers or others in sedentary occupations they are excessive. Adjustments must be made for variations in body size, age, physical activity, and environmental temperature.

[4] The Board recognizes that human milk is the natural food for infants and feels that breast feeding is the best and desired procedure for meeting nutrient requirements in the first months of life. No allowances are stated for the first month when infants show handicaps in homeostasis due to different rates of maturation of digestive, excretory, and endocrine functions. Recommendations as listed pertain to nutrient intake as afforded by cow's milk formulas and supplementary foods given the infant when breast feeding is terminated. Allowances are not given for protein during infancy.

scious trying. While it is logical and sometimes convenient to "balance" a diet by eating or serving "balanced" meals, this is by no means essential. A diet certainly does not have to be balanced daily or weekly, for the body has the capacity to store and even elaborate many of its food essentials.

Many systems for assuring a balanced diet have been worked out. A comparatively simple and convenient one was worked out during World War II and has been generally accepted under the name of the *"Basic 7."* This system of food selection assures an adequate supply of protective foods daily. *Choose one food daily from each of the following groups:*

Group 1: leafy, green, and yellow vegetables

Group 2: citrus fruits, tomatoes, raw cabbage

Group 3: potatoes and other vegetables and fruits (select 2 items from this group)

Group 4: milk and milk products

Group 5: meat, poultry, fish, eggs, nuts

Group 6: bread, flour, and cereals

Group 7: butter and fortified margarine

Special diets for treatment or prevention of disease states are numerous, and some are quite complicated. Among them are:

Diabetic diet, low in carbohydrates

Low-calorie diet, or *reducing diet,* for losing weight

High-calorie diet, for gaining weight

Salt-free diet, or *low-sodium diet,* for disease of the heart, blood vessels, or kidneys

Fat-free diet, or *low-fat diet,* often prescribed in acne

Smooth diet, or *bland diet,* to avoid gastrointestinal irritation

Low-oxalate diet (no potatoes, beans, chocolate, etc.) to avoid formation of kidney stones and gallstones

Sippy diet, chiefly milk and crackers, for peptic ulcer

Prescribing a special diet is as much the business of the doctor as prescribing any other remedy. It is no field for amateurs. *Reducing diets* are most subject to abuse.

Dieting to lose weight. Most of the two and one quarter billion people in the world do not have enough to eat; they are usually hungry. In the U.S., however, where food is plentiful, dieting to lose weight is exceptionally prevalent and often nonsensical. True obesity is undoubtedly a health hazard, but correcting it is nowhere as easy as blithe advertising claims make it seem. Following diet fads can be damaging to health.

Any intelligent program for weight reduction should be undertaken sensibly, scientifically, and usually under direct medical supervision. Many factors are involved: social, emotional, hereditary, endocrine, and dietary. Many people cannot help being overweight in terms of "standard" height-weight-age tables worked out by insurance actuaries. The psychological component is of tremendous importance. Nervous eating or overeating is often a substitute for other life satisfactions, and the fat person deprived of this outlet may divert his unconscious conflicts into other neurotic channels. See table of DESIRABLE WEIGHTS in Appendix, page 611.

The best reducing diet is a balanced diet in which the total calories taken in are cut down to a low-calorie level simply by reducing portions to a fraction (¾ or ½) their usual size! This is the method usually called "eat and stay thin."

The *amount* of food eaten, not the kind of food, determines the caloric intake. In this sense it is silly to call one food "fattening" and another "slimming." It is true, however, that caloric values are more highly concentrated in some foods than in others. A pound of fat has about 4,000 calories, or roughly 2¼ times as many as a pound of protein or a pound of carbohydrate, each of which contains about 1,800 calories.

The menu for a reducing diet can be simplified by leaving out starchy vegetables (potatoes); fried, fatty, and greasy foods (fat pork, salad dressing); heavy desserts; nuts; cream and sugar. Lean meats, all visible fat removed, fruits, vegetables, and unsweetened beverages, as well as milk, bread, and butter, all have a place on the intelligent reducing menu.

The weight of a food is not a good index to its caloric value, because all foods contain varying amounts of *water*, which has no calories. Fruits and vegetables are over 80% water; fish, about 75%; meat, including steak, over 50%; bread, about 35%; butter, 15%. You get the same number of calories from a ½-ounce pat of butter as from a medium-sized potato (5 ounces), a large orange (10 ounces), or 33 lettuce leaves.

If the daily caloric intake is cut by about 25%—that is, by about 600 or 700 calories—weight reduction of 1 to 2 pounds a week may be expected, after one or two weeks. More rapid reduction should not be attempted without medical supervision. If the balanced diet is maintained, there is no need for vitamin pills or minerals. Complete fasting or regular skipping of meals is extremely inadvisable. See CALORIE COUNTER in Appendix, pages 612-617.

Exercise is a good means of redistributing body fat and achieving firmer muscle tone, but of little value in reducing body weight. It usually whets the appetite and increases food intake. Weight loss through perspiration is quickly regained upon responding to the sensation of thirst and drinking water.

Hunger pangs are what make reducing diets difficult and usually wear away the original motivation to lose weight. These pangs can be partly controlled by tightening the belt, drinking water freely, eating some food between meals, and choosing *bulky*, low-calorie foods (e.g. grapefruit and celery).

DIGESTION

Digestion is the process by which the DIGESTIVE SYSTEM breaks down and prepares food substances taken by mouth into simpler chemical substances that can be absorbed into the blood stream and assimilated by cells and tissues. The process is partly mechanical but chiefly chemical.

Mechanics of digestion. Food is chewed (masticated) in the mouth and swallowed into the esophagus by action of muscles in the throat and neck. However, the food tube is essentially walled by smooth muscle tissues also capable of contracting. The rhythmic contraction of these muscles squeezes the food, in various stages of digestion, bit by bit, along the food tube. This is called *peristalsis*. It takes place along the entire alimentary canal, but is most evident in the intestines. It is involuntary, but can be stimulated by eating, by the smell of food, by drugs, and by irritating foods in the digestive tract. The peristaltic action is usually transmitted along the entire length of the alimentary canal. That is why the urge to have a bowel movement frequently occurs shortly after eating.

Chemistry of digestion. This is a complex process, not yet fully understood. Chemical digestion breaks ingested food down into very tiny particles, about one twenty-five millionth of an inch in diameter. This is accomplished largely through *enzymes* contained in the gastric juice after being secreted by the glands along the digestive tract.

The gastric juices work specifically on the food components taken indiscriminately into the body; that is, on proteins, carbohydrates, fats, vitamins, minerals, and water. The end products of chemical digestion are chiefly *amino acids* (the building blocks of protein), simple sugars, and tiny globules of neutral fat. The sim-

ple (or single) sugars are the end products of carbohydrate digestion. They are carried to the liver, where they are transformed into
glycogen and redistributed to provide energy, or fuel, for the body
cells. Fat digestion ends in fatty acids and glycerol, which are
quickly recombined into neutral fat. Some is immediately burned
for body fuel; the rest is stored in fatty tissues.

How digestion works. Digestion begins in the mouth. The enzymes secreted by the three salivary glands immediately go to
work to split starches into sugars. This is one reason why food
should be well-chewed and not bolted. The swallowed food moves
down the esophagus into the stomach. Since the esophagus is
made up of a series of concentric rings of muscle, it can shut off
the passage of food. That is why you can eat while standing on
your head.

The stomach is a distensible pear-shaped pouch that can hold 2
to 3 pints of food. The 5 million or more glands in its walls secrete
about 3 quarts of gastric juice a day. This includes a weak solution of hydrochloric acid (0.2 to 0.5%) and the enzymes pepsin,
rennin, and lipase. Food stays in the stomach 2 to 4 hours, sometimes longer. There it is churned into a mushy semi-solid mass
called *chyme,* which passes through the *pylorus,* a ring of muscle at
the lower end of the stomach, and enters the duodenum.

Of all the substances that get into the stomach, very few are
absorbed directly into the blood stream from the stomach. The
notable exceptions are honey and alcohol.

In the *duodenum* the partly digested food (chyme) is acted on
by more enzymes, arriving from the pancreas, and by bile, essentially a fat solvent, coming from the liver and gall bladder. Some
absorption takes place here, but this is primarily the function of
the small intestine.

Projecting from the inner surface of the *small intestine* are millions of little fingerlike projections, called *villi,* whose particular
task is to absorb nutrients from the food stream and deliver it to
the blood stream. Each villus includes a network of tiny blood
vessels surrounding a short tube called a lacteal.

By the time the food stream has reached the large bowel, practically all the nutrient substances dissolved in it have been absorbed by the villi. What is left is indigestible residue and water.
The water is absorbed by the large bowel, and the residue is excreted as feces. Harmless bacteria swarm in the lower reaches of

the large bowel; indeed, about a third of the mass of a bowel movement is made up of these bacterial swarms.

Although the time taken for food to pass through the gastro-intestinal tract can vary considerably, depending on the food and the state of the body and emotions, it usually takes 24 to 30 hours.

Exercise, bathing, and digestion. The digestive process makes special demands on the circulatory system and the blood stream. For this reason vigorous exercise should be postponed for an hour or two after meals, although moderate exercise may aid digestion. The cooling of skin caused by swimming or bathing summons blood to that area. Hence swimming and bathing (except for a quick shower) immediately after meals is likely to interfere with digestion.

Meals should be pleasurable, and when they are, digestion improves.

Digestive System—The digestive, or alimentary, system has the task of turning food taken into the mouth into nutrient particles that can be assimilated by the cells of the body. Food provides the building blocks for cell growth, the energy for body function, and the substances necessary (e.g. VITAMINS) for the regulation of body processes.

The digestive system consists essentially of a long *tube,* about 24 to 36 feet long, winding through the body from the mouth to the anus. Into this tube various *glands* pour chemical substances necessary for digestion. See illustrations on pages 128 and 129.

The segments of the alimentary canal are designated as (1) mouth and throat, (2) esophagus or gullet, (3) stomach, (4) small bowel or intestine, and (5) large bowel. The three parts of the small intestine are the *duodenum, jejunum,* and *ileum.* The large bowel consists of the *cecum, ascending colon, transverse colon, sigmoid flexure, rectum,* and *anus.* The vermiform *appendix* is attached to the cecum.

The glands that pour secretions into the alimentary canal are the SALIVARY GLANDS in the mouth, the LIVER and GALL BLADDER, and the PANCREAS. In addition, numerous small glands in the walls of the stomach and duodenum manufacture gastric juice. Bile from the liver and gall bladder enters the duodenum through a *common duct.*

(See DIGESTION for description of the functions of the different parts of the digestive system. Any part of the system may be subject to disease or disorder; these are discussed under separate headings; for example, INDIGESTION, STOMACH TROUBLE, LIVER TROUBLE, CONSTIPATION, COLITIS, GALLSTONES, APPENDICITIS, DIARRHEA.)

THE HUMAN DIGESTIVE SYSTEM

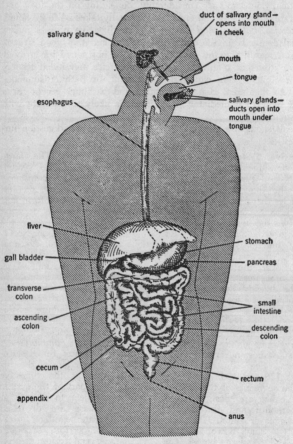

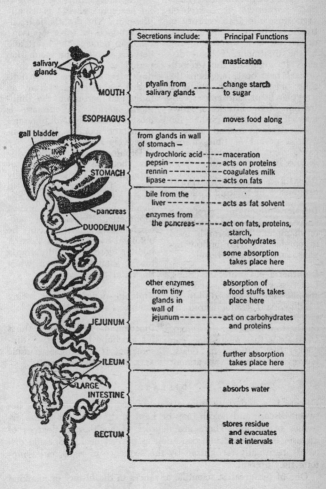

	Secretions include:	Principal Functions
MOUTH	ptyalin from salivary glands	mastication
		change starch to sugar
ESOPHAGUS		moves food along
STOMACH	from glands in wall of stomach — hydrochloric acid pepsin rennin lipase	maceration acts on proteins coagulates milk acts on fats
DUODENUM	bile from the liver enzymes from the pancreas	acts as fat solvent act on fats, proteins, starch, carbohydrates some absorption takes place here
JEJUNUM	other enzymes from tiny glands in wall of jejunum	absorption of food stuffs takes place here act on carbohydrates and proteins
ILEUM		further absorption takes place here
LARGE INTESTINE		absorbs water
RECTUM		stores residue and evacuates it at intervals

salivary glands

gall bladder

pancreas

Digitalis—a drug derived from the leaves of the foxglove (*Digitalis purpurea*). It has been used since the 18th century in treating heart failure and dropsy. It is a sovereign drug in the treatment of heart disease. It augments the strength of each heartbeat, lengthens the time between beats, abolishes irregular beats, and causes contraction of the arterioles. However, if the drug is pushed too hard, either in a single dose or over a period of time, it can cause *digitalis poisoning*, with serious heart symptoms.

Dilantin—an anticonvulsant drug used in treating epilepsy.

Dilation—dilatation; stretching or expanding beyond usual bore or diameter. The term is used in connection with hollow organs, such as blood vessels.

Diphtheria—an acute, infectious, unnecessary disease caused by a specific germ, the diphtheria bacillus, and characterized by patches of a grayish membrane on the tonsils and in the throat. Untreated, this membrane can choke the patient to death. However, prompt treatment with diphtheria antitoxin or an appropriate antibiotic (penicillin has some effect) is usually lifesaving. The diphtheria bacillus produces a toxin (poison) that can damage the heart and nervous system. The incubation period is short, from 2 to 5 days after exposure to an individual or discharges from an individual harboring the diphtheria germ. The disease is most common in children and in winter months. It is comparatively rare in the U.S.

Diphtheria is a needless disease, because administration of *antidiphtheria toxoid* practically assures immunity against it. Every infant at 6 months of age should be immunized against diphtheria. Evidence of successful immunization can be obtained by the SCHICK TEST. A booster dose of antidiphtheria toxoid should be given when the child enters school.

Diplopia—double vision; seeing double. (See EYE TROUBLE.)

Dipsomania—insatiable thirst for alcoholic beverages. A dipsomaniac is a victim of chronic ALCOHOLISM, which see.

DISEASE

Disease is a departure from a state of health. The distinction between disease and health may be hard to draw, except at the extremes of disease. There are degrees of health and degrees of disease; there is no such condition as perfect health. Specific diseases are usually recognized by the sequence of signs and symptoms they present.

One of the greatest scientific advances in the history of mankind was the demonstration in the 19th century by Pasteur, Koch, and others that germs, or MICROBES, cause disease. However, the germ theory no longer suffices to explain the principal deadly diseases that afflict the civilized world—heart disease, cancer, stroke, premature birth. We know that the causes of disease are multiple. We must give consideration to the host of the disease, the agent of the disease, and the environment of both.

The agents of disease may be deprivations (like lack of vitamins) or stresses (like warfare) that upset the normal balance and function of the body, as well as invading germs or poisons. Indeed, in the cycle of disease, all these factors are likely to be present.

There are innumerable classifications of disease. A very simple one is the following:

1. Germ diseases, about 80 in number, amounting to the uncontrolled invasion of the body by a disease-producing germ. These are all *communicable diseases,* transferred directly or *indirectly* from one host or victim to another. Indirectly is important; some of them, like malaria, are transmitted from man to man by insects. Contagious, or *catching, diseases* are those transmitted by direct contact with the sick person or some immediate discharge from him; TUBERCULOSIS and SYPHILIS, for example, are contagious.

2. Degenerative diseases, in which some part of the body wears out, fails to function, or functions improperly. In CANCER, for example, the mechanisms regulating cell growth no longer function properly. *Cardiovascularenal diseases* represent deterioration, with failure of function, of the heart, blood vessels, and kidneys. In DIABETES, the pancreas fails to work properly.

3. Psychosomatic diseases, in which the effect of the mind and the emotions on bodily function is a critical and controlling factor in the onset or perpetuation of the disease. MENTAL ILLNESS is the chief entry in this category; but it also includes such conditions as peptic ulcer, hysterical paralysis, and COLITIS.

Control of disease is effected by removing the agents of disease from the environment (for example, mosquito control), by treating patients who have the disease (for example, contact tracing and treatment of individuals spreading venereal disease), by acquiring specific artificial immunity to a disease (for example, vaccination against smallpox or paralytic polio), and by building up general resistance to disease processes through good food, adequate rest and exercise, and tranquillity of spirit.

Disinfectants—agents that kill disease-producing MICROBES outside the body. Heat (sterilization or incineration), sunlight, and chemical agents are the principal practical disinfectants. Phenol, or carbolic acid, first used by Lister as a disinfectant, is the standard against which other disinfectants are measured. Other common disinfectants are formaldehyde (formalin), various alcohols (most effective in 70% solution), chlorine-releasing compounds (for example, chlorinated lime or bleaching powder), mercury compounds (bichloride of mercury or corrosive sublimate), and various dyes (which is what the original sulfa drug was synthesized to be). See ANTISEPTICS.

Disk—(or disc) any round, flat, platelike organ or thing. Such disks, composed of cartilage, are found between the vertebrae of the spinal column (intervertebral disks), where they function more or less as little cushions to take up shock on the spine.

Slipped disk is a condition in which one of these intervertebral disks, usually in the lower back, has slipped out of place. Sometimes also the disks break (rupture or herniate). The result is low-back pain, often severe, running down the back of the leg and into the heel. Bending over often becomes exceedingly painful. Surgery may be needed to correct this condition, but it is not the only treatment.

Slipped disk has been a fashionable diagnosis in recent years, but it is only one of scores of causes of BACKACHE, which see.

Dislocation or displacement of bones follows violence and often accompanies FRACTURES and sprains. Joints are usually disrupted. For full discussion, see JOINTS and FRACTURES.

Disorientation—a state of mental confusion marked by inability to recognize where one is, who he is, or what time it is.

Diuretic—anything that promotes excretion of urine. Coffee, tea, alcohol, excitement, and worry are more or less mild diuretics. More powerful diuretic drugs are often prescribed in *heart disease* and *kidney trouble* to prevent or overcome the accumulation of excess fluids in the body tissues. Some of these diuretics contain mercury, which has a specific effect on kidney cells.

Diverticulitis—a disease of the large bowel (colon), in which small pouches (diverticula) on its inner surface become packed with feces, irritated and inflamed, and sometimes cause abscesses. See DIGESTIVE SYSTEM.

Diverticulum—a little pouch or pocket leading off a hollow tube or organ, most commonly the lower bowel. These pockets may be present at birth or arise in later life as part of a disease process. Fecal matter may accumulate in bowel diverticula and give rise to distressing symptoms. *Meckel's diverticulum* is a pouch sometimes found protruding from the small bowel. Surgery is sometimes necessary to relieve inflammation of diverticula (diverticulitis).

Dizziness—vertigo; the sensation that one is whirling around or the environment turning around him. It is a common symptom of disease or bodily disturbance, and is frequently associated (as in seasickness) with headache, nausea, and vomiting. The sense of balance comes partly from the sense of touch, partly from the sense of sight, and partly from the mechanisms of the semicircular canals of the inner EAR. (See EAR TROUBLE.)

When a person feels dizzy or giddy, there is usually some disturbance in the mechanism of the ear canals or the brain centers connected with them.

The simplest and most obvious cause of dizziness is abnormal motion of the body, as in motion sickness. Disease of the inner ear (for example, Ménière's disease) or sudden bleeding into the ear or pressure on the ear (possibly from earwax) can cause severe dizziness. Other causes include disturbance of the blood supply to the brain (dizziness and fainting are often associated), hysteria, EPILEPSY, a sudden decrease in the amount of sugar in the blood, MIGRAINE, or uncorrected refractive errors in the eyes.

An occasional dizzy spell can be managed simply by lying down in a quiet room. Repeated dizzy spells demand competent medical investigation, for this can be a symptom of serious illness. But annoying and anxiety-producing though they are, dizzy spells rarely herald a fatal disease.

Dorsal—the back side of anything, as opposed to the *ventral*—front or belly—side.

Douche usually refers to irrigation or "cleansing" of the vagina with a solution of some chemical in tepid water. Two points of importance are (1) douching is a highly unreliable method of avoiding pregnancy and (2) repeated use of chemical disinfectants, even in low concentrations, is likely to be injurious to the vagina. High concentrations, of course, can be even more quickly damaging.

A *Scotch douche* is a shower bath with alternating hot and cold streams of water.

Drain usually means a tubing wrapped around gauze that is inserted or left in a traumatic or operative wound as an exit for fluids discharging from the wound.

Dressing—a bandage, usually sterilized gauze, for laying over and protecting a wound.

Dribbling—incontinence, or inability to withhold the flow of urine. It is a sign of BLADDER TROUBLE or KIDNEY TROUBLE, which see.

Dropsy—a fairly old-fashioned term indicating the excessive accumulation of fluid in body tissues. This condition is now known to be most commonly associated with disorders of the heart, blood vessels, or kidneys. Digitalis is the old-time remedy for dropsy. Swollen ankles (indicating edema) and a swollen abdomen (ascites) are common symptoms of dropsy.

DRUGS

Drugs are medicines, but they are not all of medicine. Drugs represent only one of many methods by which doctors treat disease. SURGERY, PSYCHOTHERAPY, PHYSICAL MEDICINE, and X-RAY treatment, properly prescribed, are just as important.

Drug is also used to mean "narcotic," and *drug fiend* to mean "narcotics addict." (See NARCOTICS.) In this article, *drug* is used only in its wider sense of "medicine" or "remedy."

A revolution in medical treatment (therapy) has taken place within the lifetime of most physicians now in practice. It can be summed up in one word, CHEMOTHERAPY, which is the application of drugs produced by chemistry to the treatment of disease. This has given the doctor weapons of healing more powerful and effective than he ever had before and increased manyfold his efficiency.

A century ago the number of "specific" drugs could be counted on the fingers of one hand. As late as 1910, according to Keefer, the 10 most important drugs in medical practice were (1) ether, (2) morphine, (3) digitalis, (4) diphtheria antitoxin, (5) smallpox vaccine, (6) iron, (7) quinine, (8) iodine, (9) alcohol, and (10) mercury.

A list of the most important drugs compiled in 1945 by Fishbein dramatically revealed the chemotherapeutic revolution. He listed (1) penicillin, the sulfa drugs, and antibiotics; (2) whole blood, blood plasma, and blood derivatives; (3) quinacrine and other antimalarial synthetics; (4) ether and other anesthetics; (5) digitalis; (6) arsphenamines; (7) immunizing agents, specific sera and vaccines; (8) insulin and other extracts; (9) hormones; and (10) vitamins.

In the few years since World War II, many more important new drugs have been added. We have, for example, many new ANTIBIOTICS: streptomycin, first reported in 1944; chloromycetin, 1947; polymyxin, 1947; aureomycin, 1948; neomycin, 1949; terramycin,

1950. We must also note such new drugs as CORTISONE and ACTH, useful in arthritis; anticoagulants, like heparin and dicumarol; thiouracil and radioactive iodine, for treatment of thyroid disease; BAL (British Anti-Lewisite), an antidote for heavy metal poisoning; morphine substitutes; antihistamines (useful despite their introduction as abortives for the common cold); isoniazid, for TUBERCULOSIS; all the new tranquillizing drugs (chlorpromazine and rauwolfia derivates), for use in MENTAL ILLNESS; and polio vaccine. (See "MIRACLE DRUGS.")

The new drugs have decreased human suffering and extended the useful span of human life. The average life expectancy at birth in the United States has been extended from 47 years in 1900 to close to 70 today. But though doctors of medicine prescribe medicine, they do not make medicine. The laboratory scientist deserves a large share of credit. Ralph W. Gerard has pointedly pleaded:

"Not only as a matter of justice but also as a matter of enlightened self-interest in the long run, doctors should make it clear to the public that the great successes in the conquest of disease—penicillin, cortisone, plasmochin—have come from the biological laboratory and not from the practicing physician. . . . The poor devils in the laboratories not only deserve and should have credit; but more important, they need the support of the public to keep up their work, to continue to supply the medical profession with ever more effective tools for the practice of medicine."

The success of chemotherapy has changed the character of medical practice enormously. The fact is reflected in mortality statistics. In 1900, in the United States, the principal causes of death were, in order, (1) tuberculosis, (2) pneumonia, (3) diarrhea and enteritis, (4) heart disease, and (5) diseases and malformations of infants.

Now the list runs (1) heart disease, (2) cancer, (3) stroke, (4) accidents, and (5) noncommunicable diseases of infancy for which no specific drug treatment is available.

New drugs for treatment of disease (and possibly improvement of health) will continue to be sought and found. We can now be sure that new drugs will not be released to the public until the U.S. Public Health Service and the Federal Food and Drug Administration (FDA) are convinced that the products are safe, pure, and potent.

The cost of drugs: The cost of many of the new drugs looks pretty high to the man who has to foot the bill. However, this cost has taken over medical expenses that otherwise might have to be met. The *average* price of a prescription (drug) in the U.S. is about $2.25. Obviously, to make this average, some cost a great deal more.

The difficulty in justifying the cost of many modern drugs is that the patient can never know how much money the drug saves him. For example, the early prescription of antibiotic drugs for ear and throat infections has made MASTOID operations so rare that surgeons have a hard time finding cases on which to demonstrate the operation to medical students. Can't it be figured that the cost of the drug saves the much higher cost of operation?

An important part of the price of modern drugs is the cost of the research that goes into developing them. For example, 5,000 compounds were screened to track down isoniazid. It cost $20,-000,000 to find out how to produce penicillin in large quantities (although the U.S. Government paid most of this bill). Originally 100,000 units of penicillin sold for $20. The same amount can now be bought in tablet form for about 20 cents. Part of the money that you pay for drugs is your bet on the race among pharmaceutical manufacturers that their large-scale research departments will soon come up with still better drugs to treat your disease.

Prescriptions: Prescription drugs now account for about 25% of the average drugstore's business. A generation ago the figure was only about 5%. Why? Because of the quiet revolution in drug treatment.

Probably 90% of the total of 1,200,000 prescriptions filled *every day* in the 56,000 drugstores in the United States could not have been filled before World War II. The drugs simply did not exist! (U.S. drugstores sell more than half of the $3.5 to $4 *billion* worth of health goods purchased every year by the American public and supplied by drug, pharmaceutical, and allied industries.)

Why are so many modern drugs sold only on prescription? Because they are so powerful and effective. Many of the much cheaper old-time drugs (patent medicines) could be sold freely to anybody, because they couldn't do much harm—or much good, either. The principal and active ingredient in some of the most popular old-time patent medicines was ALCOHOL. No wonder the teetotaler old lady insisted on taking her "vegetable tonic" every day because it "made her feel so good." A glass of sherry wine would have done the same thing. Alcohol content now must appear on the drug label.

When a doctor prescribes a drug, he knows quite accurately what it is supposed to do—what MICROBES, for example, it is supposed to knock out and which ones it won't touch. The right drug in the right dosage has become more and more important in modern medicine.

Simple classification of drugs: Drugs can be classified in many ways; for example, (1) by source, (2) by method of administration, and (3) by anticipated effect. Thus, for example, phenolphthalein is a (1) synthetic chemical, (2) oral, (3) laxative. Some drugs are safe for external use only; that is, when applied to the skin. Others can be taken internally, but *in prescribed dosages.*

From drugs sometimes applied to the skin, the following effects are expected:

Corrosives destroy tissue.

DISINFECTANTS destroy microbes.

ANTISEPTICS inhibit bacterial growth (e.g. tincture of iodine).

LOCAL ANESTHETICS diminish pain.

Astringents tighten mucous membranes, diminish secretions.

Emollients soften skin (e.g. glycerine).

Caustics "burn" tissues slowly (e.g. silver nitrate).

Drugs used in the alimentary tract include ANTACIDS (e.g. sodium bicarbonate) to neutralize (temporarily!) excess acid in the STOMACH; *cathartics, purges,* and *laxatives* (e.g. castor oil, Epsom salts). See CONSTIPATION.

DIURETICS increase the flow of urine.

Antispasmodics relax muscle tone.

ANALGESICS, SEDATIVES, HYPNOTICS, NARCOTICS, and general ANESTHETICS act on the central nervous system (brain) to reduce pain and produce varying degrees of unconsciousness.

ANTIBIOTICS attack and eliminate microbial invaders of the body (e.g. penicillin).

DT'S—DELIRIUM TREMENS.

Duct—a well-defined tube or canal through which something flows; for example, bile duct, lymph duct, tear duct.

Ductless Gland—ENDOCRINE gland, which pours its secre-

tions (hormones) directly into the blood stream without their passing through any specific duct.

Duodenum—that 8-to-10-inch length of the alimentary canal or DIGESTIVE SYSTEM that follows immediately after the stomach proper. It is the site of *duodenal* ULCER.

Dysentery—any of a number of bowel disorders characterized by pain in the abdomen, diarrhea, cramps, and sometimes bloody or mucus-filled stools. Something is irritating the bowel; possibly amebae *(amebic dysentery)*, bacteria *(bacillary dysentery)*, WORMS, or chemical poisons. Dysentery is usually readily curable by getting rid of the bowel irritant with properly prescribed drugs and other treatment.

Dysmenorrhea—painful MENSTRUATION; see FEMALE TROUBLES.

Dyspareunia—painful (to the female) sexual intercourse.

Dyspepsia—indigestion; impaired digestion.

Dysphagia—difficult swallowing.

Dyspnea—shortness of breath; difficult or labored breathing, often due to heart disease. When it comes on suddenly, especially at night, making the patient feel suffocated (paroxysmal dyspnea), it is usually a sign of heart failure.

E

Any word printed in SMALL CAPITALS *can be looked up under its own alphabetical listing for further information.*

EARS

The human ear is divided into three main parts: the outer, middle, and inner ear. The function of the ears is, obviously, to provide the highly important sense of hearing and, less well known, to enable us to maintain our equilibrium, or sense of balance. Trouble in the ears may become evident through partial or complete loss of hearing (see DEAFNESS); pain in the ear *(earache);* discharges from the ear (a running ear or bleeding from the ear); noises in the ear, such as ringing (tinnitus), humming, or roaring; and dizziness, giddiness, or vertigo, usually accompanied by nausea. The medical specialty that deals with ear trouble is called *otology* and the specialist an *otologist.*

The best way to take care of the ears is to leave them alone. There is much truth in the old adage, "Never put anything in your ear except your elbow." Particularly to be deplored is digging into the ears with finger nails, matches, or hairpins. When any

THE PARTS OF THE HUMAN EAR

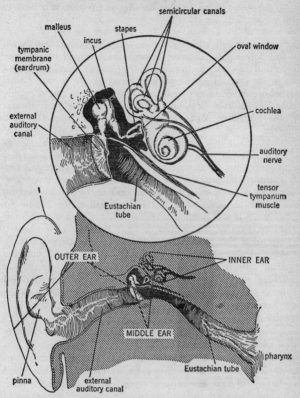

The upper circle shows details of the structure of the comparatively small middle and inner ear. The middle ear has been opened up to show the three little bones of the ear, as held in place by small ligaments and the tensor tympanum muscle.

signs or symptoms of ear trouble develop and persist, it is wise to consult a physician.

The parts of the human ear: The *outer ear* consists of a shell of cartilage, covered with tightly drawn skin, and a small open canal traveling a short distance through the temporal bone of the skull until it reaches the *eardrum* (tympanum). Modified sweat glands in the skin lining the auditory canal secrete earwax (cerumen), whose function is to catch dirt or dust that might invade the ear. The eardrum, a tightly stretched membrane that vibrates under the impact of sound waves, separates the outer from the middle ear.

The *middle ear* is a small, irregular cavity, lined with mucous membrane. On the wall opposite the eardrum, it is separated from the inner ear by a thin, bony wall in which there are two small openings, called the oval window and the round window. In back there is an opening into the air cells of the porous MASTOID process of the temporal bone. In the front wall of the middle-ear chamber there is still another opening—this one into the auditory or EUSTACHIAN TUBE, which runs down to the back of the throat. The purpose of this tube is to admit air, so that air pressure on both sides of the eardrum is equalized. Air is forced into the Eustachian tube whenever a person swallows.

Stretching across the middle ear, from the eardrum to the oval window, are three tiny movable bones. These three little bones are named, according to their shapes, *malleus* (hammer), *incus* (anvil), and *stapes* (stirrup). They are held in place by very small ligaments and muscles. They convey vibrations on the eardrum to the oval window of the inner ear.

The *inner ear,* the most essential part of the hearing apparatus, is a complicated structure set deep in the temporal bone. Filled with a lymphlike fluid, it consists of three peculiarly shaped cavities or chambers. These are called the *vestibule;* the *cochlea* (so named because it is shaped like a snail shell, which is about the size of a pea); and the *semicircular canals,* which are concerned with body equilibrium. Lining part of the cochlea is a delicate, sound-sensitive membrane (organ of Corti) from which project tiny "hair cells" that bend and sway to the vibrations in the lymph fluid transmitted through the oval window. As these hair cells respond to different frequencies of vibrations, they stimulate the fibers of the acoustic, or *auditory,* NERVE that enter the cochlea from the BRAIN. When these nerve impulses reach the brain, they are interpreted as the sensation of sound.

How we hear. Anything that produces a sound does so because it is vibrating (or oscillating). These vibrations are transmitted to the air that they are in contact with, and they set up sound waves that travel through air (or, less rapidly, through water).

The outer ear, acting something like a trumpet, picks up these sound waves and helps transmit them through the external auditory canal to the *eardrum,* which is immediately set to vibrating. Its vibrations are carried across the middle ear by the chain of three little bones, which transmit them as vibrations through the oval window to the lymph fluid of the inner ear. This fluid takes up the rhythmical oscillations and transmits them to the bending and swaying hair cells of the organ of Corti. Here they selectively stimulate nerve endings (end plates) and become nerve impulses that are carried up to the hearing center in the brain. Anything that disturbs or upsets any part of the hearing mechanism—such as a box on the ears—may stimulate the auditory nerve and give rise to sounds or noises in the ear.

Maintaining equilibrium. The semicircular canals, a set of three to each ear, are set at right angles to each other. Interconnected, they too are partly filled with fluid into which hair cells project. Whenever the head turns in any direction, it causes movement of the fluid. This movement bends the hairs and thus stimulates the nerve endings attached to them. These endings attach to the vestibulatory branch of the auditory nerve, and the stimuli (nerve impulses) to which they respond are conveyed to the *cerebellum,* the part of the brain concerned with body equilibrium. From here signals go out to muscles of the neck and bring the head back to its normal or desired position.

When the end organs of the semicircular canals are overstimulated or confused, the reflexes that maintain balance are thrown out of gear, and the result is dizziness, vertigo, nausea, and vomiting. This is what happens in *motion sickness* (air sickness, car sickness, train sickness, seasickness), when the head is subjected to many *unaccustomed changes* in the direction of motion. When the individual becomes accustomed to the changes in motion, motion sickness disappears. The condition can often be prevented by taking the antihistamine drug, dramamine, shortly before and immediately after starting on a plane, train, car, or boat trip.

The sense of sight is also concerned with maintaining equilibrium and a sense of spatial relationships. A person is less apt to get airsick if he can see the ground or the horizon. Children get carsick sometimes because they cannot see out of the car and hence lose visual contact with their environment.

EAR TROUBLE

Fortunately, the commonest form of ear trouble is the least serious and the easiest to remedy: the accumulation of *wax in the ears.* Many of the most frequent symptoms of ear trouble turn out to be caused by wax, namely DEAFNESS, *earache, running ear, ringing in the ear,* and other head noises. Competent medical attention is demanded for more serious causes and types of ear trouble, such as infection and inflammation in the middle ear *(otitis media),* *mastoid*-bone infection, *foreign bodies* in the ear, *Ménière's disease,* and progressive deafness *(otosclerosis).*

The inner ear and the auditory nerve can be damaged by systemic infections originating elsewhere in the body, notably syphilis and some virus infections. The outer ear presents some problems of its own, beyond earwax; notably boils, frostbite, stubborn fungus infections, lop ear, and tin ear or cauliflower ear. But it is the middle ear that presents the most frequent risk of infection and the greatest opportunity for preventing serious consequences.

Troubles in the outer ear: Wax in the ears (cerumen) is best removed by gentle syringing with warm water. It may be necessary to first dissolve hardened wax plugs by dropping in a few drops of warm oil (for example, olive oil). The procedure is more complicated than it sounds and often requires expert medical assistance. Above all, the amateur physician should not attempt to dig out the wax with a nail file, hair pin, or other hard object. This may force the wax plug in tighter and even scratch or perforate the eardrum.

Foreign bodies in the ear: The same rules for treatment apply to a foreign body in the ear, such as a bean or piece of chalk that a child has forced into his ear, or even an insect that has gotten there under its own power. The amateur should not try to extract it with crude home-made instruments. Physicians have special instruments for extracting foreign bodies; these are probes with some adhesive substance on the end that can pick up any foreign body that cannot be easily syringed out. Furthermore, they are inserted through an ear speculum, with illumination provided by an otoscope (lighted instrument for looking into the ears).

BOILS in the outer ear are not uncommon and may be exquisitely painful because the skin in this area is tightly drawn. They should not be meddled with. Some relief of pain may be obtained by instilling warm water or salt solution, but it is frequently necessary to have the boil lanced by a doctor.

FUNGUS *infections* of the outer-ear canal sometimes occur, cracking the skin and inciting an intense itching and desire to scratch. These infections can be stubborn and prolonged, especially under tropical conditions, though many yield promptly to regular application of fungicidal ointments, usually containing some antibiotic. Such ointments must be prescribed by a doctor.

Cauliflower ears, or tin ears, as they are called in boxing, where they represent a special occupational hazard, are the result of repeated pounding on the ear. Blood vessels are broken, and the blood accumulates in the tissues under the skin. In severe cases surgery may be necessary to remove the unabsorbed clots and reconstruct the tissues into a semblance of a normal ear.

Lop ears, and other ear deformities, whether congenital or acquired, require competent *plastic surgery* for their correction. This is the only rational and successful procedure for people who do not like the appearance of their ears or the angle at which they stick out from their head. No change in the position of the ears can be expected from simply bandaging them back against the head.

Earache may be due to wax, foreign bodies, boils, inflammation, or other troubles of the outer ear. It may also be a reflection of pain in the jaw or toothache. An acute earache, however, is usually caused by acute infection of the middle ear. The treatment of earache depends on the underlying cause, and this demands competent medical diagnosis and treatment.

For the immediate relief of pain, applying heat (a hot-water bottle or electric heating pad) to the ear and side of the head may be helpful. Pain-killing drugs, such as aspirin or cough medicines containing codeine, may also be indicated. The time-honored home remedy of putting a few drops of warm oil into the ear rarely helps. Nor should the ear be syringed. Nothing should be put into a discharging ear without express medical orders.

Trouble in the middle ear: The middle ear is frequently subject to infection (otitis media) arising from bacterial invasion by way of the Eustachian tube. Mild ear infections are especially common in young children, because the tube is shorter and wider in children. The infection may become an abscess, pouring out pus and mucus. As the accumulation of pus presses against the eardrum, pain (earache), a sense of fullness in the ears, fever, and temporary loss of hearing usually appear. Occasionally the pressure is so great that the pus bursts through the eardrum. This gives relief from pain, but it does not mean that the infection has subsided.

Good medical attention is necessary for middle-ear infection. The physician will prefer to incise the eardrum for drainage of pus rather than wait for it to perforate. The clean line of the surgical incision always heals better than the ragged edges of a perforation. A *perforated eardrum* does not cause deafness, but it may lead to later infections.

A *running ear* is a sign of chronic infection. The continuation of discharges (usually foul-smelling) indicates that infection and inflammation in the middle ear has not been cleared up. This condition should not be neglected, as it sometimes is, on the false premise that the discharge is a trifling matter that will disappear of its own accord. Proper treatment should be sought before serious damage occurs. Especially to be deplored is the tight plugging of the ear with a wad of cotton to catch the discharge.

In *mastoiditis,* a possible serious complication of middle-ear infection, the infection advances from the middle-ear chamber to the cells of the mastoid bone and may be communicated to the brain. The signs of mastoiditis are somewhat vague. Besides earache and discharge from the ear, they usually include swelling and tenderness of the skin behind the ear, pain in the bone on slight pressure, headache, and fever. Extreme cases may require a surgical operation (mastoidectomy) to drain pus away from the ear and brain. Once common, this operation is rare today because ear infections can now be very successfully treated with drugs.

Middle-ear infections, and their consequences, are less common now because the microbes that generally cause them are controlled and eliminated from the nose and throat before they get to the ears by prompt administration of penicillin and other antibiotic drugs.

How to avoid middle-ear infection. This depends chiefly on attending to and clearing up infections in the nose and throat. Sore throats and common colds should not be neglected. Particularly in children, diseased tonsils and adenoids may have to be removed. Attention should also be given to preventing and treating common childhood diseases. Ear infections occur in perhaps 10% of the cases of scarlet fever or measles; in about 5% of diphtheria cases; and less often following mumps, whooping cough, typhoid fever, and other infectious diseases.

Adults may become subject to ear infections because of chronic sinusitis or uncorrected nasal obstructions.

Indiscriminate use of nasal drops and sprays, and improper, overforceful blowing of the nose may force infection up the Eustachian tube to the middle and inner ear. Especially when you have a cold, *blow your nose gently,* one nostril at a time.

Swimming and diving are responsible for some ear trouble. Water taken into the mouth and nose may force infection up the Eustachian tubes. Diving and underwater swimming subjects the eardrums to unusual pressure. Ear plugs and bathing caps do not always offer sufficient protection. Individuals with perforated eardrums, chronic sinusitis, or a history of repeated ear trouble may have to give up aquatic sports, especially if they complain of hearing difficulties or water in the ears almost every time they try swimming. If the sensation of water in the ears persists for a long time after swimming it usually means (1) that the Eustachian tube has become blocked up (yawn deeply to open it up) or (2) that a wax plug in the auditory canal has floated up to the point where it stops up the opening.

Trouble in the inner ear: Middle-ear infections may also invade the inner ear, disrupting the senses of hearing and balance. Some secondary infections of the inner ear result from generalized infection elsewhere in the body, notably syphilis, whose spirochetes may attack and impair the auditory nerve. Three special troubles associated with the inner ear are ringing in the ears, *otosclerosis* (including progressive deafness), and *Ménière's disease.*

Ringing in the ears (tinnitus) and buzzing, humming, roaring, or other head noises are also basically associated with the inner ear, since they are subjective symptoms that represent a response of the auditory nerve to some irritation or stimulation (which may arise in the middle or outer ear). These noises should be distinguished from auditory hallucinations, the "voices" that people with severe MENTAL ILLNESS sometimes hear. Some head noises occur as the result of taking large doses of drugs, notably quinine and salicylates. They stop when the drug is discontinued. HIGH BLOOD PRESSURE, *rheumatic ailments,* and many of the ear troubles already discussed may also cause head noises, which clear up when the underlying condition is treated.

Otosclerosis describes the formation of spongy bone in the inner ear. It is usually associated with a firm fixation of the tiny stirrup bone in the oval window so that it no longer transmits sound. An early symptom is ringing in the ears, but the serious symptom is progressive loss of hearing, that is, increasing DEAFNESS. It has been estimated that 10 million people in the U.S. are more or less afflicted with otosclerosis. Women are involved about twice as often as men.

The cause of otosclerosis is unknown, though theories abound. Some relate it to chronic inflammation of the inner ear; others to heredity, vitamin deficiency, and changes in the activity of the endocrine glands. A gradual hearing loss over a period of months or years raises a suspicion of otosclerosis. In this condition high-pitched tones are usually heard more clearly than low-pitched ones. Otosclerosis usually begins in one ear but eventually involves both.

There is no specific and effective treatment for otosclerosis, but something can usually be done to offset the progressive deafness. For many people suitable electronic *hearing aids* are most helpful. In a certain number of carefully selected cases, a considerable degree of hearing can be restored by a surgical operation known as the *fenestration* operation or the Lempert operation (after the ear surgeon who devised it). A new window, which does not close shortly after the operation, is cut in the bone between the middle and inner ear. This works because the bones of the skull can conduct sounds to the inner ear.

Bone conduction of sound can be demonstrated by the following simple experiment: plug your ears, gently but tightly, and place a vibrating tuning fork to your teeth or the bones of the skull. You will hear the note clearly—unless, of course, your auditory nerve or your inner ear is severely impaired. *Tuning-fork tests* are used to help determine the type and site of deafness. The phenomenon of bone conduction makes possible the successful use of improved electronic hearing aids.

Ménière's disease, named after the French physician who described it in 1861, is an annoying, aggravating, and sometimes agonizing set of symptoms that can be traced to disturbance of the inner ear. The symptoms include repeated attacks of dizziness and vertigo, nausea and vomiting, ringing in the ears, side-to-side eye movements, and progressive deafness. This syndrome rarely afflicts people under thirty or over sixty. Once the attacks have begun, they seem to return with increasing frequency. In some cases, however, they diminish, even without treatment. In still other cases, severe and light attacks alternate. Jonathan Swift (author of *Gulliver's Travels*) was apparently a victim of Ménière's disease.

The exact causes are still obscure and probably multiple. Hence there are a wide variety of treatments that have helped some victims, but there is no certainty that any one treatment will be of value to a patient. Among the treatments are low-salt diets (on the theory that water balance is disturbed), antihistamine drugs (on an allergy theory), complicated surgery directed to the auditory nerve, and a variety of throat and sinus operations.

Ecchymosis—a black-and-blue spot or other discolored patch on the skin resulting from the escape of blood into the tissues just under the skin.

Eclampsia—a type of *convulsion* that occurs shortly before or after childbirth in about 1 in 500 pregnancies. The cause is unknown, though it is related to the toxemias of PREGNANCY. Good prenatal care can often, and usually does, prevent full-blown eclampsia. The warning signs are headache, failing vision, dizziness, rising and high blood pressure, and albuminuria.

Ecthyma—SKIN ailment; red blotches covered with pustules, which, upon bursting and discharging pus, often leave small scar spots.

-ectomy—a word ending that always means that something has been cut out or removed; for example, *tonsillectomy*, removal of the tonsils; *appendectomy*, removal of the appendix.

Ectopic—out of place. For example, an *ectopic pregnancy* is one in which the fertilized ovum attaches itself and begins to grow somewhere in the abdomen *outside* the womb, where it normally should develop.

Eczema—a SKIN disease or disorder. It is a name conveniently slapped on a great many skin disorders whose cause or origin is doubtful or unknown. A famous European skin specialist when asked to define eczema exclaimed, "Eczema? Eczema is what looks like eczema!"

The descriptive term *eczema* is applied to rough, red skin rashes that come in patches. It may or may not itch or burn. The skin may be swollen, blistered, scaly, or oozing ("weeping eczema").

A skin specialist is often needed to trace down the origin of what is called eczema. The basic cause of the inflammation is not an infection (though an infection may be superimposed on it). Sometimes it is an irritant outside the body (such as poison ivy or a wool blanket) to which the individual is particularly susceptible. These cases are really *contact dermatitis.* Quite often the eczema is a *psychosomatic* reaction; Alvarez cites the rare case of a woman who got a skin eruption on the side of her neck when her husband was caught stealing.

Most cases of eczema, especially in infants, are really *food allergies;* they are the reactions of the skin, at a particular time, to particular foods. The treatment of such cases is prevention: discovery and avoidance of the particular food.

Many cases of eczema disappear without any specific treatment. In others the physician may prescribe any one of a host of powders, lotions, ointments, salves, and pastes to dry, moisten, soften, toughen, or soothe the skin, as the particular condition dictates.

Edema—swelling of body tissues as a result of being waterlogged with fluid. A bump or bruise is often followed by edema. The other causes of edema are numerous, including allergy, malnutrition, and disease. In its more extreme and serious forms, popularly called "dropsy," edema is usually a sign of heart or kidney disease. Arms, legs, and ankles especially become overloaded with fluid. This is often relieved by *diuretics,* given by mouth or injection.

EENT stands for "eye, ear, nose, and throat." This abbreviation is popularly used to indicate a doctor or clinic specially concerned with disorders of these organs. More technically, the eye specialist is an OPHTHAL-MOLOGIST; the ear, nose, and throat specialist, an *otorhinolaryngologist.*

Effusion—pouring out of body fluids from the organs that usually contain them; for example, effusion of blood from the blood vessels into body cavities, such as the abdomen or skull. The accumulation of fluid in the pleural cavity is called pleural effusion.

Ego—the conscious self *and* the integrating, directing force of the unconscious mind. The term has important meaning only in the construct of psychology (originating with Freud) that divides the human mind up into *id, ego,* and *superego.* The ego is that part of the mind that makes contact with the outer world (through perceptions), that learns by experience, that interposes thought between wish and act, that integrates and unifies perceptions and memories, that is the throne of man's reason, that interposes between the instinctual demands of the *id* and the realities of life, that is whipped by the *superego* (conscience), and that must constantly find defenses to protect itself from pain and hurt. The ego strikes the ever-changing balance or compromise between the id, the superego, and external reality. The relationship of the ego to the id is like that of the rider to the horse. See PSYCHOANALYSIS.

Ejaculation—the expulsion of semen from the MALE SEX ORGANS. Overanxiety and other psychic disturbances may incite *premature ejaculation* when the sex act is barely begun or may cause delayed ejaculation.

Elbow—the highly movable JOINT in the middle of the arm. It is subject to all diseases that affect any other joints, and is particularly vulnerable in many sports, as the terms tennis elbow and pitcher's elbow suggest. A sore elbow is usually the result of *bursitis* in the elbow or the breaking off of a small fragment from the bones that make up the joint. An acutely or persistently sore elbow should be carefully investigated by a physician; often he will have it X-rayed. Most elbow disorders and injuries respond well to appropriate treatment, medical or surgical. (See illustration for JOINTS.)

Electricity in high voltage often causes serious bodily injury; these injuries can be classed as BURNS, ASPHYXIA (choking because of paralysis of breathing muscles) and SHOCK. For first aid treatment, look up under these alphabetical entries.

Electrocardiogram, often abbreviated as EKG or ECG. When the heart muscle beats, it generates a small electric current. By placing electrical contact points (electrodes) at suitable places on the body, this current can be detected and amplified by an instrument called an *electrocardiograph*. The graph or "picture" that it records of the electrical action of the heart muscle is called an *electrocardiogram*. This picture tells with some accuracy whether the heart is beating normally or whether and where it may be damaged. It also reveals how a once-damaged heart is healing or has healed. When properly interpreted by a physician, who adds everything he knows about the patient to what he sees in the electrocardiogram, a series of electrocardiograms are of great value in diagnosing, managing, and treating HEART DISEASE.

A normal electrocardiogram.

In the conventional scheme of an electrocardiogram, P (or the P-wave) tells what is happening in the auricles of the heart. Q, R, S, and T waves picture the contractions of the ventricles.

An electrocardiogram can only tell what a heart is doing

and what has happened to it; it cannot predict what will happen. A "normal" electrocardiogram is no guarantee that damage to a heart muscle will not subsequently occur.

Electroencephalogram. The cortex of the BRAIN (like the muscle of the heart, see ELECTROCARDIOGRAM) puts out electrical impulses that can be detected and recorded when greatly amplified. A graphic picture of these electrical impulses, sometimes known as *"brain waves,"* is called an electroencephalogram. The interpretation, by a specially trained physician, of the shape and length of these brain waves is often of great help in diagnosing and treating brain disorders, notably EPILEPSY.

Electrolysis—method of removing unwanted HAIR.

Electroshock—safe, proved, accepted method of treating some forms of MENTAL ILLNESS. A harmless current of electricity is passed through the brain.

Elephantiasis—persistent and chronic swelling of the legs so that they become as large, round, and ungainly as an elephant's leg. Anything that consistently blocks the *lymph channels,* through which lymph fluid discharged from body cells normally returns to circulation in the veins, may bring about elephantiasis—not only in the legs but also in other dependent parts, notably the arms and scrotum. Most cases result from lymph-channel blockage by threadlike worms *(filaria).* This parasite is conveyed to man by the bite of the mosquito. The disease is most common in tropical, coastal regions. Cases have been reported in which the scrotum has been enlarged to the size of a watermelon. In elephantiasis of the legs, relief can be obtained by rest, elevation of the legs, and pressure or elastic bandages.

Elixir—a pleasant-tasting solution, such as tincture of aloes or sweet orange peel, now used as a vehicle to disguise the taste of bitter or potent medicines.

Emaciation—wasting away of body tissue. It occurs as a result of *digestive* disorders in which food cannot be absorbed; of long-continued *fevers,* in which high body temperatures gradually burn up body substance (for example, tuberculosis, typhoid fever); and often of CANCER, in which normal body tissues are starved while the growing malignant cells absorb their nourishment.

Emasculation—castration of the male; removal of testes or testes and penis.

Embolism—sudden blocking or plugging of a vein or artery by an EMBOLUS carried in the blood stream.

Embolus—anything carried along in the blood stream that causes the sudden blocking of a vein or artery, that is, an embolism. An embolus may be a clot of blood (thrombus) broken off from the spot where it was formed, fragments of cancer cells, bits of fat or oil, an air bubble in a vein, clumps of bacteria, or any other foreign body in the blood stream.

Embryo—any living organism in its earliest stages where a fertilized seed or egg is in the process of growing and becoming a new individual member of the species. Embryo describes the new-fledged human being in its mother's womb from the time of conception to about the third month of pregnancy. Thereafter, until birth, it is called a FETUS.

Embryology—the fascinating and difficult science of tracing the development of new life from conception to birth; the study of life before birth. See PREGNANCY.

Emetic—anything that induces VOMITING.

Emollient—anything that soothes or softens the skin or soothes irritated internal membranes. Common skin emollients, used on dry, hard, cracked, or painful skin, include glycerin, olive oil, and dusting powders. Internal emollients include gelatin, gum arabic, tragacanth, and marshmallow.

Emotions—feelings, usually with some physical sign of their presence, such as the sweating that indicates fear. Many emotions are distorted, concealed or masked under others. The fundamental emotions are anger (at frustrations of all sorts) and fear. There is a great difference between *feeling* an emotion, which is as inescapable a reflex as blinking the eye when a light is flashed in it; *revealing* the emotion; and *acting out* the emotion. One may feel angry—yet give a soft answer. Many so-called mental illnesses are really emotional disturbances, with emotions buried and tangled in the unconscious mind. See MENTAL ILLNESS; PSYCHO-ANALYSIS; ANXIETY.

Empathy goes beyond sympathy. It implies acting out the feelings that one has for another person or a set of circumstances. For example, when a person riding next to the driver of an automobile presses his foot to the floor as the driver applies the brakes, he is acting in empathy.

Emphysema—a lung disease, most common in older people, in which the walls of the air sacs (alveoli) have been stretched too thin and broken down. As a result "air pockets" form in the lung tissue. Glassblowers, who overstrain their lungs, are particularly subject to emphysema. When the contractile power of the lungs is destroyed by overstretching, the lungs become permanently enlarged, giving a characteristic barrel shape to the chest.

Emphysema also denotes swelling or inflation caused by the presence of air between the cell walls of any connective tissue.

Empiric—essentially practical, based on observation and experience rather than on reasoning. It applies largely to methods of treatment; those for which there is a good reason are called rational or scientific; those that work despite ignorance as to why they work are called empiric.

Empyema—a collection of pus in a body cavity. The chest cavity is most commonly involved, pus accumulating between the lung and its outer lining (the pleura). This compresses the lung and limits its vital capacity. The patient becomes weak and emaciated, runs a fever, and has difficulty in breathing. It is sometimes necessary to cut into the pleura to drain out the pus. Empyema of the chest is a form of purulent PLEURISY, itself a complication of PNEUMONIA.

Encephalitis—inflammation of the brain (see BRAIN DAMAGE). There are many kinds and causes of this condition. It sometimes follows other infectious diseases, especially MUMPS, SMALLPOX, and MEASLES.

In a great many cases a *virus* has invaded the brain tissue. The disease is popularly called *sleeping sickness* or *brain fever*.

Occasionally the disease occurs in epidemic form (*epidemic encephalitis, lethargic en-*cephalitis). Epidemics of encephalitis are usually the result of a specific virus invasion in a specific locality.

Attacks of epidemic encephalitis usually begin with increasing drowsiness and lethargy (sometimes with restless excitement) and a high temperature, then go on to more or less complete unconsciousness. Muscular weakness and paralysis also occur. There is no specific treatment. The patient must be kept in bed and may benefit by physical therapy. Extended convalescence—at least three months—is recommended to prevent relapse. The effects of the disease, such as lethargy, muscular weakness and rigidity, and easy fatigability, may last for many months. Sometimes, even when physical recovery is complete, mental deterioration persists.

The viruses that cause encephalitis also invade wild and domestic animals (especially horses), birds (sparrows and chickens, for example), and insects. They can be spread by ticks, mites, and mosquitoes, but are not exclusively transmitted in this way. A special case of epidemic encephalitis is African sleeping sickness, carried by the tsetse fly.

Encephalogram—an X-ray picture of the brain.

Endarteritis—an inflammation of the inner lining of an artery. This process may sometimes eventually block and close off some BLOOD VESSELS, especially the smaller ones, thus producing the condition called *endarteritis obliterans*.

Endemic—confined to a particular group of people or locality. Certain diseases are said to be endemic to certain localities. For example, cholera is endemic in some parts of Asia; there are always a few cases around. From its endemic source the disease may spread widely, affecting many people and reaching EPIDEMIC proportions.

Endocarditis—inflammation of the lining of the heart and usually the heart valves. A form of HEART DISEASE, it is often associated with RHEUMATIC FEVER. In *bacterial endocarditis*, which may be acute or chronic, the heart lining is directly attacked by infecting microbes.

Endocrine—see ENDOCRINE GLANDS.

ENDOCRINE GLANDS

Practically all bodily activities are regulated and controlled in part by the *endocrine,* or *ductless, glands,* so called because their secretions (hormones) do not pass through tubes or ducts but pour out directly into the blood stream. The seven important endocrines, from the head downward, are the pituitary, thyroid, parathyroids, thymus, adrenals, islet cells of the pancreas, and gonads.

These glands exert their influence over the body by their secretions, chemical substances called *hormones* (from the Greek word *hormaein,* to excite). Even a small amount of a hormone may produce a major effect on such activities as growth and development, tissue nutrition, rhythms of sexual function, muscular tone, and resistance to fatigue. In addition to the hormones produced by the endocrines, hormonelike substances, such as gastrin and secretin, are elaborated in the digestive system.

Production of hormones is regulated by the emotions as well as by physical condition. Thus they act as mediators between mind and body.

When an endocrine is out of order, it produces too much or too little hormone. Though the amounts involved are minute, they affect activity, growth, and development in strange ways.

The *pituitary* gland, about the size of a pea, hangs from a short stalk at the base of the brain. Though tiny, the pituitary is sometimes called the "master gland," because its three lobes secrete at least nine known hormones, with more, and more complex, functions than are known for any other endocrine.

Hormones from the posterior lobe of the pituitary stimulate

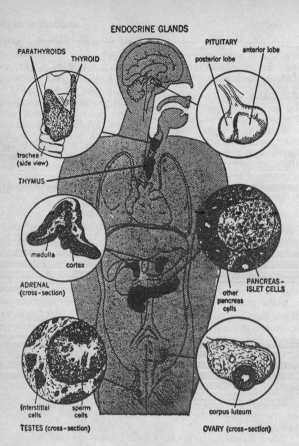

ENDOCRINE GLANDS

PARATHYROIDS

THYROID

trachea
(side view)

THYMUS

PITUITARY

posterior lobe

anterior lobe

medulla

cortex

ADRENAL
(cross-section)

**PANCREAS -
ISLET CELLS**

other
pancreas
cells

interstitial
cells

sperm
cells

TESTES (cross-section)

corpus luteum

OVARY (cross-section)

Locations of the endocrine glands are shown on the diagram of the human body. The enlargements of all or part of the glands (in the circles) are on the following scales: pituitary (2 times actual size), thyroid (⅔ times actual size), parathyroid (⅔ times actual size), adrenals (⅔ times actual size), pancreas cells (magnified 135 times), and ovary (⅔ times actual size) or testes cells (magnified 135 times).

smooth muscle, regulate water balance, and help control kidney function. *Pituitrin,* an extract of these hormones from meat animals, is used to prevent BLEEDING after CHILDBIRTH and to treat *diabetes insipidus,* the "thirsty disease," resulting from disfunction of the pituitary.

A hormone produced by the intermediate lobe possibly helps determine skin color.

The anterior lobe secretes at least six hormones needed for normal growth and development. One of these, *somatropin,* controls body size; too much produces a giant, too little a dwarf. Another hormone, *mammotropin,* induces milk production from the female breast. Still others of these hormones have to do with storage and distribution of fat; an imbalance among them may produce gross OBESITY.

Several of the anterior pituitary hormones regulate the functioning of other endocrine glands. ACTH (the abbreviation for adrenal cortex trophic hormone), for example, stimulates the adrenal cortex to secrete a complex set of hormones, including cortin and cortisone. ACTH is used to treat many conditions that are treated with cortisone.

The gonads, a pair of glands that appear as testes in men and as ovaries in women, manufacture hormones in addition to producing sperm and ova. (See SEX ORGANS, MALE AND FEMALE.) The male gonads produce the male sex hormone *testosterone,* whose presence is evidenced by the development of such secondary sex characteristics as hair distribution and body shape. The female gonads produce female sex hormones that prepare the body for pregnancy, childbirth, and motherhood, in addition to affecting the secondary sex characteristics. (See MENSTRUATION.)

The *adrenals,* a pair of glands shaped something like Brazil nuts, sit astride each kidney. Each adrenal consists of two portions, the outer shell or *cortex,* and the core or *medulla.* These differ greatly both in action and structure.

The medulla, which produces *adrenalin,* or *epinephrine,* called the emergency hormone, is connected directly with the automatic nervous system. In times of danger or emotional stress, extra adrenalin is released into the blood stream, where it quickens the heartbeat, increases the energy-yielding sugar in the blood, slows up or stops digestion, sluices blood into the big muscles, dilates the pupils of the eye, and may even cause the hair to stand on end. All this prepares the body to meet emergency—by fight or flight.

Adrenalin, used as an emergency drug, is often injected into patients suffering from shock or collapse, as in *heart failure* or *asthma.*

The adrenal cortex produces an entirely different set of hormones. Several of these, including *cortin* and *cortisone*, have been isolated. These hormones, essential to life, help regulate the distribution of potassium, sodium, and chlorine, and also the utilization of fat, carbohydrate, and protein. They are related also to the action of the sex hormones.

Insufficient adrenal-cortex activity causes *Addison's disease.* Symptoms are insufficient blood sugar, fatigue, low blood pressure, low temperature, and a distinctive bronze skin-color. It is treated with an extract of adrenal cortex called *desoxycorticosterone acetate.*

Cortisone is the name given two hormones produced by the adrenal cortex. It is used to treat some forms of ARTHRITIS; acute RHEUMATIC FEVER; diseases of the connective tissues, such as lupus erythematosus; allergic reactions, like HAY FEVER; and other conditions. The drug, which often relieves pain, must be used with caution under supervision of a doctor.

The *thyroid,* a two-part endocrine gland that looks like a butterfly, rests against the front of the windpipe. It secretes an important hormone, *thyroxin,* that stimulates the activity, or metabolism, of body cells. This is evidenced by the rate at which the body consumes oxygen and burns up its foodstuffs. Too much thyroxin (hyperthyroidism) speeds up METABOLISM; too little (hypothyroidism) slows it down.

Hyperthyroidism may result in loss of weight, rapid pulse and breathing, goiter, eye bulging, and extreme nervousness. It may be treated by cutting away part of the thyroid or with drugs such as radioactive iodine.

Goiter, which means enlargement of the thyroid, along with increased thyroid secretion, causes a bulge at the throat. *Exophthalmic* goiter is accompanied by bulging or "pop" eyes. Goiter is prevented by use of iodized salt or of diets that include sea food.

Hypothyroidism, on the other hand, causes *myxedema* in older persons and *cretinism* in children. A *cretin* is a dwarfish, misshapen, flat-nosed, usually deaf human being, physically and mentally retarded since birth, whose condition results from congenital deficiency of the thyroid gland, owing to lack of iodine. In myxedema the metabolism is decreased, the skin becomes thick, puffy, and dry, and mental and physical reactions are slowed down. Both cretinism and myxedema are treated with *thyroid extract.* The creation of a cretin can usually be prevented by making sure that the pregnant woman has a diet adequate in iodine.

Thyroid extract is a dry, powdered substance derived from the thyroid of meat animals. It is present in some reducing remedies, but it should never be taken except under doctor's supervision.

The *parathyroids,* each about the size of a pea, are located at four corners of the thyroid. They secrete *parathormone,* which helps regulate the body's use of calcium and phosphorus. Too little parathormone may cause *tetany,* a condition of muscle spasms, cramps, and convulsions, which is treated by administering calcium, Vitamin D or related substances, or by injecting parathormone. Too much parathormone may bring about calcium deposits in other than bone tissues, as in circus freaks said to be "turning to stone."

The *islet cells* are part of the PANCREAS, a much larger organ that manufactures important digestive juices. These cells produce INSULIN, which enables the body to make proper use of starch and sugar. When the cells fail to produce enough insulin, *diabetes mellitus* results.

The thymus, situated on the windpipe below the thyroids, is thought by some scientists to secrete hormones that may be necessary for normal growth. Large at birth, it generally withers and shrinks until at puberty it has practically disappeared.

Endometrium—the membrane that lines the cavity of the uterus. Inflammation of this lining is called *endometritis.* (See SEX ORGANS, FEMALE, and MENSTRUATION.)

ENEMA

Enema, the instillation of fluid into the rectum, is an ancient treatment. Enemas have their uses and abuses. The regular, self-prescribed home use of enemas to "cleanse the bowel" is to be deplored; it encourages a morbid, hypochondriac interest in the action of the bowels, and it eventually increases the constipation it is undertaken to prevent (see CONSTIPATION). Children should be given enemas only on the advice of a doctor.

How to give (or take) an enema on doctor's orders. Prepare the enema mixture as ordered; it may be a plain-water enema, or it may have soap, starch, glycerine, or even other substances dissolved in it. For a soap-suds enema the usual proportion is about 1 ounce of mild soap to 1 pint of water; a teaspoon of baking soda may be substituted.

The temperature of the instilled liquid should be tepid, as close to body temperature as possible. An adult can take 1 to 2 pints of instilled fluid; a child about 4 to 8 ounces, depending on age. The fluid should be instilled through a rubber tube with a soft tip, well lubricated (as with petrolatum) before inserting into the rectum. The upper end of the tube is attached to an enema bag, suspended about 1 to 2 feet above the anal orifice. The fluid should be allowed to run in slowly. Once instilled, it should be retained for a few minutes before being expelled. There is no danger from an enema's staying in. In children the enema is best given through a small ear syringe, with the child lying on his side.

Why give enemas? In hospitals cleansing enemas are routinely given in preoperative preparation for surgery—imperatively for bowel surgery—and for obstetrical deliveries. They also precede the administration of drugs, notably some anesthetics, given by rectal instillation. Nutrient enemas, usually containing 5% dextrose (sugar) in normal salt solution, must sometimes be administered to patients who cannot take any nourishment by mouth. Sedative, or healing, enemas, containing laudanum and silver-nitrate solutions, are occasionally given to treat inflammatory conditions in the lower bowel. *Barium enemas*, containing barium, which is opaque to the passage of X rays, are employed to take X-ray pictures of the lower bowel.

Many patients are frightened or embarrassed by the prospect of an enema. Relax. They won't hurt you. Just do what the nurse tells you. Millions of people have had them.

Enteralgia—gut pain.

Enteric—relating to the intestines.

Enteritis—inflammation of the intestines.

Enucleate—remove whole, as to enucleate the eye from its socket or to remove a tumor without cutting into it.

Enuresis—bed wetting; involuntary discharge of urine. In children the condition is usually due to psychological factors; it is often an unconscious attack against rejection and lack of tender loving care. The permanent cure lies in improving the parent-child relationship. Temporizing devices, such as a bell that rings when the bed is wet, may abate the household annoyance of wet beds. Enuresis in adults usually results from BLADDER TROUBLE or damage to the parts of the nervous system (spinal cord) that control bladder function.

Enzymes—delicate chemical substances, mostly proteins, that enter into and bring about chemical reactions in living organisms. A great many are importantly concerned with DIGESTION. In many cases VITAMINS enter into the composition and action of enzymes. Most digestive enzymes act specifically; that is, they have just one job to do. There is, for example, the starch-splitting enzyme called amylase. If pure, this enzyme will break down 20,000 times its own volume of starch in half an hour. Only small quantities of enzymes are needed because they act as CATALYSTS.

Eosinophil—a particular type of white BLOOD CELL that can be easily stained red by the dye *eosin*.

Ephedrine—an important drug, with action like epinephrine or adrenalin. It is often used in emergency conditions to counteract shock and stimulate the heart muscle.

Epidemic—the widespread attack of a particular disease in a community. How many cases constitute an epidemic is not an easy question. Epidemic conditions (and dangers) are often exaggerated in newspaper reports. It is the specific business of *public-health* authorities to prevent epidemics of infectious and communicable diseases and, if they do occur, to investigate them and enforce measures for their control. Many epidemics have a seasonal incidence (for example, poliomyelitis), and many are largely confined to particular age groups (for example, an epidemic of mumps among children).

Epidemiology—the study of disease as it spreads and involves large groups (crowds) of people. There is also an "epidemiology of health," which investigates the conditions under which health can be maintained and improved.

Epidermis—the outer layer of the SKIN.

Epidermophytosis—a FUNGUS infection of the SKIN; for example, athlete's foot.

Epididymitis—inflammation of the epididymis, the twisted mass of little tubules attached to the testicles. (See SEX ORGANS, MALE.) Gonorrhea is the most frequent cause.

Epiglottis—the lid of the voice box. It is a piece of elastic cartilage, far back of the tongue, that closes to prevent swallowed food or liquid from slipping into the larynx ("going down the wrong way" as it is popularly said). (See illustration for THROAT.)

Epilepsy—a condition characterized by sudden disturbances of BRAIN function, resulting in temporary impairment of consciousness. The attacks range from major to minor reactions (from *grand mal* to *petit mal*). The popular and mistaken concept of the epileptic is that he frequently goes into violent "fits" or convulsions. This is, however, only rarely the case; for there are now many drugs that control epileptic seizures. Under adequate medical supervision a patient may remain completely free from seizures.

There are approximately 1,500,000 epileptics in the U.S. Many of them needlessly face situations based on blind fear and superstition and on outdated laws (for example, laws in some places forbid epileptics to marry). There is also needless discrimination against epileptics in employment, though statistical studies show that the accident rate among epileptics is no higher than among other groups.

The chance that an epileptic parent will produce an epileptic child is perhaps 1 in 40; but this risk is reduced in various ways. For example, if seizures did not begin until adult life, if there are no mental symptoms, if the mate's family has no history of epilepsy, the risk is decreased.

The underlying causes of epilepsy are still being explored. It was once called the "divine disease" and seemed utterly mysterious. It is now known that epilepsy may be caused by a brain injury, disease in other organs reacting upon the brain, emotional disturbances, and alcoholic excesses. The predisposition to epilepsy is inherited, but the disease cannot be considered primarily hereditary.

The battle for further understanding of this disease and a fair break for those afflicted with it has been carried forward by cogent research in electroencephalography (brain waves).

Epinephrine—ADRENALIN.

Episiotomy—a minor bit of surgery sometimes performed on mothers during childbirth. It means cutting the vaginal walls to facilitate childbirth and prevent tearing of the tissues. The incision is promptly repaired by the obstetrician with a few stitches.

Epistaxis—nosebleed. See NOSE.

Epithelial—a type of body CELL that makes up the skin, mucous membranes lining body organs, and glands. Tumors arising from the *epithelium* are called *epithelioma*.

Epizoötic—an epidemic of disease among animals.

Epsom Salts—magnesium sulfate, commonly used in various doses to move the bowels. (See CONSTIPATION.) A 5 to 25% solution is sometimes applied externally to relieve rheumatic pains. A paste of epsom salts dissolved in glycerin may be useful in treating boils.

Erection—the enlarged, rigid

penis of the male (or clitoris of the female) under stimulus of sexual excitement is said to be in a state of erection. (See SEX ORGANS.) Given the stimulus, whether psychic or physical, voluntary or involuntary, it is normal and natural for erection to occur.

Ergot—a fungus that infests cereal grasses, particularly rye. Taken into the human body, it causes smooth muscle tissue to tighten up. Hence it is sometimes used as a drug to stop internal bleeding, to induce contractions of the uterus before and after childbirth. It has been used in obstetrics since the 16th century.

Ergotism—chronic ergot poisoning, which occurs as a result of misguided medication or from eating bread made with diseased rye flour. The principal symptoms are muscular spasms and cramps and the gradual production of dry gangrene affecting the fingers, toes, and ear tips. Severe epidemics of *ergotism* occurred in Germany and France in the Middle Ages.

Eructation—belching.

Eruption—a SKIN rash.

Erysipelas—a SKIN disease caused by infection with the streptococcus germ. It is highly contagious. Usually not only the skin but also the tissues just under the skin are infected. The skin looks fiery red, glazed, and swollen. The patient feels and is quite sick.

The infection tends to spread but often stops, or at least slows down, when it comes to a hair line or a place where the skin fits fairly tightly over the underlying bones. Men are affected more often than women. The disease often starts with a small scratch on the skin. Cheeks and ears are often involved.

Prompt treatment with sulfa drugs or antibiotics usually arrests the infection, but it can recur.

Erythema—reddening of the skin. The causes are many; for example, infections, allergies, drugs, sunburn, X-ray irradiation, contact with toxins (poison ivy). Many forms of SKIN disease, some serious, some not so serious, are classified as erythema; for example, *erythema multiforme*, a brief acute skin disease in which raised red patches appear, and *erythema nodosum*, an acute inflammatory skin disease marked by red nodules and severe itching and burning that lasts for several weeks.

Erythroblastosis Fetalis—a blood disease of newborn infants, who sometimes appear so jaundiced they are called "yellow babies." The cause is the Rh factor. "Yellow babies" can now be saved to grow up into healthy normal adults by massive blood transfusions and other treatments. See RH FACTOR.

Erythrocyte—red BLOOD CELL.

Eschar—a bit of body tissue destroyed by a strong caustic chemical or heat; a slough. An *escharotic* is a corrosive substance, like lye or acids, that kills the tissue and produces the eschar.

Esophagus—the food tube, or gullet. About 9 inches long, it conveys swallowed food and liquid from the back of the throat to the stomach. Its walls are composed of concentric rings of muscle and connective tissue, lined with mucous membrane. (See DIGESTIVE SYSTEM; illustrations for THROAT and URINARY SYSTEM.)

Estrogen—a general name for a large group of closely related *female sex hormones.* These hormones are normally secreted by the ovaries, and are stimulated by hormones from other ENDOCRINE glands, notably the pituitary. The menstrual and ovulatory cycle (menstruation) is importantly regulated by estrogenic hormones. The estrogen level rises high during pregnancy, so high in fact that a considerable amount is excreted in the urine. Estrogenic hormones are extracted from the urine of pregnant mares for use as an injectable drug in women who have an estrogen deficiency. These hormones are often of great value in relieving some of the disturbing symptoms that may occur at the MENOPAUSE.

Estrus—the period of heat, rut, and sexual desire in female animals, marked by changes in the SEX ORGANS, FEMALE, and ENDOCRINE pattern.

Ether—the chemical substance, ethyl oxide, obtained by the action of sulfuric acid on ordinary alcohol. A highly volatile liquid, it has a characteristic odor. When used as a general ANESTHETIC, it is given by inhalation, a few drops being poured on a mask. Ether dissolves many substances and is commonly used in making chemical preparations.

Ethmoid—a spongy bone at the base and front of the skull that forms the upper part of the nose. It has many cavities, air spaces, or sinuses. The olfactory nerve, giving the sense of smell, passes through it. The *ethmoid sinuses* can become infected and inflamed, producing ethmoiditis or sinusitis.

Ethmoiditis—ETHMOID inflammation; sinusitis.

Etiology—the study or knowledge of the *causes* of disease. While specific infecting microbes are known to be *etiological agents,* or causative factors, in many specific diseases, nevertheless the *causes of disease are always multiple.* The factors that make up the resistance of the host to the MICROBE are as important as those that transmit it or induce it to multiply in the body. For many diseases, there is no known infecting agent. Medical research is constantly digging at the etiology of disease, because this permits more accurate diagnosis and treatment, as well as raising the possibilities of prevention. For many diseases, notably CANCER, the etiology is still unknown, obscure, or uncertain.

Eugenics—the effort to improve the human race by attention to mating and breeding. The aim of eugenics is laudable, but the scientific problems are far more complex and the practical difficulties far more profound than imagined by its early enthusiasts.

Eunuch—a castrated male; one whose testes or testes and penis have been removed. (See CASTRATION.) Eunuchs lack secondary sex characteristics of the male; they are often beardless and have a peculiar distribution of body fat.

Euphoria—a sense of well-being, sometimes exaggerated and unwarranted. Patients with far-advanced and possibly hopeless diseases (notably tuberculosis) are sometimes protected against recognizing the seriousness of their condition by a fortunate euphoria.

Eustachian Tubes—short passages, about 1½ inches long, one on each side, leading from the back of the throat to the middle ear. They equalize the air pressure on both sides of the eardrum. When they are clogged, hearing is impaired. The temporary loss of acute hearing sometimes accompanying airplane travel is often the result of closure of the Eustachian tubes. They can be opened up again by yawning or swallowing. Infection often ascends from the throat to the middle ear by these tubes, especially in children. (See EARS; illustrations for NOSE and THROAT.)

Euthanasia—so-called "mercy-killing" of a patient with a hopeless, pain-racking disease to "put him out of misery" or "spare him suffering." Though frequently advocated, euthanasia has never been accepted by the medical profession.

Evacuant—a purgative medicine, particularly a powerful laxative that empties the bowel.

Exacerbation means that a disease condition, or the symptoms accompanying it, is getting worse or more severe, at least for a time.

Exanthem—a SKIN eruption characteristic of an infectious disease; a fever rash.

Excoriation—damage and destruction to the skin surface by rubbing or chafing. A skinned knee is excoriated.

EXERCISE

It is extremely difficult to get too little exercise. Most of the vague feelings of poor health ascribed to lack of exercise stem from other conditions. In the normal course of their everyday living most people get as much exercise as they need.

How much exercise should I take? This depends on age, sex, inclination, and physical condition. An old man should not attempt a young boy's tricks. The measure of exercise is *fatigue*. Exercise up to but not beyond your own fatigue point. You will know— *for future reference*—that you have exercised too much if you are still breathing heavily 15 minutes after you stop exercising, if you still feel weak and fatigued 2 hours afterward, if you sleep poorly that night and are "washed out" or tired the next day.

What kind of exercise should I take? The best choice is that which gives you satisfaction, is fun for you. Don't take exercise as punishment. Calisthenics, gymnastics, a "daily dozen," and deep-breathing exercises are not the least bit essential to good health. Walking, swimming, and dancing are excellent exercise. Physical training for athletic sports or military occupations should not be considered the ideal or norm for type or amount of exercise.

What good is exercise? A reasonable amount tones up the muscles, improves the circulation, and stimulates the appetite and the mind.

Is exercise good for reducing weight? Rarely, if ever. Since exercise often sharpens appetites, it usually invites the intake of more calories than it burns up. So-called "reducing exercises" have more value in redistributing body fat around the contour of a plump figure than in burning up the fat.

Should a woman exercise during her menstrual period? Yes, if she wants to, but obviously not too strenuously and beyond the point of fatigue. MENSTRUATION should not normally interfere with accustomed physical effort and activity.

What about exercising after illness, injury, or operation? The present tendency is to get patients back on their feet and walking around just as soon as possible after surgical operations or childbirth. The abuse of bed rest is properly decried. Following many weakening and debilitating illnesses, a period of convalescence with restricted but gradually increasing physical activity is advisable. Short-term virus infections are often more debilitating than the patient realizes, and he should not immediately plunge into strenuous physical activity. In conditions like HEART DISEASE, RHEUMATIC FEVER, and DIABETES the allowable amount of exercise must be carefully prescribed by the attending physician. To gain the fullest possible use of muscles damaged by disease (for example, poliomyelitis) or accidental injury, carefully prescribed and graded exercises are often of vital importance. This is *therapeutic exercise,* which is closely linked with PHYSICAL THERAPY, PHYSICAL MEDICINE, and REHABILITATION.

Exhaustion—the state of being emptied out or worn out, extreme FATIGUE. *Nervous exhaustion* is another name for NERVOUS BREAKDOWN or *neurasthenia. Heat exhaustion,* or prostration, is the result of exposure to excessive heat in the environment; for example, working in a boiler room or in the hot sun. See SUNSTROKE.

Exhibitionism—a not uncommon sexual deviation in which there is a compulsion to exhibit the body, or parts of it, particularly the sex organs, to obtain sexual gratification.

Exophthalmos—popeyes; usually the result of thyroid enlargement (goiter).

Exostosis—a bony outgrowth from the surface of a bone.

Expectorant—any remedy that helps a patient bring up and spit out excessive secretions (phlegm) accumulating in his lungs and windpipe.

Extrasystole—extra heartbeats; usually of no importance.

Extravasation—escape of fluid from a vessel that ought to contain it and its discharge into surrounding tissues, particularly the escape of blood from a broken blood vessel.

Extrovert—a personality type that turns to the outside world, feverish activity, and unreflective action to escape his own inner thoughts and emotional conflicts. He does not look before he leaps. He is the inwardly unhappy "life of the party" who needs people. The terms extrovert and INTROVERT were introduced by Carl Jung, a student of Freud's, to describe two opposite types of personality. The introvert looks into himself too much, does not act promptly. Most people are *ambiverts,* which means that they sometimes act like introverts and at other times like extroverts.

Exudate—anything sweated out by body tissues, usually blood vessels, as a result of natural or disease processes. An accumulation of pus is an exudate; so is normal perspiration on the skin.

EYES

The eyes may be a "mirror of the soul" to lovers and poets, but they are often a mirror of disease elsewhere in the body to the physician, who looks into the eye through an instrument made with mirrors (the ophthalmoscope). The human eye is essentially an apparatus for focusing and registering light rays on a light-

PARTS OF THE HUMAN EYE

sensitive membrane, the retina. It is like a camera whose images are actually recorded, interpreted, and "seen" in the brain.

The total visual apparatus, which makes sight possible, includes the eyeball, optic nerve, and visual centers in the brain. The eyeball is a ball filled with transparent fluid. In addition to its "film" of nerve endings (the retina), the eye has a shutter arrangement (the iris), which partially opens and closes to admit or exclude light rays. It has a lens, more or less self-adjusting, which focuses light rays on the retina to produce a normally clear image of what is seen. The stimulation of the millions of NERVE endings in the retina by the image seen sets up nerve impulses that are transmitted by way of the optic nerve to the brain.

How is the eye formed? The eyeball has three coats, or layers of membrane, enclosing its fluids. It is divided into two chambers, or cavities. The larger, spherical chamber in back is filled with a fluid, jellylike in consistency, called the *vitreous fluid*. The front chamber, which is the bulge of the eye we see, contains a lymph-like fluid called the *aqueous fluid*.

The outer of the three coats of the eyeball is the *sclera*. It is a tough, fibrous membrane that gives form to the eyeball and serves for the attachment of eye muscles. It appears as the white of the eye, except at the very front of the eye, where it becomes the almost perfectly transparent tissue called the *cornea*.

The middle coat is the *choroid*, composed largely of blood vessels. It is pigmented and gives color to the eye. It appears as the *iris*, which opens and closes to admit light through its central opening, the pupil. The opening and closing is controlled by tiny muscles.

The inner coat, or lining, is the *retina*, a delicate membrane that contains the nerve endings, called *rods* and *cones*, that connect with the optic nerve, which attaches to the back of the eyeball. The retina contains a coloring matter, known as *visual purple*, which must be constantly regenerated and probably requires vitamin A for this purpose.

The important *crystalline lens* is situated just behind the iris, and it separates the two chambers of the eye. The lens is transparent and refracts light. By changing its shape from flatter to thinner (becoming more or less convex), it focuses light rays on the retina. These changes are actually effected by small muscles called ciliary muscles. Fatigue in these muscles sometimes brings about *eyestrain*. The most common eye defects are defects of focus.

The eyes are protected partly by being set in sockets within the bones of the skull and partly by the eyelids and eyelashes. The cornea, in front, is covered by a mucous membrane, the *conjunctiva*, which merges into the under surfaces of the eyelids. The surface of the eye is constantly covered by a thin film of moisture from the *tear ducts* (lacrimal glands), located at the side of each eyeball. The excess fluid, except for tears, is normally drained off through small openings in the eyelids that lead into the nose. This connection explains partly why a head cold makes a person red-eyed. Small glands on the inner surface of the eyelids (Meibomian glands) secrete an oily liquid that keeps the lids from sticking together.

The eye has muscles inside, which work the iris and the crystalline lens. It also has muscles outside, which hold it in place and control its movements. There are six of these extrinsic (outside) muscles, so arranged and innervated that both eyes move together instead of independently. The proper working of these muscles gives human beings the advantages of binocular (two-eyed) vision, which gives a sense of perspective and permits judgment of speed, distance, and the like. The failure, or imbalance, of these muscles is what results in *cross-eye* (strabismus).

Eye care. In spite of the complex structure of the eye, the care of the eyes can be reduced to a few simple principles:

1. Avoid infection by keeping face and eyes *clean*. Wash hands before touching eyes. Don't use other people's towels and handkerchiefs. But daily eyewashes are so much "eyewash."

2. Don't meddle with the eyes. Don't put "drops" into the eyes for cosmetic reasons. Be careful about using dyes on the eyelashes and eyebrows; they may be dangerous.

3. Avoid eyestrain. Wear properly fitted glasses to correct vision defects. If doing much reading or close work, rest the eyes by glancing into the distance at least once every half hour.

4. See that you have sufficient light when you read or work. Avoid direct glare of light into the eyes. (Reading in bed is quite all right, provided the lighting is satisfactory.)

5. Be alert for any changes in the way you see. Whenever you notice any vision changes or abnormalities, such as failing sight or seeing double, promptly consult a competent physician or eye specialist (OPHTHALMOLOGIST).

EYE TROUBLE

A cinder in the eye can be so troublesomely annoying that it blots out all other thoughts and feelings—including symptoms of far more serious disorders. It is a mistake to consider eye diseases and disorders as limited to this organ. Eyestrain, for example, can induce fatigue in the rest of the body and thus, presumably, lower resistance to all manner of disease. Conversely, the condition of the eyes often reflects disease elsewhere in the body—for example, HIGH BLOOD PRESSURE, brain tumor, and infection. Any eye trouble, therefore, should be a signal to seek proper *medical* attention. The doctor will, if necessary, refer the patient to an eye specialist (ophthalmologist or oculist) or other medical specialist, as indicated. Although a conscientious OPTOMETRIST will promptly refer cases to a doctor of medicine, it is unwise when eye troubles arise to depend on companies or individuals who advertise, "Eyes Examined Free!"

What are the signs of eye trouble? There are many: pain, itching, or burning sensations in the eyes; bloodshot eyes; fear of light; excessive flow of tears; drooping eyelids; red-rimmed eyelids; headache; and all *changes* in ability to see. Among the vision changes that should prompt immediate medical attention are *seeing double, seeing blurred outlines, seeing halos* or *rainbows around lights,* and *seeing poorly in the dark.* Some people first discover that their night vision is failing when they are unable to see vacant seats in a darkened movie house.

Other signs of faulty or failing vision include inability to see things at a distance (nearsightedness); blurred images; difficulty in focusing on nearby objects, such as a printed page (farsightedness); distorted images (astigmatism); dimness of vision; and inability to distinguish colors (color blindness). Spots before the eyes are usually of no significance.

Many people have eye trouble without knowing it. They have accepted their visual defects for many years as normal sight and have not bothered to have them corrected. These defects are often discovered during a routine eye examination as part of an insurance medical examination or a test for a driver's license.

What can happen to the eyes? Many things—most but not all of which can be treated, corrected, and cured. Some eye defects are present at birth; for example, the shape and proportions of the whole eyeball and its crystalline lens may be such that nearsightedness or farsightedness must result. (Babies are born farsighted.)

Some infections occur during birth. Most common and serious at one time was gonorrheal infection of the conjunctiva. This condition (*gonorrheal ophthalmia* or *"babies' sore eyes"*) was once the leading cause of blindness. It has been largely eliminated by the legally required practice of putting drops of silver nitrate or other germ-killing solution, such as penicillin, into the newborn infant's eyes immediately after birth.

In recent years an exceptionally high number of premature infants were being blinded by the growth of embryonic tissue behind the lens (retrolental fibroplasia). It was then discovered that this condition was being caused, or at least perpetuated, by one part of the special care that doctors ordered for premature infants: the administration of oxygen in an oxygenated crib. Too much oxygen absorbed in the blood was responsible for this eye condition, which has now been almost entirely eliminated.

SIMPLIFIED OPTICS OF VISION

NORMAL VISION

FARSIGHTEDNESS (HYPEROPIA)

FARSIGHTEDNESS
CORRECTED WITH CONVEX LENS

NEARSIGHTEDNESS (MYOPIA)

NEARSIGHTEDNESS
CORRECTED WITH CONCAVE LENS

This series of illustrations presents the simplified optics of normal and defective vision, uncorrected and corrected with glasses. In each drawing, light rays are shown entering the eye and being bent (refracted) by the crystalline lens of the eye as well as by glass lenses in the two corrected cases.

In childhood direct injury to the eyes is common. In old age degenerative changes in the eye may dim sight. At any age part of the eye may be subject to infection.

The tragic end result of eye injury or disease can be total or partial BLINDNESS. There are approximately 260,000 "legally" or "industrially" blind people in the United States, and it is estimated that half of these cases might easily have been prevented. It must also be recognized that many blinded persons have risen heroically above this handicap and managed to achieve fruitful and well adjusted lives.

Most cases of poor eyesight are the result of defects in focus; that is, the lens of the eye fails to focus the incoming light rays sharply and exactly on the retina. This results in *nearsightedness, farsightedness, "old-sightedness"* and *astigmatism.*

Other physical abnormalities include *bulging eyes* (exophthalmos), *glaucoma, cataract, squint* (strabismus), *color blindness, night blindness, rapid eye movements* (nystagmus), *growth on the cornea* (pterygium), blocking of the *tear ducts,* and disorders of the *eyelids* and *eyelashes.*

Among the other serious noninfectious diseases of the eye are *atrophy of the optic nerve, detachment of the retina,* and *bleeding into the retina.*

Infection and inflammation of the cornea is called *keratitis;* of the iris, *iritis;* of the conjunctiva, *conjunctivitis* (which may be as mild as *pink eye* or as serious as *trachoma);* of the retina, *retinitis;* of the optic nerve, *optic neuritis;* of the eyelids, *blepharitis;* of the hair follicles in the eyelids, *stye* or hordeolum; of the oil glands on the inside of the eyelids, *chalazion.*

A *black eye* is simply a BRUISE and should be treated as such. The time-honored raw-beefsteak compress has its merits.

• *First aid for eye injuries.* Don't meddle is the first rule. Except in the simplest cases of removing something from the eye, leave the job to a doctor. Removal of glass or metal splinters usually requires very special procedures, sometimes including anesthetizing the eye and using an electromagnet. Remember that the eye is easily infected and scratches on the cornea can become scars that interfere with seeing. If you are not specially trained in managing eye injuries, do not attempt to remove anything other than a particle of dust, a cinder, or an eyelash that is visible, movable, and not on the cornea. Cover the eye with a sterile bandage or clean handkerchief and go to the doctor. *Don't rub the eye;* that usually makes things worse.

If the offending particle is floating freely in the conjunctival sac, which can be determined by its moving about, it may be possible to remove it easily by these procedures:

1. Shut both eyes for a few minutes. The accumulation of tears may wash out the particle.

2. Lift the upper lid gently by the eyelashes until it is out over the lower lashes; then let go. The lower lashes may brush the particle off. This and all other simple maneuvers should obviously be performed with *clean hands*.

3. Instill a few drops of clean water in the eye.

4. Wash out the eye by blinking it in an eyecup filled with clean water or boric-acid solution.

5. Finally, and cautiously, try removing the speck—if it can be seen and is movable—with the corner of a clean handkerchief or a piece of sterile gauze, or cotton. To see and find the particle, the lower lid may have to be pulled down or the upper lid turned up by grasping the lashes and pulling gently upward and outward. Anything more elaborate, such as rolling the upper eyelid over a matchstick, should be left to an expert.

When possibly damaging *liquids* have been *splashed in the eye,* the only sensible first-aid procedure is to wash the eye out with lots of clean water immediately. The victim may put his head in a sink or bowl of clean, tepid water and keep blinking the eye for a few minutes. Then see a doctor.

Must I wear glasses? Only if you want to see as well as you can and avoid eyestrain and other eye troubles. However, it is not necessary to wear them every waking minute. It is certainly permissible for a nearsighted young woman not to wear glasses when she goes out on a date. The idea that one can avoid wearing glasses by taking certain eye exercises (discussed below) is not valid.

The purpose of eyeglasses, or spectacles, is to correct defects in *focus* or, another way of saying the same thing, errors in *refraction* in the lens system of the human eye. Wonderful as it is, the human eye is rarely a perfect optical instrument. A lens, whether in the eye or in the glasses in front of the eye, refracts light. That means that it bends incoming light rays in a definite direction. The purpose of bending the light rays is to get them to focus exactly where they should—in this case, on the retina.

Glasses must be prescribed by an expert, which means a physician, eye specialist, or optometrist. Wearing glasses obtained without a competent eye examination is likely to be dangerous.

Glasses must be accurately adjusted to the eyes, and this includes proper fitting of the frames. Since the optical centers of the lens may be distorted by bending or other careless handling of the glasses, they should be frequently checked and, if needed, the frames realigned. CONTACT LENSES, which fit in the eye, have other problems.

Glasses are commonly prescribed to correct nearsightedness, farsightedness, "old-sightedness," and astigmatism.

Nearsightedness (myopia) means that the eyes can focus on nearby objects but vision at a distance is blurred. There are many degrees of nearsightedness. The cause is unknown, although in many people it seems to be hereditary.

In nearsightedness, the light rays are improperly focused and fall in front of the retina. It can be said that the eyeball is too long. This condition is corrected by wearing glasses with *concave* lenses (thinner in the middle).

Nearsighted children often tend to get increasingly nearsighted as they grow up, until about the age of 18 or 20. After this age they usually do not get any more nearsighted.

Most nearsighted people tend to squint, narrowing their eye slits. Squinting tends to reduce the amount of light coming in through the pupil and causes tears to accumulate in such a way that they create a concave-lens effect. Hence the observed images come into sharper focus on the retinal screen.

Nearsightedness, if uncorrected, may have definite psychological effects and, especially in children, may impair normal psychosocial development. Like the partially deaf, the nearsighted (myopic) may tend to be withdrawn and suspicious of events outside the narrow limits of their uncorrected vision.

Farsightedness (hyperopia) is perhaps ten times as common as nearsightedness. The farsighted person can see clearly at varying distances, but his close vision is likely to be blurred. He needs reading glasses. Many farsighted people are irked by close work and tend to choose occupations that do not require it.

In farsightedness, the light rays entering the eye are so focused that they fall behind the retina. This can be corrected by wearing glasses with *convex* lenses (thicker in the middle than at the edges), which give a magnifying-glass effect.

Many farsighted people are not aware of their eye defect because they do not see blurred images in doing close work or in reading. This is because the little muscles (ciliary muscles) that control the shape of the crystalline lens are persistently at work contracting. The farsighted person expects to see well, and he often overtaxes his ciliary muscles before he knows it. The result of this is *eyestrain*, reflected in pain in the eyes, headache, and nervous tension. A more extreme outcome may be cross-eyes (strabismus). The symptoms disappear when properly prescribed glasses are worn for reading and other close work.

"Old-sightedness" (presbyopia) is a type of farsightedness that comes on normally and gradually with age. The crystalline lens of the eye tends to lose its elasticity. Even though the ciliary muscles do their work, the lens fails to thicken properly and casts images behind instead of on the retina.

Sometime in their forties or later, most people discover that they have to hold a newspaper farther and farther away to read it. This is the common indication of presbyopia and the need for reading glasses.

"Bifocals." Because it is a nuisance to constantly change glasses as one shifts from reading a newspaper to looking out a window or the like, many people prefer to have glasses in which two prescriptions are ground into one lens. These are called bifocals, and were invented by Benjamin Franklin. The lower lens is convex, for reading or close work (by the farsighted); the upper lens is shaped as necessary to correct astigmatism.

"Second sight" sometimes happens to farsighted people as they grow older. They unexpectedly discover that they can read and see better than they previously could. Some of them actually can give up their reading glasses.

The reason for second sight is that the crystalline lens of the eye is gradually swelling and thickening, improving its focus on the retina. This swelling is usually a forerunner of *cataract* (see below). Nevertheless many old people enjoy second sight for a number of years before definite, perhaps surgical, treatment of cataract is necessary. A white ring around the cornea (arcus senilis) is still another common change in the aging eye. It does no harm.

Astigmatism. Practically every human eye has some degree of astigmatism, which produces distorted images, fuzzy and out of shape. Many people take their astigmatic vision for normal and do not know they have it until glasses correct it. Most instances of astigmatism, whether naturally occurring or acquired, are mild and minor and require no specific attention. In more serious cases, where both near and far vision appears to be impaired, serious eyestrain may occur and corrective lenses must be worn. Astigmatism may, and usually does, occur along with either farsightedness or nearsightedness.

Astigmatism occurs because the cornea and lens of the eye are not perfectly rounded; they have irregularities. In some spots they may be flattened out a little, in others slightly curved in one direction or another. As a result the light rays entering the eye are not evenly or perfectly distributed on the retina. Some are scattered ahead, some behind.

Astigmatism is corrected by glasses with lenses prescribed and ground to counteract each specific optical distortion in the lens system of the eye. The glass lenses curve the light rays to the proper degree in the opposite direction to that produced by the defects in the refractive surfaces of the eyes. Such lenses are called *cylindrical*. When the correction for astigmatism is ground right into glasses that also compensate for nearsightedness or farsightedness, as it usually is, the lenses are *compound*.

Cataract is a clouding of the crystalline lens of the eye or its capsule. Light then fails to reach the retina in sufficient quantity to stimulate vision. The degree of vision loss, which is, however, often preceded temporarily by better second sight (see above), depends on the location and extent of the cataract.

Cataract has been known to medicine since ancient times; effective treatment is modern. Cataract is usually a concomitant of growing old, but it may be induced by a disease such as diabetes and is an occupational hazard in industries, like glassblowing, in which the eyes are exposed to intense heat and light.

A cataract usually develops in one eye before the other. When it is "ripe" for operation, in the judgment of an eye surgeon, the crystalline lens can be safely removed. The operation is swift, painless, and almost always successful. With the opacity gone, usable vision is restored by wearing thick lenses in front of the eye.

Glaucoma, a serious eye disease of unknown cause, begins in the fluids encased in the eyeball. The pressure that these fluids exert against the other parts of the eye increases, suddenly or gradually. If this pressure is not relieved, it may make the eyeball hard, damage the retina, and even destroy fibers of the optic nerve, causing blindness. About 15% of all cases of blindness in the U.S. (and about half of those in adults) are caused by glaucoma.

The onset is often slow and insidious. At first it may be painless. Among the early symptoms are bloodshot eyes, blurred or steamy vision, inability to see to the side (that is, loss of peripheral vision), and frequent need for changing glasses. Sometimes glaucoma is not discovered until a person can hardly see out of one eye. Women are more likely to suffer from glaucoma than men. The condition can be detected by a simple instrument called a tonometer.

The blinding effects of glaucoma can often be averted by prompt treatment. Certain drugs lower the pressure; among them are those that cause the iris (pupil) to contract. These drugs are given as daily "drops" in the eyes, sometimes for a period of years. When drugs fail, there are surgical procedures that may relieve the intraocular pressure. Among them is that of boring a little hole in the outer coat (sclera) of the eye.

Glaucoma is one eye condition for which glasses do no good.

Bulging eyes, "popeyes" *(exophthalmos),* are usually the result of too much thyroid-gland hormone in the body (hyperthyroidism, goiter). Sometimes an *eye tumor* causes bulging, but these are comparatively rare.

Squint (strabismus), cross-eye, and *wall-eye* all result from essentially the same condition: an imbalance in the eye muscles. Instead of "pulling together" so that one three-dimensional image is registered in the brain, they pull in opposite directions so that two images are registered. This is fatiguing and uncomfortable. Hence the cross-eyed or wall-eyed person begins to do all his seeing with one eye, ignoring or suppressing the other. If this goes on too long, the unused eye may become partially or wholly blinded.

There is a mistaken opinion that young children, in whom squint is most commonly observed, eventually outgrow the condition. This may sometimes happen, but it is nothing to take a chance on. The afflicted child should be taken to an eye specialist promptly. He may be both physically and psychologically damaged by neglect of this highly curable eye defect.

In some cases squint can be corrected by eyeglasses. These are usually the cases in which the underlying factor of the eye-muscle imbalance is either extreme nearsightedness or a difference in the sightedness of the two eyes (one farsighted, the other near-sighted). In a few cases, up to about the age of 7, eye exercises prescribed by a specialist may help to correct squint. In these cases the defect is usually very slight. In most cases it will prove advisable to have a surgical operation that lengthens, shortens, or reattaches the eye muscles to provide proper binocular vision. This surgery is almost certain of good results.

Night blindness means inability to see well under conditions of limited illumination; in other words, poor dark adaptation of the eyes at night or twilight. This can be a serious deficiency in driving an automobile or piloting an airplane. Various disease conditions in the eye may foster night blindness. It is sometimes associated with a lack of vitamin A; such cases are often corrected by a diet rich in vitamin A.

Color blindness. This condition is hereditary and incurable. It occurs more commonly in males than in females but is usually passed on from mothers to sons. There are all degrees of color blindness. Most common is red-green color blindness, that is, inability to distinguish between red and green. This is a serious defect in our civilization, where traffic signals operate on a red-green system. Most people who are color-blind fail to recognize this defect until they are specially tested by sorting out colored yarns or finding a patterned number among a scattering of colored dots. A color-blind man may have to give up driving and have his wife pick out his shirts and ties, but he is not likely to be otherwise seriously discommoded. He will not be accepted in the Navy or Air Force.

Rapid eye movements (nystagmus). Some people involuntarily move their eyes rapidly from side to side, or up and down, or around and around. This is far more often a nervous tic than an eye disorder. It is due to lack of control over the part of the nervous system that innervates the extrinsic muscles of the eye. Treatment is likely to be psychiatric.

Growth over the cornea (pterygium). A thickened, fan-shaped patch of conjunctiva on the front of the eyeball sometimes begins to spread so that it covers the cornea and blocks out part of the visual field. Such growths can be readily removed by surgery—and should be removed, as they tend to spread over the entire eyeball if unchecked.

Optic atrophy. Sight may be impaired or irrevocably lost by damage to the optic nerve from causes outside the eye. Among these are syphilitic infection, increased intracranial pressure arising from a tumor of the BRAIN or the pituitary gland, degenerative nerve diseases (e.g. MULTIPLE SCLEROSIS), and drug or chemical poisoning. Overdoses of quinine or drinking methyl (wood) alcohol can cause atrophy of the optic nerve and blindness.

Detachment of the retina is a comparatively rare but exceedingly serious eye disorder, often resulting in total blindness. The detachment of the nerve-studded inner coat of the eye from its bed usually follows some jar or injury to the head, but this is not the whole story of its causation. It usually affects older rather than younger people (the average age at onset is about forty) and males somewhat more often than females.

Such cases were once thought hopeless, but progress has recently been made in delicate operative procedures aimed at reattaching the membrane. This procedure employs cauterization with chemicals or heat, both of which produce scar tissue. The aim is for the scar tissue to pull the retina back into the field where it should be. Cases for operation have to be carefully selected by a highly competent surgeon.

Bleeding into the retina (retinal hemorrhage) means breaking of the small blood vessels in the retina. This may be due to HEART DISEASE, KIDNEY TROUBLE, SYPHILIS, or other causes. It is the retinal (inner-lining) coat that the doctor sees when he looks into the eye with an ophthalmoscope. It is this inner appearance that has the name of *eyegrounds*. Hence retinal bleeding may lead to the discovery or more accurate diagnosis by eyegrounds of disease conditions elsewhere in the body.

Eye infections must be taken seriously and treated promptly by a physician. Usually more than one part of the eye is infected and inflamed, as the conjunctiva *and* the cornea. Infections in one eye, unless immediately taken care of, usually spread to the other eye. The systemic diseases that most frequently affect the eyes are syphilis, gonorrhea, tuberculosis, measles, and scarlet fever. Reddened eyes, a mild form of conjunctivitis, usually accompany the upper-respiratory infections, from the common cold up. Infections that attack the interior of the eye (keratitis, iritis, retinitis) are the most serious, but even those that get a foothold in the exterior surroundings of the eyeball can be damaging. Inability to look at light (photophobia) is a common sign of infections that have gone to the interior of the eye.

Conjunctivitis arises from many kinds of irritation, for example, specific bacilli and viruses; allergies, as in hay fever; drugs, such as atropine, too frequently used in the eyes; bright lights, such as Klieg lights and acetylene torches; lack of vitamin A (xerophthalmia); water, as in swimming pools; wind and dust, as found on the prairies; and chemicals encountered in many industries. Infection and irritation usually go together. Treatment usually includes bathing the eyes with a mild antiseptic solution, shielding the eyes from too much light (but not bandaging them), applications if necessary of ophthalmic ointments or lotions containing penicillin or other antibiotics, and rest.

Pink eye is an epidemic form of conjunctivitis, highly communicable and contagious. It is usually caused by a specific germ (Koch-Weeks bacillus). It may be spread rapidly in a household or school by use of a common towel or possibly by hand-to-hand and hand-to-eye contact. Cleanliness is the key to protection against pink eye. In this condition the eyes are usually inflamed and bloodshot; they itch and feel as if there were something in them; the lids are often stuck together at night.

Trachoma is a far more serious form of conjunctivitis; it is caused by a specific virus (*Chlamydozoön trachomatis*). It is highly contagious. In some parts of the world, notably Egypt and India, it is an almost universal disease, and is responsible for an immense amount of blindness. In the U.S. it is comparatively rare except among certain foreign-born populations and tribes of American Indians. The disease is sometimes called "granulated eyelids," because the infection causes severe scarring and turning out of the eyelids, which gives the eyes an ugly look. Early treatment with sulfa drugs stops the progress of the disease, but advanced cases often require careful application of mild caustics (copper sulfate and silver nitrate) to remove the blinding granules from the eyelids.

Styes are usually infections of the lash roots and associated glands in the margins of the eyelids. They usually come in crops and are often associated with uncorrected errors of refraction, eyestrain, and general poor health. Styes may be considered little pimples or boils along the course of a hair root. They usually soften in a day or two, discharge some infectious material, and then go on to recover. A hot compress may speed the stye's coming to a head. The hair around which it forms may be pulled out and an antiseptic lotion or ointment, harmless to the eye, applied to the spot.

Eye exercises, known as *orthoptics,* have definite but limited usefulness. They certainly cannot provide "sight without glasses" when organic defects exist—for example, cataract, optic atrophy, scars on the cornea. The value of eye exercises is often subjective. People who go to the trouble and expense of taking them often think that they are seeing better even when they are not.

Properly prescribed eye exercises may have particular value in nonsurgical treatment of eye-muscle imbalance. Nearsighted people and those with corneal scars can sometimes be helped by exercises, and the educational process that goes along with them, to adopt better habits of looking at and thus seeing things, so that they make the most of their vision. The education of color-blind people may help them to discriminate a little better between colors (by observing degrees of brightness rather than shade), though it will not cure color blindness.

"Eye banks" store under refrigeration in saline solution healthy eyes removed from deceased individuals. The corneas from such eyes can be successfully transplanted into eyes of living individuals whose sight has been lost or damaged by corneal disease, injury, or scarring.

F

Any word printed in SMALL CAPITALS *can be looked up under its own alphabetical listing for further information.*

FAINTING

Fainting, technically *syncope,* is a temporary loss of consciousness as the result of a diminished supply of blood to the brain.

First-aid treatment of a person who has fainted: Lay him flat on his back, with his head lower than the rest of the body (so that blood will flow to the brain). If necessary, elevate the legs. Or sit him in a chair and bend his body forward so that the head falls below the knees and between the legs. Loosen tight clothing. Stimulate the patient by applying cold water to the face, slapping the hands, pinching the cheeks, passing smelling salts (or burnt feathers) under the nose. After consciousness returns, which should be in a few minutes, give stimulants by mouth: hot coffee or tea.

To prevent fainting when one feels faint: Lie down flat on your back, with your head lower than the rest of your body; or sit down on a chair and drop your head below your knees. Have somebody douse your face with cold water, bring you smelling salts and a stimulating drink, or even a drink of cold water. Loosen your clothing. Get away from the cause of the fainting feeling, if possible.

The symptoms that warn of going into a faint are sudden paleness of the face; a feeble pulse; a sinking feeling; dizziness, giddiness, or lightheadedness; and a diminution in vision and hearing.

When a person has fainted, he lies motionless and unconscious, his breathing weak, his pulse feeble, his face pale, with beads of perspiration usually standing out on his head. There are many causes besides fainting for a person's being *unconscious*—for example, poisoning (as with an overdose of sleeping pills), diabetic *coma, stroke.* See UNCONSCIOUSNESS. If the person who has fainted does not promptly regain consciousness, call a doctor.

The causes of fainting are usually obvious: an emotional shock; a disgusting sight; the sight of blood; getting up too soon from a sick bed; an overlong, too hot bath, bringing on too much muscular relaxation; extreme pain; serious violence to the body (in which case the fainting may really be SHOCK); standing on one's feet too long, especially standing at attention on military parade; having taken drugs that lower the blood pressure; first experiences with alcohol and tobacco.

People of hysterical or unstable temperament are more likely to faint. Fainting or swooning is sometimes a learned reaction, practiced for its effect. This was the case with some Victorian young ladies. However, frequent fits of fainting, if they are not accidentally on purpose, demand a thorough medical check-up. This may reveal some correctable disease in the heart, blood vessels, ears, or elsewhere.

Fallopian Tubes—the tubes from the ovaries to the womb. See SEX ORGANS, FEMALE and FEMALE TROUBLES.

FAMILY DOCTOR

A family doctor is a physician who engages in the general practice of medicine. His specialty is the patient himself in his family environment. Despite the rise of specialties in medical practice (and perhaps on account of it), the role of the family doctor in the American medical scene is now deservedly getting more attention.

Specialists should be obtained through referral from the family doctor.

The role and status of the physician in a society has always reflected the character of the society. In ancient Greece, he was a free man, a priest-physician, an Aesclepiad; in imperial Rome, at the height of the Roman Empire, he was most likely a Greek slave. In democratic, industrialized American society, dependent on experts, the physician is (on the average) the highest-paid professional and, in general, enjoys a high social status.

The doctor alone is not responsible for his present high status. Factors beyond his control have altered his status. These factors are (1) *advances in science,* physical and chemical as well as psychological and biological; (2) *technological and industrial progress,* particularly in communication and transportation; (3) *sociological trends* set in motion by population trends and two world wars; and (4) the increasing support of *medical research,* first from philanthropy, then from industry, then from government.

The general practitioner is the heir and symbol of the long tradition of the healing arts. The picture—call it stereotype if you will—that the public holds of the physician is still the "family doctor with his little black bag"—not the specialist with his varied and intricate equipment.

General practitioners see more patients than specialists do. Hence the general practitioner is praised (or blamed) for the triumphs of modern medicine in all its aspects. He is, unfortunately, given credit for things he has little to do with, such as present-day sanitary practice, and blamed for things that are not his fault, such as the cost of drugs.

But by and large, the public has come to accord the physician greater and greater respect. High-school students usually vote medicine the field they would most like to enter.

The family doctor will be with us as long as there are families to seek his services. The character of the American family has changed considerably in the past century. Up until World War II, the American family was growing progressively smaller and the American birth rate was falling. Since World War II, the trends have been the other way and the demand for the family doctor may therefore be expected to become more insistent.

Farsightedness—hyperopia: long-sightedness. See EYE TROUBLE.

Fascia—the sheets or bands of tough, fibrous tissue that lie under the skin and serve as coverings for most muscles and many internal organs. The *fascia lata*, for example, is the broad, thick sheath of tissue covering the big muscles of the thigh.

FAT

There is a prejudice against fat—both fat on the body and fat as food—in the United States. Some of this is carried to ridiculous extremes. A good balanced diet (see DIET) should include fat; fat should supply 20 to 25% of the calories needed by the body. Weight for weight, fat has about 2¼ times as many calories as carbohydrates and proteins; it is the most concentrated energy food. It is also the vehicle of other food substances, notably fat-soluble vitamins, needed by the body. In its chemical composition fat is a combination of glycerin (glycerol) and various "fatty acids" (stearic, linoleic, palmitic, and other acids).

There is a delusion that "eating fat makes you fat." This is not true; it all depends on *how much* fat you consume. It is usually easier to cut fat out of the diet than any other common foodstuff. The total number of calories consumed, not the amount of fat, determines whether you lose weight.

Actually the animal body (including the human) can manufacture its own fat out of carbohydrates and proteins eaten. The best example is the cow, which eats grass and produces butterfat.

Sources of fat in the human diet are animal fats (such as lard and fat on meat), dairy products (especially butterfat), and plant oils (such as olive oil, soy-bean, corn, and cottonseed oil). Plant oils are often hydrogenated to make them firm; they then become *oleomargarine*. Nuts and seeds are exceptionally rich sources of fat—for example, peanuts made into peanut butter.

Will a fat-free diet prevent heart disease? No. Overweight people usually ingest more calories than they should, both as fat and other food substances. There is an association between overweight and heart disease; but the overweight does not cause the heart disease. There is also a theory, *unproved*, that a low-fat diet will prevent or slow down the deposit of fat (cholesterol) on the inner lining of the arteries, a condition (atherosclerosis) definitely associated with heart disease. However, this theory breaks down because the body manufactures its own fat (cholesterol). It is wise to keep one's weight at a sensible level as a precaution against heart and blood-vessel disorders, but completely avoiding fat is not the way to do it.

Are high-fat diets dangerous? To some extent. They usually are associated with the intake of too many calories. Fats must be consumed along with a proportion of proteins and carbohydrates; otherwise the fats are not completely digested and become ketone bodies, producing a condition of *ketosis*. This sometimes occurs in patients on high-fat diabetic diets.

A *low-fat diet* sometimes helps in treating oily skin conditions, notably acne.

Are fats indigestible? Not at all. Fried and fat foods often appear to be indigestible because they have been overcooked. The fat globules have been so molded together by the heat that it is difficult for the fat solvents in the digestive tract, gastric juice, and bile, to break them down into small globules for complete digestion.

Too much fat in the diet is neither appetizing nor assimilable; but there is no reason for avoiding fat altogether.

Fatigue, that "tired feeling," "loss of pep," is the most readily abused and yet one of the most important symptoms of disease and poor health. True fatigue cannot be relieved by taking vitamin pills, pick-up drugs, tonics (most of which contain varying amounts of alcohol), deep-breathing exercises, or by any other simple cure-all.

Fatigue is both normal and abnormal (that is, physiological and pathological). It is normal to be fatigued, and feel fatigued, after a hard day's work, vigorous exercise, or an emotionally trying experience. The relief for such fatigue is simply rest—several relaxed days and one or more good nights' sleep. Muscular fatigue is normal; muscles can be worked only so long. When they reach the fatigue point, they slow down their contractions and sometimes stop working altogether.

With rest, they recuperate. Children tire faster and recuperate faster than adults. If rest and sleep fairly quickly correct your fatigue, you need not worry about it. See EXERCISE.

Pathological fatigue is present when adequate rest does not relieve persistent tiredness. This is an important symptom of illness and calls for a medical check-up.

Fauces—the back of the mouth; the open passage, rather narrow, between mouth and throat.

Favus—a FUNGUS infection of the skin, usually the scalp. "Honeycomb" yellow crusts form, and they usually have a musty odor. This is a form of RINGWORM. It is highly contagious and difficult to treat.

Fecal Impaction—retention of a sticky or hard mass of stool in the lower bowel See ENEMA.

Feces—bowel movement; the excrement discharged from the anus.

FEEBLE-MINDEDNESS

Feeble-mindedness is a popular but old-fashioned term for mental deficiency or mental defectiveness. This condition should not be confused with MENTAL ILLNESS.

Feeble-mindedness is arrested or incomplete mental development, existing before adolescence, caused by disease or genetic constitution (HEREDITY) and resulting in social incompetence.

Feeble-mindedness is graded in both legal and psychological terms as idiot, imbecile, and moron. An idiot has a mental age below 2 years and is unable to guard himself from physical danger. An imbecile has a mental age between 2 and 7 years and is incapable of managing himself or his own affairs—or of being taught to do so. A moron ranges from 8 to 12 years in mental age and requires the care and supervision of other people to get along in the world and be protected from harming himself or others.

About 1% of the population of the United States is judged to be feeble-minded; but this judgment, of course, depends on where you draw the line between morons and dull normals. There are comparatively few idiots and imbeciles, perhaps 2 in 1,000 population.

It is estimated that at least 10,000,000 perfectly normal people in the United States carry genes for feeble-mindedness, to the extent that this is a hereditary weakness; so the hope of breeding it out of the population is a pretty weak one. However, much less importance is now attached to heredity as a cause of feeble-mindedness. Prenatal environment—special but sometimes uncontrollable conditions of life in the womb before birth—is often considered a more probable cause.

Mental defectiveness is often associated with other more or less noticeable physical abnormalities present at birth, such as an abnormally small head (microcephalism), water on the brain (hydrocephalus), CRETINISM, and MONGOLIAN IDIOCY. Convulsions in early infancy are sometimes associated with mental deficiency. The condition is discovered in a normal-appearing infant when he fails to develop habits and skills normal for his age.

Although the range of development is wide, and many children are comparatively slow learners, it usually comes as one of the sharpest pangs that life can bring to discover—and admit—that one has a retarded child.

If a specific cause for feeble-mindedness can be discovered, such as congenital syphilis, thyroid lack (cretinism), or hearing and vision defects, treatment of it may improve the mental outlook. Tragically, however, it is rarely possible to hold out any hope for the cure of mental deficiency. But proper educational guidance and resources may help these children to adjust to a way of life satisfactory to them, if not to their parents.

Morons, at least, can usually be trained for simple, routine occupations. They are better off in the country than in the city.

Should feeble-minded children be kept at home? There is no rule; this is a completely individual matter that parents must decide. While the children are young, this is often possible. Later they become a terrible drag on the family and are themselves unhappy in the atmosphere of normal children, with whom they cannot compete. At this point they are often better off in schools or institutions with other children near their own intelligence. To the extent that such schools are staffed and supported to individualize instruction and care, they do an excellent job.

Feet—see FOOT and FOOT TROUBLE.

Fellatio—insertion of the male sex organ into the mouth of a fellator (male) or fellatrice (female).

Fellowship (medical)—a form of graduate training, similar in nature to a *residency* but usually offering opportunity for teaching, study in the basic sciences and research. It is usually considered a medical school rather than a hospital appointment.

Felon—whitlow; a bad and usually painful abscess at the tip of a finger. It usually starts as a small puncture wound and infection at the base or side of a finger nail. It may result from an accident, unsanitary manicuring practices, or tearing off a cuticle, or hangnail. The infecting germ is usually the staphylococcus, but it may be any other. The infection may work its way inward, even to the bone, producing pus that has nowhere to drain off. This causes swelling, redness, and pain. At this point the standard home remedies—applying skin antiseptics and soaking the finger in hot water—are usually of no avail. The felon has to be lanced and the pus drained. Thereafter hot packs give relief. An untreated felon can be dangerous, spreading infection through the rest of the body.

Female Sex Organs—See SEX ORGANS, FEMALE.

FEMALE TROUBLES

Female troubles cover a wide variety of complaints, ailments, and disorders that affect or are reflected in the female SEX ORGANS. These disorders fall in the field of *gynecology,* though the family doctor can successfully treat most of them. It is most important to consult a physician and not resort to drugstore remedies. The advice of well-meaning friends is apt to be dangerous.

Female troubles are usually—and ignorantly—ascribed to the womb, but any female sex organ may be involved. The most common female troubles concern MENSTRUATION. However, female troubles also include infections and inflammations, tumors and new growths, and congenital malformations (such as unperforated MAIDENHEAD, double uterus, or misplaced ovary).

The most common symptoms are painful periods (dysmenorrhea), missed periods (amenorrhea), abnormal vaginal bleeding or spotting between periods (metrorrhagia), excessive bleeding (menorrhagia), abnormal vaginal discharges (leukorrhea, "the whites"), itching of the external genitals, feelings of heaviness in the pelvis, loss of libido, and inability to conceive (barrenness, STERILITY, infertility).

Painful menstruation (dysmenorrhea) is usually functional in origin, especially in young women. It often reflects a hidden, resentful attitude toward MENSTRUATION ("the curse"), toward being a woman instead of a man, and toward sex. But sometimes it is caused by hormone imbalance, tumors or infections, mechanical factors, or other constitutional disorders. Normal menstruation is not painful.

Sedentary women are more subject to menstrual cramps and discomfort than those who are physically active. Improvement in posture and regular exercise are often helpful. A heating pad or hot-water bottle may be used to relieve occasional pains, but persistent, serious pains demand medical attention. Pain-killing drugs are ill-advised.

Amenorrhea, absence of menstrual periods, is normal before puberty, after the menopause, and during pregnancy and lactation (breast-feeding). Bleeding after the menopause should always invite prompt medical investigation.

Disorders of any of the endocrine glands may produce menstrual abnormalities.

Tumors and new growths can occur almost anywhere in the female sex organs. Most commonly, however, they are *fibroids* of the uterus, *polyps* of its lining, and *cysts* of the ovaries. Most commonly dangerous is CANCER of the cervix of the uterus.

Fibroids are new growths of smooth muscle and connective tissue on the walls of the uterus. About 40% of all women have fibroid growths, but only a few are bothered by them. They vary in size from a peanut to a football. The symptoms of fibroids include vaginal bleeding, pain, sensations of pressure, and irritation. Fibroids can occur at any age, but usually appear at the MENOPAUSE. Surgical removal is the only effective treatment, though X-ray treatment may stop the bleeding.

Cysts of the ovaries are collections of fluid enclosed in a sac of membrane. Their cause is unknown, and there are many different types. They can become enormous, weighing more than the woman from whom they are removed. The treatment is surgical removal. There is great historical interest in ovarian cysts, because one of the first successful abdominal operations ever performed was the removal of such a cyst. This was done in 1809, without anesthesia and without formal asepsis, by a backwoods Kentucky surgeon, Dr. Ephraim McDowell, who thus earned the title "father of abdominal surgery."

The cervix of the uterus is one of the commonest sites of cancer in the female. It frequently arises in an inflamed or injured cervix, and it is more common in women who have borne many children. The onset usually occurs in the forties. In the early stages it does not produce pain, but may induce vaginal bleeding or other discharge. Periodic medical examinations of women in their forties reveal cases in the early stage, when they are highly curable. Cancer can occur at other sites in the female SEX ORGANS.

Infections and inflammations often cause female troubles. GONORRHEA is a particularly common and potentially serious infection. The gonococci may invade any part of the sex organs, including the glands and Fallopian tubes, where they set up an inflammation called *salpingitis*. This may result in closure of the tubes and subsequent sterility. In young female children a gonococcal infection may be innocently acquired and set up a true inflammation of the vagina.

Another common and often stubborn infection of the female sex organs is caused by the organism known as *trichomonas vaginalis*. Husbands and wives can infect and reinfect each other with this trichomonad. The symptoms are usually itching (pruritus), burning, thick vaginal discharges, and abdominal tenderness. Treatment is with a wide variety of drugs, often in vaginal suppositories.

Itching of the vulva may arise from many causes, including diabetic urine, irritating discharges from the internal sex organs, and degeneration of tissues *(kraurosis)* that sometimes occurs after the menopause.

Tipped womb, or retrodisplacement of the uterus, was once a common and fashionable diagnosis for many female troubles. Operations were performed to correct this. It is now recognized that most tipped wombs are congenital in origin and require no treatment.

Some female troubles are symptoms or disorders of early pregnancy and are related to spontaneous ABORTIONS or miscarriages. They require skilled medical attention. Other female troubles are the aftermath of CHILDBIRTH, and these, too, require professional diagnosis and treatment. See PREGNANCY.

When properly indicated and performed, surgery on the female sex organs is usually highly successful and effective. However, many women want to rush into gynecological operations for the relief of female troubles that surgery cannot cure.

Femur—the thigh bone. In elderly people the upper end (head or neck) of this bone is often broken and sometimes must be nailed or wired together. See FRACTURES and BONES.

Fertility—the state of being fertile or fecund; able to sire, conceive, or bear offspring. It is the opposite state, STERILITY or barrenness, that requires medical attention.

Fetus—the unborn offspring of any animal that bears its young alive. In human beings the newly developing individual within the mother's womb is called a fetus from about the second or third month of PREGNANCY until birth. Before that it is referred to as an EMBRYO.

FEVER

Fever is a body *temperature* above its regular or normal level. In adults the average normal body temperature is 98.6° Fahrenheit, when measured by a fever thermometer placed in the mouth (oral temperature). When a rectal temperature is taken, with the thermometer inserted in the anus, the normal temperature is usually about 1 degree higher (99.6° F.). The temperature taken under the armpits is about 1 degree lower (97.5° F.).

It is not absolutely necessary to take a temperature to determine the presence of fever. The skin feels hot, especially on the brow and the back of the neck. For borderline cases, however, there is nothing more valuable than a good fever thermometer (also called a clinical thermometer) kept in the family medicine chest and used to help decide (1) when to call or see a doctor, (2) whether to go to work, and (3) whether to send a child to school.

Some otherwise healthy children and adults normally have a subnormal or abnormal temperature. This can be determined only by a series of temperature readings over a period of time. Normal temperature also fluctuates during a 24-hour period, being higher in the later afternoon and evening, lower at night during sleep. This reflects the amount of heat being produced by the body; that is, its METABOLISM. (See TEMPERATURE.)

Generally speaking, a rise in body temperature indicates an IN-FECTION with some germ or MICROBE, which must be banished before the fever will go down. There are some exceptions, but only expert medical diagnosis can reveal them. And there is still a category of "fever of obscure or unexplained origin" that taxes the skill of the best diagnosticians.

What is fever? Fever is a *sign* of disease; it is not the disease. It is usually accompanied by other signs and symptoms of disease—a hot, dry, flushed SKIN; a more rapid PULSE; changes in breathing; a sense of being chilled; a feeling of restlessness, malaise (a sick feeling), and nausea; sometimes VOMITING, DIARRHEA, and HEADACHE. In high fever UNCONSCIOUSNESS or DELIRIUM may occur.

Fever is not always a bad thing; it is the cause of the fever that must be indicted. Fever is part of the body's defense against an invasion of microbes. It indicates that the body is speeding up its counterattack—rushing white blood cells to the site of invasion, removing the debris of germ battle (PUS), and generally speeding up its metabolism to conquer the invaders.

Many germs die when the body temperature is raised above its normal level; for example, the gonococcus and the spirochete of syphilis. That is why *artificial-* or *induced-fever* treatment in, for example, a sweatbox (hypertherm), can be used to treat certain venereal or other diseases. Since the coming of sulfa drugs and antibiotics, however, which attack the metabolism of the invading germs, fever treatment is rarely used.

Fever often reaches its highest point just before it breaks and falls sharply. On the other hand, rising fever is always a sign of increasing seriousness of disease or infection and should never be neglected. Always call a doctor.

How to reduce fever: Fever can usually be reduced by antipyretic (fever-reducing) drugs and good nursing procedures. But it may not always be desirable to reduce the fever immediately. The picture of the fever's course may be necessary for an accurate diagnosis of the underlying disease, and must not, therefore, be masked by antipyretic drugs. Again, the fever may be helpful in killing the invading microbes.

The most common antipyretic drug is aspirin, followed by other salicylates. Except for the occasional aspirin, they should not be taken indiscriminately. These drugs act on the heat-regulating center in the brain.

A high fever that is interfering seriously with a patient's rest and comfort can often be reduced by a tepid bath (temperature of bath water 85 to 90° Fahrenheit), by a sponge bath at the same temperatures, or by an alcohol rub. The rubbing brings the blood to the surface of the body; the evaporation of the water or alcohol from the skin surface cools it. Bathe or rub in a warm room.

If a patient is heavily covered with blankets, his temperature is more likely to remain elevated than if he is covered lightly with sheets.

How high is high fever? A temperature of 110° F., prolonged for any length of time, is usually incompatible with life and signals impending death. In a few rare cases fever has risen even higher and the patient has lived. The height of the fever is not always the measure of the seriousness of the underlying disease. For example, in typhoid fever and pneumonia, before treatment, the temperature usually reaches 105° F. On the other hand, in rheumatic fever and diphtheria, the fever rarely exceeds 103°; hence a temperature of 104° in these conditions must be observed with concern.

When is fever fever? This is often a hard question. If (1) a person's usual temperature is close to the average temperature (98.6° orally), (2) his present temperature has been taken correctly—at least 20 minutes after eating or smoking or vigorous exercise, and with the thermometer in place for at least 2 to 3 minutes, and (3) some other mild symptoms of illness or distress accompany the fever, it may be assumed that an oral temperature of around 100° in an adult and 101° in a child indicates illness, infectious or otherwise, and should receive prompt and adequate treatment. At these temperatures, stay home from work, keep a child home from school, and consult a doctor.

Starve a fever? Nonsense! Many people with high or prolonged fevers lack appetite and eat poorly. They need adequate nourishment and a balanced diet. Often they need excesses of PROTEINS and VITAMINS. The more rapid metabolism characteristic of diseases marked by fever burns up foodstuff—especially protein—and body tissues more rapidly than normal. As much as a pound a day may be lost. Hence prolonged fevers are often wasting diseases and bring about considerable weight loss. In some high fevers, where hair roots are damaged, loss of hair may follow. High fevers often overload the kidneys and urine with nitrogen-containing waste products (ALBUMINURIA).

Types of fever. Certain types or patterns of fever are characteristic of certain diseases. If the temperature is taken every 4 (or every 2) hours and plotted on square-ruled paper, it often shows a pattern so characteristic that diagnosis can be made by a glance at the fever chart. Temperature is a ready method of determining how well a patient is recovering from an illness or surgical operation. Hence every hospital patient has a fever chart kept by the nurses. (It used to hang at the foot of the patient's bed.)

The type of fever produced by a disease depends on the habits and nature of the infecting MICROBE. The fever pattern produced by the pneumococcus in the lungs in pneumonia is quite different, for example, from that produced by parasites in the blood stream, which invoke a variety of malarial fevers (every day, every 2 days, every 3 days). Similarly, the low-grade fever of chronic tuberculosis makes a different pattern from the acute, high fever of typhoid.

As already noted, not only infections produce fever. Rarely, for example, a brain tumor affects the heat-regulatory mechanism of the brain and engenders an exceptionally high fever. Fevers that result from infection include:

Blackwater fever (MALARIA), brain fever (MENINGITIS), childbed or puerperal fever (SEPTICEMIA), hospital fever (TYPHUS), parrot fever (PSITTACOSIS), cat-bite or rat-bite fever, jail fever (TYPHUS or DENGUE), Q FEVER, relapsing fever, RHEUMATIC FEVER, malarial fever, Rocky Mountain spotted fever (similar to tick fever or spotted fever, caused by *rickettsia*), SCARLET FEVER (scarlatina), TYPHOID FEVER, TYPHUS FEVER, TRENCH FEVER, UNDULANT FEVER, YELLOW FEVER, and valley fever (coccidioidomycosis).

Fever Blister—a mild virus infection requiring no treatment. See HERPES.

Fibrillation—tremor of a muscle. The term is usually applied to the heart muscle (auricular or ventricular fibrillation). It is responsible for rapid and irregular pulse and heartbeats. The drug *quinidine* usually corrects the condition.

Fibroid—generally describes a comparatively harmless and benign tumor or new growth inside the uterus. See FEMALE TROUBLES.

Fibrositis—a form of muscular rheumatism. (See RHEUMATISM.) More exactly, it means inflammation of the white fibrous connective tissue that forms muscle sheaths and merges into muscle attachments. However, *fibrositis* is often applied to any soft-tissue disorder that causes aches and pains in and around the muscles and joints. Tendon sheaths and *bursae* may also be involved. The muscle that runs over the top of the shoulder is often involved, becoming stiff and painful. Fibrositis is also responsible for many cases of backache.

Fortunately, fibrositis rarely produces any deformity or much disability, even though it sparks annoying episodes for a lifetime. The treatment is generally simple: application of heat, massage, light exercise, and aspirin.

Fibula—one of the two bones of the lower leg; the more slender bone on the outer aspect. The other bone is the TIBIA. (See illustrations for BONES.)

Filariasis—the name for any one of a number of diseases, usually tropical, caused by long thread-worms (filaria, nematodes). When these worms block the lymph channels, they can cause enormous swellings of legs, arms, and scrotum (see ELEPHANTIASIS). In Central Africa there is a species of filaria, carried by the mango fly, that particularly attacks the eye. This disease is called loa loa.

Finger Nails—see NAILS, also CUTICLE.

First Aid—or what to do until the doctor comes. See EMERGENCY! FIRST-AID INDEX on pages xvii-xviii.

First-Aid Kit—see MEDICINE CHEST.

Fish is not brain food. It is a valuable source of PROTEIN and should be eaten for this purpose. Generally speaking, it is low-cost protein, despite its high water content. In most fish the fat is concentrated in the liver, from which, for example, cod-liver oil is extracted. But the tastier fish, such as salmon, mackerel, sardines, and herring, have about 10% fat in the parts of the fish meat that are usually consumed. Fish are a good source of phosphorus, iodine, and vitamins A and D.

Fish-Skin Disease—ichthyosis, a SKIN disorder.

Fissure—normally a fold, groove, or cleft, such as those regularly found in the BRAIN and LIVER. Abnormally speaking, small narrow ulcers are also called fissures. These usually occur at the corners of the mouth, sometimes in association with *vitamin* deficiencies, and around the anus, often in connection with PILES.

Fistula—a false opening, a passageway between body parts that should not be there. Of the many kinds of fistulas, the most common are *fistula in ano; vesicovaginal* fistula, between the bladder and the vagina, sometimes the result of childbirth injury; *arteriovenous fistula,* an abnormal connection between an artery and a vein, caused by either a congenital malformation or a wound to the artery; a *salivary fistula,* through which saliva dribbles out on the cheek instead of going into the mouth.

A fistula may be the end result of injury or accident; of infection ending in an abscess that does not drain through normal lymph channels and so forces its way to the surface of

the skin or into another organ; of disease, such as tuberculosis; or of blockage of a duct, like the salivary ducts.

Fistulas are often difficult to treat and often require surgery. The basic idea is to obliterate the false channel and re-establish the normal one. This is sometimes done by cauterizing the false channel.

Fistula in ano is an open and needless passage from the lower end of the bowel to the surface of the skin, by-passing the normal opening of the anus. It is commonly the end result of a bowel abscess. Such fistulas usually heal slowly, even after competent surgery, because material from the bowel is constantly flowing into them. They have to be packed daily until healed.

"Fits"—CONVULSIONS, which see.

Flat Foot—see FOOT TROUBLE.

Flatulence—the accumulation of gas or air on the stomach or in the bowels, where its presence may be indicated by rumbling sounds (borborygmus). It is not cured, corrected, or prevented by gobbling a few breath-sweetening chalk tablets or taking "bicarb" (sodium bicarbonate) after each meal.

Flatulence is usually aggravated by the bad habit of swallowing air with or between meals. Most people who do this are unaware of the habit until it is pointed out to them. When the habit is broken, by conscious effort, the flatulence often disappears. Sometimes, however, there is a psychological factor, and this is not so easily eliminated.

Gas on the stomach is usually associated with a distension (ballooning) of the stomach and with some mild, or possibly severe, STOMACH TROUBLE (indigestion), which must be treated before the flatulence and its sequel, belching, can be eliminated.

Gas in the bowels is usually the result of the bacteria normally present in the bowel acting on undigested food products in the far end of the bowel. The gas produced is usually hydrogen sulfide, which has the smell of sewer gas or rotten eggs when expelled from the rectum. Correction of this condition often demands a change of diet, eliminating foods that are high in cellulose and carbohydrate content, such as green vegetables and excessive starches.

Flatus—gas or air on the stomach or in the intestines, sometimes expelled from the mouth as a belch or from the anus as "passing wind."

Fleas—see INSECTS.

Flexor—any muscle that bends or flexes a part of the body. The biceps of the upper arm are flexors; they bend the elbow and draw up the forearm.

"Flu"—short for INFLUENZA, a virus disease.

Fluoridation of drinking water is a safe and effective means of helping to prevent tooth decay (dental caries), especially in children. The amount of fluorine (really fluorides) in the water is the crucial point. The concentration should not exceed 1 part of fluorine to 1,000,000 parts of water. Years of accumulated evidence show that this amount cannot harm or poison anyone. When there is more than this amount, as naturally occurs in some parts of the United States, no poisonous effects are noted but the tooth enamel may become mottled. There has been much needless controversy over fluoridation of public water supplies. To oppose it is to deny all scientific evidence that it does safely reduce the incidence of tooth decay.

Fluorine—a chemical element, normally a gas; it is a halogen related to chlorine and iodine.

Fluoroscope—a type of X-ray machine in which the shadows of the interior of the body cast by the X-ray tube fall on a *fluorescent screen* instead of a photographic plate. The fluoroscope does not take a picture, but it enables the examiner to view parts of the interior of the body in action—especially the heart and lungs.

Flush—reddening of skin on face and neck. "Hot flushes" sometimes accompany the MENOPAUSE. They can be readily controlled with properly pre-scribed medication, if needed.

Flutter—a heart condition, re-lated to FIBRILLATION, in which the auricles of the heart may beat at the rate of 200 to 400 times a minute. The drug quinidine may slow them down.

Folic Acid—a constituent of the VITAMIN B complex; it is relat-ed to but not identical with vitamin B₁₂; it is especially use-ful in treating pernicious ANE-MIA.

Follicle—a little bag, sac, or gland. The hair follicles are the hair roots, the little oil-secreting glands from which hair grows. (See illustration for SKIN.)

Folliculitis—inflammation of a follicle, or more usually, a group of them. BOILS and STYES are forms of folliculitis; that is, infections around hair roots. So is "barber's itch."

Fontanel—the soft spots on a baby's skull; actually the areas where the bones of the skull have not yet grown firmly to-gether.

Food Poisoning—Considering the amount of food safely con-sumed every day by billions of people, food poisoning may be considered one of the rarest of diseases or accidents. Many people are sensitive to certain foods and suffer a *food allergy* when they eat them; the un-pleasant symptoms in the di-gestive tract may be similar to, but are not true cases of, food poisoning. The term *ptomaine poisoning* was once used to de-scribe food poisoning, but is a complete misnomer.

Millions of dollars and much brain power and footwork is ex-pended annually in the United States to protect people from the risk of foods that may be injurious to their health. The safeguarding of the public against unsanitary foods is one of the primary responsibilities of the public-health authori-ties, including state and local public-health departments, the U.S. Public Health Service, and the Federal Food and Drug Ad-ministration.

The usual symptoms of true food poisoning are severe vom-iting, diarrhea, and abdominal pain coming on from 4 to 30 hours after eating the infected food. To these may be added headache, cold sweats, prostra-tion, collapse, and—rarely—death. These are the symptoms of a severe intestinal infection (dysentery), which is what food poisoning usually is. The germ or microbe that causes it usually belongs to the group called *Salmonella*, though staphylococci and other germs are occasionally responsible. The most dangerous is the rar-est, botulinus. (See BOTULISM.)

One cannot go through life with a constant fear of food poisoning. The only possible rule is to avoid foods that smell or taste peculiar—especially in summer.

Foot—The human foot is de-signed and engineered for forward locomotion. Except for accident and congenital malformation (see CLUBFOOT), most FOOT TROUBLE is self-inflicted by abuse of the feet and bad footwear.

The unique parts of the human foot are its "springs," called arches, which take up the shock from walking, running, and jumping. There are two springs, or arches; the *longitudinal arch* runs from the ball of the foot to the heel; the *metatarsal arch* runs crosswise at the instep. These arches are supported by ligaments and tendons that run to the bones of the foot and the muscles of

the leg. When the arches break down, the result is flat foot (see FOOT TROUBLE).

The foot's anatomical structure is very much like the hand's (as might be expected, since the hand is an evolutionary adaptation of the foot). However, the proportions and sizes of the bones, muscles, and ligaments are different. Each foot has 26 bones, including the calcaneus (heel bone), which is one of 7 tarsal bones; 5 metatarsal bones, above the instep; and 14 phalanges, in the toes. The big toe, like the thumb, has 2 phalanges; all other digits have 3.

FOOT TROUBLE

Foot trouble may originate in the skin, bones, muscles, ligaments, bursae, or nails (toenails) of the FOOT. Most foot trouble is easily prevented. There are many effective means of relieving tired, aching, itching, burning, sweating, swollen, painful, lame, infected, or deformed feet.

Home care and drugstore remedies do more for foot trouble than almost any other group of annoying bodily ailments. A CHIROPODIST (podiatrist) can also be of great help in relieving or preventing foot trouble. But there are advanced, extreme cases that require medical attention from the general practitioner, the skin specialist (dermatologist), or the orthopedic surgeon. The diabetic patient, the pregnant woman, and other people whose foot trouble reflects disease conditions elsewhere in the body should certainly be under direct medical care.

How to prevent foot trouble: Abuse and neglect of the feet and ignorance of their proper care is the principal cause of foot trouble. Even when treated, these troubles will recur unless simple preventive measures are immediately taken; namely:

Keep your feet clean and dry. For older people especially, it is essential to wash the feet daily with soap and water. Dry them thoroughly, particularly between the toes. Put on clean socks or stockings daily. Change socks and shoes whenever they become damp. Dusting (talcum) powder sprinkled on the feet or shaken into the socks or stockings often relieves the discomfort of sweaty feet.

Walk and stand properly. Walk toeing in (slightly pigeon-toed) rather than toeing-out. Lifts on heels or soles of shoes may be necessary to get or restore proper walking. Stand in the posture most relaxing for you. Let the weight of your body be evenly supported on four points—the balls and heels of *both* feet. Military standing (at attention) and drill marching is physiologically wrong and fatiguing. (See POSTURE.)

Select and wear the right kind of shoes and stockings. Fashion is often a cruel mistress, and vanity her handmaid, when it comes to buying shoes. Despite countless warnings, men and women persist in buying, for themselves or their children, shoes that are too small or too tight. Improperly fitted shoes that pinch or squeeze either foot cause or aggravate all forms of foot trouble.

The best test of shoes is *how they feel* on your feet after *you* have stood or walked in them a few minutes. The feet spread when you walk. Don't take the word of the shoe salesman; he is not wearing the shoes.

Always try on *both* shoes. Your left foot and right foot are not exactly the same size and shape. If there is a great difference between them, you should have your shoes custom-made.

What makes a comfortable, properly fitted shoe?

1. It is at least a *half inch longer* than your longest toe when you are standing in it.

2. The *outline* of the shoe is *everywhere larger* than the outline of the foot when bearing body weight.

3. The inner *line of the sole,* from heel to big toe, is *straight* or *flares out.*

4. There is *room for toes to spread* out.

5. The *ball of the foot* presses down *on the widest part* of the shoe.

6. The *back* of the shoe fits snugly, but *not too tightly.*

7. The shoe allows for *ventilation of the foot* so that it does not become excessively damp. The style and material of the shoe govern this factor. Real leather, which has pores, is often preferable to composition materials, however "tough."

8. Rubber *heels* absorb shock when walking; leather heels are permissible. The height of the heel should be from ⅜ to 1½ inches.

High heels. Some women wear high heels all their adult life and have no trouble; they are walking downhill all the time but don't mind it. Nevertheless high-heeled shoes often predispose to foot trouble.

High heels relieve the muscles of the back of the leg of some of their normal function. These muscles tend to weaken from under-use and may fail to give normal support to the arches. Furthermore high-heeled shoes must be built with a rigid shank. This acts as an arch support and further weakens the muscles and ligaments that hold up the arch.

High heels change the center of gravity of the body and the line of weight-bearing on the soles and heels. This often strains the *metatarsal arch*, where a great many foot troubles begin in women.

The descent from high to lower heels may have to be gradual because the calf muscles have become weakened and the heel cord (Achilles tendon) shortened by long wearing of high heels. The response to stretching them by immediately wearing low heels may be pain and discomfort.

Tight socks and stockings are a more common cause of foot trouble than generally recognized. They may pinch and squeeze the feet; they may interfere with ventilation, since many of the new synthetic fabrics do not absorb water. In particular, the new "stretch yarn" hosiery may be purchased too small so that it cramps the toes. A particular risk is pressing the little toe against the fourth toe so that the space between constantly remains a dank reservoir of *fungus* infection of the feet.

Common foot troubles that concern primarily the SKIN are *corns, calluses, bunions, soft corns, blisters,* CHILBLAINS, RINGWORM (athlete's foot), *plantar warts,* and *excessive sweating*.

The foot troubles that originate in the bones, ligaments, and joints include hammertoe, CLUBFOOT (which see), *flat foot, fallen arches, painful heel,* and *foot strain ("tired feet")*.

The feet (and the ankle) are also subject to FRACTURES, dislocations, sprains, bruises, and strains, often as a result of athletic injuries. See JOINTS.

GOUT sometimes produces an exquisitely sensitive big toe. Other forms of RHEUMATISM and ARTHRITIS may also plague the foot joints.

INFECTIONS of any sort may strike the feet; they are often secondary to FUNGUS infections (ringworm). Foot infections are particularly dangerous in diabetics. They may terminate in gangrene and the loss of toes or part of the feet. Careless and dirty cutting of corns, calluses, and toenails may invite infection.

Swelling is caused by FATIGUE, late PREGNANCY, and some forms of HEART DISEASE. If the feet remain swollen even after being rested, medical attention should be promptly sought.

Ingrown toenail is usually the result of tight shoes and improper pedicure. Toenails should be cut straight across. (See NAILS.)

How can foot troubles be relieved?

Corns (clavus) and *calluses* (callosity) are thickenings of the outer layers of the skin in response to persistent friction and pressure. They are irritating and painful because the overgrowth of horny, hardened skin presses on nerve endings. The corn is usually cone-shaped, with the point of the cone, called the "eye," directed inward. A callus is a thickening over a wider area.

Corns and calluses may be pared or cut away with a razor blade or a sharp knife. This process usually must be repeated at intervals. Corn pads and corn plasters are also useful. The corn pad is a ring of felt that surrounds the corn and protects it from pressure and irritation. The corn plaster contains a mixture of salicylic acid in solution; it softens the skin so that the horny layer will come off and can be picked away. The corn may also be rubbed down with pumice stone.

Soft corns occur between cramped toes, usually between the little toe and the fourth toe. They are usually accompanied by ringworm (fungus) infection. They, too, can be carefully cut away. To relieve pain and swelling, the leg may be elevated and hot, wet packs, with a mild antiseptic, applied. When a small spicule of bone causes the constant pressure that results in the corn, surgical removal of this bit of bone may be necessary for complete relief.

Bunions occur on the ball of the foot at the base of the big toe. The overlying skin is thickened, the underlying bursa is swollen, the metatarsal bone of the great toe is displaced, and the toe is forced into a painful position in the direction of the little toe. Treatment consists, first, of separating the big toe from the second toe by inserting cotton wool or a rubber pad between the toes or having a "toe-post" built into the shoe. Stubborn cases may require surgery on the joint for permanent relief.

In *hammertoe*, the affected toe (usually the second toe) has been cramped by tight shoes and bent over at its two joints so that it looks like a hammer or claw. Corns have usually formed at the bends. Padding between the toes sometimes brings relief, but severe, long-standing, painful cases demand surgery.

Painful *blisters* on the feet may be punctured with a sterilized needle at the base of the blister. The skin should be treated with a skin antiseptic (swabbed with alcohol, for example) before this home operation. An adhesive-tape bandage may be placed over the blister area to prevent further irritation or infection.

Warts (plantar warts) on the soles can be exceedingly painful and are often difficult to cure. They should not be cut off or meddled with at home. These warts, like others, are probably specific virus infections, in which irritated tissues are attacked. There are numerous medical and surgical treatments, but none guarantee against a return once warts have been removed. Among the treatments are surgical curettage, cauterizing solutions (formalin) and electrocautery, X-ray and radium treatment, application of podophyllin or salicylates, freezing solutions (carbon-dioxide snow and liquid nitrogen), and suggestion therapy.

Athlete's foot is a misnomer, created by advertising copywriters. Athletes are no more subject to it than anyone else; it is not picked up primarily in gymnasiums or swimming pools; it is not primarily a foot disease; it occurs on other parts of the body, especially under the armpits and in the groin. The scientific name is *dermatophytosis*, which means a *fungus* infection of the skin.

Such fungus infections of the skin of the feet are extremely common and mildly contagious, but are not serious unless secondary bacterial infections follow in the cracked surfaces.

Whether or not you get athlete's foot depends more on your personal resistance to fungi than your exposure to them. They are everywhere. They thrive in a moist, dark, warm environment. That is why athlete's foot occurs more commonly in warm weather (when the feet sweat) and between the fourth and little toe (which are usually cramped together). The first sign of athlete's foot is often blisters on the soles or toes. The soggy macerated superficial layers of skin in which the fungi have grown can usually be picked off easily, but the growing fungi have usually penetrated deeper.

Keeping the feet dry relieves many cases. Too vigorous treatment, or the application of too powerful fungicides (iodine, mercurial compounds, phenol-camphor) whose repeated application seriously damages the skin, makes things worse instead of better.

Salicylic and benzoic acid (Whitfield's ointment) are *not* recommended.

A number of organic acids (undecylenic, caprylic, propionic acid and their salts) are now available for home treatment. They are sold in drugstores under various brand names. It makes little difference whether you use an ointment, lotion, solution, or powder containing the organic acid or its salt. The treatment procedure is simple, though tedious:

Wash the feet with soap and water night and morning. Apply the ointment, powder, or solution. Change socks or stockings daily. Continue treatment at least 3 weeks.

Scaling of the skin is not necessarily caused by a fungus infection. It may result from contact dermatitis caused by some substances in the shoes, hosiery, or household; or it may even be due to simple physical abrasion from poorly fitting shoes or hosiery.

Flat feet and fallen arches: Each foot has two arches (see FOOT). One runs lengthwise, from the ball to the heel (longitudinal arch). The other runs crosswise, in the middle of the foot (metatarsal arch). When these arches sag, the condition is called *fallen arches.* If the sagging is not painful, does not interfere with walking or running, and is not progressing, no special treatment is needed. When the arches have sagged so that the entire sole touches the ground, we have the condition called *flat foot* (pes planus). Flat feet, however, are not necessarily weak or painful and may require no treatment.

You can tell whether or not you have flat feet by looking at your *footprint.* You can usually see the outline of your footprint if you step lightly on a flat surface with bare, wet feet. For the record put your feet in water colored with a few drops of ink or children's water-color paints and step firmly on a sheet of white paper.

If your arches are normal, your footprint will be wide at the heel and toes and narrow across the instep. If you have flat feet, the footprint will be just as wide at the instep as elsewhere.

The height of the instep does not guarantee the strength of the arches. In fact, arches that are too high may make for painful foot trouble.

Flat feet and fallen arches are usually the result of excessive and prolonged weight-bearing on the soles of the feet, that is, more walking and standing, without rest, than the particular arches can take. Hence these conditions may be occupational diseases in work that demands much walking and standing (for example, police work or selling). In some extreme, severe, prolonged, and repeated cases, only a change in occupation can give permanent relief.

Poor POSTURE in standing or walking can aggravate arch weakness. This can be corrected. Toe in when you walk. Relax when standing.

Tiptoe exercises, performed barefoot for at least 10 minutes a day, often help. These include rising on tiptoes, walking on tiptoes, picking up marbles with the feet, rolling the feet outward.

Arch supports must be used with caution—and on the recommendation of a physician only, not a shoe salesman. In older people rigid arch supports are sometimes justified. In younger people they may aggravate flat feet by weakening the foot muscles through disuse. A properly fitted sponge-rubber pad is sometimes an effective arch support. Carefully constructed special shoes, in which the inner side of the sole is ¼ to ½ inch higher than the outer edge, also help relieve flat feet by throwing the weight of the body to the outer edge of the feet. Such shoes need not be hideous.

Orthopedic surgery and splinting of the foot in a plaster cast may be a final resort.

The first, as well as the last, step in treating fallen arches and flat feet is to give them rest.

"Tired feet," also described as lame or painful feet or foot strain, may result from any of the foot troubles described, especially in their early and incipient stages. The first thing to do is to rest the feet, usually by elevating them on a chair or footstool. The next step is to massage them gently every night. Alcohol rubs are helpful. A third procedure is contrast baths, which stimulate the blood circulation in the feet. For 15 to 30 minutes, put your feet alternately—2 to 5 minutes at a time—in tubs or bowls of *hot and cold water* (about as hot or cold as you can comfortably stand).

The itching and burning often accompanying painful feet can be further relieved by talcum powder dusted on the feet and in the hose.

Be sure your shoes and hose fit properly, change your hose often, and keep your feet clean and dry. If all these simple home measures do not relieve your tired feet, see your doctor.

Painful heel may be the result of a severe bruise that has affected the heel bone (calcaneus) or its covering (periosteum); of pulled ligaments in the heel cord; of plantar warts on the skin of the heel; of walking heavily on the heels; and of other causes. The condition can be corrected by adequate medical diagnosis and treatment. Sometimes a change to rubber heels is enough; at other times surgery on the heel bone or heel cords is required.

Forceps—surgical instruments, which vary greatly in design, used to clamp bleeding arteries, cut bones, deliver babies, and do other things. They are essentially pliers, having two handles and two blades, with a pin-hinge or other joint in the middle of the two rigid parts. The *obstetric forceps,* secretly invented in the 16th century by Peter Chamberlen, a Huguenot refugee in England, is essentially a pair of large spoons joined together in the middle. The spoon end is inserted in the birth canal and cups over the infant's head. The attending obstetrician can then help draw the baby out. Obstetricians discourage the use of forceps unless absolutely needed to facilitate a difficult childbirth. The forceps can be applied low, medium, or high—meaning to reach far inside the birth canal to draw out the baby. Such use is sometimes associated with birth injuries to the infant, possibly resulting in CEREBRAL PALSY.

Formaldehyde—a strong disinfectant gas (chemical formula, HCHO) sometimes used to fumigate rooms and clothing. It is irritant to the eyes and nose. A solution of 40% gas in liquid, called *formalin,* is also a powerful germ and virus killer. It is, for example, used in killing polio viruses to make the Salk polio vaccine. In low concentrations, e.g. 1%, formaldehyde is a very useful germicide. In higher concentrations it is an excellent tissue preservative and is commonly used in *embalming* fluids.

Fornication—sexual intercourse outside of wedlock.

Four-day Disease—a peculiar lung disease of newborn infants, in which the lungs become clogged with a hyaline membrane. The disease always begins in the first 24 hours of life, its primary indication being breathing difficulties. If the infant survives for 4 days, it is a good sign that he will completely recover.

Foxglove—the plant from which the heart drug DIGITALIS is extracted.

FRACTURES

Fractures are broken BONES. Treatment by "bone-setters" was one of the oldest medical specialties. The treatment now available from a well-trained general practitioner or surgeon backed up by the facilities of a modern hospital usually makes possible good results in even the most severe fractures.

Types of fracture. There are many types. In a *simple fracture* the overlying skin remains intact. In a *compound* or *open fracture,* bone fragments stick through the skin, making a wound. In a *green-stick fracture,* most common in children with still flexible bones, the bone is split like the end of a green stick, one side being broken and the other bent. *Colles' fracture* is a break in the lower end of the large bone of the forearm (radius) near the wrist; the lower fragment is so displaced that the hand and wrist look like a reversed silver fork. *Bumper fracture* is the break of one or both legs immediately below the knee, as the result of being hit by an automobile bumper. In some diseases bones break without application of violence; these are called *spontaneous fractures* or *pathological fractures.*

Fractures of the skull, neck, or spine are usually the most dangerous. In skull fractures the brain is often injured; *bleeding from the ears,* mouth, nose, or into the eyes is often a sign of skull fracture. In neck or spine fractures the spinal cord or the nerves coming out of it are crushed and pinched between fragments of the vertebrae. If the victim cannot move his fingers, his neck may be broken; if he cannot move his legs, his back may be broken.

First-aid for fractures is not simple. The most important thing is not to meddle in any way that might make matters worse; for example, to keep a simple fracture from becoming compound and to avoid damaging the spinal cord. Severe *bleeding,* of course, must be controlled. The patient should be kept warm and quiet, lying down, until professional help arrives.

Do not transport a fracture victim unless absolutely necessary. Do not move a person with broken limb until splints are applied. "Splint 'em where they lie." Any long enough rigid object—broom handle, board, stick—can be used as an emergency splint. The splint should be padded and tied loosely so that it does not interfere with blood circulation. Do not attempt to set a broken bone.

The victim of a broken back must be transported *face downward.* The victim of a broken neck must be carried *face upward.* Never tilt his head forward or sideways.

Treatment of fractures is threefold: (1) The fracture is first reduced, that is, the broken bones aligned in proper position by manipulation, traction (pulling), or surgery. This usually requires X-RAY observation and ANESTHESIA. (2) Reduced fragments must be held in place until they unite, a process that may take a few to many weeks. This may require plaster casts, splints, traction frames, and insertion of metal nails, wires, screws, or plates in the bones. Complications must be prevented; for example, pressure sores and infections. (3) The function of the muscles and joints around the broken bone must be maintained and restored. This may require much *physical therapy*, including massage, graded exercise, application of heat.

Fractures generally heal more slowly in older persons. A particularly disabling and often slow-healing fracture common in older people is fracture of the neck or head of the femur (thigh bone). With continued proper treatment, however, these fractures do eventually heal. Discouragement is unwarranted.

Precaution. X-ray diagnosis is essential to proper fracture treatment. If you suspect that a bruise or blow has resulted in an underlying bone crack or "chip fracture," go to a doctor and take his advice about having the bruised part X-rayed.

Frambesia—YAWS; a tropical disease.

Freckles—the small yellow and brown pigmented spots on the skin. They are the result of changes in the pigmented layer of the true SKIN. Exposure to sun and wind apparently stimulates this layer of the skin to put forth spots of pigment. Certainly freckles appear more commonly in spring and summer than in winter. People with delicate skins, and often those with red hair, appear to be more subject to freckles.

How to remove freckles: DON'T TRY. So-called "freckle removers" contain dangerous substances that cause the whole skin to peel off and may bring about a condition far more serious than freckles. Consult a doctor or skin specialist (dermatologist) if your freckles are a severe psychological hazard to you. Don't leave the treatment, if any, and advice to your barber or beauty-shop operator.

To prevent freckles, avoid undue exposure to sun and wind. Ointments for face and hands that shield against the sun's ultraviolet rays may prevent freckles.

Skin-colored ointments, powder bases, and liquids can conceal freckles if they are psychologically annoying. Some people *enjoy* having freckles.

Freezing—see FROSTBITE. Freezing temperatures are sometimes used for their temporary ANESTHETIC effects, as in spraying the skin with carbon-dioxide snow. The use of ice bags to reduce swelling and relieve pain is well-known. Some experiments have been made in reducing the entire body temperature to deter the spreading of disease processes. Use of cold for healing is called *cryotherapy*.

Freud—Sigmund Freud (1856-1939), an Austrian physician and neurologist, called the "father of PSYCHOANALYSIS." His great contribution was his insistence on the importance of the *unconscious mind* as a controlling factor in human conduct, thought, and feeling. He portrayed the unconscious mind as including an id (driving force), ego (controlling force, or self), and superego (crudely, the conscience). He is often misquoted as saying that "sex is the basis of everything." A Freudian is a believer in Freud's theories and doctrines; a *strict* Freudian does not accept modifications of Freudian psychology as laid down by the "master." In particular, he insists on long-term, orthodox methods of psychoanalysis for treatment of NEUROSES. A *"Freudian slip"* is a slip of the tongue in which a person blurts out some fact that he would prefer to have kept quiet; such a slip often reveals what he is really thinking in spite of what he otherwise says.

Frigidity in the female implies a lack of normal interest in, or sometimes a definite aversion to, sex play and sexual intercourse. The reasons are usually psychological, based largely on childhood fears and impressions or frightening sex experiences in childhood and adolescence. It is used as an ego defense; a defense against the risk of pregnancy and motherhood. It is often a symptom of NEUROSIS.

With proper and adequate psychiatric treatment, as well as a loving and understanding male companion (husband), the condition is usually curable. But self-prescribed drugs—most commonly alcohol and aphrodisiacs —usually bring results worse than frigidity.

"Frog Breathing" is taught to patients with respiratory difficulty as a help in freeing them from dependence on mechanical breathing aids ("iron lung"). Air is forced down the throat with the tongue.

Frostbite results from exposure to severe cold. Its seriousness depends on the extent of the part (or parts) of the body frozen, the length of time they have been exposed to the cold, and the depth or intensity of cold. Blood circulation in the frozen part is always impaired. The danger is that it cannot be restored and that the frozen part will be damaged or even lost by dry or moist GANGRENE. Medical and hospital treatment, if needed, should be promptly obtained in severe frostbite or freezing.

The general rules for the immediate treatment of frostbite are:

1. Take the frozen person out of the extreme cold. Put him in a warm room.

2. If he is conscious, give him a warm, stimulating drink, such as hot coffee, but not an alcoholic liquor. (Alcohol may induce the frozen blood vessels to expand [dilate] too rapidly.)

3. Keep the affected parts at a cool temperature; about 60 to 70° Fahrenheit, which is slightly below comfortable room temperature.

4. Be careful of the skin. If it is massaged at all, it should be done very gently. Keep the skin dry.

5. Do not open blisters.

The key to successful treatment of frostbite and freezing is proper control of the reaction of the blood vessels as they thaw out. In thawing, they become widely dilated and the parts of the body that they feed become red, swollen, and exceedingly painful. A gradual rather than sudden rise in temperature is required, and full supportive treatment is needed. In 1955 a 2-year-old girl successfully recovered from an exposure to freezing that had driven her body temperature down to 59° Fahrenheit.

Fumigation—the process of destroying insects, such as mosquitoes, bedbugs, lice, and fleas, or animals, such as rats, by exposing them to gaseous fumes. It was once common practice to fumigate with ill-smelling fumes (often formaldehyde) the sickrooms of patients recovered from contagious and infectious diseases. This practice has been abandoned as a useless and almost superstitious means of preventing the spread of communicable disease. (It doesn't work; the disease has spread before the fumes get there.)

Functional—a word used to describe many disease conditions in which no visible or laboratory evidence can be found by the doctor to explain the complaints and conduct of the patient. Headache and backache are often *functional* ailments. The opposite of functional in this sense is *organic;* in organic disease something definitely wrong with a part or organ can be located.

While the term *functional illness* is still used, the concept behind it is falling into disrepute. The thought is that all illnesses are ORGANIC, but medical science has not yet been able to find the cause. See ORGANIC DISEASE.

Fungicide—anything that kills *fungi.* Iodine, for example, is a good fungicide (but its repeated application to skin tissues is harmful).

Fungus (plural, *fungi*). Fungi are older than man; they were on earth before he was. Essentially a fungus is a low form of plant life. Most commonly it is a microscopically small vegetable organism, although mushrooms and toadstools are also fungi. The mold that collects on bread and the slime on ponds are fungous growths, huge collections of tiny plants. The yeast that causes bread to rise and the mold (*Penicillium notatum*) from which penicillin is derived are both fungi.

There is a class of fungi, however, that are MICROBES and cause annoying and sometimes dangerous INFECTIONS. These *fungus infections* must be distinguished from infections by bacteria, viruses, parasites, and worms, which, roughly speaking, live, grow, and reproduce more like animals than vegetables. Among the infecting fungi are many different classes, with different names such as *Candida,* "*-myces*" (*Blastomyces*), and "*-phyton*" (*Trichophyton*).

Generally speaking, microscopic fungi, like their larger kin, the mushroom, grow best in moist, warm, dark places. Most fungus infections are on the *skin,* particularly between the folds of the skin. Athlete's foot is the classical example (see FOOT TROUBLE). The scalp, the groin, and the inside of the outer ear are other common sites.

Some fungi penetrate more deeply into the body, entering, for example, the mouth and lungs. The fungus known as *Monilia* often infests the mouth ("thrush") and the vagina. Actinomyces penetrate the jaw, causing draining nodules ("lumpy jaw"). Fungus infections of the lungs (histoplasmosis, coccidioidomycosis) are sometimes mistaken for TUBERCULOSIS.

Treatment of fungus infections of the skin consists primarily in drying up the sites of infection. This is not always easy, so long as the skin exudes perspiration. Fungus-killing drugs that do not harm the skin (mainly organic acids, such as propionic acid) may be applied. There are many other fungus-killers (fungicides), among which iodine is one of the best; however repeated application of these drugs to the skin is harmful. For deep-seated fungus infection, antibiotic and sulfa drugs by mouth or injection are often effective.

Furuncle—a small BOIL. See BOILS.

Furunculosis—a crop of BOILS.

Fusion in medicine usually refers to *spinal fusion.* This means the joining or union of two originally separate spinal vertebrae. Sometimes this results from disease. However, spinal fusion more commonly describes a surgical operation in which two vertebrae are deliberately joined together to immobilize a part of the spine (and, of course, make it more rigid and less bendable).

G

Any word printed in SMALL CAPITALS *can be looked up under its own alphabetical listing for further information.*

Gait—the manner of walking; it is POSTURE in action. Gait often indicates disease, such as the jerky gait of spastic paralysis, the stamping gait of locomotor ataxia, the reeling gait of acute alcoholism.

Galactorrhea—excessive flow of milk from the breasts.

Galenical—a class of drugs containing organic ingredients (i.e. not purely synthetic chemicals) that are standard products and listed in official pharmacopoeias. Originally a galenical was a drug or medicine formulated according to prescription of the ancient Greek-Roman physician Galen (130-210 A.D.).

Gall Bladder—a pear-shaped pouch on the undersurface of the *liver.* Its function is to store and concentrate *bile,* which comes from the liver through a cystic duct and is delivered to the intestines through the *common bile duct.* Since the liver also dicharges bile through this duct directly into the duodenum, a diseased gall bladder can be safely removed by surgery without impairing bile flow. The gall bladder is subject to acute and chronic inflammations, usually in conjunction with gallstones. (See illustrations for ABDOMEN; DIGESTIVE SYSTEM.)

GALLSTONES

Gallstones—biliary calculi—are concretions of elements that make up the bile (for example, cholesterol) that have backed up and accumulated in the gall bladder. Exactly why gallstones form is not known, but they are often associated with conditions, such as infections or digestive changes, that cause the bile to stagnate in, rather than flow freely from, the gall bladder. Gallstones vary in size from small particles ("gall sand"), of which hundreds may be present, to single stones as large as a goose egg. Gallstones are often present without causing any trouble at all; but sometimes they provoke severe and painful symptoms (gall-bladder colic).

Who has gallstones? An estimated 5 to 10% of the adult population has gallstones—principally, however, of the "silent," untroublesome kind. Women are afflicted about 5 times as frequently as men. Gall-bladder attacks usually come on in middle age. The typical victim is often "fair, fat, and 40; fertile and flatulent."

What are the symptoms of gall-bladder trouble? These differ considerably in degree, depending on whether it is acute or chronic. Pain and tenderness over the region of the gall bladder become increasingly severe in some chronic cases. There is pain under the ribs and a sense of fullness in the stomach. The pains are more liable to come on after eating fatty food.

When a large gallstone lodges in the small end of the gall bladder, the cystic duct, or the common bile duct, it may bring on an agonizing, sudden attack of acute *gall-bladder colic.* The pain may shoot up to the shoulder blade, and it may be accompanied by nausea, vomiting, and slight fever. The attack usually subsides in a few hours, as the obstructing stone passes into the intestines or falls back into the gall bladder. Such attacks may recur at short intervals, in which case the symptom of jaundice appears, or may not recur for months or years.

A gallstone may not pass but become impacted in a bile duct. This is a serious condition, often demanding surgery. The acuteness of the pain gradually subsides, but jaundice increases. Opiates may be needed to relieve pain.

In general, the symptoms of chronic gall-bladder trouble are very much like those of chronic indigestion.

How is gall-bladder trouble diagnosed? This is not always easy, for the symptoms may be vague. However, it is possible to visualize the gall bladder in X-ray pictures by first administering by mouth or injection an iodine-containing dye that dissolves in bile. Such X-ray pictures reveal the presence of gallstones, and a series of them tells how long it takes for the gall bladder to fill and empty its contents.

How is gall-bladder trouble treated? The medical treatment includes rest in bed, a low-fat diet, and administration of drugs that increase bile flow (cholagogues). If attacks are severe and frequent, surgical removal of the gall bladder (cholecystectomy) may be needed.

Gamma Globulin—see GLOBULIN.

Ganglion has two distinct meanings: (1) a collection or aggregate of NERVE cells and (2) an enlargement of the sheath of a tendon, usually a fluid-filled sac or cyst and most often located on the back of the wrist. It usually starts small, about the size of a pea, and may remain this size for years without giving any trouble. Then, as more synovial (lubricating) fluid tends to collect in it, the lump grows larger and the wrist may begin to feel weak. The ganglion may often be burst by striking it sharply (as with a heavy book). The wrist should then be bandaged with an elastic or pressure bandage to prevent reaccumulation of fluid. A large ganglion may resist rupture by blows and have to be punctured or removed by surgical dissection.

Gangrene—death of body tissue over an area large enough to be visible. When the circulation of blood to a part of the body is so damaged that the tissues can no longer get nourishment or dispose of their waste products, the result is gangrene. Among the principal causes are conditions that block blood flow for any length of time, such as crushing injuries, freezing cold (FROSTBITE), BURNS, caustic chemicals (e.g. phenol), mechanical pressure (e.g. a tight tourniquet kept on too long), ERGOT poisoning, Raynaud's disease, KIDNEY TROUBLE, and DIABETES, which may have serious effects on the blood vessels.

Dry gangrene occurs most commonly in older people and diabetics and principally affects feet and toes. There is quite a sharp line of demarcation, marked by a red ring, between living and dead tissue. In *moist gangrene* the affected part is swollen, blistered, green or black in some areas, usually offensively odorous, and the line of demarcation is not so sharp. INFECTION, which can enter the blood stream and become generalized, is usually present.

Treatment for dry gangrene is to keep the part as dry and comfortable as possible. In moist gangrene the first step is to cleanse the gangrenous surface; then thick antiseptic dressings (sometimes a plaster cast) are applied to dry it up. But when the gangrene is apparently spreading, the only successful treatment is *amputation* well above the inflamed or involved part.

So-called *hospital gangrene*, associated with pus, infection, and failure of wounds to heal, is never seen in a modern hospital where aseptic surgery is practiced.

Gas gangrene is the result of the infection of dirty, lacerated wounds by any one of several air-hating (anaerobic) gasforming microbes, notably *Clostridium welchii*. The gas spreads through the muscles so that they give off a crackling sound when touched. The tissues become an angry red color at first, then turn yellow, finally black. Gas gangrene was an exceedingly serious problem of military surgery in World War I (when the condition was called "red death") and in the Spanish Civil War of 1936. In World War II the problem of gas gangrene was generally solved by early surgical cleansing of wounds (debridement), penicillin, sulfonamide drugs, specific antitoxins against gas bacilli, and whole-blood transfusions.

Gargle—any liquid brought into contact with the throat without being swallowed. For many people gargling is a much-abused pastime. It is unnecessary and may be harmful if strong, medicated solutions are indiscriminately and regularly used without medical supervision. Gargling will not keep the mouth, nose, and throat "free from germs"; nor is this necessary.

In treating sore throat or loss of voice, gargling with hot solutions—as hot as you can stand—is sometimes comforting. The heat brings blood to the throat and helps to relieve a feeling of congestion. Common salt in hot water is usually as good a gargle as any. Gargling with hot water is annoying, and most people do not continue it long enough to do themselves any real good. At least 2 to 5 minutes is needed.

If infection is present, it should of course be treated specifically. When the voice is lost, rest for the vocal apparatus (no speaking) is also advisable.

Some people, especially children, just cannot master the art of gargling. It is a small matter. Heat can be applied to the throat with hot compresses around the neck.

Gas on the stomach or in the bowels is called FLATULENCE.

Gas Gangrene—see GANGRENE

Gas Poisoning—see ASPHYXIA

and CARBON MONOXIDE poisoning.

Gastralgia—bellyache; see STOMACH TROUBLE.

Gastrectomy—surgical removal of the stomach. Subtotal gastrectomy, which is the more common operation, leaves part of the STOMACH in place.

Gastric—relating to the *stomach*, as *gastric juice* or *gastric ulcer*. See STOMACH TROUBLE.

Gastritis—inflammation of the stomach. See STOMACH TROUBLE.

Gastrocnemius—the large muscle that appears as the calf of the leg. Its lower end is attached to the heel cord (Achilles tendon). This is the muscle that bulges out in professional dancers. (See illustration for MUSCLES.)

Gastroenteritis—inflammation of the stomach and intestines (bowels). See STOMACH TROUBLE and COLITIS.

Gastroenterologist—a medical specialist in diseases of the stomach and intestines.

Gastroenterostomy—a surgical operation in which the stomach is made to open directly into the small intestine. The usual purpose is to detour the flow of food around a peptic ulcer. (See STOMACH TROUBLE.)

Gastrointestinal—refers to the stomach and intestines; the major part of the DIGESTIVE SYSTEM.

Gastroscope—an instrument for examining the inside of the stomach. A flexible tube with an ingenious arrangement of mirrors and a light and sometimes a miniature camera at the end, it is inserted through the mouth, down the food tube, and into the stomach.

Gavage—forced feeding; putting liquid nourishment directly into the stomach by stomach tube.

"Gehrig's Disease," named after the popular baseball hero, Lou Gehrig, who died of it, is a wasting disease of the muscles technically known as *amyotrophic lateral sclerosis*. It is related to *multiple sclerosis* (MS) and *muscular dystrophy* but it is not the same thing. The underlying causes of all three of these wasting diseases remain unknown, although they are the subjects of intense research interest.

The chief symptoms of "Gehrig's disease" are progressive twitching, weakness and wasting away of the muscles, often preceded by vague feelings of numbness, cramps and exhaustion. The hands are usually noticed twitching first. The disease generally comes on insidiously in middle age, or earlier, and is often associated with degeneration of the substance of the spinal cord (see NERVES). It is rarely painful.

Treatment is directed to keeping the patient comfortable, maintaining or improving his muscle tone, and helping him to accept his unfortunate weakness in the most realistic and cheerful spirit.

General Practitioner—GP, a physician who engages in the general practice of medicine; not a specialist. See FAMILY DOCTOR.

Genes—the ultimate biological units of HEREDITY; the part of or place (locus) on the CHROMOSOME that determines physical inheritance and constitution.

Genetics—the study of HEREDITY as determined by genes.

Genitalia—SEX ORGANS, MALE or FEMALE.

Genitourinary—refers to the combined body system that includes the SEX ORGANS, MALE or FEMALE, and the BLADDER, KIDNEYS and their accessory organs. (See illustration for URINARY SYSTEM.)

GERIATRICS

Geriatrics is that relatively new branch of medicine that specializes in diseases, disorders, and disabilities of *older people*. This is far more than a medical problem; it is, as Osler once said of tuberculosis, a "social problem with medical aspects." Good health in old age can be attained (1) by looking forward in youth to this goal and (2) by accepting every age of life, old age as well as infancy, as equally valid. One age is not more important than another.

Simple rules for aging comfortably: Enjoy yourself. Do not give up the pleasures of life that you can still enjoy nor seek youthful pleasures that you cannot tolerate. In other words, accept, admit, and be your age. But age is not measured only in years. It is measured in spirit. "If youth but knew, if age but could."

Beware of INFECTIONS. The aging body does not throw off infections as readily as it did years before. Simple cleanliness, using soap and water, is of great and sometimes forgotten importance. A boy at camp may not wash his feet for a couple of weeks. But an older person may suffer a prolonged and troublesome foot infection from such neglect. Colds, and their dangerous sequel, pneumonia, can often be avoided by the simple precaution of wearing warm enough and dry clothing in cold and damp weather.

Watch your DIET. People who have the right to pick their own food sometimes have peculiar ideas about what they should eat. Older people tend to neglect protein foods—meat, fish, eggs—because they are more difficult to prepare and chew and more expensive than fats and carbohydrates. Older women tend to overdo fresh fruits and vegetables. Older men often eat too many starches and completely ignore vitamins.

Drink enough WATER. In some disease conditions, such as certain diseases of the HEART, BLOOD VESSELS, and KIDNEYS, water intake must be limited. But many older people fail to drink enough water. Normal thirst is the best guide. Too little water may cause highly concentrated urine, passed with burning and itching sensations, and hard-stool CONSTIPATION. Sufficient water will usually produce a soft stool and eliminate constipation.

Respect your aches and pains—but don't overindulge them. Everyone over 40 has touches of RHEUMATISM (ARTHRITIS), although some people feel them more than others. Don't become so accustomed to your old aches and pains that you neglect new ones. Every new pain, if it is persistent or repeated, should be challenged by competent medical check-up. Often it is a danger signal of a disease that can be corrected and arrested if caught early.

Avoid FATIGUE. Respect your "fatigue point" and stop working, playing, or exercising when you reach it. Age reduces your powers of recuperation. Muscles, including the smooth muscles of the blood vessels and the diagonally striped muscles of the heart, gradually lose their elasticity with age. But this is no reason for giving up all activity.

SLEEP as long as you need to arise refreshed in the morning. This may require fewer *or more* hours of sleep than you took in earlier years.

Trust your doctor. See him regularly for check-ups and immediately when new pains or other symptoms bother you. He can quickly prescribe drugs or other treatment that will nip in the bud possibly serious and disabling ailments. Surgery in the aged is now quite safe. New and potent medicines—for example, ANTIBIOTICS, HORMONES, and TRANQUILIZERS—not available to earlier older generations, are on hand now. Trust your doctor to do the prescribing. For he who has himself for a physician has a fool for a patient.

Germ Plasm—that unique hereditary substance present in the single germ or sex cell (egg or sperm cell) through which new individuals are conceived and by means of which hereditary characteristics are transmitted from one generation to the next. (See HEREDITY.)

German Measles, technically known as *rubella* and not true MEASLES, is one of the mildest of acute infectious diseases. It is caused by a virus and spread by contact with infected individuals. Its symptoms are mild headache, running nose, slight fever, and diagnostically important, temporary enlargement (swelling) of the glands in the neck. This is followed in a day or two by a mild pink rash, beginning on the face and spreading over the rest of the body. The only treatment is bed rest and isolation until the symptoms disappear.

The incubation period averages about 17 or 18 days (range 9 to 21 days) after contact with the infecting agent. The disease is most infectious for the few days just before the rash appears.

The most important thing about German measles is this: If a *pregnant* woman catches German measles during the first few (about 4) months of her pregnancy, it may mar her unborn fetus, causing the baby to be born with congenital MALFORMATIONS, notably eye and ear defects. Hence pregnant women should keep away from any children or households harboring German measles.

Germicide—anything that kills germs in, on, or outside the body. ANTISEPTICS kill germs when applied to the skin or taken internally. ANTIBIOTICS, SULFA DRUGS, and many other medicines have the unique action of arresting or killing germs in the body without harming the patient. Chemical germicides for use outside the body are called DISINFECTANTS and should never be taken internally. Heat, sunlight, ultraviolet light, and other electromagnetic radiations in sufficient quantity are also *germicidal*. See also BACTERICIDE and FUNGICIDE.

Germs—MICROBES, or microörganisms, that cause disease. The germ theory of disease was established in the late 19th century, largely by the work of Pasteur and Koch. Anything that kills germs is called a GERMICIDE. The RESISTANCE of the host to disease-producing germs is what usually determines whether an individual actually comes down with the disease caused by a specific germ. See MICROBES, INFECTION.

Gerontology—the study of the processes of aging, with particular attention to the later ages and stages of life. It is the science on which the practice of geriatrics must be based.

Gingivitis—inflammation of the GUMS.

Glands. A gland is any body organ that manufactures some liquid product that it secretes from its cells. Most glands go on to excrete their product through one or more well-defined ducts or channels. A few glands, notably the ductless, or *endocrine*, glands, do not excrete their product but leave it to be picked up and distributed to other parts of the body by the blood stream.

There are a few large glands in the human body (the liver is the largest). Most of them, numbering in the millions, are microscopically small, like the sweat glands.

Swollen glands beneath the jaw and down each side of the neck, in the armpits and in the groin, are *lymphatic glands*, key points in the circulation of lymph fluid throughout the body. These glands or nodes filter the lymph circulation and tend to keep microbes and other impurities from entering the blood system. They also form lymph corpuscles, which are akin to white *blood* cells, and serve as garrisons of these infection-fighting agents. The enlargement of lymph glands is usually a sign of some sort of INFECTION in the body, although not all infections produce visible swelling of the lymph glands.

The *endocrine*, or ductless, glands which secrete hormones are: pituitary, thyroid, parathyroids, thymus, pancreas (one part only, other parts secrete through ducts), adrenals and gonads (testes, which also has ducts, and ovaries). See ENDOCRINE GLANDS.

Other glands of the body include:

On the SKIN, *sweat glands* and *sebaceous glands,* which secrete an oily substance.

In the mouth, *salivary glands,* which secrete saliva. These are called *parotid,* submaxillary, and sublingual glands. MUMPS is a swelling of the parotids.

On all MUCOUS MEMBRANES, glands that secrete mucus.

In the STOMACH, glands that secrete gastric juice.

In the intestines, *lacteal glands* that absorb fat particles (see DIGESTION).

Above the EYES, tear (lacrimal) glands.

The BREASTS, which are mammary glands, secreting milk.

In the SEX ORGANS, MALE, Cowper's glands and the PROSTATE GLAND.

In the SEX ORGANS, FEMALE, Bartholin's and Skene's glands.

Glandular Fever—a fairly common ailment of young people technically called *infectious mononucleosis*. The diagnostically important finding in this disease is an exceptionally high number of abnormal white blood cells in the blood stream. This is generally an acute infection, coming on quite suddenly, with high or moderate fever. The *lymph glands*, especially in the neck, are usually inflamed and swollen. (See GLANDS.) Painful sore throat involving lymph tissue in the throat (adenoids, tonsil remnants) may also be a symptom.

The cause of infectious mononucleosis is not known, but it is presumed to be a virus. The incubation period varies from 4 to 14 days. The illness usually hangs on for a few weeks and then disappears without any specific treatment and without any aftereffects. Because epidemics are common in schools, colleges, and hospitals (among student nurses), glandular fever is sometimes called "student's disease."

Glasses—eyeglasses or spectacles. See EYE TROUBLE.

Glaucoma—a serious EYE TROUBLE in which fluid pressure within the eyeball is markedly increased.

Gleet—chronic, discharging GONORRHEA; rare today

Globulin—a special kind of PROTEIN, closely related to ALBUMIN. Globulins of various kinds are found in BLOOD serum and blood plasma. The different kinds of globulin can be separated from each other because of their electrical properties. The process of separating them is called electrophoresis. The different kinds of globulin have been given Greek letter names: alpha, beta, and gamma globulin.

Gamma globulin, the best known, contains the disease-fighting *antibodies* that were built up in the blood stream of the persons from whom the blood was taken. Hence gamma-globulin injections can produce passive immunity and give temporary protection against certain diseases. The *same* gamma globulin (blood fraction) is used for all diseases. Among those for which it is most useful are MEASLES and HEPATITIS. It provides about 8 weeks temporary protection against paralytic polio, but a better means of protection is now available, the *Salk vaccine*.

Glomerulonephritis — inflammation of the kidney *glomeruli*, the tufts or clusters of blood vessels in the kidney that filter blood. See KIDNEY TROUBLE.

Glossitis—inflammation of the TONGUE.

Glucose—SUGAR in the form in which it usually appears in the blood stream (blood sugar) and in certain fruits (fruit sugar); *d*-glucose is the same as dextrose. For tube feeding of patients who cannot take enough, if any, nourishment by mouth, a 5% solution of glucose in water or normal salt solution is dripped slowly into the veins.

Glutamic Acid—an amino acid whose use has been unsuccessfully advocated for EPILEPSY and FEEBLE-MINDEDNESS.

Gluteal—related to the buttocks, which are made up of the large gluteus maximus muscles. The upper, outer gluteal quadrant is the favorite site for intramuscular injections, especially if a large quantity of fluid is to be injected.

Glycerin(e)—the clear, colorless, syrupy, slightly sweet, oily liquid that is used as a solvent for many drugs, as a sweetening agent, demulcent and skin-softener. Glycerin suppositories often induce gentle evacuations from the lower bowel (rectum).

Glycogen—animal starch, stored principally in the liver. When this carbohydrate substance is released to give muscular energy, it is re-formed into GLUCOSE (blood sugar), from which it was derived.

Glycosuria—SUGAR in the URINE. See DIABETES.

Glycyrrhiza—licorice root; usually a flavoring to disguise the taste of bitter drugs.

Goiter—enlargement of the thyroid (ENDOCRINE) gland in the neck. See HYPERTROPHY.

Gonads—a general term meaning the testicles in the male and the ovaries in the female; that is, the "seed glands" in each sex. (See SEX ORGANS, MALE and FEMALE; also ENDOCRINES.)

Gonococcus—the MICROBE that causes gonorrhea (*Neisseria gonorrhoeae*).

GONORRHEA

Gonorrhea is the most common and most curable VENEREAL DISEASE. It is caused by a specific MICROBE, the gonococcus, spread from person to person, almost always by illicit sexual intercourse. Gonorrhea is most common at those ages and in those social groups in which premarital and extramarital sexual activities are most frequent.

The only source of gonorrheal infection is discharges from lesions of the mucous membranes or lymph nodes of persons currently afflicted. Hence the disease is almost always transmitted by sexual contact or direct personal contact with the discharges. In rare instances articles freshly soiled with discharges—washcloths, towels, and other bathroom accessories—may transmit the disease. Little girls, under 6, are especially susceptible to vaginal infection with such discharges, and epidemics of vulvovaginitis sometimes occur in girls' schools. These are the principal instances in which gonorrhea is innocently acquired.

The mucous membranes of the eye are particularly susceptible to gonorrheal infection. Newborn babies were once frequently infected during the process of birth. "Babies' sore eyes"—gonorrheal ophthalmia—was once a common cause of BLINDNESS. (See EYE TROUBLE.) This condition has been practically eliminated by laws requiring silver nitrate or other equally effective gonococcus-killing drugs to be instilled in infants' eyes immediately after birth.

Symptoms: The symptoms of gonorrhea appear from 1 day to 2 or 3 weeks (usually 3 to 5 days) after exposure. In the male the symptoms of the early and acute disease include pain—stinging or burning—when urinating, some slight swelling and discomfort in the urinary region, and the discharge of a few drops of pus from the open end of the penis (urinary meatus). These symptoms grow worse as the infection of the mucous membranes of the urinary system and adjacent organs progresses. In women the early symptoms are likely to be less acute; in addition to pain on urination (which is less acute because the female urinary tract is shorter than the male), the early symptoms may include a yellowish vaginal discharge and a painful swelling or abscess of the glands (Bartholin's glands) at the mouth of the vulva. (See SEX ORGANS, MALE and FEMALE.)

Complications: Untreated gonorrhea, which lapses into chronic gonorrhea (gleet) and remains infectious so long as gonococci are being discharged from lesions (which can be a long time after the initial infection), produces a host of complications. These include blockage of the Fallopian tubes and sperm ducts, thus causing sterility; gonorrheal rheumatism or arthritis, a very intractable form of joint ailment and stiffness; inflammation of the heart valves (endocarditis); cystitis; prostate trouble; and blindness. Gonorrhea was long called the "crippler" among diseases.

Treatment: Present-day treatment is swift and sure. Cure rates approaching almost 100% have been reported. Any doctor can give the treatment. Most cases can be cleared up in a day or two by a single injection of delayed-action penicillin or administration by mouth of some other antibiotic drugs. Sulfa drugs also are effective killers of the gonococcus, but the antibiotics are better.

Prevention: See VENEREAL DISEASE. It should be noted that both gonorrhea and syphilis, an entirely different disease, are often caught from the same person at the same time. Antibiotic treatment must continue until the syphilis as well as the gonorrhea is eradicated.

Gout—a metabolic disease in which the body fails to get rid of uric acid, one of the end products of protein food breakdown. The typical picture of gout is that of a man with an exquisitely tender big toe. However, gout is a form of ARTHRITIS which may affect other joints, making them suddenly painful, red, and tender. The excess uric acid may crystallize in deposits in various parts of the body. These chalky deposits, called *tophi*, can be found in the ear lobes, elbows, skin about the finger nails, and in the cartilages inside joints. After a sudden attack of gout the patient may be free of pain and symptoms for months or years. Gout can be prevented and treated. Certain drugs, such as colchicine, have a strong tendency to rid the body of uric acid.

Gout is a man's disease; about 97 men are afflicted to every 3 women. The victims are usually past 45, overweight, and with habits of overeating and not exercising. Preventing attacks requires cutting down on food and weight and avoiding protein foods that foster the formation of uric acid; for ex-

ample, kidney, liver, and sweetbreads. There is a condition called "poor man's gout," ascribed to hard work, poor food, exposure to the elements, and overindulgence in beer and ale.

GP—GENERAL PRACTITIONER.

Graft—the transplantation of skin or other body tissues from one place in the body to another, or from one person to another. PLASTIC SURGERY employs many kinds of skin and tissue grafts. Grafts do not always "take," but often give support until new tissue can be formed. Bone grafts are sometimes done to make orthopedic repairs. One of the rarest cases of grafting on record is the transplantation, in 1954, of a whole kidney from one identical twin to the other.

Gram—a unit of weight in the metric system. The abbreviation is g, G, gm, or Gm. About 30 grams equal 1 ounce. Grams should never be confused with *grains* in measuring or taking medicine. A gram equals about 15.4 grains. The abbreviation for grain is gr or Gr.

Gramicidin—one of the first ANTIBIOTICS, preceding penicillin, but now rarely used.

Gram-Positive—a class of bacteria (MICROBES) that can be stained, fixed, and colored with dyes according to a valuable method first described, in 1884, by a Danish physician and bacteriologist named Hans Christian Joachim *Gram*. *Gram-negative* bacteria are those that don't take Gram's stain.

Grand Mal—a bad fit; a severe attack of EPILEPSY. A minor or less severe convulsion is called *petit mal.*

Granulocytopenia — AGRANULO-CYTOSIS; white BLOOD CELL disease.

Granuloma Inguinale—a VENEREAL DISEASE, most common in the tropics and among dark-skinned races. Deep skin ulcers often appear on the external SEX ORGANS. The cause is a specific microbe (Donovan body).

Gravel—KIDNEY STONES or GALL-STONES of extremely small size, which may be passed in the urine or accumulated in the gall bladder (gall sand).

Graves' Disease—GOITER with popeye.

Gravid—pregnant.

Green Sickness—*chlorosis;* a peculiar nutritional ANEMIA, found mostly in young teen-age girls. Their skin has a greenish tinge, they lack appetite, they are weak and nervous.

Grippe—INFLUENZA.

Groin—the area of the body where the legs meet the trunk.

Growing Pains in children who complain repeatedly of pains in their legs and back are usually attacks of rheumatism associated with RHEUMATIC FEVER. They are serious and will not be "outgrown." The complaining child should have a complete medical examination.

Gumboil—abscess at the root of a decayed tooth. (See TEETH.)

Gumma—a small, rubbery tumor or new growth that is one of the end results of untreated late SYPHILIS. Gumma appear on the skin and in the heart, brain, and liver.

Gums—see TEETH. Bleeding gums are often a sign of systemic disease, notably *scurvy,* and other conditions in which VITAMIN C is lacking and the capillaries break easily (capillary fragility). Lead and other metallic poisons often leave early, tell-tale signs on the gum-line just below the teeth. The care of the gums is as essential as that of the teeth. The gums should not, however, be regularly scratched and abraded with a toothbrush.

Gynecologist—specialist in diseases of women (see FEMALE TROUBLES). This specialty is often combined with OBSTETRICS.

Gynecomastia—enlargement of breasts in the male. It frequently occurs on just one side. It is often associated with disturbances in the ENDOCRINE glands, especially tumors of the adrenal glands or testicles.

H

Any word printed in SMALL CAPITALS *can be looked up under its own alphabetical listing for further information.*

HAIR

Visible hair is dead tissue which can be cut without any pain. The distribution and growth of hair on the head and other parts of the body is definitely linked to the ENDOCRINE glands. It is a secondary sex characteristic, and its relationship to sexual attractiveness has long been recognized. PSYCHOANALYSIS has uncovered a great deal of symbolism relating to the hair. The Biblical story of Samson and Delilah emphasizes the ancient superstition that cutting the hair means loss of manhood. Of course this is not true.

People begin to worry about their hair when they have too little (BALDNESS) or too much (superfluous hair, hypertrichosis) in the wrong places.

Hair grows out from hair follicles, also called hair roots, located at the bottom of the layer of true SKIN and sometimes penetrating into the layer of fat underneath the skin. Along the tubes from which the growing hair shaft emerges are situated one or more tiny oil glands (sebaceous glands), which excrete an oily substance (sebum). These excretions give the hair its luster and sheen. When mild or severe disorders in the body affect these glands and dry them up, the hair becomes dry and brittle. When these glands are overstimulated the hair and skin may be too oily. (See illustration for SKIN.)

The natural color of the hair results from the transfer of body pigments, which determine skin color, to the hair. This takes place in the hair roots.

The hair is not hollow, but it is harder on the outside than in the center of the hair shaft. Hairs differ in shape. *Straight* hair is *round* in cross-section; *curly* hair *oval*-shaped, elliptical.

The shape and color of individual hairs as well as the general pattern of hair distribution is determined chiefly by HEREDITY. The hair (dead tissue) that appears above the surface of the skin can be treated and manipulated in a variety of ways, but this does not change the color and shape of the new hairs that keep growing. They, too, have to be treated.

Human hair normally grows about an inch in 6 weeks. A

woman's hair may, if uncut, reach a length of about 2 feet in 3 to 4 years. Cutting the hair has no effect on the rate at which it grows.

Practically the only way to slightly speed up hair growth, if the hair roots are intact, is to stimulate the SCALP by massage or applying heat (for example, exposure to sunshine). However, this may dry up the hair oils and leave it looking coarse and lusterless. Scalp massage is of no permanent help in hereditary baldness (*alopecia*).

Babies are born with a fine, downy hair, called *lanugo*, which disappears shortly after birth. Normal hair on the scalp and other parts of the body (for example, the *beard*) becomes thicker and coarser (increases in diameter) with increasing age. In middle age men often discover hairs growing in their ears, and women, especially about the time of the menopause, may find excess hair on their faces. This is the result of the normal change in the endocrine pattern.

Disorders of the endocrine system, especially the adrenal gland, may produce unexpected and unwanted hair growth—as found, for example, in the bearded lady of the circus or the "dog-faced boy." Medical, rather than cosmetic, treatment is essential.

In some diseases of the *thyroid gland,* the hair becomes thin and coarse and the scalp excessively dry.

Gray hair. There is no treatment except to dye it or admire it.

Most *hair-dyes* are safe enough for normal use. However, there is no telling when a specific individual will have an allergy or idiosyncrasy to the chemicals in the particular dye. *Vegetable hair dyes* are now appearing on the market, and significant skin reactions to these dyes is unlikely. However, many people are sensitive to the chemical substances, such as paraphenylendiamine, that are commonly found in other hair dyes. Skin reaction to the hair dye should always be tested before the dye is used. (See COSMETICS.) *Hydrogen peroxide* for bleach-blonding the hair is comparatively safe.

Superfluous (unwanted) hair can be removed in a variety of ways. The only safe and permanent way is by *electrolysis,* in which the hair root is destroyed with a small electric current passed through a fine needle inserted in the hair root. This takes an expert operator, but even with the best operator some hairs are bound to return. The procedure is long and tedious. An upper lip may have as many as 1,500 separate hairs, and not more than 15 to 20 can be removed at a single sitting.

Other ways of removing superfluous hair, temporarily, are by shaving it (more women shave than admit it), rubbing with pumice stone, or yanking it out with wax. Face hairs, of course, may be bleached with peroxide to make them less visible.

Ingrown hairs are the result of shaving hair shafts too short. An ingrown hair acts like a splinter; it may cause an INFECTION.

Bald spots (alopecia areata) on the scalp or beard come suddenly upon about 2 or 3 people in every 100, for reasons still obscure but often associated with emotional shock or tension. In 99 out of 100 cases, the hair returns. Treatment that stimulates the hair follicles, such as guarded applications of ultraviolet light, may speed up regrowth. Bald spots can appear at any age, but they are commonest in the twenties and thirties. The younger the patient, the better the chance for recovery. The new growth of hair usually comes in at first as gray or white and of fine texture. However, as regrowth continues, the color and texture return to normal.

The receding hairline of hereditary BALDNESS, an entirely different condition, does not respond to treatment.

Halitosis—bad breath. The cause is usually infected teeth or gums, infections of the nose and throat (for example, chronic TONSILLITIS), certain lung diseases (especially BRONCHIECTASIS), indigestion, and eating odorous foods and spices, notably garlic. Bad breath will not really disappear until the underlying causes are corrected. Meanwhile the effects can be temporarily abated by rinsing the mouth or gargling with a mouth wash (salt water is as effective as any preparation) and by chewing breath sweeteners.

Hallucination—hearing, seeing, or feeling things that are not really there; a mental mirage. Hallucinations commonly occur in some forms of MENTAL ILLNESS and in DELIRIUM TREMENS.

Hamamelis—WITCH HAZEL.

Hammertoe—cramped, bent-over toe. See FOOT TROUBLE.

HANGOVER

Hangover from excessive indulgence in alcoholic beverages is a combination of factors related both to the physiological effects of alcohol (see ALCOHOLISM) and the circumstances under which it is consumed. We shall distinguish the typical morning-after hangover from alcoholic coma or drunken stupor immediately following consumption of great quantities of alcohol. Coma may require heroic stimulatory treatment if it is not slept off, and even better treatment if it is followed by DELIRIUM TREMENS.

Morning-after hangover is usually a combination of headache, dehydration, fatigue, and slight gastric upset and irritation. Almost all these symptoms would disappear if the person who wakes up with a hangover would drink several glasses of water, take an aspirin tablet or two, and go back to bed to sleep or doze until his unpleasant symptoms disappear. The problem is complicated because the victim wants to get up and go to work or must fulfill other immediate responsibilities.

How to handle a hangover: The headache of a hangover is of the vascular type, related to hypertension headache. Alcohol dilates the blood vessels in the brain as well as in other parts of the body. As the alcohol is gradually burned up, these stretched vessels return to their normal bore. But in doing so they tend to put the nerves that serve them a little on stretch, and this creates the sensation of pain in the head. There is some justification for the immediate relief of this type of headache by taking another drink ("hair of the dog that bit me") because it again begins to dilate the blood vessels. However, the treatment may set up another vicious cycle of indulgence and hangover. See HEADACHE for a list of other ways to get rid of a headache.

Dehydration is the second factor to be corrected in a morning-after hangover. This is the cause of the "dark brown taste" in the mouth. Alcohol is an excellent diuretic; it stimulates the kidneys. Hence the person who has been drinking heavily usually loses more liquids than he imbibes, thus changing his internal water balance and becoming dehydrated. The remedy is simply to drink water freely—as many as 8 or 10 glasses in the course of 2 to 4 hours. Fruit juice and tomato juice have no special virtue, except that they taste better.

FATIGUE, muscular fatigue, and loss of sleep are usually the third factor in producing a hangover, since alcoholic indulgence is usually begun when a person is already physically tired and is often continued for a long period that shortens available time for sleep, rest, and recuperation. This fatigue produces headache (tension headache) from unrelieved pull on the muscles at the back of the neck. The best way to relieve this fatigue is by rest. The worst way is to whip up the fatigued muscles with more stimulants, such as amphetamine, or to continue with a depressant drug such as alcohol. This is a strong argument against the "hair of the dog" treatment.

Stomach upset and irritation may arise from several circumstances. Alcohol in small quantities is an aperient, stimulating appetite. Hence, early in the alcoholic evening the victim may have been stimulated to eat an excessively large meal, which is being slowly and poorly digested. Or he may have omitted eating and have a hunger headache. Alcohol is one of the few substances absorbed directly from the stomach into the blood stream, and when this occurs in great volume, the secretion of gastric juice is altered. Bland foods, such as milk toast, help overcome the gastric factor in hangover.

Hansen's Disease—LEPROSY.

Hardening of the Arteries—*arteriosclerosis;* a condition marked by thickening, hardening, and loss of elasticity in the walls of the arteries. An important distinction must be made between arteriosclerosis, in which the deposit of lime salts and hardening takes place chiefly in the *middle* layer of the arteries, and *atherosclerosis,* in which fat deposits occur in the *inner* lining of the arteries, roughening and thickening them. Atherosclerosis of the coronary arteries is what usually induces a heart attack (see HEART DISEASE).

Hardening of the arteries is associated with HIGH BLOOD PRESSURE, HEART DISEASE, and STROKE. When the arteries of the brain harden, rigidity of thought processes may occur. Hardening of the arteries in the kidneys may gradually induce serious kidney disease. When arteriosclerosis affects the legs, the arteries may become as stiff as pipestems; this condition sometimes causes a cramp or dull ache in the calves after a short walk or sometimes even while at rest. Arteries in the arms and those bringing blood to the face can also harden, producing symptoms of mild discomfort, but this is less frequent.

Treatment of arteriosclerosis includes exercise, which keeps the blood flow at a maximum and stimulates the collateral circulation; application of heat, which has the same effects; alcohol, which dilates the blood vessels; and the prohibition of tobacco, which constricts them.

Whose arteries harden? Anyone who lives for any length of time is gradually subject to hardening of the arteries. However, men's arteries begin to harden 10 to 15 years before women's, for reasons still obscure. This partly explains why women live longer. Cardiovascular renal changes set in at a later period in women's lives. Diabetics are subject to earlier hardening of the arteries.

Harelip—a notch in the upper lip, giving it the appearance of a rabbit's (hare's) lip. This is a defect that a person is born with (congenital malformation). It is usually accompanied by CLEFT PALATE, which see. The treatment is surgery.

Hay Fever—a catarrhal inflammation of the nose and eyes, caused by ALLERGY to various plant pollens, especially ragweed. It can be quite mild or so severe as to cause loss of sleep and weight. Hay fever occurs most commonly in late summer and fall, but sometimes also in spring and early summer, when it may be called rose fever. See ALLERGY.

Some patients are relieved by ANTIHISTAMINES, others by desensitizing injections of the pollen to which they are sensitive (after this has been determined by skin tests). Still others go to resorts more or less free of irritating pollens, or try to stay in air-conditioned rooms during their hay-fever season. No single treatment relieves all sufferers.

HEADACHE

Headache—probably the commonest complaint a doctor hears—is a symptom, not a disease, and as such is almost always accompanied by other signs and symptoms that help point toward the underlying causes. Sometimes the explanation is obvious—for example, a severe blow on the head (CONCUSSION headache), a drinking spree (HANGOVER headache), or a recent shocking emotional experience. But usually less obvious causes have to be traced down and treated for permanent relief from headache and its recurrence. Temporary relief is often easy to accomplish.

Getting rid of a headache. An occasional mild headache can be treated at home. A good night's sleep or even a few hours' nap are often enough to relieve a simple headache, especially one induced by fatigue. Eating and drinking sometimes relieves a headache, especially if brought on by skipping a meal. A cup of coffee helps some people, but increases headache in others. A warm (not too hot!) bath or a cold shower, two forms of hydrotherapy, may also work. Headache sometimes disappears following a good bowel movement (but this is no argument for the regular use of self-prescribed laxatives). Change of position sometimes helps; sitting up may be more comfortable than lying down. Quietly reclining is generally valuable.

Other maneuvers that may be safely tried for immediate relief of an occasional headache include:

Dousing the face with cold water. Applying mild astringent lotions (e.g. after-shave lotions) to the face. Gently massaging the scalp. Combing and brushing the hair. Comfortably massaging the muscles at the back of the neck. Applying a cold compress (even a wet handkerchief or washcloth) to the forehead. Applying an ice bag to the front, side, back, or top of the head. Taking aspirin, if you know you are not sensitive to aspirin; two 5-grain tablets (10 grains) followed, if necessary, with another 5-grain tablet 2 hours later and another 4 hours later, is usually a safe adult dose. Children from 8 to 15 years old may be given 1 dose of ½ or ⅔ a 5-grain tablet. Younger children should not be given aspirin without a doctor's specific order. Aspirin should be followed by at least a few swallows of water, preferably more.

Headache remedies. Numerous headache remedies are on the market, sold in drugstores without medical prescription. Some fizz; some do not. The fizz is no therapeutic advantage. Few, if any, of these remedies are more effective than plain aspirin; they just cost more. Their active ingredient is usually the same as that in aspirin, a form of salicylic acid. Caffeine, the active drug in coffee and tea, is sometimes added. Some so-called headache remedies contain sedative drugs, like salts of bromine (bromides), whose continued use in excessive doses can be harmful.

Types of headaches. Running to a doctor with every little headache sometimes indicates a morbid anxiety about one's health (hypochondria). But medical attention should be sought with reasonable promptness if headaches are frequent, severe enough to interfere with sleep, or accompanied by other symptoms, particularly changes in vision. A severe headache is usually accompanied by a feeling of nausea, often by vomiting.

Headaches run the gamut from mild to severe. The most excruciating sudden head pain is caused by a break in blood vessels on the surface of the brain (subarachnoid bleeding); this is a true, though rare, medical emergency. Headaches may be constant, intermittent, or on-and-off. The pain may be dull, sharp, pulsating, splitting, one-sided, all over, or have other qualities. In seeking the underlying causes, the doctor considers these facts and all other factors.

Since the possible underlying causes are so numerous (one *simple* classification lists over 200) and since it is a symptom reported in so many different diseases, no one should try to diagnose the cause of his own headaches. To find it, the doctor will give him a complete medical check-up and, if necessary, call in other specialists and order laboratory tests which appear indicated.

The exact mechanism by which head pain is produced and the headache felt is still not absolutely clear. Brain tissue, surprisingly enough, is insensitive to pain, although the brain interprets the sensation of pain. The best theory of what produces headache is that it comes from swelling (dilatation), pressure on, or pulling (traction) of the blood vessels that feed the brain. These effects may be produced by reflex action along many nerve pathways (but particularly the vagus nerve). The reflex stimulus may originate in the stomach, bowels, eyes, or almost any other bodily organ. Other places where pulling, pressure on, and swelling of the arteries and veins of the brain may originate are the inside of the brain (e.g. brain tumor), skull, scalp, neck, and face.

Tension headache. This is the most common type of headache, and it has many names: "anxious headache," "psychosomatic headache," and so forth. A fundamental mechanism in this type of headache is constant tension and pull on the muscles at the back of the neck. Anxiety in its many guises keeps these muscles constantly on the alert, rarely relaxed, almost in spasm. Patients with tension headaches usually have many other vague, though serious, complaints; most importantly, inability to sleep well. The relief of tension headache may require all the weapons of psychotherapy. Many people respond to mild sedative drugs (barbiturates), the new tranquilizing drugs (RAUWOLFIA and CHLORPROMAZINE), and to an explanation and understanding of what causes their headaches.

Headaches following injuries to the head or other parts of the body (post-traumatic headache) follow the same general pattern as tension headaches. However, sensitivity to noise and dizziness are often added symptoms (see EAR TROUBLE).

Migraine or "sick headaches" or "bilious headaches" are the second large class of headaches. They are usually one-sided, repetitive, pulsating; but they do not interrupt sleep as decidedly as tension headaches. For fuller information and treatment, see MIGRAINE.

Histamine, or *Horton's, headache* has many characteristics in common with migraine—except that it usually comes on in the middle of the night. Treatment includes HISTAMINE injections and sometimes ANTIHISTAMINE drugs.

HIGH BLOOD PRESSURE (hypertension) is the next great cause of headaches. But not all people with high blood pressure suffer headaches, and people with low blood pressure can suffer similar types of headache. These headaches tend to occur at the back of the head, to be worse in the morning, and to disappear during the day. They appear to be the result of a stretching or dilatation of the brain arteries, which thus become vulnerable to pain production. The treatment of hypertension headaches is much like that of migraine. Mild sedatives alone are often helpful, and the high blood pressure must be looked after.

Dilatation of the blood vessels also appears to be the provoking factor in headaches related to hunger, ALLERGY, MENSTRUATION (premenstrual tension), EPILEPSY, FEVER (INFECTION), LIVER TROUBLE, KIDNEY TROUBLE, and the sudden giving up of drinking COFFEE by previously heavy coffee drinkers.

EYE TROUBLE, especially farsightedness, astigmatism, and glaucoma, brings on headaches because the pull and strain on eye muscles exerts pressures on facial nerve tracts. These headaches are readily corrected (except glaucoma) by wearing the right eyeglasses. (See EYE TROUBLE.) Though eye trouble is a frequent cause of headache, many tension headaches are falsely attributed to this cause and are *not* cured by a change of glasses.

SINUS TROUBLE, infection, and inflammation in the air spaces of the bones of the skull communicating with the nose, can produce a dull, throbbing headache—like the driving rods of a locomotive pounding on the forehead. Relief of sinus irritation, sometimes by so simple a procedure as sleeping with the windows closed in cold and damp weather, will correct this type of headache. It is usually worst about noon and wears off during the afternoon.

Even a toothache may become a headache.

Sometimes the cause of a headache cannot be located by even the best diagnostician. But if your headaches are anything but occasional and obviously explicable, you will do wisely to help your doctor keep searching for the causes.

Health—"the rich man's blessing, the poor man's wealth." Good health is not the mere absence of disease; it means mental and emotional health as well as the normal functioning of the body sometimes called "physical health." Health is not an end in itself; it is an attribute of a human being which enables him to live with the greatest satisfaction to himself within the framework of the society to which he belongs. A person can have a healthy attitude toward life despite pain and physical handicaps. Health and disease are not complete opposites, or antonyms. There are degrees of each. Even the sickest person retains a number of normal functions and even the "healthiest" has some flaws. There is no such thing as "perfect health" and it is not a valid or useful ideal toward which to work.

On the other hand, there is a high level of health whose possession makes life zestful and meaningful and whose absence depletes, prevents, and sometimes embitters total life achievements. Personal health in this sense is difficult to achieve in an unhealthy, disease-ridden community. Hence the person who would himself be healthy must take some responsibility for community health.

Through long experience science and mankind have identified a large number of specific hazards to health; for example, microbes, and their means of transmission. Knowledge about health hazards, if acted upon, can reduce the risk of disease and disability. Such information is included in this book.

HEALTH INSURANCE

The term "health insurance" means many different things to different people. Sometimes it is called "sickness insurance," or "medical-surgical protection," or "disability benefits"; and it has many other names. In general, however, health insurance describes a variety of prepayment plans by means of which individuals, families, and much larger groups can more comfortably meet the unpredictable costs of illness, accident, and medical care.

Health insurance is inextricably related to the broad and complex problem of medical economics—the development of ways and means of delivering a high quality of medical care to millions of people throughout the world. It is not a panacea for the ills of mankind. It is financial protection against some of the costs of disease. Health insurance is not a means of guaranteeing good health, although it can be one important factor contributing to this desirable end.

Discussions of health insurance are often complicated by the fact that it is sometimes an emotionally charged political issue. This has been true not only in the United States abut also in a number of European countries. Beginning with Germany in the 1870's, many European countries have adopted various kinds of health insurance plans. England now has a national health insurance program which has been subject to criticism almost since its inception soon after World War II, but which also has its stanch defenders.

The fundamental political question regarding health insurance is whether it is *voluntary* or *compulsory*. Numerous attempts have been made to enact national compulsory sickness insurance legislation in the United States. They have all been defeated. Arguments have been prolonged and heated. The proponents have argued that the health of the people is the *direct* concern of the government; therefore everyone should be insured and additional taxes collected to meet this cost. The opponents of compulsory sickness insurance have branded it as "socialized medicine" and pointed out that the intervention of government into medicine would make medical care "a political football," resulting in worse care at higher cost for everyone. The problem is exceedingly complex. The fact is that the U.S. Government does foot a number of bills for health care (for example, of veterans) and for medical research.

On the other hand, voluntary health insurance in the United States has shot ahead at a rapid pace. At the beginning of 1957 over 110,000,000 Americans—nearly 70% of the population—had some form of health insurance protection. Only 4% were protected in 1940. Voluntary health insurance agencies were in 1956 already paying about $2.5 billion (22%) of the nation's current annual expenditure of $11.3 billion for all kinds of health care.

Where do these health dollars go? About 27% to doctors; 28% to hospitals; 10% to dentists; 15% for drugs; 12% for other goods (e.g., surgical appliances) and services (e.g., nursing).

On the average, over the years an American family spends 4 to 5% of its yearly income for medical care and related services. This, incidentally, is about ⅔ as much as it spends on alcohol and tobacco, and about 3 times as much as it pays out in support of its religious and welfare activities.

There would be no serious family problem of financing medical care costs in the United States if every family could be assured that these costs would not exceed the average 4 to 5% of its income in any given year. But this is not the case; sickness costs are not predictable. Some families are struck with catastrophic expenses in a given year; about 7% of American families have medical expenses amounting to 20% or more of their income for the year. Higher costs are associated with increasing age. Women, on the average, have greater medical expenses than men—$80 a year as compared with $51.

Voluntary health insurance spreads the risk of medical costs over large numbers of families, thereby reducing the chance that any one family will suffer undue financial hardship or beggary as the result of catastrophic illness. There has been a considerable growth in the number of organizations in the United States that issue health insurance policies. Prompted often by the early experience of BLUE CROSS and, later, BLUE SHIELD plans, several hundred commercial insurance companies and a number of "independent" plans have become active.

Health insurance can be purchased either in individual policies or as group insurance. The individual policies, bought through an insurance agent, can be tailored to meet specific family needs. Group insurance premiums are usually lower for the same amount of insurance coverage but the individual is bound by the terms of the master policy (contract) issued to the group under which he joins.

What a person gets when he buys health insurance is governed strictly by the terms of the written policy, fine print and all. Many so-called "low-cost" policies have so many conditions and exclusions that they offer very little financial protection. Purchase your health insurance only from a reputable company and a reliable agent. Read the actual policy submitted and compare it for benefits, extent of coverage, cancellation clauses, rates, and the like with other similar policies. Choose the one that fits your needs best.

Types of voluntary health insurance protection. Despite the great variety of individual policies, there are basically five types of voluntary health insurance protection now available, namely:

1. Hospital expense protection. These policies pay wholly or in part the hospital charges for room, board, miscellaneous and special services, such as general nursing, use of operating room, X-ray, laboratory and drugs. The payment is either in the form of *service* rendered by the hospital or *cash* indemnity paid to the patient or the hospital.

2. Surgical expense protection. Surgical benefits are paid according to a predetermined fee schedule for each type of operation, usually including both preoperative and postoperative care.

3. Regular medical expense protection. These policies pay for medical expenses other than surgical, including home, office, and hospital calls. Diagnostic examinations, consultations, and periodic health examinations may be included; but usually benefits do not begin until the second or third call on or from the doctor.

4. Major medical expense protection. This fairly new type of

policy is designed to protect against unusually large, "catastrophic" medical expenses. It pays 75 to 80% of all medical costs above a "deductible" minimum—from $100 to $500—and up to a high maximum—$2,500 to $10,000. The patient or family, called "co-insurers," pays the other 20 to 25% of the medical and hospital bills.

5. Loss of income protection. This type of policy is sometimes called sickness and accident indemnity or disability insurance. It pays cash benefits, usually weekly, to compensate partially for loss of income owing to sickness and accident. This money can be used to pay medical costs or living expenses.

These different types of insurance protection are combined in various ways to make different "packages," expressly set down in policies. There are also other types of insurance in force which protect against the economic risks of disease and accident. Among them are workmen's compensation insurance, which covers occupational injuries and illnesses "arising in and out of the course of employment"; individual and group accident policies, which provide benefits for injuries from accidents; and liability insurance, which covers medical expenses of injured victims of the legally liable party.

It cannot be said that the final pattern of health insurance has been reached in the United States, or anywhere else. Serious consideration must be given especially to coverage of older people and those in low-income groups. The outlook for increased voluntary health insurance of all types is promising.

Hearing—see EARS, EAR TROUBLE, DEAFNESS.

HEART

The heart is a hollow muscle that pumps or circulates BLOOD through the blood vessels in all parts of the body at the rate of about 4,000 gallons a day (or 5 ounces at each beat). About the size and shape of a clenched fist, it is located in the chest between the lungs, just above the diaphragm. It is in the midline of the body, with its apex (lower point) directed slightly to the left side.

The heart muscle itself (*myocardium*) does the work; it is composed of a special kind of striped muscle tissue. This muscle is lined on the outside with a strong, fibrous membrane called the *pericardium*, on the inside with a delicate membrane called the *endocardium*.

THE CIRCULATORY SYSTEM

superior vena cava — to neck and head — aorta

pulmonary artery

to chest, shoulder and arm

pulmonary artery

pulmonary veins

pulmonary vein

LUNG

LUNG

right auricle

left auricle

inferior vena cava

LIVER

left ventricle

portal vein

KIDNEY

right ventricle

STOMACH PANCREAS SPLEEN

SMALL INTESTINE

renal artery and vein

inferior vena cava

aorta

LARGE INTESTINE

heart

C — coronary artery and vein

veins and pulmonary artery carrying unoxygenated blood

arteries and pulmonary veins carrying oxygenated blood

to leg

The essential elements of the human circulatory system are presented here in semidiagrammatic fashion. Arrows show the direction of blood flow to and from the heart. The arteries and veins leading to the digestive system have been drawn as if pulled over to the left side.

The heart is a four-chambered, double-acting pump. A septum down the middle separates it into a "right" and "left" heart. It has five *valves,* which control the flow of blood. The heart muscle is nourished by arteries called *coronary arteries.*

The septum down the middle of the heart is normally open before birth. There is a little window (foramen ovale) between the right and left heart. This window normally closes at the time of birth so that venous and arterial blood no longer mix. But in a few instances it fails to close, and a "BLUE BABY" is the result.

Each side of the heart is subdivided into two chambers, separated by valves. The upper chambers are called *auricles* (or atria), the lower chambers, *ventricles.* The left ventricle is the largest. The *mitral,* or *bicuspid,* valve stands between the left auricle and the left ventricle, the *tricuspid* valve between the right auricle and ventricle.

Blood enters the right auricle from the veins coming from the rest of the body and from the heart itself, that is, from the superior and inferior venae cavae and from the coronary sinus. There is a valve shaped like a half-moon *(semilunar valve)* at the point where the inferior vena cava empties into the right auricle.

At the first beat of the heart, the venous blood is pumped from the right auricle into the right ventricle (and simultaneously from the left auricle into the left ventricle). From the right ventricle the venous blood is forced past the *pulmonary valve* through the pulmonary arteries into the right and left lungs. There it drops its carbon dioxide and picks up oxygen, becoming redder, arterial blood. From the lungs it returns to the heart through two pulmonary veins, which open into the left auricle. The last stop in the heart is the left ventricle. At its contraction, or stroke, the blood is pumped into the large artery at the top of the heart, the aorta. It passes the *aortic valve* on the way.

From the aorta the blood passes into the arteries, arterioles, and capillaries in all parts of the body. From the capillaries, which are the tiniest blood vessels, it returns through venules, and then veins to the right auricle, having made a complete circuit of the body.

The heart normally beats from 60 to 90 times a minute, about four times the breathing (respiration) rate in a normal, healthy person. The delicately timed sequence of the heartbeat is controlled by nerve impulses from the central nervous system and by special nerve centers within the heart. One of these nerve centers

THE HUMAN HEART I

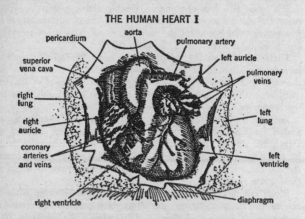

This drawing presents the exterior appearance of the human heart as it lies in the chest cavity. This is a view from the front, with the pericardial sac opened up.

in the heart (bundle of His) is called the pacemaker. One set of autonomic nerves speeds up the heartbeat; its antagonistic set slows it down. Excitement and physical exercise speed up the heartbeat because, under these conditions, there is a greater demand for blood and oxygen in the tissues.

The wave of contraction in the beating heart (its period of systole) starts with the auricles and passes on to the ventricles. In the "lub-dub" sound of the heart, the auricles are heard beating first. There are timed pauses in this process. The auricles are at rest when the ventricles contract, and vice versa. But there is also a time between beats (the period of diastole) when both auricles and ventricles are at rest. During sleep the heart rests nearly half the time (28 seconds out of 60). Infants have a much faster heartbeat than adults; it starts at a rate of about 120 beats a minute.

The heart sounds heard by placing an ear or stethoscope to the chest are made principally by the opening and closing of the heart valves. When there is some defect in the valves, the sound is said to be a "murmur." But not all murmurs indicate heart disease.

THE HUMAN HEART II

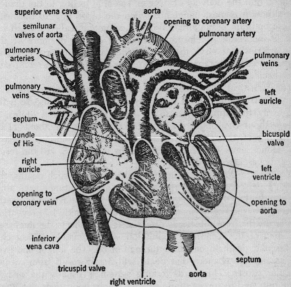

This drawing shows the interior of the human heart. A semidiagrammatic drawing, it reveals the internal structure of the heart, including its chambers and valves.

See also BLOOD, BLOOD VESSELS, HEART DISEASE, KIDNEYS, KIDNEY TROUBLE. The heart, blood vessels, and kidneys together make up the vital but vulnerable *cardiovascularenal system.*

HEART DISEASE

Heart disease is not one but many diseases. Nor is the heart alone involved. The blood vessels and the kidneys, and sometimes other organs, are also affected. When we talk about heart disease, we usually mean cardiovascular or cardiovascularenal disease, "cardio" for heart, "vascular" for blood vessels, "renal" for kidneys. When damage or change occurs in any part of this system, it is reflected in the other parts.

The net effect of cardiovascular disease is to diminish the flow of blood and the delivery of oxygen, essential to life, to the tissues. The situation is most dangerous when the blood flow to the heart muscle or brain is impaired. What is commonly called a *heart attack* is the result of closure or clogging of one or more of the little arteries that serve the heart. When a brain artery breaks or clogs, the condition known as STROKE or *apoplexy* or *cerebral vascular accident* occurs.

The statistical picture of heart disease in the United States is apt to be frightening until it is fully analyzed. Heart disease is far and away the principal cause of death in the United States; it causes about 37% of all deaths. Stroke accounts for about 11½%; hardening of the arteries (arteriosclerosis), 2%; kidney disease, 1½%. Hence more than half of all deaths in the U.S. are the result of cardiovascularenal diseases.

Yet despite the increase in the total number of such deaths, the average person faces less risk of dying at an untimely age than his grandfather did in 1900. The increase in cardiovascular deaths reflects the success of medicine and public health in preventing earlier deaths from infectious diseases. It also reflects the increased life span of the American population. Approximately 60% of cardiovascular deaths occur after the age of 65. The longer one lives the greater the chances that death will finally result from cardiovascular causes. This hard-working system is usually the first to wear out; as life forces diminish, the whole body does not go to pieces at one time, like the famous "one-hoss shay." Obviously, when the heart stops beating, a person dies. Cardiovascular disease in later life is a *degenerative disease.* Effective treatment and management can prolong life and make it comfortable, but there is no way to halt the eventual wearing-out process.

Great progress has been made in the diagnosis, classification, and treatment of heart disease. Improved drugs and more daring surgery have both helped, along with a better understanding of the nature of the disease. Those forms of heart disease due to infections such as diphtheria and syphilis, to a disordered thyroid gland, or to lack of vitamin B_1 are now almost completely preventable. Even heart attacks are more effectively controlled. They are not sentences to permanent invalidism. The average length of life after a heart attack is at least 10 years.

What kinds of heart disease are there? There are at least 20 kinds of *organic* heart disease that actually affect the heart muscle, the valves of the heart, or its inner or outer lining. There are also a number of *functional* disorders of the heart in which its function or action is altered, or in which symptoms are referred to the heart, but in which no actual damage to or lesions in the heart are discoverable. Heart trouble may be primary, or secondary to other diseases.

The most common and serious forms of organic heart disease are those affecting the coronary arteries, which supply blood to the heart. These diseases are usually associated with HIGH BLOOD PRESSURE (hypertension) and HARDENING OF THE ARTERIES (arteriosclerosis). A heart attack is usually a case of *coronary thrombosis* (described on page 242). *Heart failure* may be a late consequence of any of these conditions, or others. This group of heart troubles is predominantly, but not exclusively, associated with the middle and later years of life.

Infections present the second large class of causes of organic heart disease. RHEUMATIC FEVER, or rheumatic heart disease, associated with certain streptococcal ("strep") infections, heads the list. Syphilis, diphtheria, tuberculosis, typhoid, and other fevers can injure the heart. Fortunately, these diseases can usually be treated (or prevented) before they cause heart damage. Before the advent of antibiotics, *bacterial endocarditis,* in which the inner lining of the heart, the endocardium, is directly infected, was usually fatal. Now, with penicillin and other drugs, it is curable in 80% or better of the cases. The outer membrane, or sac, that contains the heart may also become inflamed, then thicken and harden so that it binds the heart too tightly and interferes with its work. This condition, known as constrictive *pericarditis,* can be relieved by cutting away strips of the scarred and hardened tissue. Infections are the chief cause of heart disease in childhood and early adult life.

Congenital heart defects, which develop before birth and are usually discovered shortly thereafter, account for about 2% of all heart defects. "Blue babies" have a congenital defect that permits the bluer venous blood to mix with arterial blood.

Other forms of organic heart disease are associated with or the result of poor functioning of the endocrine glands, especially the thyroid gland; with chronic lung disease that overtaxes the heart; with severe anemias; with some nutritional diseases, notably *beriberi;* with poisoning from heavy metals or kidney wastes (uremia); and with direct injuries or wounds to the heart.

Functional disorders of the heart include such conditions as heart murmurs; palpitation; premature beats; skipped beats; rapid beating, up to 250 beats a minute (paroxysmal tachycardia); slow beating, under 60 beats a minute (bradycardia); irregular rhythms; and rapid flutter. Other functional disorders are heart disturbances of psychic or emotional origin. In these cases the patient fears and believes that he has heart disease and develops symptoms associated with it, such as palpitation, shortness of breath, extreme fatigue, and dizzy spells. This condition has many names: *"soldier's heart,"* as it was labeled in World War I; *cardiac neurosis; effort syndrome;* and *neurocirculatory asthenia* (weakness of the nervous and circulatory systems). Here the doctor's job is to persuade the patient that he does not have organic heart disease. Psychiatric treatment is sometimes necessary.

Because heart disease can be so specifically classified and so much more accurately diagnosed today, more specific and effective treatment is possible for each kind of heart disease. Not so many years ago coronary thrombosis was often diagnosed as acute indigestion.

What is a heart attack? Heart attack is the popular term for what physicians call *coronary thrombosis* (also coronary occlusion, coronary closure, and myocardial infarction). Heart attacks can be suddenly fatal, but the great majority—an estimated 85%—are not. The patient recovers under proper treatment and goes on to live many useful years. The younger the victim, the greater his life expectancy.

Although the attack is sudden, the conditions underlying it have been developing for years. For reasons still obscure, the inner linings (intima) of the arteries gradually become thickened and roughened, a condition known as *atherosclerosis.* The coronary arteries, which supply blood to the heart, are subject to these changes more than other arteries. The narrowed channel slows down the flow of blood, and the roughened surface provides greater opportunity for a blood clot to form on the wall. This stationary clot is called a thrombus. At the moment such a clot cuts off the blood supply to part of the heart the heart attack occurs.

If a large coronary artery is suddenly closed up, the attack may be fatal. However, in most cases, the blood detours around the blocked artery by way of other blood vessels that compensate for the blockage. This is called *collateral circulation,* and it is the road to recovery. The immediate treatment of a heart attack includes the administration of drugs, like atropine, that will relax otherwise healthy arteries and encourage collateral circulation.

It takes about a month for this new circulation pathway to be established. During this period the heart's work must be kept to a minimum, so the patient must remain at rest in bed. Oxygen may be given through an oxygen tent or mask. The risk of other blood clots forming can be reduced by administering anticoagulant drugs, like dicumarol. A take-it-easy, convalescent period should follow the first month to six weeks of bed rest. If the patient avoids excessive strain on the heart during the healing process, recovery usually proceeds to the point where he can resume his normal life. In some cases, however, the damaged area of the heart muscle, gradually replaced by scar tissue, is so large that the heart is weakened and symptoms of distress appear.

Most heart attacks occur while a patient is at rest in bed or working quietly. Vigorous exercise by a person unaccustomed to it may perhaps precipitate the final blood clotting in the coronary artery, but even if he had not exercised strenuously, the chances are the clot would soon have appeared. Hence it is foolish to indict any single event as the cause of a heart attack.

The condition leading to heart attack is atherosclerosis in the lining of the coronary arteries, and the reasons for this are still uncertain. The deposit of fatty substances, notably *cholesterol*, under the lining appears to be a critical factor, but there is no agreement yet on why this takes place. Since heart attacks are far more common in men than in women, it has been said, "Women deposit their fat under the skin, while men deposit it in the walls of their coronary arteries." Because the body itself is able to manufacture large amounts of cholesterol from foods that contain none, the use of fat-free or other special diets cannot be depended on to prevent atherosclerosis or heart attack.

What is angina pectoris? The words mean "pain or strangling in the chest," and probably 95% of all instances occur in patients with coronary-artery disease. At one time all chest pains due to heart conditions were called angina, and the word has taken on a needlessly frightening connotation. As now understood, angina or anginal pain is a relatively mild discomfort, compared to coronary thrombosis. The pain arises because the heart muscle is being partially deprived of its normal oxygen supply. It may not be a severe pain, but simply a feeling of tightness or pressure in the chest.

Anginal pain may be considered a type of heart failure in which the heart is being asked to put out more work than it is given fuel (oxygen) to do. Narrowing or contraction of the little arteries of the heart (arterioles) accompanies the chest pain or pressure. The pain may be brought on by exercise, especially after a meal, emotional excitement, or cold weather. Experienced patients know how much of each they can take and avoid the excess that induces pain.

The sovereign remedy to relieve anginal pain is nitroglycerin. A small pellet placed under the tongue is immediately absorbed and carried to the heart's arterioles, which are quickly dilated (opened up) by the nitrite. The pain disappears, but the treatment may have to be repeated in 15 to 30 minutes. Alcohol also dilates the small blood vessels; the effect is not so quick, but it lasts longer.

What is heart failure? When the heart is unable to pump blood efficiently to all parts of the body, the condition is described as *heart failure.* It may accompany or be the result of coronary-artery disease or other types of heart disease, such as rheumatic, congenital, or hypertensive heart disease. Though serious, the condition is not necessarily rapidly fatal. Many patients live 10 to 20 years after congestive heart failure is first noted.

The cardinal symptom of heart failure is shortness of breath or difficult breathing (dyspnea). This complicated symptom involves not only the heart but also the lungs, certain veins and nerve reflexes. Breathing difficulties increase as the underlying condition progresses. At first the patient notices that he is out of breath following slight exertion, such as climbing a flight of stairs. He must sit down and rest whenever he makes any unaccustomed physical effort, and recovery is slow. He requires an extra pillow at night; eventually he may find that he can sleep comfortably only when he is sitting up. At length he pants even when he is resting, and his chest may heave deeply. With effective treatment and management, this progress toward invalidism can be interrupted.

Another common and often early sign of congestive heart failure is swelling of the ankles, usually at the end of the day. This sign certainly does not always betoken heart disease. When it is related to heart failure, however, it occurs because the heart is not pumping efficiently enough to get fluids out of the spaces between and within the body cells. This intracellular fluid is also responsible for the congestion of the lungs that occurs with advanced congestive heart failure.

To get rid of the accumulated fluids in cell spaces and body cavities, a condition once commonly called dropsy, a large group of *diuretic* drugs are now available. Diuretics increase the outflow of urine and thus draw off excess body fluids. Reduction of the amount of sodium in the body also helps to prevent the accumulation of fluids; this is the rationale of the salt-free diet. Common table salt is sodium chloride. One of the earliest-discovered and still widely used heart-stimulant drugs, *digitalis,* is also a diuretic and was originally used to treat dropsy. Diuretic drugs often bring dramatic relief to patients suffering from congestive heart failure.

The failing heart makes every effort to keep up with its responsibilities. It enlarges, as can often be seen in X-ray pictures, both by stretching its muscle fibers and by dilating so that the size of its cavities increases. There is a limit, however, to its ability to compensate for failing circulation. Irregularity of its rhythms occurs when the burden gets too heavy. Anginalike pains and digestive symptoms, referred to the abdomen, may occur.

The treatment of the failing heart comprises efforts to reduce its work load, improve its action, and get rid of excess body fluids. The patient must truly learn to live within his physical means, his cardiac reserve. This means as much rest and relaxation as possible, avoidance of physical exertion and emotional tensions, reduction of overweight, faithful adherence to medication schedules, moderation in the use of stimulants and tobacco, and intelligent, quiet recreation.

What are the symptoms of heart disease? It is a unique fact about heart disease that, in general, the more serious the condition the more remote from the heart are the symptoms. Among danger signals that may, but not necessarily do, betoken heart disease and should invite prompt medical attention are:

  Shortness of breath after slight exertion
  Pain or tightness in the chest, often running down the left arm
  Swelling in the ankles or abdomen
  Dizziness, light-headedness, or vertigo
  Seeing double (a particularly dangerous sign)
  Indigestion that is vague and hangs on
  Persistent headache
  Fatigue without otherwise explained origin

How can you guard your heart? For people over 40 and those who have had any previous trouble with the cardiovascular system, periodic medical examinations offer one line of defense against heart troubles. Prompt attention to the danger signals of heart disease is a second approach. Instruments greatly help the physician in spotting trouble in the cardiovascular system. These include that commonest of medical tools, the stethoscope, and also blood-pressure apparatus (sphygmomanometer), X-ray pictures and fluoroscopic screens, and the electrocardiograph. Early treatment of infections and other conditions that may eventuate in heart disease offers protection against it.

The simple rules of hygiene also help. Be moderate in diet, exercise, and use of tobacco and alcohol. Keep your weight within normal limits. Get reasonable amounts of rest in the rhythm of daily living. Avoid nervous tension so far as possible—and don't worry about getting heart disease.

Heartburn—a burning sensation in the food tube (esophagus), which passes near the heart in its passage from stomach to throat. Heartburn has nothing to do with the heart. The cause is STOMACH TROUBLE, commonly "ACID STOMACH." Temporary relief can be obtained with alkaline substances, such as bicarbonate of soda. But if heartburn is a regular and repeated event, full medical investigation should be made.

Heat and hot weather make many people uncomfortable, although individuals vary greatly in tolerance to external temperature. (See TEMPERATURE.) The best protection against hot weather is air-conditioning. There should not be too great a difference between the temperature in an air-conditioned room or vehicle and the temperature outside, no more than 10 to 15°. Circulation of air by an electric fan that does not produce a direct draft is also helpful.

The excessive perspiration that takes place in hot weather causes a loss not only of body water but also of body MINERALS. Too large a loss causes *heat cramps.* These can be prevented or relieved by taking plenty of fluids and common table salt. This is often provided as *salt tablets.* Two 5-grain tablets every 2 hours are enough. *Alcoholic beverages* usually increase the sensation of body heat; even cool beer does it.

Good rules for hot-weather living are: (1) Drink plenty of water. *Sip* the ice-cold drinks. (2) Stay out of the sun. (3) Avoid vigorous exercise or hard physical labor. (4) Wear cool, loose, lightweight clothing. (5) Eat sparingly. Concentrate on light foods, not heavy meals.

Heat Stroke, or heat prostration, results from exposure to excessive heat, either indoors or outdoors. If the head is unprotected from the direct glare of the tropical sun by a pith helmet, turban, or burnoose, heat stroke may occur. The principal symptom is a very high body temperature, usually 105° F. or over, with unconsciousness and convulsions. Treatment includes cooling the body with cool baths, ice packs or rubs. See SUNSTROKE.

Hebephrenia—SCHIZOPHRENIA with silly and infantile symptoms, such as senseless laughter and giggling; a form of MENTAL ILLNESS.

Heliotherapy—treatment by sunlight; once popular in treating tuberculosis of the bones and joints.

Helminth—a WORM or wormlike parasite that infests the human or animal body, generally in the intestine.

Hemangioma—a growth of unnecessary blood vessels, usually on the surface of the skin. These are often angry-looking but benign tumors. The *strawberry birthmark* is an example.

Hematology—study of the BLOOD and the blood-forming organs.

Hematoma—a bulge or growth in which BLOOD accumulates; occasionally found on the ear and around the SEX ORGANS, FEMALE. It is *not* a form of cancer.

Hematuria—blood in the urine (see KIDNEY TROUBLE).

Hemiplegia—PARALYSIS on one side of the body, commonly the result of STROKE or damage to blood vessels in the brain. If the damage is on the left side of the brain, the paralysis will be on the right side of the body, and vice versa. Adequate REHABILITATION can do a great deal to improve the outlook for hemiplegics.

Hemoglobin—the red coloring matter of the blood; it carries the oxygen. See BLOOD; also ANEMIA.

Hemolysis—breakdown of red blood cells with liberation of hemoglobin. Some snake venoms and some bacteria, among other substances, are *hemolytic*.

Hemophilia—BLEEDER'S DISEASE.

Hemoptysis—bleeding from the lungs, spitting blood, or blood-stained sputum. This is always a serious warning sign of illness, demanding prompt medical investigation.

Hemorrhage—see BLEEDING.

Hemorrhoidectomy—surgical removal of PILES.

Hemorrhoids—PILES, which see.

Hemostat—anything that stops bleeding. In surgery it refers to a metal clamp or forceps pinched onto severed blood vessels to keep them from bleeding.

Heparin—an anticoagulant drug, derived from liver, which is given to slow down the coagulation of blood inside the veins. It is used in preventing and treating various diseases of the heart and blood vessels; notably coronary thrombosis and pulmonary embolism. See BLOOD CLOTTING.

Hepatic—refers to the LIVER.

Hepatitis—inflammation of the liver. *Infectious hepatitis* has been rapidly increasing in the U.S. Approximately 50,000 cases were reported in 1954. This is a virus infection, generally spread in person-to-person contacts. Contaminated food and water may also account for outbreaks. Infectious viral hepatitis is related to *serum hepatitis*, transmitted by way of blood and blood products, for example, by blood transfusions. Gamma globulin is useful in preventing secondary cases of infectious hepatitis among family and household contacts. (See LIVER TROUBLE.)

HEREDITY

"Like father, like son" tells half the exciting story of heredity. "As the twig is bent, so the tree inclines" tells the other half. We know sons who are like their fathers and follow in their fathers' footsteps—and the same can be said of mothers and daughters. The common phrase for this is "a chip off the old block." But we also know sons and daughters who are extremely unlike their parents and unlike each other.

The study of heredity is the scientific attempt to explain both likenesses and differences between parents and offspring. In human beings this is exceedingly difficult. It is much easier with lower forms of life, such as the sweet pea or the fruit fly *(Drosophila)*. Most of what we know about the mechanisms of human heredity is based on the study of these lower forms.

The great key to the mechanism of heredity was provided in the mid-19th century by the Austrian abbot, Gregor Mendel, working with sweet peas in his monastery garden. The science of heredity, also called *genetics*, goes back to his work—which was lost but rediscovered in 1900—and is sometimes referred to as *Mendelism*.

What an individual turns out to be is determined not only by his *physical heredity* (genetic constitution) but also by his environment, his *cultural heredity*. Heredity can be described as "the way an individual reacts to his environment." Characteristics that environment cannot alter are hereditary. But in the human being hereditary characteristics are not easy to determine. For example, hair color can be changed by hair dye, although the results are not permanent. But no treatment can keep some men from getting as bald as their fathers and grandfathers.

Much nonsense is still believed about heredity. It is a complete myth that heredity is "carried"—transmitted—by the blood, even though we speak of blood relatives. On the other hand, blood type is inherited, along with other bodily characteristics. This is what makes possible blood tests for ruling out paternity. There is no evidence whatsoever that moral traits or weaknesses—criminality, laziness, drunkenness—are inherited. But of course the same type of environment and family that encouraged these traits in a father may encourage them in a son. The infamous story of the Jukes and Kallikak families, purporting to show that "degenerate" parents invariably produce "degenerate" offspring, is a pure lie, a scientific-sounding fabrication that has been passed off on unsuspecting students for years as true.

Heredity has long been used to explain circumstances and events concerning which true knowledge was lacking. It has been a scientific wastebasket. But now we have at least two other reasonable explanations for many conditions formerly attributed to heredity. These are (1) prenatal environment and (2) early-childhood development.

Prenatal environment means the conditions met by the fetus growing inside its mother's womb. It has been quite definitely shown, for example, that if a mother suffers from German measles early in her pregnancy, her child may be born with congenital defects; for example, cataracts of the eye or hearing deficiencies. An even more definite example is congenital SYPHILIS.

Early-childhood development prescribes the dominant emotional patterns that a child will have for the rest of his life. His relationship with his mother, particularly, and other members of his family determines his emotional reaction patterns for the rest of his life. Children deprived of their mothers in infancy—more exactly, of the tender, loving care that a true mother or mother substitute can give—literally sicken and sometimes die. Many psychosomatic illnesses (for example, a tendency to stomach ulcers) arise in childhood-development patterns. The role of the ENDOCRINE GLANDS in mediating between emotional states and physical illness must also be considered.

"Diseases run in families" in a much different sense than most people think. It is true mainly to the extent that the family is the unit of living. It was once thought, for example, that, in some mysterious way, some families were more susceptible to certain diseases than others. This is not provable in terms of physical heredity; it has more validity in terms of cultural heredity.

Members of the same family tend to contract and suffer from the same diseases largely because they are all exposed to the same physical, social, and environmental influences. Parents and children all get PELLAGRA, for example, because they are all eating the same VITAMIN-deficient diet. Children may contract infectious and contagious diseases from their parents (and vice versa) because they live in close contact. TUBERCULOSIS, for example, is sometimes properly described as a household epidemic. However, if this disease were truly inherited, all members of the household would get it, which rarely happens. There appear to be great individual differences in resistance to infectious disease.

There is a body of opinion which holds that the condition known as HUNTINGTON'S CHOREA is definitely hereditary; that heredity is possibly a factor in the development of HIGH BLOOD PRESSURE and some other degenerative diseases. But the evidence is not unassailable. The role of physical heredity in the etiology of human disease is exceedingly difficult to prove with statistical finality. It cannot be categorically denied, but it is too easy to offer it as an "explanation" that really means, "We do not know."

Cancer and insanity are not inherited. It is true that some strains of *mice* appear more susceptible to cancer than other strains, but mice are not men. Any personal fear of inheriting or transmitting CANCER is completely unjustified. On this point Dr. Clarence C. Little, a distinguished scientist in cancer research, declares: "The role which heredity plays is so complex, so well concealed, and so difficult of evaluation that it is both unnecessary and unwise for individuals to consider it a personal problem."

Insanity is the legal term for what is now more properly called MENTAL ILLNESS, neuroses and psychoses. It is true that much remains obscure and unknown about the origin of mental illness. But it is ignorant and superstitious to attribute much, if any, of this to heredity when it is so much more clearly known that what happens to a child in the early years of his life sets the emotional patterns from which later mental illness may emerge. An outstanding psychiatrist, Dr. Jules H. Masserman, declares: "While there might be a tendency to inherit FEEBLE-MINDEDNESS and perhaps EPILEPSY, there is no reliable evidence for definite hereditary factors in behavioral aberrations less directly dependent on organic or neurologic functions. Rather, controlled genetic-environment studies indicate that parents influence their children's patterns of behavior less by genes than by the nature of parental care, precept, and example."[*]

[*]Dr. Jules H. Masserman, *Principles of Dynamic Psychiatry* (Philadelphia W. B. Saunders Company, 1946), p. 11. Quoted by permission of the author and the publisher.

Furthermore, both cancer and mental illness are so common in modern American society that it is almost impossible to find any family tree completely free of them.

The mechanism of heredity: genes and chromosomes. The hereditary characteristics transmitted from parents to offspring are all present in the "seed" from which the vegetable plant, animal, or human being develops. We know that the living body is an aggregate of CELLS, trillions of them in the human being; and we also know that even the biggest or brightest individual who ever lived began life as a *single cell,* a sperm-fertilized human egg cell. This one cell divided into two, the two into four, and so on up to the finished human body. Whatever was in the first cell to determine its way of development must also be in the last cells produced. Hence the constitution of the complete human being arises out of the controlling factors in that first cell. This is his physical inheritance, with all its potentialities and limitations. In this sense human heredity and human constitution are the same thing.

Now science has learned what happens when a cell divides, when a "mother cell" breaks up into two "daughter cells." The controlling factor is the nucleus of the cell. In effect the ball that was the nucleus splits up into two identical sets of "threads" or "rods" that move to the opposite poles of the globe of the mother cell. Each one of these sets of rods shrinks again into a ball and forms a new nucleus. Then the old cell splits in half in the middle, and we have two new identical cells—each capable of splitting up again. All this can be seen under a high-power microscope, when these little threads are stained. They are called *chromosomes* (colored bodies).

Now, these chromosomes can be divided into still smaller bits of protoplasm, which fit into the chromosome threads like numbered links on a chain. These smaller bits, these links, are called *genes.* In the case of the fruit fly, for example, it is possible to map the insect's chromosomes and specify just where on the chromosome are the sets of genes that control particular characteristics in the grown insect (for example, color of eyes, shape of bristles). *The genes are the ultimate units of heredity.* They determine what the daughter cells are to be like; cells make up tissues; tissues make up organs; and organs, taken all together, comprise the human being.

Every living organism has a definite and constant number of

chromosomes in each of his body cells. The number of chromosomes differs with different living species. In man it is 48; in some worms it is only 2; in sugar cane it is over 200.

In the so-called sex or germ cells, for example, the human egg cell and the human sperm cell, the number of chromosomes is 24, just half that found in the body cells. When the human egg cell and sperm cell unite, the full complement of 48 chromosomes appears, half from the mother and half from the father.

However, one chromosome from the *father* determines at the instant of conception and wholly by chance the sex of the child-to-be. Genes other than those determining sex appear in this same sex-determining chromosome. The characteristics determined by these genes are called *sex-linked characteristics*. They can be traced through successive generations.

Among the sex-linked characteristics that have been noted and especially studied in man are *red-green* COLOR BLINDNESS, BLEEDER'S DISEASE, wasting of muscles (progressive muscular dystrophy), and webbed toes. Webbed toes are always passed on from father to son. A father can transmit the defective gene that causes color blindness only to his daughters; a mother can transmit this gene to either sons or daughters.

Mutation of genes. Genes sometimes change, although rarely under natural conditions. The process is called mutation of genes, and it is still very obscure. In the laboratory it has been shown that the frequency of gene mutations can be changed in fruit flies, animals, and plants by exposing them to irradiation (X rays), atomic energy, heat, and some chemicals. In human populations, present evidence seems to show that even if we could attain a human stock free of all deleterious genes, these unfavorable genes or others like them would again arise by the mysterious process called mutation of genes.

What can you inherit? You can inherit from your parents and transmit to your offspring only those bodily shapes and characteristics present in the genes of the specific sex-cells from which the new individual is formed. Some of these genes are throwbacks to remote ancestors. You cannot inherit or transmit acquired characteristics—those attained during your life.

The most obvious thing inherited through the germ cells is color of skin, eyes, and hair. Next comes body build, in its broadest sense—that is, body size and arrangement and structure of specific parts of the body. The shape and size of the eyeball is such a structure, for example, so that a tendency to nearsightedness can be inherited (see EYE TROUBLE). The composition of the blood is also inherited. Sex-linked defects of bodily function, such as color blindness, bleeder's disease, and baldness in the male, are obviously inherited. What else it is hard to be sure.

Hermaphrodite—"half man, half woman." True hermaphrodites, having the *sex organs* of both male and female, are very rare; pseudohermaphrodites are much more common. Pseudohermaphrodites are individuals of doubtful or obscure sex. Their sex organs are so imperfectly or incompletely developed that it is difficult to decide which sex nature intended them to be. This decision is properly made early in infancy. The child should be brought up one way or the other, boy *or* girl.

Occasionally a bad guess is made, and the male organs develop more extensively in an individual brought up as a girl (or vice versa). These people often become transvestites, delighting abnormally in wearing the clothes and adopting the mannerisms of the sex opposite that in which they were brought up.

For some pseudohermaphrodites a decision must be made in adult life to change their life pattern from male to female, or vice versa. This decision is often accompanied by a desire for plastic surgery to remove the vestiges of the sex they are leaving and give them the outward appearance of the sex they are entering. It is possible, for example, for a surgeon to construct an artificial vagina.

These people have not really changed sex, for they were neither one sex nor the other to begin with. Since their sex apparatus was and is imperfectly developed, hermaphrodites cannot bear or sire children. Rare exceptions among pseudohermaphrodites may occur.

Hernia—the protrusion of a loop or part of some internal organ of the body through an abnormal hole or slit. There are many kinds of hernias. Most common, however, is the *inguinal hernia* (see RUPTURE), in which a loop of bowel protrudes into the scrotum. Hernia usually results from weakness or absence of muscles, ligaments, and other connective tissues that should hold organs in place. A rare but well-publicized form of hernia is the protrusion of the stomach and other parts of the upper abdomen into the lungs through a hole or weak spot in the *diaphragm* muscle, which separates the chest cavity from the abdominal cavity. Technically known as a *diaphragmatic hernia*, it is popularly called *"upside-down stomach."* Usually found in young infants, it can be relieved by not-too-difficult surgery.

Heroin—a NARCOTIC drug.

Herpes—a VIRUS INFECTION in which blisters develop on the skin and the mucous membranes. *Herpes simplex* is the technical name for *cold sores* and *fever blisters*. These can occur anywhere, but the most common sites are the lips and external sex organs. The virus that causes them is probably present on or in the body most of the time, but does not get a chance to develop except when tissues have been weakened by high body temperatures (fever) or other irritations, such as cold weather, too much exposure to sunlight, or constant rubbing of a particular spot of skin or mucous membrane.

Herpes simplex is a self-limited disease or condition; it disappears shortly with no treatment. Application of a camphorated ointment occasionally brings some relief. But the best treatment is contempt. Leave the cold sores and fever blisters alone and they will go away. Don't pick at them or overtreat them with lotions, ointments, salves, and dabs.

Herpes zoster (SHINGLES) is a more serious condition.

Heterosexual—love directed to the *opposite* sex; the normal love of man for woman, and vice versa. Compare with HOMOSEXUAL.

Hexylresorcinol—a drug used as a topical antiseptic on the skin, a urinary antiseptic and as a vermifuge (to drive out worms, for which it is given in pill form). This drug can irritate the respiratory system.

Hiccup (Hiccough)—is caused by anything that disturbs the nerves that go to the DIA-PHRAGM, the large circular muscle that separates the chest from the abdomen and works the lungs up and down in the normal process of breathing. In hiccups this muscle contracts suddenly and irregularly instead of gradually and in rhythm. At the same time the normally silent opening and closing of the windpipe becomes irregular; after a half-drawn breath, the windpipe may close suddenly, which is what gives the characteristic noise of a hiccup.

The diaphragm's nerves can be irritated by a number of things; notably, an overloaded stomach pushing up on the diaphragm or simple indigestion. Other possibilities are disturbances of the breathing center in the brain (as may occur in UREMIA and typhoid fever); actual irritation or inflammation of the phrenic nerves (which is usually what happens in unusual cases of hiccups prolonged for days or weeks); and worry, anxiety, and emotional shock, which provoke psychosomatic reaction. Prolonged hiccups can be exhausting and may require medical or even surgical attention.

To get rid of hiccups before calling a doctor, the following simple maneuvers may be tried:

1. Hold your breath as long as you can.

2. Slowly sip one or more glasses of cold water.

3. Gargle with plain water, hot or cold, for at least a minute.

4. Pull on your tongue.

5. Sneeze once or twice. Tickle your nose with a feath-er to make yourself sneeze.

6. Breath into a paper or plastic bag for at least 2 minutes. The purpose of this is to rebreathe the carbon-dioxide gas your lungs normally exhale. This stimulates the breathing center in the brain.

HIGH BLOOD PRESSURE

High blood pressure, hypertension, is consistent elevation of the pressure of blood pulsing against the walls of the arteries and other blood vessels. High blood pressure may be diagnosed when, after repeated examinations, the blood-pressure measurements continue to stand above the normal range. See BLOOD PRESSURE.

High blood pressure is a serious condition insofar as it is the underlying factor that brings about other *cardiovascularenal* disorders, such as STROKE, HEART DISEASE, KIDNEY TROUBLE, and HARDENING OF THE ARTERIES.

Nevertheless, much of the fear created by a diagnosis of high blood pressure is groundless. The understanding, management, and treatment of this condition has progressed greatly in recent years; new drugs have proved highly effective in controlling hypertension. Furthermore, the disability associated with hypertension often arises from sheer fright of it. Finally, the condition may exist without producing either mild or serious symptoms. Complacency about high blood pressure is not warranted, but neither is undue anxiety. The wise course of action is to remain under the management of a competent physician and to slow down a too strenuous or exhausting way of life.

Who gets high blood pressure? Millions of people in the U.S. It is estimated that 1 in every 20 adults (about 6,000,000 people) in the U.S. actually has hypertension. Perhaps another 9,000,000 are in an early stage of it. Three quarters of these pre-hypertensives will progress to hypertension unless properly managed, and sometimes in spite of treatment. No age is exempt; high blood pressure is sometimes seen even in babies. The average age at onset is the early thirties. Aging does not cause hypertension.

Heredity appears to be a factor. The disease runs in some families, though not always with equal severity. Certain types of individuals seem more likely to acquire it, and this again may reflect heredity. Essential hypertension appears more commonly among short, stocky, overweight people and among those who are emotionally tense, easily excited, and highly irritable. The nervous, emotional, or psychic factors, mediated by the endocrine glands, are exceedingly important. It is common knowledge that evident fear, anger, excitement, or other strong emotions can temporarily shoot the blood pressure up. Hidden emotional conflicts have the same effect, and are more serious because they persist longer.

What causes high blood pressure? Although the hereditary, emotional, and endocrine factors already mentioned play a part in causing high blood pressure, many other factors may be concerned, and no one has the final answer. Chemical substances manufactured in various body organs may raise blood pressure. In particular, a substance elaborated by the kidneys (angiotonin) has this effect. The adrenal and other endocrine glands also liberate substances concerned in the mechanism of hypertension. When we speak of *essential hypertension,* the commonest form of high blood pressure, we are speaking of a condition whose essential or critical cause is still unknown. *Malignant hypertension* is a rapidly progressing form of essential hypertension.

High blood pressure is also secondary to a number of other diseases, for example, kidney infections. A count of 63 such diseases has been made. When the underlying disease is cured, the high blood pressure usually disappears.

In general, anything that constricts the arteries and arterioles (little arteries) brings about an increase in blood pressure. This is the same mechanical effect that can be observed in a garden hose. When you screw down the nozzle, you increase the water pressure in the hose.

What are the results of high blood pressure? High blood pressure affects first the heart and blood vessels and then, indirectly, other organs. The heart must work harder to pump blood through the narrowed vessels. To maintain blood flow, the heart muscle must grow larger and stronger. At first the enlarged heart may be very efficient, but as the muscle fibers of the heart continue to stretch, the time comes when its own coronary arteries can no longer nourish it adequately and *heart disease* develops.

Hardening of the arteries (arteriosclerosis) is perhaps the chief danger of continuing hypertension. The damage to the arteries depends on how high the blood pressure is, how long the high blood pressure lasts, and, most important, whether the blood vessels can stand the strain of the increased pressure. Some people's arteries withstand high blood pressure for years without noticeable effects.

The brain and kidneys are the organs most endangered by high blood pressure and hardened arteries. Rupture or closure of a small artery in the brain may produce a *stroke*. Damage to the arterioles of the kidneys throws the filtering mechanism of the kidneys out of order and results in the accumulation of body wastes in the blood stream, causing *uremia*. A vicious cycle can be set up here; for the internal blood flow in the kidneys has an effect on blood pressure in the rest of the body.

HEADACHE, so-called hypertensive headache, is the commonest and most disabling symptom of high blood pressure. These headaches can usually be controlled by proper treatment. Not all headaches, obviously, indicate hypertension. Other possible symptoms of high blood pressure are dizziness or light-headedness, vertigo, easy fatigue, and frequent blushing accompanied by rumbling of the bowels, palpitation of the heart, and sweating.

What can be done about high blood pressure? The physician today can do a great deal more for the person with high blood pressure than he formerly could. But the patient must do something for himself: evolve an attitude or philosophy of life keynoted by moderation and tranquility. Adequate rest and relaxation are essential. Sleeping for as long as 10 hours a night is an excellent habit; blood pressure is at its lowest during sleep. Mild exercise, without competition or fatigue, is desirable. A well-balanced diet, low enough in calories to avoid overweight, is indicated. In some cases a reduced-salt or salt-free diet may be prescribed with good effect. (The "rice diet" is a low-calorie, salt-free diet.) The use of coffee, tea, liquor, and tobacco may usually be continued in moderation, so long as they do not provoke symptoms.

Patients whose high blood pressure is definitely traced to a diseased kidney may have this kidney surgically removed. In selected cases a nerve-cutting operation (sympathectomy or removal of a portion of the sympathetic nerve chains near the spinal cord) may be warranted. This operation, while reducing blood pressure for longer or shorter periods, has certain annoying side-effects that for many people make it an unwarranted gamble.

The great recent advances in the control of hypertension are in the new drugs that lower blood pressure without causing dangerous side-effects. Among these drugs are hexamethonium, 1-hydrazinophthalazine (Apresoline), chlorpromazine (Thorazine), and rauwolfia serpentina. Rauwolfia, or Indian snakeroot, was an herb medicine used in India for many years before its active and important ingredients were recently isolated and identified by Western chemists. This class of drugs is known as TRAN-QUILIZERS.

Hip—see JOINTS and FRACTURES.

Hippocratic Oath—see page 259.

Histamine—a complex chemical substance (beta-imidazolylethyl-amine) occurring in all animal and vegetable tissues. Sometimes the human body becomes oversensitive to the quantity of histamine it contains, and the result may be some form of *allergy* or a typical, one-sided *histamine headache.* Histamine powerfully stimulates stomach secretions and the muscles of the uterus. It also dilates the *capillaries.* The effect of histamine can be counteracted by the enzyme *histaminase* and by antihistaminic drugs.

Histology—the study of minute anatomy; the observation, through a microscope, of normal and diseased CELLS and tissues. The histologist is closely related to the PATHOLOGIST.

Histoplasmosis—a systemic fungus infection, sometimes misdiagnosed as tuberculosis.

Hives, or *urticaria,* often come as a shock to those who get them for the first time. They look and feel more dangerous than they are, especially "giant hives," which may be 2 to 3 inches in diameter. Along with hives usually comes ITCHING, sometimes intense.

Small or ordinary hives look something like mosquito bites, except that there are lots of them in one small area. They are white, pink, or red wheals that may appear anywhere on the body surface. The only place that they can be dangerous is in the mouth or throat, where they may seriously interfere with breathing *(angioneurotic edema).* Hives are an AL-LERGY that comes out on the SKIN. So are some skin RASHES.

What causes hives? Hives are brought about by the passage of fluid into the skin, causing a kind of uneven swelling of the skin. The fluid collects in the *lower* layers of the skin instead of the upper layers, as it does in a vesicle or blister.

Even an acute case of hives may last for only 2 or 3 hours, then disappear without leaving a trace. New crops of hives may reappear at intervals for several days. Chronic hives may persist for several months.

The cause of hives is usually something the person has eaten —chocolate, sea food, green apples, strawberries, or any other food to which he is especially sensitive (allergic). Sometimes hives follow injections of drugs,

THE HIPPOCRATIC OATH[*]

 SWEAR by Apollo Physician and Aesculapius and Hygeia and Panacea and all the gods and goddesses, making them my witnesses, that I will fulfill according to my ability and judgment this oath and covenant:

TO HOLD HIM WHO HAS TAUGHT me this art as equal to my parents and to live my life in partnership with him, and if he is in need of money to give him a share of mine, and to regard his offspring as equal to my brothers in male lineage and to teach them this art—if they desire to learn it—without fee and covenant; to give a share of precepts and oral instruction and all the other learning to my sons and to the sons of him who has instructed me and to pupils who have signed the covenant and who have taken an oath according to the medical law, but to no one else.

I will apply dietetic measures for the benefit of the sick according to my ability and judgment; I will keep them from harm and injustice.

I will neither give a deadly drug to anybody if asked for it, nor will I make a suggestion to this effect. Similarly I will not give to a woman an abortive remedy. In purity and holiness I will guard my life and my art.

I will not use the knife, not even on sufferers from stone, but will withdraw in favor of such men as are [skilled] in this work.

Whatever houses I may visit, I will come for the benefit of the sick, remaining free of all intentional injustice, of all mischief and in particular of sexual relations with both male and female persons, be they free or slaves.

What I may see or hear in the course of treatment or even outside of the treatment in regard to the life of men, which on no account ought to be spread abroad, I will keep to myself, holding such things shameful to be spoken about.

If I fulfill this oath and do not violate it, may it be granted to me to enjoy life and art, being honored with fame among all men for all time to come; if I transgress it and swear falsely, may the opposite of all this be my lot.

* Translation by Ludwig Edelstein, published in Supplement 1, 1943, to the Bulletin of the History of Medicine, Johns Hopkins Press.

medicine, serums. Some people are so sensitive to light, cold, and heat that they break out in hives after undue exposure. Emotional tension may also show up as hives. (See MENTAL ILLNESS; NEUROSES.) The way to stop hives is to avoid the foods, drugs, and people to whom you are allergic. This, however, is not always easy to find out.

Treatment of hives, once their cause is known, is not too difficult. Most cases respond promptly to ANTIHISTAMINE drugs, given by mouth. Antihistamine ointments applied to the skin are often helpful in relieving itching. One dose of a good saline cathartic (e.g. epsom salts) often cleans out the food substances causing the skin reaction.

Hoarseness—the result of inflammation or swelling of the vocal cords, most often due to local infection (laryngitis) or irritation (overuse of the voice or too much smoking), but sometimes to general or systemic infections like TUBERCULOSIS and SYPHILIS, and occasionally to cancer of the larynx. This is a highly curable form of cancer if caught early. Hence any persistent hoarseness, lasting 2 weeks or longer, is a signal for a careful medical examination, including a good look down the throat with a laryngoscope. Singers sometimes develop nodules on their vocal cords, with resultant hoarseness. The treatment for or-dinary hoarseness from overusing the voice usually includes hot gargles (5 minutes every hour) or other application of heat to the throat and a day or so of obedience to a vow of silence.

Hodgkin's Disease, named after the English physician who first described it, in 1852, causes swelling of the LYMPH glands in many parts of the body. The cause is unknown. The only way it can be positively diagnosed is by removing bits of lymph-gland tissue and examining them under a microscope.

The swelling in the lymph glands of the neck is usually the first to be noticed, and the swelling (hyperplasia) persists. The disease usually brings anemia in its train, and the patient gets weaker and weaker. Since the disease is malignant, death eventually ensues, in an average of 2 or 3 years. However, patients have survived as long as 15 years after diagnosis.

Surgery is of no help. The best available treatment is irradiation with deep X RAY, RADIUM, or radioactive isotopes. Nitrogen mustard sometimes gives temporary relief. Other treatments include arsenic, iron, liver extracts, and whole-blood transfusions.

Homeopathy—a system of medical practice, now obsolete, based on the theory that "like cures like." It was founded in the late 18th century by Samuel Hahnemann. The theory is that disease conditions can be cured by giving the patient *very small amounts* of drugs that produce, in healthy people, symptoms like the symptoms found in the disease under treatment.

Homosexual describes love for one of the *same* sex; man for man, woman for woman. Female homosexuality is called Lesbianism. In one stage of the psychosexual development of children, homosexual love is both normal and natural. As a result some homosexual *feelings* persist in many perfectly normal individuals. The occasional homosexual *feeling* should not be confused with adult homosexual *practice*. No one need be afraid that he is "becoming a homo" because he sometimes feels strongly attracted toward a member of his own sex or because he has the capacity to enter into genuine friendships with his own sex. Such feelings are in a sense throwbacks to normal childhood reactions. But the almost complete substitution of homosexual feelings and practices for HETEROSEXUAL

love is a serious derangement that may verge on, if it has not already reached, MENTAL ILLNESS. The treatment is PSYCHOTHERAPY, possibly with the help of ENDOCRINE therapy. It is never "smart" to be homosexual; it is a social affliction with which some people must forever struggle. A few try to make the best of their affliction by calling it normal, but this is just another version of the old fable about the fox without a tail. The attempt to seduce others, especially the young, into homosexual practice is criminal. It is common for homosexuals to feel and practice heterosexual love as well.

Hookworm—infestation and illness caused by the intestinal parasite, or hookworm (*Necator americanus,* for example). See WORMS.

Hordeolum—stye. See EYE TROUBLE.

Hormones—chemical substances secreted by the ENDOCRINE GLANDS, exerting influence over practically all body activities.

HOSPITALS

Hospitals of one sort or another have been in existence since antiquity; the ancient Greeks had pleasant "temples of healing." The modern hospital is at one and the same time a doctor's—particularly the surgeon's—workshop, a center for convalescence and rehabilitation, a school for doctors and nurses, and a hotel. Except for some emergencies and some minor office surgery, practically all SURGERY is performed in hospitals. CHILDBIRTH too has left home for the hospital. Over 3 million babies a year are now born in American hospitals.

Modern hospitals enjoy a good reputation, reflecting the profound advances in medicine and surgery of the 20th century. Patients nowadays go to the hospital almost willingly, knowing that they will return home relieved of pain and illness. Yet half a century ago many people looked upon the hospital as a charnel house—a place to go to die. The principal public complaint against hospitals today is their ever-increasing costs and charges. These, however, reflect increased services and higher labor costs. About 60% of a hospital's operating budget goes toward paying wages—of nurses, cooks, maintenance men, and scores of other necessary employees whom patients never see.

Hospitals also have "house officers"—physicians known as residents or interns—who are not strictly hospital "employees." They are generally students and assistants to the doctors who make up the medical staff of the institution.

There are approximately 7,000 hospitals in the United States, ranging in size from a few beds behind a doctor's office in a small town up to 3,500-bed metropolitan county hospitals. Half of the hospitals are voluntary, nonprofit hospitals; but nearly half of the total bed capacity of about 1,600,000 beds in American hospitals is in state hospitals, ministering to the mentally ill and other patients with long-term, chronic illnesses, notably tuberculosis. The value or reported assets of America's hospitals are about $12 billion, making hospitals the country's largest fixed asset in health resources.

You cannot check into a hospital as you would into a hotel. You must be admitted (except in emergencies) on the order of a physician. Your doctor sends you to the hospital—with your permission, of course, unless you are unable to give it.

When you go to the hospital. Your doctor also arranges with the hospital for you to be admitted when he thinks it necessary. When you enter the hospital, unless you are too ill or disturbed to manage it for yourself, you will be directed to the admitting office. There the admitting officer will make arrangements with you for your hospital stay. Then a nurse or other aide will take you in charge, bring you and your bag of belongings to the bed you will occupy, and help you get settled. Thereafter, until you are discharged, you will be served by the hospital personnel—and your own doctor, of course, who will come to see you. But you will have to abide by hospital rules.

If some things seem strange to you in the hospital, remember that it is a complex institution dedicated to following doctors' orders. The routines will undoubtedly be different from those you follow in your own home. There is nothing to be afraid of, however, in these arrangements. They are part of the process that guarantees your safety and organizes the forces directed to your recovery. You will soon become accustomed to the routine.

When you pack your bag—and make it a small one—to go to the hospital, these are the few things that you will need to include: pajamas or nightgown, slippers and bathrobe, comb and brush, toothbrush and tooth paste, shaving kit or cosmetic bag, pen, pencil, stationery and stamps, and whatever small personal items you may need to make yourself comfortable.

Do not bring jewelry or other valuables. Such items will have to be checked in for safeguarding at the admitting office. An inexpensive watch or other timepiece and just a few dollars in cash will suffice at your bedside.

However, it is important to make arrangements for paying for hospital care in advance. You should bring a checkbook with you, or sufficient money to make an advance payment on your hospital stay. This will not be necessary if you bring, as of course you should, a BLUE CROSS or other recognized hospital insurance identification card.

Humpback or Hunchback—see CURVATURE OF THE SPINE and BONE DISEASES.

Huntington's Chorea—a disease of the *nervous system*, quite definitely *hereditary*. Oddly, it does not usually show up until middle life, when slowly but inexorably it damages the nervous system. The result is twitching muscles, a drunken gait, speech disturbances, and loss of mind. Patients usually live about 15 or 16 years after the disease is diagnosed; early diagnosis usually requires the help of a specialist in nervous diseases. An estimated 25,000 persons a year are stricken with this disease. People in families in which this disease persists should be wary about having children.

Hydrocele—a limited accumulation of fluid in the scrotal sac, causing it to swell. (See SEX ORGANS, MALE.) A hydrocele is sometimes mistaken for a hernia or RUPTURE, and diagnosis may be difficult. A hydrocele is nothing to worry about. In infants and children it usually goes away; in adults it can be treated by the simple operation of removing the accumulated fluid through a hollow needle. Hydroceles sometimes disappear and return. A hernia usually changes size upon changes in body position; a hydrocele stays about the same size.

Hydrocephalus—water on the BRAIN. See BRAIN DAMAGE.

Hydrochloric Acid—a normal part of the stomach juices to the amount of about 2 parts per 1,000. In large and concentrated amounts it is a corrosive poison.

Hydrogen—the lightest chemical element; found in water (H_2O), carbohydrates, and all organic substances. Pure hydrogen is a colorless, odorless, tasteless, inflammable gas. *Hydrogen peroxide* (H_2O_2) is used as a disinfectant, skin antiseptic, and HAIR bleach.

Hydronephrosis—a chronic disease with excess accumulation of water in the kidney. It is usually caused by a blockage of the ureter leading from the kidney. In early stages it may be possible to unblock the ureter, but in later stages removal of the kidney may be necessary. See KIDNEY TROUBLE; URINARY SYSTEM.

Hydrophobia—literally means fear of water. It is the common name for the VIRUS disease RABIES as it appears in human beings.

Hydrotherapy—any treatment with water; usually hot and cold baths (balneotherapy), alternate hot-and-cold needle showers (Scotch douche), wet packs, underwater exercise (as in a Hubbard Tank).

Hymen—MAIDENHEAD.

Hyoid—U-shaped bone at the root of the tongue.

Hyper—a prefix meaning too much, above normal.

Hyperacidity—too much acid; sometimes used to describe the condition of ACID STOMACH.

Hyperchlorhydria—too much hydrochloric acid in the stomach. See STOMACH TROUBLE.

Hyperemia—an excess amount of blood in any part of the body. Blushing is an example of temporary hyperemia of the skin of the face.

Hyperesthesia—exceeding sensitivity; particularly, the abnormally exquisite sensitivity of the SKIN to touch.

Hyperglycemia — concentration of SUGAR in the blood above normal limits. See DIABETES.

Hyperinsulinism—either (1) INSULIN shock from too much insulin administered in the course of treating DIABETES; or (2) too much insulin secreted by the PANCREAS.

Hyperopia—farsightedness. See EYE TROUBLE.

Hyperplasia—excess growth of CELLS. See HYPERTROPHY.

Hyperpyrexia—high FEVER.

Hypertension—HIGH BLOOD PRESSURE.

Hyperthyroidism — overactivity of the thyroid (ENDOCRINE) gland. It is associated with the enlargement in the neck called goiter. See HYPERTROPHY.

Hypertrophy—enlargement of a bodily organ because its constituent cells are getting bigger than they should be. In *hyperplasia* the organ enlarges because there is an abnormal increase in the number of cells present. *Goiter* is one example of enlargement of a gland (the thyroid gland in the neck) because of either hyperplasia or hypertrophy or both. In either case there is an increase in the amount of thyroid tissue and an increase in the amount of thyroxin, the thyroid hormone, secreted. This condition is called hyperthyroidism.

Hypnotic—anything that induces SLEEP, or that produces the effects ascribed to HYPNOTISM. There is a large class of drugs called hypnotics, including BARBITURATES, NARCOTICS, and ANESTHETICS, such as CHLOROFORM and ETHER.

HYPNOTISM

Hypnotism is the process of putting a person into a trance, or partially asleep. In this state of artificially induced hypnosis or partial sleep, the subject may feel no pain, speak out things he would not otherwise say, and take suggestions that he would not otherwise follow—without realizing that he is following somebody else's suggestions and not his own directions.

Hypnotism is an ancient form of medical treatment. It was used by the priests of Aesculapius in ancient Greece to produce what was called "temple sleep." It was studied in the 17th century by Athanasius Kircher; it was employed in the 18th century by Anton Mesmer (and got the name of *mesmerism*); it was investigated in the 19th century by Charcot and Freud, who found it a springboard to psychoanalysis; it has been both damned and praised in the 20th century, sometimes being considered a valuable and respectable adjunct to medical practice and sometimes not.

In the hands of a qualified specialist, hypnotism can be a valuable tool of PSYCHOTHERAPY; it is useful in treating certain neuroses and it can be used to produce partial ANESTHESIA. (It has even been used to achieve painless childbirth.)

Hypnotism cures nothing. It is useful only for temporary relief of some symptoms.

Should I allow myself to be hypnotized? Never, except by a qualified PSYCHIATRIST. Not everyone can be hypnotized. Women are more easily hypnotized than men. The more often a person has been hypnotized, generally speaking, the easier it is. The willingness of a person to be hypnotized and his strained attention to the process may make it easier for him to be put in a hypnotic trance, sometimes in a few seconds; but it is not absolutely essential to the process.

Being hypnotized is like falling asleep in some parts of the brain instead of sinking gradually into a state of natural sleep involving all parts of the brain. The full mechanism of hypnotism is not understood.

The hypnotic state is usually induced by asking the subject to concentrate on a bright object before his eyes, thus putting a fatigue-inducing strain on the muscles of the eyes and the eyelids. The relaxation of the eye muscles is usually the final stage of muscular relaxation before falling naturally to sleep.

Hypnotism can be dangerous and harmful when practiced by amateurs and unscrupulous quacks. The story of Trilby and her Svengali is a classical example. Since hypnotism sometimes achieves apparent cures with astonishing speed, quacks in fancy treatment are having a field day with it. Many people are subjected to hypnotism under a different name with some pseudoscientific or pseudoreligious mumbo-jumbo attached to it.

"Hypo"—a *hypodermic* syringe for giving an injection under the skin (usually an injection of morphine or other NARCOTIC to kill pain; see "SHOTS"). The word is also used as an abbreviation for HYPOCHONDRIAC. As a prefix to medical words, it usually signifies too little, not enough, underneath, or below normal.

Hypochondriac—a person who *enjoys* poor health. He hugs his symptoms. He embraces every opportunity to complain about his poor health. He sees invalidism in every ache; doom in every scratch; a heart attack in every missed beat of his heart; self-poisoning if his bowels don't move on schedule; germs, germs everywhere. A hypochondriac is overanxious about his health. He has catapulted a virtue—reasonable concern about and attention to health—into a vice, hypochondria. Prolonged hypochondria is a NEUROSIS, often a most difficult type of MENTAL ILLNESS to treat. The confirmed hypochondriac doesn't want to feel well, though he may be perfectly well in that demonstrable organic ailments cannot be found or demonstrated. Hypochondriacs often travel from doctor to doctor, seeking new diagnoses and treatments, and believing none.

Further knowledge about the nature, cause, and cure of disease, such as we have set forth in this book, will not make a hypochondriac of anyone who was not so inclined before. But the mere acquisition of scientific information will not cure hypochondria, either. If a hypochondriac finally becomes convinced that he hasn't got one disease, he will soon find another, with a new set of vague symptoms, to cling to. The treatment of hypochondria is adequate PSYCHOTHERAPY.

Hypodermic—under the skin; the same as *subcutaneous*. It commonly refers to a hypodermic needle, fitted to a syringe, for making an injection ("SHOT") under the skin. See "HYPO."

Hypoglycemia—too little SUGAR in the blood; sometimes associated with FATIGUE. See also HYPERINSULINISM.

Hypophysis—the pituitary (ENDOCRINE) gland.

Hypospadias—a *congenital malformation*, existing from birth, in the URINARY SYSTEM. In the male with hypospadias, urine is discharged from an opening on the under side of the penis rather than at the tip, as normally. In the female, hypospadias brings about abnormal discharge of urine into the vagina. Hypospadias can usually be corrected by surgery.

Hypotension—low BLOOD PRESSURE.

Hypothyroidism — underactivity of the thyroid (ENDOCRINE) gland. It causes myxedema.

Hysterectomy—surgical removal of the uterus. It is performed either through the abdomen or through the vagina. *Panhysterectomy* is an even more complete operation.

Hysteria—one of many forms of MENTAL ILLNESS, usually classified as a NEUROSIS. What most people call hysteria, however—shouting, gesticulating, wild weeping, and other behavior that suggests a child's temper tantrum in an adult body—is more properly described as MANIA. The word hysteria comes from the Greek word for womb; but men are just as subject to hysteria, if not hysterics, as women.

Hysteria is the great mimic among diseases. The hysterical patient often converts his emotional conflicts into physical symptoms, *conversion hysteria*. He may believe he suffers from any combination of symptoms known to medicine. Hysterical blindness, deafness, paralysis, choking, convulsions, pains, and fever are not uncommon. Shell shock is a form of hysteria. Many so-called miracle cures are the result of relieving hysteria and not of curing an organic disease.

The treatment of hysteria lies in the wide range of PSYCHOTHERAPY. It is one of the few conditions in which suppressive psychotherapy (the opposite of psychoanalysis) is often successful. The old-fashioned ducking stool probably cured hysteria in many cases.

I

Any word printed in SMALL CAPITALS *can be looked up under its own alphabetical listing for further information.*

Iatrogenic—caused by the doctor. For example, iatrogenic heart disease has left people acting like cardiac invalids when they didn't have heart disease at all. The classic example of iatrogenic disease is childbed fever, a "private pestilence" that was conveyed to mothers by doctors in the 19th century. Ignaz Semmelweis and Oliver Wendell Holmes were persecuted by the medical profession for daring to say so.

Ichthyosis—a SKIN disorder; scaly skin; fish-skin disease.

Icterus—JAUNDICE.

Id—the prime mover of the UNCONSCIOUS MIND, out of which develop the EGO and the SUPEREGO. See PSYCHOANALYSIS.

Idiopathic—disease that originates "in itself." When a disease is called idiopathic, the doctor doesn't know what is causing it.

Idiosyncrasy—a special susceptibility to a particular drug or other foreign substance introduced into the body; a drug idiosyncrasy. It is like ALLERGY but not exactly the same. Some people, for example, cannot take aspirin without getting an unpleasant or serious side-reaction such as tissue swelling and a skin rash.

Idiot—the lowest classification of FEEBLE-MINDEDNESS.

Ileitis—inflammation of the lower part of the small bowel.

Ileum—the small bowel below the jejunum. See DIGESTIVE SYSTEM.

Ileus—bowel obstruction.

Iliac—pertaining to the ILIUM.

Ilium—the upper part of the innominate bone; the haunch or flank.

Illusion—a false impression of what is really seen, heard, felt, tasted, or smelled. Compare with DELUSION and HALLUCINATION.

Imbecile—a classification of FEEBLE-MINDEDNESS just above idiot.

Immobilize—to hold still, as a splint or plaster cast holds a broken bone.

IMMUNITY

Immunity is the inability to catch a particular disease. It is relative, not absolute—often high but never quite 100%. In many infectious diseases, particularly those of childhood, a previous attack of the disease confers a high degree of immunity. A person is unlikely to contract his childhood diseases a second time, but there is no guarantee that he will not. Many other infectious diseases confer scarcely any immunity or only a relatively low degree of immunity for a very short period. Notable among these are the VENEREAL DISEASES, the COMMON COLD, and MALARIA.

Immunity is one component of RESISTANCE to disease. It usually refers to resistance against specific MICROBES and the diseases they cause.

One of the great triumphs of modern medical science has been to provide *artificial*, or *induced, immunity* against a great number of diseases. A most notable recent triumph was the Salk vaccine for prevention of paralytic *polio*. This vaccine does not prevent people from being infected with any of the three known polio viruses, but it does keep the virus from getting into the nerve cells and causing paralysis. The first practical success in providing artificial immunity against a disease was vaccination against SMALLPOX, introduced in England by Edward Jenner in 1798.

Different kinds of immunity. Immunity is described as natural or acquired, and active or passive.

Natural immunity simply means that certain species of living creatures just cannot get certain types of infection; the microbes causing them can't or won't live in that species. Thus fish don't get measles, horses don't get polio, and human beings don't get hog cholera. This species-specific natural immunity has only one disadvantage. It is sometimes difficult or impossible for research scientists to find experimental animals on which they can try to acquire new knowledge about human diseases. For example, only the monkey, chimpanzee, and cotton rat can be infected with any human polio virus.

Acquired immunity can be obtained in several ways: (1) from a previous attack of disease, within the limitations already noted; (2) from one's mother, for about 6 months after birth; and (3) from deliberate artificial immunity, such as smallpox vaccination or polio shots.

The secret of immunity is this: Once exposed to an infecting agent in some form, alive or dead, certain body cells acquire experience enabling them to fight off any later invasions by this same microbe. These cells become sensitized—suspicious, alert—to even the smallest amounts of this microbe or its products (e.g. toxins) on subsequent visits. Under such a threat they immediately mobilize *antibodies* to fight off the invader. The blood-forming organs and the white blood cells (the so-called reticulo-endothelial system) are in the front line of this fight.

Antibodies are biological and chemical substances produced by the living organism in response to a threat by a particular microbial invader that has been in the body before. The specific threat that sets off antibody production is called its *antigen*. The chemical formulas and structure of antibodies are not exactly known, but their presence in the body and in the blood stream can be quite accurately measured by testing them against their antigens.

Antibodies are carried in the blood stream, in the blood serum (not blood cells), and particularly in that fraction of the blood called GAMMA GLOBULIN. A person whose blood is deficient in gamma globulin is likely to suffer from repeated infections. A mother's blood stream carries the antibodies of all the diseases to which she has already acquired relative immunity, and these antibodies are passed along to her newborn infant. Unfortunately, these maternal antibodies disappear in about 6 months, and the infant's body cells have to learn how to make antibodies for themselves. The infant gets "shots" to help them.

Passive immunity is the transfer of ready-made antibodies from one person (or animal) to another, such as the transfer of maternal antibodies to the infant. Direct injections of gamma globulin or human-blood serum can also confer passive immunity to some diseases. Passive immunization is sometimes indicated under special circumstances in treatment of patients exposed to diphtheria (antitoxin); lockjaw (tetanus antitoxin); whooping cough; measles, mumps, polio, and chickenpox (gamma globulin); botulism; and gas gangrene. Since antibodies delivered from the outside are used up quickly, passive immunity generally lasts a comparatively short time, from hours to months.

Active immunity results when body cells are stimulated to produce their own antibodies against specific antigens. Active immunity, if it occurs, is the kind of immunity produced by attacks of the disease. It can also be artificially induced by the application or injection of appropriate antigens (see "SHOTS"). Active immunity develops slowly (a week to a month or more), but lasts much longer than passive immunity. The time varies with different diseases, antibodies, and antigens. See IMMUNIZATION.

Active immunity can be reinforced later by giving *booster shots*, reinjections, of the original antigen.

Immunization—vaccination (the two words now mean practically the same thing); providing IMMUNITY against infectious diseases by injections or "SHOTS." Among the diseases for which immunization is now considered practical are:

Routinely, for infants and children:

SMALLPOX: Vaccination at 3 to 12 months, repeated every 3 to 7 years, or oftener if risk is great.

POLIO: Salk vaccine at 6 to 12 months; second injection 2 to 6 weeks after first injection; third injection 7 to 12 months later.

DIPHTHERIA: Toxoid at 6 to 9 months; possibly repeated in 12 months; definitely advisable again before entering school.

TETANUS *(lockjaw)*: Toxoid at 6 to 9 months; repeated a year later; possibly again following injury or wound in which contamination is likely.

WHOOPING COUGH: Inoculation at 3 to 6 months; repeated annually through 5 years of age if fullest protection is desired.

For adults or children, at any age, if exposed to great risk:

CHOLERA, PLAGUE, TYPHUS FEVER (repeat shots in 6 months).

TYPHOID and PARATYPHOID FEVER, *Rocky Mountain spotted fever, pneumococcal infections,* INFLUENZA (repeat immunization in 12 months).

YELLOW FEVER: Vaccine provides suitable immunity for about 4 years.

RABIES: Vaccine should be given to anyone bitten by an animal known or strongly suspected to have rabies.

Impacted usually refers to firmly wedged-in bone splinters following a fracture, or to teeth (mostly wisdom teeth) so firmly embedded in the jawbone that they do not erupt above the gumline normally.

Impetigo—a SKIN disorder. It is a rapidly spreading, highly contagious infection that attacks principally newborn babies and young children. Red spots, which turn into pustules and blisters, appear on the face and neck and in the folds of the body. Touching the blisters usually spreads the infection. Fortunately, impetigo can be quickly brought under control —often in two days—by any of a number of ANTIBIOTIC drugs, given by mouth or by injection.

Impotence—inability of the male to have an erection of the penis so that he can have sexual intercourse. Occasionally this is the result of nerve injuries, but it is far more commonly a deep-seated psychic problem requiring psychiatric help. Impotence should not be confused with infertility, or STERILITY. A man capable of sexual intercourse may still be sterile; that is, unable to deliver viable SPERM. Impotence is usually associated with loss of LIBIDO.

Incision—the cut made on the skin by the surgeon in performing a surgical operation. It is also the line of the scar left by the surgical wound. A surgeon makes his incision where it will show least, provided that it will permit him to perform the surgery most effectively.

Incompatible—don't mix; said of drugs, treatments, and marriage partners.

Incontinence—inability to hold back urine (dribbling) or bowel movements.

Incubation Period—the time between contact with a source of infection and outbreak of recognizable symptoms of a specific infectious disease. During this time the infecting microbe is getting a foothold and multiplying in the host (body). The length of time varies greatly with different diseases and different infecting microbes. In polio, for example, the incubation period is from 4 days to 3 weeks; in scarlet fever, usually 2 to 5 days.

Indication has a special meaning in medicine; namely, that of a sign which points toward a specific line of treatment or toward the particular cause of a disease. See CONTRAINDICATION, the opposite of indication.

Indigestion—a mild pain in the stomach (dyspepsia); a vague feeling of distress in the abdomen. It is a symptom, not a disease. See STOMACH, STOMACH ACHE, and STOMACH TROUBLE. An occasional bout of mild indigestion following overeating, drinking too much, or emotional disturbance is not serious and may be treated by rest, 1 dose of a mild laxative, 1 or 2 doses of sodium bicarbonate, and a bland diet (tea and toast, gelatin, etc.) for a day or two.

Severe indigestion, that is, serious abdominal pain, or *repeated* indigestion demands prompt medical examination. Acute indigestion is often not indigestion at all. It may be a heart attack. Persistent indigestion may be a food allergy—or worse. Never take a laxative in the presence of severe abdominal pain!

Induration—a hard or hardened spot or area of tissue normally soft.

Inebriation—drunkenness. See ALCOHOLISM.

Infant: For care of infants and children, the reader is respectfully referred to Dr. Benjamin Spock's excellent *Baby and Child Care*. In the book you now have in your hand, diseases of childhood are arranged alphabetically by disease; for example, CHICKEN POX, DIPHTHERIA, MEASLES. Principles of feeding both adults and children are covered in such headings as DIET, DIGESTIVE SYSTEM,

MINERALS, VITAMINS. Behavior problems are reflected in entries dealing with psychological and psychiatric problems; for example, MASTURBATION, MENTAL ILLNESS, PSYCHOANALYSIS. Preparation for motherhood (and fatherhood) is treated in such entries as MENSTRUATION, PREGNANCY, SEX ORGANS, MALE and FEMALE, and STERILITY.

Infantile—childish; undeveloped, as an infantile uterus.

Infantile Paralysis—see POLIO.

Infarct—an area of dead or damaged tissue resulting from failure of blood to reach the part. Something has blocked the blood flow. Infarcts are commonly found in the heart muscle following HEART attacks.

Infection—the entry, presence, and multiplication of disease-producing MICROBES (germs, pathogenic microörganisms) in the human, animal, fish, bird, or insect body. Signs and symptoms of infection in the human being run the whole gamut of ailment and discomfort, but they are most commonly inflammation, redness, and swelling of tissues (and individual CELLS) at the sites where the germ is present and multiplying. Any part of the body may become infected, even the blood stream.

The microbes that cause human infections come from somewhere, and they can be transmitted by contact with human excretions (URINE, FECES, pus, and sputum or nasal mu-

cus in droplets); by contaminated water, food, and air; and by insect and animal carriers. For modes of transmission of specific infectious diseases, see the heading of the particular disease.

It takes much more than the disease-producing microbes to cause disease. The conditions within the body, which is the host to the microbes, must be such that they can flourish. A great deal remains unknown as to why resistance to infection occurs at one time and susceptibility at another time. But it is known that infection is more likely to produce recognizable disease at a time when the body has been subjected to unusual stress, physical or psychic, and is deprived of vital substances; for example, vitamins.

Unrecognized, subclinical attacks of disease are very common. In POLIOMYELITIS, for example, the number of unrecognized infections runs several hundred times the number of cases of paralytic or nonparalytic polio actually diagnosed.

We know also that the disease germs that cause the common cold or "strep throat" are present in the mouth most of the time. But we do not know exactly the conditions or circumstances under which they flourish and cause evident disease.

See RESISTANCE.

Infertility—see STERILITY.

Inflammation—the reaction of body tissue to injury, whether

by INFECTION or TRAUMA (violence). The inflamed area is
red, swollen, hot, and usually
painful. Body defenses are mo-
bilized and localized in inflamed areas. More blood than

usual, carrying both red and
white blood cells, collects there.
There are changes in the walls
of the small blood vessels and
more fluid than usual (exudate)
escapes into the inflamed tissue.

INFLUENZA

Influenza is also known as flu or grippe—a virus disease that may
attack the respiratory, nervous, or gastrointestinal system ("stomach flu"). Rarely fatal itself, it often opens the door to PNEUMONIA,
eye and ear infections, and brain inflammations that do threaten
life.

Influenza usually occurs in epidemic form, many people in a
community being struck at the same time. The epidemic generally
reaches its peak in 2 to 3 weeks, then subsides in another month
or two. A devastating world-wide epidemic (pandemic) of influenza occurred in the summer and fall of 1918, killing somewhere
between 6 and 10 million people, including a half million in the
United States. No such widely fatal epidemic has since occurred.

Two types of influenza virus, A and B, have been identified. Attempts to produce a vaccine against the disease have not been too
successful, partly because the virus seems to change character between epidemics. The virus is spread by droplet infection, being
sneezed, coughed, and talked out of the mouths, throats, lungs,
and noses of people whom it infects. The influenza virus is around
most of the time, harbored by many human beings. They fall ill
when their resistance is lowered. Epidemics begin when circumstances for the spread of the virus are favorable.

What are the symptoms of influenza? Influenza usually comes on
suddenly, after an incubation period of 12 to 72 hours. The victim
usually feels quite sick and uncomfortable, unwilling to work, unable to play. The early symptoms may be much like those of a
common cold, except that the running nose is less common and
the feeling of weakness much greater. Other common complaints
are headache, fatigue, drowsiness, general aches and pains, and
chills and fever (usually not too high). A dry cough and painful
eyes may also be present.

The course of the disease may run from 2 days to many weeks,
and weakness persists for some time thereafter. Relapses often
occur, and the patient is "softened up" for complicating infections.

How is influenza treated? The antibiotic and sulfa drugs that work against so many bacteria have no effect on the influenza virus. They may be given to control or ward off secondary invaders, especially the pneumococcus germ that causes pneumonia. The basic treatment for influenza is rest in bed, for as long as necessary to regain strength and avoid complications. The worst way to treat influenza is to fight it on your feet. Symptomatic treatment, which is still the best that can be offered to influenza victims, may also include aspirin, cough-control medicines, and sleeping pills.

Infra-red—the range of electromagnetic waves beyond red in the visible spectrum of light. Infra-red rays provide intense heat and provide heat treatment in the form of infra-red lamps and bulbs. These are an excellent source of dry heat; but precaution must always be taken that they are not used either too long or too close and hence cause needless, and even dangerous, burns. Children or invalids on whom an infra-red lamp is playing should be kept under constant supervision.

Infusion—a medicinal preparation made by steeping the crude product in hot water to extract its active ingredients. DIGITALIS and TEA are infusions from leaves. Infusion also means to administer any fluid by vein, when it is allowed to drip or flow in by the force of gravity. An INJECTION is forced in with a syringe.

Inguinal describes the region of the groin, as in inguinal HERNIA (see RUPTURE).

Inhalant—anything inhaled or breathed in. It can be an ANES-THETIC or other drug adminis-

tered for treatment purposes, or, on the other hand, a poison gas unwittingly breathed in.

Inhaler—an apparatus for breathing in volatile drugs in vapor state. Hand inhalers are often ridiculously overused by people with stuffed noses.

Injection—a "SHOT"; anything forced into the body through a hollow needle with a syringe and plunger behind it.

Injury—damage or harm to the body as the result of violence *(trauma)*, infection, degenerative disease, or anything else that produces a *lesion. Internal injuries* can mean any amount or kind of damage, not necessarily severe, to the soft organs inside the chest, abdomen, or pelvis.

Ink Blot Test—see RORSCHACH TEST.

Inoculation—an INJECTION, a "SHOT."

Inoperable—the judgment of a surgeon that it will do no good to operate on a patient for the condition that ails him. It usually means that it is too late for operation, especially in CANCER. It should be noted, however, (1) that surgeons may differ on what is operable and inoperable so that a second surgical opinion should be sought when a diagnosis of inoperable is made; and (2) that treatment other than surgery may get end results just as good as could be expected from surgery. Only the best surgical judgment should be relied on to determine operability of a specific case.

Insanity—the *legal term* for some aspects of what doctors call MENTAL ILLNESS or PSYCHOSIS. A person may be legally adjudged insane or incompetent if his judgment and action are so unreliable and uncontrollable as to render him, at the time, a danger to himself and others. He may be committed to a mental hospital or ward of a general hospital for observation and treatment. Quick recovery is the rule; most so-called insanity is temporary. Insanity is not inherited (see HEREDITY). It is not the same as FEEBLE-MINDEDNESS.

INSECTS

Insects are both friends and enemies of man. Some simply annoy by their *bites* and *stings,* but a few carry disease-causing microbes. The suspicion that insects were in some way associated with disease in man and animals is centuries old. The *proof* that insects transmit disease, and the demonstration of how they do it, was given less than a century ago.

In 1893 Theobald Smith, of the U.S. Department of Agriculture, published a classic paper proving that ticks transmitted Texas fever in cattle. Within 10 years Sir Ronald Ross, a British army surgeon in India, and others proved that MALARIA was carried by the mosquito, the female *Anopheles* mosquito; Walter Reed and his associates in the U.S. Army Medical Department proved that YELLOW FEVER was also carried by the mosquito—*Aedes egypti,* in this case—a discovery that made possible the building of the Panama Canal; David Bruce showed that African SLEEPING SICKNESS was transmitted by the tsetse fly; Yersin, a Frenchman, and Kitasato, a Japanese, showed that PLAGUE was carried by the fleas that infest rats.

Among the many other known insect vectors (carriers) of diseases are the louse, which transmits TYPHUS *fever* ("jail fever"), trench fever, relapsing fever; the gnat, carrier of FILARIASIS; the sand fly, carrier of sand-fly fever; and the house fly, one vector of TYPHOID FEVER.

Insect control is now standard practice in public health and military medicine. The newer insecticides, of which DDT is the prototype, have worked wonders in insect control, particularly when used as residual sprays in dwellings.

Treatment of insect bites: Some insects bite and run (if they can get away); others bite and stay. If you are bitten by a black-widow spider or suffer multiple bee, wasp, or hornet stings, see a doctor. These can be serious because there is venom in the stings. Of course, see a doctor for treatment of any disease transmitted by an insect. Other insect bites can usually be successfully managed with home remedies and drugstore products.

Stingers should be lifted or scraped, not pinched, out.

To relieve the *pain* of insect bites, apply cold water, ice, wet dressings, anesthetic ointments (sunburn ointment).

To relieve the *itching,* in addition, apply rubbing alcohol, after-shave lotion, household hand lotion, calamine lotion (with or without 1 or 2% menthol, phenol, or camphor), or antihistaminic ointments. These can be bought at the drugstore. See ITCHING.

Mosquitoes prefer some people to others: adults to children, men to women, dirty to clean, light to dark, warm to cold, many to few. Protective clothing, screened buildings, and mosquito repellents, such as oil of citronella and DDT-pyrethrum mixtures, help to keep them from biting.

Bedbugs and fleas: The difficulty here is diagnosis. Most people refuse to believe that they have been bitten. Social position is no protection. Anyone's dog or other pet can have fleas. Bedbugs do not consult the social register when looking for food; they like old mansions. Suspect bedbugs if you go to bed unbitten and wake up the next morning itching and scratching. Characteristically bed-bugs leave a row of three or four bites in areas not covered by sleeping garments.

Ticks imbed themselves in the skin. Don't yank them off. Instead: (1) Hold a lighted match or cigarette close to the tick's back. (2) Coat the tick with vaseline or any other grease or oil. (3) Put gasoline, kerosene, or turpentine on the tick and nearby skin. (4) Pick the tick off gently with a tweezers. Wash the skin with soap and water and apply any skin antiseptic.

Black-widow spiders (also called "shoe-button" and "hourglass" spiders) are the only venomous species in North America. Other spiders' bites are usually trivial, in spite of the size of the spider (except the black tarantula of Panama, the so-called banana spider). Black widows often infest outhouses; hence they often bite the buttocks and sex organs.

When a black-widow spider bites, the victim knows it. He feels a sharp pain. The site of the bite swells and reddens. The victim feels dizzy, weak in the legs, cramped in the abdomen. Children bitten may find difficulty in breathing or go into fits.

The immediate treatment is to apply suction to the area and get out as much poison as possible. Then apply a skin antiseptic. Keep the victim quiet and call a doctor, who may or may not find it advisable to give the serum or antitoxin that has been developed against the black widow's bite.

Itch mites burrow under the skin and lay eggs there. For treatment, see ITCH (scabies). JIGGERS, or sand fleas, also burrow under the skin.

Lice can infest the head (head lice), the body (body lice), or the pubic area (CRABS). Such infestation is called pediculosis. The old-fashioned treatment for head lice and their nits was to soak the hair overnight with gasoline or kerosene dissolved in oil or hot vinegar, and then go over the head with a fine-tooth comb. Modern louse killers (pediculocides), which are usually some variant of benzene hexachloride, are quicker, more effective, less irritating, and can be bought at any drugstore.

Body lice ("cooties") live primarily in clothing and come out to suck blood for 3 to 10 minutes at a time several times a day. The bite at first is only a pin-point in size, but after a week or so sensitization can occur and something like HIVES appears. The itching often induces scratching and secondary infection.

The treatment is delousing of the body, *clothing*, and bedding. This can be done in several ways; for example, by heat sterilization. However, the effective use of DDT powder and other insecticides greatly simplifies the process. Benzyl benzoate is an effective remedy. The big problem is to prevent reinfestation.

For treatment of pubic lice, see CRABS.

The *early* diagnosis of pediculosis is rarely made, except in institutions. Most people refuse to think themselves lousy. They prefer to believe that they have some exotic skin ailment.

A sympathetic portrait of the louse, and his importance, has been painted by Hans Zinsser in the wonderful book *Rats, Lice and History*.

Insemination—fertilization of an OVUM by a SPERM; CONCEPTION. *Artificial insemination* means introduction of semen into the female genital tract by means other than direct sexual intercourse. This is the process that produces "test-tube babies." See STERILITY.

Insomnia—sleeplessness. See SLEEP.

Insufflation—blowing anything into a body cavity. The lungs may be insufflated with air in artificial respiration. The uterine tubes are tested for patency (whether or not open) by blowing air into them (uterotubal insufflation).

Insulin—the hormone secreted by the islet cells (ENDOCRINE GLANDS) of the PANCREAS. It is used in treating DIABETES MELLITUS.

An overdose of injected insulin can produce a serious reaction (hyperinsulinism) in a diabetic patient. The treatment is the ingestion of sugar or candy in any form, or, if the patient is unconscious, the injection of sugar-solutions into the vein.

Commercial insulin is now produced in many long-acting forms, for greater convenience of the diabetic patient. Medical supervision when taking insulin is always necessary, although patients readily learn to give themselves insulin injections on prescribed schedules.

Insulin injections are sometimes used to produce a hypoglycemic shock for psychiatric treatment purposes, although electric shock treatment is now much more common. See MENTAL ILLNESS.

Intelligence—that peculiar and probably inborn ability of a human being to understand and comprehend what he senses and to put these impressions together in personally and socially useful ways. We also speak of intelligence among the lower animals, but this is not quite the same as human intelligence.

Psychologists are most concerned with measuring intelligence, and this is no easy matter. At best it is only possible to measure *relative intelligence;* that is, to compare individual scores on intelligence tests with the average of scores made by other people.

Intelligence should not be confused with information and education. There is much truth in the saying "Never underestimate a man's intelligence and never overestimate his information." Judgment of intelligent action requires full appraisal and understanding of the social circumstances in which it is taken.

Common measures of intelligence are quoted in terms of mental age and intelligence quotient (I.Q.). When a person—child or adult—has attained a certain mental age, it simply means that he can think as well as average, normal people of this same age have been found to think. *Intelligence quotient* can then be arrived at by dividing the mental age by the chronological age (age in years). The classifications, which must be used with great discretion, are:

Under 70—mental deficiency or retardation (see FEEBLE-MINDEDNESS)
70 to 90—dull normal
90 to 110—normal
110 to 125—superior
125 to 140—very superior
Above 140—genius

There is nothing profound or unchangeable about these classifications. Some people are always smarter than others.

Intern—a medical-school graduate who is working, and usually living, in a hospital to get at least a year of practical training before he receives a full license to practice medicine. He may or may not have already received his M.D. (Doctor of Medicine) degree. The intern is in the hospital both to learn and to serve. See RESIDENT.

Internist—a physician who specializes in treating internal organs. He is often especially skillful in diagnosing obscure and troubling conditions.

Intertrigo—a SKIN disorder. It occurs where moist skin surfaces rub together, as between the cheeks of the buttocks, in the folds of the neck, or under the breasts. The rubbed area reddens, itches, often becomes infected. Prevention and treatment lies in keeping the parts dry. Talcum powder may help.

Greasy ointments make the condition worse. "Diaper rash" is a form of intertrigo.

Intestine—bowel. See DIGESTIVE SYSTEM. (See illustrations for ABDOMEN; APPENDICITIS; HEART.)

Intima—the inner lining of the BLOOD VESSELS.

Intoxication—means either drunkenness (see ALCOHOLISM) or poisoning. There is a condition known as *water intoxication,* in which the water balance of the body is gravely disturbed and too much water is held in the tissues. Sodium and potassium balance are upset along with it. The symptoms include vomiting, low body temperatures, fits, unconsciousness, and possibly death.

Intracranial—inside the skull (cranium).

Intrauterine—inside the uterus; intrauterine life describes the life of the fetus, embryo, and unborn child inside its mother's womb.

Intravenous—into or inside the vein; used in connection with injections ("shots"), INFUSIONS, and instillation (by drops) of fluids or medication into the vein. The arm or leg veins are usually used. They are pierced with an upward movement of a pointed needle. Patients who cannot (or will not) eat may have to be fed by sugar solutions dripped into their veins. Blood transfusions are intravenous infusions or injections.

Introspection—the business of looking into oneself—usually too much and too often. The classic example is Hamlet's soliloquy, "To be or not to be." A little introspection is a good thing, but too much is a symptom of ANXIETY, NEUROSIS, or MELANCHOLIA.

Introvert—a person who is too much with himself; who looks into himself too intensely rather than to the outside world for solution of his problems; who substitutes thought for action, plan for deed, his own company for friends and companions. See EXTROVERT; MENTAL ILLNESS.

Intussusception—a peculiar form of bowel obstruction, most common in infants, in which the bowel collapses in such a way that one part telescopes into the following part of the intestine. The symptoms are severe, recurring pain; vomiting; and usually the passage of bloodstained mucus from the rectum. The treatment is immediate surgery.

Inunction—a method of giving drugs by rubbing them into the skin; it is not common.

In Vitro—"in glass." This refers to experiments performed in test tubes rather than on living organisms; such experiments often concern the action of drugs on microbes. The opposite term is *in vivo*, which means that the experiments have been performed on living creatures. What works *in vitro* often fails *in vivo*.

In Vivo—see IN VITRO.

Involution—turning inward, or on itself, as *involutional* MELANCHOLIA. Also a backward step, the opposite of EVOLUTION.

Iodine—a chemical element, derived from seaweed, in dark violet-brown scales. Tincture of iodine is a solution of 3% iodine in alcohol. An excellent skin antiseptic, it is used both in surgery, for preoperative preparation, and in the household, for emergency first-aid treatment of cuts and contusions. It is the alcohol not the iodine that burns when the solution is applied to an open cut; the iodine gives the brown stain. High concentrations of iodine applied to the skin irritate and blister it. Frequent application of iodine to the same skin area is inadvisable.

Taken internally, large doses of iodine are an irritant to the mucous membranes of the digestive tract and hence a poison. Starch solution is an *antidote* for iodine poisoning.

A minute amount of iodine is essential to the proper functioning of the body. It is necessary for the manufacture of the thyroid hormone, thyroxin. See ENDOCRINE glands; CRETIN; GOITER.

Ipecac—a drug derived from the root of a South American shrub (*Cephaëlis ipecacuanha*), containing the alkaloid emetine. In large doses it is an irritant and induces *vomiting;* in smaller doses it is a gentle stimulant to the mucous membranes of the DIGESTIVE SYSTEM and the LUNGS.

I.Q.—intelligence quotient. See INTELLIGENCE.

Iridectomy—surgical removal of a part of the IRIS of the EYE.

Iris—the colored part of the EYE; the circular shutter that opens and closes to admit more or less light through its central opening, the pupil. (See illustration for EYES.)

Iritis—inflammation of the iris of the EYE. See EYE TROUBLE.

Iron—the chemical element that appears in the oxygen-carrying *hemoglobin* fraction of the red BLOOD cell. Lack of iron causes iron-deficiency ANEMIA. See ANEMIA; MINERALS.

Iron Lung—a tank RESPIRATOR with alternating positive and negative pressures, used to treat patients whose breathing apparatus has been damaged, usually by POLIO. There are other types of respirators.

Irradiation—treatment with any form of radiant energy to which all or some part of the patient is exposed. Radiant energy includes heat, light (sunlight), X RAY, and RADIUM emanations.

Irrigation—washing out wounds or body cavities (e.g. the bladder) with a copious supply of running water or other irrigating solution.

Irritation—popularly, a mild IN-FLAMMATION on the SKIN, a sense of discomfort in the THROAT or LUNGS, something in the EYE, or an upset in the DI-GESTIVE SYSTEM.

Ischemia—loss of blood supply to a particular part of the body, usually caused by some damage to BLOOD VESSELS.

Ischium—the hind part of the oddly shaped innominate bone. It forms the back of the PELVIS and is the bone you sit down on.

Ishihara Test—a test for COLOR BLINDNESS; see EYE TROUBLE. From a series of colored dots of various sizes, those with normal vision can see and pick out patterns and figures that the color-blind cannot see.

Islet Cells—also known as "islands of Langerhans," they are ENDOCRINE GLANDS that form part of the PANCREAS.

Isolation—the separation and segregation of a person having an acute contagious disease, as in the *isolation ward* of a hospital.

Isoniazid—a group of drugs, given by mouth, which are effective in treating TUBERCU-LOSIS. They are relatively safe. They hold the tubercle bacillus in check and make home or hospital treatment of tuberculosis more effective than it has ever been. But isoniazid is not the whole answer to the problem of treating tuberculosis effectively.

Isotope. Chemical elements are composed of isotopes; that is, the different parts of the element have the same chemical properties but different atomic weights. Separation of the isotopes of uranium makes possible ATOMIC ENERGY. The developments in atomic-energy research (nuclear physics) have made it possible to make *radioactive isotopes* of common elements; e.g. carbon, iodine. Radioactive tracer elements make it possible to study in more intimate detail the workings of the human and animal body. Radioactive iodine has a place in treatment of thyroid-gland dis-

eases (goiter). Radioactive cobalt is used in CANCER treatment.

Itch—"*the* itch," the "seven-year itch," scabies, is caused by the itch mite, which burrows into the skin, lays eggs, puts out an irritating excrement. The mites, about 1/30th inch in diameter, can be dug out with a sterilized needle or pin point, as French fishwives taught learned doctors to do. However, the eggs are often missed and the infestation of mites returns. Applications of sulfur ointments, benzyl benzoate solution, or benzene hexachloride effectively kill the itch mite and its eggs. However, treatment must not be prolonged unnecessarily or it will damage the skin.

ITCHING

Itching, or pruritus, is the unpleasant sensation that provokes the desire to scratch. Unfortunately, scratching often makes the itching worse; so does indiscriminate application of ointments, lotions, and powders. Itching is a combination of the senses of touch and pain, for which the skin has many sensory nerve endings. Itching is also a defense reaction of the skin; it indicates that the skin is working hard at its job of defending the rest of the body against fungus, bacteria, or virus infections from the outside or cellular irritation on the inside. (See SKIN TROUBLE.)

Itching is a symptom of some trouble, some assault on the skin. It is a one-alarm symptom as compared with more severe skin reactions, such as redness and swelling, skin rash, blisters and wheals. Itching may be local or general, confined to one area of the body or present all over.

Some people naturally itch more easily than others; their pain threshold is probably lower. Trouble hits them on the skin; worry may hit other people in the back (backache), head (headache), or teeth (toothache). Itching is usually temporary; but it may become chronic, especially if the skin is overtreated or mistreated with medication and if scratching and the underlying causes of the itching are not corrected. Old people itch more readily than young people.

Itching may be mild or severe. Constant, severe itching can be maddening torture. With correct and properly timed medical treatment, *itching can always be relieved.* The most important part of the treatment is the diagnosis, finding out what is really causing the itching. Except for mild and occasional itching, the help of a competent physician and often a skin specialist (dermatologist) is needed to get rid of it. Do not attempt to treat your own itches with advertised remedies, friendly advice, and gross ignorance.

Some unfortunate people experience waves of itching (orgiastic itching). The itching sensation comes on in waves of increasing intensity until it reaches a climax not unlike that of a sexual ORGASM. Then the tension and itching disappear for a variable time, only to return again.

What causes itching? Any assault or insult to the skin. The possible causes are many, and often the problem is to find them. Treatment, obviously, must be directed to the cause.

Some generalized diseases are often expressed in skin itching; notably DIABETES, KIDNEY TROUBLE, LIVER TROUBLE, and ALLERGY. Itching usually accompanies HIVES and JAUNDICE. Itching around the urinary organs is often caused by undisclosed diabetes, which is marked by a high concentration of sugar in the urine.

Allergy or sensitivity to foods, drugs, and contactants is a frequent cause of itching. Usually some undiscovered allergen in the everyday environment is responsible for this form of itching. It may be the heat of a cooking stove; cold weather; irritating soap or other cosmetic; a household animal pet; eggs, wheat, milk, chocolate—or anything else—in the diet; woolen underwear; nylon stocking; the chemicals in a wrist-watch band—or anything else. Until the allergen is discovered and removed or avoided, itching will continue.

NEUROSES also cause itching *(neurodermatitis)*. The treatment here is PSYCHOTHERAPY, which may include recommendations for a change of job, residence, and other habits. Itching for no evident reason is a very convenient symptom; the itching part is scratched and gets red and swollen, sometimes infected. Then the neurotic has physical evidence that something definite is causing him to feel terrible.

Contact dermatitis usually causes itching; the common causes are poison ivy, poison oak, industrial chemicals, household chemicals (soap, detergents, cosmetics), and drugs and ointments used too freely in treating skin troubles.

Weather conditions both bring on and relieve itching. "Winter itch," if not due to sensitivity to wool clothing, is usually the result of drying of the skin. It disappears in warm weather, when perspiration moistens the skin. Some oily-skinned people itch more in warm weather and under tropical conditions. These conditions, such as prickly heat, apparently result when the blood vessels of the skin change size. The moist condition of the skin also encourages FUNGUS infections. Repeated FROSTBITE and SUNBURN cause itching.

INSECTS cause itching; notably *lice*, the *itch mite* (scabies), and mosquito or other insect bites.

For immediate relief of itching many household and a few drugstore remedies may be tried. But for persistent itching a complete medical check-up is requisite. Don't treat your own itches more than a day or two. Try the following remedies in order:

1. Apply cold water or an ice bag to the itching area.

2. Apply hot water.

3. Draw a warm bath. Add 4 pounds of bran or a half box of baking soda (sodium bicarbonate) and soak in tub for about a half hour.

4. Dry the body gently but completely. Apply talcum powder.

5. Apply a mild lotion, such as witch hazel, rubbing alcohol, after-shave lotion, ordinary hand lotion, calamine lotion.

6. Stop scratching and stop worrying as much as possible. Go to bed and get a good nap or night's sleep if possible. Or try distracting yourself by reading a good book, seeing a movie, visiting friends, playing cards. Or go back to work.

7. Take 1 *dose* of a mild laxative with plenty of water.

The physician may prescribe other treatments for your itching. Every case is *individual*. What helped your friend may make you worse. Among treatments that may be prescribed are drying or wetting agents; lanolin, tar, sulfur, or antihistamine drugs (ointments or tablets); X-ray treatments; even tattooing of the itching area with special drugs. Do not use any prescribed drugs after the time for which they have been prescribed; they may bring back the itching.

Pruritus ani and *pruritus vulvae*, which means severe, prolonged, repeated itching around the ANUS and the SEX ORGANS (FEMALE), do not usually respond to home or drugstore remedies. However, in full cooperation with a competent doctor, they can be relieved. Any of the causes and treatments already mentioned may apply, alone or in combination.

The psychological factor is often very important; guilt feelings are frequently centered on the anogenital region and itching and scratching may represent self-inflicted punishment.

Other complicating causes of anogenital pruritus, which must be sought out and corrected, commonly include such conditions as PILES (hemorrhoids), *fungus* infections, *overtreatment* with anti-itch drugs, undiscovered *diabetes, threadworms,* and *allergy* to one's own feces. Any change in treatment, or new treatment, of pruritus ani usually brings temporary relief, but it does not last unless the underlying causes are corrected.

-itis—a suffix denoting inflammation and disease, possibly infection, in a specific body organ; for example, APPENDICITIS, COLITIS, NEPHRITIS, MENINGITIS, TONSILLITIS.

J

Any word printed in SMALL CAPITALS *can be looked up under its own alphabetical listing for further information.*

Jail Fever—TYPHUS fever.

Jalap—a drastic laxative; from jalap root.

Jaundice—icterus; a serious symptom of disease that causes the skin, the whites of the eyes, and even the mucous membranes to turn yellow. The degree of yellow coloring depends on the amount of bile or bile pigments getting into the blood stream. The underlying causes of jaundice are numerous, and the diagnosis must be made by a physician.

The liver makes bile, and jaundice usually betokens some kind of LIVER TROUBLE. Or the cause may be an unusual destruction of red blood cells, which produce the yellow coloring matter *(bilirubin)* that goes into bile; or an obstruction to flow of bile from the liver to the duodenum (obstructive jaundice). Gallstones and cancer of the pancreas are possible causes of obstructive jaundice.

Jaundice is seen in such diseases as yellow fever, acute malaria, typhoid, and typhus fever. Virus disease of the liver and infectious *hepatitis,* also called *human serum jaundice,* produces the yellowing symptom. Spirochetal jaundice is caused by an acute infectious disease engendered by a spirochete (leptospirosis, Weil's disease). Picric-acid poisoning induces jaundice.

Jaw—the bones that hold the teeth. The maxilla is the upper jaw; mandible, the lower jaw. For dislocation of the lower jaw, see JOINTS. (See illustrations for TEETH.)

Jejunum—the part of the small intestine just after the duodenum. See DIGESTIVE SYSTEM.

Jiggers—sand fleas, abundant in subtropical regions of the southern United States. The pregnant female burrows into the skin of a human host, usually between the toes, on the soles of the feet, or under the toenails, producing intense irritation and even small ulcers unless removed (with a sterile needle). Not the same condition as CHIGGERS.

Jock(ey) Strap—a suspensory, an elastic supporter, sometimes including a metal "cup," worn for the support and protection of the scrotum, particularly by athletes in body-contact sports. "Jock-strap itch" (tinea cruris) is an angry red, scaly inflammation of the groin, where surfaces rub together. This is more than chafing. It is a FUNGUS *infection* closely related to athlete's foot and cannot be permanently cleared up until the feet are cleared.

JOINTS

Joints occur where the BONES of the body fit together. There are three kinds: *immovable,* like the joints between the bones of the skull; *slightly movable,* like the articulations of the vertebrae of the SPINE; and *freely movable,* in certain directions, like the shoulder, elbow, wrist, finger, hip, knee, ankle, and toe joints. The freely movable joints are of different mechanical types, reflecting the movements required of them. Knees, fingers, wrists, and toes, for example, are *hinge joints.* The hip and shoulder joints are of the *ball-and-socket* type.

Pads of cartilage are found between the slightly movable joints, like the DISKS between the vertebrae. The freely movable joints are completely enveloped in a capsule, variously called joint capsule, articular capsule, synovial capsule. The capsule has a strong outside layer of *fibrous* connective tissue, which is attached to the ends of each bone making up the joint.

The inner layer of the capsule is a synovial membrane that secretes *synovial fluid* to lubricate the joint. The integrity of the joint capsule is necessary to the proper movement of the joint.

Most joints are further lashed together and supported by tough, fibrous bands called LIGAMENTS. Muscle TENDONS that cross the

TWO TYPES OF BODY JOINTS

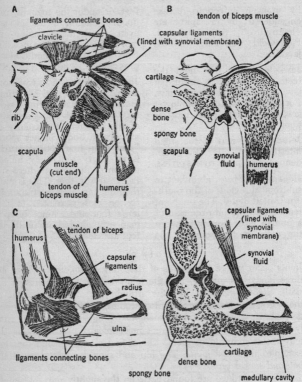

(*Top.*) Ball and socket joint in the shoulder.
A. *The joint is shown with ligaments and joint capsule intact.* B. *The same joint is shown as if it were cut through on the long axis of the humerus.*

Bottom.) Hinge joint in the elbow.

C. *The joint is again shown with ligaments and joint capsule intact.* D. *The joint has been cut through to reveal its inner working.*

Note also in B *and* D *the areas of dense bone, spongy bone, and medullary cavities, containing blood-forming marrow.*

joint give additional support. Some joints, such as those in the jaw and knee, contain plates of cartilage *(menisci)* that more or less completely divide the joint cavity.

Trouble in the joints is evidenced by pain, stiffness, swelling, redness, heat, and loss of motion. The causes are either disease, infectious or degenerative, or injury (trauma, violence). The diseases that affect the joints are discussed under the topics of ARTHRITIS, RHEUMATISM, BONE DISEASE, GOUT, and BACKACHE.

Joints fail to work properly because something has happened to the bones, muscles, ligaments, tendons, or nerves that make them up. In hysterical paralysis, for example, joints fail to function because of the emotional state of HYSTERIA. In paralytic POLIO the joints don't work because of damage to the nerves to the muscles that work the joints. When bones are broken or dislocated, when ligaments are torn from their moorings or strained, when muscles are permanently contracted, or when tendons are broken or detached, normal joint movement is prevented or interrupted.

Stiff joints, which may or may not be swollen and painful, may arise from any of the systemic diseases and other conditions already mentioned. Fractures and dislocations of bones, and the immobilization with casts and splints that usually is necessary, often leave stiff joints in their wake. That is why early movement is usually attempted and recommended by the doctor. The stiffened joint may be loosened by gradually increasing exercise, active and passive (physical therapy), and helped by massage and application of heat.

Repeated small shocks to the joint sometimes set up an inflammation inside the joint capsule. Handling an air hammer, for example, can do it quickly. The inflammation may produce adhesions inside the joint capsule, painfully limiting motion. These adhesions can be broken up by forcible movements of the limb, followed by prompt relief and recovery.

"Locking joints," particularly in the knee, are the result of loose substances (called "joint mice") floating around inside the joint capsule. They may suddenly become wedged in between the surfaces of the bone, thus locking the joint. Gently flexing, extending, or turning the limb usually causes the loose bodies to fall out of the locking position. In the knee the "lock" is often caused by a twisting or wrenching of the leg that pushes the normal joint dividers (semilunar cartilages) out of normal position and in between the bone surfaces. This is a common athletic injury.

When locked joints are a nuisance, surgery can remove the tags of cartilage, joint mice, menisci or other loose bodies that are causing the trouble.

Sprain is the rather loose description for a painfully twisted or wrenched joint, usually the result of some kind of violence. The same kind of violence may also *strain* the ligaments, muscles, and tendons that bind and operate the joint, overextending them and pulling them partly away from their normal attachments. The violence may also dislocate or fracture the ends of the bones that make up the joint.

Following any severe or troublesome sprain, therefore, X-ray pictures from several angles should be taken to make sure that the bones have not been fractured or chipped or dislocated.

A sprain means that the ligament around the joint has been torn or stretched, so that there may be some blood or other fluid that seeps around the joint and discolors the skin. It also means that the synovial membranes are slightly inflamed and reacting by pouring out fluid, thus stretching the joint capsule and accounting for part of the pain and swelling.

The immediate treatment for a sprain or strain is application of cold wet bandages or ice bags to keep down the swelling. Medical attention (and X rays) should be immediately obtained to be sure that the sprain is just a sprain.

If the pain is severe, the doctor may inject a local anesthetic directly into or around the joint capsule.

A tight or elastic bandage is smoothly applied to give the joint support. Then the patient is usually allowed to move the joint as much as he wants or dares without inducing further pain. At first, this will be very little, but with healing, more and more movement will naturally come. The general rule is, when it begins to hurt or ache, stop moving and rest. Application of heat in any form usually speeds healing. Light massage at first, gradually increased to firm massage, to improve the blood circulation is also a help.

If healing is not proceeding satisfactorily with motion permitted, the doctor may immobilize the joint temporarily with a cast or splint and forbid needless movements.

Dislocations of bones are caused by the same types of violence that produce sprains, strains, and FRACTURES. There is usually less pain, but the joint cannot be moved, the limb may be in an odd position, and its contours may differ from those of the other limb. Amateur bone-setters (including athletic trainers) should not tinker with dislocations; the reduction of dislocations, getting bones back into their proper position, is a business for experts.

First-aid treatment for dislocations is the same as that for FRACTURES. In fact, fractures often accompany dislocations. Put on a splint, bandage, or sling to immobilize the injured part, and keep the patient quiet. Resetting a dislocation must often be done in a hospital operating room. The family doctor or general surgeon can usually do it; but sometimes an *orthopedic* surgeon may have to be called in consultation.

When the dislocated bones are reset in their natural position, they are usually immobilized for a length of time with casts or splints, then heavy bandages, to prevent recurrence. Early and immediate movement of the parts is *not* indicated.

Massage and passive exercise of the part may begin in a few days, and gentle active movements be permitted in a week or 10 days, depending on the severity of the case. Casts or splints, if used, are usually taken off at this time; but elastic bandages may be advisable for at least another 2 to 3 weeks. The dislocated limb must be favored for a considerable time thereafter.

Dislocations occur most commonly at the shoulder and elbow and in the fingers and toes.

Congenital dislocation of the hip is more frequent in women than men. The head of the femur (thigh bone) lies outside the socket of the pelvic bone (acetabulum), in which it is supposed to fit. If this occurs on one side only, the person walks with a limp; if on both sides, with a waddling gait. The treatment is competent orthopedic surgery, preferably early in life.

Dislocation of the jaw forward sometimes follows a wide yawn or other too-wide opening of the mouth. It can sometimes be snapped back into place by pressing down hard with the thumbs on the teeth at the back of the mouth while at the same time pressing up on the chin, being careful not to get the thumbs bitten. This is the only dislocation that an amateur should risk reducing.

TUBERCULOSIS of the bones and joints sometimes results in bone and joint deformities. One successful method of treatment is by sunlight (heliotherapy). Erosion of the ends of the bones sometimes follows untreated SYPHILIS and other systemic diseases, producing disability in the joints (*Charcot's joints*).

When the synovial membrane, for reason of repeated trauma or other cause, becomes inflamed and secretes an excessive amount of fluid, this produces "water in the joint" (synovitis, hydrarthrosis), commonly seen in water on the knee.

All joint injuries and diseases should have prompt attention from a physician, who will call in an orthopedist if needed. Such conditions should not be allowed to drag on and become chronic. This prolongs both disability and treatment.

Some joints are partly protected by bursae outside the joint capsule. Inflammation of these bursae (BURSITIS) is sometimes mistaken for inflammation inside the joint capsule (ARTHRITIS).

Jugular—pertaining to the neck, such as the readily observable, large *jugular veins* in the front of the neck. They convey blood from the head and neck to the inside of the chest.

Jungle Rot—any FUNGUS infection of the skin aggravated by tropical conditions of heat, humidity, no baths, and overtreatment. This is no bizarre Oriental infection.

K

Any word printed in SMALL CAPITALS *can be looked up under its own alphabetical listing for further information.*

Kala-azar—a serious, infectious tropical disease, transmitted to man by the bite of the sand fly (Phlebotomus). The infecting microbe is the parasite *Leishmania donovani*. The disease is characterized by enlargement of the SPLEEN (up to 10 pounds), where the parasite delights to feast; enlargement of the liver; progressive anemia; intermittent malarialike fever; and swelling of the legs. Diagnosis is made by finding the parasite in the blood stream or bone marrow (by puncture of the sternum). The disease, once established, used to be almost universally fatal. New drugs—pentavalent antimony compounds and di-

amidines—appear to cure up to 90% of the cases.

Kanamycin—new antibiotic from Japan.

Kaolin—Chinese clay; a finely ground, smooth white powder (aluminum silicate). In doses of ½ to 2 ounces in milk or water, it is an excellent remedy for DIARRHEA. It is also used as a dusting powder in various SKIN troubles.

Keloid—an overgrown scar, usually forming an elevated white ridge, at first hard and shiny, on the skin. It is most common in young adults and among Negroes. No one knows why keloids come or tend to recur if removed by surgery. Sometimes they are tender and painful, but usually not. The treatment most successful in disintegrating a keloid without recurrence is irradiation with X ray or radium. Only a well-qualified specialist in radiology or dermatology should give this treatment.

Keratin—the hard protein substance, containing sulfur, that is the chief constituent of such hard body tissues as hair, nails, horns (in animals), and the outer layer of the skin (epidermis).

Keratitis—inflammation and infection of the cornea of the EYE. See EYE TROUBLE.

Keratoconjunctivitis—a form of EYE TROUBLE, in which the cornea and conjunctival membranes become inflamed (conjunctivitis). Excessive exposure to ultraviolet light, as in welding torches, may be a cause. Protective goggles should always be worn in occupations where such exposure is common.

Ketogenic Diet—a diet rich in fats, low in carbohydrates, intended to produce ketone (acetone) in the blood and urine. This diet is sometimes used in treating EPILEPSY and infections of the urinary system with colon bacillus.

Ketosis—"vinegar breath"; a disturbance in the normal acid-base and water-balance relationships of the body. It is a kind of ACIDOSIS in which too many ketone bodies are present (ketones are chemical compounds containing the CO radical). This is the radical found in acetic acid (of which vinegar is a dilute form) and acetone. Hence the breath smells like vinegar. Ketosis sometimes accompanies DIABETES, and can be deliberately induced by a KETOGENIC DIET.

Kidneys—the two large glands in the small of the back that filter the blood stream and remove impurities, released as URINE. For fuller description, see URINARY SYSTEM, KIDNEY STONES, KIDNEY TROUBLE. (See illustrations for HEART.)

Kidney Stones—a common form of KIDNEY TROUBLE. They often induce BLADDER TROUBLE and infections in the URINARY SYSTEM. These stones are composed of elements always present in the urine, that is, the urates, phosphates, oxalates, and other salts in solution in the urine. Most kidney stones are calcium oxalate. The stones form by crystallization of the dissolved salts about bits of foreign matter that find their way into the urine; for example, bacteria, and shreds of mucus. Stones formed in the collecting chamber of the kidney (renal pelvis) often assume a rough "stag-horn" shape. If they pass down into the tubes leading to the bladder, they may obstruct the flow of urine, scratch the lining of the tubes and bladder to the extent that it bleeds and becomes infected, and produce a colicky pain of the most agonizing sort. Kidney stones are often treated by surgical incision of the kidney and removal of the stones. People subject to recurrent attacks of kidney stones are usually put on diets free of foods containing large amounts of oxalic acid.

Small stones frequently pass and can be managed by increased fluid intake and dietary restrictions.

KIDNEY TROUBLE

Kidney trouble describes a variety of diseases and disorders affecting the kidneys and causing renal failure or insufficiency. This means the kidneys are failing in their vital job of filtering waste products out of the blood stream. Complete failure spells death from waste-product poisoning (*uremia*). Partial failure produces a host of signs and symptoms, described below. Fortunately the body has a great reserve of kidney tissue. One kidney is enough to sustain life. If the other kidney is healthy, a diseased kidney can be removed without harm.

What are the signs of kidney trouble? Difficulties in urination and abnormalities of urine are among the most significant. The patient may pass too much or too little water; the process may be painful and too frequent. *Urinalysis* may disclose blood, pus, casts, albumin, and other abnormal things in the urine. Another important sign of kidney trouble is swelling and puffiness of body tissues, due to an excess accumulation of fluids in them, the condition now called *edema* and once known as *dropsy.* Backache in the small of the back, the lumbar region in which the kidneys are located, is another frequent sign of kidney trouble. Still others are excruciating pain in the kidney, usually associated with kidney stones, and fever, when kidney trouble is acute.

All these are relatively serious symptoms worthy of prompt medical investigation. They should not be disregarded or masked with self-prescribed patent medicines. Most such medicines, incidentally, have little effect beyond encouraging the patient to drink greater quantities of water, which may dilute the urine and render it less irritating.

Not all urinary difficulties are the result of kidney trouble. Inflammations and infections of the lower part of the urinary tract (bladder, urethra) can also be responsible. Anxiety and excitement often induce frequent urination. Obstruction of urine flow, as by an enlarged *prostate gland,* can make urination painful.

"Weak kidneys," meaning the need to pass water very frequently, may not be a kidney problem at all. More often the basic difficulty is psychological, and the real problem is bladder control. See BLADDER TROUBLE.

What causes kidney trouble? There are many causes for kidney trouble, not all of them yet thoroughly understood. Kidney diseases are among the principal causes of death in the United States, accounting for around 20,000 deaths a year. The kidneys can be damaged by infection, drugs and poisons, obstruction to urine outflow, tumors, malformations, and degenerative changes, such as hardening of the arteries.

Infections that harm the kidneys may be localized in the kidneys or take their origin in other parts of the body. Infected teeth or tonsils, for example, produce toxic substances that the kidneys are called upon to eliminate. Diphtheria, scarlet fever, and other infections, particularly those involving the hemolytic streptococcus, sometimes do irreparable damage to the kidneys without directly infecting them. Localized infections often ascend to the kidneys from the bladder.

Kidney cells are particularly susceptible to destruction by certain poisons, notably the heavy metals such as mercury and lead, taken into the body. The sulfa drugs and some others, if not properly administered, can cause kidney damage.

When the outflow of urine from the kidney and bladder is obstructed, a condition that encourages urinary infection, harm can come to the kidneys. There are a number of causes of urinary obstruction: kidney stones (urinary calculi), movable (floating) kidney, enlargement of the prostate, increased fluid pressure inside the kidney (hydronephrosis), spinal-cord injury, narrowing of the tubes that carry urine away from the kidney (ureteral or urethral stricture), and new growths in the kidney.

Tumors in the kidneys may be benign or malignant, primary or, rarely, secondary.

Some people are born with congenital malformation of the kidneys. The *horse-shoe kidney*, in which the lower poles of the kidneys have grown together, is a common anomaly. In other cases the kidneys are filled with numerous small cysts (polycystic kidney). These greatly enlarge the kidney, compress the functioning renal tissue, induce a gradual renal failure, and predispose to many other kidney diseases.

Pregnancy throws a special burden on the kidneys, which must for a time eliminate the waste products of two individuals, mother and unborn child. The toxemias (poisonings) of pregnancy are associated with kidney changes, failure, and damage.

Degenerative changes in the kidneys are not understood any better than similar changes in other organs, particularly the heart and blood vessels. This whole pattern of cardiovascularenal degeneration is associated with high blood pressure and hardening of the arteries. The kidneys appear to elaborate chemical substances that increase blood pressure, and the complex network of arteries in the kidneys (glomeruli) is one of the first places where hardening of the arteries shows up.

How are kidney troubles classified? Usually by the agent that causes them, the part of the kidney affected, and the symptoms produced. A large share of kidney disease can be classified as *nephritis,* or inflammation of the kidney. Another name for nephritis is *Bright's disease,* which describes any of a group of kidney diseases marked by albumin in the urine and swelling of body tissues (edema). Richard Bright was an English physician who, in 1827, first detected albumin in the urine, by heating urine in a pewter spoon held over a candle flame. He described the class of kidney diseases now associated with his name. A great deal more has been learned about the function and failures of the kidneys since his time, but not how to prevent hardening of the renal arteries (*nephrosclerosis*) or degeneration of the kidney tubules (*nephrosis*). The situation is a little better with respect to the most common form of nephritis (*glomerulonephritis*), which primarily affects the tufts of tiny blood vessels (glomeruli) in the kidneys. It can often be prevented by prompt, effective treatment of the infections in the kidney and remote from it that might bring on the disease in acute or chronic form.

How are kidney diseases diagnosed? There have been great improvements in recent years in diagnosing kidney diseases. This has long depended in part on *urinalysis* and the patient's history, but it has been improved by kidney-function tests, X-ray pictures of the kidney, and instruments (for example, the cystoscope, with which the doctor can look into the bladder). The ability of the kidney to excrete noxious materials can be judged by injecting a harmless dye into the veins or muscles and timing how long it takes the dye to appear in the urine.

How are kidney troubles treated? Sometimes by surgery, usually otherwise. A diseased kidney can be completely removed (nephrectomy), and it can be cut into for removal of kidney stones.

"Cutting for stone" is one of the oldest surgical operations, because the kidneys (and bladder) lie outside the peritoneal cavity that surgeons in the preaseptic era were properly loath to enter. Nonsurgical treatment of kidney troubles relies heavily on clearing up infections with antibiotics and other drugs; on various kinds of diet; on promoting rest, relaxation, and generally good hygiene.

For further information, consult entries on URINARY SYSTEM, URINALYSIS, UREMIA, KIDNEY STONES, HIGH BLOOD PRESSURE, and HARDENING OF THE ARTERIES.

Kinesiology—the science that deals with human motion and locomotion, particularly the conditions of harmonious, co-ordinated action of brain, nerves, muscles, and limbs.

Kinesthesia—"muscle sense"; the combination of sense perceptions and judgment (experience) by which a human being "feels" muscle tension and thus judges in himself and others muscular motion, weight, position, and so forth.

Kleptomania—stealing repeated for the fun, thrill, and psychological relief it affords and not for the value of the objects stolen. The kleptomaniac feels an irresistible compulsion to steal; he—or more often she—is not a common thief or criminal. Kleptomania is a form of MENTAL ILLNESS.

Knee—a hinge JOINT where the bottom end of the thigh bone (femur) and the top end of the leg bones (tibia and fibula) meet together with the kneecap (patella). The trick knee that sometimes locks in place is usually the result of loose bodies ("joint mice") floating in the fluid secreted by the inner synovial lining of the joint capsule. (See JOINTS.) Water on the knee is an accumulation of synovial fluid inside the joint capsule. It may have to be withdrawn through a hollow needle.

Kneecap—the patella; a disk of bone in the front of the knee. It is sometimes fractured. Some cases heal quickly with proper orthopedic treatment; in others with equally good treatment, it may be months before the knee joint returns to normal.

Knee Jerk—a reflex action in which tapping under the knee causes the leg to jerk forward. Its purpose is to test the integrity of NERVES.

Knock-Knees are practically always the result of RICKETS in childhood. In children the deformity can sometimes be overcome with splints. In adults it is necessary to perform an orthopedic operation in which the end of the thigh bone is broken and reset to form a straight leg.

Kraurosis—the drying up and

shriveling away of SKIN and mucous membranes. It occurs most frequently in the external sex organs of elderly women, often accompanied by intense ITCHING, which can be relieved. HORMONES sometimes help.

Krebiozen—an alleged cancer cure, of unrevealed chemical structure, introduced into the United States from Argentina in 1949 or 1950 by a Yugoslav doctor. Since then it has been the subject of violent medical controversy at the University of Illinois, where it has caused staff resignations. A committee of cancer experts found the drug of no value in treating cancer.

Kyphosis—hunchback; backward CURVATURE OF THE SPINE.

L

Any word printed in SMALL CAPITALS *can be looked up under its own alphabetical listing for further information.*

Labia—LIPS. See SEX ORGANS, FEMALE.

Labor—a mother's role in CHILDBIRTH.

Labyrinth—a twisted maze of passageways. There is a labyrinth of the human ear, concerned with both hearing and balance. See EAR.

Labyrinthitis—inflammation of the inner EAR; see EAR TROUBLE.

Laceration—a tear; any wound or injury in which skin, muscle, or other tissue is torn. Compare with CONTUSION, a bruise.

Lacrimation—crying; shedding tears (see EYE).

Lactation—the act and time of giving milk from the breasts.

Lacteal refers either to milk or the small lymphatic ducts within the bowel that take up digested food particles. See DIGESTION.

Lactic Acid—a thick, almost odorless, colorless liquid that sours milk, kills sperm, disinfects wounds, and accumulates in MUSCLES as they become fatigued.

Lactobacillus—a harmless MICROBE that can be used to ferment starches and sugars. According to some theorists, it plays a role in tooth decay, but this has not been established. *Lactobacillus acidophilus* is a strain that sours milk and is related to *Lactobacillus bulgaricus,* which is used to make Bulgarian buttermilk, or yoghurt. Many ridiculous claims have been set forth about the health-giving qualities of such milk. Its value is no greater than that of ordinary buttermilk.

Lactose—milk SUGAR.

Lameness results from many causes, some obvious, some not, which may affect the bones, muscles, joints, nerves, ligaments, tendons, or blood supply (intermittent claudication) of the legs and feet. See JOINTS, MUSCLES, FRACTURES, BONE DISEASES, CLUBFOOT, POLIO, CHARLEY HORSE, FOOT TROUBLE.

Lancet—a surgeon's knife; double-edged, pointed, of various sizes.

Lanolin—wool fat. It is used in some cosmetics and ointments; it has the valuable property of taking up water.

Lanugo—the fine downy HAIR that covers the body of the fetus. See PREGNANCY.

Laparotomy—any surgical operation in which the abdomen is opened up. A variety of surgical procedures inside the abdomen may follow the incision.

Larkspur—powdered seed of larkspur (Delphinium) for external use to get rid of bodylice, especially pubic lice ("crabs").

Laryngitis—inflammation of the larynx, usually denoted by HOARSENESS and dryness in the throat and difficulty in swallowing. See THROAT.

Laryngology—the medical specialty that deals with the diseases and disorders of the THROAT It is usually combined with treatment of diseases of the NOSE and EARS, sometimes with ophthalmology in addition.

Laryngoscope—an instrument with mirrors for looking into the larynx. It does not go down as far as a bronchoscope. Many people have great difficulty in allowing the doctor to get a good look at their larynx; they gag and gag. Sometimes the throat has to be lightly anesthetized.

Larynx—voice box. See THROAT.

Lateral—on the side.

Laudanum—OPIUM (10 to 20%) dissolved in alcohol. See NARCOTICS.

Laughing Gas—the popular name for nitrous oxide, used for inhalation anesthesia.

Lavage—washing out or irrigating a hollow body organ, such as the stomach, bowel, sinuses.

Laxative—the most abused class of drugs known to self-prescribers, quacks, and charlatans. See CONSTIPATION. A laxative is supposed to make the bowels move gently; purgatives and cathartics, drastically. There is no choice among laxatives used when they are not really needed. Those in common use include epsom salts (in small doses); castor oil; cascara (made from the bark of a tree); mineral oil, with or without modifiers; agar, a form of seaweed; psyllium seed, and other mucilaginous materials that swell up with the absorption of water and add bulk to the stool; and phenolphthalein, a red coal-tar dye, which is the basis of most advertised proprietary laxatives, including the candy-coated kind.

"Candy laxatives" have the danger that young children will eat them indiscriminately with disastrous results.

Except in rare and occasional instances, laxatives should be taken only on the prescription of a physician. Self-prescribed, they are more likely to cause CONSTIPATION than to cure it. It is not necessary to be regular in one's stool habits.

Bulky foods have a slightly laxative effect; but rough foods, with much cellulose content, like bran, that threaten to scratch the inside of the intestine should be used with much caution. Prune and lemon juice have a slightly laxative effect for some people.

Never give or take a laxative in the presence of an abdominal pain that lasts for more than an hour! It can be fatal.

Lead Poisoning—the result of ingestion, inhalation, or inunction of damaging amounts of the metal lead or any of its numerous poisonous compounds or salts—for example, sugar of lead (lead acetate); white lead, used in paints; arsenate of lead, used as an insecticide; and tetra-ethyl lead ("loony gas," because it produces mental symptoms), the antiknock ingredient in ethyl gasoline.

Lead poisoning was once common in trades and industries that used lead, that is, among printers, plumbers, pottery workers, painters, and others. But knowledge of the danger and application of safety measures have eliminated much of this hazard. Infants sometimes get lead poisoning by chewing paint off toys or furniture. Most infants' toys today are colored without lead paints.

The risk of lead poisoning today resides largely in the ingestion of lead and its salts from sources where its presence is not suspected. Old lead plumbing, foods processed with lead, or lead dissolved from soldered containers are examples. It was an historic discovery many years ago that "Devonshire colic" was actually lead poisoning coming from cider processed in leaden presses. Small doses of lead accumulate in the body, so that chronic lead poisoning may occur.

The characteristic symptoms of chronic lead poisoning are severe COLIC, sometimes lasting for days; a blue line on the gums (lead line); constipation; muscle weakness and paralysis, including wrist drop and foot drop; and mental confusion. Nerves, blood, and bones are primarily affected.

Most patients recover once exposure to lead is discovered and thereafter avoided. Calcium gluconate intravenously relieves the pain of lead colic promptly. A number of drugs (for example, sodium citrate, potassium iodide) combine with lead and promote its excretion from the body.

Left-handedness is perfectly normal for individuals who from early childhood (or later necessity arising from accident) are inclined to be left-handed. These people also give slight preference to their left eye, ear, and leg. There is no point in changing a person's handedness against his will. When this is done to children, they often respond unfavorably with the type of neuromuscular incoordination seen in stuttering, stammering, and bodily awkwardness. There is nothing wrong with a lefty. Some people are more or less ambidextrous; some can even use both hands with almost equal dexterity.

Leg Injuries—see LAMENESS and other topics listed under this heading.

Leishmaniasis—any one of a number of tropical diseases caused by infection with the protozoan parasite called *Leishmania* (after the English army surgeon, Sir William Leishman). The South and Central American type of the disease attacks principally the mucous membranes of the mouth, nose, and throat. The Asiatic, African, and Middle Eastern types produce skin ulcers almost anywhere on the body. The disease has some spectacular names: Bagdad sore, Aleppo boil, Biskra button, furunculus orientalis, and (when it attacks internal organs) KALA-AZAR. The sand fly transmits the disease to man.

Lens—any transparent body (glass, crystal, etc.) shaped so that it focuses rays of light. Glass lenses are, of course, the basis of eyeglasses, microscopes, telescopes, and all other optical instruments. Each EYE has its own crystalline lens. See EYES, EYE TROUBLE, CONTACT LENSES.

Lentigo—another name for FRECKLES.

LEPROSY

Leprosy is an ancient and awesome disease. The term *leper* is almost synonymous with social outcast. However, this disease is not so much to be feared as its reputation suggests.

The United States, Canada, and Western Europe (except Norway) are practically free of leprosy, except for a rare case. In the whole United States in 1949, for example, there were just 4 deaths from leprosy, as against over 500,000 from heart disease and associated conditions. Leprosy in the United States has been limited to a few areas in the Gulf states.

For generations it has been customary for known lepers to live together in their own colonies. A National Leprosarium, under management of the U.S. Public Health Service, has been operated since 1921 at Carville, Louisiana. Before that time it was the Louisiana Leper Home, established in 1900. In a half century fewer than 1,400 patients were admitted for treatment. Compare this with admissions to state hospitals for the mentally ill.

It is difficult to discuss leprosy without conjuring up vague terrors. Part of this arises from the severe scourging of leprosy in the Old Testament. However, it is highly probable that many skin diseases were wrongly called leprosy and their unhappy victims banished into lifelong isolation. With the limited knowledge of infectious and communicable diseases then available, before the germ theory of disease, isolation was the best way that society could devise to preserve itself.

Leprosy is still widespread in Africa, Asia, the Pacific islands. It has existed in India since the beginning of recorded history. Southern China is called the "cradle of leprosy." Leprosy is still found in Mexico, Brazil, the West Indies.

Cause and course of leprosy. The germ associated with leprosy was discovered in 1874 by Hansen, and is called Hansen's bacillus, *Bacillus leprae,* or *Mycobacterium leprae.* Leprosy is sometimes called Hansen's disease. There is some resemblance between the germ of TUBERCULOSIS and that of leprosy, although the two diseases, as commonly known today, are utterly different.

There are two recognized forms of leprosy, though they are sometimes mixed. In one form the skin becomes thickened and irregular, is covered with large nodules (which may ulcerate). These nodules sometimes give the face a repulsive, lionlike expression and spread into the nose and throat, causing breathing difficulties. Life may be snuffed out in 5 to 10 years.

The second form of leprosy appears to begin in and affect primarily the nerves. The skin areas served by these nerves become large white patches, dead to feeling. The most distressing feature of this disease in its chronic form is that it causes fingers and toes and even larger parts of the limbs to shrivel up and fall off—relatively painlessly. Many patients with this form of leprosy live for 20 to 30 years.

How catching is leprosy? Not very. It takes intimate and prolonged contact with infected individuals over a period of years—and something else, still unknown—to contract leprosy. The disease begins very slowly, insidiously, and the time between infection and outbreak or diagnosis is at least 1 to 3 years, often much longer. The disease is not hereditary. Prevention and control of leprosy is primarily a public-health problem in relatively undeveloped tropic and subtropical countries. More rigid enforcement of isolation procedures (such as removing children of lepers from their leprous surroundings at birth) would probably help.

In the United States, at least, there can be no reasonable objection to admitting a leper temporarily to a general hospital, if proper nursing and medical precautions are taken.

The disease is most often discovered in young adults, 25 to 35—women only half as often as men.

Treatment of leprosy. Chaulmoogra oil has long been used as a remedy for leprosy. Chemical derivatives of chaulmoogra are also used. Sulfonamide drugs appear to be useful, but they do not cure the disease. As in the treatment of tuberculosis, general hygiene—good food, cleanliness, and so forth—seem important. Drugs that prove useful in controlling tuberculosis, such as isoniazids, may turn out to be very helpful in leprosy control. Several promising new drugs for leprosy have recently been developed.

Leptospirosis—a disease caused by a spirochete. Found in many parts of the world, including the U.S., it is carried by rats, dogs, cows, and other animals. It may also be contracted from contaminated water. Jaundice may or may not accompany the disease.

Lesbian—female HOMOSEXUAL.

Lesion—an injury to any part of the body *from any cause* that results in damage, loss of structure or function of the body tissue involved. This is one of the hardest words in the medical vocabulary to understand and appreciate. A lesion may be caused by violence, poison, infection, dysfunction, or anything else. Wherever there is a lesion, something is wrong with the body. Mosquito bites, broken bones, running sores, severed nerves, bleeding piles, are all lesions. Compare with TRAUMA.

Lethargy—that "tired feeling"; see FATIGUE and NEUROSIS.

Leukemia—a BLOOD DISEASE, too many white blood cells; sometimes called CANCER of the blood.

Leukocyte—white BLOOD CELL.

Leukocytosis—an abnormal increase in the number of white BLOOD CELLS. Except during pregnancy and menstruation and after vigorous exercise, demonstrable leukocytosis is almost invariably a sign of INFECTION or other serious disease.

Leukopenia—a serious reduction in the number of white BLOOD CELLS. This occurs in some forms of allergy, in the late stages of leukemia, and as a result of sensitivity in certain people to particular drugs (e.g.

pyramidon). See AGRANULOCY-
TOSIS.

Leukoplakia—white patches
sometimes found on the mouth,
cheek, gum, and tongue (geographical tongue). The condition is chronic, the cause obscure. It may be related to continued irritation, which, if long
persistent, may lead to CANCER.

Leukorrhea—"the whites"; a
white flow from the vagina. See
FEMALE TROUBLES.

Leukotomy—surgical cutting of
white nerve fibers in the frontal
lobe of the brain. This operation is sometimes performed to
relieve some forms of MENTAL
ILLNESS; notably psychoses attended with severe mental depression and anxious obsessions.
The patient sacrifices some of
his higher mental powers for a
more cheerful and relaxed
mood. (See LOBOTOMY.)

Libido—commonly misinterpreted to mean only sexual urge, inclination, longing or desire. But
this is only a small part of the
total libido. Libido is the
prime mover of the unconscious
mind, the driving force of the
lust for life that animates a
human being. In terms of psychoanalysis, it is the *id* in action. See PSYCHOANALYSIS, UN-
CONSCIOUS MIND.

Lice infest body, hair, and
clothing. See INSECTS; CRABS.

Ligaments—tough bands or
cords of fibrous connective tissue that hold together JOINTS
and support body organs. A

broad ligament, for example,
supports the uterus. Whole sets
of ligaments lash and bind together different joints of the
body. We speak of ligaments of
the neck, spine, shoulder, elbow, hand, pelvis, knee, and
foot. Ligaments rarely contain
elastic tissue; they should be
distinguished from TENDONS,
which are attached to muscles.

Ligaments can be pulled,
sprained, strained, torn from
their moorings, and broken by
the same kind of violence that
produces fractures, dislocations,
sprains, and other joint injuries.
See JOINTS. The treatment of a
pulled or torn ligament is usually rest, bandaging or splinting, gentle massage, and application of heat until the tear has
repaired itself or the BRUISE resolved.

Ligate—to apply a LIGATURE.

Ligature—a thread, of silk, catgut or other material, or wire
used to tie off and close up a
bleeding blood vessel. Applying
ligatures and tying knots in
them is a large part of the essential routine of SURGERY.

Lightening—the slight sinking
of the pregnant uterus into the
pelvic cavity during the middle
of the ninth month of PREG-
NANCY.

Lime—the small green citrus
fruit, rich in vitamin C, and a
preventive of scurvy; also the
element CALCIUM, particularly
as calcium oxide.

Limp—see LAMENESS.

Liniment—a liquid which is rubbed on the skin. Most liniments contain some irritant ingredient (for example, turpentine or ammonia) that, along with the massage effected by applying the liniment, may bring more blood temporarily to the aching or painful part. Liniments may give some relief to muscular aches and pains (RHEUMATISM), but they cure nothing. Though they have a long history, liniments usually have no more value than that accomplished by massage and the application of wet or dry heat. Repeated applications of liniments with strong and blistering ingredients ("horse liniments") may dangerously damage the skin.

Lipoma—a fatty tumor. Such tumors are usually painless and harmless, although sometimes unsightly. There are other types of tumors, also containing fat cells, which may be more dangerous (see CANCER).

Lips of the mouth are muscles covered by mucous membrane. Lips are subject to congenital malformation, notably HARELIP, in which the incompletely closed upper lip is notched like a rabbit's (see CLEFT PALATE). A thick overgrown lower lip (Hapsburg lip) may appear along with a jutting jaw, a deformity due to HEREDITY. An overgrowth of the upper lip also sometimes occurs, often in women as a result of ENDOCRINE-gland disturbances. Misshapen lips can be corrected by PLASTIC SURGERY if cosmetics are not adequate.

ALLERGY or idiosyncrasy to the dyes and other chemical substances contained in lipstick or other cosmetics may cause the lips to become swollen and puffed. Treatment depends primarily on discovering and avoiding the offending allergen.

Chapped and cracked lips are often caused by exposure to cold or too much sunlight. A mild protective ointment usually brings relief. Any household hand lotion (if not swallowed) generally suffices. Glycerine in rose water is an old stand-by.

Persistent cracks at the corners of the lips are often associated with VITAMIN deficiencies and can be cured by any vitamin pills containing adequate amounts of vitamin B complex (specifically, riboflavin).

BOILS sometimes appear on the lips. Those on the upper lip especially should be handled gently and with the utmost care —never squeezed or pinched, lest their infective core be carried directly to the brain.

Chronic irritation of the lips may be a factor in inducing CANCER of the lip. This is one of the most visible and therefore curable types of cancer. A spreading spot of irritation on the lips should always be checked promptly.

Lithiasis—the formation of *stones*. See KIDNEY STONES and GALLSTONES.

Lithotomy—"cutting for stone." The term is primarily applied to cutting into the bladder for removal of kidney stones that have passed into it. This operation is of great historical interest. It was the only common and generally successful operation on the internal organs undertaken by surgeons before aseptic surgery.

Liver—the largest gland in the body. The liver weighs from 3 to 4 pounds, and is situated in the right upper part of the abdomen, just below the diaphragm. Its outer border can sometimes be felt under the ribs. In a slight depression on the undersurface of the liver lies the gall bladder. Ducts from the liver join with the duct from the gall bladder to form a common bile duct that empties into the duodenum. The liver is essential to life. Fortunately, a human being has about 7 times as much liver tissue as he needs, and a damaged liver can regenerate itself if given the opportunity.

What does the liver do? Functions of the liver are numerous; it acts as a factory, warehouse, and detoxifying station. It manufactures (about a pint a day) and secretes *bile,* which is essential to the process of digesting food, especially fats. It stores *carbohydrates,* in the form of *glycogen,* and re-leases this body sugar into the blood stream when it is needed in other parts of the body, particularly by the muscles. It plays an essential role in fat storage and utilization.

All the veins from the stomach and intestines run through the liver (portal vein) on the way back to the heart. The portal vein breaks up into numerous small capillaries inside the liver. Hence the harmful substances that might appear in the blood stream are abstracted in the liver and destroyed.

Chemical reactions that take place in the liver are an important source of body heat. Among its other tasks are assisting in the build-up and breakdown of red blood cells, forming substances essential to blood clotting (fibrinogen), storing iron and copper, producing and storing vitamins, splitting proteins (amino acids). See LIVER TROUBLE. (See illustrations for ABDOMEN; DIGESTIVE SYSTEM; HEART.)

Liver Extract, processed from the livers of meat animals, contains essential blood-building elements needed by individuals suffering from pernicious ANEMIA. Liver extract can be given by mouth or intramuscular injection.

LIVER TROUBLE

Liver trouble, or biliousness, is a fairly common complaint. The best acknowledged symptom is JAUNDICE, or yellow coloration of the skin. What looks like liver trouble may actually be caused by disease of the heart, gall bladder, or pancreas. Also, liver disease may be fairly far advanced before it produces any distressing symptoms. A *sluggish liver* may describe either a *congested liver*, which is associated with heart failure and results from blood backing up into the liver, or *poor* DIGESTION, in which some obstruction to bile flow makes it difficult to assimilate fried or fatty foods.

Among serious liver diseases and disorders are *cirrhosis*, or hardening, of the liver; *atrophy*, or wasting, of the liver; *hepatitis*, or inflammation of the liver, caused by a wide variety of microbes, including viruses; *fatty degeneration* of the liver; and *congestion* of the liver. Since it is a large and prominent organ, the liver may also be injured by *violence* to the abdomen. Certain drugs also may harm the liver, notably chloroform, arsenic, and phosphorus compounds. Carbon tetrachloride, often used in dry cleaning, is a liver poison.

In *cirrhosis* of the liver the normal functioning cells are replaced by harder, fibrous tissue, like scar tissue. In *hobnail liver* the hardening process has reached such an extreme that nail-like projections appear on the outer surface of the liver.

The causes of cirrhosis are still not clear, and certainly not single. Infection, poison (toxins), and nutritional deficiency are probably all involved. In particular, a deficiency of vitamin B_1 (thiamine) seems to be concerned. The classical role of alcohol in producing cirrhosis of the liver is now considered to be very indirect. Alcoholic cirrhosis is primarily the result of nutritional deficiency; the heavy drinker simply does not get an adequate DIET. Treatment calls for a high-protein, high-carbohydrate diet, supplemented by vitamin B complex and liver extract.

Hepatitis, or inflammation of the liver, may occur as the result of infection elsewhere in the body or it may be confined to the liver. It is a frequent complication of tropical diseases, notably malaria, yellow fever, and amebic dysentery. Sometimes the inflammation goes on to abscess formation.

Infectious hepatitis is a virus infection of the liver. Before the virus factor was known, this condition was called *catarrhal jaundice*. The virus is probably spread by droplet infections from nose and throat and by contaminated food and water. Closely related to this condition, especially in symptoms, is *homologous serum jaundice.* This disease follows blood transfusions, serum injections, and unsterile injections of any kind when the donor (or needle) harbors the virus that attacks the liver.

Both conditions have long incubation periods—3 to 6 weeks following infection for infectious hepatitis; 7 to 20 weeks for homologous serum jaundice.

The seriousness of infectious hepatitis seems to be related to the protein metabolism of the patient. When the protein intake is low, or proteins are drained off, as in pregnancy, the liver damage may be severe.

Jaundice is the characteristic symptom. It may be preceded by gastrointestinal symptoms, nausea, vomiting, and loss of appetite. The liver is sometimes swollen and tender.

Jaundice and other symptoms of infectious hepatitis usually subside in 1 to 3 weeks under a regime of treatment that includes rest in bed and a diet high in proteins and vitamins B and C. This is a debilitating disease, and convalescence cannot be hurried too fast or relapses may occur. Return to a full schedule of activity must be gradual.

Congestion of the liver, more exactly, chronic passive congestion, arises as a result of the close connection of the blood circulation in the liver with that of the right side of the heart and of the lungs. When the right side of the heart is dilated, or the pulmonary circulation impeded, blood backs up into the liver. The liver becomes enlarged and tender; gastrointestinal symptoms, headache, and depression may appear. The treatment of this condition is essentially the treatment of the heart or lung conditions bringing it on. This usually means bed rest and administration of digitalis and diuretics.

In *fatty disease or degeneration of the liver* the cells of the liver become infiltrated with fatty tissue. This may be the result of wasting disease, but it more commonly follows upon a diet too rich in fat. The liver enlarges, but is not painful. This condition usually produces some indigestion, constipation, and discomfort in breathing, particularly after eating.

Liver tests. Many tests have been devised to determine liver function. These depend chiefly on the amount of bile found in the blood or urine and the amount of sugar in the blood. Since damaged liver cells pour out their glycogen, the treatment of many cases of liver damage requires injection of glucose into the veins.

Lobe—a rounded part of a body organ, more or less divided from the other parts. LUNGS, LIVER, and BRAIN are divided into lobes. The ear, too, has its lobe.

Lobectomy—removal of a lobe by surgery. It usually refers to the lobes of the lungs. This operation is most often performed for BRONCHIECTASIS and lung CANCER.

Lobotomy—cut into a lobe. It usually refers to the lobes of the brain (see LEUKOTOMY). A prefrontal or frontal lobotomy is performed by drilling holes into the skull and cutting the white fibers of the brain with a sharp, pointed instrument. In a transorbital lobotomy the entrance into the skull and brain is made just above the eye(s). This is the "ice-pick" operation. Lobotomies are performed for certain types of MENTAL ILLNESS.

Local Anesthetic—see ANESTHESIA.

Localized—restricted to one spot or area in the body and not spread all through it (which would be SYSTEMIC or generalized). Some infections or other conditions localize themselves and do not spread. In other cases great efforts must be made to keep an infection or cancer localized and not allow it to spread. Some conditions that *seem* localized in one area may actually be spread, via the blood and lymph streams, through the whole body; for example, syphilis.

LOCKJAW

Lockjaw, or tetanus, is not caused by stepping on a rusty nail unless that event introduces into the body the specific disease-causing microbe called the tetanus bacillus (*Clostridium tetani*). Any wound that brings this germ into the body—and the deeper the worse, because tetanus bacilli grow better without oxygen—can bring on lockjaw, a serious, often fatal, disease with symptoms something like hydrophobia (RABIES) and strychnine poisoning.

The risk of getting lockjaw, which was a scourge of armies in earlier generations, is not very great in today's civilized and motor-transported populations, because it is now possible to immunize with *tetanus toxoid*. Every infant at the age of 6 months should get *tetanus shots* (usually combined with DIPHTHERIA and WHOOP-ING-COUGH inoculations). Military personnel are routinely inoculated against tetanus; hence there was not a single death from tetanus in the U.S. armed forces in World War II.

Furthermore, the tetanus bacillus is found most frequently in soil contaminated with horse, cattle, or human excrement, and people don't have much contact with such soil nowadays. The bacillus lives and multiplies in the intestines of animals, with whom most people have little contact.

What is lockjaw? Lockjaw is an acute, infectious disease, When the germ invades the body, almost invariably through a puncture, laceration or gunshot wound, it multiplies and produces a powerful poison (or toxin) that irritates and excites the NERVES of the spinal cord. Symptoms may come on from 2 days to a month after infection, but usually within a week. All of them are MUSCLE spasms or contractions, more or less violent, resulting from nerve irritability. The commonest symptom, of course, is the tightening of the jaw muscles (trismus), baring the teeth and giving the appearance of a sardonic smile (risus sardonicus). The body may be rigidly bowed or arched backward or sideward. Painful, exhausting convulsions frequently appear, following the slightest stimuli. The mind usually remains clear, though anxious.

Treatment: With the best of modern treatment, something better than half the victims can be saved. Treatment includes administration of tetanus antitoxin, that is, immune serum (observing precautions for serum sensitivity); administration of sedatives and calcium; cleansing of the wound; and absolute rest and quiet. Tetanus toxoid is more efficient and less dangerous in persons who have been previously immunized.

Tetanus toxoid should be given immediately when there is any real risk that a wound may be infected with the tetanus bacillus.

Locomotor Ataxia—tabes dorsalis; a manifestation of late SYPHILIS. It is the result of syphilitic attack on the nerves of the spinal cord. The characteristic symptom is a heavy-footed, stumbling, uncoordinated gait. With modern PENICILLIN treatment, the distressing picture of locomotor ataxia has become exceedingly rare. See TABES.

Loin—the middle part of the back, the lumbar region, reaching from the bottom of the lowest rib to the top of the SACRUM.

Lordosis—swayback; forward CURVATURE OF THE SPINE.

"Lost Manhood"—a completely false term used to describe the perfectly normal event of nocturnal emission of semen (*"wet dream"*) experienced by practically all males from puberty onward. Unscrupulous quacks sometimes try to frighten young men into believing that if they "waste" their sperm early in life, the supply will soon run out. This is untrue. Until very old age the testes continue to manufacture sperm in the billions.

Lues—a politer name for SYPH-
ILIS. The adjective is LUETIC.

Lumbago—pain in the middle
part of the back, the lumbar
region. See BACKACHE, RHEU-
MATISM, LINIMENT, ARTHRITIS,
JOINTS.

Lumbar Puncture—a spinal tap;
that is, inserting a hollow needle
into the spinal canal and withdrawing spinal fluid. This is
done between the lumbar VER-
TEBRAE. The purpose of lumbar
puncture is to obtain spinal
fluid for diagnosis, relieve pressure from excess spinal fluid
(as in meningitis), or introduce
a drug or anesthetic solution
(spinal ANESTHESIA).

Luminal—a NARCOTIC drug used
in sleeping pills.

Lungs—left and right, are situated in the chest cavity (thoracic cage) and are enclosed by
the ribs, diaphragm, and chest
and back muscles. The heart is
located between the lungs. The
right lung has three lobes (or
parts): upper, middle, and lower. The left lung has two lobes:
upper and lower. The upper
part of the lung is called its
apex; the lower part its *base;*
the upper middle, inner aspect
where the bronchi and blood
vessels enter, the *hilus.* Each
lung is covered with a thin,
delicate membrane, the *pleura.*

The terminal portion of the
human breathing apparatus
(respiratory system) is made
up of the air sacs (alveoli) of
the lungs. These lie in lung tissue richly endowed with tiny

blood vessels (capillaries) coming from the pulmonary veins
and arteries that lead directly
to the heart. The exchange of
oxygen from the outside air to
the hemoglobin of the red
blood cells takes place between
the *alveoli* and the capillaries.
The lungs are worked for
breathing purposes by the diaphragm below them and the intercostal muscles that lie between the ribs. (See RESPIR-
ATORY SYSTEM; illustrations for
HEART.)

Lung Troubles are among the
commonest of serious human
ailments. The lungs are especially subject to infections. In
the early diagnosis and discovery of such troubles, the chest
X ray is a great boon.

The following diseases and
disorders of the lung or affect-
ing it are discussed under sep-
arate headings: TUBERCULOSIS,
PNEUMONIA, INFLUENZA, EMPY-
EMA (lung abscess), EMPHYSE-
MA (distended air sacs),
ATELECTASIS (collapse of the
lung), lung CANCER, BRONCHI-
ECTASIS, BRONCHITIS, ASTHMA,
PNEUMOTHORAX (gas in the
pleural cavity), and PLEURISY.

Lupus Erythematosus—a rare
COLLAGEN DISEASE.

Lupus Vulgaris—a disfiguring
SKIN disease, which is really the
reaction of the skin to infection
with the tubercle bacillus (skin
TUBERCULOSIS). The characteristic lesion is a soft, small, painless, yellow group of lumps on
the skin, so-called apple-butter

nodules. When they disappear, unsightly scars often remain. Strong ultraviolet light sometimes helps, and the apple-butter nodules can sometimes be surgically removed. However, vitamin D₂, isoniazid, and general lung hygiene are the best available remedies.

Luxation—a dislocation. See JOINTS.

Lymph—the fluid, outside the blood vessels, in which the cells and tissues are constantly bathed. It is much like the fluid part of the blood (blood plasma), except that it is the part that has oozed through thin walls of the smallest blood vessels. In it are dissolved proteins, fats, sugar, and everything else, brought by the blood stream, that the cells need for their life processes. Also in the lymph are the waste products given off by the cells, such as urea, uric acid, and large numbers of white BLOOD CELLS, mostly *lymphocytes*.

Lymphadenitis—acute or chronic inflammation and swelling of the lymph nodes.

Lymphatics—the channels and vessels that collect tissue fluid, lymph, and transport it back to the veins, so that it re-enters the circulating blood. The lymphatic vessels are something like blood vessels, but they are not blood vessels. For one thing, they have much thinner walls. The lymphatics are associated with the capillaries. Like the veins, they join together

into larger and larger lymphatic vessels, which eventually lead into a large vessel, called the *thoracic duct*. This duct empties into one of the large veins near the heart. At intervals along the lymph channels are situated oval masses of lymphoid tissue called lymph nodes or lymph glands (see GLANDS).

Lymph Nodes and glands are located at frequent intervals along the lymph channels. The larger ones, called glands (and sometimes noted as "swollen glands"), are found in the neck, groin, and armpits. These nodes are masses of lymphoid tissue whose function is to produce *lymphocytes* (white BLOOD CELLS) and act more or less as filters removing impurities and microbes from the lymph stream. (See GLANDS.)

Lymphogranuloma Venereum (Inguinale)—the "fifth VENEREAL DISEASE." It is also called climatic, or tropical, *bubo* and many other names. It is a specific virus infection, spread from person to person by sexual intercourse, and from the site of the infection to the groin and sometimes other parts of the body by way of the lymph channels. The early symptoms—swelling, stiffness and aching in the groin—occur about 10 to 30 days after exposure. Untreated, the condition may proceed to the development of slow-healing abscesses (sores, buboes) in the groin and to ELEPHANTIASIS of the pendent SEX ORGANS,

MALE. There is a diagnostic skin test for this disease, and vaccines derived from the infected lymph glands themselves (autogenous vaccines) are often helpful. Both men and women can be infected.

Lymphoma—any abnormal growth involving lymphoid tissue.

Lymphosarcoma—see HODGKIN'S DISEASE.

Lysis comes from the Greek word meaning "to dissolve." In medicine it is applied to the *gradual* disappearance of DISEASE symptoms (as contrasted with crisis, or sudden disappearance) and to the breakdown and destruction of cells, particularly red BLOOD CELLS.

M

Any word printed in SMALL CAPITALS can be looked up under its own alphabetical listing for further information.

Magnesia—popularly called "milk of magnesia," correctly magnesium citrate solution, is an agreeable, effervescent, lemon-flavored, saline LAXATIVE.

Magnesium Sulfate—Epsom salts.

Maidenhead—*hymen;* a thin, perforated mucous membrane stretching across the opening of the vagina. Its biological purpose is unknown. It varies greatly in size, thickness, and extent. In many women it is merely rudimentary. It has one or more holes in it that permit the escape of menstrual blood. The hymen is usually broken by first sexual intercourse, but it may be ruptured in other ways. Despite superstition and opinion to the contrary, an unbroken hymen is not an absolute sign of virginity, nor is its absence proof of the opposite. (See illustration for SEX ORGANS, FEMALE.)

Malaise—a sick feeling, often accompanied by NAUSEA and HEADACHE.

MALARIA

Malaria is a mosquito-borne disease that remains the world's greatest public-health problem. Every year approximately 300,000,000 new cases of malaria occur and perhaps 3,000,000 people die of it (about 1% of the cases). While the disease has been practically eliminated from the United States, it continues as a scourge and menace in most tropical and subtropical countries.

Malaria has a long history. It was known to Hippocrates in the

4th century B.C.; it played a role in the decline and fall of the Roman Empire; it attacked a million Union soldiers during the American Civil War. However, the proof that it was transmitted from one human being to another by the bite of the *Anopheles* mosquito was not shown till the end of the 19th century. Credit for this discovery goes largely to Sir Ronald Ross, a British army surgeon stationed in India, and Battista Grassi, an Italian scientist. However, Alphonse Laveran had previously discovered the malarial parasite in the blood of patients (1880). Malaria has been known by many names, such as "jungle fever," "blackwater fever" (a very severe form of the disease), "marsh miasma," and "the ague."

The characteristic symptoms of malaria are shaking chills, high fever, and profuse sweating, often accompanied by headache, nausea, mental confusion and extreme thirst. The attacks, or paroxysms, are periodic; they usually begin in the early afternoon and last for several hours, after which the patient is free of symptoms until the next attack begins. The symptoms and their periodicity vary in accordance with the particular species of the malarial parasite present. The attacks may come on daily (quotidian), every other day (tertian), or at intervals of four days (quartan). Malaria wears its victims down, leaving them frail and exhausted. Because the parasite attacks the red blood cells, anemia and enlargement of the spleen are common consequences.

What causes malaria? The one-celled parasite (protozoön) that causes malaria belongs to the genus *Plasmodium.* The four species that affect man are named *P. vivax, P. falciparum, P. malariae,* and *P. ovale. P. vivax* is the cause of benign tertian malaria, the most common type of the disease; *P. falciparum,* of estivo-autumnal or subtertian malaria; *P. malariae,* of quartan malaria.

The malarial parasite has a complicated life cycle, which required a high order of scientific research to unravel. Human beings are, in fact, only intermediate hosts of the parasite; the *Anopheles* mosquito is the primary, or obligatory, host. The mosquito becomes infected by biting a person suffering from acute or chronic malaria at a time when the victim has the right proportion of male and female malarial parasites in his circulating blood. These forms mate in the stomach of the mosquito and produce a different (spore) form of the parasite (sporozoite). In about 10 days to 3 weeks these spore forms find their way into the salivary glands of the mosquito, from which they can be transmitted to human beings by the bite of the mosquito. These spore forms develop, mature, and split up in the blood stream of the human being. It is this *repeated process,* beginning about 10 days to 2 weeks after the mosquito bite, that brings about the periodic attacks of chills and fever in the infected individual.

The treatment of malaria depended for centuries on the QUININE contained in the bark of certain trees. In 1926 the first of the synthetic antimalarial drugs, plasmochin (plasmoquine), was introduced in Germany and since then hundreds of synthetic antimalarials have been formulated. Among those which have been widely used are atabrine, quinacrine, primaquine, and chloroquin (chloraquine). These antimalarial drugs are used not only to treat active cases of malaria but also to suppress the symptoms of the disease. In the suppressive treatment the drug must be given over long periods of time because symptoms may return when the drug is discontinued.

The prevention of malaria depends upon individual vigilance against *Anopheles* mosquito bites, plus the taking of suppressive drugs, and wide-scale public-health measures directed at mosquito control. Theoretically the disease could be controlled if *Anopheles* mosquitoes could be kept from biting people who already harbor the malarial parasites. But this is not quite practical. In some areas 20% of the population harbors the parasites. The *Anopheles* mosquito roams abroad particularly in the early evening. Individual protection includes wearing of proper clothing (especially leg covering), application of strong insect repellents, use of mosquito netting inside and outside sleeping quarters, and tight screening of such quarters.

The World Health Organization (WHO) places malaria control high on its agenda. The public-health attack on the *Anopheles* mosquito and its larvae takes many forms. The draining and cleaning up of swamps, rain holes, and other breeding places, the spraying of such places with oils and insecticides, the introduction of fish that eat larvae—all these measures are important and must be repeated. However, the great new hope in mosquito control is found in the newer insecticides, of which DDT is the prototype. These have a residual action that lasts for a long time. The spray-painting at intervals of walls and ceilings of homes and other buildings where mosquitoes come to rest knocks the insects out by the millions and is a primary malaria control measure. See INSECTS.

Male Sex Hormone—testosterone, produced in the testicles. Its chemical structure is known, and it can be produced synthetically for administration by injection or under the tongue. Its function is to induce and maintain secondary sex characteristics of the male. It induces growth and formation of muscle and bone. A tumor of the testicular cells producing an oversupply of male sex hormone in infancy results in a "little Hercules," a rapidly growing, deep-voiced child with a large penis and pubic hair.

As a drug, testosterone is used to speed up delayed puberty; promote muscle-building in patients with wasting diseases; stimulate growth in the thin, retarded child; strengthen porous bones (osteoporosis); substitute for lack of naturally produced hormone (eunuchoidism); encourage the descent of undescended testes (cryptorchidism); and treat certain female troubles, such as senile inflammation of the vagina. Too much male sex hormone given to a woman masculinizes her, bringing about growth of hair on the face, a lowered pitch of voice, and increased libido.

Unfortunately, testosterone appears to be of little use in increasing sperm production in the sterile or infertile male. Also, it is without value in treatment of IMPOTENCE, diminishing or decreasing sexual desire, and weak or incomplete erections—provided there is no testicular failure. These conditions are usually psychic in origin. In the normal male, testosterone has no discernible effect on LIBIDO. It may benefit some patients who are going through the gradual and ill-defined male climacteric, but it has no effect on pure personality disorders exhibited in the same symptoms of fatigue, irritability, depression, and nervousness.

Male Sex Organs—see SEX ORGANS, MALE.

Malformation—a deformity; for example, clubfoot, cleft palate, harelip, hunchback. *Congenital malformations* are those present at birth. They represent a failure of the fetus to develop properly. There is no adequate explanation for such failures, and no blame can attach to them.

Malignant in medical terminology refers primarily to CANCER. A true cancerous growth or neoplasm is called malignant. This means that it will tend to grow relentlessly, crowding out normal tissues, unless removed by surgery and/or treated by irradiation. However, there are degrees of malignancy; some growths are much less malignant than others. The diagnosis of malignancy must usually be made by a pathologist who examines the new-growing tissue under a microscope. The term usually used in distinction to malignant is *benign*, which means that the tumor is self-limited in its growth.

Malnutrition—failure to receive

adequate nourishment. This may be due to an inadequate DIET, the most common cause, or to some disease state or other abnormal condition that makes it difficult or impossible for the body to absorb, assimilate, and metabolize an adequate food intake. Vitamin, mineral, and protein deficiencies in the diet can induce various degrees of malnutrition even though a person is getting enough calories to sustain life.

Malocclusion—failure of the TEETH of the upper and lower jaws to meet properly for chewing and appearance.

Malpractice on the part of a physician or surgeon means failure to treat a patient with the skill and attention that could reasonably be expected of him. This is a question for expert witnesses, for only physicians can attest what reasonable skill in a particular situation may be. Most physicians are insured against malpractice. No physician is expected to guarantee a cure. While malpractice does occasionally occur, most malpractice suits are brought for the wrong reasons: grievance against a physician, failure to understand what the physician is expected to perform, anger at a fee charged, countersuit against suit for payment of a bill, or hope of collecting money from the physician. Most malpractice suits fail. If a patient feels he has a legitimate grievance against a physician, he should present this matter to the grievance committee of his local county medical society before hastening into a lawsuit.

Malta Fever—UNDULANT FEVER.

Mammary—relating to the *breasts*, which are mammary glands.

Mandelic Acid—an excellent urinary antiseptic.

Mandible—the lower jawbone.

Mania—frenzy or madness, a sign of MENTAL ILLNESS or disorder. It may be characterized by extreme violence of behavior, overtalkativeness, wildness, excitement, grandiose flights of ideas, or excessively high spirits. Mania may be temporary or prolonged, leading to complete exhaustion. It may be cyclic, or periodic, as in manic-depressive psychoses. It can be induced by purely emotional stimuli, organic disease (such as the delirium of high fevers), and drugs (such as alcohol). *Monomania* is excessive preoccupation with one idea. *Dipsomania* is incessant indulgence in alcoholic beverages. *Nymphomania* is excessive and abnormal desire for sexual gratification on the part of the female.

Mantoux Test—a simple and common test used in TUBERCULOSIS case-finding. To perform the test a very small amount (0.05 cc.) of diluted old tuberculin is injected into or between the superficial layers of the skin. If the site around the injection turns red, the test is called *positive*. It indicates that the person has *at some time* been infected with tubercle bacilli. It does not mean that the person has active tuberculosis. However, it is worthwhile getting a chest X-ray immediately if one has a positive Mantoux test. (This is also called Mendel's test.)

Manubrium—the top of the breastbone (a handle).

"Maphrodite"—see HERMAPHRODITE.

Marasmus—a disease state in infants in which they are unable to assimilate food. They gradually waste away and often die. No specific cause can be found.

Marihuana—a NARCOTIC drug.

Marrow—the soft, fatty substance found in the hollow inner spaces of the bones. Some of the cells in the bone marrow are importantly concerned with the manufacture of BLOOD CELLS. The breastbone is sometimes punctured (sternal puncture) to remove marrow cells for study.

Masculinization — development in the female of secondary sex characteristics of the male, such as hair on the face or even a heavy beard, a lower voice, baldness, and shrunken breasts. This condition, also called virilism, results from a change in the ENDOCRINE system, the male sex hormone becoming excessive. It often appears after the menopause and very markedly in the presence of certain tumors of the adrenal glands.

Masochism—the psychological tendency to take pleasure in receiving pain. In its extreme forms masochism is a sexual perversion in which satisfaction can be obtained only through receiving "cruel and inhuman treatment"; for example, whipping (flagellation), kicking, beating, and biting. The name derives from a 19th century Austrian novelist, Leopold Masoch, who described such scenes. The opposite of masochism is SADISM.

Massage. Even cavemen must have known that rubbing or stroking a sore part of the body made it feel better. But proper, intelligent application of massage as a part of modern medical treatment requires adequate training, skill, and real knowledge of the intended effects. Massage is just one of the techniques of PHYSICAL THERAPY (physiotherapy), and rarely, if ever, stands alone.

The purposes of massage are to relieve pain, decrease swelling, and increase the capabilities of movement in affected joints and muscles. If massage does not prove beneficial in these ways, or seems to make the condition worse, it should be discontinued, at least for the time being.

Gentle massage, superficial and rhythmical, soothes the nerves of sensation. It can relieve pain and put a person to sleep. Deep massage quickens the circulation of blood and lymph, bringing about speedier removal of waste products from affected areas. Deep stroking is done in the direction of the blood and lymph flow, that is, toward the center of the body. It serves to relax muscles and reduce swelling.

A number of massage movements are practiced by the skilled masseur or masseuse. The two principal ones are *stroking*, or *effleurage*, which is gentle pressure of the hand in one direction, and *kneading*, or *pétrissage*, which includes squeezing, kneading, or rolling movements applied with greater pressure. Other massage movements include *pressing, tapping* (with the finger tips), *thrusting* (into deeper parts), and *hacking* (striking muscles with the inner edge of the hand). *Vibratory movements* can also be made by hand or motor-driven machine.

Massage for treatment of body illness, such as arthritis, should be specifically prescribed by a physician, not taken casually.

Mastalgia—pain in the breasts.

Mastication—act of chewing food.

Mastitis—inflammation of the breasts. It is usually caused by specific infection and can be treated by administration of antibiotic drugs. Sometimes, however, abscesses form that have to be surgically drained. A stagnation mastitis, or "caked breast," in which painful lumps form in the breast, may occur in the early stages of milk-production and nursing.

Mastoid—the breast-shaped bone directly behind the ear. More exactly, the mastoid process is a part of the temporal bone of the skull. There are numerous cavities (air cells) in the mastoid bone. Some of these communicate with the middle ear, so infection in the EAR may pass on to the mastoid bone, causing MASTOIDITIS.

Mastoiditis—inflammation and infection of the mastoid. It is brought about by the same conditions that cause *middle-ear infections*. It frequently follows such diseases as measles, scarlet fever, and diphtheria. Symptoms include earache, a clinking sound in the ears, swelling behind the ear, and pain on pressure to the mastoid bone.

Since the mastoid bone touches on the coverings of the brain (meninges), as well as communicating with the ear, infection in this bone must always be taken seriously. It was formerly often necessary to operate on the mastoid bone to remove infected cells and thus prevent dangerous extension of infection from the ear to the brain. But since the advent of sulfa drugs and antibiotics, which control infection and are now used early in the course of a developing mastoiditis, mastoid operations have become rare.

Masturbation — self-stimulation of the sexual organs, usually to the point of orgasm. Contrary to some popular misconceptions, masturbation does not cause insanity, pimples, or any other damaging physical effects. Since the practice has long been judged wrong, it frequently invites feelings of fear, guilt, and shame. However, most of this is needless, since it is now known that touching of the genitals begins in infancy and that the practice of masturbation is exceedingly widespread.

When other interests are fostered, this substitution will often take a child's mind off masturbatory practice. Sometimes masturbation reflects the child's feeling of being neglected or rejected. In adolescence a morbid concentration on the subject, prompted by guilt, and the accompanying effort to fight it is one of the surest ways of effecting its continuance. Most people, sooner or later, simply outgrow their masturbatory needs and practices.

Maturation—the process of becoming fully developed, mature, "ripe." The word often refers to the development of body cells, particularly germ cells and blood cells.

Maturity—a common word in modern psychological vocabularies, it is used in contradistinction to *immature* and *childish*. Maturity describes the ideal pattern of everyday living in which an individual responds most favorably and appropriately, in terms of the society in which he lives, to the demands, stimuli, pressures, and frustrations that are the inescapable normal allotment of human beings.

Maxilla—the upper jaw bone. The lower jaw bone is called the *mandible,* or sometimes the inferior maxilla.

M.D.—doctor of medicine; a graduate and licensed practitioner of medicine. See FAMILY DOCTOR.

MEASLES

Measles, or rubeola, is an acute, infectious disease, usually of childhood. It is one of the most contagious diseases known. The cause is a specific virus *(Briareus morbillorum).* The disease is more feared for its complications than for itself; it is of greatest risk to children between 6 months and 5 years of age. Young children should not be exposed to measles on the specious grounds that "they will get it anyway."

Measles catches from measles; that is, from exposure to the oral or nasal discharges of an individual who has the disease. The incubation period of measles is from 7 to 14 days, usually about 9 or 10 days after exposure.

What are the symptoms of measles? The disease comes on suddenly, acting like a bad cold getting worse. The nose runs, the eyes are red and watery, a hard dry cough occurs, and fever goes up a bit every day for 3 or 4 days. On the third day of fever little white spots (Koplik's spots) can be recognized inside the mouth by an experienced observer. On the fourth day a characteristic rash or skin eruption occurs. This usually begins behind the ears, spreads rapidly to the face and body. The rash comes out fully in 2 or 3 days, and the patient is sickest during this time. Then the skin eruption begins to fade, and the "spots" may become little dry scabs. With the disappearance of the spots, the patient usually improves rapidly. A child can be allowed out of bed 2 days after his fever is down and permitted to play with other children within the week. The disease is most contagious in its *early* stages, from about 4 days before until 5 days after the appearance of the rash.

What are the complications of measles? Most commonly they are pneumonia, bronchitis, and ear abscesses. They come on after the rash in most cases and are heralded by the fact that the fever does not come down promptly, as expected. Children with measles should be protected from adults and other children with colds or sore throats, for these are the usual agents of the complications. Fortunately, the complications of measles can be effectively treated with antibiotic drugs.

What can be done about measles? The disease can be modified by injections of *gamma globulin,* which offers temporary protection. It is recommended for children under 5 and those in rundown condition. During the course of the disease the patient can be kept comfortable, often in a slightly darkened room. The young child can be protected from exposure. Complications can be watched for and promptly treated.

An attack of true measles usually confers permanent immunity to subsequent attacks.

Measles should not be confused with GERMAN MEASLES (rubella), an entirely different disease.

Meconium—newborn infant's first bowel movements; it is composed of bile, mucus, and other secretions that have accumulated in the intestines during intrauterine life.

Medical Social Service—a professional service to patients, physicians, hospital administration and the community. It has been developed in hospitals, clinics and convalescent homes to help patients out of environmental, emotional and personal difficulties related to their illness, recovery and preservation of health.

Medicine—the art, based on science, of treating disease. It is the province, responsibility, and dedication of the physician —the doctor of medicine, whether FAMILY DOCTOR or specialist. *Medicine* also refers to that branch of medical practice more fully known as internal medicine—in contrast to SURGERY, for example. A surgeon must be a physician and doctor of medicine, but many physicians do no surgery. *Medicine* also refers to the drug or remedy prescribed by the doctor, or bought at the drugstore without prescription, to alleviate pain or promote healing. See DRUGS.

Medicine Chest—The medicine chest or first-aid kit for home, office, factory, travel, or outdoor use should contain those minimal essential supplies necessary to take care of emergencies before or until a doctor arrives on the scene. The more isolated the locality, the more complete the medicine chest must be. In the average American home or office, just a few minutes away from a drugstore, it would be well to keep on hand the following:

Roller BANDAGES—1″, 2″, and 3″ sizes (width)

A triangular bandage—which can be folded into a cravat (a square yard of muslin cut diagonally will make two)

Sterile gauze pads—2″ x 2″ and 3″ x 3″ square

Adhesive tape—1″ width

Adhesive bandages and patches—assorted sizes

Sterile absorbent cotton—½-oz. box

Cotton-tipped wooden applicators—box of 50

Small bottle of ANTISEPTIC—e.g., iodine, mercurochrome

Tube of BURN ointment or petroleum jelly (petrolatum)

ASPIRIN tablets (or equivalent)—5-grain tablets

Bicarbonate of soda (baking soda)—4-oz. box

EPSOM SALTS—1 lb.

Aromatic spirits of ammonia—small (2-oz.) bottle

Rubbing alcohol (isopropyl alcohol)—small bottle, half-pint

Common table SALT—a small package (or salt tablets)

"Universal antidote" against POISON—1 package

Thermometers—1 oral and 1 rectal clinical (or FEVER) thermometer

Talcum powder

Hot-water bottle

Ice bag

Scissors

Safety pins

Tweezers

Eye cup and eye dropper

Paper cups

Teaspoon

Megacolon—an exceptionally large, "giant" colon (lower bowel), usually discovered in infancy or early childhood (*Hirschsprung's disease*). The symptoms include CONSTIPATION and fecal impaction. Treatment includes ENEMAS, PSYCHOTHERAPY (in adults), and sometimes SURGERY for removal of part of the lower bowel. See DIGESTIVE SYSTEM.

Megalomania—irrational belief in one's own overpowering greatness; the delusion of grandeur often seen in SCHIZOPHRENIA.

Melancholia—the deeply melancholy state of mind and body in which fear, anxiety, worry, indecision, pessimism, brooding, and unwillingness to act dominate the individual's mental outlook. There are many degrees of melancholia, which is also called *depression*. Only the extreme forms need be regarded as MENTAL ILLNESS. Everyone has days when life hardly seems worth-while.

Involutional melancholia is a condition that appears in late middle age, 3 times more commonly in women than in men, and appears to have some relationship with the change in the endocrine pattern that follows the change of life. The acuteness of this condition, however, often responds favorably to the administration of endocrine substances and stimulating or sedative drugs, to psychotherapy, and to a redirection of a pattern of life into new and constructive hobbies and activities.

Melena—dark, bloody stools.

Membrane—a sheet or layer of tissue that covers body surfaces or lines and divides body cavities. Typical are *mucous membranes*, as found on the lips and the lining of the digestive and respiratory tracts; *serous membranes*, such as those that separate parts of the chest cavity; and *synovial membranes*, fluid-secreting membranes that line joints. See MUCUS; JOINTS.

Menarche—onset of MENSTRUATION.

Mendelism—HEREDITY as predicted by scientific principles originally uncovered by Gregor Mendel.

Ménière's Disease, or syndrome, consists of repeated attacks of dizziness, nausea, ringing in the ears, and progressive deafness, all associated with inner-ear disturbances. See EAR TROUBLES.

Meninges—the membranes that cover the brain and spinal cord. There are 3 of them, called dura mater, pia mater, and arachnoid. (See illustration for BRAIN.)

Meningitis—inflammation of the meningeal membranes that envelop the brain and spinal cord. This inflammation can be secondary to a great many types of infection—for example, syphilis, tuberculosis, and pneumonia —but it is more commonly the result of infection with the *meningococcus* germ.

Meningococcal meningitis, also called cerebrospinal fever and spotted fever, is an acute infectious disease, usually of sudden onset and in epidemic circumstances. The early symptoms include fever, nausea, vomiting, headache, and sometimes coma or delirium. A dusky red skin rash, varying from little points to large blotches, then appears. Later symptoms include severe headache, muscle rigidity, stiff neck, and arched back.

The disease is transmitted by droplet infection from the nose and throat of patients or "healthy carriers," of whom there are a great number. It has sometimes been associated in epidemic form with military training camps or other institutions in which overcrowding occurs. It is most common in the late winter and early spring, most dangerous to infants. The incubation period ranges from 2 to 10 days after exposure, and the patient remains infectious to others as long as the bacteria remain in his nose and throat.

The diagnosis is usually confirmed by drawing fluid from the spinal cord (spinal puncture). The germ may also be found in the blood stream.

While meningococcal meningitis is a very serious disease, there are several favorable points about it. Most adults and many children are immune to it. Furthermore, the meningococcus germ is extremely vulnerable to sulfa drugs, penicillin, and other antibiotics, so prompt treatment with these usually controls the disease quickly. Before they were available, meningitis carried an extremely high death rate. Now it is down to from 3 to 5%.

Menopause—*change of life,* or *climacteric.* It is the time when normal MENSTRUATION ceases, and marks the end of the potential childbearing period. The menopause comes on anywhere from the early forties to the late fifties; on the average at about the age of 47. It usually comes on earlier in women who began to menstruate in their late rather than their early teens.

Just as the beginning of the menstrual cycle is marked by an increase in the hormones produced in the ovary, so the menopause is characterized by a gradual decrease in ovarian hormones. The menstrual and ovulatory cycle does not come to a sudden stop. It first becomes irregular and then stops. During this transition period, which may last 2 or 3 years, the menstrual flow becomes scantier.

In about 85 out of 100 cases there are no unusual symptoms, other than cessation of menstruation, at the menopause. Others endure a few "hot flashes," lasting a minute or two, occasional feelings of fatigue, or mild pains in the joints. Some women have feelings of depression and irritability. Fortunately, most symptoms associated with the menopause can now be quickly relieved by ovarian hormones. However, psychotherapy is sometimes required.

Mental attitude is most im-

portant in approaching the
menopause. It should be regarded as a normal event, not
something to be feared. Many
women find the years after the
menopause "the best years of
their lives." Sexual feelings
(libido) are not necessarily lost
at the menopause; they are
often heightened.

Menorrhagia—profuse menstrual bleeding; see MENSTRUATION;
FEMALE TROUBLES.

MENSTRUATION

Menstruation, also known as the *menses* or monthly *period*, is the
periodic discharge of blood from the vagina. The onset of menstruation (menarche) occurs normally in a girl's early teens, and
menstruation continues, unless interrupted by pregnancy or disease, until the late forties or early fifties, that is, until the
MENOPAUSE, or change of life. These are the years in which women
are able to bear children. The menstrual cycle, or as it might also
be called, the ovulatory cycle, is a part of the pattern of human reproduction for which the SEX ORGANS, FEMALE are designed.

On the *average*, menstruation occurs every 28 days, counted
from the first day of menstrual flow. However, many perfectly
normal women have regular cycles of 21 to 35 days, and occasionally even longer or shorter ones. Rarely, if ever, are women
as regular as clockwork in their menstrual cycle; a few days' irregularity is quite normal. The cycle can be upset by disease, physical
shock, or emotional excitement. A truly missed period may be an
early sign of pregnancy, but this is by no means always so.

On the *average*, again, a normal menstrual period lasts 3 to 5
days, but 2 to 7 days is still within normal range. The blood loss
is usually 1 to 2 ounces, and is quickly restored.

Excessive bleeding, or bleeding between periods (spotting), or
any other menstrual irregularities should invite a prompt medical
check-up. Painful menstruation (dysmenorrhea) is a common
FEMALE TROUBLE but need not be. A change in attitude toward
the menstrual process often may relieve the intensity of discomfort.
Slight cramps are magnified into intolerable pain by a hostile,
resentful attitude toward this normal phenomenon.

Myths and misconceptions about menstruation are many, dating
back to ignorance of the scientific facts. To the ancient Hebrews,
Greeks, Romans, and early Christians, the menstruating woman
was "unclean." To correct a few of these misconceptions, it may
be said:

Menstruation is *not* a sickness; it is a normal physiological process. It is *not* necessary to go to bed.

Exercise during the menstrual period is *not* harmful. An intelligent woman will take her period in stride, engaging in normal activities but avoiding extremes.

It is quite all right to bathe, shower, set or shampoo the hair, or even go swimming (except in very cold water).

The menstrual or ovulatory cycle is a complex process that involves the uterus, ovaries, and endocrine glands—especially the pituitary gland. The whole process is controlled by hormones. The most evident changes during the cycle occur in the inner lining (endometrium) of the uterus.

During the menstrual flow this lining is being shed, torn away from the underlying uterine tissues to which it is attached. Small blood vessels (capillaries) are broken as this takes place, and this is the menstrual blood. But even as this old lining is being shed, a new lining is commencing to grow. It gets thicker and thicker, soft and velvety, and enlaced with blood vessels for the next 3 weeks.

The function of this lining is to receive a fertilized ovum, if one should appear. If none appears, which is usually the case, the lining is again shed, with bleeding, and still another begins to grow. If a fertilized ovum *is* present to embed itself in endometrium, the menstrual cycle comes to an abrupt halt, to resume after childbirth.

OVULATION occurs at about the midpoint of the menstrual cycle. This is the time when a ripened egg cell bursts out of the tiny sac, or Graafian follicle, in which it has been maturing. This follicle manufactures ovarian hormones; it is a kind of "temporary endocrine gland." Most amazing, it makes one kind of hormone before the egg erupts, another kind afterward. The emptied follicle is called *corpus luteum* (literally, yellow body). Its hormone influences the endometrial lining to degenerate and disappear as part of the menstrual flow. But it also influences the pituitary gland to issue hormones that speed another egg cell to maturity and another Graafian follicle to open up, thus starting the whole cycle of events over again.

MENTAL ILLNESS

Mental illness is the exaggeration of personal behavior to the point where it strikes other people as queer, odd, abnormal, or dangerous. The distinction between mental health and mental illness, disease, or disorder is a very practical one: a person is mentally ill to the extent that he cannot love or work. The bulk of so-called mental illness is really *emotional maladjustment*. It represents the individual's failure to resolve emotional conflicts in his unconscious mind, and his unconscious choice of behavior patterns that he feels will protect him, more or less, against the intolerable inner pain of this continuing conflict. This pattern stands out clearly in the chronic alcoholic who drinks to "drown his sorrows." In this sense, mental illness is a reaction against and an escape from inner pain and conflict.

There are all degrees of mental illness, from mild to exceptionally severe. The person who becomes mentally ill continues to feel as he has basically felt before. However, his reactions and behavior become exaggerated and inappropriate, as viewed by the outside world. He may feel guilty about blunders forgotten and forgiven years before. He may hear voices, distorted symbols of the commands and warnings issued to him by his parents in his childhood; these voices may urge him to acts of folly or aggression. Under such circumstances he may become dangerous to himself and others and require professional psychiatric help, perhaps hospitalization. Contrary to popular misconceptions, the mentally ill are not so different from the mentally healthy. Indeed, they are often the same people at different times!

Is mental illness curable? Decidedly yes. There are some incurable cases, particularly those in which there has been irreversible damage to the brain cells; but on the whole mental illness responds to psychiatric treatment and is curable in a very high percentage of cases. "No branch of medical science, except obstetrics, is blessed by so many recoveries as psychiatry," declares Dr. Karl Menninger, an outstanding American psychiatrist. In mental hospitals that specialize in intensive treatment of selected cases, improvement and recovery rates run as high as 85%.

Few mental hospitals, it is true, are staffed and equipped to give such intensive treatment; but even at that about 45% of the patients admitted to state hospitals (which get about 90% of all patients admitted to mental hospitals) are discharged as improved or recovered. When a person has recovered from a bout of mental illness, whether spontaneously or with the help of treatment, he is just as capable of going about his business as he was before he took ill, and he should not be stigmatized for his illness.

Most patients admitted to mental hospitals require only a few weeks or months of hospitalization. About 60% of those admitted to public hospitals are discharged within a year; from private hospitals discharges are made even earlier.

What mental illness is NOT. There are a great many popular misconceptions about people who suffer from mental illness. We shall attempt to correct some of them here:

Insanity and mental illness, though related, are *not* the same thing. Insanity is a legal rather than medical term and implies that the person is incapable of determining between right and wrong and further that his actions are so unreliable that he is a danger to himself and others. Both circumstances are sometimes the case, but most mentally ill people are *not* insane.

The mentally ill person does *not* "lose his mind," except in rare instances. *Temporary* distortions of some mental faculties, such as memory and power of concentration, frequently occur. Real or permanent deterioration of the intellect is exceptional.

Mental illness is *not* mental deficiency, mental defectiveness, or FEEBLE-MINDEDNESS. The mentally defective person never develops average intelligence, whereas many people who suffer from mental illness are far above normal in intelligence.

Mental illness is *not* caused by masturbation, is *not* punishment for sin, is *not* directly inherited. There has been much speculation on the subject, but there is no convincing scientific evidence that mental illness is passed along from parent to child in the germ plasm. Considering how widespread mental illness really is, the appearance of several cases in the same family need not be considered particularly remarkable. It is much more reasonable to account for several cases of mental illness in one family on the grounds of social and cultural, rather than purely physical, heredity. All the members of the family have been exposed to the same cultural heritage and the same anxiety-provoking personalities and environment.

What causes mental illness? (1) Actual, demonstrable brain damage and (2) stress beyond the breaking point of the individual's particular personality structure. Even the most stable personalities have a breaking point, as World War II experiences often demonstrated.

A distinction can be made between "organic" and "functional" mental illness. In organic cases damage or destruction of nerve cells can be demonstrated, postulated, or even located. In "functional" disorders purely psychological mechanisms initiate the condition. However, the intimate relationship of mind and body must always be taken into account. No illness is altogether psychological or altogether physical. Still it must be noted that in a large proportion of mental illnesses no definite changes in the physical structure or function of the nervous system can be found. And yet many cases of functional illness respond to physical treatment; for example, electroshock and administration of drugs.

The causes of damage to brain cells, with accompanying symptoms of mental disorder, include head injuries, infections, toxins, drugs, tumors, and clogging or hardening of the arteries of the brain ("little strokes"), which are part of the aging process. Infections sometimes produce the delirium found in high fever. Late syphilitic infection (see TABES) is responsible for general *paresis*. Alcoholic psychoses are typical of brain damage induced by drugs or poisons. (See DELIRIUM TREMENS.)

In the functional, or psychogenic, mental illnesses, the least that can be said is that the causes are multiple. These conditions are long in developing; they reflect faults in personality development and structure. They are usually the culmination of unsuccessful and inappropriate reactions to life problems and repeated failure to adjust to reality. The underlying cause of functional mental illness is previous emotional conditioning, with special emphasis on a whole chain of emotional experiences in infancy and childhood, when reaction patterns were unconsciously set.

But there often exists an immediate or exciting cause of mental illness that can be more exactly identified. This usually turns out to be unusual stress (for example, a more responsible job, threat of death, or subjection to a domineering personality) or sudden deprivation of previous emotional support (for example, loss of a job, death of a spouse, removal to an unfamiliar environment).

How is mental illness classified? The basic classification in mental illness depends on the severity of symptoms and the degree to which they incapacitate the individual. Severe types of mental illness, those which may require hospitalization, are called *psychoses*. Milder degrees of illness are called *neuroses*. In between is a category of *psychoneuroses*, but this term has become practically synonymous with neuroses. The differences between psychoses and neuroses are of degree. The American Psychiatric Association has a standard classification of about 60 categories of mental illness. However, there is now a trend in psychiatry toward avoiding diagnostic labels for mental illness.

SCHIZOPHRENIA (split personality), also called dementia praecox, is the most common and least understood psychosis. Others include manic-depressive psychoses (see MANIA), with extreme mood swings; PARANOIA; involutional MELANCHOLIA; toxic psychoses; senile dementia (the childishness that sometimes occurs in old age).

Mental illnesses more likely to fall in the milder categories of neuroses go by the names of HYSTERIA, NEURASTHENIA, psychasthenia, anxiety state, shell shock, combat fatigue, soldier's heart (neurocirculatory asthenia), and hypochondria (abnormal preoccupation with the state of one's health). *Nervous breakdown* is a popular term applied to any mental illness that incapacitates a person and removes him from his usual sphere of activity.

How widespread is mental illness? If a broad definition of mental illness is taken, the number runs high into the millions. It has been estimated that 70% of medical practice in the U.S. is taken up with nervous and emotional disorders, alone or in combination with organic disease.

It is further estimated that at any one time about 1 person in every 20 in the U.S. is suffering from some serious mental or nervous disorder, that 1 in 10 will at some time be hospitalized for mental illness. This means that 8 to 10 million Americans are now in the throes of mental illness; that nearly 750,000 are in or under care of the nation's mental hospitals; that 250,000 new patients are admitted each year; that there are probably 1 million (0.6% of the population) psychotics in the U.S.

Nearly half (48%) of all hospital patients are in mental hospitals, and more than half of these are suffering from schizophrenia. Most of these patients (90%) are in state hospitals, of which there are about 360 in the U.S. Most of these are large hospitals, averaging 1,100 beds and running as high as 12,000 beds, and most are woefully understaffed. All psychiatric (mental) hospitals in the U.S. now maintain nearly 775,000 beds.

The cost of caring for these patients is high. Approximately 25% of tax income of some states must be appropriated for the care of the mentally ill (and the feeble-minded, who are about 1% of the population). It costs U.S. taxpayers over $1 billion a year to care for mentally ill patients. (In strange contrast, only a comparatively few million dollars a year are spent on research in mental illness.

How is mental illness treated? Modern psychiatry has a great many strings to its bow for treating mental illness, especially of functional origin. Central to all is PSYCHOTHERAPY, which includes PSYCHOANALYSIS, reassurance, suggestion, persuasion, and—the sum of all methods of expressive psychotherapy—re-education of the patient toward adopting more constructive attitudes toward himself and other people. Other methods of psychiatric treatment include hypnosis, narcosynthesis (the patient is given a sedative drug that puts him in a twilight state in which he talks freely), group psychotherapy, the protected environment of a mental hospital, shock therapy, drug therapy, and, most drastic, psychosurgery.

Even though its rationale is not yet completely understood, electroshock treatments have proved of great value in treating mental illness, particularly depressed and melancholy patients. A mild electrical current is passed between the frontal lobes of the brain; it is quite safe. Shock treatment may be repeated in a series of 8 to 10 or more treatments.

Stimulating (e.g. amphetamine) and sedative (e.g. barbiturate) drugs have long been used in treating mentally ill patients. "Tranquilizing drugs," in psychiatric use since 1950, often give even more remarkable results. Among these drugs are CHLORPROMAZINE and RAUWOLFIA derivatives. They are of particular value in quieting and relaxing agitated patients. Beginning in 1956, these new drugs reversed the long-time trend of increasing population in mental hospitals.

How can mental illness be prevented? This is a large order, which goes under the label of *mental hygiene.* It must be considered not only a personal problem but also a family, community, and public-health problem. As an individual, you can make conscious efforts toward leading a well-balanced life, including work, play, love, and worship, and toward understanding yourself, which means accepting the fact that there is a worse side to your nature, as to everyone else's. As a parent, you can help prevent mental illness in your children by bringing them up wisely with a balance of tender, loving care and discipline that sets limits for action. The roots of mental illness are set in childhood; emotional patterns are set before intelligence takes over. Hence mental health becomes a family affair. As a citizen you can support the mental-hygiene movement, lend a voice toward adequately staffed mental hospitals, mental-hygiene clinics, and child-guidance centers, both within and without the school system. You can speak up for an intelligent, well-informed attitude toward mental illness and break down prejudices against the mentally ill. If a relative, friend, employee or fellow-worker seems to be "losing his grip," you can urge professional psychiatric attention. Mental illness is, after all, an illness, not a shame or disgrace.

See also PSYCHOANALYSIS; NEUROSIS; SCHIZOPHRENIA.

Menthol—a secondary alcohol derived from oil of peppermint or made synthetically. Solid or in alcoholic solution, it is a cooling counterirritant, useful for application to the skin in mild neuralgias and headaches. It also relieves ITCHING and the burning sensation of fungus infections on the feet and hands when applied in an oily solution or ointment containing ½% to 1% menthol. It is an antiseptic and stimulant to inflamed mucous membranes, especially in the nose and throat, where it is used in 1% petrolatum solution. Menthol imparts a tingling sensation to the skin; it is used in many after-shave lotions and so-called "skin-fresheners."

Mercury—quicksilver; the well-known "heavy metal," liquid at ordinary temperatures, commonly used in fever and other thermometers. Compounds of mercury are found in many drugs, called *mercurials*, particularly ANTISEPTICS, antisyphilitics (no longer commonly used), and DIURETICS. Calomel is mercurous chloride. Mercury can be given in ointment form, because it is directly absorbed by the skin. Mercury poisoning occurs in both acute and chronic

form (as by ingestion of bichloride of mercury tablets). BAL is a specific antidote. One of the early symptoms of chronic mercury poisoning is a metallic taste in the mouth. Mercury wreaks special havoc on the kidneys.

Metabolism describes the physical and chemical changes, even in the smallest degree, that are constantly taking place in the billions of cells that make up the living body. It is the normal building up and breaking down of cells and tissues as they perform their allotted task and run their life span. In this process heat energy is released. The building-up process is called *anabolism;* the breaking-down process, which releases energy for the use of the body, is called *catabolism*. Oxygen is of supreme importance for maintenance of body metabolism. The individual body cells' use of oxygen and the end products of digestion is the essence of metabolic processes.

Some change in body metabolism occurs in all disease states. A high fever, for example, burns up an excess amount of chemical energy stored in the body as sugar and fat. In a number of diseases, however, notably DIABETES, GOUT, and OBESITY, failure of metabolism is the central factor. These are often called *metabolic diseases*. Endocrine glands are frequently involved.

See also BASAL METABOLISM.

Metastasis—spread of disease *within* the body, usually by way of the blood stream or lymph channels. The word is particularly used to describe the migration of CANCER cells from the site of their original growth to other parts of the body. Thus a bone cancer may metastasize to the liver.

Metatarsal—any one of the 5 more or less parallel bones of the feet that reach from the ankle joint to the toes. When in proper position, the metatarsal bones form a strong *metatarsal arch*, extending from the out-

side border of the foot to the instep. The breakdown of this arch (as well as the longitudinal arch, extending from the ball of the foot to the heel) is known as *flat feet* or *fallen arches*. Cramping of the metatarsal bones by improper footwear can result in sudden, extreme, burning pain (metatarsalgia), relieved only by removing the shoe and massaging the foot. (See FOOT TROUBLE; illustrations for BONES.)

Metrazol—proprietary name for a drug that powerfully stimulates the central NERVOUS SYSTEM. It has been used in the treatment of MENTAL ILLNESS.

Metrorrhagia—abnormal menstrual bleeding, especially between anticipated "normal" menstrual periods. See MENSTRUATION; FEMALE TROUBLES.

MICROBE

A microbe is a tiny living organism, a microörganism, visible only through a microscope. (The very smallest microbes can be seen only through an electron microscope, which magnifies up to 20,000 diameters or more.) Many microbes have been identified as *germs* causing disease in man and animals. However, in comparison to the total known number of microbes, only a few are disease-producing (pathogenic).

Smallest of the disease-producing microbes are VIRUSES (which see), responsible for such diseases as smallpox, the common cold, and polio. Slightly larger are RICKETTSIA, which cause such illnesses as typhus fever and Q fever. (Rickettsia are named after an American research worker, Howard Taylor Ricketts, 1871-1910, who first identified them and died investigating them.) Still bigger are BACTERIA, which bring on a great number of infectious diseases; for example, tuberculosis, pneumonia, and the venereal diseases. Next up the scale are FUNGI, including yeasts and molds, which cause fungus infections, such as athlete's foot. Then come PROTOZOA, which are tiny one-celled animals and parasites; notably the malarial parasites.

Under favorable conditions microbes multiply with great rapidity, and this is what makes them dangerous to man. An INFECTION, often evidenced by inflammation, is the result of rapidly increasing numbers of microbes at some places in the body.

Microbes commonly reproduce by simple cell division, called fission. One cell divides into 2, 2 into 4, and so on. Many microbes begin reproducing themselves when they are less than a half hour old. At this rate a single bacterium, if unchecked, could turn into more than 16 million bacteria in 12 hours! However, there are checks on such growth; for instance, a limited supply of nutrient, accumulation of waste products, and special microbe-fighting white blood cells.

Microbes require a variety of special conditions favorable to their growth and reproduction. Among their requirements are adequate nourishment from their host cells, proper temperature (usually close to body temperature), moisture, either the presence or absence of air and oxygen, absence of direct sunlight or chemical or biological antagonists. In general, disease-producing microbes can be considered unwelcome parasites on their host cells.

Man's attack on his microbial enemies, since he discovered their existence, has been manifold. Many methods have been devised to destroy them and interfere with their life cycle, both inside and outside the human host. A great problem has been to devise drugs that would destroy or inhibit bacteria without harming the patient. Antibiotics, like penicillin and the sulfa drugs, have gone a long way in this direction. Heat sterilization, the principle of pasteurization, makes unlivable temperatures for microbes. The operating-room rituals of *aseptic* surgery are designed to keep microbes out of the operative field. The control of communicable disease demands many techniques of breaking the chains of microbial infection.

Micturition—urination.

MIGRAINE

A migraine, or sick HEADACHE, is generally confined to one side of the head, often preceded by warning signals, such as flashes of light before the eyes or other visual disturbances. Unfortunately, it often recurs in an individual with a migrainous temperament or inheritance. Few conditions that do not kill can make a person as miserable as a severe migraine attack.

Moderate to severe migraine headaches are usually accompanied by pain in the eyes, nausea, and vomiting. Sometimes the head pain is mild, while that in the abdomen is so severe as to suggest an acute abdominal emergency. However, abdominal surgery never cures migraine.

Women appear to suffer from migraine headaches far more frequently than men. The migraine type is usually a keen, sensitive, imaginative, intelligent, serious, and ambitious person, but a perfectionist and a worrier. She is often a little woman, with thin nostrils, a smooth complexion, and fine hair.

What causes migraine? Nobody really knows, although there are plenty of theories. Heredity seems to be an important factor, but only one of many. There is some evidence that migraine is *associated* with dilatation of the blood vessels of the neck and brain, but this does not solve the problem. Psychic strain and emotional conflict undoubtedly play a part. Given a migraine temperament, any number of psychic or physiological events (e.g. the prospect of divorce or the arrival of a menstrual period) can set off (trigger) an attack.

What can be done about migraine? This is a stubborn but not insoluble problem. There are no sure-fire or miracle cures. A sympathetic physician who helps the patient adjust herself to the conditions that induce migraine attacks can be of inestimable help. The idea is to avoid circumstances that trigger attacks. Since fatigue is one of these, genuine rest and relaxation often help, not to mention avoidance of fatigue. Sensitivity to certain foods may also be a trigger (though doubtfully a cause) of migraine. Hence it is a good idea to keep a record of foods that bring on attacks and henceforth avoid them. A change of habits, reducing needless pressures and fruitless worrying, is also of value.

When an attack is imminent, numerous drugs may relieve or abort it. What works for one may not work for another, and this is what has to be worked out by experience with the help of the sympathetic physician. Among the drugs used to control migraine are caffeine (even a few cups of strong coffee), amphetamine, aspirin, ergotamine, barbiturates, and oxygen and carbon dioxide (by inhalation). Treatment must be prompt and adequate.

Miltown—a TRANQUILIZER.

Minerals considered necessary to the nutrition and function of the human body are, in order of amount: calcium, phosphorus, potassium, sulfur, chlorine, sodium, magnesium, iron, iodine, copper, and—possibly—cobalt, manganese, molybdenum, and zinc. Collectively they make up 4 to 5% of the body weight. There is enough lime (calcium) in an adult to whitewash a goodsize basement, enough phosphorus (2 pounds) to keep a man in matches for months, enough iron to make a large nail, enough sodium and chlorine to provide a shaker of table salt.

The mineral elements most likely to be deficient in the American DIET are calcium, iron, and iodine. When these 3 elements are included in adequate amounts in a mixed diet of foods from natural sources, the other mineral elements are also usually present.

CALCIUM is found in the BONES and TEETH; it is essential to BLOOD CLOTTING; it helps regulate the acid-base balance of the body, the heartbeat, and the irritability of the neuromuscular system (see TETANY). The best dietary source of calcium is milk.

PHOSPHORUS usually goes along with calcium and plays a complementary role to calcium. It, too, is found in bones and teeth. Phosphorus (phosphates) is also concerned with metabolism of fats and carbohydrates.

Iron is concentrated in the hemoglobin of the BLOOD. Its lack causes ANEMIA, which see. The best dietary sources of iron are variety meats, like liver, and molasses. *Copper* goes along with iron.

Sodium and *potassium* are another pair of minerals that complement each other's actions in body function. They are largely concerned with water balance. Sodium is found in common table salt (sodium chloride) along with *chlorine*, which shows up in the hydrochloric acid of the gastric juice.

IODINE, in minute amounts, is essential to the function of the *thyroid gland* (see ENDOCRINE GLANDS). It is found in sea food and iodized salt.

The trace elements—minerals found in tiny amounts in the human body—have not yet been assigned any clearly defined role or any vital level of intake.

"Miracle Drugs"—there are none; this is a newspaper term for any number of drugs that appear to yield unexpectedly good results in treatment. In the 1930's the sulfa (sulfonamide) drugs had the title; in the 1940's, it was the antibiotics, beginning with penicillin; in the 1950's, the designation has gone to ACTH and cortisone (for arthritis), later isoniazid (for tuberculosis), still later rauwolfia and chlorpromazine (for mental illness). The newest drug usually gets the miracle title. Actually all drugs introduced for use have undergone careful scientific study for their pharmacological action before release.

Miscarriage—spontaneous ABORTION. See PREGNANCY and CHILDBIRTH.

Moles—SKIN abnormalities. An enlarging mole should always get prompt medical attention; it may be a forerunner of skin CANCER.

Mongolian Idiot—a child born with serious mental and physical defects, most notable of which (and from which the condition gets its name) is an upward, oblique slant of the eyes, like an Oriental's. The unfortunate Mongoloid child usually has a flat face, stubby nose, a protruding tongue, small or deformed ears, limp muscles, short thumbs, and an abnormal heart. Such children develop slowly and their intelligence is never high. However, they may be quite lively and imitative. Most of them die young. Placement in a special home or institution is recommended by many physicians.

The reasons for this particular congenital deformity of mind and body are not known; certainly no blame can attach to mother or father. Chances of a subsequent child being Mongoloid are extremely small, almost negligible.

Moniliasis—specific FUNGUS infection by monilia (Candida), which may involve the mouth (thrush), skin, intestines, lungs, or vagina.

Mononucleosis—the presence in the blood stream of an exceptionally large number of white BLOOD CELLS with but one nucleus. *Infectious mononucleosis* is an acute, infectious disease also called GLANDULAR FEVER.

Monster—a badly deformed fetus incapable of living if born. Monsters usually lack a vital part, such as heart or head, or have extra parts, such as two heads and four legs. Monster births are exceedingly rare, because badly deformed fetuses are usually spontaneously aborted. Parents are in no way to blame for siring or bearing monsters.

Mons Veneris—"mount of Venus"; the pad of rounded, fatty tissue just above the SEX ORGANS, FEMALE, covered with pubic hair.

Morbidity—sickness. The *morbidity rate* is the ratio of the number of sick people in a community to the total population. It is exceedingly difficult to determine the general or specific morbidity rates with great accuracy (except for a few specific, reportable diseases).

Moron—a person of low intelligence, smarter than an imbecile and just below a dull normal. By some reckonings a moron has a mental age of 8 to 12 and an intelligence quotient (I.Q.) between 50 and 74.

Morphine—a NARCOTIC drug, derived from opium. Though addiction to it must be guarded against, an injection of it is still the physician's sovereign remedy for prompt relief of many kinds of agonizing pain. It is contraindicated in some painful conditions.

Mortality—the death rate; the ratio of total number of deaths to the total population. The mortality rate of a specific disease is usually reported as the number of deaths per 100,000 population.

Mosquito Bites—see INSECTS.

Motion Sickness—dizziness, headache, nausea, and vomiting produced by unaccustomed motions of vehicles of transportation; also called seasick-ness, car sickness, airsickness. See EARS, where the seat of the trouble really lies.

MS—MULTIPLE SCLEROSIS.

Mucus—the thick, slippery fluid normally secreted by *mucous membranes,* which line the hollow organs of the body, notably the nose, mouth, stomach, intestines, bronchial tubes, urinary tract, and vagina. Mucus contains *mucin* (a sugar and protein compound), water, salts, and some sloughed-off cells. Its principal function is lubrication of the parts. A large flow of mucus usually signifies an underlying infection. Mucus raised from the bronchial tubes of the lungs is called *phlegm;* that which flows from the running nose, *snot.*

MULTIPLE SCLEROSIS

Multiple sclerosis, commonly called MS, is a chronic, crippling disease of the central nervous system, usually attacking young adults. The insulating tissue that covers the nerve fibers, that is, the myelin sheath, degenerates in patches and is replaced by scar tissue, which gives the disease its name. (MS is sometimes roughly translated as "many scars"—on the nervous system, of course.)

In patients suffering from multiple sclerosis, nerve messages from the brain to muscles and organs are "short-circuited." Hence normal nervous system control is lost over many different parts of the body, notably the muscles of locomotion.

Signs and symptoms of the disease vary greatly, depending on the degree and location of nerve damage. Among the most common signs are staggering gait (some patients walk as if they were drunk), blurred or double vision, tremors, paralysis, pins-and-needles sensations, numbness, slurred speech (some patients talk as if they had a hot potato in their mouth), bowel and bladder difficulties.

What causes MS is not yet known, but it is known that the disease is not contagious. Most authorities agree it is not hereditary. Many theories regarding its origin are now being explored. Some scientists think it is caused by a *virus;* others that it has a different infectious origin. Disturbances of *metabolism, blood clotting,* and even *allergies* have been suspected.

MS should not be confused with amyotrophic lateral sclerosis ("GEHRIG'S DISEASE.")

Who has MS? About a quarter-million Americans and hundreds of thousands of people in other countries. MS usually strikes young adults in the prime of life, between the ages of 20 and 40. It seems to be more common in cold climates than in warm ones.

What are an MS patient's prospects? MS can attack fatally, but usually it does not. Many patients live close to a normal life span. Often they have *remissions* of the disease, during which their physical condition improves significantly—sometimes for a few weeks or months, sometimes for years. In general, though, the course of the disease is progressive; a patient who can at first walk alone must later use a cane, then a wheel chair, and may finally become bedridden. Even so, it is usually much better for these patients to remain in their homes than to go to hospitals, except for temporary, specialized treatment.

Whatever the stage of the disease, the rehabilitation procedures can help the patient to live as efficiently and happily as possible within the limits of his disability. It is especially important that the families of MS patients know something about the disease and make adequate plans for keeping the patient in the family circle without overprotecting him or allowing him to become too great a burden on the family routine and resources. A matter-of-fact, take-it-in-stride, guilt-free attitude toward the patient will help him to achieve his maximum usefulness with the least drain on the family.

What is the treatment for MS? Unfortunately no specific treatment has yet been found to cure the disease or halt all its symptoms. The situation is complicated by the fact that no two cases of MS are exactly alike. Nevertheless—

Physical therapy is often recommended to maintain muscle tone. Along with this often go *rehabilitation* procedures that permit the patient to master the activities of daily living with far less trouble to himself and his family than anyone had previously imagined.

Psychotherapy has proved helpful to many patients—and their families. Avoidance of undue emotional disturbances, along with good food and carefully graded and selected exercise, may help to control the effects of the disease.

What should a person do if he thinks he has MS? He should visit his family doctor immediately. After a careful examination the doctor will, if he thinks it necessary, refer the patient to a nerve specialist or to one of several multiple-sclerosis clinics in the United States for a neurological examination. There is no quick, simple way for a doctor to diagnose MS.

What is being done about MS? Research is the most hopeful approach toward understanding and curing or preventing any disease, and this is true of MS, with its many still-baffling factors. The disease was first scientifically recognized (in the case of a young servant girl) and described in 1870 by the famous French nerve specialist Jean *Charcot,* but comparatively little research was done on it until MS patients and their friends organized the *National Multiple Sclerosis Society* in 1946. This society now supports and encourages many research projects.

Mumps—infectious *parotitis;* an acute contagious disease, serious only in its complications. It is caused by a specific virus (*Rabula inflans*), and its characteristic mark is inflammation, swelling, and tenderness of the parotid glands, which lie just behind the lobe of the ear. Sometimes the other salivary glands, submaxillary and sublingual, are involved. The swelling usually begins on one side and spreads to the other in a few days. It lasts, on the average, from a week to 10 days. There is usually some fever in the early course of the disease, highest on the second or third day. There is no specific treatment; the patient is made as comfortable as possible, and kept in bed as long as fever and swelling persist. Chewing and swallowing are often painful; tart foods, like pickles and lemon juice, may cause great discomfort.

Mumps is essentially a childhood disease, occurring most frequently between the ages of 5 and 15. It is somewhat less prevalent than measles and chickenpox, and less contagious. It is spread by discharges from the nose and throat. The incubation period ranges from 12 to 26 days. Immunity follows an attack, but mumps can be caught more than once.

Complications: The serious complication of mumps is involvement of the sex glands—testes in men, ovaries in women. This is far more common after puberty than before. While mumps has complications in perhaps 1 in 100 cases, its advent in *adult males* brings about swelling and inflammation of the testicles (*orchitis*) in about 10 to 15% of the cases.

Sometimes atrophy of the testicles and sterility result. Involvement of the testicles demands special treatment to reduce pain and risk of damage. Fathers and big brothers of children with mumps should not needlessly expose themselves to the disease. The mumps virus may also invade the breasts, labia majora, pancreas, and meninges (causing *mumps meningitis* with a stiff neck and high fever).

Murmur—medically, a gentle, blowing sound heard through a stethoscope. It is one of many heart sounds, and there are many kinds of murmurs. Sometimes the murmurs come and go. The presence of a heart murmur does not necessarily indicate heart disease or any serious heart damage.

MUSCLES

Muscles are the flesh of the body, making up about 40% of its total weight. Their particular function is to move themselves and other parts. There are two main types of muscle: (1) *voluntary* or *striped* (striated) muscle, which is the bulk of the skeletal muscle; and (2) *involuntary* or *smooth* muscle, such as that making up the muscular layers of the intestines, blood vessels, and bladder. The heart (cardiac) muscle is in a class by itself: striated but involuntary.

There are about 620 voluntary muscles, each with its own name, nerve supply, function, and points of origin and insertion. Muscles vary greatly in size and shape—from the gluteus maximus, which makes up the substance of the buttocks and moves the thighs, to the arrectores pilorum, which are attached to hair follicles and elevate the hairs of the skin. Muscles are named from location, direction of fibers, uses, shape, and points of attachment.

Each muscle is a separate organ, controlled by a special nerve or set of nerves that connect it with the spinal cord and the brain. No muscle acts alone. There is, in general, this coordinated set of actions: (1) the signaled muscle contracts; (2) the muscle or muscles opposing it, its antagonist, relaxes; and (3) adjoining muscles spontaneously contract to increase the efficiency of the contracting muscle.

When a muscle's nerve supply is interrupted, the muscle becomes paralyzed and will not be under voluntary control again unless and until the nerve function is restored. When the nerve coordination of the muscles fails (in the brain or along the line of nerve impulse transmission), tremors, twitchings, and uncontrolled movements result. The nerves, not the muscles, are at fault.

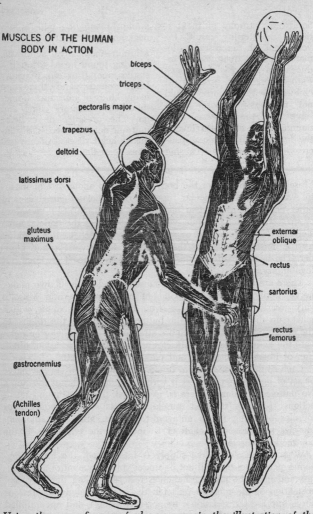

MUSCLES OF THE HUMAN BODY IN ACTION

biceps

triceps

pectoralis major

trapezius

deltoid

latissimus dorsi

gluteus maximus

gastrocnemius

(Achilles tendon)

external oblique

rectus

sartorius

rectus femorus

Using the same figures of players seen in the illustration of the skeleton in action 'p 58', this drawing shows in action the superficial layer of muscles directly under the skin Only some of these muscles, the largest and most familiar, have been labeled. There are many other muscles underneath this top layer.

What muscles can do: A muscle is composed of muscle fibers, the soft contractile tissue, enclosed in a tubular sheath (sarcolemma). All muscular tissue has these properties: it can contract; it can stretch; it is elastic, snapping back to its original length after stretching; it responds to nerve stimuli. Also, it normally has tone. This means that it is not completely relaxed; it is always partially contracted and on the alert to contract more. Cold can stimulate muscle tone to the point of involuntary contraction, that is, shivering. This is one reason for the stimulating effect of a cold shower.

A muscle can be viewed as an elaborate system for producing heat and energy, that is, mechanical work. Even when muscles are not apparently working, they are consuming energy and producing heat necessary to preserve total body heat. The large skeletal muscles are the heating plant of the body.

The energy of muscular contractions is obtained from a complicated series of chemical reactions, involving, among other substances, oxygen and glycogen. The muscles are about 25% efficient in converting fuel (chemical energy) into work (motions performed), more efficient than the best steam engine.

Muscular fatigue and sore muscles: When muscle fibers contract, the chemical events that take place leave certain waste products, notably carbon dioxide and lactic acid. When the amount of exercise or number of contractions a muscle is forced to perform exceed a certain limit, the lactic acid cannot be removed as fast as it is formed. This affects the end plates (nerve endings) of the muscle. Muscular fatigue occurs when lactic acid accumulates in the muscle and spills over into the blood stream.

If enough time is allowed to lapse between muscular contractions, the fatigue effects are diminished because the waste products are adequately removed. An ordinary sore muscle is more likely to be the result of fatigue products accumulating in the muscle than of sudden violence or strain on it. Gentle massage, heat, and rest usually relieve the soreness.

Building muscles: The voluntary muscles are among the most educable parts of the body. Exercise and practice can produce enormous skills, as seen in the athlete and concert pianist. Constant practice is essential to maintenance of muscular skills. Graded exercise produces muscular development. EXERCISE should not be carried beyond the point of ready recovery from the fatigue produced. The principle of overload can be applied in training muscles for quick reaction and strength. For example, a batter swings several bats before he goes to the plate, but hits with only one. Grace and skill are more desirable in muscular development than bulging biceps. Strength must be useful.

Muscular ailments and disorders: Comparatively few diseases or disorders affect the muscles themselves. Some forms of RHEUMA-TISM (myositis) are really inflammations of the muscles. Most muscular disorders are really attributable to the nerves that activate them, as in the palsies. Such is not the case in MUSCULAR DYSTRO-PHY or muscular atrophy, in which muscles waste away. The muscles are sometimes invaded by trichinae, from uncooked pork, and become the site of the disease TRICHINOSIS. Muscular rigidity occurs in such diseases as rabies and lockjaw. TETANY may result from overactivity of the parathyroid gland.

(See illustration for JOINTS.)

MUSCULAR DYSTROPHY

Muscular dystrophy is a progressive disease whose principal and tragic characteristic is a wasting away of the striped or striated voluntary muscles. An estimated 200,000 people in the U.S., mostly children, are victims of progressive muscular dystrophy. In this disease the striped muscles gradually degenerate and are replaced by fat or fibrous tissue. Any skeletal muscles may be involved, but most commonly they are the shoulder muscles together with those of the face, then the muscles at the back of the thighs (buttocks) and in the calves of the legs.

In the most common form of the disease (pseudohypertrophic) some of these muscles at first appear to enlarge. Within a variable number of years after onset, generally 6 to 12 years, the victim usually becomes a helpless cripple, and dies of respiratory infection or failure or heart failure before he reaches the age of 20.

Who gets muscular dystrophy? The progressive pseudohypertrophic form almost invariably strikes little boys between 2 and 5 years. Though he may look like a healthy child, the boy falls easily, has difficulty getting up, waddles when he walks, is sway-backed and has trouble climbing stairs. Obvious and symmetrical (two-sided) muscular weakness soon appears. When someone attempts to lift the child by putting hands under his armpits, he slips through because of weakness of chest and shoulder muscles. Wasting and weakness of the muscles continues inexorably until death intervenes. There are practically no remissions or improvements.

In another common form of progressive muscular dystrophy (facio-scapulo-humeral), the disease usually appears at puberty, in the early teens, and strikes girls as often as boys. The patient often first complains of being unable to raise his arms above the head—because of weakness in the shoulder girdle muscles. Because of weakness of facial muscles, he may not be able to close his eyes completely and he cannot smile. This form of muscular dystrophy is also generalized and progressive, but the disability may be mild and is compatible with a long and useful life.

What causes muscular dystrophy? Nobody yet knows for sure. The disease runs in families, and heredity seems to be an important factor. Much research on muscle function is now going on, and it has been suggested that muscular dystrophy is a metabolic deficiency disease (like diabetes) that can eventually be corrected by replacement therapy (like insulin). But what has to be replaced is not yet known. Research in this field is promising.

What can be done for muscular dystrophy? Much can be done to prolong life and promote well-being. There is great value in orthopedic measures that prevent or minimize deformities, though corrective surgery is rarely indicated. The patient may take regular muscle-stretching exercises; he should not be kept in bed for a prolonged period, for this encourages muscle weakness. If a stay in bed is necessary, the muscle exercises should be kept up. Anything that builds a patient's morale is also a worth-while contribution to his welfare.

Continuing research and greater understanding of muscle function and action is of course the great hope in this disease. Research is being vigorously promoted and supported by, among others, the *Muscular Dystrophy Associations of America, Inc.*

Myalgia—pain in the muscles. See RHEUMATISM.

Myasthenia—muscular weakness. *Myasthenia gravis* is a rare disease in which some muscles, particularly those of the face, lips, eyes, tongue, and neck, gradually or suddenly become weakened, easily fatigued, and eventually, if the disease progresses, exhausted and paralyzed. The muscles improve with rest, but weaken again on slight exertion. They do not waste away. The actual cause is not known, but it is associated with a decrease in certain substances (acetylcholine, cholinesterase) necessary for muscular contraction. Injections of prostigmine (neostigmine) help many patients, for whom a regime of rest is also necessary.

Mycosis—a FUNGUS infection, or

any disease caused by it; for example, barber's itch, athlete's foot, ACTINOMYCOSIS.

Myelin—a white, fatty substance that envelops nerve fibers. It can be compared to the insulation on electric wires. Destruction of the *myelin sheath* from causes still unknown is the mechanism by which MULTIPLE SCLEROSIS occurs. (See illustrations for NERVES AND THE NERVOUS SYSTEM.)

Myelitis—inflammation of the spinal cord, as in POLIOMYELITIS, or of the bone marrow, as in OSTEOMYELITIS.

Myeloma—any abnormal growth of cells found in the bone marrow. When such malignant growths appear in many places, the condition is known as *multiple myeloma;* it is a form of CANCER. Anemia and some pain from nerve roots usually accompany this condition. Spontaneous fractures of bones occur in perhaps 1 out of 5 cases.

Myocardium—the HEART muscle.

Myocardial Infarction means damage to some part of the heart muscle (myocardium) be-

cause it has been deprived of its blood supply, usually but not always as a result of blockage or closure of the CORONARY blood vessels that normally supply it. Hence myocardial infarction is the outcome of coronary occlusion or coronary thrombosis. See HEART DISEASE.

Myocarditis—inflammation of the heart muscle.

Myopia—nearsightedness; inability to see clearly at a distance. See EYE TROUBLE.

Myositis—inflammation of voluntary MUSCLES; often associated with FIBROSITIS. See ARTHRITIS.

Myringitis—inflammation of the eardrum. See EAR.

Myringotomy—piercing the eardrum.

Myxedema—an ENDOCRINE disorder, caused by thyroid deficiency. Administration of thyroid completely controls the condition. Unlike cretinism, myxedema usually arises in middle life. It is far more common in women than in men. Puffy face and hands, low body temperature, and low basal metabolism are characteristic.

N

Any word printed in SMALL CAPITALS *can be looked up under its own alphabetical listing for further information.*

Nails—Finger nails and toenails are, like hair, outgrowths of the true skin. They are flat, horny plates composed of epithelial cells. Nails grow outward in a straight line from a nail bed at the rate of about 1/16th of an inch a week.

Nails are affected by general body conditions of health or disease, and are subject to localized disease or injury. If the nail bed is severely involved, permanent damage may occur. With somewhat lesser injury, the nail merely pits. Purplish or black-and-blue areas usually appear under an injured nail, and the nail is often shed. It takes about 6 months for a new nail to grow, during which time the tip of the finger requires some protection.

Shedding of the nails sometimes occurs following scarlet fever, typhoid fever, severe DERMATITIS, or an abscess at the base of the nail.

Some people are born with deficient nails, and they never look normal. "*Spoon nails*," depressed in the center and high at the edges, are often associated with anemia, especially in middle-aged women. The nails regain their normal shape when the anemia is treated. Low humidity may cause brittle nails. Excessively hot water can loosen them. Exposure to chemicals damages them, as does constant biting or picking at them. PSORIASIS causes all types of malformation—detachment of the nail plate, partial destruction, discoloration, and commonly pitting.

The nails may suffer bacterial INFECTION or FUNGUS invasion, which obstinately resists treatment. The treatment is that of the underlying condition.

Nail polish or lacquer rarely damages the nails, but the solvent fluid in it is a frequent cause of skin rashes (dermatitis) on the cheeks and eyelids. *Nail-polish removers* often tend to make the nails brittle and the finger tips dry and lifeless.

Ingrown toenail usually involves the big toe. It is caused by tight shoes plus the bad habit of cutting the edges of the nail too short. The nail then grows into the skin, producing a tender toe that may become infected. Ingrown toenails can be avoided by cutting the nails straight across and not removing the corners.

If an ingrown toenail has reached serious proportions, evidenced by exquisite tenderness, swelling, inflammation, and redness, it should be treated by a physician or competent CHIROPODIST. Very minor surgery is sometimes necessary. The pressure of the corner of

[347]

the nail on the underlying skin can sometimes be relieved by repeatedly inserting bits of sterile cotton between the nail and the skin. A V-shaped or U-shaped notch may be cut in the center of the nail. (See FOOT TROUBLE.)

Narcissism—self-love. Narcissus, a character in Greek mythology, fell in love with his own image reflected in a pool of water. Narcissism is an arrested state of personality development. See PSYCHOANALYSIS; MENTAL ILLNESS.

Narcolepsy—an uncontrollable desire to sleep at any time of the day or night; the habit of repeatedly falling asleep, usually for short periods, during normal waking hours. A loss of muscle tone and muscular weakness often accompanies attacks of narcolepsy. This condition is pathological and must be distinguished from fatigue due to prolonged lack of sleep. The cause of narcolepsy is sometimes purely psychological. However, it may also be a symptom of brain tumor, endocrine disturbance, brain inflammation, or epilepsy. The danger in narcolepsy is that the person will fall asleep under conditions that produce an accident, for example, while driving an automobile. Drugs that stimulate the central nervous system, notably caffeine, ephedrine, Benzedrine (amphetamine), may be used under medical supervision to ward off narcolepsy.

Narcosynthesis—a method of psychiatric treatment that became prominent in World War II for treatment of psychoneuroses, often of combat origin. The patient is given a light dose of some BARBITURATE drug, usually sodium amytal, until he is in a twilight state in which he talks freely about things suppressed into his unconscious mind that he would not otherwise dare mention. The facts he reveals about himself under these conditions are then discussed when he is fully awake and can be brought to understand the basis for his neurotic symptoms. This treatment has produced excellent results in properly selected cases. See MENTAL ILLNESS.

Narcotics—drugs that put you to sleep, completely or partially. As pain relievers, they have an important place in medicine. But self-medication with any narcotic, for any purpose, is dangerous and damaging.

There are four classes of narcotics whose continued use brings about deterioration: opium and its derivatives; cocaine; barbiturates; and marihuana.

Opium and its products—*morphine, codeine, papaverine,* and *heroin*—derive from the poppy. All produce addiction; heroin is the most dangerous. At first these drugs relieve pain and produce a false sense of well-being. The addict may feel like Superman. Later, however, he suffers excruciating mental and physical pain unless he can get ever-increasing doses.

Cocaine, or *"snow,"* is extracted from the South American coca plant. At first it stimulates and exhilarates the victim, but soon he suffers from hallucinations and sleeplessness.

Barbiturates, the active ingredient of most sleeping pills, are synthetic chemical drugs sold under a variety of trade names. Though indiscriminate use and self-medication may produce dependency, these drugs are safe to use, even over long periods, *when prescribed and supervised by a physician.*

Marihuana is obtained from the Indian hemp plant, which grows wild in many parts of the world, including the United States. Commonly smoked in cigarettes known as *"reefers"* or *"muggers,"* the drug produces a variety of effects, including exaltation, recklessness, or violent delirium. It is not habit-forming in the sense of causing agonizing withdrawal symptoms, as other narcotics are. But crimes are frequently committed by persons under the influence of marihuana.

Narcotic addiction is much easier to acquire than it is to cure. However, the Federal government and some state and city authorities maintain facilities for treating addicts.

Nasal—refers to the NOSE.

Nasal Congestion—see NOSE; COMMON COLD.

Nasopharyngitis—a fancy name for a bad cold. See COMMON COLD; NOSE; THROAT.

Nasopharynx—NOSE and THROAT taken together. (See illustrations for NOSE; RESPIRATORY SYSTEM.)

Nausea—the queasy feeling of being sick at the stomach and ready to VOMIT.

Navel—umbilicus; belly button; the scar left on the abdomen after the umbilical cord, which attaches the unborn and newborn infant to his mother, is cut and healed. (See CHILDBIRTH.) Not everyone has a navel for his whole lifetime; it is sometimes removed during abdominal surgery.

Nearsightedness—myopia. See EYE TROUBLE.

Necrophilia—sexual intercourse with a corpse; an abnormal desire for dead bodies; altogether an extreme sexual deviation.

Necropsy—a post-mortem examination of a body, an AUTOPSY. The purpose is to determine accurately, if possible, the exact cause (or causes) of death and to correlate this information with the symptoms of disease or accident previously noted. Relatives of deceased persons are well advised to permit a necropsy when requested.

Necrosis—the death or destruction of body tissue (or cells) while still in place and surrounded by living tissue. *Gangrene* and *bedsores* are examples.

Needle, usually referred to as "the needle," is a hollow, pointed, steel needle, attached to a syringe, through which injections can be given under (hypodermic or subcutaneous) or into (intradermal) the skin, veins (intravenous), or muscles (intramuscular). Fear of "the needle" is quite common among children and adults who do not understand that many medications must be given by injection to be effective. This fear is quite normal, though needless, and should not be allowed to block necessary injections for treating or preventing disease. See "SHOTS."

Hollow needles are also used for taking samples or donations of blood and for obtaining spinal fluid (spinal tap).

Surgeons use many kinds of needles, straight and curved, with and without sutures attached, to sew up wounds. Surgical needles are not hollow.

Neisserian—usually a polite term for the venereal disease GONORRHEA. The name is derived from that of the German physician, Albert Neisser, who discovered the gonococcus.

Nematodes—roundworms or threadworms.

Neoplasm—literally a new growth among the tissues of the body; a tumor. Neoplasms may be MALIGNANT or BENIGN. A malignant neoplasm is a form of CANCER, but not necessarily incurable.

Neostigmine—a drug used in the treatment of *myasthenia gravis*, a MUSCLE-weakness disease.

Nephrectomy—surgical removal of a kidney. (See KIDNEY TROUBLE.)

Nephritis—inflammation in the kidneys. See KIDNEY TROUBLE.

Nephrosis—KIDNEY TROUBLE of any kind. However, it usually refers to degeneration of the KIDNEY tubules without primary infection, accompanied by swelling (EDEMA), ALBUMIN in the urine, and a decrease in the amount of albumin in the blood.

NERVES AND THE NERVOUS SYSTEM

The human nervous system is made up of nerve cells (neurons), which differ decidedly from all other cells in the body. Collectively, they control the thought, feeling, and action of the human being; they are, however, acted on by other cells, so it is fair to say that we "think" with the whole body. The nervous system is the communication system of the body, and it functions like a vast, interconnected telephone system. It commands all the rest of the cells to perform their tasks at the right time and in the right way. The nervous system, like the rest of the body systems, is all of one piece. However, for descriptive purposes, the nervous sys-

NERVE CELL

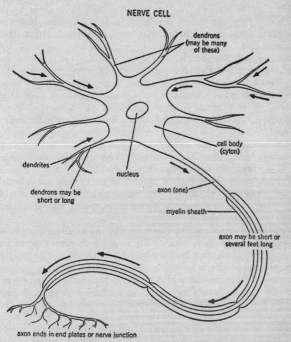

A typical nerve cell (neuron). Arrows show the direction of nerve impulses within the nerve cell to and from the cell body (cyton).

tem can be broken down into three main divisions: (1) the central nervous system, (2) the autonomic nervous system, and (3) the peripheral nervous system.

Nerve cells. The nerve cell is the fundamental unit of the nervous system. Nerve cells vary greatly in size, shape, and branching out; a few, such as the cells of the sciatic nerve, have processes stretching 2 or 3 feet. Typically, a nerve cell looks like an octopus. It has a central *cell body* from which tentacles extend. One of these extensions, or tentacles, carries impulses *away* from the cell body; it is called the *axon*. The other tentacles or fibers, which vary in number, receive impulses and carry them *to* the cell body; they are called *dendrons,* and in *their* far branches, *dendrites.* These nerve fibers are covered, "insulated," by a white myelin sheath.

As they run the length and breadth of the body, axons and dendrons often parallel each other, forming nerve pathways. Like telephone wires running underground, they form a kind of cable, which is enclosed in a flexible tube of connective tissue. This whole cable of nerve fibers is what we ordinarily call a nerve. When a nerve is injured, a great many nerve fibers are actually cut or crushed.

Nerve *cells* have the serious disadvantage of not being able to regenerate once they are destroyed. The nerve fibers growing out from them will regenerate, though slowly.

In some parts of the body a number of nerve cells are collected in one spot; such collections are called ganglia. The vulnerable solar plexus on the stomach (sometimes called the abdominal brain) is an example.

How the nervous system operates. The outstanding capacity of nerve cells and fibers is their ability to carry or convey nerve impulses to and from other body cells and *to each other.* The junction between nerve cells is called a *synapse.* What happens at these junctions is still something of a mystery, because it is here that a sensation is transformed into an order for action. A nerve impulse can be compared to the transmission of an electric current in a wire, though it is not exactly the same. In the first place, nerve impulses travel more slowly; only about 200 to 300 feet a second. This is why it takes time to react to signals relayed by the nervous system.

Motor nerves carry orders or messages *away* from the central nervous system; they command muscles, glands, and other parts of the body to action. Sensory nerves convey sensations of all kinds *to* the central nervous system; they carry the sensations that the brain translates into such senses as sight, hearing, pain, and the like. In between sensory and motor nerves are intermediate or associative nerve cells. These are packed into all nerve ganglia and are most plentiful in the brain. These intermediate nerve cells connect with each other and with the motor and sensory nerves. They can be compared with the switchboards and relays of a telephone system, but they are much more mysterious.

These associative neurons encompass the human being's ability to select and interpret the sensations (nerve impulses) carried by the sensory nerves and to translate them into orders for action carried by the motor nerves. They are what enables a person to remember, perceive, think. The vast bulk of the activity of the intermediate nerve cells is, of course, carried on without our being aware of it; that is, below the level of consciousness.

Reflexes: The basic mechanism of nerve-cell action is described as a reflex. In simplest terms this means that whenever a nerve cell is stimulated, some sort of response is elicited. Stimulus always brings response. However, both stimulus and response may be below the conscious level.

In the simplest case, a stimulus sets off a nerve impulse in the end plate of a sensory nerve. This impulse is carried along the axon of the nerve to its cell body and thence out along one or more dendrons. At the appropriate nerve junction (synapse) the impulse "jumps" to an associative neuron or group of them. There it is transformed into a message for action; how we do not know. Then the transformed impulse "jumps" back to a motor nerve that goes back to the spot where the original stimulus came from and excites muscles or cells to appropriate action.

Reflexes operate from the simplest to the most complex actions, from blinking the eyes when a light is flashed into them to composing sonatas.

The *central nervous system* consists of the *brain,* the *spinal cord,* and their interconnections.

The *autonomic nervous system* is a part of the central nervous system, but its key units include a series of ganglia strung along the spinal column *outside* its bony structure.

The *peripheral nervous system* includes the nerve trunks or pathways, their end organs (such as the retina of the eye), their spinal roots, and 12 pairs of so-called cranial (or cerebral) nerves that issue from the base of the brain.

The central nervous system can be considered the central office, with innumerable switchboards, of the body's communication system. It directs, coordinates, and controls the activities of the rest of the body. Whatever we *consciously* feel or do is the concern of the central nervous system. Our unconscious thoughts, feelings, and conflicts are also resident here; and the whole host of body functions, like breathing and digesting food, by which we live but which we are rarely aware of and do not consciously direct,

THE NERVOUS SYSTEM

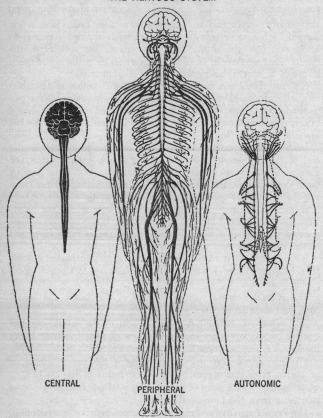

CENTRAL   PERIPHERAL   AUTONOMIC

The central nervous system includes the brain and spinal cord. The peripheral includes the cranial nerves, shown here coming out from the base of the brain and as though cut short, and the spinal nerves, only the main branches of which are shown.

The autonomic system includes a chain of ganglia on each side of the spinal cord and nerves to other organs. The general arrangement of these nerves is indicated but their size is much exaggerated. Solid lines are sympathetic and dotted lines are parasympathetic nerves.

are also controlled by the central nervous system. These automatic functions are directed by the autonomic nervous system.

The *brain* is the largest and most specialized mass of nerve cells in the body. Located inside the skull, it is well protected from possible injury. The brain consists of the cerebrum, the largest part; the cerebellum; the pons, or bridge connecting them; and the medulla oblongata, which terminates in the spinal cord. (See BRAIN for fuller description.)

The *spinal cord* runs through the bony vertebrae that make up the spinal column. It ends in a thin thread of nerve, but just before its termination it gives off a series of nerves running to the lower extremities. This is called the cauda equina ("horse's tail").

At different intervals, or segments, on its way down the spinal column, the spinal cord gives off spinal nerves. There are 31 pairs of spinal nerves, named from the portion of the spinal column through which they emerge (for example, 5 pairs of lumbar nerves). Most of these spinal nerves are mixed; that is, they contain both motor and sensory fibers.

The roots of the motor nerves are in the front (anterior) portion of the spinal cord; the sensory roots are at the back (posterior) portion. After leaving the spinal cord, the spinal nerves often unite in plexuses and ganglia, through which nerve impulses are received from and directed toward various parts of the body.

Most importantly these spinal nerves connect up with the chain of ganglia outside the spinal column that are the key units of the autonomic nervous system.

The *autonomic nervous system* has several names. It is called autonomic because when first investigated it seemed to be a law unto itself; now it is known to be intimately associated with the rest of the nervous system. It is also called the *vegetative* nervous system, because it controls man's most elementary functions. Since it responds to the stress of feelings and emotions, one part of it is designated as the *sympathetic* nervous system and another part, usually antagonistic, the *parasympathetic* nervous system.

The autonomic system innervates all smooth muscle tissue in the body, the heart and the glands. To most of these organs both sympathetic and parasympathetic fibers go. How the organs react depends on which of these systems is in control. Thus, for example, when the sympathetic impulses are in the ascendant, the heart beats faster, the pupils of the eyes dilate, the blood pressure goes up, the sweat glands dry up, the contractions of the gastrointestinal tract are decreased. When the parasympathetic system is in command, the opposite things happen: the heart beats slower, the pupils contract and so on.

Certain drugs are known to have a selective action on the autonomic nervous system; they hold back sympathetic-nerve impulses and encourage parasympathetic effects, or vice versa. For example, the drug *atropine* to a certain extent paralyzes the parasympathetic nervous system, leaving the sympathetic system in control. When this drug is given, therefore, the heart beats faster, the pupils dilate, blood pressure goes up, and so forth. The hormone *adrenalin* also stimulates the sympathetic nervous system, with similar results.

Most of the innumerable reflex acts by which the body functions are controlled by the autonomic nervous system; that is to say, at the level of the spinal cord and the ganglia outside it. They do not come to the *conscious* attention of the brain, though it cannot be said that the brain is completely unaware of what is going on. It is the intensity of stimulus that usually determines whether or not a particular event rises to the level of consciousness.

The *peripheral nervous system* operates at the outside end, or periphery, of the total nervous system. It, of course, connects with the central nervous system, bringing its sensations to it and taking orders from it. At the far, or outside, end of the nerve trunks are *end plates* or *end organs,* capable of picking up stimuli (heat, cold, pressure, sound, and so forth) and of delivering orders for action to the glands, muscles, and other cells to which they are attached.

The end organs may be compared to the mouthpiece and receiver of a telephone instrument. The end organs that pick up sensations or stimuli are called *receptors;* those that deliver orders, *effectors.*

The end organs are *specific* for the stimuli to which they respond. Thus, the retina of the eye reacts to light, the ear to sound, the taste buds of the tongue to chemicals in solution. There are end organs for hot and cold sensations, for pain, for pressure; there are combinations of impacts on end organs that give the sensations of fullness or tension, a sense of balance, and the feelings of hunger, thirst, or sexual desire.

Of course, all sense organs eventually convey the stimuli to which they respond to the brain or lower levels of the central nervous system, where the interpretation, or "meaning," is actually made. A blow on the eye is recorded as "seeing stars" because the retina is able to react only in terms of visual images to any stimulus it receives.

Cranial nerves. The 12 pairs of cranial (or cerebral) nerves that pass from the base of the brain to various parts of the body, without going through the spinal cord, may be considered as part of the peripheral nervous system. They include both motor and sensory nerves, and mixed. They are concerned with the senses of smell, sight, taste, and the movements of the muscles of eyes, face, tongue, jaws, and digestive tract. In the order in which they arise from the brain, they are (1) olfactory, (2) optic, (3) oculomotor, (4) trochlear, (5) trigeminal, (6) abducens, (7) facial, (8) acoustic, (9) glossopharyngeal, (10) vagus, (11) accessory, and (12) hypoglossal.

Nervous Breakdown—popular name for any sort of MENTAL ILLNESS serious and prolonged enough to take a person away from his usual activities and environment. The symptoms may be mild or extreme. Usually there is a precipitating event—for example, the death of a loved one, military combat experience—that finally puts more stress on an individual's personality structure than he can bear. It is important that a person suffering from a nervous breakdown get the best of modern psychiatric treatment, for prompt and effective psychotherapy in most instances brings early relief of the troubled state of mind and restores the individual at least to the degree of mental health he enjoyed before his nervous breakdown.

Nettle Rash—HIVES.

NEURALGIA

Neuralgia means pain in a nerve, usually a pain arising from a specific nerve and running along its course. Neuralgia is a pretty loose term. When a pain is described as neuralgia, it is often a sign that its exact cause is not known. Neuralgia differs from NEURITIS in that the pain in neuralgia usually comes in spurts (paroxysms), which may be more or less severe, whereas in neuritis it is generally more constant.

A toothache is a kind of neuralgia (dental neuralgia), and so is a headache, especially a MIGRAINE headache. SCIATICA is neuralgia along the course of the sciatic nerve in the back and thigh. Neuralgia often accompanies certain degenerative and infectious diseases; notably, ANEMIA, DIABETES, GOUT, ARTHRITIS, MALARIA, and

SYPHILIS. In these cases relief of the nerve pain depends primarily on treatment of the underlying condition.

Many cases of neuralgia are of psychosomatic origin, more closely allied to MENTAL ILLNESS than to physical disorder. The person with psychosomatic neuralgia is usually the last one to believe it. There is no questioning of pain, however, in the case of two of the most common and serious forms of neuralgia: trigeminal neuralgia and intercostal neuralgia.

Trigeminal neuralgia, also called *trifacial neuralgia* and *tic douloureux,* is one of the most distressingly painful conditions known to medicine, although it has no serious side-effects beyond the exhaustion caused by sleepless nights from repeated bouts of pain. It affects the nerve that carries sensations to the face, the trigeminal nerve, and may occur in any one or all three branches of this nerve. Head, forehead, eyes, eyelids, cheeks, and jaws may be shot through with burning, cutting, piercing, stabbing pains. The pain may be periodic, recurring at certain hours, or it may be brought on by the mildest sort of stimulus, for example, a breath of air on the cheek or a mouthful of hot soup or cold milk.

Nobody knows why trigeminal neuralgia occurs. It usually comes on after middle age and affects women more often than men. Sometimes the condition disappears, without treatment, for reasons as obscure as those of its origin. In other cases strenuous treatment may be needed to relieve pain. Various pain-killing drugs are usually prescribed, although habit-forming narcotics are avoided, if possible. Inhalations of the drug trichlorethylene sometimes gives temporary relief. Injections of alcohol into the nerve roots provide longer respite from pain. In depressingly intractable cases surgery, actually cutting the roots of the nerves along which the pain sensations are carried, may be necessary. In a few instances very simple remedies such as aspirin and hot compresses to the face may make the pain tolerable.

Intercostal neuralgia affects the nerves that run along the ribs from the spinal cord to the front of the body. This condition is sometimes mistaken for PLEURISY or other lung conditions, but there is actually nothing wrong with the lungs or pleura. This type of neuralgia is often preceded or followed by an attack of SHINGLES (herpes zoster). It sometimes responds to hot applications or counterirritants (e.g. liniments), but in other cases techniques for blocking or destroying the sensory nerves must be employed.

Neurasthenia literally means nervous weakness or exhaustion. It is one of the milder forms of MENTAL ILLNESS. The principal symptom is excessive fatigue and loss of energy or "pep." Neurasthenia is a form of NEUROSIS and usually responds well to expert treatment and guidance. See NERVOUS BREAKDOWN.

Neuritis—inflammation of a nerve. In this condition, the body areas served by the nerve are usually painful and tender. Sometimes there is a loss of sensation in the area; sometimes loss of nerve reflexes, paralysis, and wasting of the muscles. Neuritis arises from many causes, including alcoholism, poisons like lead, diabetes, arthritis, vitamin B deficiency (beriberi), and specific infections, particularly malaria, syphilis (the tabes of late syphilis), diphtheria, and leprosy. Multiple neuritis (polyneuritis) occurs when more than one set of nerve tracts is inflamed.

Treatment of neuritis depends on effective treatment of the underlying condition. Relief is sometimes obtained from sedative drugs, application of heat to the affected parts, and keeping them at rest—even with splints, if need be.

Compare with NEURALGIA.

Neurodermatitis—a chronic SKIN ailment of uncertain origin, possibly neurotic. Well-defined patches of dry skin, particularly in the armpits and around the genital organs, itch persistently. See ITCHING. With proper treatment this condition can be greatly alleviated.

Neurologist—a specialist in diseases of the nervous system. This specialty is often combined with that of PSYCHIATRY; the specialist with this extra training is called a neuropsychiatrist. For some of the conditions that the neurologist is especially competent to diagnose and treat see NERVES AND THE NERVOUS SYSTEM, BRAIN, BRAIN DAMAGE, and MENTAL ILLNESS.

Neuron—a nerve cell. See NERVES.

Neuropsychiatrist — a medical specialist with special training in *both* neurology (NERVE disorders) and psychiatry (MENTAL ILLNESS).

NEUROSIS

Neurosis is a comparatively mild and lesser MENTAL ILLNESS and *emotional disorder*. It is equivalent to *psychoneurosis*, which is sometimes considered a slightly more aggravated and stubborn form of neurosis. It stands in contrast to PSYCHOSIS, which indicates more severe mental illness, and to NEURITIS, which connotes physical damage and inflammation of a definite nerve tract.

The origin of neurosis is in previous life experience, invariably dating back to childhood. It is the outcome of reaction to frustrations, as viewed in the unconscious mind, and the unresolved emotional conflicts that persist in the unconscious mind.

Everyone has frustrations, so everyone at some times suffers from neurosis. All human beings, from childhood on, have some neurotic streak, some prejudices, whims, unreasoning anxieties.

In some people, however, inner conflicts are so persistent and severe as to cripple their enjoyment of life and to steal their freedom of action. Their emotional energy is so bound up in fighting themselves that they cannot respond effectively to other people. They cannot fully love and work. Though these people are neurotic, their inner guilts and fears may drive them to action that gives their lives the outer picture of success.

The basic nature of neuroses was first revealed in the early 20th century by Sigmund Freud, through the technique of PSYCHOANALYSIS. The theory of neuroses is the essential element of psychoanalysis, both as a treatment instrument and a research tool. Neuroses may be relieved by other treatment than the classical psychoanalysis.

The neurotic person tries to hide and mask his true feelings—particularly from himself. They are too painful. He resists talking about them, even to his analyst. He hugs them as the lesser of evils and dangers that he unconsciously fears.

The relief of neurosis depends partly on getting the victim to see and accept himself as he really is, admit his shortcomings, find and build on his strengths, and face the world as he must find it. This is often a time-consuming process. Emotional habits built up over the years cannot be changed overnight. The neurotic must re-educate himself. He must develop more satisfying and constructive reaction patterns.

Neuroses go by many names; for example, nervous breakdown, neurasthenia, anxiety, hysteria, combat fatigue, obsessions, compulsions. Many have physical symptoms relating to a particular set of body organs, such as the heart (cardiac neurosis, "soldier's heart"), intestines (colitis), limbs (hysterical paralysis), sex organs (impotence in the male, frigidity in the female).

When emotional conflicts are converted into physical symptoms, one speaks of a *conversion neurosis.* For some people intense aversion to their occupation or profession produces *occupational neuroses;* for example, writer's cramp. Anxiety neuroses are extremely common.

A good doctor (or sometimes even a good friend) can be of immense help in enabling a person to live successfully in spite of his neurosis. Much is gained by talking out what troubles you.

Neurosurgeon—a surgical specialist highly trained to operate on the nervous system and the brain. He is sometimes called a brain surgeon.

Neurosyphilis—SYPHILIS affecting the nervous system; usually in the later stages of the disease. See SYPHILIS; PARESIS; LOCOMOTOR ATAXIA; TABES; BRAIN DAMAGE.

Neutropenia — AGRANULOCYTOSIS; white BLOOD CELL disease.

Nevus—BIRTHMARK or MOLE; a limited new growth on the skin of a newborn infant, often an overgrowth of blood vessels.

Newborn—see INFANTS; CHILDBIRTH; PREGNANCY.

Niacin—nicotinic acid; the PELLAGRA-preventive factor of the vitamin B complex. See VITAMINS.

Nicotine—the principal active alkaloid in TOBACCO. *Pure* nicotine, even in very small doses, is a dangerous poison.

Nicotinic Acid—niacin; a part of the VITAMIN B complex. It is used in treating and preventing PELLAGRA. Nicotinic acid has no relation to the nicotine found in tobacco.

Night Blindness—see EYE TROUBLE.

Nipple—outlet for milk from breast or bottle; teat. See PREGNANCY; CHILDBIRTH.

Nitrofurans—a class of antimicrobial drugs.

Nitrogen—a chemical element; the highly inert gas that makes up about 4/5ths of the atmospheric air. It is a necessary constituent of PROTEIN substances, so that it is essential to all plant and animal life. Soil fertilizers have nitrogen in them. In the human body, nitrogen combines to form AMINO ACIDS, UREA, and other substances. It is found in ammonia.

In diagnosing and treating many diseases, particularly those concerning the kidneys, it is often useful to determine by laboratory tests the *nonprotein nitrogen* (NPN) content of the blood stream. (See KIDNEY TROUBLE.)

Nitrogen gas bubbles dissolved in the blood stream are responsible for the symptoms of compressed-air disease (the BENDS).

Nitroglycerin—one of the most important drugs used in treating and relieving the spasms of chest pain called *angina pectoris*. (See HEART DISEASE.) The effect of nitroglycerin (and many other nitrite substances) is to dilate the small blood vessels. A pellet of nitroglycerin placed under the tongue is almost immediately absorbed into the blood stream, and is carried in a few seconds to the small arteries of the heart, which immediately dilate under its influence. Pain disappears. Nitroglycerin can be taken repeatedly, as needed, without harm.

Nitrous Oxide—laughing gas, a short-acting ANESTHETIC given by inhalation.

Nocardiosis—an infectious disease, related to ACTINOMYCOSIS; specifically caused by the microbe *Nocardia*, named after the French veterinarian Edmund Nocard.

Nocturia—strong need to pass urine at night. See ENURESIS.

Noise—the unpleasant impact on the nervous system conveyed through the EARS and the rest of the hearing apparatus. Sudden, explosive noises and repeated loud noises, as encountered in some industries, can produce total or partial DEAFNESS (see EAR TROUBLE). Newborn infants instinctively fear loud noises. At the cost of some wear and tear on the nervous system, most people eventually get to tolerate the repeated and inescapable noises they are constantly subjected to—for example, street noises. But some people are more highly sensitive to noise than others and never quite tolerate it. They may have to wear ear plugs or "ear defenders."

Sensitivity to noise, which unconsciously always implies a *threat*, increases when general health is lowered or when a person is in the state of temporary helpless debility that follows a severe illness or surgery. That is why hospitals insist on *quiet zones* around them.

Constant noise increases blood pressure and muscular tension. It puts the body in a state of false alarm. Hence, working efficiency is usually reduced by noisy surroundings, and sleep is sometimes long delayed. The rhythmical, gentler sound that we call *music* has the opposite effect.

Normal—OK; within the usual pattern; neither too much nor too little, too high nor too low; what you would expect to find in a healthy, well-adjusted body and personality. The range of the normal is very wide.

NOSE

The human nose is an organ of smell, respiration, and some beauty. It is subject to malformation, accident, infection, new growths, and other damage. We shall consider here the running nose, the stuffed-up nose, the red nose, the bloody nose, and the misshapen nose.

The nose consists of a few small bones, some cartilage, lined on the outside with skin and on the inside with a sensitive mucous membrane generously endowed with blood vessels. Together they form two hollow cavities (nostrils or nares) divided by a *septum* of bone and cartilage.

The upper part contains the end organs (chemoreceptors) of the olfactory nerve and provides the sense of smell, which is closely allied with the sense of taste. The lower part, lined with hairs, serves to filter and warm inhaled air before it proceeds into the rest of the respiratory tract.

The nose communicates with the EYES, EARS, and THROAT, as well as the so-called nasal and *paranasal sinuses,* which are air spaces in the bones of the skull. The tear ducts of the *eye* drain eventually into the nose; that is why a person who is crying has to blow his nose.

The communication with the *ears* is by way of the EUSTACHIAN TUBES, which open in the back of the throat. The back of the nose opens into the upper part of the throat just about at the point where *adenoid* tissue commonly grows. Violent blowing of the nose may force infectious material into the throat, the Eustachian tubes (and the ears), and the eyes. *Always blow your nose gently* into a clean handkerchief or, especially if you have a cold, a disposable paper tissue.

A *running nose* is usually the first sign of a COMMON COLD or HAY FEVER. The nasal discharge of mucus ("snot") is a defensive effort to wash out infective or irritating substances. This condition is variously called *coryza, acute* or *chronic rhinitis,* or *nasal catarrh.* Treatment lies in correcting or meeting the underlying infection (e.g. common cold) or ALLERGY (e.g. hay fever).

Postnasal drip is the continual discharge of nasal mucus down the throat instead of through the nostrils. This condition is exceedingly common, varied in origin, and sometimes insignificant. It often disappears without any specific treatment; at other times it continues without producing any other symptoms or even annoyance. Among the many possible reasons for postnasal drip are low-grade chronic infections or allergies, unfavorable atmospheric environment (cold, foggy weather), and heavy smoking.

Stuffed-up nose and inability to breathe effectively through the nose (the normal way of breathing) arise from many causes; for example, *swollen mucous membrane, nasal polyps, overgrown adenoids, deviated septum,* and SINUS TROUBLE.

In colds and hay fever the stuffy nose usually follows the running nose. It signifies that the nasal mucous membranes are overworking and have become swollen with blood and tissue fluid in the effort. Immediate relief is often afforded by applying or inhaling drugs, such as ephedrine, Privine, Neosynephrine, Propa-

THE NOSE

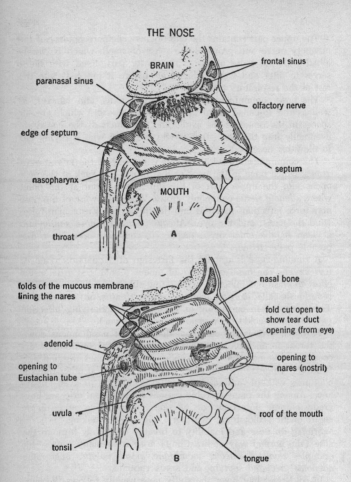

A. *Side view of the nose showing the septum between
the two nares and the branches of the olfactory nerve.*
B. *Side view of the nose, septum removed, showing the
connections to the eye, ear, and throat.*

dine, and Benzedrex, which constrict the blood vessels and thus temporarily shrink the nasal mucous membranes. Continuous use of such drugs, particularly the ever-present inhaler, can be harmful.

Self-prescribed *nose drops* and nasal sprays are not likely to help the stuffy nose. Oily nose drops may descend into the lung and cause a lipoid PNEUMONIA. Nasal sprays that subject the sensitive lining of the nose to any high pressure can be very damaging. However, physicians may prescribe antibiotics or other drugs to be administered by spray. Drugs so administered are called *aerosols*, and they may be very effective.

Nasal polyps are soft, jellylike growths, hanging from a short stem, that may develop in the back part of the nose as a result, usually, of chronic and repeated inflammation of the nasal passages. They are not dangerous but may be very annoying and interfere unpleasantly with normal breathing. They may yield a perpetual stuffed nose. Sometimes polyps disappear without treatment. They can be removed by comparatively simple surgery, being cut out with a wire snare. They tend to recur even after removal, and the operation may have to be repeated.

Enlarged adenoids often interfere with proper nasal breathing, particularly in children, and should sometimes be surgically removed along with enlarged or diseased tonsils. Skilled surgical judgment is required in each individual case to determine whether the adenoids should be taken out. Enlarged adenoids are most common between the ages of 5 and 12 and usually recede in size thereafter. They are the common cause of *mouth breathing*.

Deviated septum means that the septum of bone and cartilage that divides the nose into two chambers is not absolutely straight. It never is; it always bulges (deviates) to one side or the other, so that the two nostrils are of somewhat different size. This is usually of no importance. However, if the deviation of the septum is so extreme that it makes breathing through one side extremely difficult or impossible, a simple surgical operation to straighten the septum may be warranted. Chronic inflammation and stuffy nose may thus be corrected.

A *red nose* may be the result of chronic inflammation or infection of the nostrils, poor circulation in cold weather, chronic indigestion, various skin diseases (notably ACNE and ERYSIPELAS), or, quite commonly and evidently, chronic ALCOHOLISM. In the last case it is usually called brandy nose, or *rosacea*. Alcohol dilates the small blood vessels, and this is the reason for the bright-red appearance. In severe cases the dilated veins and capillaries may be treated by electrocautery, following abstinence from alcohol.

Nosebleed (epistaxis) is usually the result of violence, a fall or punch in the nose, or unwarranted picking at the inside of the nose. Repeated nosebleeds without such evident cause require full medical investigation. So do nosebleeds following any head injuries.

To stop a nosebleed, lie flat on your back and remain quiet there for a few minutes. Meanwhile, apply mild pressure to the bleeding nose with a towel, handkerchief, or bandage.

A cold compress or ice bag may be applied if the bleeding does not soon subside. This failing, the inside of the nose may be packed with sterile gauze or cotton.

If the bleeding still persists, call or see a doctor. He may put in special packing with the proper instruments or, if necessary, seal off bleeding points with an electrocautery. Nosebleeds can always be stopped, but proper treatment should be started before too much blood is lost.

Loss of the sense of smell (anosmia) may result from any of the conditions that cause a stuffed-up nose. Brain damage or head injuries affecting the olfactory nerve can also be responsible. Some drugs, notably phenol applied to the nose, can eliminate the sense of smell. The nerve endings of the olfactory nerve are quickly fatigued. Hence some powerful odors may paralyze the sense of smell, notably coal gas and prussic acid. (CARBON MONOXIDE is odorless.) The human nose is a poor guide to the presence of poison gases in the air.

Shall I have the shape of my nose changed? If the shape of your nose is the result of disease or accident, the answer is probably yes, if you can afford it. The injection of paraffin under the skin is a common procedure for this. If the nose that you think you want changed is the one nature endowed you with, think twice, at least. You may be no more satisfied with your new nose than your old one, and there is no reason to be sure that it will make you more popular or desirable. You may be falsely attributing your personality defects and attitude toward life solely to the shape of your nose. You must be prepared to change a great many things about yourself along with your nose. You would do well to consult a PSYCHIATRIST before you see a PLASTIC SURGEON. A new nose is no guarantee of success or happiness in life.

Modern plastic surgery, however, can safely and successfully reshape a nose to almost any desired contour. The operation is usually performed from inside the nose so that no scars appear. If you decide to have your nose "lifted" be sure that (1) the plastic surgeon is properly accredited in the surgical profession and not an incompetent quack, (2) the hospital is accredited by the joint committee on accreditation of the American Medical Association, the American Hospital Association, the American College of Surgeons, and the American College of Physicians, and (3) you can afford the operation in terms both of surgical fees and hospital costs and of time lost from work.

(See illustration for RESPIRATORY SYSTEM.)

Novocain—a trade name for procaine hydrochloride, a local ANESTHETIC. It is much used in dentistry to block nerves when working on the teeth. It is sometimes injected near joints to relieve the pain of athletic injuries; notably, sprained ankles.

Nucleus of a CELL is its *core,* center, and reproductive system. It is denser than the rest of the cell. It contains the threadlike CHROMOSOMES that separate when one cell breaks up into two cells. It also contains vital fluid substances called *nucleic acid.*

An atom also has a nucleus at its core. "Splitting the atom" is the science of nuclear physics and chemistry.

Nutrition—the life-essential process of assimilating food or nutriment. Failures in nutrition of body cells may occur not only as a result of faulty or inadequate food intake (poor diet) but also from inability of the body to absorb and utilize the ingested nourishment. See DIET, DIGESTION, DIGESTIVE SYSTEM, MINERALS, VITAMINS.

Nyctalopia—night blindness; see EYE TROUBLE.

Nymphomania—extreme sexual desire in the female, comparable to *satyriasis* in the male. Both conditions are abnormal and represent some kind of MENTAL ILLNESS, usually curable. See MANIA.

Nystagmus—rapid eye movements up and down, side to side, or around and around. See EYE TROUBLE.

O

Any word printed in SMALL CAPITALS *can be looked up under its own alphabetical listing for further information.*

OBESITY

Obesity is the accumulation of excess fat in the body. Whether or not it is unhealthy, it is certainly unfashionable in modern American society. This is not true everywhere in the world.

The treatment (and prevention) of true obesity is nowhere near as simple as the dieteers have led a gullible public to believe. There are many ways to lose weight *temporarily,* and many little gimmicks and gadgets advertised for doing so. If you reduce your food intake, you lose weight. See DIET.

Never take reducing pills or other reducing medicines without the personal advice of a doctor. Many contain substances that can be harmful; for example, THYROID extract, which speeds up metabolism; and central-nervous-system stimulants (e.g. amphetamine), which may kill the appetite but have undesirable side-effects. The will-power pill, labeled "No" and "No more," is the only safe reducing pill. Many so-called reducing pills are simply VITAMIN pills, offered to assure an adequate vitamin intake during prolonged periods of limited food intake.

The underlying causes of obesity are numerous, but the psychological ones are usually very important. Obesity may reflect failures in DIGESTION and METABOLISM. It may also represent natural HEREDITY; some people just can't help being fat; their genes make them so. The "tides of life," as expressed in changes in the ENDOCRINE glands, also account for many individual cases of obesity at different ages.

Exercise does not cure obesity. The best it can do is redistribute body fat into less conspicuous places. The only successful reducing exercise is pushing the chair away from the dinner table before you have eaten too much.

Most fat people prefer themselves that way, despite their claims to the contrary. They may diet temporarily, but they soon stop and regain (or surpass) their former weight. This is not necessarily bad. What is bad is to be unhappy about it.

Gluttony is a NEUROSIS (like nervous eating). If a person is cured of gluttony, without any change in his underlying neurotic pattern, the same disturbed feelings and motivations that drove him to overeat may take another adverse direction, such as gambling, drinking, or fanaticism. The only cure for many types of obesity is PSYCHOTHERAPY. Food gives satisfaction and relief from troubled thoughts to many people. Unless an adequate substitute for food is found, overeating is likely to continue. Some men and women get and stay fat because it protects them against normal sex feelings and relationships, which they unconsciously fear and hate. They usually put the story the other way around. They say they are unattractive to the opposite sex *because* they are fat. They are honestly fooling themselves (rationalizing). They like it the way it is—or they would change. Food has many subtle meanings to many people; it is related to their family feelings. Sometimes it is taken and given as a substitute for love.

The principal medical objection to obesity is that carrying around extra weight throws a needless burden on the heart and circulation system. With more flesh to supply blood to (and miles more of tiny blood capillaries to pump blood through), the heart has to work harder. Some hearts can take the extra work better than others. (See HEART DISEASE.)

A second medical objection is that the intake of fatty foods that often accompanies obesity may tend toward development of *atherosclerosis*, that is, a fatty lining of the inside of the blood vessels, and thus also induce heart and blood-vessel damage at an early age. This relationship between heart disease and obesity has been much studied and discussed, but it is still unresolved.

To many people a trim figure gives a psychological satisfaction, for which they are willing to sacrifice, and thus improves their muscle tone and general health and well-being. This same reasoning does not apply to the neurotic for whom obesity is an ego defense. Cut out his food and he may develop a full-blown MENTAL ILLNESS (PSYCHOSIS).

Insurance statistics show a correlation between overweight and average length of life. On the average abnormally overweight people die earlier than normal or underweight people. To protect their pocketbooks, insurance companies charge fat people more for life-insurance protection.

Unfortunately, the insurance statistics are often badly misunderstood. The obesity is not the *cause* of the average earlier death. Nor is losing weight any guarantee of increasing one's years of life. The same factors, which are highly individual and often undiscoverable, that make a person fat also create the other bodily conditions that may bring about earlier degeneration of body tissues and consequent earlier death.

Obsession—a symptom of MENTAL ILLNESS, especially paranoia. It means holding and harping on an idea or set of ideas with foolish passion and beyond reason. The borderline between faith and obsession is sometimes hard to distinguish. Many great men have seemed obsessed to most of their friends and contemporaries.

Obstetrics—the medical specialty of managing the conditions and accidents incident to CHILDBIRTH. It is called a "happy specialty," because patients consult their obstetricians for something they want, a healthy baby. See PREGNANCY; CHILDBIRTH. Obstetricians were once called "man midwives." This specialty is often combined with *gynecology*. See FEMALE TROUBLES.

Obstruction—blocking of a passageway. *Intestinal obstruction* or blocking of the bowels for any reason (for example, a strangulated hernia or RUPTURE) is always a serious emergency demanding immediate surgical treatment, usually an emergency operation. *Urinary* obstruction means impedance of the flow of urine out of the bladder; it is often associated with PROSTATE TROUBLE. *Bile* obstruction produces JAUNDICE (see GALL BLADDER).

Occipital refers to the back of the head (occiput bone of the skull).

Occlusion—closed. The closure of the small arteries of the heart is called *coronary occlusion* or coronary thrombosis; see HEART DISEASE. In dentistry occlusion describes the fit of the teeth of the upper and lower jaws together when the mouth is closed. Good occlusion is necessary to proper chewing of food. Much reparative dental work is often necessary to establish or restore it.

Occupational Diseases—those that arise out of the course of one's work or occupation, unless adequate safety and preventive measures are taken. Typical examples are BENDS in sand hogs; LEAD POISONING in painters; contact DERMATITIS, SKIN TROUBLE, in chemical factory workers; SILICOSIS in miners and workers in dusty trades; FLAT FEET in policemen; PILES in bus drivers; PROSTATE TROUBLE in judges.

Occupational Therapy—part of the process of REHABILITATION of severely ill or injured patients. It means providing the patient with interesting opportunities, in the hospital or at home, to exercise those muscles and talents that can be strengthened and lead toward a life as normal as possible. It is treatment, not diversion. It may include weaving, specialized carpentry, painting, dancing, leatherwork and other hobbycraft, reading, listening to music, and anything else undertaken to promote recovery. It may be specific—directed, for example, to improving the strength of the arm muscles through sandpapering a bird house—or nonspecific—such as the essential recreational activities useful in recovery from *mental illness*. The occupational therapist is a part of the medical team necessary for full rehabilitation. She is part teacher, part nurse, part social worker.

Oculist—eye specialist; same as OPHTHALMOLOGIST.

Oedipus Complex—a construct of Freudian PSYCHOANALYSIS. Its name comes from Oedipus Rex, king of Thebes, a character in Greek mythology who was destined by the gods to kill his father and marry his mother. The theory contends that there is a *normal* stage in the psychosocial development of the male child, usually around the ages of 5 to 7, when he wants to replace his father in the affections of his mother. Since this is impossible and the very thought brings fear of punishment, the idea is deeply repressed into the unconscious mind, where it may someday make trouble. This repression is said to be the basis of the universal horror of incest. Little girls go through the same process, wanting to possess their fathers and being intensely jealous of their mothers, but not daring to show their jealousy and therefore repressing it. This is sometimes called the Electra complex.

Most present-day psychiatrists and psychologists do not accept the Oedipus complex idea as firmly as Freud did. They point out that this complex is only likely to develop and be of importance in societies (patriarchal, middle-class, 19th-century, Viennese) like those in which Freud grew up and described, and from which he drew his patients.

Ointment—any more or less fatty or greasy substance applied to the skin for a particular purpose. Cold cream and brushless shave are typical nonmedicated ointments. The base of most ointments is lanolin, beeswax, glycerine, petroleum jelly, or any of scores of other animal and vegetable fats and oils, processed for a consistency that allows them to spread and hold readily at body temperatures. For treating and preventing SKIN TROUBLE, many kinds of medication are added to the base. Local ANESTHETICS, ANTISEPTICS, and DRYING AGENTS, for example, can be included. A *salve* is a thick ointment; a lotion is a wash, though if sticky, it may approach the consistency of an ointment.

Whitfield's ointment is a drying agent, a combination of salicylic acid (1 part), benzoic acid (2 parts), petrolatum (30 parts).

Greasy ointments should not be applied indiscriminately for SKIN TROUBLES. They usually make them worse.

Old Age—the inevitable far end of the life cycle. Since it cannot be prevented, it might just as well be enjoyed. The way to become a dear old lady or a happy old gentleman is to begin early, say at about the age of 17. For discussion of the medical problems of old age (and they are certainly not all medical), see GERIATRICS.

Olecranon—the funny bone; the top end of the arm bone (ulna) at the *elbow*.

Olfactory—related to the sense of *smell*, as the *olfactory nerve*.

Oliguria—scanty URINE.

Omentum—an apron of tissue inside the skin that hangs down from the stomach and covers the intestines from the front. It is one fold of the lining of the abdominal (peritoneal) cavity. It is usually more or less infiltrated with fat. This is where belly fat collects in the OBESITY common to middle age.

Onanism—often used as a synonym for *masturbation*. More correctly, it means withdrawal of the penis from the vagina before ejaculation (coitus interruptus). Onan, son of Judah, is a Biblical figure.

Onchocerciasis—a tropical disease, something like FILARIASIS; infection with a barb-tailed threadworm (*Onchocerca*).

Onychia—inflammation in the bed of a NAIL.

Oöphorectomy—surgical removal of one (unilateral) or both (bilateral) OVARIES. This operation is often performed in connection with hysterectomy, removal of the uterus.

Operable—a diagnostic term used by surgeons to indicate that they have reasonable hope that surgery will accomplish the treatment or prevention purpose for which it is undertaken. INOPERABLE means there is little use or hope in operating.

Operation—see SURGERY.

Ophthalmia—inflammation of the eye; conjunctivitis. See EYE TROUBLE.

Ophthalmologist—eye specialist; oculist; a doctor of medicine (M.D.) specially trained to treat eye diseases and disorders by any and all means, including surgery.

Ophthalmology—the medical specialty dealing with EYES and EYE TROUBLE.

Ophthalmoscope—an instrument for examining the inside of the EYE. It is essentially a mirror with a hole or slit in it.

Opiate—any pain killer or NARCOTIC, particularly one derived from opium.

Opium—see NARCOTICS.

Optic—relating to the EYE, as the optic nerve. (See illustration for EYES.)

Optician—a technician who

grinds lenses and adjusts the frames of eyeglasses. He is *not* an OPTOMETRIST nor an OPHTHALMOLOGIST. He must not diagnose or treat EYE TROUBLES.

Optometrist—a person licensed to give limited eye care. He is permitted to examine eyes for errors of refraction (defects of focus), prescribe lenses (eyeglasses) to correct these errors, and prescribe eye exercises and other nonmedical measures for certain eye conditions. The optometrist is *not* a physician nor an eye specialist, like the OPHTHALMOLOGIST. There are about 18,000 optometrists in the U.S.; they write about 75% of all prescriptions for glasses. Many dispense (sell) glasses as well as prescribe and fit them. When an optometrist discovers EYE TROUBLE beyond his competence, he is honor-bound to refer the patient to a physician.

Oral—relating to the mouth, as *oral medication* (given by mouth).

Orchitis—inflammation of one or both *testicles* (see SEX ORGANS, MALE). This condition is usually marked by swelling, pain, and a sense of hanging heavy. The usual causes are MUMPS, GONORRHEA, SYPHILIS, and FILARIASIS. The underlying disease condition must be treated.

Organ—an organized collection of tissues that have a special and recognized function. Stomach, liver, pancreas, spleen, and bowels, for example, are internal abdominal organs.

Organic Disease—a disease in which some change in the structure of body tissue can either be visualized or positively inferred from indirect evidence (for example, examination of blood samples). It stands in contrast to FUNCTIONAL disease, in which no such positive evidence, if any evidence at all, can be adduced in the present state of medical and scientific knowledge.

Organism—any living body, regardless of size. Anything from a polio virus to a whale is an organism. The word is commonly used to mean a *microörganism*, a living body, of one cell or more, that can be seen only through a microscope.

Organotherapy—opotherapy; the theory and practice of treating disease by administering bodily organs or extracts of these organs (organ juices) taken from animals. This practice involves both primitive superstition and empiric success. Thus primitive hunters ate the hearts of their prey to make themselves braver and stronger. This is superstition. But the use of liver extract in treating pernicious anemia and insulin (from the pancreas of meat animals) in controlling diabetes is science.

Orgasm—the climax; the moment of highest pitch of sexual excitement. In the male this is the degree of sensation that triggers the ejaculation of semen from the male *sex organs*. In the female the orgasm may be a more generalized feeling of sexual satisfaction and release of tension. It is not essential for a woman to have an orgasm to become pregnant.

Orinase—oral drug for DIABETES; tolbutamide.

Ornithosis—a term, probably on the way out, that describes the VIRUS disease PSITTACOSIS when it occurs in birds other than those of the parrot family.

Orthopedics—the medical specialty that deals primarily with disease and accident to the BONES, JOINTS, and MUSCLES. The word literally means "straightening children."

Orthopedist—primarily a surgeon "specially concerned with the preservation and restoration of the functions of the skeletal system, its articulations and associated structures." In practice orthopedists are deeply involved in REHABILITATION and often direct and employ the techniques of PHYSICAL MEDICINE.

Orthopsychiatry—an area of psychiatric interest that can be described as straightening people out by keeping them from getting crooked. It splints emotional development. Orthopsychiatrists are largely concerned with child development and techniques of promoting and encouraging mental health. This is preventive PSYCHIATRY.

Orthoptics—eye exercises. See EYE TROUBLE.

Os—a Latin word that means both *mouth* (or entrance) and *bone*. For example, *os uteri* is the entrance to the neck of the womb; *os calcis* is the calcaneus or heel bone.

Osmosis—the passage of fluid solutions through a MEMBRANE that ostensibly separates them. Popularly the phrase *by osmosis* means getting something without effort, just letting it seep in. Osmosis is not really understood by science, and it lies close to the basic mystery of life. This is why: Every CELL is surrounded and enclosed by a membrane. Nobody knows why these membranes are *selective* and let some things through and others not. The things that pass through the membrane pores are, of course, very tiny, microscopic, and molecular in size. Osmosis presents one of the great unsolved riddles of chemistry and biology.

Osmotic Pressure—the tendency of solutions separated by a porous membrane to flow in one direction or the other, that is, to mix on one side of the membrane or the other. The delicate balances of the fluid solutions in the human body depend on changes in osmotic pressure.

Ossification—formation of bone; more exactly the deposit of lime salts in the bone molds laid down originally in cartilage. This process is partly controlled by the *parathyroid* glands, depends partly on available vitamin D in the body. (See RICK-

ETS, VITAMINS, BONES, PREG-
NANCY.)

Osteitis—bone inflammation.
See BONE DISEASE.

Osteoarthritis—see ARTHRITIS.

Osteomalacia—softening of the
bones; adult RICKETS. It is
caused by a deficiency in the
presence or absorption of calcium and phosphorus and vitamin D. Rheumatic pains and
weakness are common symp-
toms. The condition sometimes
occurs among women who have
borne many children without
taking adequate care of themselves. See BONE DISEASES;
PREGNANCY.

Osteomyelitis—inflammation of
the bone and the bone-marrow
cavity. See BONE DISEASES.

Osteopath—osteopathic physician; a medical practitioner who
has been trained in and accepts
the tenets of *osteopathy*. Some
are much better prepared for
the practice of medicine than
others and hold both M.D.
(Doctor of Medicine) and D.O.
(Doctor of Osteopathy) degrees. An osteopath is *not* the
same as a CHIROPRACTOR.

Osteopathy—a system of medical treatment and practice
founded by Andrew Taylor
Still in the 19th century and
much modified since in the direction of rational, scientific
medicine. Osteopathy today labors under a jargon that sometimes conceals the fact that
many osteopaths utilize generally accepted methods of diagnosis and treatment. More of
the practices of orthodox medicine are used by the younger
osteopaths and by those who
have been trained at the better
of the six osteopathic schools in
the U.S.

Osteopathy has been de-
scribed as "that system of the
healing art which places the
chief emphasis on the structural
integrity of the body mechanism as being the most important single factor to maintain
the well-being of the organism
in health and disease." Briefly,
it pays special attention to
bones, joints, and posture. The
limitations of osteopathic practice are defined in state laws
licensing osteopaths.

Osteoporosis—too-porous BONE.

Otalgia—earache. See EARS.

Otitis—inflammation of the inner, middle, or outer ear. Of the
middle ear, it is *otitis media*.
See EAR TROUBLE.

Otolaryngologist—a medical
specialist primarily concerned
with diseases and disorders of
the ears, nose, and throat. The
more pompous title for an ear,
nose, and throat man is
oto*rhino*laryngologist.

Otologist—ear specialist.

Otosclerosis—formation of spongy bone in the inner ear, a common cause of progressive DEAF-
NESS. See EAR TROUBLE.

Otoscope—an instrument, usually electrically lighted, for

looking into the outer ear (up to the unperforated eardrum).

Ouabain—a drug with effects like DIGITALIS.

Out-patient—a patient who makes use of the diagnostic or therapeutic services of a hospital, but who does not occupy a regular hospital bed or bassinet.

Ovary—the SEX ORGAN, FEMALE where the human egg (OVUM) ripens and where the female sex hormones are produced; the female gonad. See also MENSTRUATION, OVULATION, PREGNANCY, ENDOCRINE GLANDS.

Overweight—see OBESITY.

Oviducts—the uterine, or Fallopian, tubes through which the ova descend from the ovaries to the womb. See SEX ORGANS, FEMALE; STERILITY.

Ovulation—the escape of a ripened and mature egg cell from the sac, or Graafian follicle, in which it has developed. It usually occurs about halfway between menstrual periods (see MENSTRUATION), but cannot be determined with complete accuracy. There is some evidence that at the time of ovulation the body temperature falls slightly (by a fraction of a degree), after which there is a relatively sharp, though small, rise in body temperature.

The time of ovulation is crucial to conception and pregnancy. The ripened ovum has a comparatively short life span, probably not more than 48

hours and possibly less. Unless a viable sperm meets and penetrates the egg within this time, the egg dies and is shed from the body. The meeting of egg and sperm normally takes place in the uterine tubes. (See SEX ORGANS, FEMALE.)

Ovum—egg. The human ovum, matured in the ovaries, is a spherical cell about 1/120th of an inch in diameter, but immensely bigger than a human SPERM cell. See SEX ORGANS, FEMALE; MENSTRUATION; GERM PLASM; HEREDITY; OVULATION.

Oxygen—the vital chemical element that makes up about 20% of the atmospheric air and enters into all metabolic activities of the living organism. Attached to the hemoglobin of the red blood cells, it is carried to all parts of the body by the circulation system in order to support METABOLISM. Any interruption in the distribution of oxygen damages the tissues that don't get it. Oxygen exchange is the basis of external (breathing) and internal respiration.

Oxygen tank is a heavy metal cylinder, with a valve, in which a large supply of pure oxygen can be conveniently kept for gradual release through an oxygen tent or mask. Except for perhaps a few occasional whiffs, a patient is not given pure oxygen to breathe; it is usually about 50% oxygen, 50% air. With this mixture a standard tank of oxygen lasts a patient about one day, if breathed continuously.

Oxygen is *not* a remedy of

last resort. When a doctor orders oxygen, it does not mean that the patient is ready to die. Oxygen is often administered early in an illness when a suspicion of breathing difficulty exists. It is used in treating all kinds of asphyxia and breathing difficulties; for example, pneumonia, carbon-dioxide poisoning, and respiratory paralysis. It is essential to fliers in the upper, low-oxygen regions of the earth's atmosphere and to divers under the sea. Oxygen into the lungs is useful to some patients with HEART DISEASE and not to others.

Premature infants are often given oxygen, but too much is a bad thing; it may cause an eye disease called retrolental fibroplasia.

Oxytocic—anything that stimulates uterine contractions, hastens CHILDBIRTH.

Oxyuriasis—threadworm or pinworm infestation.

Ozena, literally meaning stench or stink, is a disease of the nose in which it gives off a foul discharge and odor. The nasal mucous membranes degenerate, and the underlying bony parts are exposed, leaving crusts. The cause is probably long-continued, neglected infection.

Ozone—a more active form of *oxygen* (O_3). It has deodorant properties and a characteristic odor—the sharp smell one gets in electric power plants, where sparks cut and alter the oxygen of the air.

P

Any word printed in SMALL CAPITALS *can be looked up under its own alphabetical listing for further information.*

Pachydermia—thickening of the skin; "elephant skin."

Paget's Disease—a chronic disease of the BONES; *osteitis deformans;* cause unknown. Bones, especially of the skull, limbs and spine, become thick and soft and bend.

Pain—the warning siren that some part of the body is under stress or attack. However, the site of the pain does not explain the cause of the pain; nor is it always a very good pointer toward what ought to be done to get rid of the pain—permanently. For example, pain in the joints may be the end result of a long-forgotten or neglected venereal disease; and the treatment may consist essentially of injections into the muscles.

Pain is the spur that drives most people to seek medical attention. Some foolish people, however, pride themselves on being able to "live with pain" even though simple treatment, based on correct diagnosis, could quickly eliminate it. Others dangerously mask recurring pains—headaches, backaches, gut pains, for example—with painkilling pills and powders recommended by bad friends and drugstore clerks. Still others feel vague pains that have no rational cause and invalid themselves needlessly. All these people exemplify the old axiom: "He who has himself for a doctor has a fool for a patient."

The ability to endure pain —the so-called "pain threshold" —varies greatly among different people and in the same person at different times. That is why doctors constantly have to individualize and change dosages of DRUGS (or change one drug for another) to keep pain under control. With the host of drugs now available to the physician, and the other modalities of treatment which recent medical progress has brought (SURGERY, PHYSICAL THERAPY, PSYCHOTHERAPY, for example), no one in the United States today need live in pain—or labor in pain in CHILDBIRTH.

Painter's Colic—LEAD POISONING.

Palate—the roof of the mouth. It consists of the *hard palate* in front, a bony structure covered with mucous membrane, and a *soft palate*, composed of nine small muscles, behind. The UVULA is a prolongation of the center of the soft palate. By changing the shape of the mouth, the soft palate is an important organ in the production of *speech*. See CLEFT PALATE.

Palliative—any drug or treatment that relieves or alleviates a disease or painful condition but does not cure it and has little, if any, effect on the underlying cause of the distress.

Palpation—examination by hand; feeling with the fingers or whole hand for signs or symptoms of disease.

Palpebra—eyelid.

Palpitation—rapid heart beat of which a person is acutely aware. It is usually temporary and rarely a serious symptom. See HEART DISEASE.

Palsy—originally meant PARALYSIS, now has extended its meaning. See, for example, CEREBRAL PALSY. *Shaking palsy* is PARKINSON'S DISEASE; *wasting palsy*, MUSCULAR DYSTROPHY; *bulbar palsy*, respiratory POLIO; *printer's palsy*, antimony poisoning; *scrivener's palsy*, writer's cramp or NEUROSIS. *Bell's palsy* (named after the early 19th-century Scotch physiologist Sir Charles Bell) describes the distortion of the face that follows damage to the facial NERVE.

Pancreas—a large, long organ, or gland (called the sweetbread in animals), located behind the lower part of the stomach. It has a head and a tail. It is an important part of both the DIGESTIVE SYSTEM and the ENDO-

CRINE system. (See illustrations for ABDOMEN; HEART.)

The bulk of the pancreas is concerned with the manufacture of digestive juices, particularly enzymes, which empty out of the pancreas through the common bile duct from the LIVER.

Throughout the pancreas are found scattered islet cells ("islands of Langerhans") which secrete insulin, the hormone necessary to proper CARBOHYDRATE metabolism. Failure of the pancreas to develop adequate supplies of insulin results in DIABETES *mellitus*. Insulin extracted from the pancreas of meat animals may then be injected into the patient as a "substitution therapy."

The pancreas is richly supplied with blood vessels and nerves, which makes inflammation of the pancreas (*acute* PANCREATITIS) one of the most exquisitely painful diseases known to man. Abscesses, stones, new growths (usually CANCER which gives no early signals of pain), cysts and stones are sometimes found in the pancreas, but they are rare. If severe, surgery is usually indicated.

Pancreatitis—inflammation of the pancreas, usually the result of a back-up of bile from the LIVER and gall bladder into the ducts of the pancreas. The symptoms are generally sudden, acute pain, piercing enough to cause collapse; tenderness and swelling of the abdomen; and vomiting. The condition is serious and requires expert medical and surgical management. *Chronic pancreatitis* is often associated with GALLSTONES; jaundice is a common symptom.

Pandemic—very wide-scale EPIDEMIC. Influenza was pandemic in 1918; it swept across the whole United States and many countries in Europe.

Panhysterectomy—surgical removal of the uterus. The term is often loosely used, however, to mean removal of *all* the internal SEX ORGANS, FEMALE (except, of course, the vagina).

Pantothenic Acid—a part of the VITAMIN B complex; its significance in human beings is not yet clearly understood. It will *not* prevent hair from greying or turn grey hair back to its original color.

Papanicolaou Smear—sometimes called "Pap smear," is made up of scrapings taken from the internal SEX ORGANS, FEMALE (cervix) through a dry vaginal speculum. Examined under a microscope, these scrapings may help to detect early CANCER of the cervix or give clues to the correct diagnosis of other FEMALE TROUBLES. (George N. Papanicolaou is an American physician.)

Papaverine—a NARCOTIC drug.

Papilla—any small nipple-shaped elevation above the surface of the skin or mucous membrane. The taste-buds on the tongue are papillae (pl.)

as are the HAIR papillae on the skin.

Papillitis—usually refers to painful inflammations of the papillae around the ANUS; sometimes of the optic disk (see EYE TROUBLE).

Papule—*pimple*. See SEBORRHEA.

Paracentesis—puncture of any body cavity with a hollow needle or its equivalent, trocar and cannula, to remove an accumulation of unwanted fluids. The operation may be applied to the chest, ear, heart sac, bladder wall or other organs.

Paraldehyde—a powerful, bitter-tasting hypnotic drug, often given by mouth or rectum for the control of acute ALCOHOLISM or maniacal excitement.

Paralysis—loss of muscle function owing usually to damage to the NERVES that control the MUSCLE. The impairment of function may be minor or extreme, temporary or permanent. See POLIO, PARKINSON'S DISEASE, PARAPLEGIA, STROKE, MUSCULAR DYSTROPHY, PARESIS.

Paralysis Agitans—PARKINSON'S DISEASE.

Paranoia—a form of MENTAL ILLNESS. When the condition reaches an extreme or acute stage (PSYCHOSIS), the patient usually suffers from delusions of being persecuted or illusions of grandeur. He thinks he is Napoleon or Christ. See SCHIZOPHRENIA, of which paranoia is one manifestation.

Paraplegia—paralysis of both legs, usually accompanied by paralysis of the bowels and bladder, resulting in incontinence. Injury to the spinal cord and brain, from accident or disease, is the usual cause. With modern methods of REHABILITATION, much can be done to restore paraplegics to nearly-normal living.

Parapsychology—the outer space of psychology. It deals with psychic phenomena that are still unknown, misunderstood or misinterpreted; such as mental telepathy, clairvoyance, extra-sensory perception, psychic research.

Parasite—a plant (for example, FUNGUS or mistletoe) or animal (for example, PROTOZOA) that lives and feeds on another plant or animal, presumably at the expense and to the detriment of the host. A VIRUS is a parasite on a cell. See SAPROPHYTE.

Parasympathetic—a part of the autonomic NERVOUS SYSTEM.

Parathormone—the hormone secreted by the parathyroid (ENDOCRINE) glands.

Parathyroids — ENDOCRINE GLANDS.

Paratyphoid—a milder form of TYPHOID FEVER.

Parenchyma—the essential or functional elements of a bodily organ, the working tissue; as contrasted with the structure or framework that holds it up or together (stroma).

Parenteral—literally, outside the gut. Usually applied to the administration of medication or other substances, such as blood, by other routes than by mouth; for example, intravenous injection. See "SHOTS."

Paresis—slight or temporary paralysis; usually applied, however, to the general paralysis of the insane *(dementia paralytica)* which used to occur in about 3% of the people who became infected with SYPHILIS. With modern antibiotic treat-

ment of both early and late syphilis, paresis has become much rarer and much more amenable to successful treatment.

Paresthesia—abnormal feeling; heightened sensitivity, such as burning, prickling or crawling sensations on the skin. It is associated with diseases of the NERVES AND NERVOUS SYSTEM.

Parietal—refers to the walls of any body cavity, usually the skull.

PARKINSON'S DISEASE

Parkinson's disease, also known as *shaking palsy,* parkinsonism, or paralysis agitans, is a degenerative disease in which something goes wrong with the NERVE ganglia at the base of the brain. What, nobody knows. In some cases the palsy follows inflammation of the BRAIN (ENCEPHALITIS), HIGH BLOOD PRESSURE, or certain kinds of poisoning (CARBON MONOXIDE, for example). But in most cases the precipitating cause remains unknown. It may well turn out to be faulty metabolism in the brain and brain stem. (See BRAIN and BRAIN DAMAGE.)

The outstanding symptom is *tremor* (shaking), which continues whether the patient is at rest or moving. The tremor is usually most pronounced in one of the upper limbs, and usually starts there. With this tremor comes *rigidity,* or stiffening of the muscles. Along with this usually occurs restriction of movement, so that the patient tends more and more to reduce his activities, which damages him both physically and psychologically. He seems to respond to the insidious inner command: "Don't do something. Just stand there." In extreme cases, the posture slumps seriously, so that in advanced cases the patient loses height and becomes a stooped and bowed creature. Fluency of speech is often impaired.

What can be done about Parkinson's disease? Great advances have been made in recent years, particularly in the direction of new drugs and surgery. However, the muscle contractures and consequent needless confinement to wheel chair or bed are a severe handicap to the victim of parkinsonism. Contractures amounting to deformity (such as wry neck) can be prevented to a large extent in almost every patient by constant attention to the right medicine, regular physical therapy, and continual exercise. Early cases are comparatively easy to treat and can be kept under control. Advanced cases often need a great deal more encouragement from their family and friends than they get. Many profit tremendously by PSYCHOTHERAPY and the attention of a sympathetic psychiatrist. Many are excellent candidates for full-scale REHABILITATION.

Parkinsonism is no contraindication to work and gainful employment. Every victim of the disease should join the do-it-yourself movement and make every effort to handle his necessary activities of daily living—and more. Because of his personality structure, many a patient takes his illness for excuse. He becomes more dependent and invalided than he needs to be. Sometimes the morale of other members of the family may require psychotherapy.

Drugs used in treating parkinsonism are primarily antispasmodics, which reduce muscle spasm. They include old drugs like hyoscine and belladonna and new synthetic chemical drugs like trihexyphenidyl (Artane). Adjustment of the drug and the *dosage schedule* to the patient's needs must be done by the physician, not the patient. The name of the drug is not anywhere near so important as how and when it is used.

Surgical treatment—brain surgery—is now being done in selected cases and appears to offer new hope for many patients who could not have been helped at all a few years ago. One of the newer operations consists of injecting absolute alcohol into a small area of the brain (globus pallidus). About two-thirds of the patients who undergo this operation obtain remarkable relief from tremor and rigidity.

Paronychia—FUNGUS infection around the NAILS (finger nails or toenails).

Parotid Glands—the saliva-producing glands in the back of the mouth, near the ear.

Parotitis—MUMPS; inflammation of the parotid glands.

Paroxysm—a fit of pain, coughing, sneezing or other REFLEX action; a sudden, sharp, repeated reaction.

Parrot Fever—PSITTACOSIS.

Parturition—CHILDBIRTH.

PAS—para-aminosalicylic acid.

Pasteurization, named after Louis Pasteur (1822-95), the great French chemist and bacteriologist who formulated the germ theory of disease. It is a method of "sterilizing" milk and other substances which is not open to the objections of boiling.

The milk is heated to a moderate temperature, usually about 145 to 150 degrees F., for a period of thirty minutes and then cooled to about 55 degrees F. This heating kills most harmful bacteria and considerably impedes the growth and spread of others. There is also a high-temperature (about 165 degrees F.), fast-cooling pasteurization process.

It would be difficult to estimate the immense value of pasteurization of milk in doing away with milk-borne diseases, especially among children. Pasteurized milk has gone a long way toward eliminating from the civilized world such diseases as TUBERCULOSIS of the glands and bones (bovine tuberculosis), UNDULANT FEVER, SCARLET FEVER, TYPHOID and PARATYPHOID FEVER, and FOOD POISONING.

There are no valid arguments against pasteurization of milk as a public health measure. The slight vitamin C loss from the milk is easily made up in other foods.

Patch Test—a small patch of adhesive tape is applied to the skin. The tape contains some substance (ANTIGEN) to which it is hoped to find out whether or not the patient is sensitive (allergic). If, when the patch is removed, the skin area looks red and inflamed, the test is called "positive" and it is assumed that the patient *is* sensitive to the particular antigen.

Patella—kneecap. (See illustrations for BONES.)

Pathogenesis describes how a disease takes hold on the body; where, for example, an infecting microbe enters the body (nose? mouth? skin?), how it spreads in the body (blood stream? nerve pathways?), where it lands (lungs? liver? brain?) and what it does to the body (causes paralysis? fever? difficult breathing?).

Pathogenic—anything that causes disease, such as pathogenic bacteria.

Pathology—the study of disease processes, particularly the changes in structure and function of tissues that occur as the result of disease. Knowledge of pathology is the essence of medical practice. Compare with ANATOMY, PHYSIOLOGY, DIAGNOSIS.

Pathologist—a specialist in the examination of tissues, especially under the microscope, to determine whether or not they are diseased. An important routine assignment of pathologists is the examination of tissue removed by surgical operation to determine whether or not CANCER cells are present.

Pectoral—relating to chest or breast.

Pederasty—sexual congress *per anum* with boys.

Pediatrics—the medical specialty of child care. It usually stops at about the age of 16, sometimes earlier. Pediatrics is a comparatively new clinical specialty in medicine. It emphasizes *preventive medicine,* checking frequently on the well child to keep him well and aid his physical and emotional development.

Pediculosis—lousiness; infestation with lice. See INSECTS.

Pellagra—literally "painful skin"; a vitamin-deficiency disease once extremely common among the "poor whites" of the South. These people existed on a very limited diet, chiefly salt pork, corn meal, and molasses. About 1927 Dr. Joseph Goldberger, of the U.S. Public Health Service, demonstrated that pellagra was a dietary-deficiency disease that could be prevented by adding fresh fruits, vegetables, and milk. It was later shown that the important pellagra-preventive factor was the vitamin called *niacin,* a part of the vitamin B complex. (See VITAMINS.) The symptoms of pellagra include a sore tongue and mouth, skin eruptions (dermatitis), digestive disturbances (diarrhea), mental depression (melancholia), backache, weakness, and debility.

Pelvis—the large basin of bone, and its contents—intestines, internal sex organs, bladder and so forth—at the lower end of the trunk. The bony pelvis is composed of the two innominate bones on the sides and in front (where they join in the symphysis pubis) and the sacrum and coccyx bones behind. The pelvis rests on the legs below and supports the spinal column above. (See illustrations for ABDOMEN; BONES.)

"Pelvic Disease" usually refers to some FEMALE TROUBLE.

Pemphigus—a SKIN disease marked by repeated crops of blisters (bullae). When the blisters disappear, they may leave spots behind. The skin usually itches and burns and the patient generally feels poorly. Sometimes he is acutely ill. This disease can be very serious. Ordinarily there is a kind of cement that holds the top layers of skin to the lower layers. In serious pemphigus this cement, or "glue," does not seem to work very well and the top layer slides over the lower layers. Consultation with a well qualified skin specialist (dermatologist) is strongly urged.

Pendulous—hanging; as in pendulous breasts.

Penicillin—the first and still one of the best and cheapest of the most widely used ANTIBIOTICS. It is derived from the mold, *Penicillium notatum.* It is effective against a wide variety of microbes, including staphylococcus (boils), pneumococcus (pneumonia), streptococcus (sore throat), and gonococcus (gonorrhea). It has simplified and revolutionized the treatment of SYPHILIS and kindred venereal disease.

Penis—the male organ of copulation and urination. See SEX ORGANS, MALE and URINARY SYSTEM.

Pentothal—a barbiturate; NARCOTIC and ANESTHETIC, generally given by intravenous injection.

Pep Pill—usually contains AMPHETAMINE and often CAFFEINE; possibly dangerous if taken in repeated or excessive doses.

Peptic—refers to the stomach, as in peptic ulcer (see STOMACH TROUBLE), or DIGESTION.

Percussion—a method of DIAGNOSIS which consists of tapping parts of the body lightly with a hammer or the fingers and listening carefully to the sounds produced. The method was developed by the Austrian doctor, Leopold Auenbrugger, in the middle of the 18th century. The principle of it is the same as tapping a barrel to see how full it is. The chest and back are usually tapped.

Per Diem—per day. In usual hospital usage it indicates the average cost to a hospital for provision of a day of care to a patient in the hospital.

Perforation — a break-through; by disease, as in a perforated peptic ulcer, or by intention, as in SURGERY.

Periarteritis—inflammation of outer layers of an artery and the tissues surrounding it. *Periarteritis nodosa* is a rare COLLAGEN DISEASE affecting arteries.

Pericarditis—inflammation of the membrane or sac *(pericardium)* which holds the HEART. See HEART DISEASE. (See illustrations for HEART.)

Perineum—the anatomical region at the lower end of the trunk and between the thighs; running from buttocks to scrotum or vagina.

"Period"—see MENSTRUATION; FEMALE TROUBLES.

Periodic Medical Examinations offer many health-saving advantages. A regular check-up by a physician has much to recommend it. However, you should not rely exclusively on scheduled check-ups. You should also see your doctor whenever minor signs and symptoms of disease or discomfort appear and hang on.

Many industrial organizations now offer, or insist on, periodic medical examinations for their employees. In one industrial organization, approximately 6,000 workers were examined regularly over a 6-year period (1948-54). These favorable results were observed: occurrence of disabling or fatal heart disease dropped 15%; deaths from cancer of internal organs in men fell 33%, and deaths from cancer of the breast or pelvic organs in women decreased 50%; occupational skin diseases declined 80%. Furthermore, the employees had fewer accidents.

Periodontal—around the TEETH.

Periosteum — elastic lining around BONES; two layers of fibrous tissue.

Periostitis—inflammation, usually painful, of the PERIOSTEUM.

Peristalsis—the wave-like motion, brought about by the alternate contraction and relaxation of smooth muscle tissues of the gastro-intestinal tract, that carries food and juices along from the stomach to the anus. See DIGESTION; CONSTIPATION.

Peritoneum—the interior of the abdomen; more exactly the strong membrane that lines the abdomen and helps hold the internal organs of the body (viscera) in place. (See illustrations for ABDOMEN; APPENDICITIS.)

Peritonitis—inflammation in or of the peritoneum. The infection usually starts in one abdominal organ (for example, a perforated bowel or stomach) and spreads dangerously to others along the lines and sheets of the peritoneal lining. This is the great hazard of abdominal wounds and operations. With modern ANTIBIOTICS and BLOOD transfusions it is now possible to control much of the formerly-feared ravages of peritonitis.

Perlèche—mouth infection with FUNGUS (MONILIASIS), usually with grayish white patches and a tendency to lick the lips. May be associated with VITAMIN B deficiency.

Pernio—CHILBLAIN.

Personality Development—see PSYCHOANALYSIS.

Perspiration—sweating, a normal means of regulation of body TEMPERATURE.

Pertussis—WHOOPING COUGH.

Pessary—any one of an exceedingly great variety of metal, rubber, or even wooden instruments designed to be placed in the vagina and wholly or partly in the womb for treatment of various displacements ("tipped womb": see FEMALE TROUBLES) or with contraceptive intent. The continual or too frequent wearing of a pessary may be dangerous.

Pest—PLAGUE.

Petechiae—small black and blue spots on the skin, resulting from broken capillaries underneath.

Petit Mal—a small convulsion, as contrasted with a bad fit, or *grand mal,* in EPILEPSY.

Petrolatum—petroleum jelly, vaseline; the soft, gooey ointment and vehicle for other drugs that remains when the more volatile fractions of crude oil have been distilled off.

Peyote—an intoxicating drug obtained from Mexican cactus; it produces feelings of ecstasy. It must be considered a NARCOTIC with all its dangers.

Phagocyte—a white BLOOD CELL that engulfs and destroys MI-

CROBES and other cellular material that infects the body. It is one of the body's own microbe-hunters.

Phalanges—(singular, phalanx); the bones of the digits, fingers, and toes. Thumb and great toe have 2 phalanges each; all others, 3. (See illustrations for BONES.)

Phallus—penis; or representations of it as found in phallic worship rites.

Pharmacist—druggist; apothecary; licensed to fill doctor's PRESCRIPTIONS.

Pharmacology—the science that deals with DRUGS of all sorts. The pharmacologist is usually a research scientist, well-grounded in chemistry and PHYSIOLOGY. *Materia medica* is almost but not quite synonymous with pharmacology; it embraces the clinical art of using drugs, which the pharmacologist studies and invents, most effectively.

Pharmacopeia—an authoritative and usually official treatise or book that describes all manner of DRUGS and tells in exact detail how to make and use them. Many countries have an official pharmacopeia. The United States Pharmacopeia, abbreviated U.S.P., sets American standards for drug safety, purity, and potency. First issued in 1820, the U. S. Pharmacopeia is now revised about every five years.

Pharmacy—drug store; also the art of keeping, compounding and giving out (dispensing) DRUGS.

Pharyngitis—sore THROAT.

Pharynx—back of the THROAT; includes nasopharynx which is the upper part leading into the back of the nose, and a lower part leading into the windpipe and food tube. Tonsils and adenoids are located in the pharynx. (See illustrations for THROAT; EARS; RESPIRATORY SYSTEM.

Phenobarbital—a NARCOTIC drug used in sleeping pills.

Phimosis—tightening of the foreskin of the PENIS so that it cannot be pulled back over the head of the penis. The treatment is circumcision. Phimosis of the *clitoris* may also occur in the female. See SEX ORGANS, FEMALE and MALE.

Phlebitis—inflammation of the walls of the veins, often leading to THROMBOPHLEBITIS.

Phlebotomy—blood-letting, presumably for healing purposes, by cutting into a vein (venesection).

Phlegm—thick MUCUS, coughed up or spit out of the mouth, usually when one "clears his throat."

Phobia—abnormal fear; for example, *agoraphobia,* fear of wide open spaces. See MENTAL ILLNESS; PSYCHOANALYSIS.

Phosphorus—a chemical element; highly poisonous and inflammable in a relatively pure state. However, compounds of phosphorus, notably phosphates, are regularly and importantly present in the human and animal body and can be extracted from bones and urine.

Photomicrograph—a photograph taken through a microscope; it shows minute cellular structure.

Photophobia—abnormal fear of light.

Phrenic—related to the *diaphragm* by which we breathe or, rarely, to the mind. The *phrenic nerves* stimulate the diaphragm to its breathing action. When some of these nerves are cut *(phrenicotomy)*, one side of the diaphragm can be paralyzed. This nerve-cutting operation has sometimes been used in the treatment of TUBERCULOSIS to put one side of the lung at rest.

Phthisis—TUBERCULOSIS of the lungs; or any wasting away of body substance.

Physiatrics—PHYSICAL MEDICINE.

Physic—any drug or medicine, but usually means a laxative; see CONSTIPATION.

Physical Education—a specialty field in school and college *education*. It includes management and supervision of a wide range of activities, including water sports, camping and outing activities, competitive athletics, dancing, gymnastics, individual and team sports, stunts and tumbling, recreational exercise, and prescribed special exercises and activities. EXERCISE is the keynote of physical education, but physical education also makes great contributions to promoting mental health and preventing MENTAL ILLNESS. Only in the field of special *corrective exercises* does it impinge on medical practice. The name of honor among physical educators is not "doctor" but "*coach.*" A good coach permits his teams to do only what the doctors say is safe and proper.

Some physical educators in schools are also "health educators." However, exercise is only one small part of the total health picture. (See also POSTURE.)

Physical Medicine—employment of physical means in diagnosing and treating disease. It does not ordinarily include the use of such complicated physical instruments as the X-ray machine (radiology), the electron microscope (laboratory medicine), and other electronic diagnostic instruments (electroencephalograph, for example).

The emphasis in physical medicine is more on treatment than on diagnosis. It is directed primarily at the "third phase of medicine," the convalescent period when the problem is to restore the patient to his useful place in society.

Physical medicine is an ancient specialty, dating back to the times of Hippocrates. Physical medicine includes the use of heat, cold, water (hydrotherapy, balneotherapy), light (infra-red and ultraviolet, for example), electricity (in its simpler forms), manipulation, MASSAGE, EXERCISE (active and passive), and mechanical devices (sometimes including braces, splints, and assistive devices, such as feeding slings that permit a victim of paralysis of the upper extremities to feed himself).

Physical medicine is a well-recognized medical specialty. Because it often requires elaborate equipment, most physical medicine is practiced in hospitals and special institutes for the physically crippled and disabled. The effective practice of physical medicine often requires special skills in *administrative medicine*. The physical-medicine specialist must organize, direct, and sometimes captain a whole team of paramedical specialists and staff necessary to bring the full benefit of physical medicine to a disabled patient.

Physical medicine is not synonymous with REHABILITATION (which see), although physical medicine, since World War II, has taken great leadership in this direction. The physical-medicine specialist works in coordination and cooperation with other medical specialists (notably the orthopedist).

Physical Therapy—the treatment of disease by physical means. See PHYSICAL MEDICINE. The physical therapist is an important member of the team that provides physical therapy in the direction of rehabilitation to the disabled patient. He (or more often she) works under direction of the doctor. The physical therapist's orders come from either the physiatrist or the orthopedist or both. Most physical therapists work in hospitals, but some (like visiting nurses) make house calls. Registered physical therapists have professional training and should not be confused with old-fashioned masseurs, masseuses, and gymnastics teachers. See MASSAGE.

Physician—doctor of medicine, M.D., legally authorized to practice medicine. Surgeons are physicians who perform operations: many doctors do not. See FAMILY DOCTOR.

Physiology—the science and study of the functions or actions of living organisms in their gross or minute structures. ANATOMY describes the parts of the body; physiology seeks out and tells what each part does.

Pica—craving for strange foods; a perverted appetite; occasionally seen in pregnancy.

PILES

Piles, or hemorrhoids, are swollen or VARICOSE VEINS situated just outside, just inside, or across the walls of the anus. Two out of three adults have, or have had, them. Sedentary (sitting-down) occupations encourage their development; they are an occupational disease of judges and bus drivers.

The presence of hemorrhoids means little or nothing. The problem is to keep them from becoming annoying or seriously infected. At long last, piles can be cured by safe and simple (though sometimes delicate) surgical operations. The swollen veins can be obliterated by cutting them out, cauterizing them with an electro-cautery, or injecting them with a solution (sclerosing solution) that hardens them. Such surgery provides permanent relief for long-standing, truly bothersome cases, but is not always necessary.

Are "bleeding piles" dangerous? Not really. There is some risk of infection, but the bleeding often provides a natural cure for the piles. It fills them with little blood clots, which causes them to shrivel up and disappear. The presence of bleeding piles is usually discovered just after a bowel movement, when streaks of blood are noted in the toilet bowl or on toilet tissue.

When this bleeding arises from scratching or irritation of *external piles*, situated outside the anus, it is nothing to worry about. The bleeding from *internal piles* may appear more alarming, for several ounces of dark blood may issue forth. This usually looks like a lot more than it really is.

The problem is to be sure that the cause of the bleeding is piles and not any other more serious condition of the lower bowel. For this reason medical examination at an early date is advisable.

What makes piles itch? The ITCHING sensation that sometimes accompanies piles and is the chief complaint associated with them is usually irritation brought on by misguided efforts to relieve the itching; namely, violent scratching, overtreatment with salves and ointments, and intemperate use of cathartics or laxatives to self-treat CONSTIPATION. Itching is often the result of secondary infections superimposed on the varicose veins, particularly FUNGUS infections similar to those found in athlete's foot.

How to manage itching piles. If the piles are left alone and not fussed with, they often disappear, along with the itching, of their own accord. Large piles often occur in the course of PREGNANCY, because the return circulation of blood in the veins is slowed down by the pressure of the enlarged uterus. These piles usually disappear after childbirth, and need no special treatment.

Other conditions that piles are often associated with are constipation, overweight, sedentary living, hard seating, and diseases affecting blood circulation (HEART DISEASE and LIVER TROUBLE, for example). Prevention and relief of piles, therefore, usually depends not on some hitherto untried ointment or suppository but on correcting the underlying factors; namely, medical treatment of the heart disease or liver trouble, change of seat cushions at work (a foam-rubber seat cushion often works wonders of relief), a reasonable amount of EXERCISE to stimulate circulation, reduction of overweight (see DIET), and prevention of *hard-stool* constipation by drinking plenty of water and occasionally taking a bulk-producing laxative (psyllium seed or agar-agar; see CONSTIPATION).

For immediate relief of itching piles, a hot sitz bath usually works well—water as hot as you can stand it, tub or bowl only ¼ to ½ filled with water, sitting time at least 15 to 30 minutes.

Glycerin suppositories, inserted in the rectum, and mild skin-anesthetic ointments (like sunburn ointments) also give quick relief to itching piles. But continued use of suppositories and ointments, regardless of switches in brands, is unlikely to give permanent relief unless the underlying causes are corrected. Then the suppositories and ointments are no longer needed.

Particularly when fungus infections are responsible for the itching, careful and gentle washing and thorough drying of the anal region immediately after each bowel movement is helpful. Cotton or soft disposable paper tissues may be used. Talcum powder can also be helpful.

Pills—small balls of medicine to be swallowed. The outside of a pill (or tablet) can be any color; this is no clue to what is in it or what effect it will produce. Pills are colored for easy identification on the part of nurses and patients.

Pilonidal Cyst is a sac or cyst containing hair. The troublesome one is that found at the base of the spine, where the tail would be if human beings had tails. This cyst may become inflamed, swollen and painful and may develop into a draining *fistula*, excreting pus and other body fluids. The pilonidal cyst is actually a congenital anomaly, because most people don't have them. They represent a failure in the development process; normally there is no sac or opening at the base of the spine.

Men between 20 and 45 are most often troubled by this condition. The first and simplest treatment is a hot sitz bath. Puncture of the cyst to let out the fluid which has accumulated under pressure is usually the next step. In many instances a complete surgical operation is necessary for relief. All the abnormal tissue must be cut out. Reparative or plastic surgery may also be necessary. Sufficient time for complete healing must be allowed; hospital stay is often prolonged.

Pimples—see SEBORRHEA. Don't pick at pimples!

Pineal Gland—small, cone-shaped, presumably ENDOCRINE gland, lying at the base of the brain near the pituitary. No one is exactly sure of what it does; what purpose or function it serves. Some say it is related to the development of early sexual precocity. The ancients called it the "seat of the soul."

Pink Eye—inflammation of the conjunctiva of the EYE, a highly contagious, epidemic disease. See EYE TROUBLE.

Pinworm—see WORMS.

Pituitary—an ENDOCRINE GLAND; the "master gland." (See illustration for BRAIN.)

Pituitrin—a hormone produced by the pituitary ENDOCRINE GLAND.

Pityriasis—a SKIN disease marked by the presence of bran-like scales or flakes of skin. In its most common form, *pityriasis rosea*, a red spot, often beginning on the chest, gradually spreads and scales to cover abdomen, chest, legs and thighs. The cause is unknown, possibly a VIRUS. The condition is not serious, and only mildly contagious; however, it may continue for as long as three months. Sunbathing or exposure to ultraviolet light, if taken dur-ing the first two weeks of the attack, sometimes stops its further development.

Pityriasis rubra is a more serious form of scaling skin disease; it is an inflammatory condition, involving the whole system. The skin turns deep red and is covered with white or gray scales. This can be a long-term illness, occasionally fatal. *Pityriasis versicolor* is a fairly common FUNGUS disease, resulting in large, yellow, scaly spots on the skin of the trunk.

Placebo—sugar pill, or any other "make-believe" drug, that looks like the real thing but isn't. Placebo medication, which has no pharmacological effect, is sometimes prescribed by doctors for patients who insist that they have to take some medicine, however inert, and often feel better psychologically for going through the ritual of taking medicine.

More importantly, placebo medication is often used in the conduct of scientific experiments on drugs to provide controls for determining how effective a particular drug may be. Often neither the doctor nor the patient in the experiment knows whether the pill, tablet, fluid or other form of medication is a placebo or a potent drug.

Placenta—afterbirth; the pancake-shaped tissue attached to the uterus wall through which the fetus is nourished from its mother's blood. See PREGNANCY, CHILDBIRTH.

Plague—*bubonic* or *oriental plague,* or *pest,* is an acute infection caused by the plague bacillus *(Pasteurella pestis).* It is commonly carried by fleas that infest rats and other rodents; hence rat control is a crucial preventive measure. Some forms of plague (pneumonic plague) are transmitted directly from person to person, via infected droplets of sputum.

The disease runs a rapid, severe and often fatal course. It begins with fever and chills, soon followed by prostration, delirium, headache, vomiting and sometimes, in the severe forms, by internal bleeding into the lungs, spitting of blood, breaking of small blood vessels on the skin (petechiae), and swelling of the lymph glands in the groin, armpits and neck. These swellings which may break down into ulcers are called *buboes;* hence the name *bubonic plague.* This disease was the *black death* that terrified Europe in the 14th century.

An eye-witness, Guy de Chauliac, a French physician, has described the plague that appeared at Avignon in January, 1348. People who caught it died in 3 to 5 days. "Men died without attendants and were buried without priests. The father did not visit his son, nor the son his father. Charity was dead and hope crushed." So wrote de Chauliac.

Plague is rare in North America, though occasionally found in ground squirrels and other wild rodents. It is endemic in some parts of Asia.

Plantar—pertaining to the sole of the foot, as in plantar *warts.*

Plasma—the fluid part of the blood, in which the blood cells are suspended. Plasma is obtained from whole blood by removing the blood cells, either by letting them settle out (sedimentation) or whirling them out (centrifugation). Plasma was widely used during World War II to prevent SHOCK following battle wounds. It is still used in treating shock. Plasma is more readily available under emergency conditions than whole-blood transfusions; it is more easily stored and transported; it can be expanded in volume by certain complex chemical substances called plasma expanders. However, whole-blood is now generally preferred for many conditions in which plasma alone was formerly used.

Blood serum is not quite the same thing as blood plasma. Blood serum is the clear fluid that separates from blood when it is allowed to clot. Blood serum, therefore, is blood plasma *minus* its clotting elements, notably FIBRINOGEN.

Plasmodium—MALARIA parasites, found in the blood stream.

Plaster of Paris—calcium sulfate; when mixed with water, it quickly hardens (crystallizes) to form casts and splints used in surgery.

Plastic Surgery—the phase and specialty of surgery that deals with repair of visible defects, scars and malformations; for example, "nose-lifting." See SURGERY.

Platelet—a BLOOD platelet, essential to *blood clotting*.

Pleura—the membrane that covers the lungs and lines the inner walls of the chest cavity. Actually there are two pleura, right and left, almost completely shut off from one another. The pleura secrete a serous fluid that provides a kind of lubrication for the movement of lungs in the chest.

Pleurisy—inflammation and infection of the pleura, the membrane enveloping the lungs and lining the chest cavity. It is a frequent complication of PNEUMONIA and TUBERCULOSIS. The condition may come on suddenly—*acute pleurisy*—or it may develop more slowly and hang on for a long time—*chronic pleurisy*.

In acute pleurisy the moist, smooth surfaces of the pleura first become dry, rough, and shaggy and give off sounds like two pieces of leather being rubbed together. The disease may then progress to a second stage in which copious quantities of serous fluid exude from the pleural surfaces. This reduces the friction of lung movements. However, large amounts of pus and fluid may accumulate in the pleural spaces, causing EMPYEMA. The inflamed surfaces of the pleura tend to stick together, causing *adhesions* which are often permanent.

A stitch in the side, or a knifelike pain, is often the first symptom of pleurisy. This is followed by chills and fever and a dry cough. When the pleura again begins secreting fluid, the stabbing pains lessen but difficult breathing occurs.

Plexus—a knot or tangle, usually of nerves or veins. The *solar plexus* is a large network of nerves located on the outside of the stomach. It is painfully disturbed by sharp blows to the abdomen.

Plumbism—LEAD POISONING.

Pneumococcus—the MICROBE that causes PNEUMONIA.

Pneumoconiosis—disease of the lung as a result of the continued inhalation of various kinds of dusts and other particles. The tissues of the lung harden. See SILICOSIS.

PNEUMONIA

Pneumonia is an inflammation of the lungs; it usually refers to *lobar pneumonia*, caused by the pneumococcus germ and involving one or more lobes of the lung. If both lungs are involved, the condition is called *double pneumonia*. When the infection begins in the bronchial tubes and the inflammation involves small patches of the lung, we have *bronchopneumonia*. There are still other types of pneumonia owing to a variety of agents and causes. Some of these are described below.

Pneumonia, together with the closely allied condition *influenza* (flu), still ranks first among *infectious diseases* as a cause of death in the United States. It kills about 45,000 adults a year. However, it is no longer quite the dread disease it was before modern sulfa drugs and antibiotics. Pneumonia used to kill 1 in every 3 or 4 people it attacked. Now 19 out of 20 people recover. This decline in the pneumonia fatality rate, from 25 to 30% down to less than 5%, is one of the great triumphs of modern medicine.

Who gets pneumonia? No one is immune, for the germs that cause it are commonly present in the nose and throat. However, it is most dangerous at the extremes of life, in infancy and old age, and among alcoholics or people debilitated by other disease. Terminal pneumonia has been called the "friend of the aged," because it often carries off elderly, suffering patients quickly and with little pain. However, pneumonia is the foe of newborn and young children, often dealing death at the termination of some other disease. Males contract pneumonia more often than females.

What is the pneumonia season? In the United States the pneumonia months are January, February, and March, when the death rate may be 4 to 8 times as high as in the summer months. Cold weather, particularly a change in weather from warm to cold, influences the development of pneumonia. This is true partly because the disease is often secondary to other infections of the upper respiratory tract, which occur more frequently in cold climates and winter months. Pneumonia is rare in the tropics.

How does pneumonia begin? It usually follows a neglected cold, a mild bout of influenza—virus diseases—or other conditions that lower body resistance and permit the pneumococcus to get a foothold in the lungs. After a few days' incubation, with symptoms much like those of a common cold, pneumonia comes on suddenly and abruptly. The early symptoms are shaking chills; high and rising fever; knifelike pains in the chest, side, or shoulder, which become worse with attempts to breathe deeply; a painful cough; blood-flecked or rusty sputum; and a very marked feeling of illness. Whenever this dangerous combination of symptoms appears, medical attention should be promptly obtained. Immediate treatment modifies the course of the disease.

What is the course of pneumonia? If not treated with drugs, pneumonia runs a typical 7- to 10-day course. It comes to a turning point, or crisis, at which the patient may promptly recover, or die. During the course of the disease, the patient may get sicker and sicker and even go into delirium. Breathing is painful, rapid, and shallow. With proper modern treatment, however, the disease can be brought under control in 12 to 36 hours.

What happens when the pneumococci invade the lungs is that the lungs try to drive them out by pouring out fluids (exudates). This mixture of serum, red and white blood cells, and fibrin fills the air sacs of the lungs (alveoli) and prevents the normal and necessary transfer of oxygen to the blood stream. When great amounts of fluid fill the air spaces, parts of the lung are *consolidated* into dense tissue, visible by X ray. If a person dies of pneumonia, he has in effect drowned in his own body fluid.

When the physician listens with his stethoscope to the fluid-congested lung, he often hears a bubbly or musical sound (râles), as the air moving in and out of the lung riffles through the fluids. Because the fluids interfere with oxygen-transfer, the patient may begin to turn blue (cyanotic) and require an oxygen tank.

How is pneumonia now treated? Bed rest and good nursing care are still needed in treating pneumonia, but they are not quite so important as they used to be when only expectant and symptomatic treatment was available. The chief agent of cure is now drugs, notably penicillin and other antibiotics, such as aureomycin; and sulfa drugs, such as sulfadiazine. These are given either alone or in various combinations. Administration of these drugs can quickly stop the spread of inflammation in the lungs. Temperature and breathing may become normal in a half day. Pain rapidly disappears; if it does not, the chest may be strapped or pain-killing drugs given. The patient must be kept under observation for some days to make sure that no further complications occur.

How can pneumonia be prevented? There is no widely practical method of specific immunization. The great hope of prevention lies in obtaining prompt treatment of the less serious upper-respiratory infections, like the common cold, sinusitis, bronchitis, and middle-ear infection, which are sometimes followed by pneumonia. Fatigue, chilling, poor nutrition, alcoholism, physical exhaustion and anything else that lowers bodily resistance should be avoided.

What are the other types of pneumonia? Among them are:

Hypostatic pneumonia usually occurring in elderly, bed-ridden patients whose lungs become congested because they have been lying flat on their back for too long.

Lipoid pneumonia, once common in young children. It results from inhaling oily nose drops into the lungs. This condition can be avoided simply by not using oily drops or sprays in the nostrils of infants and young children and by care in giving them cod-liver oil and other oily vitamin preparations.

Virus pneumonia, also called *primary atypical pneumonia,* which may be caused by any one of a number of viruses. It is characterized by fever, cough, and general weakness, lasts a long time and then disappears, does not respond to sulfa drugs and antibiotics. The viruses of influenza, psittacosis (parrot fever), and Q fever may produce a similar picture of illness.

Aspiration pneumonia, which sometimes follows inhalation of irritating fumes or a general anesthetic.

Besides the pneumococcus, the infecting agent in pneumonia can be streptococcus, staphylococcus, *Hemophilus influenzae,* or Friedlander's bacillus.

Pneumothorax—the accumulation of air or gas in the pleural cavity or spaces. A penetrating wound of the chest, burrowing abscess from the lung, or infection with gas-forming microbes may cause it. Pneumothorax usually begins with sudden and severe pain, followed by increasing difficulty in breathing. *Artificial pneumothorax* is the deliberate introduction of air or inert gas into the pleural spaces (between the lung and the pleura) to collapse the lung and put it at rest. This treatment is sometimes used in pulmonary TUBERCULOSIS; it usually has to be repeated.

Podagra—GOUT.

Podiatrist—chiropodist (see FOOT TROUBLE).

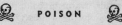

POISON

Accidental poisoning can have a tragic outcome if prompt and intelligent action is not taken. BUT most "poison scares" in a household do not turn out fatally, or even seriously. "The dose makes the poison." In other words the ingestion or inhalation of something poisonous—and perhaps clearly labeled poison—may not have serious consequences IF the dose of the poison was actually quite small, too small to do any harm. This is often the case.

One takes no chances, however, when accidental poisoning is suspected. The first thing to do is *call a doctor.* If you can't reach a doctor, call the *police department* and ask for an ambulance.

1. If the supposed poison victim is UNCONSCIOUS, *don't* try to force him to drink anything or take anything by mouth. Keep him covered and quiet until the doctor or ambulance arrives (or until you have other direct instructions from a doctor or other authority).

2. If the patient is apparently a victim of some kind of gas poisoning (CARBON MONOXIDE or cooking gas, for example), remove him from the contaminated atmosphere and see that he gets plenty of *fresh air*.

3. If the patient is in CONVULSIONS, restrain him *gently*—just enough to keep him from hurting himself. Put a mattress, rug, or coat under him.

4. If the supposed poison is something that has been swallowed, and the victim is conscious, *induce vomiting* by tickling the back of the throat. It is all right if the patient vomits many times and keeps vomiting until his stomach is empty.

5. To induce vomiting, give him any of the following drinks:

Strong salt water—Dissolve 2 tablespoons of common salt in a glass of lukewarm water. Give as many as 4 to 7 glasses, if needed, at 15-minute intervals.

Soapsuds—A warm sudsy solution of soap (or soap powder) in water. Give two or three glassfuls, and repeat in 15 minutes, if necessary.

Mustard water—One or two teaspoons of powdered mustard in a glass of lukewarm water. Repeat in 15 minutes, if necessary.

6. After the victim has vomited completely, or if he cannot soon be induced to vomit much or at all, *and remains conscious*—and medical help has not yet arrived—administer whatever *antidotes* against poison you have on hand, for example:

Milk—2 or 3 glassfuls, warm or cold.

Raw egg white—Separate the whites (mainly *protein*) from the yellows of 2 or 3 eggs. Get the victim to swallow the whites alone or mix them in milk. Egg whites and milk are especially useful when the victim has taken mercury (bichloride of mercury tablets), arsenic (rat poison), or other metallic poisons.

Flour or starch—Mix a generous quantity in a glass of milk or water so that it almost forms a paste. This is especially useful in iodine poisoning.

"Universal antidote"—This is a powder consisting of 2 parts of activated charcoal, and 1 part each of magnesium oxide and tannic

acid. It may be quickly available in a family medicine chest or at a nearby drugstore.

Hot coffee—This is a stimulant to the central nervous system rather than an antidote. It should be given every half hour. Coffee is especially important for patients who have taken an overdose of SLEEPING PILLS, i.e., BARBITURATES or other NARCOTIC drugs.

Strong tea—This, too, stimulates the central nervous system. It also contains a certain amount of tannic acid, which precipitates many alkaloid and metallic poisons.

7. If the victim stops *breathing*, give ARTIFICIAL RESPIRATION (which see for directions).

8. If it is obvious that medical assistance will be long delayed (several hours), the poison victim may take or be given a strong laxative (for example, epsom salts) after he has completed vomiting and taken antidotes.

9. Try to locate the *source* of the poison—an empty or half-emptied bottle or other container. The label may tell you what the chief poisonous ingredient is and thus help in the selection of suitable antidotes and other treatment. "Poison control centers," now operating in many states and cities, can usually identify the poison by a few words on the label of its container.

Prevention of accidental poisoning is just as important as treatment. Here are some simple hints:

Keep poisons away from children. Put them on high shelves or in locked cabinets. Educate children to their dangers. *Don't* keep any poisonous substances around the house unless they are absolutely necessary.

Beware of your own medicine cabinet. A high percentage—possibly half—of the cases of accidental poisoning arise from drugs or medicines taken in error or by mistake. *Don't* take anything from a box or bottle on which you cannot read the label. *Don't* take medicine from a box or bottle in the dark—turn on a light. *Don't* keep poisonous drugs near other medicines. Identify poison bottles with a pin through the cork or a thumbtack, point up, attached to the lid with adhesive tape. See PRESCRIPTIONS; DRUGS.

POISON IVY

Poison ivy is the itching SKIN disorder resulting from contact with the oily poison of the poison ivy plant. This powerful irritant can be conveyed to the skin in many ways—for instance, by petting a dog that has played in poison ivy. Inhalation of smoke from burn-

POISON IVY

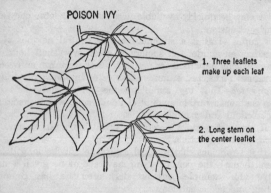

1. Three leaflets make up each leaf

2. Long stem on the center leaflet

Poison ivy can be distinguished from other shrubs and vines by these two characteristics.

ing leaves of the poison ivy plant has also been known to introduce the poison into the body.

The symptoms of ivy poisoning usually occur from 24 to 48 hours after exposure, but may appear in 6 hours or be delayed as long as a week. The skin itches and burns. Red patches and, later, blisters appear. Avoid scratching the affected area, as this may spread the damage. See ITCHING.

Some people are more sensitive than others to ivy poisoning (and other skin irritants). The best protection is to stay away from the irritants. Desensitization to poison ivy by injections of increasing amounts of extracts from the plant is sometimes warranted and effective.

Whenever you fear you have been exposed to poison ivy or other skin irritant, wash off the parts promptly with soap and water. That may get rid of the irritants before they poison the skin.

The greatest risk you run from ivy poisoning is that it will induce you to daub your skin with useless and potentially dangerous lotions, salves, ointments, unguents, powders, and liquids that contain irritant chemicals. By doing this, on the advice of misleading advertisements, misinformed relatives, or enthusiastically misguided friends who know "just the treatment for your itch," you can turn a 48-hour inconvenience into a 2-week hospital stay and worse.

Poison ivy is not the only skin trouble maker. Other irritants that you might be susceptible to include poison oak, crab grass (especially during seeding time), tumble grass, ragweed, dog fennel, hollyhock, Indian mallow, goldenrod, and horse nettle. Different people are affected by different plants. Many common household and garden chemicals can also induce contact dermatitis in susceptible people.

Maltreatment, mistreatment, and overtreatment of the simple itch caused by poison ivy and other contact dermatitis sometimes reaches fantastic proportions. One patient brought his doctor a whole bushel basket full of useless remedies that he had used to make his skin condition worse. The basket was so heavy his wife had to help him carry it.

Costly and disastrous results occur when attempts are made to "tan the skin in the living state with chemicals disguised as remedies."

The skin is clean when the water-soluble substances have been washed off its surface with warm water. What remains on the skin is a flat-film, insoluble in water, which protects the outside covering of the skin. Take this film away and the skin becomes more vulnerable to irritants.

Every serious case of skin poisoning should be treated by a physician. The important thing is not to undertake any home treatment that will make the condition worse.

Poison Oak—see POISON IVY; SKIN TROUBLE.

Poison Sumac—see POISON IVY; SKIN TROUBLE.

POLIO

Polio—poliomyelitis, infantile paralysis—is an acute, infectious disease that sometimes kills and sometimes cripples. The paralytic form of the disease can now be largely prevented by administration of polio vaccine. See VACCINE.

Paralytic polio occurs chiefly in infants and children, but older persons are not exempt. About 25% of the cases occur in people over 20; about 2% in those over 40. The paralytic involvement is generally more severe in older patients.

The cause of polio is the polio virus, of which 3 types are known. The very important point must be made that infection with polio virus rarely causes the paralytic disease. In fact, paralysis appears in only one out of several hundred infections.

In the presence of a polio epidemic, for example, the virus spreads in ways not altogether clear from person to person until practically everyone in the community harbors it. The virus apparently multiplies in the intestine, then appears briefly in the blood stream. Finally, in the paralytic case, the virus crosses the blood-brain barrier and gets into the central nervous system.

Its damaging effects are caused by its attacks on the anterior horns of the gray matter in the spinal cord; that is, the motor neurons. These may be temporarily or permanently damaged, causing motor paralysis of the limbs or other parts of the body served by the nerve cells attacked. Most serious, and fatal, are those instances in which the virus attacks the bulb of the brain (medulla oblongata), where the nerve center controlling the muscles of breathing is located. In these so-called *bulbar* cases, a paralysis of the respiratory muscles occurs and the patient must usually be put in an iron lung (tank respirator) to save his life.

Of all patients stricken with paralytic polio, about half recover completely; another 30% recover with slight aftereffects that do not interfere seriously with normal living; about 15% are extensively and permanently crippled; and 5% die. Largely because of the improved care given to patients in the early and acute stage of the disease, the death rate has been cut radically and the incidence of crippling disabilities and deformities reduced.

Polio virus and polio infection are found throughout the world, but the paralytic cases occur far more frequently in the temperate zones. From an epidemic standpoint, a great deal remains to be discovered. No one yet knows why an epidemic starts or why the disease has its highest incidence in the summer months. It has been demonstrated, however, that epidemics of paralytic polio can be arrested through vaccinating a large percentage of the exposed population at an early enough date.

Many people have attained an immunity to at least one type of polio virus as a result of undiagnosed, subclinical, abortive infection at some earlier time in their lives. *Abortive polio* is a brief illness, with fever, headache and other vague discomforts. In *nonparalytic polio* the symptoms are fever, headache, stiff neck, and increase in the number of cells in the spinal fluid. Loss of appetite, nausea, vomiting, constipation, and abdominal pain may also be present. The patient recovers from nonparalytic polio in about a week, and has no residual symptoms. Polio-like virus diseases sometimes simulate nonparalytic polio.

The most famous victim of paralytic polio was Franklin D. Roosevelt, President of the United States. In 1938 he founded the National Foundation for Infantile Paralysis to "lead, direct and unify" the fight against polio. This organization, generously supported by the American people, crowned its efforts with the development of the Salk vaccine.

The National Foundation, as it is now called, undertook in 1958 an expanded program of research, education, and service in the areas of virus diseases, birth defects, neurological diseases, and arthritis.

Conquest of polio as a threat to life and limb now seems almost certain as a result of widespread use of the Salk vaccine (see VACCINE). Scarcely 2,500 cases of paralytic polio—and at least half of these too slight to leave any later paralysis—were reported in the United States in 1957. Five years earlier, in 1952, there were ten times as many paralytic cases.

Polyarthritis—ARTHRITIS in many joints.

Polycythemia—too many red blood cells; see BLOOD DISEASES.

Polymyxin—an ANTIBIOTIC drug.

Polyneuritis—the uncomfortable inflammation of many NERVES at the same time. Lack of VITAMIN B complex factors is sometimes a cause.

Polyps are new growths of body tissue, overgrowths of the mucous membranes that line many body cavities. They have a smooth surface and a strange shape—looking more or less like a small mushroom growing up or hanging down. They are most commonly found in the nose (nasal polyps), where they may block efficient breathing; in the uterus from which they often disappear without treatment; in the large bowel, where they are usually discovered by accident of X-raying for something else; and in the rectum, from which they can easily be removed by simple electrical desiccation.

Polyps rarely cause any symptoms and are in general more worrisome than dangerous. The risk is that what looks like a harmless polyp may actually be the beginning of a CANCER. The person who has polyps should therefore keep in touch with his physician so that the condition can be frequently observed and the risk of cancer ruled out. Nasal polyps are often allergic in nature. See NOSE.

Pores—the openings of the sweat glands in the SKIN.

Posterior—in back of or behind, the opposite of ANTERIOR. Thus, the molar teeth of the mouth are posterior to the front teeth; also, the backside, rump, or gluteus maximus muscle is posterior to the belly.

Postmortem—after death; usually refers to postmortem examination of a body; that is, necropsy or AUTOPSY.

Postnasal Drip—a common affliction in humid, temperate and cold climates. Sometimes little can or need be done about it. However, if the drip is due to sensitivity, low grade infection, polyps, or allergy, appropriate treatment of the underlying condition can do much to correct the annoyance. See NOSE.

Postnatal—following CHILD-BIRTH.

Postoperative—following operation. See SURGERY.

Postpartum — following CHILD-BIRTH.

Posture is as posture does. Good posture is natural posture; bad posture more often *reflects* disease or discomfort than causes it.

Posture, or position, is constantly controlled by the force of gravity, a sometimes neglected fact. Many muscles must remain at work to overcome this invisible force. Hence a person has not one but many postures, which may be conveniently grouped as standing, sitting, reclining, and moving (walking or running) posture. In athletics posture is often called stance or form; in dance it is called style.

Standing and reclining posture is essentially controlled by body build and body weight, factors that go back to the skeletal bone-and-joint structure an individual inherits. Sitting and moving postures can be learned. There is no one posture for everybody. Military postures, especially standing at attention, should be recognized for what they are—methods of military discipline. They are physiologically wrong and should not be taken as ideals of good posture. Nor should the stylized poses of dress models (mannequins) be misinterpreted as representing either good or normal posture for the average woman.

Every individual finds for himself the postures that are most comfortable as he goes about his daily work. Posture, gait, and carriage often reflect psychological attitudes, whether it be the "gangster's swagger" or the "debutante's slouch." All advice for achieving a conventionally "good posture" boils down to two phrases: *stand tall* and *sit straight*. Corrective exercises for changing postural habits should be taken only after consultation with a physician.

Many occupations, especially that of housewife, invite habitual, needless overstrain of muscle groups. For example, many women stand to iron clothes when they could just as easily sit down. Such strain induces muscle fatigue, and this is expressed as poor posture, which may give symptoms of FOOT TROUBLE or BACKACHE.

Poor posture and muscular FATIGUE can also result from faulty nutrition (see DIET), chronic low-grade INFECTION, bad seating, bad lighting, and

defects of vision or hearing that
require a person to strain to
hear or see (see EYE TROUBLE
and EAR TROUBLE). These possible causes of poor posture
suggest why no one should enter into indiscriminate exercise to correct poor posture before he has a thorough medical
check-up.

Potassium—a soft metal or alkali earth; a chemical element,
whose salts are essentially present in the human body in some
kind of balance with SODIUM
salts. They are commonly used
in drug combinations; for example *potassium iodide.*

Pot-Belly—the fairly normal collection of fat in the OMENTUM
under the skin of the abdomen,

common in middle-aged males.
See OBESITY; DIET.

Pott's Disease—TUBERCULOSIS of
the spine; SPONDYLITIS.

Pott's Fracture—serious FRAC-
TURE of the leg just above the
foot.

Preclinical—the course of a disease before it can be recognized
or diagnosed; also, the preliminary phase of modern medical
education, the instruction given
before the medical student deals
with patients.

Precordial—the region of the
body situated in front of the
heart or the stomach; the lower
chest and upper abdomen. *Precordial pains* do not necessarily
arise from the heart.

PREGNANCY

Pregnancy begins with CONCEPTION and ends with CHILDBIRTH
(labor) or ABORTION (miscarriage).

Given enough time—nine months—any fool can diagnose pregnancy. In the early stages of pregnancy, however, even the wisest
doctor may find it difficult to make a positive diagnosis. False or
spurious pregnancies, with many of the classic symptoms of pregnancy, are sometimes discovered in women who have an overwhelming fear or desire of having a child; this is a psychosomatic
ailment, a form of conversion HYSTERIA, an exhibition of MENTAL
ILLNESS. Women who are not pregnant at all sometimes tragically
submit themselves to criminal abortions. Tumors sometimes mimic
pregnancy.

A delayed or missed menstrual period may raise a *suspicion* of
pregnancy, but it should not be taken as a certainty that pregnancy has occurred. If *two* periods are missed, the woman should
consult her doctor.

Sometime during the second month of pregnancy, the condition
can usually be confirmed by a laboratory test: the "mouse" or
"rabbit test." These tests are about 98% accurate, but they do give

THE FIGURE IN PREGNANCY

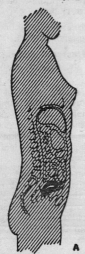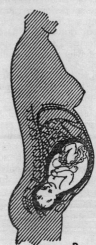

A. *This is a diagrammatic cross section of the mother's body at the beginning of pregnancy.*
B. *This is the same figure at full term, just before the child is to be born. The wall of the uterus and the placenta are shown in black; the uterine contents in white.*

a few false positives and false negatives. In the rabbit (Friedman) test, a sample of the woman's urine is injected into the ear of a virgin rabbit. If the woman is pregnant, changes in the rabbit's ovaries can be detected within 24 to 48 hours.

The rabbit and mouse tests, and all others depending on reactions in test animals (for example, toads and fish), are based on this fact: when pregnancy occurs, there is a drastic change in the HORMONE and ENDOCRINE balance of the body. This, incidentally, explains in part why many women feel different during pregnancy; some may feel wonderful, others depressed.

In particular, large quantities of gonad-stimulating hormones are made and released into the blood stream in early pregnancy. Excess quantities of this hormone spill over into the urine; that is, the kidneys extract it from the blood stream and release it into the urine. It is this hormone that stimulates the changes in the sex organs of the test animals, such as the virgin rabbit.

Time-table of pregnancy. The following time-table suggests what a woman going through a normal, uneventful pregnancy may look forward to, although, needless to say, not all women have the same experience:

1st month: Conception occurs. There is no way of knowing on this first day that it has actually occurred. Within about 7 to 10 days after conception, the fertilized egg cell implants itself in the lining of the uterus (see SEX ORGANS, FEMALE and MENSTRUATION), but again there is no way to tell.

Within 2 to 3 weeks after conception, the suspicion of missing a period must arise. Some of the early symptoms of pregnancy, described below, may appear at this time, but they usually come on somewhat later.

2nd month—dating, as always, from the time of conception: Morning sickness—nausea and vomiting—may develop; it is not inevitable. Easy fatigue, extreme sleepiness, full and sensitive breasts, frequent urination often appear—but not all these symptoms in all women.

3rd month: The breasts begin to enlarge; the ring around the nipples may darken. The abdomen is not yet noticeably extended, but the uterus can be felt either as a small hard ball or softening and enlarging. The feeling of fatigue may be tremendous. An appetite for "strange and naughty foods," often a test of the husband, may begin. Neither of these symptoms is essential.

4th month: The pregnancy usually begins to show on the abdomen, unless concealed by obesity or artful dressing. Gain in weight commences. This usually continues at the rate of about 3 *pounds a month,* with considerable variation in different women.

5th and 6th months: The quickening of the baby is felt by the mother; these at first are light, fluttery movements. Later they can be felt as definite kicks against the wall of the enlarged abdomen. The baby's rapid heartbeat can be definitely heard by the doctor. The bones of the skeleton of the infant in the womb can be visualized on an X-ray picture. These are *positive* signs of pregnancy.

7th and 8th months: The rapidly growing baby kicks vigorously against the still enlarging abdomen, on which striations, or stretch

OBSTETRICAL TABLE TO ESTIMATE WHEN BABY WILL BE BORN

The date on the top line is the first day of the LAST menstruation before pregnancy. The date immediately underneath it is the *theoretical* date when the baby should be born. Practically, however, the theoretical date will rarely be hit. The baby will usually arrive within two weeks before or two weeks after this date. Thus, if the date of the last menstruation was Jan. 1, the baby will be born somewhere between September 24 and October 23.

	1	2	3	4	5	6	7	8	9	10	11	12	13	14	15	16	17	18	19	20	21	22	23	24	25	26	27	28	29	30	31	
Jan.	1	2	3	4	5	6	7	8	9	10	11	12	13	14	15	16	17	18	19	20	21	22	23	24	25	26	27	28	29	30	31	
Oct.	8	9	10	11	12	13	14	15	16	17	18	19	20	21	22	23	24	25	26	27	28	29	30	31	1	2	3	4	5	6	7	Nov.
Feb.	1	2	3	4	5	6	7	8	9	10	11	12	13	14	15	16	17	18	19	20	21	22	23	24	25	26	27	28				
Nov.	8	9	10	11	12	13	14	15	16	17	18	19	20	21	22	23	24	25	26	27	28	29	30	1	2	3	4	5				Dec.
Mar.	1	2	3	4	5	6	7	8	9	10	11	12	13	14	15	16	17	18	19	20	21	22	23	24	25	26	27	28	29	30	31	
Dec.	6	7	8	9	10	11	12	13	14	15	16	17	18	19	20	21	22	23	24	25	26	27	28	29	30	31	1	2	3	4	5	Jan.
Apr.	1	2	3	4	5	6	7	8	9	10	11	12	13	14	15	16	17	18	19	20	21	22	23	24	25	26	27	28	29	30		
Jan.	6	7	8	9	10	11	12	13	14	15	16	17	18	19	20	21	22	23	24	25	26	27	28	29	30	31	1	2	3	4		Feb.
May	1	2	3	4	5	6	7	8	9	10	11	12	13	14	15	16	17	18	19	20	21	22	23	24	25	26	27	28	29	30	31	
Feb.	5	6	7	8	9	10	11	12	13	14	15	16	17	18	19	20	21	22	23	24	25	26	27	28	1	2	3	4	5	6	7	Mar.
June	1	2	3	4	5	6	7	8	9	10	11	12	13	14	15	16	17	18	19	20	21	22	23	24	25	26	27	28	29	30		
Mar.	8	9	10	11	12	13	14	15	16	17	18	19	20	21	22	23	24	25	26	27	28	29	30	31	1	2	3	4	5	6		Apr.
July	1	2	3	4	5	6	7	8	9	10	11	12	13	14	15	16	17	18	19	20	21	22	23	24	25	26	27	28	29	30	31	
Apr.	7	8	9	10	11	12	13	14	15	16	17	18	19	20	21	22	23	24	25	26	27	28	29	30	1	2	3	4	5	6	7	May
Aug.	1	2	3	4	5	6	7	8	9	10	11	12	13	14	15	16	17	18	19	20	21	22	23	24	25	26	27	28	29	30	31	
May	8	9	10	11	12	13	14	15	16	17	18	19	20	21	22	23	24	25	26	27	28	29	30	31	1	2	3	4	5	6	7	June
Sept.	1	2	3	4	5	6	7	8	9	10	11	12	13	14	15	16	17	18	19	20	21	22	23	24	25	26	27	28	29	30		
June	8	9	10	11	12	13	14	15	16	17	18	19	20	21	22	23	24	25	26	27	28	29	30	1	2	3	4	5	6	7		July
Oct.	1	2	3	4	5	6	7	8	9	10	11	12	13	14	15	16	17	18	19	20	21	22	23	24	25	26	27	28	29	30	31	
July	8	9	10	11	12	13	14	15	16	17	18	19	20	21	22	23	24	25	26	27	28	29	30	31	1	2	3	4	5	6	7	Aug.
Nov.	1	2	3	4	5	6	7	8	9	10	11	12	13	14	15	16	17	18	19	20	21	22	23	24	25	26	27	28	29	30		
Aug.	8	9	10	11	12	13	14	15	16	17	18	19	20	21	22	23	24	25	26	27	28	29	30	31	1	2	3	4	5	6		Sept.
Dec.	1	2	3	4	5	6	7	8	9	10	11	12	13	14	15	16	17	18	19	20	21	22	23	24	25	26	27	28	29	30	31	
Sept.	7	8	9	10	11	12	13	14	15	16	17	18	19	20	21	22	23	24	25	26	27	28	29	30	1	2	3	4	5	6	7	Oct.

marks, usually appear. Skin color on the abdomen and face may darken slightly, but not permanently. A few drops of fluid—colostrum, a precursor of mother's milk—may begin to flow from the breasts. Weight gain continues.

9th month: The abdomen no longer enlarges. The fetal movements are felt less often, less vigorously. This is nothing to worry about. The enlarged uterus may cause pressure symptoms on other abdominal organs and on the veins, giving symptoms of temporary enlarged veins in the legs (and often hemorrhoids, which disappear after childbirth). The need for frequent urination is common. However the mother-soon-to-be is often filled with unusual energy at this time; cleans house, buys clothes, gets ready for the baby.

About 2 weeks before childbirth, the infant's head begins to sink into the pelvic cavity (he is normally upside down), and the uterus correspondingly descends with it. This is the lightening. The woman usually feels more comfortable.

At last, somewhere around 280 days after conception, labor begins and the baby is born. (See CHILDBIRTH.)

When will the baby be born? In round numbers, 280 days, 40 weeks, or 9 months after the day of conception. But there is no way of foretelling this *exactly,* because no one yet knows what sets off the trigger mechanism of normal labor. Unless the labor is artificially induced or Caesarean section done, the date of birth cannot be assured. A common method of predicting birth date (Nägele's rule) is to add 7 days to the date of the first day of the last menstruation and then count back 3 months. Only 1 in 10 babies are born on this calculated calendar date. But 75% are born within 2 weeks of this time. See OBSTETRICAL TABLE on page 408.

A PREMATURE infant is judged premature by his *weight* at birth; if it is under 2,500 grams (about 5½ pounds), the infant is called premature. Truly late (postmature) babies are rare, and they are a hazard to themselves and their mothers. Most late babies represent an error in calculation.

The inside story of pregnancy: While the mother-to-be is carrying and nurturing her infant-to-be, this tiny living creature is also going through the most fateful days of its existence.

Life before birth, which is the story unfolded by the science of *embryology,* begins at the instant of conception, when only one of many sperm pierces the ripe and ready ovum and fertilizes it.

This also is the instant when the future sex of the person-to-be is irrevocably determined, and by the father of the child. It is de-

termined by the chance of whether the single sperm that penetrates the egg happens to be carrying in its *chromosomes* a male-
making or a female-making *gene*. (See HEREDITY.) In this sex-determining chromosome, there are also other genes. These carry
sex-linked human characteristics; for example, the tendency to red-
green COLOR BLINDNESS.

Time-table of life before birth (embryology): At the instant of
conception the new baby-to-be is much smaller than a dot on this
page. It is even smaller than the egg (1/120th of an inch in diameter), because the egg must develop into accessory structures for
the infant in the womb as well as the infant itself.

At the age of 1 month, dating from the time of conception, the
infant-to-be, that is, the embryo, is only about ¼ inch long; at 2
months, 1 inch long; at 3 months, 3 inches long; at 6 months, a
little over a foot long; at 9 months, the time of birth, somewhere
around 1½ to 2 feet long.

The embryo weighs less than an ounce until it is 3 months old.
At 4 months the infant-to-be weighs around 6 ounces; at 5 months,
about 1 pound; at 6 months, about 2 pounds; at 9 months, that is,
at birth or term, about 7½ pounds.

1st month: The fertilized egg cell *(zygote)* quickly divides into 2
cells, the 2 into 4, the 4 into 8, and so on. (See CELLS.) While
multiplying, it moves down the uterine tube, about a 3-day journey, and enters the cavity of the uterus. For a week or 10 days it
may float, as it were, in this cavity; then it embeds itself in the
lining of the uterine wall (endometrium), rich with blood vessels
and prepared for its reception. By this time the zygote is a tiny,
hollow ball of cells, and it is called the *morula* ("mulberry").

Some parts of the morula develop into the placenta, umbilical
cord, and "bag of waters." From one tiny spot on its inner layer
of cells the embryo arises. This tiny spot is called the embryonic
disk. Out of it develop the billions of differentiated cells that make
up the finished living creature.

The *placenta,* called the *afterbirth* following delivery of the
child, is a flat disk of tissue by which the infant is attached to the
mother's womb and through which it is nourished. It grows along
with the embryo and fetus. At term it is a pancake-shaped tissue,
an inch or two thick, 6 to 9 inches in diameter.

The placenta interlocks with the tissues of the uterus. The nourishment for the growing child in the womb seeps through the
membranes of the placenta from the maternal blood stream. These

membranes filter out many things that might harm the infant. But some things, like the spirochete of syphilis, certain viruses (like that of GERMAN MEASLES), blood elements like the RH FACTOR, and some drugs (including ANESTHETICS), can get through this membrane. The growing fetus has its own blood supply, and circulatory system, and does not use the mother's blood as such.

THE UTERUS IN PREGNANCY

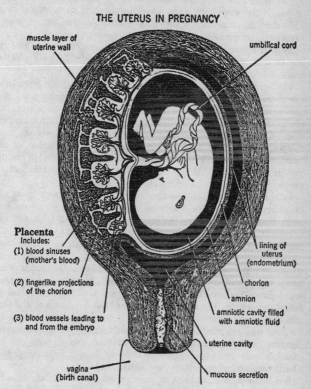

muscle layer of
uterine wall

umbilical cord

Placenta
Includes:

(1) blood sinuses
(mother's blood)

(2) fingerlike projections
of the chorion

(3) blood vessels leading to
and from the embryo

lining of
uterus
(endometrium)

chorion

amnion

amniotic cavity filled
with amniotic fluid

uterine cavity

vagina
(birth canal)

mucous secretion

This is a diagrammatic cross section of the uterus containing a fetus about three months old. The cross section of the placenta is very much simplified.

The *umbilical cord* runs from the middle of the placenta to the navel (umbilicus) of the developing infant. The cord increases in size as the placenta and infant grow. At birth the cord is usually about 2 feet long, ⅜ to 1 inch in diameter. It is usually twisted, and on rare occasions a loop of it may snare the neck or limbs of the fetus.

The *"bag of waters,"* or amniotic sac, is a kind of elastic bottle in which the growing infant develops, floating in amniotic fluid. This fluid is secreted by the inner lining of the bag of waters (amnion). It protects the child from pressures on the mother's body and helps regulate the infant's temperature. Just before the bag of waters breaks at term, it carries between 1 and 2 pints of fluid.

The embryonic disk, which is something like a rolled-up tube, has three layers of cells: endoderm, inside layer; mesoderm, middle; ectoderm, outside. The first specialized cells to appear are young blood cells, which show up about 17 days after conception. Within about a week thereafter, tiny blood vessels have merged together to form a "heart tube," the forerunner of the heart. On about the 25th day after conception this "heart" begins pulsating or beating. At the same time the nervous system and digestive system begin to take place and shape.

In the first month of life the infant-to-be progresses from egg to embryo. It looks like a human tadpole, one quarter of an inch long. Its head is one third its total length. Two leg-buds and two arm-buds may be barely visible. Along its back are 38 little bundles of tissue (somites), from which the muscles will develop.

2nd month—dating from conception: During the second month the human tadpole loses its tail and gets a face. The tail was not more than 2 millimeters long. It also begins to get a brain, a neck, some bones and connective tissue, fingers and toes, skin and internal sex organs. The face forms around the head end of the foregut. The eyes, formerly on the side of the head, converge to the forward-looking position above the rudimentary nose and mouth. Somites swell into muscles. The patterns of many bones are laid down in soft cartilage (gristle), later to harden with absorption of calcium and phosphorus (see MINERALS).

3rd month: the embryo is now a reasonable facsimile of a human being, although out of all proportion, like a child's drawing of the human figure. In the third month, the sex of the infant-to-be emerges, more evident in the male than the female. Tooth buds begin to sprout inside the dental arch (though some teeth will not appear above the gumline for many years). Ears are formed. Finger nails and toenails appear. Liver, stomach, and kidneys begin to work. Mouth and jaws, nose, throat and vocal cords become more fully fashioned.

4th month: the embryo is now called a *fetus*—by custom, not reason. It begins to move about in its bag of waters. This is the sign of life that the mother recognizes as the quickening, although she may not feel these fetal movements for another month. The fetal heartbeat gets much stronger. The forebrain begins to develop rapidly, gets its first "wrinkles," or convolutions. External sex organs become more sharply delineated into male or female. Eyebrows, eyelashes, fingerprints (whorls and ridges of skin on toes and fingers), are usually formed. A soft downy hair, called *lanugo,* covers the gnomelike body, especially the face.

5th month: Real hair appears on the head. Finger nails and toenails grow out. Sweat glands and sebaceous glands appear on the wine-colored skin. All internal organs are present, but not in the shape or position they will later assume.

6th month: The fetus begins to open its eyes, formerly shut. As the trunk lengthens and the back straightens, the internal organs settle more and more into their proper places.

7th month: The unborn child, the infant-to-be, now rarely called a fetus, fills out and develops in all directions. In the male, the testes normally descend into the scrotum.

8th and 9th months: The infant gains much weight and strength. It waxes fat. Its skin color improves; blood vessels no longer show through the skin. The infant moves around in the uterus. About 95% of the time, however, it grows head down. It is getting ready for entrance into the outside world, for passage through the birth canal and expulsion from its mother's body. At last labor calls and CHILDBIRTH begins.

Prenatal care: Pregnancy is a natural, normal physiological process: it is not a disease and should not be treated as such. Nature is on the side of the pregnant woman and seeks a happy outcome as fervently as she herself. The hazards of pregnancy are, in fact, comparatively few, and the discomforts are more often determined by the woman's own psychological attitude toward her particular pregnancy than by anything else.

Some women are depressed by their pregnancies, especially if they have had any trouble before or have borne many children.

Other women find their health improved during pregnancy (relief from arthritis and migraine, for example, often occurs). It is a happy time of their lives.

Nulliparas (women who have not had a child or have not been pregnant before) are likely to be overenthusiastic, overmeticulous, and overfearful. Such anxiety in the presence of what is, after all, a profoundly important experience is natural, normal, and to be anticipated. Sometimes the pregnancy is harder on family and friends than on the mother-to-be herself. "Look, honey," a sharp-tongued friend may finally be pushed to say, "you're not the first woman in the world to have a baby."

From the standpoint of the patient, prenatal care looks deceptively simple. From the doctor's standpoint it often requires consummate skill to keep the patient and her human freight out of trouble.

Personal hygiene during pregnancy is the same as good health care at any other time, magnified by the responsibility for the life and health of two (or more) lives instead of one.

A patient receiving adequate prenatal care from a private physician or a clinic is expected to:

1. See the doctor regularly—once a month during the early months of pregnancy; twice a month, or oftener, in the later stages.

2. Bring urine samples when requested.

3. Do what her doctor tells her and not listen to "old wives' tales," the misinformation peddled by well-meaning friends or half-baked books.

4. Report promptly to the doctor any unusual signs or symptoms of disease or any sudden changes in her condition.

Little danger signals in pregnancy, to be promptly reported to the doctor, include:

SWELLING of hands, feet, wrists, or eyelids on arising. Swelling of the feet, late in pregnancy and late in the day, is common and not significant.

HEADACHES, if prolonged, severe, or repeated.

PAIN in the abdomen or chest.

DIZZINESS, lightheadedness, or vertigo at any time.

BLEEDING from the vagina—even if it is just a spot or blood-stained mucus.

EYE TROUBLE, particularly seeing double or blurred vision.

BLADDER TROUBLE—especially scant, frequent, or painful urination; blood-tinged or otherwise discolored urine.

NAUSEA and VOMITING, if at all severe.

CHILLS and FEVER.

FATIGUE, if exceptional.

Gush of fluid from the vagina, which means breaking of the bag of waters.

Many women experience *none* of these danger signals. If one or more occurs and is promptly reported, it enables the doctor to institute treatment to keep the patient out of trouble. However, it should be remembered that a pregnant woman can suffer any of the diseases that attack a nonpregnant woman: anemia, heart disease, kidney disease, tuberculosis, diabetes, sore throat, polio, and venereal disease, to name a few. Good prenatal care can carry many "poor risk" cases through to successful full-term childbirth with a healthy baby.

Prenatal care from the doctor's standpoint begins with making a presumptive diagnosis of pregnancy and then confirming it, with hormonal tests described above if necessary. He takes a complete medical history and gives a complete physical examination. Vaginal and rectal examination is included and must sometimes be repeated to feel the condition of the uterus. Weight, BLOOD PRESSURE, and URINE are repeatedly checked. BLOOD samples are taken to check for SYPHILIS and ANEMIA and to classify BLOOD TYPES, in case a BLOOD TRANSFUSION is needed or RH FACTOR (which see) is involved. The chance is only 1 in 250 that any child will be affected by Rh factors. Prenatal blood tests for syphilis are required in many states. Repeated urinalyses are performed because the kidneys are under special strain in pregnancy; the waste products from the fetal circulation are passed back into the mother's blood stream by way of the placenta, and these wastes are removed from the maternal blood by the kidneys.

X-ray pictures of the chest and pelvis may sometimes be ordered. Chest X rays help determine the condition of heart and lungs. Pelvic X rays permit accurate measurements of the pelvic opening through which the infant must descend; and in cases of small and deformed pelvic-bone structure, may help to determine the type of delivery, for example, the desirability of Caesarean section. Pelvic X rays, revealing fetal-bone structure, also help establish a positive diagnosis of pregnancy, determine the stage of the pregnancy, and may reveal TWINS!

Salk poliomyelitis vaccine will and should be administered to all pregnant women who have not already received it. The pregnant woman is nearly twice as susceptible to paralytic polio as the nonpregnant woman of the same age group.

Discomforts and hazards of pregnancy are suprisingly few for the woman who receives adequate prenatal care.

Morning sickness—nausea and vomiting—occurs in fewer than half the cases. Worry and anxiety appear to induce it. An excellent preventive treatment is to eat some dry food, such as soda crackers, immediately on awakening in the morning and go back to bed for at least another half hour. It is also helpful to eat small morsels of food frequently during the day so that the stomach is not empty.

Fatigue and *sleepiness* can be treated also by simple rest in bed. A half-hour to an hour's nap in the middle of the day is a good idea, if it is needed and feasible. Don't take "pep pills."

Muscular fatigue, strain, and cramps are sometimes brought on by women who are active beyond their normal fatigue point. They forget that they are carrying an added weight burden.

The enlarged uterus in late pregnancy displaces other abdominal organs. Pressure on the bladder may cause *frequent urination*. Upward pressure on the diaphragm may result in *shortness of breath* until the lightening. Pressure on the veins carrying blood back from the legs may result in temporary VARI-COSE VEINS or "milk leg." To avoid this do not wear elastic around-the-leg garters or tightly rolled stockings.

ANEMIA of pregnancy responds readily to treatment. RH FACTOR is a hazard to the infant, not the mother. GERMAN MEASLES during the first three months of pregnancy is also a risk to the fetus.

The more serious hazards of pregnancy include ectopic pregnancy, ABORTION and miscarriage, toxemias of pregnancy, premature separation of the placenta, and placenta previa. Except for induced *abortion,* the causes of these conditions are not definitely known; and, except for spontaneous ABORTION, or miscarriage, these mishaps of pregnancy are comparatively rare.

ECTOPIC PREGNANCY is a condition in which the fertilized ovum embeds itself outside the uterus, usually in the uterine tubes. The treatment is surgery.

Premature separation of the placenta is really a complication of CHILDBIRTH except in those cases where it is a cause of spontaneous, habitual ABORTION. In such cases the pregnant woman may have to spend most of her pregnancy in bed.

Placenta previa means that the placenta develops too near the mouth of the womb, closing off the opening and impeding the normal process of childbirth.

Toxemias of pregnancy are far less common now than they were in the days before adequate prenatal care. Toxemia means poisoning; but it is doubtful if toxemias of pregnancy are caused by anything like real poisoning. They may turn out to be deficiency diseases related to diet and nutrition. Toxemias of pregnancy occur in the last three months. They are often divided into pre-eclampsia and *eclampsia*, depending on the severity of the involvement. The signs and symptoms of these conditions include rising blood pressure, eye trouble, rapid weight gain, headache, swelling, diminished output of urine, albuminuria, and pain in the upper abdomen.

See also FEMALE TROUBLES.

What shall I eat? Diet is an important matter. The mother-to-be is, after all, "eating for two." The infant is in one sense a parasite, drawing from the mother's blood stream all the food elements it needs. Furthermore, a woman's BASAL METABOLISM normally goes up 5 to 10% during pregnancy, reflecting many physiological and hormonal changes in her body.

A good balanced diet (see DIET) is requisite in pregnancy and before pregnancy. There is some evidence that troubles with pregnancy arise because the woman was not well-nourished *at the time of conception.*

Eat plenty of meat, eggs, cheese, and other *protein* foods. Drink milk, if it agrees with you; fruit juices and tomato juice; lots of water—perhaps eight glasses a day. Get enough VITAMINS and body MINERALS. A good balanced diet, of about 2,500 calories a day, supplies these essentials. If you are worried about it, take any good vitamin and mineral supplement to the diet. It's expensive but harmless. Calcium tablets alone are not enough.

Too many women do not change their previous faulty eating habits and prejudices when they are pregnant. You can't keep your weight down when you are pregnant, so don't try any reducing diets.

Some women take the occasion of their pregnancy for deliberately getting overweight. They pamper themselves with an excess of food they would feel guilty about gorging at any other time. An excess of calories in the form of carbohydrates and fats is not essential in pregnancy—and, in fact, should be guarded against.

Will I lose my figure? Only for the time being. Within a few months afterward you will probably have a better figure—if pregnancy has taught you anything about diet and health care generally. With multiple and frequently repeated childbearing, the abdominal muscles tend to lose tone and sag, but it takes a lot of pregnancies for this. Because of the hormone change that pregnancy induces, the body contours following pregnancy are often fuller and more appealing. Figure is, after all, a social and psychological ideal. In modern American society the choice lies between Diana and Venus—the goddess of the chase and the goddess of love.

What about exercise? If your pregnancy is proceeding normally, any kind of physical exercise or activity within reason is permissible: walking, dancing, gardening, bowling, golf, driving, and light housework. Bending and squatting exercises are particularly good, as they strengthen the muscles used in childbirth. The only rule is: don't overdo! Respect your fatigue point and stop. Avoid violent exercise on general principles and not because you think it will cause you to lose your baby. But don't treat yourself as an invalid or shut-in. And remember, your own doctor may have good and special reasons sometimes for recommending that you take little if any exercise and get plenty of rest in bed.

What about bathing, smoking, drinking, sexual intercourse? While every case must be individualized, and some doctors have different opinions, the consensus runs about as follows:

Shower anytime, but don't take tub baths after the eighth month. Wash your hair whenever you want to. During the last two months you may clean your nipples daily and gently with soap and water.

If you are accustomed to smoking and drinking, you may continue in moderation—up to about 10 cigarettes a day and one or two drinks at a party.

Sexual intercourse is usually permissible up to the last month of pregnancy.

What about teeth? The old saying, "For every child a tooth," is probably the result of neglect of teeth during pregnancy. Dental care is both permissible and advisable. The gums often swell and bleed easily during pregnancy (pregnancy gingivitis) in response to hormone changes.

What shall I wear? Anything loose and comfortable—and as stylish as you want or can afford. Some multiparas (women who have had many children) may require a special corset or girdle for their own comfort. In general, however, constricting garments and tight garters should not be worn. Brassieres should support the breasts from underneath, not pull them up. Wide shoulder straps are usually more comfortable. Low, broad-heeled shoes will make for greater comfort and less muscle fatigue, but it may take time to get used to them. (See FOOT TROUBLE; POSTURE.)

Attitude. How you feel about your pregnancy is the most important thing. It will determine in part your attitude toward your child-to-come, your other children, if any, your husband and family. Eat well, sleep well, and enjoy yourself. Take your questions and problems to your doctor and respect his advice. The world respects the pregnant figure and nature is on your side in helping you to produce, without trouble, a healthy, normal infant.

See CHILDBIRTH.

Premature—too soon, too early. A premature infant is one born before full term as judged primarily by weight (under about 5½ pounds at birth). See PREGNANCY; CHILDBIRTH. Premature ejaculation is a psychosexual disability of some men; see ANXIETY, PSYCHOANALYSIS.

Premenstrual Tension—see MENSTRUATION; FEMALE TROUBLE.

Prenatal—before birth. See PREGNANCY.

Preoperative—before operation; see SURGERY.

Prepuce—foreskin. (See illustration for SEX ORGANS, MALE.)

Presbyopia—"old sightedness"; a type of farsightedness that comes with advancing years. See EYE TROUBLE.

Prescription—an order, signed by a physician, to a pharmacist to provide an exactly specified amount of an exactly specified drug or medicine. The name and the address of the patient must be on the prescription. The directions or instructions for taking the medicine are also included. These are copied by the pharmacist and placed on the label of the box or bottle in which the medicine is supplied.

Some doctor's prescriptions can be refilled by the druggist, but in most cases they *cannot* be refilled. The druggist is bound by law to obey the doctor's order, and the doctor may write on the prescription *non repet*—which means, in Latin, "Don't repeat."

Do not blame the druggist

if he refuses to refill a prescription. He must obey the law.

Medicine prescribed by a doctor for one illness should not be kept and used for another. In the first place, most drugs deteriorate with age; in the second place, only another diagnosis by the doctor can tell whether the medicine, even if it hasn't deteriorated, is still the right thing to use. Clean out your medicine chest at least once every three months. Throw away old medicine.

Don't use prescription drugs that have not been particularly ordered for you. And don't give anyone else in your family a drug prescribed for you. Old drugs can be useless and dangerous. One man's drug may be his child's poison. See DRUGS.

Priapism—constant erection of the penis; often painful and unaccompanied by sexual interest. It may result from spinal cord injury, bladder stones, leukemia or some injuries to the penis itself.

Prickly Heat—a SKIN condition which sometimes bothers infants in hot weather and frequently annoys Americans or Europeans who go to live in tropical climates. In infants it is a mild skin rash, generally amenable to the same treatment as diaper rash. In the tropics it appears to arise, sometimes with intolerable itching, from a clogging of the channels of the sweat glands. Anything that induces perspiration makes it worse; for example, the consumption of large quantities of fluids. Calamine or other soothing skin lotions may give temporary relief.

Primigravida—a woman carrying her first child.

Primipara—a woman who is delivering her first child, or one who has borne one child.

Probe—a medical or surgical instrument for poking into or around a wound or body cavity; usually a short, bent, metal rod.

Procaine—a local or topical ANESTHETIC; novocain is procaine hydrochloride.

Process—a word sometimes used to describe a particular part of a bone; for example, the mastoid process (or portion) of the temporal bone of the skull. Process also means a sequence of events, as in *disease process*.

Proctitis—inflammation of the RECTUM or ANUS.

Proctoclysis—rectal feeding.

Proctology—the medical and surgical specialty especially concerned with diseases and disorders of the RECTUM and ANUS.

Proctoscope—instrument, of smooth metal, inserted through the ANUS so the doctor can get a good look at the inside of the bowel.

Prodrome—the preliminary or warning symptoms of an oncoming disease or attack. MI-

GRAINE headaches often have a prodrome.

Progeria—premature aging.

Progesterone—a female sex HORMONE.

Prognathism—a jutting jaw—like Mussolini's.

Prognosis—the doctor's estimate, based on experience, of the outcome of a disease or injury. A good or favorable prognosis means that the patient is expected to recover. A poor or unfavorable prognosis means that he is likely to die or suffer from severe residual disability.

A guarded prognosis means that the doctor does not yet have enough information or evidence to make a reasonable forecast. There is almost never such a thing as an absolutely certain prognosis; no man can surely foretell the future. Many patients with an apparently poor prognosis nevertheless get well.

The *pronouncing of a prognosis,* "You will recover!" is often an integral part of successful medical treatment. The patient is speeded to recovery because both he and his doctor believe he will quickly get well again.

Sometimes relatives are more interested than the patient himself in the doctor's prognosis. It is not good practice to force a physician into the position of giving anything more than a guarded prognosis before he is ready or able to make it. The doctor himself is always ready to call in consultants if he feels the patient himself will benefit.

Projection—a mental mechanism by which a person unconsciously blames someone else or something else for his own faults or failures; see PSYCHOANALYSIS.

Prolapse—the slipping or sinking of some bodily part or organ. Most common is *prolapse of the uterus,* in which part of it abnormally protrudes into the vagina; and *prolapse of the rectum,* in which it slips into itself or slips partially through the anus.

Pronate—to turn the forearm so that the palm of the hand faces down.

Prone—lying face down; opposite of SUPINE.

Prophylactic—*anything* that tends to prevent disease. The term is very commonly used to describe the rubber sheath worn for the prevention of venereal disease; but it has a much wider meaning.

Prophylaxis—the art and science of preventing disease and injury; the practice of staying out of trouble. Preventive medicine in all its aspects is prophylaxis; this includes "SHOTS" for the prevention of such diseases as diphtheria and paralytic polio; environmental sanitation and public health practices generally; and even the thorough cleaning of the teeth to avoid dental troubles (*dental prophylaxis*).

Proprietary—drug that can be sold without a doctor's prescription.

Prostate Trouble occurs in the prostate gland, a fairly useless SEX ORGAN, MALE, located just below the bladder and encircling the urethra where it exits from the bladder. It occurs most often in older men. The principal symptom is difficulty in passing URINE. Enlargement or overgrowth (hypertrophy) is the most frequent cause of trouble. It is estimated that 1 in every 12 men who reach the age of 60 will suffer prostatic enlargement. By blocking urine flow the enlarged prostate encourages many kinds of KIDNEY TROUBLE and BLADDER TROUBLE, and generally upsets the URINARY SYSTEM. Other prostate troubles include cancer of the gland, which also causes enlargement, and infection and inflammation. Infection usually comes by way of the urethra; as for example, GONORRHEA, which used to be the most common cause of *prostatitis.*

Since the prostate gland is located immediately in front of the rectum, the examining finger of the physician in the rectum can feel the gland, determine its size and shape. *Prostatic massage,* "milking" fluid and pus out of the gland, is also performed rectally.

Antibiotics and other drugs clear up many prostate infections. Female sex hormones may help to bring some regression of prostatic cancer. Surgery, however, is often needed to reduce prostatic enlargement and the urinary obstruction it causes. The gland can be reached by incision through the abdomen. It is also accessible through the urethra. An electrically lighted instrument, called a *cystoscope,* is passed through the urethra. The surgeon then manipulates cutting loops and small blades through the inner shaft of the cystoscope and removes part or all of the enlarged prostate piecemeal. This operation is called transurethral resection of the prostate.

(See illustration for SEX ORGANS, MALE.)

Prostatectomy—removal of the prostate gland or part of it by surgical operation performed through incision in the lower abdomen or perineum or through the urethra with aid of a CYSTOSCOPE. See SEX ORGANS, MALE.

Prostatitis—see PROSTATE TROUBLE.

Prosthesis—any artificial replacement or substitute for a part of the body that has been lost or is missing. Such a substitute may be a false tooth, a glass eye, a wooden leg or a plastic arm. Great strides have been made in recent years in the construction, operation and effective fitting of all kinds of prosthetic devices; notably, arms that can be effectively worked by the patient.

Prostration—complete exhaustion.

Protein—"meat"; the prime and principal component of the flesh of any living organism, from the one-celled ameba to the whale. Some form of protein, or its "building blocks," the AMINO ACIDS, are essential to a life-sustaining diet. When chemically analyzed, proteins are complex organic compounds, containing, among other things, the element NITROGEN. *Simple proteins* are such substances as ALBUMIN and globulin.

The best sources of protein in the human diet are milk and milk products, such as cheese; meat; fish; poultry; eggs; nuts; and some vegetables, such as peas, beans (especially soy beans), and lentils. About 10 to 12% of the human diet should be protein.

Protoplasm—living matter.

Protozoa—one-celled "animals" of a variety of shapes, sizes and forms; usually larger than most bacteria or microbes. Many of them cause human diseases; notably, the plasmodium of MALARIA; the ameba of amebic dysentery; the trypanosome of African sleeping sickness.

Prurigo—a chronic SKIN ailment, marked by small papules and ITCHING; sometimes related to HIVES.

Pruritus—same as ITCHING.

Pseudocyesis—false PREGNANCY.

Pseudohermaphrodite—an individual of uncertain sex who has the gonads (testes or ovaries) of one sex but the external sex organs and perhaps the secondary sex characteristics of the opposite sex. These are the people who are sometimes apparently transformed by surgical operation and endocrine therapy from man to woman or vice versa. True hermaphrodites ("half man, half woman") have complete sets of sex organs of both sexes, though often in a rudimentary stage of development; they are exceedingly rare. See HERMAPHRODITE.

Psittacosis—"parrot fever"; a virus disease that produces atypical pneumonia. The incidence of the disease is rising in the United States. Parakeets and domestic fowl can transmit the disease to man. Diseased birds must be destroyed.

Psoriasis—a SKIN disorder of unknown cause, usually beginning in the teens or twenties, and persisting off and on for years. Reddish-brown areas or patches appear on the skin and these are soon covered with silvery-white or grayish scales of dead skin, which drop off. The affected areas may range in size from a small circle, ¼ inch in diameter, on the scalp, elbows, or knees, to involvement of the entire back or thighs. Treatments are legion, but none seems to keep psoriasis from recurring. It often gets better in the summer, then comes back in the fall and winter—or sometimes the other way around. Psoriasis has been called "a healthy man's disease" and is more annoying than dangerous. It does, however, often produce disorders of the NAILS, commonly pitting.

Psychasthenia—NEUROSIS with FATIGUE. See NEURASTHENIA; MENTAL ILLNESS.

Psyche—the mind. The word is from the Greek and originally stood for the concept of intelligence. Since PSYCHOANALYSIS came in, psyche has become the goddess of the conscious and unconscious minds.

Psychiatry—that branch of medicine that deals primarily with MENTAL ILLNESS and the restoration and maintenance of mental health. This specialty is often practiced along with NEUROLOGY.

Psychiatrist—popularly, a "head doctor." A psychiatrist is first of all a physician, holder of an M.D. degree from a recognized medical school. Many psychiatrists also hold a diploma from the American Board of Psychiatry and Neurology, certifying their competence. There are about 10,000 genuine psychiatrists in the United States.

"Psycho"—slang expression for a person afflicted with MENTAL ILLNESS.

PSYCHOANALYSIS

Psychoanalysis—the creation of Sigmund FREUD—is a method of *treatment* for some forms of MENTAL ILLNESS, notably NEUROSES; a method of *research* for throwing light both on mental illness and on the nature of man's mind, conscious and unconscious; and, finally, the name for a *theory* about how the human mind and personality with its emotional underpinning seems to operate.

Psychoanalysis is only one of many methods of treating mental illness (psychotherapy). It is not necessary or suitable for all patients with mental illness. Besides, it is time-consuming and expensive, and there are nowhere near enough competent psychoanalysts to treat all people who theoretically might benefit by it.

Psychoanalysts are usually doctors of medicine, M.D.'s, who specialize in psychiatry. But there is another group of nonmedical psychoanalysts who, if properly trained, are equally competent in applying this method of treatment. They are sometimes called lay analysts. Some are clinical psychologists, with training and degrees (Ph.D.) from graduate schools of psychology in recognized universities.

The success of a particular course of psychoanalysis often depends largely on the character and personality structure of the analyst and on how well the patient fits with that analyst.

Psychoanalysis as treatment: In classical Freudian analysis, the troubled patient lies on a couch in a semidarkened room and the analyst sits behind him, listening and interpreting. The patient is encouraged to speak out everything—*everything*—that comes into his mind—his dreams, fears, loves, hates, childhood memories, current problems. This is called "free association."

From this disjointed conversation the patient is encouraged, with the help of hints, if needed, from the analyst, to see himself as he really is. His inner, repressed fears, doubts, and hates—the things he has never dared to admit to himself—gradually come out to the light of consciousness. When these ideas, often childhood fears, come up from the deep shadows of the unconscious mind to the light of reason, they can be dealt with constructively and often banished. One's fears are usually masked and distorted.

By way of very crude example, a patient may report that he feels very uneasy, almost panicky, whenever he sees a traffic policeman, but the deep-seated reason behind this "I-don't-know-why-I-feel-it" panic may stem from repressed fear and hatred of his father long ago. As a helpless child, he did not dare admit he hated his father and thought of killing him. This would be unthinkable to the child who needed his father. Therefore he pushed the hate down into the cavern of his unconscious mind, where it was stored away and "forgotten." But the sight of the policeman—a symbol of authority, like his father—triggers, tickles, and evokes this buried memory and gives rise to the feeling of uneasiness.

It takes a long time for a patient to dare to see and talk out openly what is really bothering him. The admission is too painful. He resists making it and hugs instead a less frightening picture of himself—a picture whose continual repainting is draining away his emotional energy and making him sick, depressed, neurotic, unhappy. This reticence is called "resistance."

Another thing happens to the patient. He transfers to the analyst many of the feelings toward other people, especially long-repressed feelings about his family members. Hence he may alternately hate and despise, or adore and fall in love with, the analyst. This phenomenon of *transference* is well understood by the analyst. He deals with it objectively, because it is part of the healing process.

The analyst helps the patient to re-educate himself, to discover new attitudes toward himself and other people, and to take these attitudes out into the world and put them into practice in real-life situations. The doctor cannot give the patient a new personality; he can only help him to accept his personality and make the most and best of it. But this is often enough to transform chronic woe into a reasonable opportunity for happier living, tinged with the inevitable everyday unhappiness and frustration to which all human beings are recurrently subject.

A true psychoanalysis can rarely be completed in less than 250 hours and may run to 600 to 800 hours. These "hours," or visits to the analyst, must be made three, four, or five times a week, at a cost of about $15 to $25 an hour.

Psychoanalysis as a method of research was introduced by Freud to uncover the nature of mental processes, originally in sick (neurotic, hysterical) people, later in normal people. The fundamental discovery was the vast power of the unconscious mind.

Modifications of Freud's theory and practice were made as early as 1911 by two of his early students, Alfred Adler, who described the *inferiority complex*, and Carl Jung, who postulated a "collective unconscious." Still other "schools" of psychoanalysis came into being—and conflict—later; notably, those of Karen Horney and Harry Stack Sullivan, which place more emphasis on a patient's current problems. But Freud's formulations remain the basis of orthodox psychoanalysis.

Psychoanalysis as a theory of human conduct makes the following construct of human personality structure and development:

The newborn baby is born with a lust for life, with an innate desire to live and complete a life cycle of growth and reproduction. This lust for life (which may later express itself in particular lusts for particular love objects) is called the *libido*. To that part of the mind, or psyche, animated by the crafty, uncontrolled, always pleasure-seeking libido, Freud gave the name *id*.

But the baby also makes contact with the outside world, the part of him beyond his sack of skin. He sees, feels, hears, tastes, smells what is going on around him—at first very imperfectly, gradually more and more accurately as his sense perceptions sharpen and memories accumulate. The libido forces the id to make contact with, and more or less master perception of, environment. Out of repeated perceptions gradually comes a dawn of consciousness, of awareness to the environment and appropriate response to the stimulus of this environment. Thus, at length, is formed out of part of the id another structure of the psyche to which the name *ego* is given. The ego controls the id, as a rider controls a balky horse.

The ego comprises nearly all of the conscious mind; but it has its roots in the *id*, which makes up the vast part of the unconscious and subconscious mind. A traffic of thoughts, memories, sensations, desires, passes back and forth—mysteriously along nerve pathways —between the ego and the id. One moment a thing is remembered, the next moment forgotten. But the id does not forget! This thought is filed away. Some thoughts are so painful that the ego does its best never to let them out of the unconscious mind and up to the level of consciousness. This is called ego defense.

As the child continues to grow, something else develops in the unconscious—the *superego*. This is the voice of authority and command—originally from parents and their substitutes. It is the impression of society, in the guise of the family, on the growing child. It says what is permitted and forbidden, what is "right" and "wrong," "good" and "bad." This is the voice that censors conduct and, later, thought. The child has little or no choice but to obey the commands and conditions imposed on him. In so doing, however, he develops standards of values, a sense of right and wrong, and a conscience, which is the conscious part of the *superego*.

The ever-shifting *relationship* between the id, ego, and superego makes up the hypothetical construct of the *unconscious mind*. The relationship of the conscious to the unconscious mind is about like that of the skin of an apple to the whole apple.

Psychoanalysis holds strongly to the old axioms that "the child is father to the man" and "as the twig is bent, so the tree inclines." It believes that behavior patterns are inculcated early in life on an emotional basis in the unconscious mind and persist, unless strongly altered by later experiences and events.

In the normal and inevitable frustrations of the infant are the seeds of later anger, hate, and other negative (though protective) emotions. He does not get his bottle the instant he is hungry, and he cries angrily.

In the infant's need to be loved, since he is long dependent on his parents for survival, is set in train a normal course of learning to love. The infant's first love is attached to himself and to different parts of his body (narcissistic love). This self-love gradually shifts to the outside and attaches to outside love objects: first to the mother (or her substitute), then to parents (often to the parent of the opposite sex as seen in the OEDIPUS COMPLEX), then to peers and friends (usually of the same sex, as seen in gangs of boys and tittering bevies of young girls), then to distant and ideal heroes ("pin-ups"), and finally to flesh-and-blood members of the opposite sex (heterosexual love).

Some unfortunate people never grow up emotionally and psychologically. Their capacity to love is arrested at levels below normal heterosexual love. They continue to love too much either themselves or their parents or their friends of the same sex or their unattainable ideal loves.

These people, as well as those who have become fixed in their frustrations and hates, are the ones whom psychoanalysis can often, but not always, help.

Mental mechanisms or mental dynamisms. It remains to be said that the ego has a hard time meeting and satisfying the conflicting demands of the id, the superego, and the world outside (external reality). To do this even partially successfully the ego must make certain compromises in its own defense (ego defense). These compromises, which are normal unless they are badly overworked, are called mental mechanisms or mental dynamisms. These are some of them:

Repression: burying unpleasant thoughts and memories, purposely forgetting what you don't want to do (e.g., forgetting a dental appointment).

Idealization: Uncritically overestimating people; for example, unfavorably comparing later-life loves with idealized images of one's parents.

Regression: reverting to childish behavior when one doesn't get his own way.

Fantasy: Daydreaming one's way to power and success instead of going out and getting as much of it as possible.

Rationalization: Being unwilling or unable to see or admit the real underlying motives for one's opinions and behavior.

Projection: Blaming others for one's own faults or shortcomings. (The auto accident is always the other fellow's fault.)

Symbolization: Substituting relatively harmless symbols or behavior for thoughts that would be too painful to bear; for example, the old maid's love for a cat or dog; the repeated washing of the hands to wash away a feeling of guilt.

Conversion: Converting conflicts in the unconscious mind into physical ailments; for example, hysterical paralysis, peptic ulcer, colitis, backache, or headache.

It is a sad fact that the people who overwork the mental mechanisms to their own detriment are rarely aware that they are doing it, because these compromises take place principally in the unconscious mind. Psychoanalysis often reveals these conflicts and makes the victim aware of how seriously he is damaging his own personality structure.

The theory of psychoanalysis informs and guides all modern forms of expressive psychotherapy, even when a full analysis is neither warranted nor undertaken. See PSYCHOTHERAPY; FREUD.

Psychodynamics—a slippery and often meaningless word, greatly overworked, which usually refers to some offshoot of Freudian PSYCHOANALYSIS. It has become a mumbo-jumbo word to mystify the uninitiated.

Psychogenic—"in the head"; functional. See MENTAL ILLNESS.

Psychology—broadly, the scientific study of the mind and the whole range of human and animal behavior in which the mind functions. Mind and brain are not synonymous. "Using psychology" usually means getting somebody to do something that he would not otherwise do. Abnormal psychology deals with MENTAL ILLNESS.

Psychologist—correctly speaking, an individual trained in the science of psychology. Many people who call themselves "practical psychologists" are without adequate training or experience. They can, like parlor hypnotists, do harm to their unwitting subjects or patients. A well-trained psychologist usually has a Ph.D. degree from a recognized university. One should investigate very carefully anyone who claims to be a psychologist but has no academic training or reputation. A clinical psychologist often administers intelligence tests and personality-interpretation tests, such as the Rorschach (ink-blot) test.

Some clinical psychologists give guidance, counseling, and simpler kinds of PSYCHOTHERAPY to troubled people.

Psychomotor—muscular actions triggered primarily by psychic events in and stimuli directly to the BRAIN. For example, CONVULSIONS are psychomotor discharges.

Psychoneurosis—practically the same thing as NEUROSIS. See MENTAL ILLNESS.

Psychopath—a socially delinquent person, not quite criminal and yet not normal, suffering from nondescript MENTAL ILLNESS.

Psychopathic—refers to MENTAL ILLNESS.

Psychosis—a term used to describe the more severe forms of MENTAL ILLNESS, some of which were formerly designated as insanity. Most psychoses fall under the headings of SCHIZOPHRENIA, manic-depressive psychosis, and toxic (e.g. alcoholic) psychoses. See MENTAL ILLNESS, PSYCHOANALYSIS, NEUROSIS.

Psychosomatic—an illness, disorder, or disability in which the mind appears to have an especially great or direct bearing on its origin or continuation. To a greater than usual extent the mind (emotions, unconscious conflicts) seems to be affecting the functions of the body. Classic examples of psychosomatic ailments are hysterical paralysis and stomach ulcers. *Psyche* means "mind," *soma* stands for "body."

Psychotherapy—a "planned and organized pattern of action designed to cure or alleviate a mental illness or morbid emotional state" (Whitehorn). It shades off into all kinds of efforts to help people who are sick in mind or body or both. The Indian medicine man, with his drums and rattles, and the orthodox psychoanalyst, with his couch and darkened room, are both practicing psychotherapy. So is the doctor who reassures his patient that "Everything is going to turn out all right." The question is not, What is psychotherapy? Rather it is, What is *good* psychotherapy? The only possible answer,

unfortunately, is in the nature of a round robin: Good psychotherapy is that practiced by good psychotherapists. And who are good psychotherapists? Those who actually help their patients to make the most of themselves.

To correct one popular misconception: there is a great deal more to psychotherapy than PSYCHOANALYSIS. Psychoanalysis is only one of many kinds of psychotherapy.

The physician, or other counselor, practicing psychotherapy, first tries and must obtain a feeling with and for (a rapport with) the patient. Sometimes, as in group psychotherapy or "family psychiatry," the therapist must establish his rapport with a number of people. The therapist then tries to influence or educate his patient. Among the methods of influencing are reassurance, catharsis (or confession), suggestion, interpretation of the meaning of the patient's thoughts and feelings to give the patient more insight into himself, interpreting and sometimes practically helping to change the relationship between the patient and his doctor or the patient and other people, and helping to change the environment that is damaging the patient.

For a fuller discussion of the methods of psychotherapy, see MENTAL ILLNESS (*How is mental illness treated?*) and PSYCHOANALYSIS.

Pterygium—a growth of thickened conjunctival tissue over the cornea of the eye. See EYE TROUBLE.

Ptomaine Poisoning—an old-fashioned and incorrect name for FOOD POISONING. Ptomaines are a class of substances formed in the decay or putrefaction of flesh.

Ptosis—drooping or sagging of some body part, such as drooping of the eyelid or sagging of the abdomen.

Ptyalin—the enzyme in the saliva which converts starches to sugars. See DIGESTIVE SYSTEM.

Ptyalism—SALIVA (spittle) pours out of salivary glands in the mouth too profusely. See DIGESTIVE SYSTEM.

Puberty—the teen age time of life when SEX ORGANS develop to the point where reproduction is physically possible and when secondary sex characteristics begin to burgeon. This may normally take place anywhere from 12 to 17 years of age. In the female it is most clearly marked by the onset of MENSTRUATION; in the male, by change of voice and nocturnal emissions ("wet dreams").

Public Health—the vast and vital matter, delegated to health officers and their staffs, of safeguarding the health of a community under law. Public health deals with sanitation, vital statistics, epidemic control, and many other matters which require societal rather than individual action.

Public health is one facet of *community health,* which embraces *all* agencies concerned with the health of a community. Public health law is one facet of the *police power* that people extend to their governments. Its basic activities are *tax-supported.* Its keystone is preventive medicine.

Pudenda—the external SEX ORGANS, male or female.

Puerperium—confinement following CHILDBIRTH.

Puerperal Fever—childbed fever; infection, often septicemia, after delivery. This scourge, now largely eliminated by sulfa drugs and antibiotics, was manfully fought in the 19th century by O. W. Holmes and Ignaz Semmelweis.

Pulmonary—related to the LUNGS.

Pulmonary Embolism—a not uncommon cause of death, it is the blocking or closure of the pulmonary artery by an EMBOLUS. The pulmonary artery and its branches lead from the heart to the lungs. Blood clots or other emboli entering the veins are carried along through larger and larger vessels until they come to the pulmonary artery, which is smaller. Hence this is the place where the plugs may fatally lodge. (See illustrations for HEART.)

Pulse—the tangible expansion and contraction of an artery when touched and grasped by the fingers of an examiner. It gives an indication of the ebb and flow of the blood; hence it reflects the rate and power of the heart-beat. In men the normal pulse rate is 70 to 72 beats a minute; in women, 78 to 82; in infants and children, still higher, 100 to 120. Following exercise or excitement the pulse rate is temporarily higher than normal; in sleep it is slower than while waking.

The artery in which the pulse is usually taken is the radial artery of the wrist. However it can also be detected and counted in other arteries that lie near the surface of skin in the ankle, neck, and other parts of the arm.

Purgative—a strong laxative or cathartic; see CONSTIPATION.

Purpura—"purple patches" on the skin and mucous membranes as a result of spontaneous bleeding. See BLOOD DISEASES.

Purulent—containing PUS.

Pus—the fluid that accumulates around an inflammation. It contains dead cells and many white blood cells, whose task it is to fight infections and inflammations. Before the relationship of germs to infection was clearly established, physicians used to speak of a certain kind of "laudable pus," which betokened the healing of an inflammatory process. Today we know that no pus is laudable.

Pustule—a tiny blister-like spot on or elevation of the SKIN harboring PUS.

Putrefaction—decay of once-living (organic) matter under the influence of microbial action and chemical decomposition. The event is usually accompanied by an unpleasant smell of hydrogen sulfide or ammonia.

Pyelitis—inflammation of the kidney, usually its inner core or pelvis. The common symptoms are pain in the back (loins), frequent urination (irritable bladder), pus or blood in the URINE. Treatment is usually by sulfa drugs, antibiotics or a large class of special urinary antiseptics, including mandelic acid. See URINARY SYSTEM.

Pyelogram—X-ray picture of the kidney. To get the shadows on the picture a RADIOPAQUE substance must usually be injected beforehand.

Pyelonephritis—kidney infection. See KIDNEY TROUBLE.

Pyemia—pus in the blood stream; an advanced infection; generalized septicemia ("blood poisoning").

Pylorospasm—muscular convulsions at the opening of the stomach.

Pylorus—literally, the gatekeeper of the stomach; the circular muscles, covered with mucus membrane, at the lower end of the stomach which regularly and rhythmically open and close to let food out of the stomach into the intestines.

Pyorrhea—a flow of pus. *Pyorrhea alveolaris* describes infection and inflammation of the gums and the membranes that cover the roots of the TEETH below the gum line. The treatment is adequate dental care and hygiene; general health conditions must also be looked after. No mouthwash alone will either prevent or cure pyorrhea.

Pyothorax—EMPYEMA of the chest.

Pyrexia—fever.

Pyridoxine—VITAMIN B_6; see DIET.

Pyrogen—anything that produces FEVER.

Pyuria—pus in the URINE.

Q

Any word printed in SMALL CAPITALS *can be looked up under its own alphabetical listing for further information.*

Q Fever—an infectious disease caused by a rickettsial organism. It was first described in Queensland, Australia, but sometimes occurs in the U.S., principally on the Pacific Coast and in the Southwest.

q. i. d.—four times a day.

q. s.—as much as necessary (*quantum sufficit*), a common abbreviation on prescriptions.

Quack—a fake or fraudulent healer; a charlatan; a mountebank.

Quadriceps—literally means "four-headed"; applied to the "four-headed muscle of the calf" of the leg and to the muscle in the front part of the thigh that elevates it.

Quadripara—a woman who is bearing or has borne her fourth child.

Quadriplegia—paralysis of all four extremities; both arms and both legs. See PARAPLEGIA.

Quarantine means legal, and if necessary forcible, restriction of people from entering or leaving countries, premises or quarters where a communicable or contagious disease exists. It originally meant the detention outside a port for at least forty days of ships coming into harbor from places where epidemic diseases were raging or suspected. The practice began in Italy in the 14th century. See PLAGUE. *Quarantina* is Italian for forty. Modern PUBLIC HEALTH practice relies as little as possible on quarantine for the control of communicable and epidemic disease.

Quinidine—a drug closely related to QUININE. It is especially useful in relieving irregular heart and pulse beats (FIBRILLATION and FLUTTER).

Quinine—cinchona bark; more exactly the bitter white alkaloid powder extracted from it. From the time of its introduction into Europe from South America, by the Countess of Cinchon in about 1640, until World War II, in 1940, quinine was the sovereign specific drug for treating all forms of MALARIA and was also commonly used to reduce fever in many other infectious diseases. See MALARIA.

Quinsy—sore THROAT; *tonsillitis.*

Quintuplets—five babies born at one time. Most famous in the 20th century were the Dionne sisters of Canada.

R

Any word printed in SMALL CAPITALS *can be looked up under its own alphabetical listing for further information.*

Rabbit Fever—TULAREMIA.

Rabid—pertaining to RABIES (or hydrophobia). A mad dog may be a rabid animal.

Rabies—hydrophobia; a virus disease, usually fatal, transmitted from animals (mad dogs, wolves and so forth) to human beings by *bite.* The incubation period, after the bite, may be from 1 to 6 months. The beginning of the disease itself is marked by a general feeling of illness, mental depression and swelling of the lymph glands near the site of the bite.

The neck and throat muscles necessary for breathing and swallowing are then affected; they tighten up and go into spasm. The results are a choking sensation, a husky voice, urge to drink water but inability to do so, then panic at the sight of water, delirium and death in 2 to 5 days. Hydrophobia is from the Greek words, *hydro* for water and *phobia* for fear. Postmortem examination of the brain following death from rabies reveals characteristic small particles (Negri bodies) inside a certain number of brain cells.

Death from rabies, following the bite of a truly rabid animal, can usually be prevented by a series of inoculations with anti-rabies vaccine. This type of treatment was originated by Pasteur in 1885 and is still called the Pasteur treatment even though the actual substances injected are now prepared differently from the way he made them.

This treatment is not always successful and entails some risk; but the chances of it succeeding are very great. It is certainly advisable when the biting animal has definitely been proved to be rabid, or when there is strong suspicion, if not positive proof, that this is the case. The biting animal should be kept caged, under observation, and its brain examined after death to determine whether Negri bodies or other positive signs of rabies infection are present. However some so-called "mad dogs" are not really infected with the rabies virus which causes the disease.

In *dumb rabies*, paralysis is an early and prominent symptom.

Rachitic—afflicted with *rickets*, the twisted BONE disorder owing to lack of VITAMIN D in the diet.

Radiation—emission of radiant energy; electromagnetic waves. See X RAYS and ATOMIC ENERGY.

Radiation Sickness, injury, or reaction describes the damage done to body tissues by exposure to radiation from X RAYS, gamma rays, RADIUM, radon, ATOMIC ENERGY, and other radioactive substances. The damage, of course, will depend both on the amount of exposure—the dose—and the individual's personal tolerance for or resistance to radiation. The harmful effects, if any, may be acute or delayed.

Acute radiation sickness sometimes occurs in patients who are receiving X-ray treatment for conditions that cannot be expected to respond as adequately to other kinds of treatment, if available. The symptoms are loss of appetite, nausea, vomiting, and diarrhea. The treatment is symptomatic, but the symptoms usually disappear in a day or two if no further exposure to radiation occurs.

Massive doses of radiation, as encountered in atomic bomb explosions, can produce such severe reactions that death shortly ensues. The actual cause of death in these cases, however, can usually be attributed to severe ANEMIA, since the blood-forming organs are exceptionally sensitive to radiation; to internal BLEEDING, since the capillary blood vessels are also adversely affected; to secondary INFECTIONS, since the white blood cells often are knocked out; or to severe BURNS, with changes in the body fluid balance, since radiation is a form of heat.

In *delayed radiation sickness* the same mechanisms of body damage and possible death operate; but the severe symptoms develop more slowly and insidiously, sometimes over a course of many years. Early symptoms may include easy fatigue and lethargy and (in women) cessation of MENSTRUATION. Radiation injury in peacetime can be avoided by strict obedience to safety rules and regulations in establishments where radiation is a known hazard.

See X RAYS; ATOMIC ENERGY.

Radiculitis—inflammation at the root of a nerve, especially one or more of the NERVES whose roots are in the spinal cord.

Radioactive—any element or compound that emits radioactive rays or energy as a result of its inner atomic disintegration. Radium and uranium are typical radioactive substances. See RADIUM; ISOTOPE; ATOMIC ENERGY.

Radiography—the business of taking and studying X-ray photographs.

Radioisotope—any isotope of a chemical element or its compounds that has been made radioactive by treatment in an atomic energy pile or a cyclotron. Radioactive carbon and other elements are commonly used now in medical research. They are tracer elements. Their passage through and deposit in the human and animal body can be readily traced and detected with suitable instruments (a Geiger counter).

The chemical substances into which the radioisotope enters are called "tagged" or "labeled" atoms. A few radioisotopes have been used in actual medical treatment; notably radioiodine in the treatment of GOITER and radiocobalt in CANCER.

Radiologist—a specialist in radiology. He reads X-ray pictures and gives opinions of the underlying disease condition revealed by the black and white shadows. He also arranges for and gives treatment by the careful application of X ray or RADIUM.

Radiology—sometimes called roentgenology, the specialty branch of medicine which deals with the application of X rays both to the DIAGNOSIS and treatment of *pathology,* or study of abnormalities of body tissues and fluids. When these relate to abnormal (cancerous) cell growths only, the subspecialty is sometimes designated as oncology.

Radiopaque—describes substances that do not permit the passage of X rays; such as the BARIUM taken into the gastrointestinal tract when a series of X-ray pictures of this tract is to be taken.

Radiosensitive is a word applied to cells, tissues and organs that are comparatively more sensitive to the effects or damage resulting from exposure to radiation than other similar structures. For example, CANCER cells are more radiosensitive than normal cells.

Radium—the rare, expensive, radioactive metal discovered in 1898 by Pierre and Marie Curie, who isolated it from pitchblende and recognized its rare quality. Radium spontaneously disintegrates at all times, giving off radiation as a result of intra-atomic shifts.

Radium salts emit heat, light and radioactive gas, called *radon* or radium emanation, as well as three other distinct kinds of radiation called alpha, beta and gamma rays. Gamma rays are the most powerful; they are, practically speaking, the same as X rays. They pass through many substances opaque to light.

There are many substances, however, through which they will not pass; notably, lead, which is commonly used to shield against radium and to contain it. Radium is used in the treatment of CANCER and some SKIN diseases.

Ragweed—the common American weed whose pollen brings on HAY FEVER in those especially sensitive to it. See ALLERGY, ANTIGEN.

Rale—any sound or noise in the lungs that shouldn't be there and therefore indicates that something is wrong. The physician sometimes hears rales when he listens to the chest through his STETHOSCOPE (AUSCULTATION). He may hear a kind of rattling sound (dry rales) or a gurgling sound (moist rales) as the patient breathes. The type of sound is often indicative of the type of disease in the chest cavity; for example, dry rales, with a whistling, musical or squeaky tone, are often heard in the presence of ASTHMA and BRONCHITIS. A clicking sound, or rale, is sometimes heard in early TUBERCULOSIS.

Ramus—a branch—of an artery, vein, nerve or bone.

Rash—abnormal reddish coloration or blotch on some part of the SKIN. The causes are manifold, including irritation and infection. Many childhood diseases are marked by a characteristic rash; for example, measles and scarlet fever. Effective treatment of skin rashes depends on discovering the real underlying cause and dealing with that. See POISON IVY, HIVES, ITCHING, SKIN TROUBLE.

Rat—the omnivorous rodent, black, brown and white, that is the ubiquitous enemy of man, despoiling him of food and delivering him disease.

The black, or English, rat (*Rattus rattus*) is the common carrier of plague by way of the *flea* that infests it.

The larger brown rat (*Rattus norvegicus*) and its cousins, including the white or albino rats often used in laboratory experiments, also carry at least 11 intestinal parasites that can be transmitted to man, such as tapeworms, roundworms and trichinae, and are reservoirs for the MICROBES that cause typhus fever and ratbite fever.

Rat control is an important special occupation in the field of public health; sometimes called *deratization*. In general, rat populations are controlled by shielding the food supplies (for example, garbage) rats must have to live and by poisoning them in a variety of ways.

Many powerful rat poisons are known; for example, ANTU (alpha-naphthyl-thiourea). The trick is to get enough rats to eat it and at the same time keep the poisons safely away from human beings, especially children.

Ratbite Fever—an infectious disease brought on, as its name implies, by rats which bite young infants and children. However the infecting microbe can also be transmitted through food or water contaminated with rat droppings.

There are two forms of the disease, one caused by a SPIROCHETE (*Spirillum minus*), the other by a bacterium (*Streptobacillus moniliformis*). The first one, named *sodoku* by Japanese investigators who traced it down, causes swelling and inflammation of the LYMPH glands, chills and fever, and rigidity of body parts as a result of involvement of the nervous system.

The second type, related to Haverhill fever (from Haverhill, Mass., where the disease was investigated), is marked by sore throat, fever, headache, skin rash, vomiting and joint pains and stiffness.

Any ratbite or other rodent bite should be promptly treated by a physician, who will cauterize it and apply the appropriate antiseptic.

Rationalization—a common mental mechanism, operating chiefly in the UNCONSCIOUS mind, through which one finds for himself acceptable reasons for doing things or thinking things that his conscience (SUPEREGO) does not approve. Rationalization conceals from the conscious mind basic, emotionally powered motives for action—for example, envy, jealousy and anger. It makes them appear plausible and laudable. See PSYCHOANALYSIS.

Rauwolfia—a drug derived from the plant *Rauwolfia serpentina*, which grows in India, Ceylon, Burma and Malaya. It has been used for centuries as a herb remedy for the treatment of fever, sleeplessness and excitement. It was introduced into Western medicine, in more purified forms, in the early 1950's and is now extensively used in the treatment of HIGH BLOOD PRESSURE and as a tranquilizer in mild and severe MENTAL ILLNESS.

Ray—a line of radiant energy, such as heat ray, light ray, ultra-violet ray, X ray. See SPECTRUM.

Raynaud's Disease, named after the French doctor, Maurice Raynaud, who described it in 1862, is a disease of the small blood vessels in the outlying parts of the body, notably in the fingers, toes, ears and nose. Women under forty are most commonly afflicted.

The condition is one in which spasms or blocking of

the small arteries, arterioles, and capillaries repeatedly occurs. The afflicted parts turn white, waxy and numb ("dead fingers"). They may not even bleed if pricked. The spell may last for a few minutes, several hours or even a day or two.

In a more severe form of the disease, veins as well as arteries contract and the affected parts swell, tingle and turn purple. Following repeated attacks, the circulation may be so impaired that gangrene of the skin and affected organ occurs.

To make a positive diagnosis of Raynaud's disease, the doctor must be sure that attacks have occurred for a period of at least two years.

The *treatment* of Raynaud's disease in its early stages is largely preventive. People who have or fear getting it must keep themselves warm, avoiding cold weather and cold water. They must give up smoking.

When attacks continue in spite of good medical management, surgery may be considered. The operation is some form of *sympathectomy*, cutting those parts of the sympathetic NERVOUS SYSTEM which will keep the tiny blood vessels in the affected parts from contracting unduly and thus help assure an adequate blood supply to the part. There are some disadvantages to this operation and it is more successful when the feet rather than the hands are affected.

Reaction—the thing that happens because something coming before made it happen; the response that can be observed to a specific psychological or chemical event; for example, the rage that follows frustration or the salt that comes out of mixing an acid and a base. There are numerous specific reactions known to chemistry and medicine and these are frequently taken as tests for or indexes of disease; for example, the Wassermann reaction that serves as a test for SYPHILIS.

Reagent—anything that evokes a chemical reaction. It usually refers to small amounts of index, trace or dye chemicals by which samples of body fluids (or other liquids) can be conveniently tested for the presence of certain specific chemical ingredients or qualities.

Recessive describes characteristics, traits (or GENES) of living organisms that are less likely to appear in offspring than *dominant* traits. See GENETICS; HEREDITY.

Rectocele—a bulging out of part of the rectum; *proctocele*. The bulge frequently impinges on the vagina in women who have borne several children.

Rectum—the lower part of the large bowel, terminating in the anus. It is 6 to 8 inches long, lined with mucous membrane, contains feces and intestinal flora, absorbs water from the fecal stream. See DIGESTIVE SYSTEM.

"Reefers"—NARCOTIC cigarettes made of marihuana.

Reflex—an involuntary act or movement performed in response to some stimulus, general or specific, from or to the NERVES and NERVOUS SYSTEM. A typical human reflex act is the blinking of the eyelids when light is flashed into the eye. There are numerous reflexes which are useful to the physician in diagnosing disease and testing the integrity of the nervous system; for example, the jerk of the leg that normally follows a light tap underneath the kneecap.

Refraction—(1) the deviation of light rays when they pass from one transparent medium to another; for example, from air to glass lenses in which they are bent; (2) the business of testing eyesight for errors in refraction of the crystalline lens of the eye and prescribing lenses (spectacles) to correct for the errors. This is the particular skill of the OPTOMETRIST, but is also performed by the OPHTHALMOLOGIST and the general practitioner. See EYES and EYE TROUBLE.

Regional Ileitis—inflammation, sometimes to the point of threatened blockage, in one or another region of the lengthy small intestine. This is a comparatively rare diagnosis (low grade bowel inflammation is common). It received international attention in 1956 when U. S. President Eisenhower was operated upon for it.

Regression—the unconsciously motivated psychological mechanism in which a person reverts to earlier, childish types of behavior. See PSYCHOANALYSIS. Regression also describes the disappearance of signs or symptoms of disease.

Regurgitation—backflow, such as vomiting up undigested food or backflow of blood in the chambers of the HEART because of faulty valves.

REHABILITATION

Rehabilitation—the challenge of helping disabled people to make the most of themselves—is a task, process, business, responsibility, and opportunity. It is a point of view and a technique. It is a philosophy concerning society and an attitude toward individuals. An operative definition is still in the process of being formulated through practice and experience. The unsettled practical questions are:

1. *When does rehabilitation begin?* (Some say "With diagnosis"; others, "When the doctor can do no more for the patient"; still others, "Long before the patient gets sick or is injured.")

2. *How far does rehabilitation extend?* (What is total rehabilitation?)

3. *Who does what with what to whom to make rehabilitation work and stick?* (How big is a medical team engaged in rehabilitation? Who's the captain? Who's the quarterback?)

4. *Who pays the bills for rehabilitation?* As now practiced, rehabilitation is a costly business. Patients pay part (a small part), hospitals pay part, voluntary health agencies (such as the National Foundation) pay part, government pays part (probably the biggest part).

All these questions are complicated by the sad fact that no person is completely healthy, that everyone has his own greater or lesser disabilities, handicaps, and unhappinesses. Where shall he turn for help?

The idea of rehabilitation is older than scientific medicine. It was the basic goal of the primitive medicine man, or shaman, who defined health in terms of function, and who danced, rattled, and sang to get his poor patient back on his feet and into tribal activities again. Rehabilitation as the "science of human salvage" has developed more slowly.

In the United States the responsibility for rehabilitation was first assumed by the orthopedic surgeons, who worked with physical cripples. During World War I practical working techniques for rehabilitation began to be developed to handle war casualties. The specialties of occupational therapy and physical therapy, as a help to the orthopedic surgeon, began to take organized form.

During the 1930's, when great stress was placed on the economic aspects of medicine, and when the toll of long-term chronic illnesses, like TUBERCULOSIS and MENTAL ILLNESS, got more serious attention, rehabilitation took a different focus and widened, though vaguely, its horizons.

The necessities of World War II, the manpower need to get "half-cripples" out of hospitals and back to military duty or industrial production, accentuated the need for rehabilitation, gave it an immediate goal, a set of practical working techniques, unlimited financial support (as a war-economy measure), and—thanks to the men who did the job—an inspiration for the future.

Doctor-organized and doctor-centered, rehabilitation after World War II was described in such phrases as "dynamic therapeutics," "the third phase of medicine," or "from the bed to the job." The need for specially equipped and staffed rehabilitation centers outside the military purview soon became apparent. So much more could be done for so many more people if anyone wanted to take the trouble and had the heart and skill to do it!

Specialists in PHYSICAL MEDICINE carried the ball for rehabilitation after World War II. Their enthusiastic efforts left the impression that physical medicine *was* rehabilitation. Leaders in rehabilitation had recognized from the beginning, however, that all medical specialties—and the paramedical specialties, like physical therapy, occupational therapy, medical social work, and clinical psychology—were equally concerned. The concept of the medical team, employing all specialists, came into being as the prime method of rehabilitation. The current arguments are not centered on whether there should be a team but on who should be captain.

The concept of rehabilitation is now well accepted. Techniques are still being worked out. One of the most helpful modern ideas in rehabilitation is a concentration on the necessary first steps in rehabilitation practice in a hospital or home-care setting.

Efforts are concentrated on making the disabled person capable of meeting and mastering the activities of his own daily living.

This first-step procedure in rehabilitation is eminently successful, as much accumulated experience now proves. The second-step question, Where does the patient go from the hospital or rehabilitation center? remains to be answered satisfactorily. But rehabilitation always signifies *hope.*

Relapse—getting sicker after being better.

Relapsing Fever—the name for a group of infectious diseases in which fever, lasting 5 to 7 days, comes and goes from 2 to 10 times. The disease is caused by a microbe *(Borrelia)* which is transmitted to man by the bite of louse or tick. See INSECTS.

Relaxative—a tranquilizing drug; a "don't-give-a-hang pill."

Remission—the disappearance of signs and symptoms of disease without, necessarily, the elimination of the underlying cause of the disease; the oppo-

site of RELAPSE. Remissions occur in a number of long-term diseases, such as TUBERCULOSIS and MULTIPLE SCLEROSIS.

Renal—related to the KIDNEYS.

Renin—an enzyme liberated by the kidney under certain conditions in the cycle of BLOOD PRESSURE changes.

Rennin—an enzyme that curdles milk; it is obtained commercially from the fourth stomach of calves and is the active ingredient in *rennet* used for making cheese and milk delicacies.

Repression—the fundamental

mental mechanism by which disagreeable, unpleasant or painful thoughts and feelings are submerged into the UNCONSCIOUS MIND, often to rankle there and make trouble by coming out in disguise. See PSYCHOANALYSIS.

Reproduction—see SEX ORGANS, MALE and FEMALE; PREGNANCY; CHILDBIRTH.

Resect—cut out by SURGERY.

Resident—a graduate physician, who already has his M.D. degree and license to practice, who chooses to remain on the house staff of a hospital in order to get further training that will qualify him for a medical specialty. He often lives in the hospital. A resident is higher than an INTERN on the hospital staff. Residents are sometimes classified as junior and senior, depending on how long they have served in the hospital. A *residency* that helps qualify for a specialty may run from 1 to 4 years. Residents are paid by the hospital—maintenance being counted. In some institutions resident physicians live on the premises as a matter of choice, convenience, or necessity and are not working toward specialty accreditation. Residents are allowed more or less discretion in treating patients, depending on the disposition of the attending staff and the chiefs of service. However, they always act nominally under orders of the hospital medical staff.

Resistance to disease on the part of an individual, and the reasons for this ability to resist the onslaught of MICROBES or degenerative changes in CELL tissues, are the great unsolved mysteries of modern medicine.

Specific resistance to a few infecting microbes can be built up by artificial immunization (smallpox vaccination, and diphtheria, whooping cough, tetanus, polio, yellow fever, and a few other immunizations).

A high degree of immunity to some diseases is acquired by naturally occurring attacks of the disease—notably the common childhood diseases.

But in most other infectious diseases, including the common cold, venereal disease, "strep throat," previous attacks are no barrier to subsequent INFECTION.

When it comes to the degenerative diseases—for example, heart disease, cancer, diabetes— we are even more in the dark as to why one person resists their advent and another does not. There are no easy answers. We cannot honestly fall back on such clichés as "HEREDITY, SMOKING, poor DIET, lack of EXERCISE, or a bump on the head in infancy." More accurate explanation of resistance to disease is the area in which we can confidently look forward to the greatest opportunities of new medical progress.

Respiration—breathing. See ARTIFICIAL RESPIRATION.

THE RESPIRATORY SYSTEM

nasopharynx

nasal passages

pharynx

nose

mouth

tongue

larynx

trachea

left lung

bronchus

right lung cut
away to show
inner structure

bronchiole

bronchioles
end in air sacs

blood vessels
pick up oxygen

rib

intercostal
muscles

diaphragm

blood vessels
to and from
the heart

enlarged view of end of
bronchiole with air sacs

Respirator—a mechanical device which provides physical aid for a patient with breathing difficulty. Tank respirators are often called "iron lungs." However, there are two general types: tank respirators which encase the patient's entire body, except for the head; and chest respirators. In these the shell (cuirass) fits over the patient's chest and abdomen. The chest respirator is used for transportation and weaning patients from tank respirators.

Respiratory Center—(1) an area in the brain that controls breathing; (2) a center dedicated to patient evaluation and care, clinical investigation and teaching in connection with polio patients having respiratory difficulty. These centers are in teaching hospitals associated with medical schools where demonstration care programs, teaching, clinical investigation and research are conducted. The National Foundation [for Infantile Paralysis] sponsored a number of them in the U. S.

Respiratory System consists of—in descending order—the NOSE, mouth, nasal passages, nasopharynx, PHARYNX (back of the throat), voice box (LARYNX), windpipe (TRACHEA), BRONCHI, bronchioles, air sacs (alveoli) of the LUNGS, and muscles of respiration (DIAPHRAGM and intercostal muscles). This system introduces oxygen from the air into contact with hemoglobin of red blood cells and removes carbon dioxide and water.

Resuscitation—ARTIFICIAL RESPIRATION, which see.

Rete—a network of nerves or blood vessels.

Retching—unproductive vomiting. Lie down and try to relax.

Reticulocyte—an immature red BLOOD cell, characteristically marked when viewed under the microscope.

Retina—the inner, light-sensitive lining of the eye. See EYES and EYE TROUBLE.

Retinitis—inflammation of the retina. See EYE TROUBLE.

Retractor—any surgical instrument used for drawing or holding back the edges of an incision or wound.

Retro—backward or behind, as in *retroversion,* backward tipping of the womb.

Rhagades—tiny cracks in the SKIN.

RHEUMATIC FEVER

Rheumatic fever is a COLLAGEN DISEASE that can involve any connective tissue but is most damaging when it scars the heart muscle or the valves of the heart and thus produces *rheumatic heart disease.* (See HEART DISEASE.) When the connective tissue in the brain is involved, the condition known as *St. Vitus dance* (more technically, *Sydenham's chorea*) may appear. The jerky, uncontrollable movements associated with St. Vitus dance always disappear eventually, though it may take a long time.

Damage to the heart muscle interferes with its pumping force; scarring of the heart valves impedes blood flow. The valve damage can sometimes be detected as a *heart murmur,* although not all murmurs heard through the physician's stethoscope indicate a serious malfunctioning of the heart.

One attack of rheumatic fever does not prevent another. In fact, the real damage arises out of the repeating nature of the disease. First attacks may be mild.

Parents often dismiss mild attacks of rheumatic fever as mere "growing pains" in children; but this is a dangerous attitude. Though rheumatic fever is still widespread, great progress is being made in preventing it, and its occurrence in the United States is declining.

Who gets rheumatic fever? Perhaps a million people in the United States suffer from rheumatic fever or its aftereffects. The onset, or first attack, of the disease is usually in childhood, between the ages of 6 and 8, but it may be delayed to adolescence or early adulthood. The disease is responsible for about 90% of all heart trouble in children and perhaps one-third of the crippled hearts met in adult life. Girls are not affected more frequently than boys, but women are affected more frequently than men.

What causes rheumatic fever? The exact cause is unknown, but it is unquestionably associated with, and follows by 2 or 3 weeks, infections with hemolytic (blood-destroying) streptococcus germs. A "strep infection" triggers the rheumatic response. These infections may be so mild as to escape notice; they usually appear as tonsillitis, middle-ear infection, scarlet fever, or "strep sore throat."

Rheumatic fever is not contagious, though the strep infection preceding it decidedly is. Not every child who gets a strep infection comes down with rheumatic fever; indeed, relatively few do. Other factors that predispose to the disease must be considered. Social, economic, hereditary, personality, and environmental factors have been studied. There is some evidence that impoverished, overcrowded, and disrupted homes more often breed the disease. Climate plays a role; the geography of rheumatic fever corresponds with that of strep infections. Both conditions are decidedly more common in cool than in warm or tropical climates. Rheumatic fever reaches a peak of incidence in April, a low point in November in the U. S.

What are the symptoms of rheumatic fever? Except for the characteristic twitching movements of St. Vitus dance, the symptoms of rheumatic fever are generally vague; diagnosis is not easy. Among the complaints of children or adolescents that should encourage prompt and complete medical check-up are loss of or failure to gain weight; a low but persistent fever; pallor; poor appetite; repeated nosebleeds without apparent cause; jerky body movements; repeated complaints of pain in the arms, legs, or abdomen; fatigue; and weakness.

How is rheumatic fever treated? The fundamental treatment, aimed at minimizing heart damage, is prolonged bed rest. This must continue so long as the disease is active. Rarely can patients be up in less than 4 months; 6 months to a year is more likely. Whether at home or in the hospital (which has certain things to recommend it), good and sympathetic nursing care must be provided during this prolonged convalescence. Since most children resent such enforced inactivity, great ingenuity must be exercised to keep them amused and quiet. With proper treatment, however, about two-thirds of the children and adult patients recover with little, if any, limitation on their future work and play.

How can rheumatic fever be prevented? Today positive steps can be taken to prevent rheumatic fever and its sequel, rheumatic heart disease. The first step is prompt—within 24 to 48 hours—treatment of all strep infections or potential infections evidenced by a cold or other upper-respiratory involvement. The second step is to prevent recurrences of strep infections by taking small protective doses of *sulfa* drugs or *antibiotics* on a regular schedule when these infections are around. Injections of slow-acting, long-lasting penicillin appear to be particularly useful in preventing reinfection.

RHEUMATISM

Rheumatism—"the misery"; a popular term that covers a multitude of aches and pains in the muscles, bones and joints. With improved medical diagnosis, it is now possible to pin-point many of the vague ailments called rheumatism and hence offer more specific and effective treatment. All rheumatic conditions are marked by some inflammation or other change in connective tissues. Much of what used to be called rheumatism is now diagnosed as *fibrositis,* or inflammation of the white fibrous connective tissue that forms muscle sheaths and merges into muscle attachments. Most rheumatic conditions, however, are now called *arthritis,* especially rheumatoid arthritis, which infers inflammation of a joint. (See ARTHRITIS.)

Rheumatism is the leading cause of disability and invalidism in the U.S., accounting for an estimated 10% of all prevailing illness and afflicting some 10 to 12 million Americans at any one time. Rheumatic ailments, however, are nothing new to mankind. There is bony evidence that prehistoric man suffered from arthritis.

The underlying causes of rheumatism are legion. They include hereditary disposition, specific infections (for example, gonorrhea), injury to bones and joints, overweight, poor nutrition, faulty METABOLISM (as in GOUT), ENDOCRINE disorders, ALLERGY, and poisons. The symptoms of most forms of rheumatism seem to come and go, though over the years, if untreated, the disease usually progresses. Most forms of rheumatism are made worse by emotional stress, too much exercise, overfatigue, and exposure to inclement weather. The rheumatic patient who claims he can feel it in his bones that bad weather is approaching is often right.

Among the many conditions, besides *arthritis* and fibrositis, that are often called rheumatism are *myositis,* or inflammation of a muscle; *myalgia,* or muscle pain; *gout; tenosynovitis,* or inflammation of tendon sheaths; *bursitis,* or inflammation of the bursae, the little sacs of fluid that lubricate tissues at points where they might develop friction; *neuritis,* or nerve inflammation; *sciatica,* producing pain and tenderness along the course of the sciatic nerve, prickling or burning sensations in the thigh and leg, and sometimes wasting of the calf muscles; *lumbago,* or pain in the middle back, the lumbar region; and *torticollis,* or wryneck. *Rheumatic fever,* often affecting the heart, must be classified as a cardiac as well as a rheumatic ailment.

How should rheumatism be treated? Since rheumatism is not one but many kinds of disease, there is no single treatment. The best medical diagnosis and treatment is indicated. What is good for one patient, or one kind of rheumatism, may be bad for another. For example, a patient with fibrositis may improve if he has the grit to exercise off his pain and stiffness, but a patient with rheumatoid arthritis may damage himself by inappropriate and excessive exercise. Massage helps some types of rheumatism but not others. Application of heat is usually beneficial. The commonly used drug is aspirin (or some other salicylate). However, many other forms of treatment are available, on proper indications. Endocrine therapy (often cortisone), CHEMOTHERAPY, physical therapy, and orthopedic surgery may be prescribed.

Rheumatic diseases offer a happy hunting ground for quacks and frauds, who make extravagant claims for curing them. The drugs they peddle are usually forms of aspirin sold at very high prices. These fake healers should be avoided by the patient who wants to get well.

How can rheumatism be prevented or avoided? There is no simple or guaranteed formula. But a good health regimen may help. This means good nutrition, attention to weight control, regular periods of sleep and rest, and proper mental attitudes. Avoidance of undue exposure to cold and damp is also recommended. Insofar as rheumatic ailments are due to hereditary disposition, nothing can be done about them. Where infection is a factor, avoidance or early treatment of the infection helps prevent subsequent rheumatic involvement.

Rh Factor—an invisible substance attached to red blood cells. Rh is an abbreviation standing for Rhesus monkey, because it was in this animal that the Rh factor was first discovered. The Rh factor is important practically in typing blood for transfusions and in obstetrics.

Some people (15% of white people, 7% of Negroes, 1% of Chinese and Japanese) do not have this Rh factor in their blood. They are called Rh-negative. Those who have it are designated Rh-positive.

If an Rh-negative woman gets a transfusion of Rh-positive blood, her body may react by producing antibodies against Rh-positive blood cells. This same thing may also happen, though comparatively rarely, if she has a child whose father is Rh-positive. The Rh factor is an hereditary characteristic, carried in the GERM PLASM.

Once the Rh-negative mother has become sensitized to Rh-positive blood, and has begun to produce antibodies against

it, she may have trouble with *subsequent* pregnancies. If her unborn child is Rh-positive, the mother's antibodies may become attached to its blood cells, destroying them and causing anemia with mild to severe jaundice. This condition in the infant is called *erythroblastosis*.

The Rh problem, though real, has been overpublicized. Not more than 5% of Rh-negative women will ever have any Rh problem or difficulty with their children. And these problems will not show up until second or subsequent pregnancies, unless the mother has had a previous transfusion of Rh-positive blood.

With efficient modern methods of treatment, including mass or exchange blood transfusions, the "yellow baby" (with erythroblastosis) can usually be saved and grow up healthy.

Rhinitis—inflammation, usually with some swelling, of the lining of the NOSE. It is the cardinal symptom of the COMMON

COLD, HAYFEVER, and many other kinds of ALLERGY.

Rhinoplasty—"nose lifting"; a common operation in plastic surgery.

Rhinorrhea—running NOSE.

Rhomboid—a kite-shaped group of muscles attached to the shoulderblade.

Rhonci—rattling in the throat. See RALE.

Rhubarb—the common garden plant long and reasonably employed as an herb remedy which serves as a mild laxative and gentle, if not always effective, stimulant to other parts of the digestive system.

Rhus—the general name for a large number of poison plants, trees and shrubs that produce dermatitis on contact; notably poison ivy, *Rhus toxicodendron*. See POISON IVY.

RHYTHM METHOD

The rhythm, or the so-called "safe-period," method of CON-TRACEPTION (birth control, child-spacing) is based on the assumption that the couple refrains from sexual intercourse at that point in the woman's menstrual cycle when she is most likely to conceive. It is a method of temporary abstinence. Though long suspected that there were fertile and sterile ("safe") periods in the menstrual cycle, scientific evidence on the usual spacing of these periods was not available until shortly after World War I. An Austrian physician, Knaus, and a Japanese physician, Ogino, then formulated what has since been called the rhythm theory—at first on the evidence of pregnancies in the wives of soldiers who came home on leave at different times of the month. The Roman Catholic Church accepts the rhythm method as a means of birth control to be employed under proper moral sanctions.

The physiological principles on which the rhythm theory operates are presented under the heading of MENSTRUATION. (See also SEX ORGANS, FEMALE.) The obvious occurrence of menstruation is under the control of *ovulation*, which is not obvious or readily demonstrable. Conception can occur only when a viable sperm meets a fertilizable ovum in the uterine tubes. The fertile period in the menstrual cycle includes only those few hours, not more than 48, when a fertilizable ovum is present in the uterine tubes. However, viable sperm, capable of impregnating an ovum, may remain alive in the female sex organs for as long as 3 days following deposit in the vagina. Hence there is a span of at most 5 days during the course of the menstrual cycle when impregnation is possible.

When is the "safe period"? Practical use of the rhythm method of birth control depends on the attempt to calculate in advance just which 5 days these may be and avoid intercourse at that time. The general rule (and the statistical average) is that the fertile period comes *approximately* in the middle of the menstrual cycle. The "safe periods," therefore, occur just before and just after visible menstruation.

In the course of a perfectly regular 28-day menstrual cycle (and perfect regularity is the exception), it is generally calculated that the first 8 days after the onset of menstruation and the 10 days preceding the next expected menstruation, a total of about 18 days, are the "safe period" when conception is less likely. The middle 10 days of the cycle, between the 9th and 19th days, are designated as the "fertile period." A generous margin of safety is allowed in this common calculation, since it is impossible to determine in advance on just which of these mid-cycle days ovulation may actually occur.

Use of the rhythm method requires careful calendar records to calculate the average length of a particular woman's menstrual cycle and thereafter the date of the next expected menstruation. If a woman could easily determine *for certain* the exact time of ovulation, the rhythm method would come close to being an ideal method of birth control. However, in the present state of scientific knowledge, this is not the case. Advance calculations of the time of the *next* ovulation cannot always be made with certainty on the records of past performance. Ovulation *can* occur at practically any time in the menstrual cycle, although, statistically, it usually falls in the 10 days designated as the fertile period. Many physical, emotional, and environmental conditions, acting through the mediation of the ENDOCRINE system, may induce or delay ovulation so that it does not occur when statistically expected.

The *exact* time of ovulation is difficult to determine. A slight decrease, by a fraction of a degree, in basal body temperature sometimes marks this event, and it can be noted by keeping a daily TEMPERATURE record, usually by taking rectal temperature, over a period of weeks or months. This advice is often given to couples eager to have children, who wish to determine that point in the menstrual cycle when conception is most likely. (See STERILITY.)

Riboflavin—a VITAMIN; part of the vitamin B complex.

Rice Diet—low sodium, low calorie, but unpalatable DIET sometimes prescribed in the treatment of HEART failure and HIGH BLOOD PRESSURE. Fruit, fruit juices and sugar go along with rice cooked in *unsalted* water.

Rickets—BONE deformities from lack of VITAMIN D in childhood. See BONE DISEASE.

Rickettsia—a group of MICROBES named after Howard Taylor Ricketts (1871-1910), an American research scientist who gave his life to studying them. Rickettsia are usually smaller than BACTERIA but larger than VIRUSES. They are parasites carried by INSECTS and transmitted to man. Among the diseases caused by rickettsia are TYPHUS FEVER, Q fever, and Rocky Mountain spotted fever.

Rickettsialpox—a mild feverish disease closely related to chickenpox.

Rigor—stiffening. *Rigor mortis* is the stiffening of the muscles after death.

Ringworm (tinea) is not a worm at all; it is a FUNGUS infection of the skin. It is called ringworm because the infection starts in one small spot then spreads or radiates outward to form a ring, or circle. While the infection in the center of the circle disappears, the picture of the advancing border is that of a ring. The common forms of ringworm are *ringworm of the feet* (athlete's foot, see FOOT TROUBLE), *ringworm of the scalp* (tinea capitis), and *ringworm of the groin* ("jock-strap itch," "jungle rot"). TRICHOPHYTOSIS is still another name for ringworm.

Ringworm of the scalp usually appears as moth-eaten patches on the back of the head. The infecting fungus is usually *Microsporon audouini*. It can be detected with a special ultraviolet light, Wood's light. In the presence of this light the fungus-infected area glows (fluoresces) like the radium-painted dial on a wrist watch. Children, mainly, are infected, and the infection may last six months or more. In school epidemics, some control can be obtained by having children wear disposable paper skullcaps.

The condition can be treated by plucking the infected hairs and by applying organic acids (e.g. propionic acid) or their salts to the affected areas.

Ringworm usually produces a scaly condition of the skin as the small patches of dead skin fall or peel off.

Risus—laughter; the grinning set of the muscles *(risus sardonicus)* that gives the false impression of a sardonic grin in the presence of LOCKJAW and strychnine poisoning.

Rocky Mountain Spotted Fever —a rickettsial infection somewhat akin to TYPHUS FEVER.

Rodent Ulcer—a chronic, gradually enlarging skin ulcer which often mars the face and nose of older people. Radium, X-ray or surgical treatment will all effectively correct this unsightly condition.

Roentgen, abbreviation r., named after Wilhelm Roentgen, the discoverer of x RAYS, is the international unit for measuring amounts of X-ray radiation (see ATOMIC ENERGY). It measures the quantity of radiation which, under given test conditions, increases the ability of air to conduct electricity.

Roentgenogram—X-ray picture.

Roentgenologist—X-ray specialist; RADIOLOGIST.

Rorschach Test—named after Hermann Rorschach (1884-1922), a Swiss psychiatrist. This is the inkblot test. The patient is shown a standard series of inkblots and asked to describe what he sees. From his answers, which are considered projections of his feelings and personality, the highly skilled examiner or tester is often able to get a reasonably accurate picture of and insight into the personality of the subject. This testing method has both advantages and limitations; it crucially depends upon the interpretations made by the examiner.

Rosacea—SEBORRHEA, oily skin, in middle age. The treatment is more or less the same as that for *acne* (see SEBORRHEA). Rosacea is sometimes associated with ALCOHOLISM and then called brandy face or brandy nose.

Rose Fever—a form of HAY FEVER occurring in the spring.

Roseola—a rose-red SKIN *rash*, sometimes seen in CHOLERA, SYPHILIS, TYPHOID FEVER, and MEASLES.

Rubefacient—anything that reddens the SKIN by bringing additional blood to it; for example, a mustard plaster.

Rubella—GERMAN MEASLES.

Rubeola—MEASLES.

Rubor—redness owing to inflammation, usually observed at the site of infections.

Rumbling in the stomach, or more accurately, in the bowels (borborygmus) is caused by an accumulation of gas in these hollow organs. The condition is known as FLATULENCE.

RUPTURE

Rupture (break) is the popular term for the break in the ligaments of the groin that permits an *inguinal* HERNIA to develop; and in this sense rupture means hernia. However, rupture of any other body organ can occur, such as rupture of a blood vessel in the brain, producing STROKE, or rupture of the SPLEEN. Weakness any place in the abdominal wall may result in a rupture; for example, an umbilical hernia.

Both women and men, girls and boys, are subject to rupture in the broad sense of the term; but inguinal hernia is almost always found in the male. The rupture is the break in the wall or muscle that permits something on the inside to come through; the hernia is the loop or part of the internal organ that comes through the break, hole, or opening that shouldn't be there.

More than one type of rupture can occur even in the groin, and this depends on the peculiar anatomy of this region. The inguinal canal is the natural opening through the ligaments supporting the abdomen, through which the testicles descend in early life and through which the spermatic cord runs up and back to the abdomen (see SEX ORGANS, MALE). When this opening is abnormally large or loose, a loop of the bowel may descend and protrude through it. This is true inguinal hernia. There is another natural opening in this area—called the femoral, or crural, canal— where the large blood vessels from the legs return to the abdomen. When a loop of bowel protrudes through it, we have a femoral hernia.

What causes rupture? Basically it is a weakness in the ligaments and muscles. However, a small opening can be enlarged and made troublesome by physical exertion, such as athletic contests, improper lifting of heavy objects, even violent coughing and straining at stool. The increase in the pressure inside the abdomen is just as important in pushing the loop of gut through the opening as is the tearing or stretching of the ligament through which it comes. Inguinal hernia is often present at birth (congenital hernia), and the loop of gut is found descended almost to the bottom of the scrotal sac.

It is not necessary to strain oneself violently to bring on a rupture. This condition, unnoticed, may have been occurring gradually for a long time before the sudden strain brings it to light.

The protrusion of the loop of intestine through the inguinal canal may not be discovered until a complete medical examination is given. The examiner's fingers are placed just above the scrotal sac pressing inward, and the patient is asked to cough. The coughing increases the pressure inside the abdomen and momentarily forces the intestine through the opening if it is there.

Inguinal hernias are classified as *reducible,* which means they are freely movable, can be pushed back into the abdominal cavity, but will descend again through the opening until it is closed; or *irreducible*, which means they cannot be pushed back into the abdomen.

Strangulated hernia, the real risk: When the ring of ligament and muscle surrounding the hernia begins to pinch and squeeze tightly on the loop of intestine, endangering its blood supply, the hernia is said to be strangulated. This is serious. If the blood supply is cut off for even a few hours, the strangulated portion of the bowel suffers *gangrene* and dies. The bowel becomes obstructed.

The symptoms of strangulated hernia (which may occur in a person who doesn't yet know he has a hernia) are pain in the groin and abdomen, stoppage of bowel movements (peristalsis), and vomiting. This group of symptoms brooks no delay; see a doctor immediately. Emergency surgery is usually required to correct a strangulated hernia. This may include cutting out part of the gangrenous gut and sewing the cut ends together. It also includes repair of the rupture openings.

Treatment of rupture: Every case is individual, and the best judgment of a competent physician should determine how a particular case is most effectively treated. Reliance on a truss-maker or salesman is particularly to be deplored; this gentleman will never have to operate for a strangulated hernia. The treatment may be either palliative (getting rid of the symptoms) or curative (correcting the underlying cause). In young people with small ruptures, the condition often disappears with palliative treatment, in which the reducible hernia is kept in place in the abdomen. The older the patient and the larger the rupture opening, the more likely the need for surgery.

The surgical repair of a rupture consists primarily in pushing the projecting loop back into the abdomen and sewing up the hole through which it has come down. Sometimes metallic sutures or webs are used to close the opening. This can often be done under local anesthesia. The risk of the operation is small and the percentage of good results very high. It is not an especially dangerous operation, and the person who undergoes it can usually be back on his feet and at work in a few weeks.

Another method of treating rupture calls for injecting a semi-irritating solution (sclerosing solution) through a long hollow needle at the site of the rupture. This solution causes gradual development of scar tissue at the site and closes up the opening. Several injections are usually needed, and, in most hands, the probability of a good result is nowhere near so high as with surgery.

For palliative treatment of a rupture, the wearing of a well-fitted truss may be recommended by the physician and suffice to keep the hernia reduced. Reducible and irreducible hernias take different types of trusses. If one has been wearing a truss, or other support, he should "throw it away" only on advice of a competent physician. (See TRUSS.)

S

Any word printed in SMALL CAPITALS *can be looked up under its own alphabetical listing for further information.*

Sac—any sac or pouch-like organ of the body; for example, hernial sac or conjunctival sac.

Sacroiliac—the lower part of the back; specifically, the joints between the SACRUM and ilium (hipbone) and the ligaments that join them. It is a common site of BACKACHE.

Sacrum—the lower part of the back; the last five vertebrae of the spinal column fused together to form a triangular bone, which is the back wall of the pelvis. (See illustrations for BONES; SPINE.)

Sadism—deliberate cruelty, usually for the satisfaction of open or disguised sexual impulses, as in a teacher who flogs pupils for his or her own delight. The word derives from the Marquis de Sade, a perverted 18th century nobleman, who wrote

books describing the type of practices now called sadism. The opposite of sadism is MASOCHISM, the love of being hurt.

"Safe Period" is only relatively safe. It generally comprises the 10 days before and the 8 days after the onset of visible MENSTRUATION. See RHYTHM METHOD.

St. Vitus Dance—chorea; see RHEUMATIC FEVER.

Salicylates—a large class of drugs that have the same general effects as ASPIRIN, which is one of them.

Saline—salty. Saline solutions are salt solutions. Normal saline solutions are used as a vehicle for dripping food and medicines into veins (intravenous feeding).

Saliva—spit. It is secreted by

the salivary glands in the mouth. It keeps the mucous membranes of the mouth moist and supplies enzymes that begin the digestion of food, especially starches, taken into the mouth. It can be a vehicle of bacteria in the mouth and from the respiratory system. Therefore, spitting in public places is properly prohibited.

Salmonella—a class of MICROBES (germs) sometimes responsible for FOOD POISONING.

Salpingectomy—cutting out one or both uterine tubes. (*See* SEX ORGANS, FEMALE.)

Salpingitis—usually inflammation of the uterine (Fallopian) tubes; sometimes inflammation of the Eustachian tube between the EAR and throat. (See SEX ORGANS, FEMALE; FEMALE TROUBLES.)

Saltpeter—potassium nitrate. There is a stupid myth that it is sometimes secretly served in foodstuffs at boys' schools and in army camps to cut down sexual desire and impulse. This is nonsense. The drug has no such specific effect, and it is not used for this purpose.

Sanatorium usually refers to a tuberculosis hospital (a "san") although the word, from the Latin verb "sanare" (to cure), can be applied to any institution for the resident care of sick people. *Sanitarium* means exactly the same thing; it is a less preferred word, though not wrong.

Saphenous Vein—either of the two veins of the leg, the long and the short saphenous veins, which are near the surface of the skin and are usually involved when veins become varicose. (See VARICOSE VEINS.)

Sapphism—homosexuality in women; lesbianism.

Saprophyte—a special kind of parasite; that is, any vegetable organism that lives on dead or decaying organic substances. Many BACTERIA are saprophytic.

Sarcoidosis—a disease of unknown cause in which lumps and tumors appear on the skin; in lymph nodes, salivary glands, eyes, and lungs; and sometimes at the ends of bones. The disease has many other names (such as Boeck's sarcoid). It most commonly afflicts young adults and lasts for a long time. At times it seems to go away; at other times it may flare up, along with fever and a general feeling of being sick. The outlook for complete recovery is often uncertain.

Sarcoma—CANCER arising from connective tissues; not necessarily fatal if diagnosis is made and treatment (surgery, X ray, or radium) given in time.

Satyriasis—abnormal and excessive sexual desire in the male; a frenzy for coitus. In the female this condition is called NYMPHOMANIA.

Scabies—"the ITCH"; a SKIN disorder.

Scalp—the SKIN covering the skull. See HAIR; DANDRUFF. For ringworm of the scalp, see RINGWORM, which is a FUNGUS infection.

Scalpel—the surgeon's knife; usually short and with a curved-out blade.

Scaphoid Bones—small boat-shaped bones in the hands and feet.

Scapula—the shoulder bone or blade. (See illustrations for BONES; JOINTS.)

Scarlatina—scarlet fever; usually applied to a light and mild attack of the disease with a slight rash and minor sore throat.

Scarlet Fever, or scarlatina, as the milder form of the disease is called, is an acute infectious disease caused by a particular blood-breaking (hemolytic) STREPTOCOCCUS germ. This is the same MICROBE family that is commonly responsible for sore throats and swollen glands in children.

Scarlet fever occurs most commonly in school children between 6 and 10 years of age, rarely under 1. It attacks most frequently in the winter and late spring.

The early symptoms of scarlet fever are sore throat, chills and fever, headache and vomiting. The red, scarlet rash does not come out until a day or two later, beginning on the warm, moist parts of the body; for example, in the groin and on the sides of the chest. The overall red flush is actually made up of numerous red spots. They begin to fade in two or three days and are usually gone in a week. Thereafter the skin peels in large flakes.

Full recovery from scarlet fever is slow. The child should be kept in bed a full 3 weeks and be considered a convalescent for another 3 to 4 weeks.

Complications following scarlet fever are a real risk. Most often the ears, lymph glands, kidneys and eyes may be affected. These are usually noted from 10 days to two weeks after the fever is down. Kidney inflammation (nephritis) with blood in the urine sometimes follows scarlet fever.

The child who has been exposed to scarlet fever, in school or elsewhere, will usually come down with the disease within a week after exposure—if he is going to get it.

The virulence of scarlet fever now encountered does not seem to be so great as it was years ago. Furthermore, with modern antibiotic and sulfa drugs all streptococcus infections are more readily controlled.

Schick Test, named after Béla Schick, a Hungarian physician, is a simple method of determining whether an individual is immune to DIPHTHERIA. A tiny amount of diphtheria toxin is injected into the skin of the arm. If there is *no reaction* at the site of injection, immunity may be assumed. If the injected area turns red, is inflamed, the person is not immune and should be protected with further (or an original) injection of antidiphtheria toxoid.

Schistosomiasis—a tropical disease caused by infestation with a peculiar kind of blood flukes or parasites. The serious kinds of these parasites (schistosomes) are dependent on *snails* for part of their life cycle. The eggs of the parasite are hatched in water contaminated with human feces. The hatched eggs enter into snail hosts, where they multiply and develop. These larvae then leave the snail and swim for themselves. Upon contact with human skin, the larvae penetrate it and gain access to the victim's blood stream. They next advance to the bowels, bladder, and liver, producing such symptoms as diarrhea and blood in the urine, along with inflammation of the bowels and bladder and hardening of the liver (cirrhosis). The disease is treated with many drugs, including antimony compounds.

SCHIZOPHRENIA

Schizophrenia is a MENTAL ILLNESS—the most common of the serious mental illnesses. It is the name given to dementia praecox (early madness). It is sometimes described as "split personality," but it actually covers a whole class of mental disorders (psychoses). It is the mental illness for which hospitalization is most often required.

In general terms, schizophrenia means withdrawal from the real world into a fantastic (but sometimes logically fantastic) world of one's own. Some schizophrenics *appear* sad, others happy. All, however, are in a state to daydream their lives away. They sometimes hear inner voices.

At times some schizophrenics act silly and talk childishly; they do not know who or where they are. Other schizophrenics fall into a state of stupor or muscular rigidity; they vegetate. Still others become overexcited, talkative, and sometimes combative. (These are the ones that the new tranquilizing drugs apparently slow down.)

Generally speaking, schizophrenics do not lose their minds. Their intelligence, as measured by I.Q. tests, does not deteriorate. But they do not use their minds properly. Their intelligence is divorced from other phases of their personality.

Schizophrenia usually develops gradually—appearing as a magnification of common mental mechanisms. (See PSYCHOANALYSIS.) Other members of a family gradually begin to notice that the person is acting strangely; they are usually unwilling to believe that he is on the verge of being mentally ill and they put off seeing a doctor or psychiatrist.

Paranoia is very much like schizophrenia, if not a form of it. The victim imagines that other people are out to kill, poison, or otherwise persecute him. Or he may believe that he is God, Napoleon, or Christ. Paranoia is less common than schizophrenia.

In both schizophrenia and paranoia, the victim suffers from delusions and hallucinations. Delusions are false, fixed ("paranoid") ideas. Adolf Hitler was a paranoid. Hallucinations are imaginary voices or visions. The enemies of Joan of Arc described her as a "mad peasant girl."

The causes of schizophrenia and paranoia are essentially still unknown, although research is beginning to suggest some partial answers. Of particular interest is the production of temporary artificial psychoses with the chemical known as LSD-25 (lysergic acid diethylamide). The Swiss scientist who discovered this effect declared that for twelve hours after inhaling LSD-25 he had "multicolored visions and hallucinations." "It seemed that I was floating in space outside my own body," he said.

Whatever the causes of schizophrenia turn out to be, they will almost certainly be multiple.

What can be done about schizophrenia? The outlook is much more hopeful today than ever before. Many new treatments are being devised and used. No one method of treatment is the answer, but all combined seem to have increasing significance. All forms of psychotherapy are (or have been) attempted. Emphasis today is placed on electroshock (electroconvulsive) therapy, cheerful hospital routines, and new drugs, particularly the tranquilizers, for disturbed and combative patients. Deep PSYCHOANALYSIS has also been tried; also psychodramatics (in which the patient acts out his inner feelings). Some patients respond to insulin coma treatment, originally introduced by Dr. Manfred Sakel. There are few, if any, areas of medical and social interest more urgently in need of genuine and inspired research.

Sciatica—a form of NEURALGIA or NEURITIS affecting and inducing pain along the course of the sciatic nerve, the longest nerve in the body, which runs down the back of the thigh and into the leg. There is usually tenderness in the thigh, pain along the course of the nerve, and sometimes wasting of the muscles of the calf.

A mild sciatica is usually

caused by some mild arthritic inflammation in the lower end of the spine. Cold, damp weather may aggravate it, as does any pressure on the nerve. Such pressure may arise from a tumor in the pelvic region or even from obstinate constipation. Mild cases tend to clear up with application of heat, counterirritants, massage, and aspirin. Bed rest and avoidance of exercise may be indicated in slightly more severe cases. What is called sciatica sometimes turns out to be a "slipped" or ruptured DISK in the spine, for which a surgical operation is required.

In extreme and persistent cases of sciatic pain, the most skillful medical diagnosis and treatment are necessary to get relief.

Sclera—the outer coat of the eyeball. See EYES.

Scleroderma—hardening of the skin; a rare COLLAGEN DISEASE.

Sclerosis means hardening. It is used in such terms as *arteriosclerosis* and *atherosclerosis* (HARDENING OF THE ARTERIES) and in such phrases as MULTIPLE SCLEROSIS (MS) and amyotrophic lateral sclerosis ("GEHRIG'S DISEASE"), where changes akin to hardening occur in nerve tissues and sheaths.

Scoliosis—sideward CURVATURE OF THE SPINE.

Scotoma—a blind spot in some part of the visual field; usually owing to impairment of the retina of the EYE. This word also describes the temporary effect of "spots in front of my eyes."

Scrofula—a disease; essentially TUBERCULOSIS in which the infecting tubercle bacillus primarily damages the LYMPH glands and the *skin*, sometimes the bones and joints. Once a common childhood disease, it is now exceedingly rare. In England, in the 17th and 18th centuries, it was called "the King's Evil" and was presumably cured by being touched by the King or Queen. This was a quack practice.

Scrotum—the sac of skin and muscle suspended from the groin and containing the testicles. See SEX ORGANS, MALE. In vigorous athletic contests the scrotum must usually be protected by an athletic supporter ("jock-strap").

Scurvy—a vitamin-deficiency disease. It has a long and curious history. The specific lack is vitamin C (see VITAMINS). Among the early signs of scurvy are swollen and bleeding gums and small black-and-blue spots (petechiae) on the skin. Later symptoms are loosened teeth, anemia, rapid heart, shortness of breath, sore arms and legs, and extreme weakness.

Scurvy was a disease of sailors during the days of long voyages in sailing ships. It was finally suspected that these sailors were subject to scurvy because they had no fresh fruits or vegetables. This guess turned out to be right. In the late 18th century James Lynd encouraged the admirals of the British navy to put limes, a citrus fruit rich in vitamin C, on the regular ration list. Brit- ish sailors were nicknamed "limeys," but henceforth they didn't get scurvy.

Seasickness—see MOTION SICK- NESS, EARS and EAR TROUBLE.

Sebaceous Glands—glands in the SKIN secreting sebum.

SEBORRHEA

Seborrhea is oily SKIN carried to the point of being an annoying skin disease. An excess output of *sebum* from the sebaceous glands of the skin forms greasy scales or cheesy plugs; itching and burning symptoms often occur.

In youth seborrhea, or seborrheic dermatitis, is called *acne*. Its cause is unknown; it is related to puberty, HORMONES and the de- velopment of secondary sex characteristics of youth, but no one knows exactly how. The excess oil secretion may be occurring in many parts of the body, but the place that it shows—and causes untold personal agony—is on the face.

In middle aged people seborrhea appears, or re-appears, under the name of *rosacea*. It usually affects the skin of the nose, cheeks, forehead, chin and sometimes even the eyes.

Much can be done to control acne and rosacea (seborrhea)— and there is perhaps even more that should not be done. Above all, one should avoid meddling with his skin.

The advice of a competent physician should be sought early and followed faithfully. Recommendations of drug-store clerks, glamor- ous advertisements, and so-called beauty experts should be shunned. They can ruin your skin. Don't put anything on your skin unless your doctor prescribes it.

Ointments are almost always forbidden; they overload the skin. Occasionally the doctor or skin specialist (dermatologist) will pre- scribe special cleansing lotions, containing drying agents like sul- fur and resorcin. Rarely X-ray treatments may be advised; anti- biotics and hormones are occasionally tried. But these are all pro- fessional treatment measures, never to be self-prescribed. Sunlight heals some people, makes others worse.

Eight rules for the management of acne (N. Goldsmith):

1. Do not tamper with the skin; do not pick or squeeze pustules and pimples.

2. Clean the face thoroughly but *gently;* avoid irritating soaps —however blandly advertised.

3. Watch your diet. Avoid those foods which personal experience shows has made your acne worse. Chocolates and nuts are frequent, but not inevitable, offenders. An excess of seafood containing *iodine* may sometimes make acne worse.

4. Do not put greasy ointments—or cold cream—on the skin.

5. Wash the hair frequently—preferably with a detergent shampoo—to keep the scalp free of grease.

6. Live a sensible life; get enough sleep, exercise, water, and a balanced DIET.

7. Try to control your needless worries and anxieties. Uncontrolled, they will often make your skin condition worse.

8. Get professional advice if you are worried about your skin; don't overtreat it yourself and make it worse.

Sebum—an oily substance secreted by the sebaceous glands in the SKIN.

Second-look Operation—an operation performed on cancer patients a few months after the initial operation to make sure that all cancerous tissue was removed—even though the patients do not complain of any new symptoms. Second-look cancer operations, undertaken on patients with "silent cancers" of the intestinal organs, were initiated at the University of Minnesota in 1948 and have increased the survivals of many patients.

Sedative—any drug that reduces activity and allays excitement or overt anxiety. There are literally thousands of sedative drugs, their useful effect—as sedatives—being determined largely by the doses given or taken. Most of the NARCOTICS have a sedative effect, as do the drugs also called "tranquilizers," ATARAXICS and ANESTHETICS. BARBITURATES are among the most commonly prescribed sedatives. It is common for patients to be given sedatives before administration of full anesthesia for surgical operations.

Semen—the white, slightly sticky fluid produced by the SEX ORGANS, MALE and ejaculated from them. Semen is the vehicle for SPERM. A normal ejaculate is about 2 to 5 cubic centimeters of semen, each cubic centimeter carrying 75,-000,000 to 100,000,000 sperm!

Sepsis—poisoning by MICROBES, or their by-products, in the living body. See ASEPSIS and ANTISEPTIC.

Septicemia — *blood-poisoning,* usually marked by high fever, sweating and prostration. Since sulfa drugs and antibiotics, septicemia is uncommon.

SEPTUM [464]

"Childbed fever" was once among the most killing and damaging forms of septicemia.

Septum—a wall or partition between parts of the body. Best-known is the nasal septum, the wall that runs down the middle of the NOSE and separates the left nostril from the right. It is formed of bone above and cartilage below. It is often twisted or bent—a *deviated septum*—and thus sometimes interferes with breathing efficiency. (See illustration for NOSE.)

Sequela—the sequel, the follow-after, of disease processes or accidents. Thus, for example, residual paralysis may be a sequela of acute paralytic POLIO.

Sequestrum—a small piece of dead bone that has broken loose from its mooring as a result of disease in the BONE.

Serology—the branch of science that deals with the study of ANTIGENS and ANTIBODIES that can be detected in BLOOD SERUM when blood samples are taken. The Wassermann test and other common blood tests for syphilis are serologic tests. The phrase, "Serology positive," means that disease process (usually syphilis) is still active, or that INFECTION is present. "Negative serology" means no disease detectable by serologic test.

Serum—the liquid part of the BLOOD that remains when the solid elements in it have been removed by clotting. It is *not* the same as PLASMA. Blood serum contains the ANTIBODIES and ANTIGENS that fight against disease.

Numerous serums for use in treating infections are made by immunizing animals (for example, horses) against the specific infection, withdrawing their immunized blood (containing antibodies), purifying it and then injecting it into human beings—or other animals. Serum and VACCINES, however, are *not* the same thing, although both are BIOLOGICAL products.

So-called *"truth serum"* is not a serum at all. It is a hypnotic drug, usually a BARBITURATE, injected into the veins to put the patient in a kind of semi-trance in which he will talk freely. See NARCOSYNTHESIS.

Serum Sickness—an aggravated form of ALLERGY which sometimes follows the administration of biological products containing animal SERUM. HIVES, FEVER, and skin rash are the common symptoms; usually they pass away quickly or can be readily treated. In rare instances a severe serum reaction (also called allergic shock and anaphylactic shock) may occur and cause rapid death. Horse serum is most often the offending or fatal allergen.

Sex-linked characteristics are those transmitted from parent to offspring in the same GENE, or part of the CHROMOSOME

chain, which determines whether the sex of the individual will
be male or female. Red-green
color blindness, for example, is
a sex-linked characteristic in
human HEREDITY.

SEX ORGANS, FEMALE

The female *reproductive system* (female sex organs) consists of a
pair of *ovaries,* a pair of *tubes* leading from them, the *uterus* or
womb, the *vagina, external genitals,* and some accessory *glands.*
The breasts, or mammary glands, are sometimes considered part
of this system. Since the sex organs have a close anatomical relationship to the URINARY SYSTEM, both together are often described as the *genitourinary* or *urogenital* system.

All the important female sex organs are located inside the body.
The whole system is greatly influenced at all times by hormones
produced both in the ovaries and in other ENDOCRINE glands. Any
endocrine upset has some effect on the activity of the female sex
organs.

The female sex organs have at least three functions: to produce
and yield mature ova (human eggs) for union with viable SPERM,
to shelter and nourish the fertilized egg cell until it has developed
into a newborn baby, and to elaborate female sex hormones. The
fundamental relationship of man to woman in human society is
based on the fact that, as in other mammals, the female must
bear the children who assure the perpetuation of the human race.

CONCEPTION of a new life takes place within the female sexual
apparatus (generally in the tubes). The childbearing period is
limited, running roughly from early teens to middle forties. The
onset of MENSTRUATION (menarche) at puberty marks the beginning of the childbearing years, which terminate at the MENOPAUSE,
or "change of life." A woman's ability to conceive and bear
children does not depend on the intensity of her sexual feelings,
or libido. It is not necessary for her to have an ORGASM to become
pregnant.

Ovaries: The ovaries, or female gonads, are two small glands,
each about the size and shape of an almond, set in the pelvic cavity (lower abdomen), just below the navel. One is about three
inches to the right and the other the same distance to the left of
the midline of the body. The ovaries do two jobs: they bring ova
to a point of readiness for impregnation,· and they secrete hormones.

A normal woman has about 50,000 ova, or egg cells, in her two

THE FEMALE REPRODUCTIVE SYSTEM

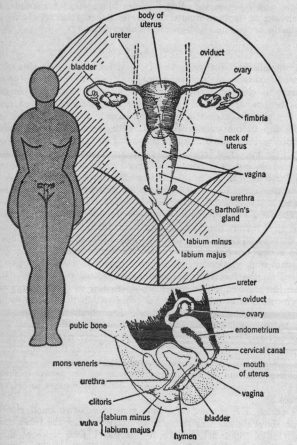

The upper diagram in the circle is a straight front view. The lower diagram is a side view, a front-to-back section through the center of the body.

ovaries. These were laid down in immature form early in the
course of her life before birth, in her mother's womb. These egg
cells do not ripen or become mature until puberty. Then, with the
onset of menstruation and ovulation, they mature at about the rate
of one a month. Each egg cell matures in its own little "nest," or
pocket, called a *Graafian follicle*. A complicated hormone pattern,
in which the follicle is greatly concerned, controls this ripening
process. It is a repeating, cyclic process, called the menstrual or
ovulatory cycle. (See MENSTRUATION.) The release of the mature
ovum from its follicle is called OVULATION. This usually occurs at
about the midpoint of the menstrual cycle. Sometimes more than
one mature ovum is released at the same time, as evidenced by
the birth of fraternal TWINS.

The hormones released by the ovaries have several functions.
They help to govern the monthly rhythm of ovulation and menstruation. They do this in part by their effect on other endocrine
glands. Furthermore, these hormones spur the development and
maintenance of secondary sex characteristics; for example, de-
positing of fat under the skin to give the characteristic feminine
curves, enlargement of the breasts, growth of pubic hair.

"The tubes": When the matured egg cell escapes from its follicle, it is caught or picked up in the far end of "the tubes," more
properly known as Fallopian tubes (after Fallopius, the Italian
anatomist who described them), uterine tubes, or oviducts. Each
of the two uterine tubes is about 3 to 5 inches long. Its lower end
clearly opens into the uterus. Its trumpet-shaped far end, however,
is not really attached to the ovary. It just lies close to it and holds
out fingerlike projections (called fimbria) toward it, reaching for
the ripened egg.

The upper, inner lining of the tubes has little hairlike organs,
called *cilia*, which by waving back and forth carry the egg down
the tube. This action is essential because the egg itself has no
power of locomotion. The journey down the tubes takes 3 to 6
days. This is the time and place at which the egg must meet and
be penetrated by a viable sperm if pregnancy is to occur.

The fertilized egg normally completes its journey to the uterus.
About once in 500 times, however, it implants itself in the tube,
causing a tubal, or *ectopic, pregnancy*. This is a serious emergency,
demanding surgery.

If both uterine tubes are blocked, usually as a result of inflammatory disease, pregnancy cannot occur. A common test to tell whether the tubes are open (patent) is to blow air into them.

The *uterus*, or womb, is the central organ of the female reproductive system. Nonpregnant, it lies just above and slightly behind the urinary bladder, in the center of the pelvic cavity. Swollen with pregnancy, the womb fills a large part of the lower abdomen, displacing other organs as it rises.

The nonpregnant womb is a hollow, pear-shaped pouch of muscle, about 3 inches long and 2 inches wide. The stem of the pear points down. This narrower, lower end is called the *cervix*, or neck, of the womb. The upper round portion, where the embryo actually grows, is called the body, or fundus, of the womb. The uterus is held in place, loosely, by a number of ligaments. This looseness of attachment is essential, because it permits the changes in shape, size, and position of the womb that occur during pregnancy. It is also the reason why the womb can be "tipped" (uterine displacement).

The uterine muscle is one of the strongest in the body. It has to be to expel a full-grown, newborn infant when the time comes.

The inner lining (*endometrium*) of the womb is one of the most unusual tissues in the body. A soft, velvety tissue, greatly influenced by hormones, heavily interlaced with blood vessels, it grows and degenerates in the monthly cycle of ovulation and menstruation. It is prepared monthly for the reception of a fertilized ovum. When this fails to arrive, the inner lining degenerates and sloughs off, breaking some small blood vessels in the process. This is the source of menstrual bleeding, sometimes described as "the tears of a disappointed womb."

When a fertilized ovum does arrive in the uterus, it embeds itself in the uterine wall. Then it forms the structures that feed and protect it—the placenta, interlocked with the blood vessels of the womb; and the amniotic sac, the "bag of waters" or elastic bottle, inside which the embryo and fetus develop.

The lower end of the cervix, called its os or mouth, extends into the upper vault of the vagina. A short cervical canal passes through it. Male sperm must get through this canal to reach the uterus and the uterine tubes above it. If this canal is plugged with mucus, or otherwise blocked, conception cannot occur.

The uterus is generally blamed for all FEMALE TROUBLES (which see), but this is not true. Any of the internal female sex organs can be responsible for female trouble or STERILITY.

The *vagina* serves both as the female organ of intercourse and the birth canal through which the newborn infant enters the world. It is a tubular cavity, about 3 or 4 inches long, extending from the cleft of the legs to and beyond the mouth of the womb. It is set at an angle of about 45 degrees to the front of the abdomen, and just below the bladder. The muscles that make up the vaginal tube can be greatly stretched without harm. The inner lining is mucous membrane, which liberally secretes mucus during sexual excitation.

Accessory glands also secrete mucus during sexual excitation, thus lubricating the vagina. These are *Bartholin's glands,* two small oval glands located on each side of the vagina, near its external opening; and *Skene's glands,* multiple small secreting glands located near the opening of the urethra into the vaginal vestibule.

External genitals of the female, also called the vulva, include the *labia* ("lips") and the *clitoris.* The labia consist of elongated folds of skin covering fatty tissue. The outer pair, *labia majora,* are covered with hair in the adult woman. The inner pair, *labia minora,* are thinner folds of tissue covered with mucous membrane. At the far forward fold of labia minora is the clitoris. This organ is the homologue (similar structure) of the male penis, though much smaller and *not* a passageway for urine. The clitoris consists of erectile tissue which responds, like the penis, to sexual stimulation by becoming engorged with blood. It is usually, but not necessarily, the most sexually sensitive (erogenous) organ in the female body.

The *mons veneris* (mount of Venus) is a mound of fatty tissue just above the external genitals. It is covered with pubic hair. The *hymen,* or MAIDENHEAD, is a membrane that partly closes the vagina.

SEX ORGANS, MALE

The male sex organs comprise the male *reproductive system,* whose design and purpose is to deliver a living SPERM to fertilize the OVUM (egg) produced in the SEX ORGANS, FEMALE. Since it is linked in some places with the URINARY SYSTEM, the whole apparatus is sometimes called the *genitourinary* or the *urogenital system.*

The male sex organs, located partly inside and partly outside the body proper, include the *testes* (also called male gonads), *epididymes, spermatic cords, prostate gland, seminal vesicles, urethra, penis,* and *accessory glands.*

Testes: Two testes, or testicles, each about the size of a walnut, are enclosed in a sac of skin, called the *scrotum,* suspended from the groin. Hanging outside the body, between the legs, the scrotum has a temperature slightly lower than the rest of the body; this appears to be an essential condition for production of sperm. The testes normally descend from the abdomen into the cooler scrotum just before or shortly after birth. If they fail to descend (undescended testes, cryptorchidism), medical or surgical treatment may be needed.

The first important function of the testes is to manufacture sperm. This takes place, so far as is known, in a series of little twisted (convoluted) tubules, where the sperm develop from immature sex cells laid down in these membranes early in the life of the embryo. Mature sperm, capable of fertilizing an ovum, do not appear until puberty. The testes may continue producing sperm, though at a slower rate, well into old age, as is evidenced by the not infrequent birth of children to aged fathers. From collecting tubes in the testes, the sperm move on to a series of ducts, beginning with the epididymes, through which they are eventually conveyed outside the body.

The second important task of the testes is to manufacture the *male sex hormone, testosterone,* which brings about development of secondary sex characteristics at puberty: growth of beard and pubic hair, deeper voice, comparatively rapid increase in size of the male sex organs, and general muscular development. The male sex hormone is produced in a set of specialized cells located in the tissues that support the tubules making sperm; a lesser amount is elaborated by the *adrenal glands.* The testes are part of the *endocrine* system. They are not absolutely essential, however, to the feeling of sexual desire or the performance of the sex act. Eunuchs, or castrates, whose testicles have been removed, are still capable of sexual intercourse.

Epididymes: These are coiled-up tubes, several feet long but looking like a twisted ball of string, attached like a hood or pouch to the outer surface of each testicle. They collect and store sperm. In them the sperm become mature and motile, that is, capable of moving under their own power. However, they do not do this until they are discharged from the body. They are propelled

THE MALE REPRODUCTIVE SYSTEM

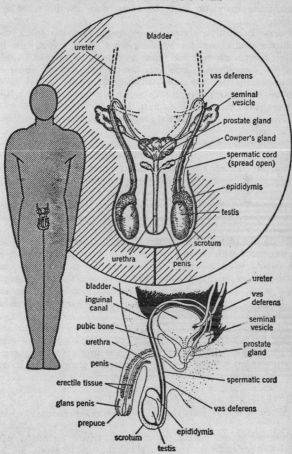

The upper diagram in the circle is a straight front view. The lower diagram is a side view shown as if a section had been made a little to one side of the center of the body, from front to back.

through the spermatic ducts by contractions of the tubes and tubules.

Spermatic cords, or *ducts,* convey sperm from the epididymes up to the seminal vesicles. Winding tubes, about a foot long, including the *vas deferens* and other structures, the spermatic cords, one from each testicle, issue from the scrotum into the abdomen by way of the inguinal canal—which, incidentally, is the site of inguinal *hernia* or RUPTURE. Spermatic cords can be felt where they pass over the pubic bone near the base of the penis. Cutting the cords near this point is the simplest operation for *sterilization* of the male.

Seminal vesicles are the upper outlets of the spermatic cord. They are two small pouches or sacs located in the abdomen just behind the bladder. They secrete a large part of the thick, white, alkaline fluid, *semen,* in which the sperm float. Like the rubber bulb on an eye dropper, they can contract vigorously and spurt or squirt semen out into the *urethra,* the mucus-lined tube that traverses the penis and carries urine as well as semen. (See URINARY SYSTEM.)

Ejaculation of semen from the seminal vesicles is a nerve-reflex act, associated with the sensation called *orgasm.* The motor nerves that control orgasm respond to both physiological and psychic stimuli. The stimulating impulses usually arise in the head (glans) of the penis. The distention of the seminal vesicles with an accumulation of semen may also prompt the discharge of semen as a nocturnal emission ("wet dream").

The *prostate gland,* normally about the size of a walnut and roughly heart-shaped, is located just below the bladder and seminal vesicles. It encircles the neck of the urethra as it emerges from the bladder. Anatomically, the prostate gland is the homologue (similar structure) of the female womb. But the function of the prostate gland is not very important, and it can be dispensed with. The gland secretes an alkaline fluid that makes up part of the semen. It is frequently the source of PROSTATE TROUBLE, which see.

Accessory glands among the male sex organs include a pair called *Cowper's glands.* They are about the size of a pea, are located near the base of the penis, and open into the urethra. They secrete a clear, oily lubricating fluid. A few drops of this fluid may come out of the penis following sexual excitation not carried to the point of orgasm.

The *penis*, a cylindrical organ suspended from the front and sides of the groin, is the male organ of intercourse, designed for delivery of semen into the vagina. Enlargement, or erection, of the penis is necessary for this function. This occurs when the normally retracted and flaccid organ becomes engorged with blood. The shaft and head of the penis are composed of a spongy, cavernous, erectile tissue, traversed by many blood channels. When stimulated, these channels become filled with blood, whose immediate return to the rest of the circulation is temporarily cut off by constriction of the veins leading away from the penis. Under conditions of adequate sexual excitation, erection of the penis is a normal, natural, and inescapable reaction of the male animal—part of nature's design to assure perpetuation of the species.

The penis is covered with loose folds of skin, allowing for enlargement. The extra skin at the tip, or glans, is called the *foreskin* or *prepuce*. The operation for its removal is known as *circumcision*. The size of the penis increases markedly at puberty. Except in rare cases where this development fails, the size of the penis has no relationship with ability to obtain and give satisfaction in marital relations.

Disorders of the male sex organs: The ability of the male sex organs to produce and deliver viable sperm may be impaired by malformations, disease, and accident. Several types of congenital malformation of the penis occur; notably a condition (hypospadias) in which the urethra opens on the under surface of the penis instead of at its tip. Again, the foreskin may be or become so tight that it cannot be pulled back over the tip of the penis (phimosis), a condition usually requiring circumcision for correction. Sometimes fluid accumulates in the scrotal sac (hydrocele) or the veins in the spermatic cord become greatly and evidently dilated (varicocele). Enlargement of the prostate is common at older ages.

The urethra and all the other ducts through which sperm and semen flow are subject to infection and inflammation. Before sulfa drugs and antibiotics, *gonorrhea* was the most common cause of chronic *urethritis* and *epididymitis,* often resulting in male sterility.

Formation of sperm in the testes may be temporarily arrested by any disease that induces a high fever. Greater and more lasting damage to the sperm-forming tubules can result from certain liver diseases, excessive exposure to radiation, and chronic alcoholism. Any chronic wasting disease may cause atrophy of the testes. Inflammation of the testes (orchitis) may occur as a result of MUMPS, a common virus disease of childhood, or other severe infectious diseases, such as typhoid fever.

Shaking Palsy—PARKINSON'S DISEASE.

Shigella—a MICROBE, BACTE-RIUM, which causes diarrhea, dysentery, and other bowel ailments.

Shingles—*herpes zoster; zona;* a virus infection, perhaps caused by the same virus *(Briareus varicella)* that brings on CHICKEN POX. The disease is mild in children, becomes increasingly serious and severe with age. In old people it can be a long-lasting, painful, and distressing affliction. Except for pain (neuralgia), the principal symptoms appear on the skin. However, it is essentially a disease of the NERVES. The invading virus concentrates its attack on nerve ganglia, particularly the spinal nerves that supply the chest and one of the nerves (5th cranial) that supplies the face.

The skin lesions appear along the sites supplied by the infected nerve centers. The first symptom is usually a crop of small blisters on reddened bases. They can appear anywhere on the body, but they generally come out first on one side of the chest or face. There is an ancient superstition that if the crop of blisters completely encircles the chest, the patient will die. This is nonsense. When the nerves that supply the side of the face and the forehead are attacked by the

virus, the eye also may be involved. This can be followed by damage to the cornea.

Sometimes the little blisters are so numerous that they run together to form large blisters and even ulcers, which leave scars when healing. Usually, however, if the skin is kept clean, the blisters dry up and heal in 2 to 4 weeks. In older people, however, the neuralgic pain often persists for weeks or months after the blisters heal.

There is no specific treatment for shingles. A variety of symptomatic treatments relieve the pains; e.g. heat to the spinal cord, pain-killing injections, ACTH and cortisone, and antihistaminic drugs.

Shock has many meanings: primarily, the rapid and sometimes fatal *fall in* BLOOD PRESSURE following injury, operation or the administration of anesthesia. It also means ELECTRIC *shock,* caused by a passage of electricity through the body, and the electric-shock or insulin-shock treatment ("shock therapy") given in some cases of MENTAL ILLNESS.

The word also refers to *psychic shock,* the emotional experience that follows a sudden, terrorizing event; to *anaphylactic shock,* the violent and fatal reaction to a second dose of some drug or serum to which a person has become abnormally sensitized; and to many other kinds of shock, like *"shell shock,"* which is a form of mental illness.

The basic reasons for the occurrence of shock following injury—such as a skull fracture —or surgery remain unknown, despite great and continuing research attention to the problem. Main effort today is given .to preventing and treating shock promptly, if it should occur.

The well-observed basic mechanism in the presence of shock is a decrease in the circulating fluids of the BLOOD; that is why extreme, uncontrolled bleeding and large blood loss also produce shock.

When a patient goes into shock, he turns pale, his skin becomes moist and clammy, his blood pressure falls, his pulse becomes fast and feeble, his breathing slows down, he often complains of thirst, he becomes restless, anxious and sometimes unconscious.

The *immediate treatment* of shock is to keep the patient lying down at rest and warm— but not too warm. The legs may be elevated, the limbs loosely bandaged (to improve the circulation). PLASMA or whole BLOOD infusions into the veins are often required to restore blood volume. This was the common use for Red-Cross-collected blood and plasma on the battlefield; and it is one of the commonest indications for blood bank usage in a hospital. Drugs that raise blood pressure (for example, adrenalin) must often be administered to combat shock.

Shoes—see FOOT TROUBLE.

"SHOTS"

"Shots" is the popular term for *injections*. Such shots are given to treat and prevent disease and to relieve pain. Most shots are given into the muscles (intramuscular injection), usually in big muscles like the buttocks or the upper arm. Some are given under the skin (subcutaneous or hypodermic), some between the layers of the skin (intradermal), a few directly into the veins (intravenous).

Do shots do any good? It all depends on what's in them and when they are given. And how the person reacts!

A shot ("hypo") of MORPHINE, ¼ gr., or other painkilling drug, if not contraindicated, is almost certain to relieve pain promptly. (See NARCOTICS.)

Young babies, beginning at about the 3rd month of life, should get shots to protect them against DIPHTHERIA, WHOOPING COUGH, LOCKJAW (tetanus), and POLIO; also SMALLPOX vaccine.

Under special circumstances, when they are exposed to undue risk of infection, adults can get protection against a number of diseases by taking shots; namely, CHOLERA, PLAGUE, TYPHUS FEVER, TYPHOID and PARATYPHOID FEVER, YELLOW FEVER, ROCKY MOUNTAIN SPOTTED FEVER; possibly INFLUENZA, pneumococcal infections, and TUBERCULOSIS.

RABIES shots should be taken by anyone bitten by an animal known or strongly suspected to have rabies.

(See IMMUNITY and IMMUNIZATION.)

Cold shots given for prevention of the COMMON COLD are usually *autogenous* VACCINES and not usually effective.

Hay-fever shots, given in a series of injections before the hay-fever season, include increasingly large doses of the pollens to which the individual is presumably sensitive. This process is called desensitization. It works for some people but not for others. (See HAY FEVER; ALLERGY.)

Most people prefer to take pills or liquids if they need medicine, but there are a few people who feel that they have not been properly treated unless the doctor gives them a shot. This is nonsense. The reasons for giving shots instead of pills are several, as follows:

Some medicines, particularly biologicals (e.g. insulin, liver extract), cannot be given by mouth because they are largely destroyed or rendered impotent by the stomach juices and are very poorly absorbed through the gastrointestinal tract.

Drugs given by injection are more quickly and certainly absorbed in the blood stream, and they take effect more quickly. Conversely, by adding certain fats and oils to some injected drugs, their rate of absorption into the blood stream can be controlled and spread evenly over a fairly long and definite period of time. Examples are PENICILLIN in peanut oil, and slow-acting INSULIN.

In many cases the dose of a drug given by mouth must be 5 or 10 times higher than the same drug given by injection. If it is an expensive drug, the shot is much cheaper.

Shoulder—the large joint where the upper limbs join the trunk. It is subject to the same kind of troubles that assail other JOINTS. See ARTHRITIS, JOINTS, FRACTURE, BURSITIS, etc. The simple treatment for a bruised or painful shoulder is usually gentle MASSAGE and heat. A *frozen shoulder* is one which greatly limits the excursions of the arm because the joint capsule itself has suffered some kind of damage (usually fibrositis, a form of ARTHRITIS). In some athletic events the shoulder muscles themselves are severely overtaxed, pushed too far beyond their normal stretch. Baseball pitchers often have sore arms for this reason. The fundamental treatment is *rest* of the arm, often reinforced with a shoulder sling or splinting, with pain eased by drugs (for example, aspirin) and the application of moist or dry heat.

Sialorrhea—secretion, presumably excessive, of SALIVA.

Siderosis—lung disease resulting from inhalation of iron dust or other metallic particles.

Sigmoid—the S-shaped curve of the large bowel; the part of the intestine just before the rectum. See DIGESTIVE SYSTEM.

Sign—an indication that disease or disorder of some sort is present. A sign is always an objective signal. It can be seen or elicited by the examining physician; for example, a skin rash is a sign of disease. Doctors use signs to make or confirm diagnosis of disease. Signs differ from SYMPTOMS, which are what the patient feels—for example, nausea and headache. These cannot be seen or felt.

Silicosis—lung disease caused by inhalation of stone or sand dust, containing silicon dioxide. It is an ancient, and once common, occupational or industrial disease found in stone-cutters, quarry workers, grinders using unprotected grinding wheels. It is often complicated by TUBERCULOSIS; the constant assault of the lungs by the dust particles softens them up for increasing activity on the part of tubercle bacilli that may be present. Modern safety engineering has eliminated most of the industrial hazards that once commonly produced silicosis.

Singultus—HICCUP (HICCOUGH).

Sinus—a channel or cavity. This word has many medical meanings, including—most commonly—air cavities in the frontal bones of the skull (the paranasal sinuses), widened channels for venous blood, and even fistulas, particularly of the anus. (See illustration for NOSE.)

Sinusitis—inflammation of a SINUS; most commonly refers to the paranasal sinuses.

SINUS TROUBLE

Sinus trouble, or sinusitis, is a common affliction among people who live in temperate or cold climates where the common cold and other upper respiratory infections are frequently encountered. Seasonal and even daily changes of weather often have an adverse effect upon sinus trouble.

The nasal sinuses are part of the respiratory system. They are cavities in the face and skull bones where inspired air is slightly warmed before proceeding to the lungs. The cavities are lined with mucous membrane, like the canals of the nostrils to which the sinuses are connected. The sinus in the cheekbone is designated as the *antrum;* that above the eyes, the *frontal sinus;* the deep one, behind the nose, the *ethmoidal sinus.*

Sinus trouble is often indicated when pressure against the upper socket of the eye gives a pain response out of proportion to the pressure applied.

The discomfort of sinus trouble originates principally from the inflammation and swelling of the mucous membranes lining the sinuses. This, in turn, is a response to acute or long-standing infection. The first problem in sinusitis therefore is to get rid of the underlying infection. Antibiotic and sulfa drugs, given by mouth, are often prescribed. Local topical applications of medicine to the inside of the sinuses are not likely to do much good. In fact, they sometimes irritate the mucous membrane to the point where it remains uncomfortably swollen as a result of chemical injury.

However, the withdrawal of accumulated mucus in the sinuses is often necessary to relieve the headache and pressure symptoms resulting from the disease. A gentle cleansing with mild saline solution is often required. Negative pressure apparatus which, like a small vacuum cleaner, sucks the mucus and pus, if any, out of the sinus cavity must often be used by the doctor.

The shrinking of the mucous membranes of the nose and sinus can often be accomplished by the application of drugs like adrenalin, amphetamine and ephedrine. Occasionally these drugs are given by inhalation. The inhaler frequently used by people with colds, if used too frequently, may do more harm than good. It will give immediate temporary relief, but, by irritating the mucous membranes, leave the inflammatory condition worse than it was before.

Sinus sufferers, especially those with chronic or recurrent sinusitis, must unhappily recognize that it sometimes takes weeks or months to relieve the condition. A well-balanced diet and a good regime of living are helpful. It is especially inadvisable to demand surgery for immediate relief.

The prevention of sinus trouble is of first importance. People subject to this condition should avoid swimming, diving, and overtaxing outdoor exercise. When the weather is cold, they should *sleep with the windows closed.* Cold air irritates and overstimulates the mucous membranes of the sinuses, especially during the period of lowered metabolism characteristic of sleep. (See illustration for NOSE.)

Sippy Diet—a 28-day diet prescribed for some patients with peptic ulcer (see STOMACH TROUBLE). It begins with milk alone, to which are gradually added in increasing amounts crackers, cereals, eggs, and homogenized vegetables. It was

named after an early 20th-century Chicago doctor, Bertram W. Sippy.

Skeleton—the bones of the body when fastened in their usual relative position to each other. (See illustrations for BONES.)

SKIN

The skin is really the largest organ in the body and one of the most complex. It has an area of approximately 17 square feet and weighs about 5 pounds.

Dr. Logan Clendening described the skin as "one of the most interesting and mystic of structures . . . that outer rampart which separates us from the rest of the universe, the sack which contains that juice or essence which is me, or which is you, a moat defensive against insects, poisons, germs. . . . The very storms of the soul are recorded upon it."

The epidermis, or outer skin, consists of two layers—the horny top layer of dry dead cells, constantly being shed, and the growing layer that replaces the dead cells with new cells. This growing layer includes the pigmented Malpighian cells, which help to determine the skin color.

Directly beneath the epidermis, and several times thicker, is the *dermis,* or *true skin,* also called the *corium.* It consists of tough, fibrous, living tissue, with an undulating surface that is reflected in the distinctive ridges of the outer skin.

The dermis contains millions of capillary BLOOD vessels, LYMPH vessels, NERVE endings, sebaceous glands, and sweat glands. Hair follicles also start here.

The capillaries nourish the skin, and deliver waste products to the sweat glands.

The nerve endings report to the brain sensations of pressure, roughness or smoothness, heat, cold, and pain.

The HAIR follicles are tiny tubes, each harboring a hair root. Close by lie the *sebaceous glands,* which secrete an oily substance called *sebum* that helps keep the hair lustrous and the skin soft. The conditions known as *dry skin* and *oily skin* result from too little or too much activity of these glands.

The skin has from 2 to 3 million *sweat glands,* with special concentrations in the armpits, on the hands and feet, and on the fore-

THE HUMAN SKIN

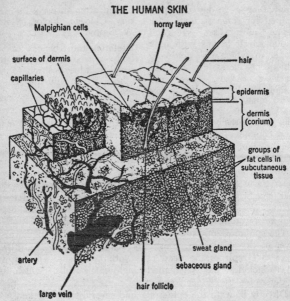

Malpighian cells

horny layer

surface of dermis

capillaries

hair

epidermis

dermis (corium)

groups of fat cells in subcutaneous tissue

artery

sweat gland

sebaceous gland

large vein

hair follicle

The skin has a more complicated structure than appears on the surface of the body. This neatly blocked-out piece of skin tissue reveals the various layers and underlying structures of the human skin. The blood vessels, shown in black and white, are very numerous; however, they are shown only in the left half of the drawing.

head. These glands extract water, salt, and waste substances from the capillaries, and release them at the skin surfaces through small openings, or *pores*.

We sweat all the time, even when we don't feel it. Our invisible perspiration, evaporated as quickly as it appears, may amount to a quart a day.

The dermis rests on a thick layer of *subcutaneous tissue*, infiltrated with fat cells. This layer softens the contours of the body, and serves as a cushion between muscles and skin.

The skin is the body's maid-of-all-work. Besides separating us from the outside world, it regulates our temperature, warns us of dangers in the immediate environment, resists bacteria, and eliminates waste products. Because the skin mirrors both physical and mental states, it also serves doctors as a general health indicator.

Body temperature is regulated by means of the capillaries and sweat glands. When we are hot the capillaries expand, spreading the blood out over a wider surface. At the same time we sweat. The sweat evaporates, producing a drop in temperature at the skin surface and cooling the blood.

The odor of perspiration is caused by the small amounts of waste products it carries. Attempts to neutralize this odor should not check perspiration, for it is a natural and healthy process.

Bacterial resistance of the skin and the mucous membranes is quite high. So long as the skin is clean and whole, it quickly rids itself of most unwelcome bacteria.

Another protective device is the release of melanin pigment produced by the Malpighian cells, to shield against skin injury from the sun. The result is a coat of *tan,* or sometimes a crop of *freckles.* Since the cells produce pigment only gradually, an attempt to get tanned all at once may produce a *sunburn.* This is as dangerous as any other BURN, and should be treated similarly.

Moderate doses of sun help the body produce vitamin D, and also stimulate the growth of red blood corpuscles. But excessive exposure, even when it doesn't cause burns, may lead to dryness and even, occasionally, to precancerous growths.

The best *skin care* for most persons is regular use of ordinary, nonmedicated soap and water. No better cleansing agent has been devised. Cleanliness, rather than special soaps, is the best preventive of *body odor.*

The skin can't be "nourished" by creams or lotions or "skin foods" applied from outside because, like all body tissues, it is nourished only through its blood supply. Plain cold cream may be useful as a cleanser and lubricant for dry skin, but adding vitamins or hormones to cold cream or other skin preparations is useless.

There's no reason why a woman shouldn't use COSMETICS to cover up defects and bring herself closer to her beauty ideals. But good health is by far the most potent cosmetic. No rouge or foundation cream can rival the ruddy glow of a healthy skin.

Don't fall for miracle promises in cosmetic advertising. The following types of products, for example, are misleadingly labeled, for no product known can fulfill the promises their names imply: contour cream, crow's-foot cream, deep pore cleaner, enlarged pore preparation, eye-wrinkle cream, miracle oil, nourishing cream, pore paste, rejuvenating cream, scalp food, skin conditioner, skin firm, skin food, skin tonic, eyelash grower, wrinkle eradicator, spot reducer, bust developer, bust reducer. See SKIN TROUBLES.

SKIN TROUBLES

Skin troubles are technically described as dermatosis and dermatitis. Hundreds of skin disorders have been named and classified; many have long and complicated names. All of them, however, represent the response of the skin to some insult or assault from within or without the body.

Contact dermatitis, of which poison ivy is a typical example, is the most common skin disorder produced by outside agents. To fight against such agents, the skin pours forth lymph fluid, which forms blisters. Along with the blisters may come a burning sensation, itching, redness, and swelling. Fungus infections are also common.

Skin inflammations, rashes, and pustules may arise also from systemic infections of the body—the assault from the inside. Among the systemic diseases which write their signature on the skin are smallpox, chicken pox, measles, scarlet fever, and syphilis.

Welts, wheals, and bumps sometimes appear on the skin in protest, one might say, against something in the victim or his environment to which he is peculiarly sensitive. In other words, hives are a sign of allergy.

The diagnosis and treatment of skin troubles is tricky and requires expert medical judgment. The attempt to treat skin troubles at home often makes them worse. "Overtreatment dermatitis" frequently occurs when home and drugstore remedies are applied.

For more information on specific skin ailments, see the following headings in this book: BIRTHMARKS, BOILS, DERMATOPHYTOSIS, ECZEMA, ERYSIPELAS, FOOT TROUBLE (for treatment of ATHLETE'S FOOT and WARTS), HERPES, HIVES, IMPETIGO, INTERTRIGO, ITCH (scabies), ITCHING, LUPUS, MOLES, PEMPHIGUS, PITYRIASIS, POISON IVY, PRICKLY HEAT, PSORIASIS, RASH, RINGWORM, SEBORRHEA (for ACNE and ROSACEA), SHINGLES, VITILIGO; ALLERGY, FUNGUS.

Skull—the sturdy bones that make up the head (cranium) and the face. There are 8 bones in the cranium (not counting the little bones of the ear) and 14 to shape the face.

The bones of the skull are slightly movable at birth. However, they soon become fused with one another and form a solid bony structure. (See illustration for BRAIN.)

A fractured skull is a dangerous but not necessarily fatal occurrence, the result of violence. The danger signs are UN-CONSCIOUSNESS, BLEEDING from the mouth or ears, and deranged breathing—too heavy or too shallow. Get adequate medical attention immediately when any one of these signs occurs! See FRACTURES.

SLEEP

A human being spends approximately a third of his life in sleep. Yet for an activity—or perhaps, lack of activity—so common and universal, we still know surprisingly little about its fundamental mechanisms. The most scientific explanations of the function of sleep do not surpass Shakespeare's 17th century description:

> Sleep that knits up the ravell'd sleave of care,
> The death of each day's life, sore labour's bath,
> Balm of hurt minds, great nature's second course,
> Chief nourisher in life's feast.

There are many theories about sleep, but none is universally accepted. On the other hand, many extended and acute scientific observations have been made to illuminate the nature of sleep and the effects of lack of it. The longest that a man has been known to go without sleep and survive is a little over 9 days. Why do human beings and other animals sleep? They sleep because they must rest. The rhythm of sleep and wakefulness, commonly within the 24-hour pattern of a day, comes as close as anything we know to being a law of nature.

What happens during sleep? Most obviously, the sleeper becomes unconscious, unaware, and more or less unresponsive to the environment about him. However, this is a relative matter. Some senses and some parts of the body remain more alert and more in function than others. For example, a sleeper may sleep through a loud noise but awake at the lightest touch. Again, while the lungs and heart may work more slowly during sleep, the sweat glands and some parts of the brain and nervous system may become more active. The increased, even though temporary, activity of the nervous system is the explanation of dreams, sleepwalking (somnambulism), and talking in one's sleep. Exactly why these events occur to a specific person on a given night cannot be explained. But the fact of their occurrence demonstrates that sleep and waking are both part of the same cycle of living. It is questionable whether the unconscious mind ever completely rests. Anxiety, certainly, is one of the great enemies of sleep.

Most of the measurable physiological functions of the body are diminished during sleep. Thus, the body temperature falls, indicating a decline in metabolism generally and a decrease in the tone of muscles. Indeed, muscular relaxation is one of the key components of sleep. Practically all the systems of the body take things easier during sleep, although they never give up their normal functions completely. Thus, the heart beats more slowly, blood pressure and pulse rate fall, breathing is slower, secretions from nearly all glands diminish.

But sleep is more than a time of rest and relaxation. It is also a time of recuperation and repair, of growth and regrowth. During the normal course of living, cells of the body wear out and must be replaced. This regeneration takes place more rapidly during sleep. It has been shown, for example, that the epithelial cells of the skin divide and make new cells about twice as fast during sleep.

How much sleep does a person need? There is no hard and fast answer to this question, either for children or adults. The amount of sleep a person needs is directly related to his rate of growth. Hence, rapidly growing infants need more sleep than children; children more than adults. Again in old age, when the reparative processes of the body are less active, an increase in sleep may sometimes be required. Furthermore, during the period of recovery from a debilitating illness or operation (convalescence) and in some stages of pregnancy, added increments of sleep or rest may be essential.

Research indicates that sleep requirements are a highly individual matter, governed by many factors. These include age, general state of health, current activities, emotional outlook, and previous sleeping habits. Most adults sleep 6 to 8 hours out of 24. But some need more, a few less. Occasionally a person "drugs" himself with too much sleep and fails to get his full measure of living. Victims of NARCOLEPSY cannot help falling asleep during the day.

The people who claim to get along on very little sleep at night usually do some of their sleeping during the day. They take short naps and they have usually mastered the art of relaxation.

The test of whether or not you are getting enough sleep is a simple, practical, and individual one. You are getting enough if you wake up in the morning refreshed and ready for the new day. The first half hour after arising can be discounted in applying this test, because it takes varying lengths of time for metabolism to rise to a level of full wakefulness.

Occasional loss of sleep will not have harmful effects. Under conditions of military necessity men have often gone 48 or 72 hours without sleep and recovered with 10 or 12 hours of rest and sleep. Even test subjects who have been kept awake as long as 200 hours have not suffered significant physiological changes. Of course, these subjects do exhibit some temporary psychological deficits; they become restless, irritable, and unable to do mental arithmetic accurately.

Children's sleeping habits are a matter of great concern to parents, who frequently feel that their children are not getting enough sleep. But this again is a highly individualized matter. In one study of the sleeping habits of nearly 800 children aged 2 and 3 years, it was found that they slept 13 hours, on the average. However, some slept only 8 hours, others as long as 17. A newborn infant usually sleeps 22 hours out of 24. This sleep requirement gradually dwindles down to about 12 hours at age 6, 9½ hours at age 12, and 8 hours in the later teens. Again the test is whether or not the child is sufficiently rested and does not drowse through the day.

What is the best position for sleeping? There is none. Any position in which you are comfortable will serve. It is the common practice in Western society to sleep in a bed. But there are some primitive people who sleep in a squatting position. The Japanese sleep on the ground or floor without mattresses. Sailors manage to get a good night's rest in hammocks. And, as every college student knows, almost anyone can learn to sleep sitting up.

The concept expressed in the phrase "sleeping like a log" is a complete fallacy. Many studies made with concealed cameras and other recording devices have definitely established that the sound sleeper (in a bed) changes his position frequently, sometimes every 10 or 15 minutes. These changes in position apparently operate to give different muscle groups fuller opportunity for relaxation.

What makes for sound sleep? First it must be recognized that some hours of sleep are deeper or "sounder" than others. These 2 to 4 hours of deep sleep, whether they come before or after midnight, are the important ones in the body's recuperative process. The different levels of sleep can be detected in "brain wave" patterns. The factors that make for sound sleep are many and often highly individual. They include both physical and psychological factors. For the most part we take them for granted and become aware of them only when they are missing or changed. Darkness, quiet, favorable room temperature, and an accustomed, comfortable bed favor a good night's sleep. So do regular sleeping habits—that is, going to bed about the same time almost every night—and a balanced pattern of living that is free from repeated, abnormal tensions. A satisfying day is usually an invitation to a refreshing night's sleep.

Why can't I sleep? Insomnia (sleeplessness) is a common complaint. Many people who utter this complaint are getting more sleep than they think; they remember the hours they were tossing about and forget the time they were asleep.

Everyone has occasional sleepless nights, usually after a particularly worrisome day. But persistent insomnia deserves a careful medical check-up and not frantic self-medication.

Excessive fatigue is sometimes a cause of insomnia; a person may be just too tired to sleep. On the other hand, mild exercise, like a short walk before going to bed, may induce sleep.

Eating habits may be a factor in insomnia. One person may be kept awake because he has had too heavy an evening meal, another because he is really hungry. Coffee, tea, and other cerebral stimulants taken late in the day affect different people differently. Some will not be bothered by them; others will be kept awake. Personal experience is the only test.

You may not be sleeping because your room is too hot or too cold, too noisy or too light. These factors can usually be corrected. A comfortable bed and mattress can also be obtained. If the failure to sleep has deep psychological origins, improvements in the physical factors of the sleeping quarters may not help much.

The key to falling asleep is relaxation of the mind and muscles. That is why many of the time-honored techniques of getting to sleep often work. These include: leisurely retiring, reading or listening to music before retiring, taking a warm (not hot) bath, counting sheep (or anything else), breathing deeply and rhythmically, consciously attempting to relax the muscles. A helpful technique of "progressive relaxation" has been worked out by Dr. Edmund Jacobson.

The greatest single cause of sleeplessness is simply the fear that one is not getting enough sleep. The facts about sleep already presented in this article should help to eliminate this needless fear. Remember that sleep needs differ. If you will go to bed at a regular hour every night with the confident attitude that you are going to get enough rest, whether you sleep or not, you will have taken a long first step toward relieving your insomnia.

What about sleeping pills? Don't take them unless your doctor prescribes them. The indiscriminate use of self-prescribed sleeping pills can be a dangerous and damaging practice. Proof of this is found in the fact that the sale of sleeping pills without a doctor's prescription is forbidden. The pills that can be bought without prescription usually contain ineffective drugs.

Sleeping pills are sedative and hypnotic drugs, usually but not always barbiturates. Addiction to barbiturates is possible (see NARCOTICS). Bromides and antihistamines also have a sleep-producing effect. The use of these drugs is sometimes prescribed when physical pain is an important cause of insomnia. You need not be afraid of taking sleeping pills so long as your doctor prescribes them and you keep in touch with him.

Sleeping Pills—usually BARBITURATES, which see. They should be taken only on a doctor's prescription. An overdose can cause death. The treatment of persistent sleeplessness (insomnia) requires more than pills. Those that can legally be sold without prescriptions are usually not potent enough to have any valuable effect.

Sleeping Sickness occurs as the result of some damage to or disorder in the brain. The term describes several different kinds of illness; notably, ENCEPHALITIS (especially epidemic or lethargic encephalitis), inflammation of the brain caused by a virus; *trypanosomiasis,* or African sleeping sickness, a tropical disease; and sometimes, NARCOLEPSY, the uncontrollable urge to sleep during normal waking hours.

African sleeping sickness occurs in Western and Central Africa. Characterized by weakness, lethargy, a constant tendency to sleep, and eventually emaciation and death, it is brought about by a tiny blood parasite, the trypanosome. This parasite, found in the blood of animals, both domesticated cattle and some jungle animals, is conveyed to man by the bite of the tsetse fly and kindred insects. In man these parasites invade the minute blood vessels of the brain, damaging the nervous system.

In the early stages of the disease, treatment with drugs that are compounds of antimony and arsenic (tryparsamide) may often effect a cure. However, the suppression and avoidance of the tsetse fly is the best protection.

A condition like African sleeping sickness also occurs in tropical America, notably Brazil, where it is known as American trypanosomiasis, or Chagas' disease.

Slough—dead tissue separated or separating from living tissue. As a wound heals, it sloughs off dead tissue.

Smallpox—a VIRUS disease, also called variola. The disease was once common and deadly in Western civilization but has been almost entirely eliminated by the practice of vaccination. The characteristic aftermath of the original acute, feverish infection was the presence of small pits or pock-marks on the skin, particularly on the face. The incubation period for smallpox is from 2 to 3 weeks after exposure.

VACCINATION against smallpox was the first major triumph in preventive medicine. It was first announced by Edward Jenner in England in 1798.

Often against much misinformed opposition, the practice of vaccination has now spread to most parts of the civilized world and eliminated the threat of epidemics of this great scourge.

When smallpox is introduced into primitive populations which are not immune to the infection, it often wreaks great havoc. Many American Indian villages and tribes in the 18th and 19th centuries were practically wiped out by smallpox infection brought by the white man.

Smear—a glass slide, for examination under the microscope, upon which slide has been spread a bit of blood, sputum, urine or other samples of body tissue extracted from the body by one careful means or another. The "Papanicolau smear" requires a bit of tissue from the female genital tract (sex organs) and is used to make an early diagnosis of suspected CANCER of the womb.

Smegma — unpleasant-smelling, cheesy secretions that sometimes accumulate under the foreskin (in men) and around the labia (in women).

Smoking—see TOBACCO.

"Snow"—a slang word for COCAINE.

Soda—baking soda; sodium bicarbonate. The fizz in soda drinks is created by the gas, carbon dioxide.

Sodium—a chemical element,

classified as a soft metal; a strong base that binds many acids into forming salts. It is essential to blood and body metabolism, acting in complicated patterns of chemical reaction along with other body minerals like calcium, potassium, and phosphorus.

Sodium chloride (NaCl) is common table salt.

Sodium bicarbonate (NaHCO₃) is common baking soda; "bicarb" commonly used and overused in treating ACID STOMACH.

Sodomy—usually means intercourse *per anum* or sexual traffic with lower animals, but has a variety of different legal definitions in different localities. Sodom was a sinful city of Biblical times.

Softening of the Brain—a popular term for MENTAL ILLNESS, especially in old age. See BRAIN. The usual cause of the symptoms described as "softening" is the breaking of numerous small blood vessels, multiple "STROKE."

Soldier's Heart—neurasthenia, conversion hysteria directed toward the heart. See HEART DISEASE (which soldier's heart is not); MENTAL ILLNESS; PSYCHOANALYSIS.

Soma—body; as distinct from psyche, mind. Also the substance, meat or body of tissue as distinct from its coverings, linings, secretions and fluids. *Somatic* ailments are organic illnesses, as distinguished from functional or psychosomatic illnesses.

Somnambulist—sleep-walker.

Soporific—anything that puts a person to sleep or makes him drowsy. Many NARCOTIC drugs are soporific. See also HYPNOSIS.

"Sore"—an ULCER on the skin or mucous membranes, usually accompanied by an INFECTION and often reflecting an underlying systemic disease, for example, syphilis or diabetes. *Sore,* as an adjective, describes a bruised, painful, or stiff MUSCLE, or other organ. See, for example, EYE TROUBLE, HEADACHE, BACKACHE, FOOT TROUBLE.

Sore Throat—tonsillitis, laryngitis, pharyngitis—alone or in combination. See THROAT.

"Spanish Fly"—CANTHARIDES; dangerous if taken internally.

Spasm—tightening or contraction of any sets of MUSCLES; CONVULSION. When tight and persistent, as in muscle cramps, the spasm is called *tonic.* When alternating or interrupted but recurring, it is called *clonic spasm.* Spasms may occur in striped, voluntary muscle, as in LOCKJAW and TETANY, or in smooth muscle tissue, particularly those that make up the muscular coats of the blood vessels and the alimentary canal.

Fainting and "butterflies in the stomach" are mild forms of the effects of smooth muscle spasms. Relaxation of smooth muscle spasms is achieved with a variety of *antispasmodic drugs,* many of which contain atropine or belladonna derivatives.

Spastic—marked by muscle spasms, usually recurrent. A "spastic" child or adult is usually one whose rigid, stiff muscles or awkward muscular movements reflect brain damage more commonly described as CEREBRAL PALSY or PARKINSON'S DISEASE.

Specialist—a doctor who limits his practice to a medical specialty in which he has had special training and experience. See SPECIALTIES; also FAMILY DOCTOR.

Specialties—Among the best-recognized specialties in medical practice today are the following:

Internal Medicine, which places great emphasis on DIAGNOSIS, and includes such fields as:

Cardiology, or study of diseases of the HEART; and

Gastroenterology, study of diseases of the GASTROINTESTINAL tract, down to, but not usually including, the terminal end, which is the province of:

Proctology, study of diseases of the rectum and anus, including a considerable amount of surgery.

Surgery, which has several important subdivisions (which see under SURGERY), notably: *orthopedic surgery*; *plastic surgery*; and *neurosurgery.*

Anesthesiology, a subspecialty of SURGERY, which is concerned not only with the administration of ANESTHETICS during operation but also the preoperative preparation and the postoperative care of the patient.

Obstetrics and Gynecology, which are usually practiced together, though OBSTETRICS embraces prenatal care and all the problems of PREGNANCY and CHILDBIRTH, whereas gynecology is more strictly related to diseases of the SEX ORGANS, FEMALE.

Otolaryngology, giving special attention to diseases of the EAR, NOSE, and THROAT.

Dermatology and Syphilology, concerned with diseases of the SKIN and skin manifestations of constitutional diseases, plus study of SYPHILIS and other venereal diseases (venereology). These two specialties were placed together before the causative agent of syphilis was known, when skin manifestations were the most common signs of the disease that brought the patient to the attention of the physician. Venereology, per se, is a disappearing specialty.

Neurology and Psychiatry, providing diagnosis and treatment of diseases of the nervous system and of MENTAL ILLNESS. These two specialties require training in both, though in practice a man is likely to give much more emphasis to one than to the other.

For the following specialties,

see under the respective listing: PEDIATRICS; OPHTHALMOLOGY; UROLOGY; RADIOLOGY; PHYSICAL MEDICINE; GERIATRICS; *preventive medicine and* PUBLIC HEALTH; ALLERGY; OTOLOGY.

Specific—a drug that specifically cures a particular disease or has an effect on a specific MICROBE. For example, *quinine* is a specific for MALARIA.

Specimen—a sample for further study or laboratory examination. "A specimen" usually means a small sample of URINE in a bottle—to be used for urinalysis. However, stool specimens (feces) are also sometimes needed and requested.

Spectrum—the complete band of wavelengths that make up the whole series of electromagnetic radiations translated into human experience as visible light, radio waves, heat waves and the like. The visible spectrum is the breakdown of white light into all its rainbow of colors. *Broad-spectrum antibiotics* are those which deal with a large variety of infecting MICROBES. This is a mere figure of speech.

Speculum—doctor's instrument for looking into a body cavity. They come in many sizes and some queer shapes; notably the duck-bill speculum. The little funnel-shaped instrument through which the doctor peers into your ears and nose is a speculum.

Sperm—the fully developed male sex cell formed in the testes and capable of fertilizing the female *ovum*. The term is sometimes applied to *semen*, the fluid that carries sperm. The full word is *spermatozoön* (plural: spermatozoa). The abbreviated word, sperm, is used both for singular and plural.

Human sperm are very tiny, only about 50 to 65 microns in

HUMAN SPERM CELLS

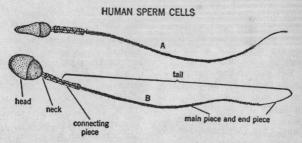

Here are two diagrammatic views of human sperm cells, magnified approximately 1,500 times actual life size. A. Side view (profile). B. Top view (looking down).

length. Each sperm consists of a spear-shaped head, a neck, and a threadlike tail, about 10 times as long as the head. As can be seen under a microscope, sperm can move or "swim," at about the rate of 1 inch in 20 minutes, by a whiplike lashing of the tail. Sperm moving at this rate, and normally shaped and proportioned, are considered *viable*, that is, alive and capable of impregnating an ovum.

Billions of sperm are formed in the testes from puberty to old age. In a normal ejaculation somewhere from 200,000,000 to 500,000,000 sperm are emitted and deposited in the female genital tract. Until ejaculated, sperm are carried through the *male sex organs* by muscular contractions of the tubes through which they pass. Deposited in the female vagina, they begin to move under their own power, pressing toward that site (usually the oviduct) where a mature ovum is most likely to be encountered. If encountered, one and only one sperm cell penetrates and fertilizes the egg. This is the moment of *conception*.

The rest of the sperm cells simply perish, like seed on barren ground. The sperm cells that enter the uterus may remain viable up to about 72 hours. (See illustration for EN-DOCRINE GLANDS.)

Sphenoid—wedge-shaped bone at the base of the skull. It has interior openings—called the sphenoid sinuses.

Sphincter—a ring of muscle that, when contracted, closes off a natural body opening. The anal sphincter, for example, normally keeps the bottom end of the alimentary canal closed tight. Sphincter muscles, of course, relax under the proper body stimulus and open up the otherwise shut orifices.

Sphygmomanometer—apparatus for measuring BLOOD PRESSURE.

Spica—a *bandage* applied in the form of a figure-of-eight where one turn crosses another. The ankle is usually bandaged spicawise.

Spider Bites—see INSECTS.

Spina Bifida—the unfortunate congenital condition in which the VERTEBRAE of the lower SPINE have failed to develop and close completely during intra-uterine life. As a result, the covering (meninges) and sometimes the actual nerve tissue of the spinal cord protrude outside the faulty vertebral opening.

Spine—the backbone; the spinal column, made up of 26 or 33 VERTEBRAE, separated by DISKS of CARTILAGE, and forming a series of slightly movable JOINTS. The child's description is most apt: "Your head sits on one end and you sit on the other." The top vertebra is appropriately called the "atlas" bone.

The vertebrae of the spine are subject to the same BONE

THE SPINE

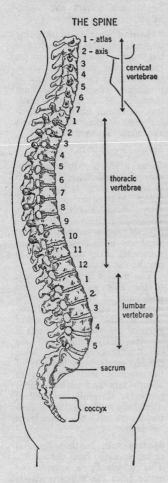

1 – atlas
2 – axis
3
4
5
6
7

cervical vertebrae

1
2
3
4
5
6
7
8
9
10
11
12

thoracic vertebrae

1
2
3
4
5

lumbar vertebrae

sacrum

coccyx

DISEASES as any other BONES, and to FRACTURES, dislocations, and fusion. CURVATURE OF THE SPINE occurs for many reasons, resulting in hunchback and poor POSTURE. Injury to the spine usually means damage to the SPINAL CORD, with temporary or permanent PARALYSIS as a result of NERVE impairment; for example, "cord BLADDER." (See SPONDYLITIS.)

When a *broken back*, spinal fracture, is suspected, the victim should always be transported face down—if it is absolutely essential to move him at all. (See FRACTURES.)

Interestingly enough, BACKACHE is not usually due to injury or disease of the spinal column or its joints.

(See illustrations for BRAIN; VERTEBRAE.)

Spirochete—any cork-screw, spiral-shaped MICROBE, ranging from 6 to 500 microns in length. It usually refers, however, to the pale, delicate infecting organism of syphilis (*Spirocheta*, or *Treponema pallida*).

Spleen—an internal organ (or gland) located high on the left side of the stomach and just underneath the diaphragm. It is a flat, spongy oblong, normally about 5 or 6 inches long and weighing about 6 ounces. It is dark purple in color and riddled with blood vessels, in which the blood circulation is somewhat slowed down.

The function of the spleen was long a mystery to medicine. Now it is known to be something like an enlarged lymph gland. (See LYMPH; GLANDS.) It is a graveyard for old red BLOOD CELLS. Sometimes it destroys red blood cells too vigorously and has to be removed (*splenectomy*). A removed spleen is not likely to be missed any more than a removed appendix. The spleen is not an essential organ, even though all its functions are not known. When the spleen is badly torn in an accident, it is good practice to remove it. Rupture of the spleen can cause fatal internal BLEEDING.

Enlargement of the spleen (splenomegaly) occurs in certain diseases affecting the liver and the blood. The enlarged spleen may reach a weight of 15 to 20 pounds when engorged with blood.

(See illustrations for ABDOMEN; HEART.)

Splenectomy—removal of the SPLEEN.

Splenomegaly—enlargement of the SPLEEN.

Spondylitis—inflammation of one or more vertebrae of the spine. It is commonly owing to TUBERCULOSIS of the spine, *Pott's disease*. *Ankylosing spondylitis* is a severe form of arthritis affecting the lower back and sometimes the hip joints. The bones "freeze" (fuse) together, producing the condition variously called stiff back, poker back, bamboo spine and Marie-Strumpell's disease. It is exceedingly disabling. Young men are most commonly affected. See BONES, JOINTS and BACKACHE.

"Spotting"—oozing or dripping of small amounts of blood from the vagina when it occurs at times of the month and under conditions of the menopause or pregnancy when it would not normally be expected. "Spotting" demands immediate medical consultation. See FEMALE TROUBLES; MENSTRUATION.

Sprain—see JOINTS.

Sprue—a chronic disease, probably of nutritional origin, which is marked primarily by the frequent evacuation of frothy, fatty, "soapy" stools. The other symptoms include a sore mouth, a raw tongue, loss of weight, weakness and a blood picture somewhat like that found in pernicious ANEMIA.

The disease is most common in the East and West Indies and parts of Asia where it is known as "hill diarrhea." However it often occurs in other parts of the world. In infants it is frequently diagnosed as CELIAC DISEASE. The basic trouble seems to be inability of the stomach and intestines to absorb fats and carbohydrates properly. Carefully prescribed diets help to bring the disease under control. See DIGESTIVE DISORDERS.

Sputum—spit; anything ejected or expectorated from the mouth. This is usually a mixture of *saliva* from the salivary glands and mucus from the air passages and lungs. However, when these organs are diseased, the sputum may also contain blood ("rusty sputum"), pus, and germs. The laws against spitting in public places are to protect against the spread of infectious organisms found in the sputum.

Squint—strabismus; cross-eye or wall-eye. See EYE TROUBLE.

Staff—the members of an institution; especially the physicians who are privileged to practice at and have their patients admitted to a particular HOSPITAL in which they have "staff privileges."

Stammering—a speech defect usually of psychologic origin; see STUTTERING.

Stain—any dye or other chemical coloring substance that will infiltrate tissues and MICROBES so that they can be more clearly seen when viewed through a microscope.

"Staining"—same as "SPOTTING"; an unusual or unexpected flow of blood from the vagina. Medical attention is necessary. See FEMALE TROUBLES.

Stapes—the stirrup-shaped little bone of the EAR.

Staphylococcus, often abbreviated to "staph," is the general name for a particular group of round, ball-shaped BACTERIA that grow in little bunches like a cluster of grapes. They cause many human infections, are commonly found in BOILS, usually produce PUS, and often cause hospital epidemics.

Stasis—stoppage of normal flow of body fluids, such as blood, lymph and intestinal contents. *Intestinal stasis* is a condition in which the tone of the muscle coats of the intestine is low, so that the bowels sag and are sluggish about carrying food and the fecal stream along.

Steatorrhea—fatty stools. See SPRUE.

Stenosis—narrowing or constriction, for any reason, of a body canal or duct. Most seriously affected, most often, are the AORTA (aortic stenosis) and the PYLORUS at the lower end of the stomach (pyloric stenosis).

STERILITY

Sterility and fertility are opposite sides of the same coin. About 1 in 10, perhaps 1 in 7, married couples who look forward to having children gradually discover after a few years of normal marriage relationships that pregnancy does not occur. They often become needlessly haunted by the specter of sterility or barrenness.

For a half to two-thirds of these childless couples, adoption is the only method by which they can have a child of their own. But in a third to a half of the couples who not so long ago would have been doomed to involuntary childlessness, advances in medical diagnosis and treatment now make possible CONCEPTION, PREGNANCY, and birth of a healthy child.

The most important things recently learned about sterility are these:

In perhaps one-third of the cases the husband rather than the wife is primarily "to blame."

The causes of sterility are multiple, and one or more local causes or constitutional factors favoring sterility may appear in both husband and wife.

Sterility is usually *relative* rather than absolute. Either mate might be able to have a child with a different partner, or after suitable treatment.

Absolute sterility means inability to sire or bear children at any time or under any circumstances.

Relative sterility means that either or both partners are incapable of contributing to conception unless and until some or all of the factors making for infertility are changed or corrected. This is exactly the point at which apparent sterility can be attacked by suitable medical advice and treatment.

Sterility in the male: Absolute sterility in the male at any given time can be determined with relative ease. A specimen of SEMEN, collected in a condom or, better, a glass jar, is examined under a microscope within a few hours. If no living sperm are found, the man is absolutely sterile at that time and probably permanently sterile. If the number of live sperm are few, if they move sluggishly (have "low motility"), if a great number of poorly or wrongly developed sperm are seen, the man is probably relatively sterile; but this diagnosis requires expert knowledge. Repeated semen examinations may be needed.

Absolute sterility occurs when *both* testes are lost by accident or operation (CASTRATION). It may also occur when the individual has been born without some crucial link in the SEX ORGANS, MALE (CONGENITAL MALFORMATION) or some part has failed to develop properly.

An occasional cause is failure of the testes to have descended into the scrotum (cryptorchidism).

When the virus that causes MUMPS descends into the testes and causes inflammation there (orchitis), the sperm-producing capacity of the testicular tissue may sometimes, but by no means always, be permanently lost.

Exposure of the body and the testes to high temperatures or to various forms of irradiation—for example, X rays, radium emanations, nuclear reactions—*may* sometimes result in absolute or relative sterility. The amount of exposure involved and the particular radiosensitivity of the individual tissues are the crucial factors. Small amounts of radiation do not cause sterility. Excessive exposure to irradiation, however, may damage or abolish fecundity. Some individuals cannot tolerate dosages of radiation that are perfectly harmless to sperm formation in others.

Safety engineers are well acquainted with the potential dangers of radiation and heat exposure. So long as the individual obeys established safety rules, he need not be afraid that he is exposing himself to sterility by working in any particular industry or under any conditions involving radiation or high temperatures.

Complete blocking (occlusion) on both sides of the ducts through which sperm normally travel from the testes to the seminal vesicles is another cause of absolute sterility. Such closure may be the result of previous disease, notably gonorrhea not promptly treated. The ducts may also be closed off by a simple surgical operation, cutting and tying off the ducts, the common operation for *sterilization* of the male. This has little or no effect on potency or libido. The claim is now made that exceptionally skillful surgery can in rare instances undo this sterilization operation.

Sterility in the female: The diagnosis of absolute sterility in the female requires much more direct physical examination than the simple semen examination of the male. Occasionally a battery of specialized tests must be run. The causes of absolute sterility in the female include some of those that account for this condition in the male; notably, congenital malformations, such as absence of the vagina or other parts of the normal sex organs; previous pelvic inflammatory disease, especially gonorrhea, which may have sealed off the uterine tubes; excessive exposure to irradiation; and surgical intervention.

The common operation for *sterilization* of the female is severing and tying off of the uterine tubes. Again, it is claimed that this operation is sometimes subject to repair. However, after surgical removal of both ovaries, both Fallopian tubes, and/or the uterus (hysterectomy), the ability to bear children cannot be restored.

Relative sterility in a couple: Relative sterility can be evaluated only with reference to the *couple* involved and not singly for either partner, unless, of course, one or the other is absolutely sterile. Fertility may be considered as a quotient, the husband's times the wife's.

If there are many factors that reduce the wife's fertility, but the husband's fertility is high (or vice versa), conception may nevertheless occur. If both partners are low in fertility for reasons that cannot be changed by medical advice and treatment, conception may never be possible.

However, correcting one or more of several minor causes of infertility in either the husband or wife, or both, can make a sterile marriage a fruitful one. This can now be accomplished in perhaps a third to a half of the couples who are denied children of their own.

To husbands whose ability to copulate remains to them positive proof that they are neither absolutely nor relatively sterile, it is sometimes difficult to demonstrate that the reason for their wife's apparent barrenness lies wholly or partially with them. If they are ignorant of the possibility of relative sterility, they may even refuse to cooperate in seeking medical examination.

The causes of relative sterility in both men and women are much more numerous than those of absolute sterility. Some of the same causes are operative—but with this difference: they have not proceeded to a point where they are no longer correctable. Thus, for example, the uterine tubes may have been sealed shut by previous inflammatory disease. But in some cases, a good many in fact, the tubes can be opened by blowing air through them (tubal insufflation).

In the male probably two-thirds of the factors resulting in relative sterility are constitutional in nature—for example, generalized INFECTIONS or ENDOCRINE disturbances. Only about one-third are found locally in the SEX ORGANS.

In women this ratio is reversed; probably two-thirds of the factors tending toward relative sterility are discovered in the sex organs. (See FEMALE TROUBLES.)

Inflammation of the neck (cervix) or body of the uterus is quite commonly found and can be readily treated. Cysts and benign tumors of either the uterus or the ovaries may be present and require treatment. The vaginal secretions may be so highly acid that they quickly kill all sperm that enter. Alkaline douches are sometimes recommended. The so-called "tipped womb" is rarely, if ever, a sole cause of sterility. Few, if any, doctors now recommend surgical treatment for this condition.

The over-all physical and mental health of either husband or wife, or both, may have an important bearing on their relative fertility. Hence the physician gives attention to their DIET and nutrition; to the possible presence of undisclosed INFECTIONS, metabolic diseases (e.g. DIABETES), endocrine disturbances, serologic incompatibilities (e.g. the Rh factor), tumors, and the like; and to mental attitudes, which may reflect psychiatric difficulties of a nature and degree sufficient to bring about serious endocrine imbalance.

The importance of mental attitude is emphasized by the not infrequent event that soon after a long-childless couple have finally adopted a child, the wife becomes pregnant. One explanation here is that parenthood effects some subtle change in body chemistry to raise a couple's fertility quotient. Exactly how this occurs is unknown.

Age is an important factor in fertility. MENARCHE and MENOPAUSE in the female limit the ages of childbearing span. In the male there is no sharp decline in ability to sire children. Probably two-thirds of men up to 70 and half the men who reach 90 can still become fathers. An authenticated case of fatherhood in a man of 94 has been reported. However sperm-producing ability does gradually recede with age.

Sheer ignorance of sexual anatomy, physiology, and functional technique account for some few cases of apparent sterility. In some couples, married for many years, the husband has never completely entered his wife; in others, coitus without ejaculation has been permanently practiced without husband or wife being aware of the simple fact that pregnancy was unlikely to occur unless a pool of fertile semen was deposited at the mouth of the uterus.

Sheer chance in the timing of marital relations may account for some cases of apparent and relative sterility. The number of hours during the monthly menstrual cycle in which the female may be impregnated is comparatively limited.

The chance factor in achieving conception is also related to the frequency of marital intercourse. This varies enormously among couples, depending on their particular sexual drives, which decrease steadily with age. According to Kinsey, married couples still in their teens average intercourse 3.9 times a week; the frequency drops steadily to 2.9 at 30; 1.8 at 50; and 0.9 at 60.

A high degree of sexual activity usually occurs immediately following marriage and gradually tapers off. In some apparently sterile marriages in which intercourse is relatively infrequent, it is quite possible that even over a number of years, intercourse has never occurred at or near the time of ovulation, the only time when conception is possible.

Artificial insemination. A few physicians have undertaken to treat infertility by artificial insemination, the procedure popularly called "producing test-tube babies." It is by no means a universally successful method of relieving human infertility. Artificial insemination has been far more accurately employed in animal husbandry. The technique of the method is certainly no secret: A pool of human semen from an acceptable donor is drawn into a syringe and deposited, via syringe, at the mouth of the uterus. The date selected for the procedure is that on which the woman is presumably ovulating. The time is apparently guessed wrong in a number of cases, demonstrating the necessity of accurately calculating the time of ovulation to achieve pregnancy.

Medically speaking, artificial insemination is still in the experimental stage. The procedure raises many serious social, moral, and legal issues. Many of the most serious of these revolve about the situation arising when the donor of the semen is not the husband of the woman.

In 1951 the Bureau of Legal Medicine and Legislation of the American Medical Association reported: "There is little that can be said with any degree of assurance concerning the medicolegal aspects of artificial insemination, for such aspects have not been explored satisfactorily by any court of appellate jurisdiction in the United States."

Sterilization has two very different meanings: (1) It means making surgical instruments and dressings absolutely sterile, or germ-free, or completely aseptic, by processes, such as autoclaving under steam, that kill all bacteria or other microbes present. It is more drastic than antisepsis.

(2) Sterilization means also making an individual incapable of further reproduction; that is, making him or her absolutely sterile. See STERILITY.

In human beings sterilization is commonly performed by simple surgical operations—cutting both spermatic cords in the male or both uterine (Fallopian) tubes in the female. It can also be achieved by heavy doses of radiation.

Under different state laws in the United States, and under different national laws throughout the world, sterilization is sometimes permitted and sometimes required to prevent further transmission of "poor HEREDITY." A famous ruling of the U. S. Supreme Court, voiced by Justice Oliver Wendell Holmes, and upholding the constitutionality of sterilization laws, declared, "Three generations of imbeciles are enough."

Enthusiasm for legalized sterilization as a means of improving the human stock has declined greatly in recent years. The complicated facts about human GENETICS have thrown out the confidence once held in this easy-to-order procedure. Furthermore, it is too easily subject to abuse, as experience in Germany under the Nazis tragically demonstrated.

Sterilizer—any apparatus for killing all the germs put inside it. Most operate by heat (steam) killing. Convenient small models can be seen in most doctors' offices. Hospitals sometimes have huge ones; e.g. large autoclaves.

Sternum—breast-bone. (See illustrations for BONES.)

Stethoscope is the instrument, almost the badge of the practicing physician, which enables him to hear better what is going on inside the body. A stethoscope conducts sound; it does not amplify it unless, as rarely, an electronic amplifying unit is included in the instrument. The same conducting effect can be gotten by rolling up a sheet of paper and listening through it. In fact, that was how the stethoscope was originally invented by the 19th century French physician, René Laennec.

What the doctor hears through the stethoscope helps him greatly in forming his *diagnosis*. He listens acutely to the sounds of the heart, the lungs, the arteries, the veins, the intestines, and even the fetal heart-beat (if present). The commonly used stethoscope is arranged to convey sounds to both ears (binaural stethoscope); but there are other models in which the doctor can listen with only one ear. See AUSCULTATION, which is listening for sounds of disease.

Stimulant usually describes a drug that excites or stimulates some organ or part of the body to greater function or activity. AMPHETAMINE, for example, and caffeine are stimulants of the central nervous system; see NERVES. The caffeine also sometimes stimulates kidney function.

Is beverage alcohol a stimulant? This depends partly on what you mean by the word, stimulant—becoming thus a semantic problem. It is generally conceded, however, that alcohol is a *depressant* drug, like NAR-

COTICS, and hence gives the pleasant feeling or effect of stimulation by depressing inhibitions and painful feelings. The net effect of depressant drugs is to inhibit or reduce feeling, often to the point of amnesia, coma, and unconsciousness.

Stomach—a pear-shaped pouch of membrane-lined muscle, capable of holding 2 to 3 pints of food. It is a key organ of the DIGESTIVE SYSTEM and plays a central role in the DIGESTION of food, but it is not the only organ of digestion. (See illustrations for ABDOMEN; HEART.)

Stomach Ache, "belly ache," and "pain in the gut" are popular phrases for any kind of *abdominal pain,* usually sharp and acute or "knifing," though often steady and continuous or "gnawing," and sometimes intermittent or recurring. More often than not, the stomach is probably not the primary source of pain. The stomach is called the "greatest liar in the anatomy," because it reflects and reacts to pain stimuli originating far outside its orbit. Vomiting, for example, may reflect brain tumor.

In a few kinds of abdominal pain, or stomach ache, the cause is obvious even to the victim; namely, great overindulgence in food or drink. This pain may be relieved by inducing vomiting and by lying down quietly with the knees drawn up.

When overeating or drinking is *not* the obvious cause of abdominal pain, whether sharp and severe or mild and continuing, medical advice should be promptly sought. Self-diagnosis and self-treatment of abdominal pain is very dangerous practice. Especially to be deplored is the persistent use of home remedies (for example, baking soda) or patent medicines without medical advice to get temporary relief from recurrent abdominal pain or discomfort.

The continuing use of alkalis, like baking soda, to relieve stomach pain or "acid stomach" may have just the opposite effect; it may stimulate the stomach to produce more hydrochloric acid, thus setting up a vicious circle of pain and temporary relief. Again, the use of patent medicines that "relieve indigestion" may cover up a serious sequence of symptoms, which, if investigated early, might save much future pain and even life. Persistent indigestion, especially after eating meat, is one of the clues that may lead to early and lifesaving discovery of stomach *cancer.*

Don't take a laxative. When an abdominal pain lasts more than an hour, or frequently recurs, don't take a laxative, cathartic, or purge. Don't eat or drink anything until you have consulted a doctor.

The reason is simple. Many serious medical and surgical emergencies are heralded by acute abdominal pain. Among them are acute APPENDICITIS, perforated gastric ulcer, rupture of gastric organs (a sudden, terrifying pain that often quickly subsides), and bowel obstruction. Every one of these conditions may be made worse by the effect of laxatives. Prompt medical attention quickly stops the pain and, if life is endangered, saves it.

Among other possible causes of abdominal pain are food allergy, food poisoning (for example, *botulism*), and psychological stress or emotional conflict (as in "nervous stomach" and COLITIS). These conditions also demand the best of medical diagnosis and treatment.

STOMACH TROUBLE

Stomach trouble describes any of many chronic ailments both of the stomach and of related parts of the DIGESTIVE SYSTEM or gastrointestinal tract. The branch of medicine that deals with these disorders is called *gastroenterology;* the specialist in them, a gastroenterologist. Stomach troubles are not confined to the stomach alone. The patient knows them by the symptoms and discomforts they produce. The doctor must look for the underlying causes.

STOMACH ACHE (which see), or abdominal pain, ranging from mild to severe, is a common denominator of practically all stomach troubles, with one big and important exception, *cancer*. Other common symptoms of digestive-tract disorders are indigestion, regurgitation of food, gas on the stomach (flatulence), heartburn, a coated or "furred" tongue, nausea, vomiting, constipation, and diarrhea. Among the many diseases or disorders of the stomach that may be responsible for some or all of these symptoms are *ulcer, cancer, inflammation, infection,* and *congenital malformations.* Emotional stress or distress can also upset the stomach.

The persistence or severity of symptoms is not necessarily correlated with the seriousness of the underlying disease.

Ulcer: A *peptic* ulcer is a breach or erosion in the inner linings and, rarely, the entire wall of the stomach or the duodenum, which immediately follows it in the digestive tract. A true stomach ulcer is called a *gastric ulcer;* the others are *duodenal ulcers.* From the standpoint of symptoms and treatment, they are pretty much alike, although differences between them must be taken into account. There is also an ulcerlike disease that displays many of the same symptoms and responds to the same treatment, but in which no ulcer can be demonstrated.

Peptic ulcer seems to be highly individualized. While there are effective general principles in its management, the sometimes long course of the disease does not follow exactly the same pattern in different individuals and the provoking factors may be utterly different.

How common is peptic ulcer? Very common. Approximately 5% of the American population have an ulcer at some time during their lives. Duodenal ulcers are perhaps 10 times as frequent as gastric ulcers. Men are about 4 times as subject to duodenal ulcer as women, although gastric ulcer is more common among women. The disease usually begins in young adulthood, disappears after treatment, then recurs with greater or less frequency.

What provokes a peptic ulcer? The cause, or causes, of peptic ulcer are not really known. Different factors provoke ulcers in different people. Some physicians believe that there is a strong familial or hereditary tendency and that there is an "ulcer type." This person is often described as the high-pressure executive or the tall, thin, highly emotional individual, tense and nervous.

It is quite clear that peptic ulcer is a *psychosomatic* disease. Worry, anxiety, and emotional stress tend to bring on ulcers (in susceptible individuals) and bring them back. They flare up under conditions of nervous tension and fatigue.

An excess secretion of hydrochloric acid from the stomach almost always accompanies peptic ulcer; and it is this acid that eats away at the site of the ulcer, causing pain and complications. But the reason for the excess acid is not really understood.

Other factors that *may* contribute to development or recurrence of peptic ulcer are infections, blood-vessel spasms, endocrine-gland disorders, poor eating habits, coarse and rough or highly spiced foods that irritate the stomach and duodenal linings, alcohol, tobacco, exercise, and—for some reason—severe burns.

Even here it must be recognized that what may be one man's meat is another man's poison. The doctor and his patient must work out, on the basis of experience, the factors that actually provoke the individual's ulcer attacks. It is usually wise for an ulcer patient to stop smoking, at least temporarily, avoid exercise more vigorous than golf or swimming, and give up hard liquor. But, as Alvarez says, "It is hard to say whether a moderate amount of well-diluted alcohol will do harm."

What are the symptoms of peptic ulcer? They are strange and varied. Sometimes there are no symptoms, the ulcer coming and going without the patient being aware of it. The classical symptom is *hunger pain,* a gnawing, burning, or aching pain in the upper part of the abdomen and sometimes radiating to the back. The pain comes on before meals and *can be relieved* by taking food or alkalis.

Among symptoms that do *not* often reflect ulcers are jittery feelings in the abdomen, regurgitation of food, soreness in the lower abdomen, belching, and nausea. These symptoms are more likely to be related to the nervous stomach or irritable bowel (see COLITIS).

Sometimes an ulcer is first revealed by its more serious complications, *bleeding* and *perforation.* The signs of bleeding may be black and tarry stools or vomiting of blood, either "coffee grounds" vomitus or, more rarely, bright blood. Ulcers are the most common cause of vomiting blood (hematemesis). Perforation may invoke a sudden, agonizing abdominal pain.

How is peptic ulcer diagnosed? By the patient's history, X-ray examinations, and therapeutic test. The X-ray diagnosis, following a barium meal, is difficult and not always definite. If the patient recovers promptly when he is put on an ulcer regime, he probably has an ulcer.

What is the treatment of peptic ulcer? The essentials of the treatment are mental and physical *rest, frequent feedings,* a carefully selected bland *diet,* medications that reduce gastric acidity (alkalis) and control intestinal spasms (for example, atropine), and escape from worry and emotional stress. In reasonably severe cases the patient is often placed on the Sippy diet (named after Dr. Bertram Sippy, of Chicago), which includes frequent feedings of milk, cream, and alkaline powders, to which other bland foods are gradually added after a few days. There is another school of medical thought that recommends a meat diet instead.

Should peptic ulcers be operated upon? Approximately 15% of recurrent peptic ulcers come to surgical operation because medical management no longer succeeds or a serious complication—bleeding or perforation—has occurred. The latter are genuine surgical emergencies. Otherwise the decision to operate should be made by a competent general practitioner, internist, or gastroenterologist in consultation with a good surgeon.

Do peptic ulcers often turn into cancers? Gastric ulcers sometimes do; duodenal ulcers rarely do. But what looks like an ulcer, especially in men past middle age, may be a beginning cancer that demands expert diagnosis and prompt surgery.

How can ulcers or their recurrence be prevented? By avoiding the individual provoking factors so far as possible. Strict dieting alone is not enough. Practically speaking, the person with an ulcer must try to reorganize his life to avoid emotional stress, worry, overfatigue. He must also respect hunger pains, making sure that he takes food immediately whenever these begin to bother him in the least.

Stomatitis—inflammation of the tissues of the *mouth,* usually including the gums. In man it is usually accompanied by pain, soreness, increased saliva and bad breath (fetor). The causes are numerous and are often related to dental conditions, decayed TEETH, poorly fitting dentures, and pyorrhea (see TEETH).

Bacterial or other microbes multiplying in the mouth may cause stomatitis; TRENCH MOUTH, or Vincent's angina, is the typical example. Poor DIET and nutritional failure, especially lack of vitamin C, may also be a partial cause. Heavy-metal poisoning, notably mercury poisoning, also causes stomatitis. The combined efforts of the dentist and the physician are often necessary to relieve this condition, if it becomes chronic. Medicated mouthwashes and drugstore remedies are usually useless.

Strabismus—squint; cross-eye or wall-eye. See EYE TROUBLE.

Streptococcus—a particular MICROBE, BACTERIUM, sometimes called "strep" and associated with many illnesses; for example, sore THROAT and RHEUMATIC FEVER.

Streptomycin—an ANTIBIOTIC, obtained from a soil mold. It was isolated in 1944 by a U. S. scientist, Dr. Selman Waksman. It was one of the very first drugs to show any effective action against the tubercle bacillus. It is also effective against a host of Gram-negative bacteria which penicillin does not readily touch. Unfortunately, the organisms to be attacked often soon become resistant to the drug; this can be overcome by carefully controlled doses and the addition of para-aminosalicylic acid (PAS) and isoniazid to the dosage schedule. In some patients unpleasant toxic side-effects occur, notably dizziness, because the drug seems to affect the balancing apparatus of the EAR.

Striated—striped; usually applied to the voluntary big MUSCLES as contrasted with smooth or non-striated involuntary muscles.

Stroke—any sudden, severe attack of illness; usually an apoplectic stroke, or apoplexy. More technically, this is described as a *cerebral vascular accident* or an *intracranial lesion of vascular origin,* under which title it ranks third among the principal causes of death in the U.S.

Stroke is usually caused by the bursting of a blood vessel in the brain, and sometimes by the clogging of an artery in the brain. This accident generally occurs late in life and is associated with HARDENING OF THE ARTERIES and HIGH BLOOD PRESSURE. Hence stroke is one of the serious cardiovascularenal diseases. The blood-vessel damage often leads to localized areas of softening in the brain.

Stroke appears as a sudden loss of consciousness (coma) followed by paralysis, generally of the side of the body opposite the side of the brain affected (hemiplegia). Face,

arm, or leg may be paralyzed. A few victims of stroke die immediately; others linger on for a few weeks, if the lesions are extensive. But many recover more or less completely and live for years. The great Louis Pasteur did some of his best work after he had suffered a stroke.

Alvarez has called attention to the frequency of "little strokes," which often go unrecognized for what they really are: brain damage. The victims of little strokes do not fall unconscious, but they lose their former mental sharpness.

See BRAIN and BRAIN DAMAGE.

STUTTERING

Stuttering is a personality defect, due to anxiety in meeting various social situations, rather than a speech defect. Except in rare instances, most stutterers can talk when they are alone, they can talk to animals, and they can often talk to people they are friendly with. Stuttering occurs only in situations arousing fear and anxiety.

Intensive studies have been made to show some organic cause for stuttering, but only in very occasional cases has there been evidence of a neurological or anatomic deformity as the cause. There have been some cases of stuttering after brain hemorrhage, but these cases are rare. There is a theory that lefthanded children who are made to write with their right hand fail to establish the speech area in one hemisphere and that there is a conflict between the two hemispheres, but most investigators do not accept this theory.

The organs used for speech are also used for other more primitive purposes, such as coughing, sneezing, sucking, breathing and vomiting. The symptoms of stuttering seem similar to these primitive actions, as though the person were trying to vomit, chew, or suck. There are about 600 speech sounds in the various languages of the world. The baby in his babble stage uses hundreds of these speech sounds, but when he begins to speak he must exclude all the sounds not used in the English language, which has only about 56 sounds. Stutterers seem to fail to make this exclusion, and retain these primitive sounds.

Stuttering is caused by the stutterer's fear of people, and can often be removed by suggestions made by a strong personality.

We know that between 1 and 1½% of people stutter. Perhaps half the children in nursery schools pass through a stuttering stage lasting a few days. The more sensitive and timid the child the more likely he is to have spells of stuttering. Treatment consists in building up the stutterer's confidence, giving him loving attention, and teaching him to adjust to the group.

In hysterical paralysis of the hand it is helpful for the person to use the hand in various ways, but the essential treatment consists in removing the unconscious barrier that caused the paralysis. In much the same way, it is helpful for the stuttering child to receive speech training, perhaps in a good speech center or public-speaking class. However, some of the results of speech training may be due less to the treatment than to the loving attention the child gets during the training. Some schools have various methods of treatment, such as speaking while waving the hands in the air, breathing in a certain way while speaking, or speaking in a scanning fashion.

In the case of the very young child who stutters, family life should be reorganized so that the child receives the right amount and kind of love and affection, so as to develop a sense of security. There is no short-cut to the treatment of stuttering. When stuttering persists into adolescence and adulthood, the person's whole personality is involved and not just the speech organs. He must be trained to understand himself and to learn to adjust to other people without fear and without tension. (The concept of the cause and care of stuttering presented here is that of Dr. Smiley Blanton and was thus outlined by him in an editorial in the *J.A.M.A.*)

Stye—a boil-like infection or inflammation of the eyelids. See EYE TROUBLE.

Subacute—an illness or condition that is not quite serious or damaging or dangerous—that is, acute—but may become so if not properly managed. A subacute condition may hang on for a long time and become irreversibly chronic.

Subarachnoid—underneath the

middle coat of tissue that sheathes the brain and spinal cord. Bleeding sometimes occurs in this lining and must be properly diagnosed promptly.

Subcutaneous Tissue—the layer, primarily of fat, beneath the SKIN.

Sublimation—the difficult but rewarding psychic process, achieved with the help of both the conscious and unconscious mind, of converting powerful libidinal energy into personally satisfying and socially useful activities. It is an important goal of treatment in all psychotherapy animated by the dynamics of Freudian PSYCHO-ANALYSIS.

Failure or inability to sublimate a large part of one's basic (sexual?) energy is often a seed or symptom of MENTAL ILLNESS. The word, sublimate, however, has gotten a bad name. To many people it means, "When you feel like love, go take a brisk walk."

Subluxation—an incomplete or partial slipping of a joint. Chiropractic gives great importance to "subluxations of the spine," a mouth-filling phrase. Most physicians, however, do not take subluxations very seriously.

Sugar—a sweet-tasting CARBO-HYDRATE, occurring in many forms, such as cane sugar, beet sugar, maple sugar, milk sugar (lactose), and blood sugar (glucose). Eating too much sugar in the form of sweets, pastries, and candy is usually associated with overweight— but it is not the "cause" of obesity. Reducing diets usually demand cutting sugar intake and substituting other nonfattening sweetening agents, such as *saccharin,* for sugar. "Non-caloric" soft drinks make such substitutions.

Sugar in the blood (glycemia) is normal if the amount of sugar (glucose) is about 80 to 120 milligrams per 100 cubic centimeters of blood. *High blood sugar* (hyperglycemia) occurs in certain disease conditions, *notably* DIABETES, and under the stress of emotional excitement. *Low blood sugar* (hypoglycemia) is exceedingly rare, although an overdose of insulin or cancer of the pancreas can produce it. Many people (but not doctors) falsely attribute spells of fatigue and headaches to low blood sugar; this is rarely true.

Sugar in the URINE is usually a symptom of DIABETES, though it can occur as a result of emotional stress, endocrine-gland disturbances, and injection of certain drugs. The term *glycosuria* (sweet urine) describes a higher than normal excretion of sugar (glucose) in the urine, especially the excretion of amounts in excess of 1 gram within 24 hours.

A number of simple tests can determine the amount of sugar in the urine. Some depend on a *change in color* of a test-tube solution or piece of paper impregnated with a reagent chemical when a few drops of sugary urine are applied.

There are no simple home remedies or secret drugs for reducing sugar in the blood or urine. When these signs of disease or body disorder occur, there is no safe or sensible course of action other than obtaining competent medical attention.

Sulfa Drugs—a great number of MICROBE-fighting drugs, all of which contain in some combination or other the chemical group called the sulfonamide radical (SO_2NH_2), which includes the chemical element sulfur. The sulfa drugs are bacteriostatic; that is, they do not actually kill bacteria but they interfere with their metabolism in a way that the bacteria can no longer grow or multiply.

The first sulfa drug was formulated as a red dye. Its usefulness as a drug for treating infections of the human and animal body was demonstrated in 1935 by the German scientist, Gerhard Domagk. He called his drug "prontosil"—but it was quickly shown by French and American chemists and bacteriologists that the sulfonamide grouping was the one that beat the bacteria. Sulfa drugs first came quickly into use for the treatment of "strep throat" and puerperal *septicemia* (childbed fever).

The introduction of sulfa drugs gave new life to the science of chemotherapy. Since that time they have been su-

perseded in many indications by the *antibiotics;* but they retain great usefulness alone and in combination for the treatment of many bacterial infections.

When the doctor selects a sulfa drug, he uses the one (or combination) known to be most effective against the particular infecting organisms. Dosages must be carefully controlled, because some sulfa drugs may have damaging side-effects, especially on the kidneys.

Among the sulfa drugs commonly used are: *sulfanilamide, sulfadiazine, sulfamerazine, sulfacetamide, sulfathiazole,* and a variety of derivatives which are less toxic and have fewer, if any, undesirable or uncomfortable side-effects. The chemical construction of improved sulfa drugs remains a subject of intense research interest.

Sulfonamide—SULFA DRUG.

Sulfur—the well-known nonmetallic chemical element that has had a long history of use in medicine and alchemy. Administered internally, in small, nontoxic doses, sulfur promotes sweating and peristalsis. In various compounds it is still extensively used for external application in treating many SKIN troubles. Sulfur is one chemical part of the SULFA DRUGS.

Sunburn—a skin burn caused by the ultraviolet rays of the sun. It should be treated like any other burn. (See BURNS, SKIN.)

SUNSTROKE

Sunstroke results from excessive exposure to direct sunlight. An analogous condition, *heat stroke,* occurs from exposure to heat rays. High humidity usually increases the risk of sunstroke or heat stroke.

True sunstroke is a serious medical *emergency.* It means that the heat-regulating mechanism of the body has been taxed to a point where it no longer operates. (See TEMPERATURE.)

Under these circumstances the following sequence of symptoms usually occurs:

The sunstroked individual becomes weak and irritable.

He seems dazed and confused.

He stops sweating—or sweats only a little bit. His skin feels dry and very hot.

Suddenly, or gradually, his temperature shoots up. It may reach 105 degrees F. or even higher.

Restlessness, then unconsciousness (coma) ensue.

The emergency treatment for true sunstroke (also called heat fever or hyperpyrexia) is to *cool the patient off quickly.* This is usually most efficiently done with cold-water dousing or baths and the application of ice-packs. The cold treatment should be stopped when the temperature has been brought down to about 102 degrees F. The patient should be removed promptly to a hospital because other complications, such as fall in blood pressure (shock), may intervene.

There are milder forms of sunstroke in which other bodily functions are deranged but the heat-controlling mechanism has not been put out of action. These are variously described as *heat collapse, heat exhaustion* and *heat cramps.*

A mild sunstroke may produce only a headache and feelings of extreme fatigue. It can be treated by retiring to a cool dark room, resting quietly on a bed with wet cold compresses and an icebag applied to the head.

When the sunstroke is more severe, the headache may be piercing, the skin dry, the pulse rapid, the temperature moderately elevated. The patient may be bothered by light, vomit and go into a delirium.

The treatment here is a cool, dark, quiet environment. Restlessness may be controlled by medication (possibly bromides). Generous quantities of fluid should be given—but no alcohol. Long convalescence and slow recovery, with occasional episodes of depression and loss of memory, are the rule.

Patients who have suffered one true or severe sunstroke, or several milder attacks, must guard themselves carefully against exposure to direct sunlight and excessive heat. They are usually well-advised to live outside tropic zones.

The risk of sunstroke is well-known to residents of the tropics, who usually protect themselves against it by suitable clothing and headgear (the pith helmet and the turban) and by social customs that forbid excessive activity in the heat of the day (noon-time siesta). But, as Noel Coward put it, "mad dogs and Englishmen go out in the mid-day sun."

The symptoms of heat cramps (in the legs, gut and elsewhere) are usually the result of excessive sweating and subsequent loss of water and salts from the body (dehydration). The essence of both the treatment and prevention of these conditions—in addition to avoiding hot places—is to drink plenty of water and take salt tablets (sodium chloride) regularly. Modern air-conditioning has reduced the incidence of these conditions.

Superego—roughly, the conscience. It is an important part of the structure of the UNCONSCIOUS MIND as constructed in Freudian *psychoanalysis*. The superego is the unconscious censor of thought, feeling and action; it controls the EGO and often gives the individual unconscious but troubling feelings of guilt and anxiety. It is an "inner voice," guiding and controlling. The origin of this voice, Freud said, lies in the consciously forgotten admonitions and warnings of parents, nurses and teachers which were visited upon the child in his early years of life. These obvious origins of the superego are often forgotten or denied, and in later years the inner threats seem to come as the voice of a hidden or supreme power. The superego reflects the ideals and values of conduct that parents held high. The superego, however, is always "behind the times" so far as the individual is concerned. See MENTAL ILLNESS; PSYCHOANALYSIS.

Supine—lying down on the back, face up; the opposite of *prone*.

Suppository—any medicated mass intended for application by insertion into the rectum (rectal suppository), vagina (vaginal suppository), or urethra. Rectal suppositories are commonly used and overused in treating PILES. Vaginal suppositories are prescribed for a variety of FEMALE TROUBLES. Suppositories are made of oils and other substances that melt at body TEMPERATURE (normally 98.6° F.). Hence in the summer they usually have to be kept in the refrigerator rather than the medicine chest. Suppositories should never be mistakenly taken by mouth

after their customary foil wrapping is removed. Glycerine and oil of theobroma are commonly used in suppositories.

Suppuration—forming PUS.

SURGERY

Surgery means the performance of a surgical *operation,* or, sometimes, the room where it is performed.

Modern surgery is safe and efficient. It "removes the disease from the patient and puts it in a bottle." It is a far cry from the "kitchen-table surgery" of the 19th century or the crude operating rooms which Lord Lister, the father of modern surgery, sprayed with carbolic acid to get rid of germs. The development of surgery has gone hand in hand with improvements in HOSPITAL facilities, for the hospital is truly the surgeon's workshop. Old-fashioned fears of surgery are not warranted. In the operating room of a modern hospital there are available the skills and facilities to make sure that the best and safest treatment can be given.

Approximately 10,000,000 surgical operations a year are now performed in the United States. Only about 1 in 650 patients fails to survive the operation. This remarkable record has been achieved despite the fact that many patients come to the operating room severely injured by accident or desperately ill.

Why is surgery so safe today? Many factors contribute to this pleasant fact. They include the improved training of surgeons; the availability of new drugs that control infection and produce other important physiological effects; improvements in anesthesia; careful preoperative preparation and postoperative care of the patient; and better hospitals.

Modern surgery is performed under the best possible *aseptic* conditions, which means exclusion of every possible source of infection. This fact accounts for much of the ritual of the operating room—masks, gowns, "scrubbing up," sterile instruments, sponges, towels, and the like.

Training to be a surgeon. Surgery is one of the best-defined specialties in medical practice and the surgeon must undergo rigorous training and apprenticeship before he can ply his art in an accredited hospital. Surgical specialists put in 5 or 6 years of surgical residency in a hospital. Then, following rigorous examinations, they may qualify as Fellows of the American College of Surgeons and diplomates of specialty boards in the various branches of surgery. A good surgeon is far more than a pair of trained hands, important as a gentle, deft touch on tissues actually is. He also has the priceless intellectual quality of "surgical judgment," which tells him when and how to operate.

Preoperative and postoperative care. Better care of patients before and after operation has played a major role in making surgery safer. Laboratory tests reveal the state of the patient's body chemistry. Preoperative deficiencies in proteins, vitamins, minerals, and sugars can be corrected by intravenous infusions. If necessary, blood transfusions can be given before operation—although it is more common to give them after operation to overcome blood loss and to combat shock.

Other preoperative medication usually includes sedative and narcotic drugs, given so the patient comes into the operating room in a relaxed, semiconscious state. These drugs are also given to control pain after operation; addiction does not occur in the short space of time needed to recuperate from a surgical operation.

Antibiotics to control and prevent infection are prescribed both before and after operation. Surgeons now make every effort to get their patients out of bed as soon as possible after operation; often the next day, sometimes a week or longer.

Anesthesia. The importance of good and correct anesthesia to safe surgical procedures can hardly be overestimated. Many types of anesthesia are available: general (nitrous oxide, cyclopropane, ether), intravenous, spinal, caudal, regional, and topical. The choice is usually left to that important member of the surgical team—the anesthetist. He is the one responsible for the condition of the patient during operation, while the surgeon himself and his assistants, if any, concentrate on the techniques of the surgery itself in the operative field. Because of the increasing complexity of anesthesia, the trend is toward the employment of private physician-anesthetists wherever available. (These physicians receive a separate fee for their services.) There are also skilled nurse-anesthetists. Incidentally, a patient need never fear that the surgeon will begin operating before the pain-relieving anesthetic effect has been completely achieved.

What types of surgery are there? There is practically no site in the human body which today is inaccessible to surgical operation, if indicated and warranted. Along with this has come an increasing definition of surgical specialties, so that most surgeons tend to confine themselves to operations on one region or system of the body.

Types of surgery can be described by the region of the body they deal with, in either simple or technical terms. Thus we have such terms as chest (thoracic), heart (cardiac), ear (aural), eye (ophthalmic), and bladder and kidney (genitourinary) surgery.

More comprehensive terms are:

Abdominal surgery, which treats with all the organs inside the ABDOMEN.

Orthopedic surgery, which is concerned with diseases of the BONES, JOINTS, and MUSCLES.

Neurosurgery, which deals with surgery on the BRAIN and the NERVES distributed along the spinal cord.

Plastic surgery, which is the reconstruction of facial and other skin and soft tissues, and sometimes their transplantation from one part of the body to another, to relieve disfigurements, deformities, and malfunctions—a specialty that developed after World War I and is sometimes inadequately described as "cosmetic surgery."

A "general surgeon" is one who tackles all kinds of surgical cases.

Surgery can also be classified by its urgency. Emergency surgery, demanded, for example, in such conditions as a fractured skull or acute bowel obstruction, brooks no delay in getting the patient to the hospital and into the operating room. Urgent surgery, as demanded by cancer or kidney stones, may be put off for a few days; required surgery, such as tonsillectomies and thyroid operations, may be postponed for a few weeks or months. There are also categories of elective surgery, such as removal of simple hemorrhoids, in which operation is strongly indicated but not imperative; and optional surgery, like "nose lifting," which the patient may choose not to have done at all. "Office surgery," or minor surgery, such as lancing a boil, is that which the doctor can perform without sending the patient to a hospital.

Except in emergency, the decision to undergo operation lies with the patient. The surgeon can only advise and counsel. The patient must have confidence in his advice. Sometimes a patient will want a second independent surgical opinion, and there can be no objection to such consultation.

The costs of surgery are high, although surgeons usually scale their own fees in accordance with the patient's ability to pay. Other costs include hospital services, special drugs, special-duty nursing (if needed), blood transfusions, anesthetist's fee, and some other possible costs. These lavish but inescapable costs have prompted the rapid development of hospital insurance and HEALTH INSURANCE, notably the BLUE CROSS and BLUE SHIELD plans.

Suture—the material for sewing up a wound, such as catgut, wire, silk or cotton thread; or the stitches made with the suture. Skilful surgeons have developed a great variety of useful and efficient stitches; for example, continuous, interrupted, blanket, mattress, double-button and figure-of-eight sutures.

Suture also describes the lines where the bones of the *skull* join together.

Sweat Glands—glands that release sweat through the SKIN. See TEMPERATURE.

Swelling—see EDEMA; GLANDS; TUMOR.

Sycosis—barber's ITCH; either a FUNGUS or STAPHYLOCOCCUS infection of the HAIR follicles, especially of the beard.

Sympathectomy—surgical operation for cutting the NERVES of the sympathetic nervous system. It has been used, among other indications, for the relief of HIGH BLOOD PRESSURE.

Symphysis—the lines where bones, originally distinct and separate, have fused and grown together. This occurs between the two halves of the lower jawbone, between the coccyx

and sacrum at the base of the spine, and between the pubic bones in the lower abdomen.

Symptom is any bit of evidence from a patient that he is sick; it may be a complaint to the doctor or an unvoiced personal feeling. To the patient, the symptoms are the essence of the disease. He feels sick. To make a *diagnosis*, however, the doctor must piece the symptoms reported to him together with the signs of disease he sees. A symptom is subjective; the patient feels his headache. A sign is objective; the doctor can see a skin rash or a pathological derangement in a blood or urine sample.

Syncope—FAINTING spell.

Syndrome—a collection, constellation, or concurrence of signs and symptoms of disease. For example, nausea and vomiting are a syndrome; they usually go together. The word syndrome is sometimes synonymous with disease; for example, Parkinson's syndrome and PARKINSON'S DISEASE mean the same thing. The word syndrome is often used to point to a set of symptoms which almost but don't quite make up a full-fledged and recognizable disease entity.

Synovial Fluid—the lubricating fluid in the JOINTS.

Synovitis—inflammation of the membranes that line joint capsules; the synovial membrane. See JOINTS.

SYPHILIS

Syphilis, also called "bad blood," lues, and "the pox," is the most dangerous of the venereal or "social" diseases, which are transmitted principally by sexual intercourse. Physicians have also called syphilis "the great imitator," for its late symptoms can mimic those of almost any other disease.

The specific cause of syphilis is a tiny corkscrew-shaped germ, the spirochete called *Spirochaeta pallida* or *Treponema pallidum*. It can be seen only under a specially arranged microscope, in which it shows up as a wriggly thread against a dark background. Spirochetes can invade all human tissues and not just the blood stream. Inside the body the spirochete is extremely sensitive to many drugs and antibiotics; outside its human host cells, it quickly perishes.

How is syphilis spread? By direct contact with infected people —well over 90% of the time by sexual intercourse. Very rarely it is spread by kissing. Only in the rarest instances is it transmitted by indirect contacts; that is, by infected objects, such as towels, toilet articles, and objects held in the mouth, like musical instruments. The object would have to be moist and handled by a second person within just a few minutes after being contaminated with discharges from an infected individual. There is no warrant for fear of catching syphilis from toilet seats, door knobs, bathtubs, or eating utensils.

Outside of direct contact, and the rare indirect contacts, the only other way of getting syphilis is congenitally. Syphilis can be passed on from an infected mother to her unborn child during intrauterine life. This is *not* by means of the germ plasm; neither syphilis nor a tendency to it is inherited. The spirochete in the mother's body simply crosses over placental barriers to enter the infant's body. Fortunately, treatment of the mother for syphilis will keep the child from being born with the disease.

The course of syphilis. This is a disease which, if acquired and untreated, runs a long course and goes through the following stages: primary, secondary, latent, and tertiary.

Primary stage: This is marked by a sore at the site where the spirochetes entered the body. It is usually found on the sex organs, but occasionally in the mouth. This sore is called a chancre (pronounced *shanker*); it is generally hard and painless; it may look like a small pimple or ulcer, ranging from pinhead size to an inch or more. It is often concealed and may pass unnoticed. The chancre appears any time from 10 days to about 3 months after exposure, but on the average in about 3 weeks. By this time the spirochetes have spread throughout the body, but there are no general symptoms of disease. Treatment of syphilis should begin promptly whenever a chancre is discovered, for this is the best time to drive out the spirochetes. The disease is highly communicable while the chancre is present.

Secondary stage: Even without treatment, the chancre disappears in about 3 to 6 weeks. The secondary stage of syphilis begins as the chancre is disappearing; at this time the spirochetes diffuse further throughout the body. They can be found in the circulating blood. The secondary stage lasts for a variable period of time, usually a few months but sometimes for several years. Common, though not inevitable, symptoms include skin eruptions and rashes, a slight falling of the hair which gives the scalp a moth-eaten appearance, mucous patches, mouth sores, headache, fever, fatigue, and pains in the bones and joints. The symptoms range from mild to severe. The disease is still readily curable in the secondary stage.

Latent stage: The signs and symptoms of secondary syphilis gradually pass away although no treatment be given. The disease then lapses into a latent or quiescent stage, which usually lasts from 5 to 20 years but may range from 2 to 50 years. There are no symptoms in the latent stage, but the spirochetes are still present in the body.

Tertiary (third) stage: In this final stage of syphilis, the untreated disease often comes to a hideous flower and imitates many other diseases. It may attack the brain and spinal cord (neurosyphilis), the heart and blood vessels, the bones and the skin. Tumorlike masses (gumma) may appear on the skin and bones. The aorta, leading from the heart, may be attacked by the spirochetes and rupture, causing death. Blindness and deafness can occur; running sores are frequent. The effects of late syphilis on the nervous system are many and varied. These conditions go under such names as paresis, general paralysis of the insane, dementia paralytica, locomotor ataxia, and tabes dorsalis. See TABES. Late syphilis can be treated—but not so effectively as the earlier stages of the disease.

The diagnosis of syphilis requires laboratory confirmation. In the primary stage it is confirmed by examining fluids from the chancre under a dark-field microscope and actually seeing the pale, wriggly spirochetes. In the subsequent stages the diagnosis is made by serologic tests, popularly called *blood tests* because they require a sample of blood as the starting point for the laboratory test. (Spinal fluid is also used.) The best-known of these laboratory tests for syphilis is the Wassermann test, but there are a great many others also named after the laboratory men who developed them; for example, the Kahn, Kline, Kolmer, Hinton, and Eagle tests. A four-plus Wassermann signifies a completely positive reaction on the test; but it does not determine how seriously involved with the disease the patient may be.

How is syphilis treated? With penicillin and other antibiotics. The treatment period is *short* and the injections can be given easily and painlessly in any doctor's office. A series of four or five injections of penicillin in the course of a week can change a positive Wassermann test to a negative Wassermann test in that time. Relapses are few, although reinfection can occur. Penicillin is used in the treatment of all stages of syphilis.

Before penicillin, the treatment period was long, and many patients failed to complete the full course of arsenical drugs (salvarsan, 606, neoarsphenamine) then prescribed. With the effectiveness of the modern medical treatment of syphilis, there is absolutely no excuse for self-medication with quack remedies.

See VENEREAL DISEASE.

Systemic—spread throughout the body; affecting all body systems and organs; not LOCALIZED in one spot or area. Syphilis and septicemia (blood poisoning), for example, are systemic infections.

Systole—the time when the heart muscle is in contraction, pumping blood at the contracting stroke into the aorta and pulmonary artery from the left ventricles. This is the moment when the blood pressure is highest in the arteries throughout the body: the *systolic blood pressure*. When the heart is not in systole—that is, working—it is in DIASTOLE—that is, at rest.

T

Any word printed in SMALL CAPITALS *can be looked up under its own alphabetical listing for further information.*

Tabes literally means a wasting away (atrophy) of some body parts or organs as the result of disease or poisoning—for example, SYPHILIS, TUBERCULOSIS or ERGOT poisoning. Most commonly, however, it refers to *tabes dorsalis,* otherwise known as *locomotor ataxia,* the demoralizing final stage of syphilis in which the spirochete insidiously attacks the nervous system *(neurosyphilis).*

The attack of the spirochetes in this late stage of syphilis is centered on the NERVES in the spinal cord. The results of this attack spell the wide and unhappy variety of symptoms that accompany tabes dorsalis; for example:

Sharp shooting pains, loss of sensation (anesthesia) or abnormal sensation (paresthesia) in parts of the body, loss of nervous reflexes, incoordinated movements, difficulty in walking (often with a characteristic, legs-wide-apart, shuffling gait), a decline in sexual desire and power, growths on the bones and skin, wasting away of muscles and joints, inability to control bladder and bowel excretions (incontinence). In the final stages, the afflicted patient becomes more of an insensible, vegetative creature than a human being.

Tabes dorsalis (neurosyphilis) comes on 15 to 50 years after a first untreated or unsuccessfully treated attack of primary syphilis. Hence tabes is predominantly a disease of middle or old age. Untreated with modern methods, the disease progresses slowly but inexorably to a miserable death. However, with efficient treatment—penicillin and other antibiotics—the ravages of both early and late syphilis can be largely eliminated. Even if complete cure is not attained, the nerve degeneration can usually be arrested and the host of disagreeable symptoms banished. Compare with PARESIS.

Tabetic—related to TABES, the final stage of SYPHILIS. A *tabetic crisis* describes the paroxysms of shooting pains and arrest of organ functions that sometimes occur with a shocking fatal outcome in *tabes dorsalis.*

Tachycardia—rapid HEART beat, and corresponding fast PULSE beat—usually over 100 per minute. In *paroxysmal tachycardia,* the spurt of heartbeats may rise at intervals to as high as 250 to 270 beats a minute. The outcome, unless checked with drugs like quinidine, may be fatal. So-called "voodoo

[520]

deaths" are sometimes caused by this condition. The victim is so frightened at having broken a taboo, or so afraid of some other voodoo threat, that his heart beats faster and faster, soon beating him to death.

Taenia—tapeworm. See WORMS.

Talc—or talcum powder, is really a soft mineral, magnesium silicate, finely ground.

Talipes—CLUBFOOT.

Talus—ankle bone; astragalus.

Tampon—a plug of cotton, or other absorbent material, introduced into a body cavity to stop bleeding or soak up secretions. Tampons are safely and comfortably inserted into the vagina to absorb menstrual flow. *Tamponade* with a tight pack of gauze stops NOSE bleed.

Tannic Acid, or *tannin*, is a yellow powder extracted from bark of trees and leaves or fruit of plants; notably, oak-tree gall. Applied to the skin or mucous membrane, tannic acid dries up secretions and shrinks it; hence it has some usefulness as an astringent and local hemostatic (stops bleeding). Given internally, it is an antidote of uncertain value against many vegetable and metallic poisons; and it is sometimes used in the treatment of DIARRHEA. Its use in the treatment of burns is *not* recommended.

Tansy—bitter oil of the plant, or herb, *Tanacetum vulgare;* sometimes used as a remedy for WORMS and as a stimulant to MENSTRUATION or urination. It can be a dangerous poison, quickly paralyzing muscles of swallowing and breathing, and causing pain in the abdomen, convulsions and death.

Tantalum—a rare metal that does not corrode and is easily worked. It is drawn into fine wire for surgical SUTURES, and easily fashioned into plates or discs to replace destroyed or removed parts of bones, especially in the skull.

Tapeworm—see WORMS.

Tar—the black, sticky, complex chemical residue left after the destructive distillation of wood or coal (coal tar). It has an antiseptic, preservative but often irritating action when applied to the SKIN or mucous membranes. *Tar water* is an expectorant, makes coughing easier; it is sometimes used in chronic BRONCHITIS.

Tarsalgia—pain in the instep of the foot; see FOOT TROUBLE.

Tarsus—the instep of the FOOT, with its seven bones that form part of the meta*tarsal* arch. (See illustrations for BONES.)

Tartar—the concretion, chiefly phosphate of lime, that accumulates on the gumline of uncleaned TEETH; dental calculus.

Tartar Emetic—an antimony compound; it induces spitting, nausea and vomiting. It must be used cautiously.

Taste is the sense dependent on the *taste-buds* in the tongue and the mouth. It is closely related to the sense of smell. See TONGUE.

Tattoo in haste, repent at leisure; this is the fate of many young men who allow themselves to be tattooed in their youth and then spend much time later worrying about how they are going to get rid of the tattoo marks. There is no easy way.

If the tattooed area is not too great, the skin can be cut away and new skin grafted on from other parts of the body. This calls for *plastic* SURGERY. Another method calls for sterilizing the skin with antiseptics, sandpapering the tattooed skin down to its base while controlling bleeding and encouraging new skin to grow. The marks can be temporarily covered with skin-colored cosmetic plasters; but these, of course, must be frequently renewed.

Tattooing is a truly primitive art. Vegetable and mineral dyes are introduced under the SKIN with needles. Tattooing has health as well as esthetic risks. If the needles are not sterile—and particularly if the tattooer moistens them with saliva—the needles may transmit infection, including venereal disease.

Tea—a beverage that is stimulating because, like COFFEE, it contains about 1½ grains of CAFFEINE per cup and even more if long brewed or steeped.

Tears—see EYES; EYE TROUBLE.

TEETH

Few people have "perfect teeth." The average American, at the age of 30, has only a dozen healthy, unfilled teeth in his mouth. Fifteen out of 100 Americans wear false teeth (artificial dentures) and another 20 in 100 could profitably use them. Even at that, Americans are better off than the residents of most other civilized countries—because the United States has more and better-trained dentists than any other country. Some people living under primitive conditions have better teeth than the populations of civilized countries, but this is not universally true.

Neglect of the teeth is the prime factor in dental decay and other dental disorders. All too often people fail to visit a dentist until they have to; that is, when they are plagued by a severe toothache. Routine dental examination and prophylaxis (cleansing) and regular care of the mouth would eliminate a high proportion of dental ills. Failure to see a dentist regularly often has a psychological root in childhood. The child is first taken to the dentist when he has a toothache; hence he thereafter unconsciously associates the dentist with pain and shuns him, if possible. Therefore,

HUMAN TEETH

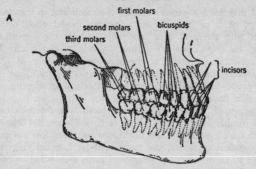

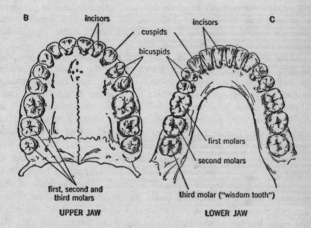

A. *A side view of the teeth in the upper and lower jaws. The dotted lines indicate how the roots of the teeth are set in the jawbones. Only about one-third of each tooth is visible above the gum margin.*

B. *The dental arch (adult upper jaw).*

C. *The dental arch (adult lower jaw).*

it is good practice for parents to take their children to the dentist at the age of 2 or 3, both for a routine dental check-up *not* associated with the pain of a toothache and for the opportunity of getting an application of sodium fluoride to the teeth. This topical application, repeated at the ages—approximately—of 7, 11, and 13, reduces the risk of tooth cavities (decay) by about 40%. Fluoride prophylaxis will not help adult teeth; it is effective only on teeth that have recently erupted.

The neglect of "baby" (deciduous) teeth is a common cause of dental trouble later in life. These teeth influence the shape of the mouth and the face. When deciduous teeth are lost too early, through accident or decay, the permanent teeth underlying them may erupt in an unnatural position and form a crowded or otherwise irregular dental arch. Furthermore, the child needs a good set of deciduous teeth to chew his food properly and to preserve a proper bite (occlusion) between the upper and lower jaws. Perhaps half the children in the United States suffer from some degree of malocclusion (faulty bite).

How teeth grow. Both the baby and permanent teeth grow out of tooth buds that were laid down under the gums fairly early in embryonic life (before birth). Baby's "first tooth" usually erupts above the gum line when he is about 6 months of age. However, there is a wide variation in the time when the first tooth comes out; generally speaking, late teething is nothing to worry about. The infant usually has his full set of 20 deciduous teeth by the time he is 2 or 2½ years old.

The child begins to lose his baby teeth when he is about 6 years old. At this age also the first of the permanent teeth come in. These are the *6-year molars* (first molars) at the back of the mouth. These four grinding teeth are extremely important. They are called the "keystone of the dental arch" and they will carry the main burden of chewing for many years. Permanent teeth replace baby teeth in the mouth at the rate of about 4 a year for 6 or 7 years.

The last teeth to erupt are the "wisdom teeth" or third molars, which are usually delayed until the late teens or early twenties. These teeth often come in crooked or "impacted" against the second molar and may have to be extracted. They are no great loss.

A full set of adult teeth numbers 32; there are 16 each in the

INNER STRUCTURE OF THE TOOTH

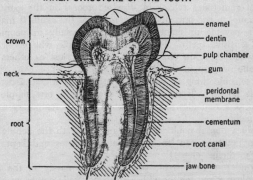

crown — enamel, dentin, pulp chamber, gum

neck — peridontal membrane

root — cementum, root canal, jaw bone

upper and lower jaws. The four sharp teeth at the front of each jaw are called *incisors*. Immediately following them in the dental arch is the *cuspid,* after which come a first and second *bicuspid,* then the first (6-year), second, and third *molars.*

The *crown* of a tooth is the part that appears above the gum line; it is only about ⅓ of the whole tooth. Underneath the gum line lie the *roots.* Incisors have only one root; other teeth, 2 or 3. The crown of each tooth is covered with dental *enamel,* the hardest substance in the body. The roots are encased in *cementum,* not quite as hard. Inside the enamel and cementum is the somewhat softer bony substance called *dentin,* which is the bulk of the tooth. The dentin surrounds a *pulp chamber,* where nerves and blood vessels of the tooth are located. The nerves and blood vessels run up or down through narrow channels, called *root canals,* through which they connect with the rest of the circulatory and nervous systems of the body. Covering the roots of the tooth is the *periodontal membrane,* which holds the tooth in its socket in the jaw and takes up some of the shock of chewing. This is why the teeth are slightly movable.

The functions of the teeth are obvious: to chew food and mix it with saliva, to aid speech, and to maintain the position of the jaws. Primarily, the teeth are part of the digestive system. It should be pointed out that human beings are able to get along without teeth, but that among the lower animals loss of teeth spells death.

A *toothache* is usually the sign of a badly decayed tooth. However, it sometimes reflects a disease process in the periodontal membrane, in the jaw, or in other parts of the skull. It may even have a psychic or emotional origin, especially in people who have "sensitive teeth." There are some people who get a toothache when they are emotionally disturbed, just as others get a headache or pain in the back.

●The sensible thing to do for a toothache is to see a dentist as soon as possible. If no dentist is available, a few simple home or drugstore remedies may be applied to give temporary relief of pain, namely:

Apply a dental poultice to the gum beneath the aching tooth. (These poultices can be bought at drugstores and kept in the home medicine chest.)

If, under a good light, you can see a cavity in the aching tooth, clean it out gently with a swab of sterile cotton on a toothpick. (These swabs, commonly used for babies, are also available ready-made at drugstores.)

Pack the cavity carefully with a bit of sterile cotton dipped in *oil of cloves.* (This can also be obtained at the drugstore.) Be careful not to drip the oil of cloves on the gum, cheek, or tongue; it will irritate.

If this is ineffective, or if you cannot locate a cavity, put an ice bag, or ice wrapped in a towel, against the jaw on the aching side. This failing, try a hot-water bottle. Sometimes cold and sometimes heat will relieve the pain. Try both, if necessary.

Take two 5-grain aspirin tablets, repeated in two to four hours —if you have taken aspirin before and know you are not sensitive to it.

Despite the fact that you have relieved pain by these measures, it will be a wise idea to consult a dentist as soon as possible. The underlying cause of the toothache must be remedied or it will return.

Dental caries, or tooth decay, is the common cause of losing teeth up to about age 35. Thereafter disease of the supporting membranes and structures of the teeth takes first place. The step-by-step mechanism of dental caries is well known; but the fundamental causes remain obscure and complex. The most widely held theory of tooth decay is this. It is associated with the presence of *Lactobacillus acidophilus* (a microbe) and lactic acid (a chemical) in the mouth. The lactic acid is a by-product of the performance of the *Lactobacillus* in its chief function of fermenting sugars and cooked starches. This acid either helps to dissolve the outer structure (enamel) of the tooth or pours through the tiniest break in it. (At this point the theory is obscure.) Once through the enamel, the lactic acid eats away at the dentin; that is, demineralizes it. The tooth may become sensitive to heat, cold, or sweets when it has just a small cavity. As the cavity enlarges, approaching the pulp chamber, the irritated nerves set up the signal of a toothache.

The dentist repairs tooth decay by removing the decayed dentin and putting in a filling of gold, silver, or dental cement. If the pulp chamber has become involved, it may be necessary to pull the tooth and replace it with a false tooth. In some cases it is possible to fill the root canals and leave the tooth in place.

Many factors beyond lactic acid are concerned in tooth decay. Among them are diet, heredity, mouth hygiene, endocrine gland activity, accumulation of tartar (dental calculus) on the teeth, character of the saliva, frequency of dental examinations, mechanical pitting and fissuring of the teeth, and the natural hardness and smoothness of particular sets of teeth.

There is as yet no single factor which in itself will assure complete control of dental decay. There is no diet that will assure good teeth or prevent decay. There is no one food or type of food that produces dental caries, although there are some who believe that excessive amounts of sugar and carbohydrates may favor decay. Toothbrushing alone, regardless of dentifrice, will not avoid caries. "Clean" teeth do decay. Research into the causes of dental caries is continuing.

Pyorrhea alveolaris is the name given to inflammation and degeneration of the periodontal membranes that surround each tooth. It is the common cause for loss of teeth after age 35. The onset and development of pyorrhea is accompanied by tender and bleeding gums (gingivitis) and loss or recession of the bony structure that supports the teeth in their sockets. As a result the teeth become loosened ("wobbly teeth") and may eventually fall out.

There is no simple home remedy for pyorrhea, but adequate dental treatment can usually correct the condition. Among the many factors which may induce pyorrhea are: a faulty "bite" (malocclusion); constant grinding of the teeth or clamping of the jaws, usually a nervous habit; accumulation of tartar on the teeth, especially at the gum line; systemic diseases, notably diabetes and blood diseases; missing teeth, especially in the back of the mouth; and faulty diet, particularly lack of vitamin C.

Both the prevention and treatment of pyorrhea call for regular dental prophylaxis, to remove tartar; correction of the faulty or shifting bite; replacement of missing teeth; change in the habit of grinding the teeth; medical treatment of underlying systemic disease; and an adequate, balanced diet with plenty of vitamin C.

Answers to some common questions about dental health and mouth care:

What toothpaste should I use? You can make your choice on the basis of flavor and price. There is no significant difference between pastes, powders, or liquid dentifrices. There is precious little scientific evidence that any of the therapeutic agents now added to dentifrices, acting alone, will control or even favorably influence pyorrhea or tooth decay.

What kind of toothbrush should I use? Any kind that you can handle easily and that feels comfortable when used in your mouth. The arrangement of the bristles is a matter of little importance, provided they do not scratch the gums. This often happens with old, well-worn toothbrushes. Teeth should be brushed away from the gums rather' than toward them; that is, up and down rather than across. The inside surfaces should be brushed with a rotary motion.

How often should I brush my teeth? Ideally, after every meal —if the full hygienic value of toothbrushing is to be realized. Most people, however, brush their teeth only once or twice a day, because for them the value of toothbrushing is more esthetic than hygienic. One should not harbor the illusion that toothbrushing alone will of itself prevent dental decay or pyorrhea.

What kind of mouthwash should I use? Since the effect of a mouthwash is primarily that of a mechanical cleanser of the teeth and mouth, it makes little difference. Warm salt water will serve as well as any. The bactericidal effect of any safe mouthwash is dubious. Flavor, price, and convenience may again be the guide.

Will the dentist hurt me? Sometimes, a little. Pain during the dental operation itself can be banished with injections of local anesthetics. Afterpain can be controlled with a wide variety of modern drugs. Apprehension about extractions and other major dental operations can be reduced by the advance prescription of tranquilizing drugs. Many of the attachments on the modern dental engine (e.g. the water jet and high-speed operation) also act to reduce pain.

What about artificial dentures? Most complaints come with respect to full lower plates, which are sometimes hard to wear. They occasionally need refitting and must be kept clean. Fixed bridgework gives the least trouble but cannot always be applied. Partial, removable dentures are second choice. The efficiency of any set of false teeth is at best only about 1/3 that of natural teeth. However, with modern dental laboratory work and special processes, their appearance rivals and sometimes surpasses that of natural teeth.

When should tooth-straightening (orthodontia) be started? Usually about the age of 12 or 13, sometimes earlier.

For additional information on mouth and teeth, see STOMATITIS, FLUORIDATION, GUMBOIL, VINCENT'S ANGINA.

Telangiectasis—swelling and dilatation of the small BLOOD vessels (capillaries) and minute arteries. Sometimes so many are swollen in one area that they form a small tumor *(angioma)*. In one hereditary form of telangiectasis, the capillaries are extremely fragile; they break and bleed easily. This is not the usual picture, however.

TEMPERATURE

Temperature of the human body is controlled by a delicate heat-regulating system, including the brain's heat-regulating center, the SKIN, LUNGS, BLOOD, MUSCLES, and GLANDS. Normally, there is a fine balance maintained between heat production by the muscles and glands and heat dispersion or loss through the skin, lungs, and—a little bit—urine and bowel movements.

When a person gets too hot, the skin signals to the thermostat in the brain, which then directs more blood to the surface of the body (the skin capillaries) and increases the release of fluid (sensible and insensible perspiration) from the sweat glands. As the perspiration evaporates, under the influence of a hot external temperature or a breeze, such as that produced by an electric fan, the sensation of cooling results.

Conversely, when a person is too cold, the thermostat closes up the little blood vessels on the skin, sending more blood to the interior of the body, and speeds up muscular metabolism. Sometimes this speed-up is evident in shivering and chattering of the teeth.

Normal and abnormal temperatures: The average normal temperature of the human body is 98.6° Fahrenheit (taken orally), equivalent to 37° Centigrade. The temperature normally fluctuates in the course of 24 hours from about 97.3° in the middle of the night to about 99.1° in the middle of the afternoon. Metabolism, which governs temperature, is of course lower during sleep. Many adults in good health have normal-for-them temperatures averaging as much as a degree higher or lower than 98.6° (orally taken temperature). Rectal temperatures average about 1° higher. People who are sluggish in the morning, "slow starters," but pick up energy momentum in the afternoon and evening, often show temperature curves revealing that their metabolism climbs more slowly during the day than other people's.

Most disease conditions are reflected in body-temperature changes. In the presence of INFECTION a rise of temperature almost invariably occurs. (See FEVER.) Exposure to heat and sunlight also brings about rises in body temperature, characteristic of heat stroke, SUNSTROKE, and heat exhaustion. In some conditions body temperature falls; notably, myxedema, diabetes, some forms of kidney disease, and shock. Exposure to cold outside temperatures may produce CHILBLAIN, FROSTBITE, or FREEZING, if the body is not protected.

Body temperatures above 106° F. or below 95° F. indicate that a patient is in grave danger. However, there is a case on record of recovery from a low temperature of 59° F., and high temperatures of 110 to 112° F. have occasionally been recorded without subsequent early death.

How to take a temperature with a clinical thermometer: Many people are needlessly stumped by this simple procedure, which should be done as follows in taking an oral adult temperature:

1. Examine the fever or clinical thermometer.

2. Take hold of the end of the thermometer opposite the mercury bulb, give the arm a full downward swing, ending with a snap of the wrist. Repeat this motion two or three times. Its purpose is to shake the mercury in the thermometer down below the mark of 97° F.

3. To see the mercury column, which is a shiny silver color, stand with your back to the light, hold the thermometer out in

front of you, and look for the mercury column—a silver streak—between the numbers and lines on the glass tube. Twist or turn the tube slightly between your fingers until the silver streak catches the light. This is the secret of *reading the thermometer*.

4. Insert the mercury end of the thermometer into the mouth and under the tongue as far as possible. Close the lips tightly.

5. Wait at least 2, preferably 3 minutes before taking the thermometer out.

6. Read the temperature as directed in No. 3 above. Stand with your back to the light.

Precautions: Take care that the thermometer is not broken when shaking it down. Do not leave the patient with a thermometer in his mouth unattended, especially if he is unconscious, irrational, or paralyzed. Children must always be watched.

Temperature should be taken at least 20 minutes after eating, drinking, smoking, or vigorous exercise.

Clean the thermometer after use with cool water, alcohol, or other cleansing solution. DO NOT USE HOT WATER. It will break the instrument.

It is a good idea to write down the temperature reading and the time it was taken immediately after doing so.

For rectal temperatures, lubricate the mercury end with soap, vaseline, or cold cream before inserting into the rectum about half the length of the thermometer. The maneuver is most easily done with the patient lying on his side. Children may be held across the knee face-down. The rectal thermometer should be held in place. Two minutes is sufficient to register a rectal temperature.

Tendinitis—inflammation of TEN-DONS and their attachments to MUSCLES.

Tendons—the glistening white fibrous connective tissues in which muscle fibers end and which attach the muscles to bones or other body organs. Tendons differ from LIGA-MENTS. (See JOINTS.) Many tendons have a sheath or covering, whose inner layer secretes a lubricating fluid that aids in their smooth action. (See MUS-CLES, BURSA.) The Achilles tendon runs from the calf muscle to the heel bone. (See FOOT, FOOT TROUBLE.)

A *pulled tendon* usually means a sore *muscle*. A pulled ligament usually means a sprained *joint*.

Tenesmus—straining at stool; the nagging feeling and effort to eliminate feces or urine but usually with little success.

Tennis Elbow—a form of *bursitis;* see JOINTS.

Tenosynovitis—inflammation of the connective tissue sheath of a tendon; usually with thickening of the tissue. It is a common cause of *painful wrists*.

Tenotomy—the surgical operation of cutting or dividing a *tendon;* usually for the correction of some such deformity as CLUBFOOT or crosseye.

Tension means putting something on the stretch. *Muscle tension* is the normal condition of the muscles, which are in a state of moderate contraction that gives them *tone. Emotional tension* is equivalent to ANXIETY; see also MENTAL ILLNESS. *Premenstrual tension* is essentially the needless fear of anticipated MENSTRUATION; it involves both *anxiety* and heightened *muscle tension*. The best treatment rarely involves the regular use or prescription of tranquilizing drugs.

Teratoma—any tumor or new growth that includes embryonic tissue; especially teeth and hair of an unborn fetus that did not completely develop. Teratomas are most commonly found in the testes and ovaries.

Terramycin—a broad-spectrum ANTIBIOTIC, isolated from a soil fungus.

Testes—TESTICLES. (See illustration for SEX ORGANS, MALE.)

Testicle—testis; the egg-shaped *male* SEX ORGAN, located in the scrotum and producing SPERM.

Testosterone—MALE SEX HORMONE.

Test Tube—thin-walled, heat-resistant glass tube closed at one end; commonly used in laboratories for chemical and biological experiments; the symbol of the laboratory. What works in a test tube (*in vitro;* literally, in glass), however, may not work in a living organism (*in vivo*).

"Test-Tube Babies" are those produced by *artificial insemination*. See STERILITY.

Tetanus—LOCKJAW. Do not confuse with TETANY.

Tetany—a disease state marked by muscular twitching, tremors, spasms, cramps, or *convulsions*. It can be traced to a fall in the amount of *calcium* in the blood stream. This leaves the muscles in a very irritable state. The fall in calcium, in turn, can be the result of lack of vitamin D, or a failure of the *parathyroid* glands, which regulate calcium metabolism, to secrete an adequate amount of hormone, or other causes. Overbreathing (hyperventilation) may also bring on tetany. The disease is treated by administering calcium, vitamin D, and parathyroid hormones. Tetany is not the same condition as *tetanus,* or LOCKJAW, which is caused by a specific germ.

Thalamus—a part of the BRAIN; the interbrain or tweenbrain, situated at the base of the brain, below the cerebrum. It is the main relay station for sensory nerve impulses to the higher centers of the cerebral cortex. In particular, emotional stimuli appear to be transmitted, transmuted and otherwise acted upon in the thalamus (and its somewhat smaller, neighboring brain substance, the *hypothalamus*). (See illustration for BRAIN.)

Thalassemia—a kind of ANEMIA that occurs in populations hailing from Mediterranean Sea countries. It is serious in infants and children, who usually need repeated blood TRANSFUSIONS, but rarely of significance in adults.

Thelitis—inflammation of the nipple.

Thenar—related to the palm of the hand.

Theobromine—the active (drug) principle, related to CAFFEINE, which is found in the cacao bean; hence in cocoa and chocolate. It is a diuretic, a HEART muscle stimulant and a dilator of small blood vessels.

Theophylline—a drug similar to THEOBROMINE; a diuretic and cardiac stimulant; derived from TEA.

Therapy—*treatment* of disease by any and all means; for example, drug .therapy, physical therapy. Rational treatment depends upon accurate DIAGNOSIS and governs PROGNOSIS.

Therapeutics—the art and science of healing the sick; motivated *treatment* of disease, based on logical (or even illogical) premises. Therapy heals or

alleviates disease; PROPHYLAXIS prevents it. A distinction is sometimes made between therapeutic (curative) and preventive medicine; but the difference tends to break down.

Thermometer. A clinical or fever thermometer is an instrument for registering body temperature accurately. It is a graduated glass tube with a mercury tip or bulb. Such thermometers are rarely in error if used properly. Every medicine chest should be equipped with one, to determine especially whether fever is present when one feels sick. An oral thermometer has a thin mercury tip, a rectal thermometer a round bulb. See TEMPERATURE, for taking a temperature with a clinical thermometer, and FEVER for interpreting what the temperature reading means.

Thiamine—part of the vitamin B complex. See VITAMINS.

"Thin Blood"—see ANEMIA.

Thiourea, and its derivative, *thiouracil,* are powerful drugs, containing sulfur, which interfere with the manufacture of *thyroxin* in the thyroid gland. See ENDOCRINE GLANDS.

Thirst is a symptom of disease, a regular feature of all conditions that raise body temperature to *fever* pitch. It also appears in disease conditions in which much water is removed from the body; notably, DIABETES, KIDNEY TROUBLE, DIARRHEA, large blood loss and physical exhaustion. Thirst is, obviously, relieved by giving water or other fluids by mouth.

Thoracectomy—cutting into the wall of the chest and removing a rib or part of one.

Thoracocentesis—the process of puncturing the chest wall, generally with a hollow needle or TROCAR, and withdrawing accumulated fluids from the chest cavity.

Thoracoplasty—a surgical operation for collapsing a lung by removing the ribs to which it adheres. The operation is employed in advanced cases of tuberculosis and bronchiectasis with excellent prospects of success.

Thorax—the chest; from the neck to the abdomen.

Thrill—a vibration felt by the fingertips or hand applied to the body in the presence of certain kinds of disturbances and disease conditions within the heart. A thrill is felt, for example, when the valve openings of the heart have been narrowed or an ANEURYSM of the aorta is present.

THROAT

The term *throat* is used indiscriminately to describe the front of the neck, or the voicebox (larynx) alone, or, most properly, the cavity in the back of the mouth. This irregularly shaped cavity is called the *pharynx;* it is the spot in the body where the respiratory and digestive systems meet, where the food line and the air line cross. The mouth and nose (nasopharynx) enter the pharynx from above; the larynx and the gullet (esophagus) depart from it below. The Eustachian tubes from the ears open into it, one on each side. A pair of tonsils flank it and adenoids may be included. In front of it hangs the soft palate (uvula). The pharynx is a busy place and it bears the brunt of the common cold and other upper-respiratory infections.

The upper end of the larynx is covered with a flap of cartilage called the *epiglottis.* During the act of swallowing, the larynx rises and contracts so that food and fluid cannot enter. When one attempts to talk while eating, this automatic mechanism may be crossed up and the food is said to "go down the wrong way"—with a choking and coughing accompaniment.

The larynx proper is a cylinder, about 2 inches high, through which air passes on its way to and from the windpipe (trachea) immediately below. The larynx is in a vulnerable position in the front of the neck; but it is protected by a series of five cartilages, notably the thyroid cartilage or "Adam's apple." Inside the larynx

THE THROAT

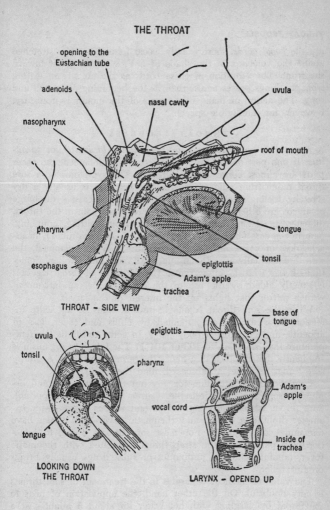

opening to the
Eustachian tube

adenoids

nasopharynx

nasal cavity

uvula

roof of mouth

pharynx

tongue

esophagus

tonsil

epiglottis

Adam's apple

trachea

THROAT – SIDE VIEW

uvula

tonsil

tongue

pharynx

LOOKING DOWN
THE THROAT

base of
tongue

epiglottis

Adam's
apple

vocal cord

inside of
trachea

LARYNX – OPENED UP

are the *vocal cords,* more exactly, vocal folds. They are stretched across the voicebox in the shape of a V, with the point toward the front. The vibration of these cords as the air stream exiting from the lungs passes across them is the beginning of speech and song. The action of many other parts of the mouth is necessary, however, for intelligible speech.

THROAT TROUBLES

A *sore throat* can be a case of *pharyngitis, laryngitis,* or *tonsillitis.* If one part of the throat is infected and inflamed, the other parts are almost certain to be affected. The symptoms of a sore throat range from mild to severe. The first one is usually a dry scratchy feeling. Hoarse or husky voice and excessive discharge of mucus are other early symptoms. Later come pain in the throat, difficulty in talking or swallowing, hawking, spitting, coughing, pain in the ears (because of the blocked Eustachian tubes), headache, loss of voice, and choking sensations. When examined, the sore throat usually appears an angry red color and swollen. Sometimes it has whitish-yellow spots. The diagnosis of throat troubles is greatly aided by the use of the *laryngoscope,* an instrument with a mirror that lights up the interior of the larynx.

When the sore throat is one of several signs of an acute infection, it is usually accompanied by chills and fever, loss of appetite, and generalized body pains. In acute tonsillitis the temperature may shoot up to 103 or 104°F. The infecting organism is frequently the streptococcus; hence the term *strep throat.* A quinsy sore throat describes an abscess behind the tonsils.

Prompt medical attention for any but the most minor and explicable sore throat is desirable. Correct diagnosis is important. Sore throat is one early sign of several serious diseases—for example, diphtheria, polio, and rheumatic fever—and it can have damaging complications. For most sore throats owing to infection, and particularly the strep throat associated with rheumatic fever, administration of antibiotics or sulfa drugs usually brings prompt relief.

The value of medicated gargles in the treatment of sore throats is very doubtful. On the other hand, the application of heat to the throat by gargling with hot water for about 5 minutes at a time may be soothing, if not curative. If the application of an anesthetic or antiseptic to the throat is indicated, the physician will usually "paint" it on with a cotton swab.

In almost every sore throat there is some touch of infection, because the microbes that can cause it are usually present in the upper-respiratory tract. However, there are numerous other factors that may be the primary cause of throat irritation. Among them are heavy smoking; dry, overheated rooms, especially sleeping rooms in the wintertime; dry, arid climates; exposure to dust and fumes; and excessive use of the voice (which the British call "clergyman's sore throat").

The loss of voice that often accompanies a severe case of laryngitis can be remedied most quickly by not using the voice for several days. The vocal cords thus get a needed rest. Hot or cold applications to the throat may be helpful. Warm, moist, "vaporized" air is also soothing to the overworked vocal cords.

Hoarseness is an extremely important symptom of possibly serious throat trouble. It is usually the first symptom of CANCER of the larynx, a site in which the cancer is very often curable by surgery if diagnosis is made sufficiently early. Other annoying, nonmalignant growths on the vocal cords also signal their presence by hoarseness. These too can be surgically removed.

See also TONSILLITIS, GARGLE, NOSE, ADENOIDS.

Thrombin—a part of normal blood which makes BLOOD-CLOTTING possible. It is an enzyme. In circulating blood, it is present as prothrombin *(thrombinogen)*. This is acted upon by *thromboplastin* and calcium salts to form the needle-like network of fibrin which holds the blood clot.

Thromboangiitis — inflammation with clotting of the inner lining of a blood vessel. *Thromboangiitis obliterans*, also known as Buerger's disease, is a condition in which the small blood vessels of the limbs, but particularly the legs, become inflamed and clog up. The process is slow, but if unchecked, it eventually leads to gangrene. Pain is the predominant symptom; whitish patches also appear on the affected parts.

The treatment is nonspecific; but anything that improves the blood circulation to the affected part usually gives much relief; so do painkilling drugs. Thromboangiitis obliterans occurs most frequently in young males. The cause is unknown; but smoking tobacco certainly makes the condition worse and must be absolutely forbidden.

Thrombocytopenia—a relative decrease in the number of red BLOOD platelets (thrombocytes). It occurs in various blood diseases, such as PURPURA.

Thrombophlebitis—a serious disease of the veins in which the formation of blood clots (thrombi) is associated with inflammation of the walls of the vein (phlebitis). Infection or injury may cause the vein walls to become inflamed, and this makes a favorable situation for clots to form. Soreness at the point where the vein is inflamed is usually the first sign of the disease.

The great risk in thrombophlebitis is that blood clots formed in the veins will break off and be carried to the heart and lungs. Here the floating clots, called *emboli*, can do serious damage by clogging the blood vessels. A large embolus in the heart or lungs (pulmonary embolism) may cause sudden death. Small emboli may cause pain in the chest, difficult breathing, or spitting of blood. Until the underlying thrombophlebitis is cleared up, the danger of recurrent emboli remains.

Prolonged inactivity, as in pregnancy and following a surgical operation, is an important factor in allowing clots to form in slightly inflamed or damaged veins. This is one of the important reasons for getting patients out of bed and back on their feet as soon as possible after childbirth or surgical operations.

With modern treatment, recovery from thrombophlebitis is usually quick and satisfactory. An important part of the treatment is use of *anticoagulant* drugs that retard blood clotting.

Thrombosis means the clogging of a blood vessel as the result of the formation of a BLOOD CLOT within the vessel itself. This narrows the lumen (channel or opening) in the vessel and may eventually shut it off entirely. The causes of thrombosis are not fully understood; they probably include such factors as slowing down of the blood circulation owing to HEART DISEASE or KIDNEY TROUBLE, inflammation or other damage to the inner walls of blood vessels, and changes in the clotting tendencies of the blood as the result of ANEMIA, wasting diseases, or altered body METABOLISM.

Coronary thrombosis (or coronary occlusion), a common cause of death, means the clogging of the coronary arteries that supply the heart itself with nourishment. The condition, however, is not always fatal; because the damaged part of the heart muscle (the area of infarction) can be made to recover by putting the patient at rest while the blood finds new channels of flow (collateral circulation) within the heart muscle. Anticoagulant drugs may be given to decrease the risk of clotting. See HEART DISEASE; also THROMBOPHLEBITIS.

Thrombus—a blood clot or plug in a blood vessel that remains at the point where it began to form. See THROMBOSIS; THROMBOPHLEBITIS. If the clot breaks off and is carried along in the blood stream, it is then called an EMBOLUS and produces EMBOLISM.

Thrush—a FUNGUS infection of infants (occasionally of adults) caused by the organism *Candida albicans*. It begins, and usually remains, in the *mouth*, showing up as patchy white spots (aphthae) on the lips, tongue and palate. Fever and gastro-intestinal distress usually accompany the infection, which may spread from the mouth to the groin, buttocks and other parts of the body. The condition is also known as *"white mouth"* and *oral moniliasis*. This condition should not be neglected, either in infants or adults. Prompt diagnosis and treatment is requisite.

Thymus—an ENDOCRINE GLAND.

Thyroid—an ENDOCRINE GLAND; it is enlarged in goiter.

Thyroidectomy—cutting out all or part of the thyroid gland. This surgical operation is performed when the thyroid gland has become enlarged and gives out too much THYROXIN. The diagnosis is usually *goiter* or *Grave's disease*. Some thyroid tissue is always left, because the body will continue to need thyroxin. Hence the operation is generally called *subtotal thyroidectomy*. The surgical skill involved in this procedure includes avoidance of any damage to the nearby nerves (laryngeal nerves) which control the operation of the voicebox. Although thyroidectomy re-

quires incision into the neck, it can be carefully done so that practically no visible scar remains on the throat. See ENDOCRINE glands.

Thyroid Extract—a substance derived from the thyroid (ENDOCRINE) glands of meat animals. It is sometimes included in reducing remedies because it speeds up metabolism, but it should be used only under a doctor's supervision.

Thyroiditis—inflammation of the thyroid gland.

Thyrotoxicosis—goiter; the condition that results when the thyroid gland enlarges and produces too much THYROXIN. See ENDOCRINE glands.

Thyroxin—the important hormone secreted by the thyroid (ENDOCRINE) gland.

Tibia—the shin bone; the larger and inner of the two bones of the lower leg. The other one is the *fibula*. (See illustrations for BONES.)

Tic—a twitching of muscles, especially of the face, constantly repeated; habit spasms. Present theory holds that many tics are expressions of NEUROSES and may have some factor of HEREDITY in their origin. They usually begin in youth. The basic treatment, therefore, is PSYCHOTHERAPY. See MENTAL ILLNESS.

Tic Douloureux—trigeminal neuralgia; lightning pains in the face. See NEURALGIA.

Tick Bites—see INSECTS.

Tincture—any solution of a drug in *alcohol*.

Tincture of Iodine—a solution of IODINE in alcohol; a commonly used SKIN antiseptic. It is the alcohol not the iodine that "stings" when swabbed on broken skin surfaces.

Tinea—RINGWORM; a FUNGUS INFECTION of the SKIN. *Tinea barbae* is barber's itch, affecting the beard; *tinea capitis*, ringworm of the scalp; *tinea cruris*, "jock-strap itch"; *tinea pedis*, athlete's foot.

Tinnitus—ringing, buzzing, roaring, or other sounds in the ears. See EAR TROUBLE.

"Tired Blood"—advertisingese for iron-deficiency ANEMIA.

Tissue—the name for a collection of body CELLS of the same kind in sufficient number to do a particular job. Thus, a great number of MUSCLE cells joined together make up *muscle tissue*. The BRAIN, an enormous aggregate of nerve cells, is *nerve tissue*.

Tissue is also used to describe the aggregate of wood-pulp fibers that make up convenient, disposable, absorbent paper *handkerchiefs*, used for a variety of sanitary purposes (cleansing tissue, toilet tissue, etc.).

Tissue Culture—a method of culturing and growing living tissues outside the body, in flasks or test tubes. The growing CELLS must be fed on a nutrient medium, which contains human or animal serum, and other ingredients necessary to the survival of cells; for example, AMINO ACIDS and VITAMINS.

Tissue culture methods of research are extremely valuable in the study of CANCER and VIRUS diseases.

Virus particles lodge in the test-tube cells and eventually kill them. This is called the *cytopathogenic effect*. However, if human or other serum containing ANTIBODIES against the particular virus is also placed in the test tube, the viruses rather than the cells are killed.

These facts make it possible for laboratories to perform tissue culture tests (neutralization tests) which detect and measure the presence of viruses or their antibodies in the blood stream. The POLIO virus, out of which polio VACCINE is made, is first grown in tissue culture.

Titer—the measurement of quantities obtained when using the chemical and biological laboratory method of TITRATION.

Titration—the laboratory method, used in chemistry and biology, of finding out the quantity of chemicals or viruses in a solution of fluid by measuring it against standard solutions. Titration depends upon an "end point," where something specific, like a color change, takes place.

TOBACCO

Tobacco consists of the dried and "cured" leaves of the plant *Nicotiana tabacum,* widely cultivated in the United States and some other parts of the world. The chemical composition of tobacco leaves varies widely. Its important and unique component is the alkaloid nicotine. Even in small doses, pure nicotine is a poison. Whether the amounts present in tobacco smoke constitute a health hazard is a moot point.

The average nicotine content in the smoke of a regular-size, nonfilter cigarette is about 2.5 milligrams. King-size cigarettes contain about 25% more. The use of the filter has little, if any, advantage in removing nicotine; but it does cut down somewhat on the amount of tar in the smoke. The average tar content in the smoke of one regular-size nonfilter cigarette is about 18 milligrams. In the opinion of most investigators, the effect of cigarette smoking on the respiratory tract—nose, throat, and lungs—arises from the tars, resins, and other combustion products rather than from the nicotine. It should be noted that a cigarette acts as its own filter. If it is not smoked too far (to less than an inch), a considerable amount of the nicotine and tar will be filtered out in the butt.

Why do people smoke? Psychologists have gone to considerable trouble to find out the answer to this question, but there is no single final answer. The answers generally given are: for pleasure, for relaxation, for sociability, for relief of nervous tension, for a sense of security (related to the feeling that an infant gets from sucking a bottle, breast, or thumb), for the feeling of being "grown-up" (among adolescents), and for the reduction of hunger cravings. Some people say they like the sight, smell, and taste of the tobacco smoke; a few admit that the habit is a sublimated pyromania (desire to set fires). The reasons given for not smoking include the belief that it is harmful, religious conviction against it, expense, and lack of desire. Once started, the smoking habit is not easy to break. All advice on this subject boils down to one word: *stop.* Mark Twain is reported to have said, "It's easy to stop smoking. I ought to know, because I've done it a thousand times."

What are the effects of smoking on health? This is an exceedingly complex question. Smoke absorbed from the mouth and lungs probably has some effect on all tissues of the body, but the extent and harm, if any, of these effects in a particular person cannot be stated with assurance. People vary a great deal in their response to tobacco. For some people 10 cigarettes a day is heavy smoking; for others, 40.

It is generally agreed that children, adolescents, athletes in training, victims of disease in the small blood vessels of the extremities (Raynaud's disease and Buerger's disease), and people with stomach ulcers or coronary heart disease should not smoke. Under any circumstances, moderation in smoking is a good rule.

Conscientious investigators have uncovered a wide variety of physiological and pharmacological effects ("symptoms") as a result of tobacco smoking. Many of the effects are transient and, as noted, individual reactions vary greatly. Nevertheless smoking is known to have effects upon the respiratory, gastrointestinal, circulatory, and nervous systems.

Absorbed nicotine acts at first as a stimulant to the cerebrum of the brain and to the autonomic nervous system. But large doses have a depressant effect. Too heavy smoking, therefore, may result in dizziness, nausea, and diarrhea (as beginning smokers discover), and sometimes overexcitement and insomnia. There is also a rare condition, known as tobacco amblyopia, in which the optic nerve is affected and vision (especially for color) is disturbed.

Smoking sometimes increases gastric acidity, which is why it is forbidden in the presence of stomach ulcers. Partly, perhaps, because it dulls the senses of taste and smell, smoking also suppresses hunger contractions and appetite. Many people who give up or cut down on their smoking find that their appetite for food increases enormously.

The effects of smoking on the circulatory system include elevation in blood pressure, increase in heart and pulse rates, constriction of the peripheral arteries, and decrease in the skin temperature, especially of the fingers and toes. Dr. Grace Roth showed that these effects were the result chiefly of nicotine and that they occurred even in habitual smokers after smoking two cigarettes. Some doctors, therefore, forbid smoking in patients with high blood pressure and hypertensive heart disease. Many others feel that moderate smoking does help these patients to overcome certain nervous tension and is therefore justifiable. Most physicians do not believe that smoking places a serious burden on the heart—except in the presence of well-defined coronary artery disease. A committee of the American Heart Association reported in March, 1956:

"The available evidence is not sufficient to define the effect of tobacco smoking upon the coronary arteries or upon the heart itself except in the small group mentioned above who already have coronary artery disease. It is believed that if smoking plays any part in the causation of heart disease, it is only one of many factors. . . . Much greater knowledge is needed before any conclusion can be drawn concerning relationship between smoking and increased death rates from coronary heart disease."

The irritant effect of smoking on the upper-respiratory tract is often evident in the condition known as "smoker's cough" or "cigarette cough." It clears up when smoking is stopped or greatly reduced. More serious conditions in the respiratory tract—bronchitis, emphysema, and cancer of the lung—have also been attributed to heavy smoking. But here the evidence is far from being indisputably positive. Whatever injury smoking may do to the respiratory tract appears to have far less to do with the nicotine content of tobacco than with the tars and resins and dust it contains and with other products of combustion that a burning cigarette yields.

Smoking and lung cancer. The relationship of smoking to CANCER of the lung has not yet been resolved. Strong opinions are held on both sides of the question. The possibility that increase in smoking practice in the United States was a "cause" of the rapidly increasing death rate from lung cancer was suggested many years ago. In June, 1954, and again in 1957, the statistical department of the American Cancer Society released an impressive study which appeared to confirm this possibility. In a study of the deaths of 187,000 American men between the ages of 50 and 70, the statisticians found, among many other things, that the death rate from lung cancer among heavy cigarette smokers (a pack a day or more) was at least five times as high as among nonsmokers. In a later refinement of this statistical study, it has been stated that lung cancer is about 27 times as frequent among men who smoke two packages of cigarettes a day as among men who have never smoked.

These statistical conclusions have been challenged on several grounds and a number of important studies are under way to adduce more definitive evidence. Dr. Clarence C. Little, chairman of the scientific advisory board of the Tobacco Industry Research Committee, has stated: "Any possible role of smoking in the etiology of lung cancer remains an unresolved question. It cannot be said that smoking has been absolved from suspicion; neither have the charges . . . been proven."

The American Cancer Society says it has no plans for a campaign against smoking, although it intends to publicize widely the facts which will enable an individual to make up his own mind whether or not to smoke.

It seems reasonable to suppose that something in the air we breathe is also playing a role in the increase in lung cancer deaths. These air pollutants may arise in varying amounts from sources other than tobacco smoke. Suggested sources of these pollutants are industrial wastes and automobile exhausts.

Toes—the five digits of the feet, analogous to the five fingers of the hand. See FOOT and FOOT TROUBLE; also JOINTS. *Pigeon-toe* (pes varus) is the condition in which the leg and foot are turned so that the toes point inward (toe-in). *Hammertoe* is a claw-like bending of the outer joints (distal phalanges) of one or more, but usually second, toes.

Toenail—see NAILS.

Tolerance—the ability of the human body, or other living organism—notably MICROBES—to resist the usually anticipated effects of drugs, poisons or other kind of stress.

Tolerance is usually acquired by previous experience with the drug or stress. If a drug is taken in gradually increasing doses, a tolerance for it often develops.

This is the principle of the desensitization treatment for various kinds of ALLERGY. It is also the reason for not taking penicillin and other ANTIBIOTIC drugs indiscriminately, when they are not really necessary. One's microbes become accustomed to the antibiotic and it no longer affects them; they tolerate it. See also RESISTANCE.

-tomy—a suffix that indicates a cutting, usually a cutting into, surgical operation; for example, *phlebotomy*, cutting into a vein. Compare with—*ectomy*, a cutting out operation; for example, THYROIDECTOMY, which means cutting out and removing part of the thyroid gland.

TONGUE

The tongue is composed of a number of highly mobile muscles covered with a special kind of mucous membrane that includes *taste-buds.* The very movable front part is called the *tip;* the more or less fixed back part, the *root.*

The tongue has many muscle attachments in the mouth. One muscle on each side connects it with the jawbone; and these muscles make it possible to stick out the tongue. Other muscles, which pull it back in the mouth, are attached to the hyoid bone, the roof of the mouth, the voicebox and bones at the sides of the skull.

Underneath the tongue is a fold of mucous membrane (frenum) that attaches to the floor of the mouth and reins in the tongue. If this frenum (rein) extends too far forward toward the tip of the tongue, it produces the condition of *"tongue-tie."* Fortunately this can be relieved by a simple surgical operation, cutting through the frenum.

The tongue is richly supplied with nerves and blood vessels. It has five nerve-supply branches on each side, coming from the cranial nerves. When the tongue is bitten, or otherwise injured, an immediate sharp pain is registered. On the other hand, because of the rich blood supply, injuries to the tongue usually heal rapidly.

The tongue is essential to the production of *speech,* to the swallowing of food and to the sense of *taste.*

While *taste-buds* are scattered in many parts of the mouth—on the palate and back in the throat—many sensitive buds are located on the tongue. The small, rounded elevations (papillae) on the tip of the tongue are taste-buds.

The finer discriminations of taste, which is a cultivated sense, depend as much upon the sense of smell as on the sense of taste. The four basic tastes, which almost everybody can discriminate, are (1) sweet, (2) salt, (3) bitter and (4) acid. Sweet is usually appreciated at the tip of the tongue, acid on the sides, bitter at the back.

Tongue signs. The condition of *the tongue reflects many kinds of disease;* but it is not wise for a physician or anyone else to make a diagnosis based solely on the appearance of the tongue.

A moist, clean tongue is generally an indication of good health—but not always so. A dry, furred (coated) tongue may indicate or point to some underlying disease. The furring may be white, brown, yellow or even black.

Fevers are often associated with a furred tongue; notably, TYPHOID FEVER. In scarlet fever a "strawberry tongue" sometimes appears; white "fur" through which angry red dots protrude.

A furred tongue, though sometimes associated with gastro-intestinal upsets, should *not,* however, be taken as a sign of CONSTIPATION or a signal for giving or taking a laxative.

A bright red and smooth tongue ("beet tongue") is often a sign of PELLAGRA or other VITAMIN-deficiency disease.

Paralysis of one side of the tongue, causing slurred or mumbling *speech,* is a frequent outcome of STROKE (apoplexy). The rapidity with which the tongue-paralysis clears up is a good indication of the general recovery from stroke. Loss of sensation and taste on one side of the tongue is also an indicator of various kinds of BRAIN damage. Tremor of the tongue, with difficult speech, is a sign of many kinds of nerve and brain damage; for example, PARKINSON'S disease. It also appears in ALCOHOLISM.

Burning tongue, usually with a smooth red appearance *(glossitis),* is a common symptom of disease. The causes, however, are numerous and must be carefully investigated. Among them are PELLAGRA, pernicious ANEMIA, STOMACH TROUBLE, bad TEETH, false teeth, and tooth fillings with metals of different electric potentials (e. g., gold and silver amalgams). When such fillings are on opposite sides of the mouth, moistened by saliva, they may turn it into a weak electric battery and leave a metallic taste in the mouth.

Raised white patches on the tongue, especially in children, may be an indication of THRUSH ("white mouth"), a FUNGUS infection.

Small, smooth white patches on the tongue, separated by deep fissures, in adults are called *leukoplakia* and are the result of continued irritation, particularly smoking. These patches usually give little trouble, if any. However, some investigators feel that they are forerunners of possible CANCER of the tongue, which will develop later in life. The evidence on this point is certainly not strong enough to warrant interdiction on smoking.

Geographical tongue is the rare condition in which the tongue displays white patches, interspersed with bare red areas and elevations and depressions of tissue so that it looks like a relief map in miniature. The cause is not known; nor is the condition serious. It usually clears up with the use of mouthwashes and DIET rich in VITAMINS, liver and iron.

(See illustrations for DIGESTIVE SYSTEM; NOSE; RESPIRATORY SYSTEM; THROAT.)

Tonic is a "pick-me-up" drug; tonics are rarely prescribed by physicians. They are the stand-by of old wives and fools who treat themselves.

When a person thinks, or is told, he needs a tonic, what he really needs in most cases is a thorough medical examination to locate the reasons or underlying disease conditions that may be weakening him. More specific and effective treatment than a shotgun tonic can then be prescribed.

The principal ingredient of all famous and successful tonics is ethyl *alcohol*. This tonic is simply a medicated cocktail; it is the alcohol, however, which usually gives the desired effect. Such tonics have had a great vogue among women who have taken them for years for "FE-MALE TROUBLES" without being aware that they were sometimes just getting a little tipsy in the process. Many of them would refuse to drink *liquor*.

Tonics have also sold well in states where the sale of alcoholic beverages is prohibited by law.

Tonsils—a pair of almond-shaped lymphoid-tissue masses in the back of the throat. Sometimes they are large, sometimes small. Like all lymph tissue, they release phagocytes that destroy bacteria. Sometimes, however, they themselves become overwhelmed with infection and are chronically diseased. This inflammation of the tonsils,

called *tonsillitis,* is usually evidenced by a sore throat. Repeated attacks suggest that the tonsils should be removed. The operation is called *tonsillectomy.* It should not be performed when there is a risk of polio in the community. (See illustrations for NOSE; THROAT.)

Tonsillectomy—surgical removal of tonsils, with snare, knife or by electrocoagulation. This is a common and highly perfected surgical operation. However, it must be performed under optimum hospital conditions because complications, such as excessive bleeding, can occur.

Tonsillectomies are no longer routinely performed on all children. Candidates for operation are more carefully selected on the basis of history of repeated colds, frequent sore throat and definite enlargement of the TONSILS.

Enlargement alone, however, is not a sufficient reason for operation. Repeated infection, tonsillitis, which cannot be readily controlled by antibiotics and other medication is the chief indication for tonsillectomy. ADENOID tissue is usually removed at the same time.

Tonsillitis—sore THROAT owing to inflammation of the TONSILS.

Toothache—see TEETH.

Tophi—chalky stone deposits (urates) found in or near joints (and sometimes in the ear) in GOUT.

Torsion—twisting. The term describes the twisting of organs in the body so that their blood supply is limited. It also describes the application of a TOURNIQUET to stop bleeding. The term is also used in OPHTHALMOLOGY to describe rotation in clockwise or counterclockwise direction.

Torticollis—wryneck; head twisted on the shoulders.

Touch. The sense of touch depends upon the presence of end-organs (exteroreceptors) of the peripheral NERVOUS SYSTEM on or near the surface of the skin and mucous membranes in all parts of the body. These sensory end-organs, or end-plates, are not, however, equally distributed. There are far more on the fingertips and on the tip of the tongue than on the other parts of the body; more on the palms of the hands than on the arms; more on the arms and legs than on the back.

The end-organs on the skin are more or less specific for the sensations they record and flash back to the brain—just as the retina of the EYE is specific for light and records all sensations upon it in terms of light.

The sense of touch includes end-organ sensitivity to *touch sense proper,* by which we feel the shape, size and texture of objects with which we come in contact; *pressure sense,* by which we judge the weight of objects laid upon the skin; *heat sense; cold sense; pain sense; muscular sense,* which enables us to judge the weight and heft of an object held in the hands; *muscular sensitivity,* which makes us react to a pinch or a squeeze; *positional sense,* by which we can without looking gauge the position of the limbs and other parts of the body; and a kind of *common sensation,* perhaps related to the pain sense, which makes us feel tickling or creeping sensations on the skin, a sense of fullness in the abdomen and even a general sense of well-being.

The sense of touch is disturbed in a number of disease conditions which affect the nervous system. In neuralgia, the skin in the affected areas may be extremely tender to touch, pressure, heat or cold; toothache—dental neuralgia—is another good example. When spinal nerves are injured, as in late syphilis (TABES), the sense of touch and pain in the arms and feet may disappear.

Tourniquet—any instrument designed to stop bleeding by exerting pressure somewhere along the line of the opened blood vessel. Most tourniquets are designed to increase pressure on the vessel by turning a screw or twisting a strap or handle. The tourniquet is often life-saving when properly applied to stop massive bleeding.

The simplest, make-shift type of tourniquet consists of a belt or strip of cloth (a folded handkerchief) looped around a badly bleeding arm or leg and twisted until the bleeding

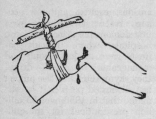

A crude tourniquet applied.

stops. The twisting can be facilitated by putting a stick through the loop of the tourniquet and turning the stick. A pad or hard object (stone) placed in the lower loop to bring pressure against the bleeding vessel is also useful.

However, *direct pressure* on the gaping wound will often serve as well as the tourniquet to stop bleeding. The tourniquet has the further risk, in the hands of amateurs, that it may be put on too tightly and not loosened soon enough or often enough. Under such conditions it may cause GANGRENE.

Toxemia -poisoning by way of the blood stream, usually from toxins released by MICROBES or by decomposition of body products.

Toxemia of pregnancy describes a number of metabolic disturbances which the pregnant woman may suffer—up to and including fits and convulsions *(eclampsia)*. The causes remain uncertain; they may be related to nutrition, endocrine disturbances, impaired kidney function. Careful medical observation and prompt treatment can materially lessen the burden and risk of toxemias of pregnancy. See PREGNANCY; CHILDBIRTH.

Toxic—poisonous.

Toxicity—the degree of poisonousness. The dose makes the poison. Every drug is a potential poison. Toxicity studies on animals are used to determine how much, or how little, of the substance under test will kill the experimental animal.

Toxicology—the scientific study of poisons and their antidotes.

Toxin—a poison. It may be a chemical substance introduced into the body (arsenic) or the end-product of MICROBES that invade the body; for example, the toxin produced by the diphtheria bacillus, the neuro*toxin* engendered by the BOTULISM microbe, or snake venom.

Toxin-Antitoxin—a neutral mixture of a bacterial toxin and its antitoxin; especially the DIPHTHERIA toxin-antitoxin (T.A.T.)

Toxoid—a form of DRUG (biological) given to produce IMMUNITY to specific diseases, notably DIPHTHERIA and TETANUS. See "SHOTS."

Toxoplasmosis—infection with the protozoan parasite *Toxoplasma gondii;* usually encountered in infants, who may suffer repeated convulsions.

Trachea—windpipe; running from the voicebox down to the

bronchi of the LUNGS. (See illustrations for ENDOCRINE GLANDS; RESPIRATORY SYSTEM; THROAT.)

Tracheitis—inflammation of the windpipe, usually accompanied by BRONCHITIS.

Tracheotomy—cutting into the trachea (windpipe) from the front of the throat to provide a temporary air passage. This is an emergency operation occasionally required by children choking to death with diphtheria or polio patients whose breathing apparatus is failing (respiratory paralysis).

Trachoma—a serious eye disease; a form of conjunctivitis. See EYE TROUBLE.

Traction—pulling, drawing or stretching action. It often refers to methods of setting broken BONES in which the limbs or head are pulled in a definite direction and kept that way by weights, pulleys and frames.

Tragacanth—gum arabic; a sticky vegetable substance that absorbs water and swells up. It is used as a demulcent and as a vehicle for drugs.

Trance—the "half-asleep, half-awake" state associated with HYPNOSIS. It also means a deep sleep from which a person cannot be easily aroused; it may be induced by HYSTERIA.

Tranquilizers—or ataraxics, are a class of drugs whose principal effect is to calm down nervous, anxious, excited, agitated people. After their use was first demonstrated in psychiatric hospitals, where difficult patients were made tranquil and manageable by these drugs, they skyrocketed into use among less disturbed people. It is estimated that in 1956 over 35 million prescriptions for tranquilizers were written. Although the tranquilizers reduce anxiety, anguish, hostility, and destructiveness in many patients, psychiatrists have urged caution in their indiscriminate use. The American Psychiatric Association stated in 1956: "These drugs have not been in use long enough to determine the full range, duration and medical significance of their side effects." The question has also been raised, How tranquil can you get?

The first of the crop of tranquilizers was reserpine, the active alkaloid of the plant *Rauwolfia serpentina*, isolated in 1952. Rauwolfia, grown in India and other parts of the Far East, had been used in India for centuries as an herb medicine (extract of the roots) for nervousness, fevers, and insomnia. Indian biochemists had reported on the use of Rauwolfia as a hypertensive drug in 1931, and its use for this purpose is still indicated. With the first hint of success, the biochemists went to work and a score of Rauwolfia derivatives or alkaloids were isolated and marketed. Other synthetic drugs with tranquilizing effects followed shortly. Most of them are central nervous system depressants. They are marketed under many trade names (of which Miltown is the best known). The chemical names of these drugs include: chlorpromazine, meprobamate, piperazine, prochlorperazine, and promazine.

Transference—a technical term in PSYCHOANALYSIS. It describes the process whereby a patient reproduces his early loves and hates during his analysis—and may fall in love with the analyst as a substitute for a long-lost parent.

Transfusion of blood has become commonplace in modern hospital and surgical practice. The fact that a patient gets a blood transfusion does not mean that he is dangerously ill or on the critical list. The value of whole blood as a treatment agent has been amply demonstrated since World War II.

Most blood transfusions today are *indirect* transfusions, that is, from blood stored under refrigeration in a hospital BLOOD BANK. To the blood given by the donor has been added a preservative, such as sodium citrate, that prevents clotting. The transfused blood is dripped into the vein of the recipient through a plastic or rubber tube and a hollow needle inserted into the vein. Arm veins are generally used because they are most accessible.

Transfusion today is safe and common because the blood of the donor is *matched* with the blood of the recipient. See BLOOD GROUPS and RH FACTOR.

Transillumination—a technic of applying a strong light close to or inside a body cavity so that it can be seen through, thus revealing some disease process, if present. A strong light in the mouth, for example, will transilluminate nasal sinuses.

Transvestism—the emotional quirk, carried to adult extremes, which induces a person to wear the clothes of the opposite sex. Compare with MENTAL ILLNESS; PSEUDO-HERMAPHRODITE.

Trapezius—the large muscle stretching over the shoulder from the back of the neck to the collarbone. It raises the shoulder and draws the shoulderblade backward. (See illustration for MUSCLES.)

Trauma—an injury or wound brought about by an outside force of greater or lesser degree. It is a medical word that is exceptionally difficult to appreciate. Generally speaking, it means injury by violence; but it may also apply to the wound produced by the surgeon's healing knife and manipulation of body tissues. *Birth trauma* means injury in the process of being born. Sometimes this produces actual BRAIN damage, with later organic symptoms. There is one school of psychiatry that holds that being born is itself a shocking and traumatic experience from which it is impossible to recover fully. *Psychic trauma* is emotional shock, the result of an event or circumstance etched tragically and unforgettably on the conscious and unconscious mind, a searing experience. Compare trauma with LESION.

Treatment—the sum of drugs, nursing, and all other attention given to a sick person with the idea of getting him well; THERAPY. Rational treatment depends upon reasonable DIAGNOSIS. The wise man avoids QUACK treatments and self-treatment. "He who has himself for a physician has a fool for a patient."

Tremor—involuntary shaking, trembling or quivering; shaking palsy. See PARKINSON'S DISEASE. This is a neuromuscular symptom of many possible origins, including alcoholism and metallic poisonings.

Trench Fever—a World War I disease, caused by a RICKETTSIA and transmitted by body lice. See INSECTS; TYPHUS.

Trench Foot—essentially frostbite of the foot, from slogging in icy water. See FOOT TROUBLE.

Trench Mouth—inflammation of the GUMS (Vincent's infection) with ulcerations that may also extend to the TONSILS (VINCENT'S ANGINA). The breath has a bad odor. The causation of this condition is complex and not thoroughly understood. Anaerobic (living without air) bacteria are usually present. It is not certain either how or whether the disease is transmitted from one person to another. Dirty mouths and unfavorable living conditions, as in wartime trenches, favor its development. Hydrogen peroxide, which releases oxygen, has been used to treat it—but without much success.

Trephine, or trepan, means either the instrument or the operation by which a circular hole is made in the skull, a round disk of bone being removed. The operation may also be applied to the outer coat of the eyeball to reduce tension (see EYE TROUBLE; GLAUCOMA).

Trephining of the skull is one of the oldest *known* surgical operations. Prehistoric people, by the evidence of skulls found in burial places, practiced it. The purpose of the operation is to get inside or to relieve pressure inside the cranial cavity.

Treponema—a class of spiral, "corkscrew" MICROBES, including that of SYPHILIS (*Treponema pallida*) and YAWS.

Triad—a group of three signs and symptoms, indicating a specific disease syndrome. For example, (1) a swollen neck, (2) a fast heartbeat and (3) pop-eyes make up *Basedow's triad* and point to exophthalmic goiter. (See THYROID.)

Trichiasis—ingrowing hairs; most commonly, ingrowing eyelashes, which can irritate and damage the eyeball. This condition may be congenital or may follow upon an inflammation of the eyelids that distorts their normal position. The condition is troublesome but can be readily controlled.

Trichinella—a class of WORMS (nematode parasites) that infest man, household and farm animals, notably pigs. It is the cause of TRICHINOSIS.

Trichinosis—a disease caused by infestation with TRICHINELLA *spiralis,* a hair-like parasite barely visible to the naked eye. The early symptoms include loose bowels, fever, griping, and nausea. Later in the course of the disease the patient may suffer from stiffness, pain and swelling in the muscles, excessive sweating, continued fever and sleeplessness. The diagnosis is difficult, but may be confirmed by an intradermal skin test, done with an extract of larvae from the trichinella.

The worm enters the human body (or that of other carnivores like the rat and the pig) in the form of cysts enclosed in the flesh (meat, muscles) eaten. The cysts are dissolved in the intestine and the parasite multiplies freely therein. Thence it travels to the muscles by way of the blood stream and again goes into its encysted capsules —causing muscle pains. Little in the way of effective treatment can be offered.

Prevention of trichinosis is simple, if practiced. *Never eat uncooked pork or pork products.* Control of trichinosis is a public health problem; swine should not be fed on uncooked garbage.

Trichitis—inflammation at the roots of the HAIR.

Trichobezoar—a hair-ball; a massed lump of hair discovered in the stomach or bowels. It may result from constant chewing of the ends of the HAIR of the head.

Trichology—the sum of knowledge about the HAIR.

Trichomonas—a class of parasites—PROTOZOA—that infest human beings, birds and animals. Each parasite is pear-shaped and has three or five little "propellors" (*flagellae*) at the head end by means of which it moves about.

In man this organism may be found in the mouth, intestines, lungs and genito-urinary tract. Sometimes it makes trouble; at other times it is just there.

Trichomonas vaginalis is the species that causes difficulty most often; it inhabits the *vagina* and brings about a VAGINITIS, inflammation of the vagina, accompanied by ITCHING and vaginal discharge (see FEMALE TROUBLES). An acid condition of the vagina favors the growth and activity of the trichomonas.

This is a troublesome condition to treat, and there is no "sure cure." The discomfort of the condition can be alleviated with a variety of medicated douches, powders, tablets and insufflations—including ANTIBIOTICS.

The treatment is usually prolonged. There is, however, a great tendency for the condition to recur—since 30% to 40% of all women harbor *Trichomonas vaginalis* (without symptoms) all the time. The parasite can invade the bladder and urethra.

Men can become infected with trichomonas organisms, with resulting discharge from the penis (sometimes mistaken for GONORRHEA) and inflammation of the PROSTATE gland (*prostatitis*). They can thus infect women with trichomonas.

Careful medical attention is necessary in the management of trichomonas infections. Home remedies are to be deplored.

Trichomoniasis — TRICHOMONAS infection.

Trichophyton—a FUNGUS that attacks skin, hair and nails, causing what is called RINGWORM.

Trichophytosis—RINGWORM of the scalp, face, beard, body, crotch or nails, caused by infection with the FUNGUS, TRICHOPHYTON. Also called *tinea*.

Tricuspid—usually refers to the three-pointed valves of the HEART.

Trigeminal Neuralgia—lightning pains in the face, along the course of the trigeminal nerve. See NEURALGIA.

Trigonitis—inflammation in the bladder; a form of cystitis; see BLADDER TROUBLE.

Trocar—a surgical instrument, a punch with a sharp point, used for piercing body cavities to remove excess fluids. It is usually employed in connection with a hollow tube—*cannula*—into which it fits tightly, except for the exposed point. When the puncture is made, the trocar is withdrawn and the accumulated fluid runs out through the cannula.

Trochanter—parts of the thighbone (femur). The trochanters are situated just below the neck of the femur. One is called the *greater trochanter;* the other, the *lesser trochanter.*

Troche—any medicated lozenge for sucking rather than swallowing.

Tropical Diseases are those which occur exclusively, or almost so, in tropical countries with hot climates, both wet and dry. Most important is MALARIA. Among others, mentioned in this book, are BERIBERI, blackwater fever, DENGUE, DYSENTERY, CHOLERA, ELEPHANTIASIS, PLAGUE, LEPROSY, SLEEPING SICKNESS, YELLOW FEVER and YAWS.

True Skin—the dermis, or lower layer of the SKIN.

Truss—any device for holding a reduced HERNIA in place. It is most commonly used in the palliative treatment of inguinal hernia or RUPTURE.

Many types of trusses for adults are available. The important thing is that they should be well-fitted and comfortable. They should be prescribed by the doctor and made and fitted by the truss-maker. The essential parts of a truss are (1) the properly shaped pad that fits over the rupture and pushes the loop of gut back into place, (2) a metal spring or belt that encircles the pelvis and keeps gently pushing on the herniated area, and (3) a strap between the legs to keep the truss in place and keep it from "working up." A poorly fitted truss is worse than none at all.

Trypanosomiasis — SLEEPING SICKNESS, caused by invasion of the blood stream by a tiny parasite, known as a *trypanosome,* and transmitted by insect bite.

Trypsin—an ENZYME, an important part of the pancreatic secretion, which breaks down protein in the DIGESTIVE SYSTEM.

Tsetse Fly—the vector of African SLEEPING SICKNESS, TRYPANOSOMIASIS.

Tsutsugamushi—a RICKETTSIA-

caused, TYPHUS-like disease of the Far East, occurring in Japan, Sumatra, Malaya and Australia. The disease is transmitted by the bite of a mite (trombicula). The disease is named after the Japanese expression for "dangerous bug." See INSECTS.

Tubercle—a nodule or small rounded lump or mass found on the skin or bones or in the lungs; especially the characteristic little nodule in the lungs produced by the tubercle bacillus and characteristic of the disease TUBERCULOSIS.

Tubercular—having small nodes or nodules; TUBERCLES. Compare with TUBERCULOUS.

Tuberculin—any one of a great variety of preparations made from the tubercle bacillus. Robert Koch made so-called "old tuberculin" in 1890 and thought it might be a cure for tuberculosis. It wasn't. Since that time, tuberculin preparations have been used principally in skin tests for the diagnosis of TUBERCULOSIS. See MANTOUX TEST.

TUBERCULOSIS

Tuberculosis, otherwise known as *phthisis, consumption,* the *"white plague,"* and once "Captain of the Men of Death," is an infectious disease caused by the tubercle bacillus (Mycobacterium tuberculosis). It was once the leading cause of death in the United States (and still is in some foreign countries), but the death rate dropped 90% in 40 years. An estimated 400,000 active cases of tuberculosis still exist in the United States, many among people who don't know it. One of the biggest tasks in controlling tuberculosis is to find these undiscovered cases, who unwittingly spread the infection.

Once the tubercle bacillus enters the body, it can settle in any part—bones and joints, bladder, kidneys and adrenal glands, for example. But in 90% of the cases, the affected organs are the lungs, so that the serious disease problem is *pulmonary tuberculosis.* Many humpbacks are victims of tuberculosis of the spine (Pott's disease).

How is tuberculosis spread? "Tuberculosis comes from tuberculosis." It spreads by contact with infected people and the germ they emit. The hardy tubercle bacillus can live outside the body, often for a considerable time. Tuberculosis is often a "household epidemic," because there are many chances for the bacillus to spread in the intimate family circle. When a patient with active tuberculosis spits, coughs, sneezes, or just talks, he can disgorge as many as 3,000,000 tubercle bacilli a day! The germs hitchhike to other lungs on droplets of moisture.

Milk from cows afflicted with bovine tuberculosis was once an important source of infection. However, with the destruction of infected herds and pasteurizing of milk, the risk of tuberculosis infection from milk is practically zero.

How does the infection act? Not everyone who gets tubercle bacilli into his body actually falls sick with tuberculosis. Indeed, comparatively few do! There is a tremendously important factor of resistance to the germ in the body of the human host. A primary, or first-infection, type of tuberculosis often occurs in childhood, and is usually so mild that it goes unnoticed. The invading bacilli are killed or surrounded and walled-off in a capsule, or tubercle, from which the disease gets its name. In later years a reinfection or adult type of tuberculosis occurs. In any event, when the body's resistance can no longer keep the bacillus in check, active tuberculosis results. This infection may be arrested by adequate and successful treatment, or it may progress toward advanced tuberculosis and possibly death. The disease may become chronic, lasting for years. "Open cases" are those capable of transmitting the infection. "Closed" or "arrested" cases are those in which the germs remain locked in the tissues. These people are a risk only to themselves. The disease may become active again if their resistance falls below a critical level.

What lowers resistance and permits tubercle bacilli to become active in the body? No one can say exactly, but the possibilities include poor food, insufficient rest, overwork, worry, other illness, and excessive emotional strain. A high level of general health offers some protection against tuberculosis.

Who gets tuberculosis? Anyone can and many do—without harm. In earlier times, active, rapidly progressing tuberculosis appeared to be primarily a disease of youth. Now it is becoming a disease of old men. In the United States there is a high concentration of the disease in nonwhite groups, Negroes, Indians, and Orientals, for whom special efforts to control the disease are warranted.

Low standards of living are associated with high death rates from tuberculosis. The disease is more prevalent in poor, underprivileged, crowded, unsanitary slum areas. Sir William Osler once said, "Tuberculosis is a social problem with a medical aspect."

Occupation plays a role in tuberculosis incidence. Workers in the dusty trades—miners, stonecutters, sandblasters—are particularly susceptible. Exposed to the inhalation of silica dust, they develop *silicosis*, upon which tuberculosis of the lungs is superimposed.

How can tuberculosis be diagnosed or discovered? The onset is often slow and insidious. Early symptoms are usually vague. Among possible early danger signals are fatigue not relieved by rest, unexplained loss of weight and energy, loss of appetite, persistent coughing and hoarseness, afternoon fever, night sweats, and spitting blood (hemoptysis) or blood-streaked sputum. None of these symptoms definitely means tuberculosis; they are signals for a medical check-up. Periodic chest X rays are the surest way of catching early tuberculosis. Skin tests with tuberculin (Mantoux test) will also reveal present or *past* infections. A positive diagnosis of active tuberculosis is made by chest X rays and by discovering tubercle bacilli in the sputum.

How is tuberculosis treated? The modern essentials in treatment of tuberculosis are bed rest, good food, and where indicated, drugs and surgery. These essentials are best supplied in a special tuberculosis hospital or sanitarium. Ailing lungs must themselves sometimes be put at rest, splinted as it were. This is accomplished by various forms of collapse therapy, which includes such surgery as cutting away parts of ribs and introduction of a measured amount of air into the pleural cavity to compress the lung (pneumothorax).

New drugs, however, are revolutionizing the treatment of tuberculosis. The antibiotic, streptomycin, was the first drug that gave promise of usefulness. However, *isoniazid* and drugs like it have provided the great changes. The need for hospital beds for tuberculosis patients is rapidly declining, because these new drugs promptly render the patient noninfectious and make it possible for him to be safely treated at home.

How can tuberculosis be controlled? By eliminating the sources or reservoirs of infection. This is done by adequate case-finding through chest X rays, tuberculin tests, and contact tracing; providing proper facilities for treatment; isolating patients with active tuberculosis when necessary; and rendering patients noninfectious by treatment, which is where the new drugs come in. Vaccination against tuberculosis with *BCG vaccine* is another control measure, but it has not been generally adopted in the United States.

Control of tuberculosis has been, and remains, one of the great challenges to the public-health movement around the world. In the U.S. great credit for the change in the tuberculosis picture belongs to the Christmas-seal-supported *National Tuberculosis Association,* the oldest voluntary health association in the country. Its program of education, research, and service looks to the day when tuberculosis may be eradicated.

Tuberculous—suffering from or resulting from infection with the tubercle bacillus; i.e., TU-BERCULOSIS.

Tuberosity—a part of a BONE that sticks out or stands out.

Tularemia—rabbit fever. The disease was originally described in Tulare County, California. Although wild rabbits are the chief reservoir of the MICROBE *(Pasteurella tularensis)* that causes the disease in human beings, it is also found among other rodents; for example, squirrels, muskrats, opossums.

The animal plague *(epizootic)* is spread and kept alive by transmission of the microbe through INSECT bites: ticks, fleas, lice. It is transmitted to human beings chiefly through handling the carcasses of infected rabbits. Well-cooked rabbit meat is safe to eat, for the tularemia microbe is killed at temperatures of 130° F.

The first sign of tularemia, among rabbit handlers, is an ulcer, occurring several days after contact, at the site where the microbe entered the body—usually some cut or skin abrasion on the hand. Swelling and inflammation of the LYMPH glands soon follow. Later symptoms may include high FEVER, aching in muscles and joints, headache, and great weakness, lasting for a few weeks. Tularemia, fortunately, responds to treatment with many of the broad-spectrum ANTIBIOTICS; e.g. aureomycin, terramycin.

Tumescence—a swelling; physiologically normal in such events as the erection of the penis, pathological in such instances as a swollen "black eye."

Tumor describes a swelling or, more commonly, a new growth of useless CELLS and tissues anywhere in the body. Most tumors are *benign* and self-limited in growth, but often should be removed. Some are *malignant*, and must be removed or otherwise treated. Tumor is *not* the same as CANCER, which see.

Turbinate—part of the inside of the NOSE. At the top of the nasal cavities, there are three small, irregularly shaped projections of bone (covered by mucous membrane) which form three small ducts, upper, middle and lower, in which air is moistened and warmed as it passes through the nose on its way to the lungs. The lower (or inferior) turbinate may become inflamed and enlarged, impeding air flow. The nasal sinuses open off the turbinates. See SINUS TROUBLE.

Turgor—swelling or fullness, especially of BLOOD VESSELS.

Twilight Sleep—a once-popular method of inducing painless CHILDBIRTH. One of the early formulas was the introduction into the rectum of a mixture of liquid ether and olive oil (Gwathmey's ANESTHESIA). This was too dangerous to the baby. The use of painkilling drugs (analgesics) during labor is still sometimes described as giving "twilight sleep."

Twins are born about once in every 80 pregnancies. (Triplets are born once in 80 times 80, and so on). Twins—or, for that matter, triplets, quadruplets or quintuplets—may be classified as *fraternal* or *identical* twins. Three out of 4 sets of twins are fraternal.

The birth of fraternal twins results because, occasionally, the ovaries release more than one ripened egg cell at about the same time. See MENSTRUATION, PREGNANCY. Each of these egg cells is fertilized by a *different* SPERM. Hence, in terms of HEREDITY, fraternal twins are no more alike than any other brothers or sisters.

Identical twins are something else again. In that case a single fertilized egg splits into two parts after it has been fertilized. Hence both identical twins come from the same egg cell and sperm cell. They are always of the same sex and usually look very much alike. They have exactly the same HEREDITY and the differences that are found between them must be attributed to differing environmental influences before and after birth.

There is some evidence that twinning tends to run in certain families.

Tympanites—bloating. The abdomen becomes so distended

with accumulated fluid or gas (in the intestines) that, when struck with the fingers, it sounds like a muffled drum.

Tympanitis—inflammation of

eardrum; otitis media; see EAR TROUBLE.

Tympanum—the EAR drum (tympanic membrane), or the middle ear, where it is located.

TYPHOID FEVER

Once greatly feared, typhoid fever is now quite a rare disease in civilized countries with good standards of public health and an understanding of hygiene and environmental sanitation. The cause of the disease is a specific MICROBE, the typhoid bacillus (*Salmonella typhosa*).

The disease is spread through excretion of this microbe in the bowel movements (feces) of those infected with it. It can be carried indirectly by milk, water, ice, food, flies, "night soil" and direct contact with sick patients or "typhoid carriers," who harbor the microbe but are not themselves sick from it.

The most famous "typhoid carrier" was "Typhoid Mary," a belligerent Irish cook, Mary Mallon, who was spotted by the New York City Health Department in 1908 and kept under observation (and sometimes confined) for 30 years thereafter.

Sanitary disposal of human excrement and safeguarding of milk, food and water supplies—the triumphs of modern sanitary engineering and public health practice—keep typhoid under control. Under emergency and disaster conditions, such as war, it tends to break out again. It was long known as the "soldier's disease." In the 19th century it killed more soldiers than did bullets. An ancient disease, Alexander the Great is presumed to have died of it at the height of his military triumphs.

Before antibiotics, typhoid had a high death rate; about 10%. The typhoid bacillus, however, is now readily knocked out with ANTIBIOTICS, notably aureomycin and chloramphenicol.

The onset of typhoid fever is insidious, generally coming on one to two weeks after infection. The incubation period, however, may be as short as 3 or as long as 38 days. Without effective (antibiotic) treatment, the disease runs a long and serious course, reaching its high point in about 2 weeks and lasting for 8 weeks.

The symptoms include high fever, splitting headache, rose-red splotches on the skin, extreme prostration. The spleen and the bowels are particularly subject to attack of the typhoid bacillus, producing conditions of gas, bloating, bloody stools, diarrhea and dysentery. Typhoid is classified as an enteric (intestinal) fever.

Some patients are infected without ever knowing it. Their symptoms are so mild that they escape detection. This condition is called *"walking typhoid"*—and is responsible for the presence of many typhoid carriers.

The presence of typhoid bacilli in the body can be determined with reasonably high accuracy by a laboratory blood test—the *Widal test.* The diagnosis can also be made from the history of the case, the course of the symptoms and careful blood studies.

Individual protection against typhoid fever is available with "typhoid shots." Unfortunately the immunization, consisting of 3 injections of killed typhoid bacilli in suspension, is limited, transient and sometimes uncomfortable. Injections between the layers of the skin (intradermal) require less vaccine and produce fewer unpleasant reactions. A "booster"—reinforcing—shot of the vaccine should be given annually if a high degree of protection is necessary (as under military conditions). Oral vaccine is of questionable value.

Paratyphoid fever is a milder form of typhoid, caused by the paratyphoid bacillus *(Salmonella paratyphi, A, B or C).* The Widal test is negative in these cases and the symptoms are much milder, so mild in fact that they may not be noticed. The chief symptom is acute DIARRHEA. Salmonella infections resemble (and are frequently the cause of) ordinary FOOD POISONING.

TYPHUS

Typhus fever is a disease with a long history of its own; and its epidemics, as pointed out by Hans Zinsser in *Rats, Lice and History,* have frequently changed the course of human history. World War I, for example, might have ended quite differently had it not been for typhus on the Eastern front. Yet positive facts about typhus are of comparatively recent origin, as history goes. The disease was not clearly differentiated from TYPHOID FEVER until 1837.

Typhus describes a large class of fevers caused by the microbes known as RICKETTSIA; they are all rickettsial diseases, and most important, they are all transmitted from man to man or from animal to man by INSECTS. There are 3 main classes of typhus, all with many local names depending upon what part of the world the disease occurs in; for example, tick fever in the United States, *tabardillo* in Mexico, *tsutsugamushi* in Japan.

1. *Classical, urban,* or *epidemic typhus* is transmitted from man to man by the bite of the *louse* or by scratching crushed body lice into skin abrasions. The infecting microbe is named *Rickettsia prowazeki*. Typhus was described by Hippocrates in 460 B.C. The disease usually kills about 5% to 20% of those it attacks; but in some epidemics 7 out of 10 have died!

The incubation period of epidemic typhus is from 5 to 15 days after the louse-bite. It comes on suddenly, striking its victims down with high and increasing fever, chills, great prostration, rapid pulse and severe headache. Apathy, delirium and convulsions may occur.

On about the fifth or sixth day a dark red eruption on the skin occurs, covering most of the body except the face. This disappears in about three days, leaving blood spots behind. At the same time blood may appear in the urine, stool and vomit. Blood clots arrest the function of vital organs. PNEUMONIA frequently appears as a complication.

The disease reaches a crisis sometime in its second week, either killing or gradually disappearing.

Treatment of louse-borne, epidemic typhus is not very satisfactory, although ANTIBIOTICS, atabrine, and hyperimmune serum sometimes interrupt the infection. The key to the control of the disease is *prevention,* through all kinds of delousing procedures. Use of DDT powder on clothing has been one of the most effective means of avoiding or stopping epidemics.

One attack of epidemic typhus usually confers a more or less permanent immunity; but a milder form of the disease (sometimes called Brill's disease, after Nathan Brill, an American physician who identified it in immigrants from southeastern Europe in 1898) occasionally occurs in people who have previously been attacked by epidemic typhus.

Since epidemic typhus usually occurs in crowded, unhygienic surroundings, it has in earlier years earned such names as *"Old World"* or *"European" typhus,* and also *jail, ship, prison, camp,* and *putrid fever.* TRENCH FEVER, of World War I, was a related, but far less serious rickettsial infection.

2. *Endemic* or *murine typhus* is transmitted from rats to man by the *flea (Xenopsylla cheopis)* and from rat to rat by fleas, rat lice and rat mites. The infecting microbe is *Rickettsia typhi*. The disease follows the distribution of rats throughout the world and hence occurs commonly on sea-coasts. This disease is less severe

than epidemic typhus (from which it cannot always be distinguished) and has a case-fatality rate of only about 2%.

3. *Scrub typhus* is transmitted from rats and mice to human beings by *mites* in the larval stage (notably *Trombiculae*). The infecting organism is *Rickettsia tsutsugamushi*. This is primarily a disease of the South Pacific, where it has such names as pseudo-typhus, Mossman's fever, flood fever, and, of course, TSUTSUGA-MUSHI. Scrub typhus responds to treatment with some ANTIBIOTICS.

Rocky Mountain spotted fever, also called *spotted fever* and *tick fever*, is a typhus-like rickettsial disease transmitted by ticks (primarily wood-ticks). The causative organism is *Rickettsia rickettsii*. This type of disease is not limited to the Rocky Mountain regions where it was first noted in 1896. Tick-borne typhus-like rickettsial diseases occur all over the world—under such names as South African tick fever, Colombian spotted fever, Kenya typhus, and Mediterranean fever. Many of them can be treated effectively with some antibiotics.

U

Any word printed in SMALL CAPITALS *can be looked up under its own alphabetical listing for further information.*

Ulcer—the destruction of skin or mucous membrane, with or without infection or pain. The tissue disintegrates and leaves a running sore. Ulcers can occur on any part of the skin or mucous linings of body organs; for example, BEDSORES (decubital ulcers), corneal ulcers, venereal ulcers, and ulcerative COLITIS. For more information on *stomach ulcers*, also called *gastric, peptic*, or *duodenal ulcers*, see STOMACH TROUBLE.

Ulceration—the process by which ulcers are formed.

Ulitis—inflammation of the GUMS; gingivitis.

Ulna—the larger and heavier of the two BONES of the forearm, running from the elbow to the wrist. The other bone of the forearm is the *radius*. (See illustrations for ENDOCRINE GLANDS; JOINTS.)

Ultraviolet Rays, or ultraviolet light, describes the electromagnetic radiations that occur beyond the violet end of the visible spectrum (rainbow) of light. These radiations stand between visible violet light and

X RAYS. They are found in the rays of the sun and have powerful properties.

Ultraviolet irradiation will bring about the formation of VITAMIN D in usable form from sterols (fatty chemical compounds) present in human and animal bodies. The Steenbock process for making vitamin D enriched milk calls for passing the milk under ultraviolet light.

Ultraviolet irradiation has been successfully used in the treatment of RICKETS, many forms of SKIN TROUBLE, and some kinds of TUBERCULOSIS.

Ultraviolet light of sufficient intensity kills MICROBES; ultraviolet lamps therefore have important industrial applications in food processing and storage. The use of ultraviolet lights in schools and hospitals, to prevent spread of infections, has been tried but is not practical—nor very important. The indiscriminate use of ultraviolet ray machines for home treatment, without strict medical supervision, is objectionable.

Umbilical Cord—the long hollow tube that runs from the middle of the abdomen of the unborn and newborn infant to the *placenta*. Through this tube or cord the infant in the womb receives nourishment from the maternal blood stream. This is the "silver cord." (See PREGNANCY and CHILDBIRTH.)

Umbilicus—NAVEL; belly-button.

Uncinaria—hookworm. See WORMS.

Uncinate Fits—the HALLUCINATION that one is tasting or smelling something that is nowhere around his mouth or nose. This derangement of the senses of taste and smell may be a manifestation of BRAIN DISEASE or damage—notably epilepsy or brain tumor—which is disturbing the centers in the brain that register tastes and smells.

Unconscious Mind, or the unconscious, refers to the hidden, or buried, part of the mind. Its importance is revealed by PSYCHOANALYSIS. The unconscious describes the theoretical abode and interrelationships between the ID (instincts), EGO (self), and SUPEREGO (conscience).

Unconsciousness—a state of being unaware of the world around. Normally induced in the process of sleep, it can also be induced by drugs (anesthetics), BRAIN injury (such as a skull fracture), brain poisoning (as by body toxins), HYPNOTISM, and FAINTING. Unconsciousness (coma) following an injury, in the course of a disease, or of sudden, unexplained cause (which may, for example, turn out to be a STROKE) is always a serious symptom demanding immediate medical attention.

Underweight—a weight lower than normal and proper for the person under consideration. In children, underweight usually reflects slow or delayed development. In adults underweight is usually a sign of some underlying, but undiagnosed, disease condition. When this is corrected, a gain in weight can be expected. A high-calorie diet alone will not put on weight if there is some pathological reason why the body cannot absorb and make flesh of the extra food ingested. A loss of weight, particularly a large or sudden loss, should prompt a thorough medical check-up. This is an important symptom of many serious diseases and should not be passed off lightly —or joyfully—without a medical examination. See DIET.

Undulant Fever — *brucellosis; Malta fever;* perhaps the most important animal disease transmitted to man. The causative agent is the *Brucella* germ, named after Sir David Bruce, who discovered it in 1887. This is the germ that causes contagious abortion in cattle. It is conveyed to human beings principally through *unpasteurized milk* and by contact with infected animals (chiefly cows, goats, pigs) and their carcasses. It is very common on the shores of the Mediterranean sea, and its importance in the United States is coming to be recognized. Though only about 5,000 cases of undulant fever are reported annually in the United States, it has been estimated that the mild and chronic cases run up in the millions.

Diagnosis of undulant fever is difficult. It mimics a great many other acute and chronic diseases; for instance, typhoid fever and malaria. Over 150 different symptoms have been associated with it. The disease comes on insidiously from 5 to 30 days after infection. It produces generalized aches and pains, headache, profuse sweating (night sweats), and a prolonged, undulating fever, which goes up and down.

The chronic form of the disease, which can last for months or years (average, about 3 months), is exceedingly tedious and debilitating. The great weakness it engenders is often reflected in mental symptoms and attitudes, particularly feelings of depression and loss of ambition. However, proper treatment can assure even the bed-ridden patient of complete recovery and return of bodily strength. The newer antibiotics —aureomycin, chloramphenicol, streptomycin, and terramycin— combined with sulfa drugs promise more effective treatment than just bed rest and good diet.

Unilateral—on one side only.

Union—the healing process; the proper growing back together again of the ends of broken BONES or the edges of cut or lacerated soft tissues.

"Upside-Down Stomach"—diaphragmatic hernia; protrusion of the stomach up through the diaphragm into the lungs. See HERNIA.

Urea — the nitrogen-containing

chemical substance, $CO(NH_2)_2$, which is the chief end-product of the decomposition of PROTEINS in the human and animal body. It is present in blood, lymph and urine. It is probably formed in the liver and delivered to the kidneys by way of the blood stream. A normal adult excretes a little more than an ounce of urea a day. Urea compounds are sometimes administered for their diuretic effect, increasing urine flow.

The synthesis of urea from non-organic substances by Friedrich Woehler in 1828 was a milestone in the history of chemistry and physiology. It proved that chemical reactions inside the body were the same as those outside.

Uremia—poisoning by the accumulation in the blood stream of waste products, like urea, that should normally be passed off into the urine by the kidneys. It sometimes occurs in pregnancy, but the usual cause is KIDNEY TROUBLE. Uremia, if it progresses, can be fatal. Serious changes occur in the blood; it becomes more acid (ACIDOSIS), it accumulates nitrogen (azotemia), and its cells are destroyed (ANEMIA). Uremia usually comes on gradually, with symptoms of headache, lethargy, and depression. Nausea, vomiting, heavy breathing, dizziness, dimness of vision, stupor, coma, and convulsions may also occur. The breath and sweat have the odor of URINE. Treatment of uremia is essentially the treatment of the underlying conditions causing suppression of urine. But generally uremia is the terminal result of failing kidney function that cannot be restored.

Ureter—either of the two pencil-thin tubes through which urine drips from the kidneys into the bladder. See URINARY SYSTEM. (See illustrations for SEX ORGANS, MALE and FEMALE.)

Urethra—the mucus-lined tube that carries urine from the bladder outside the body. It is part of the URINARY SYSTEM. In the male it runs through the penis and also conveys SEMEN, thus being a part of the male sex apparatus. (See illustrations for SEX ORGANS, MALE and FEMALE.)

Urethritis—inflammation of the urethra, usually as a result of infection, notably GONORRHEA, but occurring from other causes also, for example, GOUT.

Urinalysis—examination of the urine as an aid in detecting and diagnosing disease. It is of especial importance in *kidney trouble* and *diabetes,* but it may throw light on many other types of disease. Examination of the urine has an ancient history; Shakespeare mentions it, and the old Dutch masters painted pictures of physicians gravely examining flasks of urine. Only careful chemical and microscopic examination of the urine yields significant findings. And these must be properly interpreted by the physician in the light of the patient's entire condition. Self-diagnosis based on a drugstore urinalysis can be damaging.

A routine urinalysis calls for observing color and turbidity of the sample; testing for acid-base reaction, albumin, sugar, blood, and acetone; searching under the microscope for epithelial cells (pus), red and white blood cells, casts (small threadlike masses of protein), and crystals. A complete urinalysis also includes bacteriological study to find and identify any bacteria present. If indicated, other special tests can also be run.

URINARY SYSTEM

The urinary system includes the kidneys, ureters, bladder, and urethra. Because of its close anatomical relationship with the reproductive system (see SEX ORGANS, MALE and FEMALE), it is sometimes described as the *genitourinary* or *urogenital system*. The urinary system proper is an excretory system, removing water and waste products of metabolism from the body as *urine*. (Other organs of excretion are the skin, lungs, and rectum.)

The *kidneys* are a pair of bean-shaped organs, weighing about 5 to 6 ounces each, located deep in the small of the back, one on each side of the spinal column. Each kidney contains a million or more tiny filtering units, called nephrons. Each nephron is enclosed in a cuplike capsule in which are meshed kidney tubules and a network of tiny blood vessels (glomeruli). Blood enters the glomeruli from branches of the renal artery. The cells of the kidney tubule selectively extract from the blood the water and waste products in solution that make up the urine. The tubule follows a winding pathway, selectively restoring to the blood along the way those substances the body still needs. The tubules unite and form collecting tubules, which empty through cuplike structures called calyces into a kind of collecting chamber in the middle of the kidney, the kidney pelvis.

The *ureters* are a pair of tubes, 16 to 18 inches long and about the diameter of a pencil, that convey urine from the kidneys to the bladder. They originate in the kidney pelvis and terminate at the base of the bladder. Urine trickles down them at the rate of about a drop every 30 seconds.

The *bladder* is a collapsible, balloonlike sac composed of smooth muscle and lined with a smooth membrane. It is the reservoir for urine. It is situated in the forward part of the pelvic cavity. In the female it lies behind and above the uterus. Its size and shape

THE URINARY EXCRETORY SYSTEM

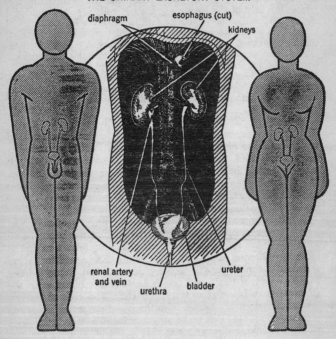

diaphragm

esophagus (cut)

kidneys

renal artery
and vein

urethra

bladder

ureter

are determined by the amount of urine it contains. The outlet of the bladder is guarded by a strong sphincter muscle, which is firmly contracted except during urination. As urine collects in the bladder, the sensory nerves in its walls are stimulated. These nerve impulses are transmitted by way of the spinal cord to the brain. The relaxation of the sphincter muscle, allowing urine to escape, is then permitted. This is partly a reflex act and partly a learned re-action.

The *urethra* is the mucous-membrane-lined tube or canal that conveys urine from the neck of the bladder to the outside world. The male urethra is about 8 or 9 inches long and terminates in the tip of the penis. It is also the passageway through which *semen is* ejaculated. The ejaculatory ducts, a part of the male reproductive system, open into it. The female urethra is short, measuring about 1½ inches. Its external opening is located just in front of the opening of the vagina.

URINE

Urine is the body water secreted by the kidneys and carrying off, by way of the bladder and urethra, the waste products of protein breakdown in the body, chiefly *urea*. A great many other organic and inorganic chemical substances are also contained in normal urine; notably, sodium chloride (common salt), ammonia, uric acid, creatinine, sulfuric acid, hormones, and phosphates. Urine is about 96% water, 4% dissolved solid materials. Normal urine is of a clear amber color, slightly acid, salty to the taste (except diabetic urine, which is sweet), and has a characteristic odor. If URINALYSIS reveals blood, pus, albumin, sugar, or anything else that should not be there, this usually indicates a disease state. The average healthy man voids about 1 to 1½ quarts of urine a day. The amount of urine voided is likely to be less in the summer, when more body water is lost in perspiration. Only about half the water taken into the body is eliminated as urine.

Urination, also called micturition, is the process of discharging or passing urine. In the infant this is altogether a reflex act. When a certain amount of urine has accumulated in the bladder, the urge to void it is felt. Gradually, usually between the ages of 2 and 3, the child learns to control this urge so that he urinates only in a socially approved place and fashion. Throughout life, bladder control remains a delicately regulated process. Involuntary urination (incontinence) can occur as the result of psychological stimuli, such as great fright, or physical factors that irritate or impair the nerve supply to bladder muscles. Spinal-cord injuries; diseases of the nervous system, like polio and multiple sclerosis; pelvic disease; and other conditions can bring about complete or lesser urinary incontinence.

Abnormalities of urination usually signal disease. Excessive urine output may betoken *diabetes*. Scanty urination (suppression of urine) may flag serious *kidney trouble*. Painful urination may indicate infection, inflammation, irritation, or stones in the bladder; the pain may also point to some obstruction of urinary flow, such as an enlarged *prostate gland* or stricture (narrowing) of the tubes that carry urine down from the kidney. Too-frequent urination may be the result of mental anxiety; overindulgence in *diuretic* stimulants like coffee, tea, and alcohol; or disease processes, like obstruction and infection, anywhere along the urinary tract. The healthy adult should not need to get up at night to pass water. Other abnormalities of urination that may be worthy of medical check-up are hesitancy, stop-and-go urine stream, retention of urine, and presence of large quantities of unvoided residual urine in the bladder. Urine should flow easily, regularly, and painlessly.

Urning—a male homosexual.

Urogenital describes the SEX ORGANS, MALE and FEMALE, in conjunction with the URINARY SYSTEM to which they are closely related in the anatomic development of the body.

Urography—X-ray pictures of the URINARY SYSTEM, taken with RADIOPAQUE dyes.

Urology—the medical specialty that deals with diseases and disorders of the UROGENITAL system (both male and female), such as KIDNEY TROUBLE, BLADDER TROUBLE. In practice the urologist deals largely with diseases of the male genital tract, a specialty which has been sometimes designated as andrology.

Urologist—a medical specialist in urogenital disorders, i.e., UROLOGY.

Urticaria—the scientific name for HIVES, a form of ALLERGY on the SKIN. Large welts or wheals usually appear—but go away.

Uterine—related to the uterus, womb.

Uterus—womb; see SEX ORGANS, FEMALE.

Uvea—the middle pigmented layer, or coat, of the EYE, including iris, ciliary body and choroid.

Uveitis—inflammation of UVEA; see EYE TROUBLE.

Uvula—the "little grape" of muscle tissue that hangs down from the roof of the mouth. It is part of the soft palate and an important organ of speech. In some throat conditions it may become elongated and hang down so far that it brushes against the tongue, setting up reflexes that make for coughing and retching. With recovery from the throat ailment, the uvula will return to its normal size and position. (See illustrations for NOSE; THROAT.)

V

Any word printed in SMALL CAPITALS *can be looked up under its own alphabetical listing for further information.*

Vaccinate, from the Latin word *vacca,* for cow, originally meant to inoculate with cowpox in order to prevent SMALLPOX. The word has since come to mean injection of or inoculation with any product of biological origin, usually a VACCINE, for the purpose of preventing either infection or the serious consequences of it. *Vaccinate* and *immunize* are practically synonyms.

Vaccination — immunization against disease by inoculation, injection or ingestion ("oral vaccine") of any product of biological origin and immunologic potency designed to prevent a specific disease. Originally vaccination meant only the process of protecting against SMALLPOX attacks by scratching cowpox (VACCINIA) virus, present in the lymph of a cow or calf, into the human skin.

VACCINE

Vaccine, like VACCINATE, originally referred to the material derived from the cow—and containing cowpox virus—which is used to protect against SMALLPOX. Today vaccine means any biological material administered to protect against microbial invasion or damage. It usually applies to preparations of VIRUS OR BACTERIA, killed or attenuated (weakened), which will stimulate the body to produce ANTIBODIES against later invaders of the same origin. In this sense a vaccine is a particular kind of ANTIGEN. The effectiveness of vaccines is relative; some last for a comparatively long time, others give but brief IMMUNITY and must be repeated.

Among the most commonly used vaccines, which generally produce a relatively high immunity at the time it is needed, are those which protect against smallpox, paralytic polio (Salk vaccine), yellow fever, whooping cough, lockjaw (tetanus), typhoid (and paratyphoid), scarlet fever and rabies.

Since the Salk polio vaccine is a very well known vaccine, a detailed history of its development will reveal pertinent facts that apply to many vaccines and also to virus diseases. See VIRUS, POLIO.

Polio vaccine. The idea that children and adults could be protected against polio by a vaccine goes back at least to the early

1900's. However, it was only after 1950 that sufficient basic scientific information became available to make this hope a practical reality.

Here, briefly, is the inside scientific story of how the threat of polio was finally conquered:

It begins in 1908, when two Austrian doctors, Karl Landsteiner and Erwin Popper, made a great step forward in knowledge about polio. They were able to transmit the disease to monkeys, and then showed that it was caused by a virus. The idea of making a vaccine against it immediately occurred. Within two years a pair of American investigators, Simon Flexner and P. A. Lewis, came forward with the suggestion that vaccination or immunization might be possible. They demonstrated that polio infection in monkeys could sometimes be prevented by giving them injections of blood serum from monkeys who had recovered from the disease.

The idea that a vaccine might prevent the disease lingered in scientific literature for a quarter of a century. Then, beginning in about 1935, a group of doctors in New York and Philadelphia brought out a vaccine that they actually tried out on human subjects.

It didn't work; it was, in fact, a dangerous experiment. Its failure discouraged other potential workers in the field, and for another 15 years no serious efforts were made to develop a vaccine against paralytic polio.

These failures convinced research workers that a great deal had yet to be learned about the disease; ignorance and mystery remained. But research was expensive, difficult, and time-consuming. The only experimental animal for polio research was the monkey, and monkeys were costly.

Then, rather abruptly, in 1949 and 1950, the picture changed. Hope for a vaccine again dared to be raised. For these years saw the culmination of advances in basic polio research: virus typing and TISSUE CULTURE.

It had begun to be suspected in the 1940's that polio was caused by more than one kind of virus. If this was true, then protection against the disease afforded by a vaccine made from one kind of virus could not be expected to protect against the disease caused by other kinds.

The National Foundation for Infantile Paralysis resolved to put the serious question about different kinds of polio viruses to a long-range scientific test. A cooperative research program was set up at four universities. Hundreds of different strains of polio virus were tested. At a cost of $1,190,000 and 17,500 monkeys, it finally became clear in 1950 that there were *three* different types of polio virus, each capable of causing paralytic disease. This meant that a polio vaccine would have to protect against all three types of virus.

Dr. Jonas E. Salk was one of the young research men engaged in the tedious virus-typing program. He quickly showed aptitude in improving the ways of doing it.

In the meantime, in Boston, another crucial step was taken. In 1949 Dr. John F. Enders and his younger associates, Dr. Thomas H. Weller and Dr. Frederick C. Robbins, discovered how to grow polio virus on non-nerve tissue in test tubes.

The secret of this discovery lay in that great scientific virtue of patience. When they seeded polio virus into bits of living tissue growing in a test tube, they waited longer than anyone else to see if the virus would multiply and grow. It did!

The polio virus, like other viruses, is a parasite on living cells. Growing the virus in special strains of living tissue maintained in glass tubes or bottles outside the body is called virus cultivation in tissue culture.

Enders, Weller, and Robbins received the 1954 Nobel Prize in Medicine and Physiology for their work. Their discovery meant:

1. It would be possible to make a safe polio vaccine. Polio virus had been grown in *nerve* tissue before, but such a mixture could not be safely injected into human beings. It would cause serious reactions.

2. It would eventually be possible to make large quantities of vaccine, because polio virus, the starting point of vaccine, could now be grown in large amounts. Actually, the techniques for large-quantity growth of polio virus in tissue culture were worked out at the Connaught Laboratories, in Toronto, Canada. This depended very importantly on the discovery of a synthetic chemical medium of about 60 ingredients, called mixture 199, which safely nourishes the test-tube tissues (cells) on which the virus grows. This is an example of the international research in poliomyelitis out of which the Salk vaccine evolved.

3. The development of tissue-culture growth of viruses, and the demonstration that the growing viruses eventually killed the tissue in which they grew, made possible a whole series of comparative-

ly simple laboratory tests for finding, identifying, and comparing both polio viruses and their antibodies.

4. The growth of polio virus in tissue culture broke the bottleneck of almost complete dependence on monkeys for polio-virus research. It opened the field to rapid progress.

Research developments leading toward a vaccine now began to pile up. Working independently, Dr. David Bodian, in Baltimore, and Dr. Dorothy Horstmann, in New Haven, showed in 1952 that there was an early stage in the development of poliomyelitis when antibodies against the disease were circulating in the blood stream.

The importance of this finding was very great. It meant that if a vaccine for stimulating the human body to produce antibodies could be worked out, the chance of its working to prevent paralytic disease would be very good.

The next year, Dr. Wm. McD. Hammon, of Pittsburgh, conducted field trials with gamma globulin, which is not a vaccine but a blood derivative containing antibodies against poliomyelitis. He showed, most significantly, that even barely detectable levels of antibody in the blood stream offered protection against paralytic polio.

Without all this knowledge, made promptly available, the rapid development and testing of a practical vaccine could not have gone forward. Indeed, Dr. Howard Howe and Dr. Isabel Morgan had already made an experimental polio vaccine by growing virus in nerve tissue and killing the virus with formaldehyde. They had even cautiously tested it in six human subjects, discovering that it did induce protective antibody formation. However, because it was grown on nerve tissue, it was, like earlier vaccines, considered too dangerous to use.

Salk had considered the possibility of putting together a safe, potent, and effective polio vaccine while he was still working on the virus-typing program. He went seriously to work on the vaccine problem in Pittsburgh in 1951.

Bulwarked by all previous research on the subject, Salk finally managed to put together all the jig-saw-puzzle pieces and arrive at a satisfactory working formula for a polio vaccine. In outline the formula was simple:

Grow each of the three types of polio virus on minced monkey kidney cells in large bottles. Kill the virus with formaldehyde. This is what makes a killed-virus vaccine out of a solution of live virus. Neutralize the formaldehyde with other chemicals. Mix the three different type pools of vaccine together to get a single vaccine effective against all three types of virus. Test the final product for safety and potency, potency meaning ability to induce the formation of antibodies when injected into a human body.

But an incredible host of technical details had to be surmounted before Dr. Salk's simple laboratory procedure could be turned into large-scale manufacture of safe, pure, and potent vaccine.

Before the Salk vaccine could be recommended for use it had to have a large-scale field test to find out how effective it might be, under conditions of natural exposure, in preventing paralytic polio in children. For this purpose an extensive field trial of the Salk vaccine was planned for early in 1954. It had to be postponed time and again because of technical difficulties in manufacture.

Finally it began, in Fairfax County, Virginia.

There, on April 26, 1954, second-grade pupil Randy Kerr got the first field trial injection of 1 cubic centimeter of Salk vaccine in the triceps muscle of his left arm.

About 440,000 children in 217 field trial areas in the United States received vaccine in the spring of 1954, and nearly 2 million had to be kept under observation for the rest of the year. The incidence of paralytic polio among the vaccinated and unvaccinated children had to be carefully observed and analyzed.

This overwhelming statistical and analytical task was entrusted to Dr. Thomas Francis and his independent evaluation center at the University of Michigan. On April 12, 1955, an historic day in the annals of medicine, Dr. Francis was at last able to issue a famous report announcing to the world that the Salk vaccine was safe and effective.

Almost everything about the Salk vaccine since that time has been reported in the newspapers. There was an overwhelming demand for and a short supply of vaccine in April and May of 1955. Then there was difficulty with some lots of vaccine provided by one manufacturer. These difficulties were overcome by excellent scientific detective work and 10 million children received one or more injections of safe and potent Salk vaccine in 1955.

With technical difficulties in vaccine manufacture ironed out, production and use of Salk vaccine was rapidly stepped up. Between April 12, 1955, and September 15, 1956, over 100,000,000 cc. of vaccine were released for use by the U.S. Public Health Service.

By January 1, 1958, among 111,000,000 U.S. residents under age 40, 35,000,000 people (31%) had received the recommended three SHOTS, properly spaced, of the vaccine. Another 25,000,000 children and adults (23%) had received two shots and an estimated 5,000,000 (5%) one shot. Altogether, therefore, 65,000,000 people under 40, or about 60% of the age group generally susceptible to paralytic attack, were already protected against it by one or more doses of vaccine.

How the vaccine works: The Salk vaccine was not intended to prevent poliomyelitis. It was intended to, and does, prevent paralytic poliomyelitis.

The vaccine prevents paralysis by stimulating production of antibodies—particles that stop polio virus after it has invaded the system and before it reaches nerve centers. The vaccine triggers the creation of antibodies within 7 to 10 days after the first injection. The second shot, given 2 to 6 weeks after the first, raises the level of antibody production to an effective preventive level within 2 weeks. The third, or booster, shot is given 7 to 12 months after the second one, and results in a very rapid rise in antibodies within 9 days. It produces a level of immunity as high as that observed in persons who have recovered from natural infection.

Stand-out facts about the Salk vaccine:
The vaccine is safe.

The vaccine's effectiveness surpasses early hopes for it. In 1955 it cut paralytic polio by about four-fifths among the children who received one or more injections. In 1956 it did even better. A full schedule of three properly spaced injections is over 90% effective in preventing paralytic polio.

Leading medical authorities in the United States are unanimous in endorsing vaccination against polio. It is evident that immunization during the second six months of life has become standard practice in pediatrics.

Vaccinia—cowpox; a VIRUS disease of cattle that can be transmitted to man, purposely by VACCINATION for protection against SMALLPOX.

Vagina—birth canal and female organ of sexual intercourse; see SEX ORGANS, FEMALE. The word *vagina* is also used to describe other sheathlike structures in the body. (See illustrations for PREGNANCY.)

Vaginismus—tight contraction or spasm of the muscles that surround the vagina. This may make it impossible for the penis to penetrate the vagina or, on rare occasions, may make it impossible for the penis introduced to be released (penis captivus), until a relaxing drug or anesthetic is administered to the woman. Extreme sensitivity (hyperesthesia) of the pudendal regions to sexual sensations is the mechanism through which vaginismus occurs. This sensitivity almost invariably reflects a psychosexual fear of coitus in the UNCONSCIOUS MIND. It is related to *frigidity* as a psychological phenomenon.

Vaginitis—inflammation of the vagina, usually accompanied by pain and discharge. See FEMALE TROUBLES; TRICHOMONAS.

Vagus—the "wandering"—tenth and largest—cranial nerve that innervates many parts of the head, neck, chest and abdomen. See NERVES AND NERVOUS SYSTEM.

Valgus means twisted or turned outward. It is applied to CLUBFOOT (talipes valgus), knock-knees or bowlegs (genu valgum), and out-of-line hips (coxa valga). The adjective for displacement in the opposite, turned inward, direction is *varus*.

Valve—usually refers to the structures of the HEART or VEINS which keep blood from flowing the wrong way. However there are valve-like arrangements in other parts of the body; notably the gastro-intestinal tract, which has an ileocecal and a pyloric valve. (See illustrations for HEART.)

Valvotomy—cutting into a valve of the body, generally into the mitral or pulmonary valves of the heart.

Valvulitis—inflammation of a valve, usually of the HEART.

Varicella—CHICKENPOX.

Varicocele—a swelling of the veins in the spermatic cord (see SEX ORGANS, MALE). The same type of varicose veins may occur in the region of the ovaries (pelvic varicocele).

Varicose Veins—dilated or swollen veins. The veins of the legs are by far the most commonly affected because, being farthest from the heart, they are subject to greater hydrostatic pressure than veins in other parts of the body. When the stretched and swollen veins are close to the surface of the legs or trunk, they can be clearly seen. They often appear knotty and tortuous, with little bumps in them.

What causes varicose veins? The walls of the veins are neither so thick nor so elastic as those of the arteries. Hence they are more apt to become distended when their walls weaken or their valves are damaged. Varicose veins appear more often in women than in men. This is partly due to pregnancy, during which the prolonged pressure of the enlarged uterus on the veins entering the pelvis may cause blood to stagnate in the veins of the legs.

Standing long hours at work

is usually the immediate cause of varicose veins. Only when a person is lying down is the high venous pressure in the legs significantly reduced. Other factors that induce varicose veins are tight garters and girdles, inflammation of the veins *(thrombophlebitis)*, pelvic tumors, and overweight. When varicose veins persist, untreated, for a long time, the result may be daily swelling of the whole lower leg and ankle, often with a badly itching eczema. At night, when the patient lies down, the swelling subsides.

How can varicose veins be treated? Temporary relief can usually be obtained by elevating the legs and wearing elastic stockings or bandages, which tend to force blood into deeper veins in the leg. In some cases, however, surgery is necessary. Most commonly this means tying off and removing the dilated veins. Very small veins can sometimes be shriveled by injections. In either case a *collateral circulation* is established in the deeper, unaffected veins.

Variola—SMALLPOX.

Variolation—a method of preventing SMALLPOX that antedated VACCINATION. Variolation called for introduction of unmodified smallpox virus, with the expectation that it would give a mild case without leaving any pox or having any serious side-effects. Variolation was introduced into England from Turkey in the 18th century by Lady Mary Wortley Montagu. It is not safe.

Varioloid—a mild form of SMALLPOX that sometimes occurs in people who have previously had the disease or have been vaccinated against it.

Varix—an enlarged and twisted (varicose) vein.

Varus—turned inward. The opposite of VALGUS, which see.

Vas—a tube or vessel, particularly a blood vessel. *Vas deferens* is the duct through which sperm leave the testicles (see SEX ORGANS, MALE).

Vascular—relating to BLOOD VESSELS. "Highly vascular" means lots of blood vessels present.

Vasectomy—a simple surgical operation for sterilizing the male by cutting through or removing part of the vas deferens in the region of the groin. See STERILITY; SEX ORGANS, MALE.

Vaseline—petroleum jelly; a lubricant.

Vasoconstrictor—anything that induces the blood vessels to constrict, tighten up, become narrower in bore. It usually describes a vasomotor nerve or a drug (e.g., adrenalin).

Vasodilator—anything, usually a nerve or a drug, that dilates or expands the blood vessels, especially the little arteries.

Vasomotor—affecting or controlling the bore of blood vessels, and hence the flow of blood through them. *Vasomotor nerves* are small peripheral nerves attached to the walls of blood vessels. They direct the expansion (vasodilation) or contraction (vasoconstriction) of the vessels which they serve.

Vasopressin—a hormone, also called pitressin, from the pituitary gland, that contracts smooth muscle tissue—e.g., blood vessels, intestinal tract.

V.D.—VENEREAL DISEASE.

Vein—BLOOD VESSEL leading *to* the heart. Veins, like *arteries*, have three coats or layers; but they are thinner. A cut vein collapses. Veins carry so-called "venous blood," darker than arterial blood because it has lost its oxygen content. Veins pass into venules and then become capillaries, which are looped and linked with the arterial system to assure circulation of the blood. Some veins, especially those near the surface of the body, have valves. These valves, reduplication of the linings of the veins, act to prevent backflow of blood by the force of gravity in dependent parts of the body. Veins are subject to inflammation—PHLEBITIS and THROMBOPHLEBITIS—and to stretching, dilating and twisting —VARICOSE VEINS, PILES, VARICOCELE. (See illustrations for HEART.)

Vena Cava—the two large VEINS, superior and inferior, that empty directly into the HEART.

Venereal Disease—disease spread principally by sexual intercourse. (Venus was the Roman goddess of love.) There are three principal venereal diseases encountered in the U.S.: SYPHILIS, GONORRHEA, and CHANCROID. In tropical and undeveloped countries a few other venereal diseases flourish; notably, lymphogranuloma venereum and granuloma inguinale. The extreme fear and horror with which venereal disease has been regarded was more justifiable in the past than now, when highly effective treatments are generally at hand.

Are syphilis and gonorrhea the same disease? Absolutely not. But they may both be contracted at the same time. Untreated syphilis is a long-time disease—and a killer. Untreated gonorrhea is usually of shorter duration—and can be a crippler. All venereal diseases are tragic sources of human suffering. Fortunately, it is possible to avoid, prevent, and cure them.

Who gets syphilis and gonorrhea? No age or race is immune. However, as might be expected, they are principally contracted in youth; in women, most commonly from 16 to 20; in men, in their early twenties. These diseases are proportionately more common in non-white races subject to lower standards of living. They are, in a sense, diseases of irresponsibility—many times more common in prison than in college populations. An estimated 95% of all prostitutes are infected with communicable venereal disease. Their clients, therefore, unless protected, run a high risk of contracting the diseases. There is no such thing as a "safe" prostitute of the commercial variety.

Venesection—blood-letting; cutting into a vein to draw out blood; phlebotomy. This was a common medical practice up to the middle of the 19th century. It probably harmed more patients than it helped. George Washington was probably bled to death.

Venipuncture—inserting a hollow needle into a vein for the purpose of taking a venous blood sample or giving an intravenous injection or infusion. Arm and leg veins are usually used.

Ventilation of sleeping, dwelling and working quarters is essential to provide adequate fresh air for healthful living. Humidity and TEMPERATURE must both be taken into account. In summer, dwelling temperatures from 70° to 85° F., with windows open, are comfortable enough. In winter, temperatures from 65° to 68° F. usually suffice, except for infants and old people, provided the relative humidity of the rooms ranges from 30% to 60%. Modern air-conditioning apparatus provides comfortable ventilation of sleeping and other rooms in summer heat; it is

perfectly safe, but should not be set at temperatures too extremely below those outside the room. The great risk in winter is that the heating of rooms will dry out the air too much; nose and throat feel dry and uncomfortable under these conditions. It is not necessary to sleep with windows open in cold weather; the cold irritates mucous membranes of the nose and throat. See SINUS TROUBLE.

Ventral—belly-side; the opposite of DORSAL, back-side.

Ventricle—a cavity or chamber, as the left and right ventricles of the HEART, and the several ventricles of the BRAIN.

Ventriculogram—X-ray picture of the head taken when fluid has been removed from the ventricles of the brain and replaced by air.

Veratrum—a drug from the plant *veratrum viride* sometimes used in the treatment of HIGH BLOOD PRESSURE.

Vermifuge—a drug that kills or expels WORMS; an anthelmintic.

Verruca—WART.

Version—an obstetrical maneuver; the turning of a baby in the course of CHILDBIRTH, usually by the hand of the obstetrician, so that it will be more safely and easily born(e).

Vertebrae—the odd-shaped BONES that, piled one on top of the other, make up the spine, or backbone. In *children* the number of vertebrae is 33—7

THE SPINAL VERTEBRAE

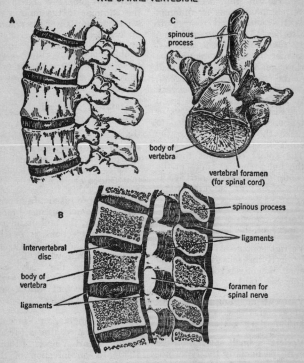

A series of lumbar vertebrae found in the lumbar (lower back) region of the flexible human spinal column (backbone).

A. Side view, showing the arrangement of vertebrae one on top of the other, separated by intervertebral discs.

B. Same group of vertebrae as in A, cut through to show internal structure. Ligaments which hold the vertebrae in place have been added in this drawing.

C. A single vertebra.

cervical in the neck (other vertebrate animals as different as the whale and the giraffe also have 7 cervical vertebrae); 12 *thoracic* or *dorsal*, attached to the ribs and completing the rib cage; 5 *lumbar*, in the small of the back, the loins; 5 *sacral*, over the rump; and 4 *coccygeal*. In adults, the last 4 are fused together to form the coccyx or tailbone; the 5 sacral fused to make the *sacrum*. Hence the adult has only 26 vertebrae. The spinal cord runs through the holes (neural ring) in the center of each vertebra. (See illustrations for BONES; BRAIN; SPINE.)

Vertex—crown of the head; top (apex) of the heart.

Vertigo—DIZZINESS. More exactly, it is the sensation that the environment is revolving around you. See EARS.

Vesicant—anything that produces BLISTERS. CANTHARIDES and mustard gas are vesicants.

Vesicle—a small BLISTER on the SKIN, particularly the type produced by virus infections like chickenpox; or a small, fluid-containing sac in the body, such as the *seminal vesicle*, a part of the SEX ORGANS, MALE. Skin vesicles in which pus accumulates become PUSTULES.

Vessel in medicine usually means a BLOOD VESSEL, vein or artery, or some other tube or channel which conveys body fluids.

Vestibule—generally refers to the entrance to the inner EAR; sometimes to that of the VAGINA or AORTA.

Viable—containing life; alive; usually refers to a sperm cell, egg cell or unborn infant (fetus).

Vibrator—a mechanical apparatus for MASSAGE.

Vibrio—a family of MICROBES shaped like short, curved rods, quarter-moons, or commas. It includes the *Vibrio comma* that causes cholera.

Villus—a protrusion from the surface of a mucous membrane; in particular, the multitudinous, hair-like projections from the inner lining of the small intestine through which food is absorbed into the body. See DIGESTIVE SYSTEM. The villi give the intestinal wall a velvety look and feel.

Vincent's Angina, or Vincent's infection, named after a French doctor, Henri Vincent (1862–1950), is an infection of the mouth, gums and throat, sometimes called TRENCH MOUTH. The cause of the disease is apparently a pair of MICROBES, a bacillus and a spirochete, acting together. Much about this disease remains obscure. The communicability is not definitely established, nor is the method of treatment. Poor living conditions, poor mouth hygiene seem to favor its development.

In advanced cases ulcers may appear on the cheeks, gums and throat. The breath has a very unpleasant odor.

Virilism—the development of physical male characteristics in the female; a beard, a deep voice, and so forth. It is usually owing to overactivity of the adrenal (ENDOCRINE) gland, sometimes as the result of an adrenal tumor, or to overdoses of male sex hormone.

Virology—the study and science of viruses and virus diseases. See VIRUS.

Virulence describes the strength of a MICROBE in attacking its host. A virulent microbe tends to multiply rapidly, damage the cells of its host quickly and badly.

VIRUS

A virus is a tiny parasite living, growing and reproducing its kind *inside* a host CELL. When viruses damage or destroy the cells they invade, they produce *virus diseases;* polio, smallpox and rabies are typical examples. Viruses are the smallest MICROBES.

"Virus," or *"the virus,"* has also become a fashionable medical diagnosis. It is usually applied to minor disturbances of the stomach or intestines ("stomach flu") and to upper respiratory tract infections related to the COMMON COLD. It is as good an explanation as any for transitory infections, of unproved origin, which make a person feel miserable and weaken him for a considerable length of time.

There is no specific treatment for "the virus." The victim is well advised to go to bed and make himself comfortable until he feels better. Good nursing, a light but balanced diet, adequate fluid intake, and careful medical observation to see that no serious complications develop are what is required.

Nature of viruses. Viruses were first discovered in 1892 by a Russian scientist, D. Iwanowski, who noted infective agents that would pass through a filter that stopped ordinary bacteria. Hence they were originally called *filterable viruses.* First to be discovered was the tobacco mosaic virus, a plant virus that puts spots on tobacco leaves.

In 1898, Loeffler and Frosch discovered the virus that causes hoof-and-mouth disease in cattle and in 1901, Walter Reed and his associates found the virus that causes yellow fever in man. Since then, a great many viruses, all parasites on the cells of plants, lower animals or human beings, have been identified. Viruses that are parasites on bacteria are called *bacteriophage* (phage).

Closely related to viruses are RICKETTSIA, microbes which are parasites on host cells but which are too large to pass through the porcelain filters that let viruses through. The principal rickettsial disease is TYPHUS.

The exact nature of viruses has not yet been settled. They are on the border-line between the living and the dead. A "live" virus can apparently be reconstituted out of inorganic chemicals (the tobacco mosaic virus) and will multiply or replicate itself within cells. This is the area where chemistry and biology seem to merge.

The crux of the matter appears to lie in the nucleus of the virus, made up of nucleic acid and nucleoproteins. The outer coat of the virus, which can be stripped, is a protein. The nucleic acids—chemicals—have a special configuration in their molecular form. They are twin spirals, like spiral springs, one turning to the right, the other to the left.

Under certain circumstances of virus reproduction, they split apart and then join together again. This is much the same process that occurs when the CHROMOSOMES in the nucleus of a living cell split apart and rejoin to form new cells (see HEREDITY). In other words, viruses act much like GENES, and greater similarities between them may be found. The process of wild multiplication of CANCER cells also has much in common with virus duplication; and research may yet show cancer to be a special kind of virus disease.

How big are viruses? They are unbelievably small—millionths of an inch in length, breadth and thickness. The largest known virus, that of parrot fever (psittacosis)—measuring 450 millimicrons—is only about 1/20th the size of a red blood cell. The smallest virus, that of hoof-and-mouth disease, measures only 10 millimicrons. The largest viruses are bigger than some of the smallest bacteria and the smaller viruses are exceeded in size by some protein molecules.

The size and shape of viruses is now determined by electron microscope and X-ray procedures. Viruses come in all kinds of shapes—spheres, balls, ovals (egg-shaped), cubes, rhomboids, commas, and rods.

Technics of TISSUE CULTURE, in which viruses are grown on living cells which are themselves growing in a nutrient (feeding) medium in glass tubes, have greatly enhanced virus research.

Virus infections engender a certain amount of immunity against subsequent re-infection with the same type of virus. In some cases immunity is high, as in polio-virus infections; in other cases, like the common cold, the immunity is temporary and limited. Some types of viruses induce the development of ANTIBODIES which protect against invasion by related viruses. That is how the cowpox induced by vaccination protects against SMALLPOX. See VACCINE.

Viruses are spread in a variety of ways. Some virus diseases, like chickenpox and measles, are spread by contact or by droplets in the air. Rabies virus is transmitted only through a wound—the bite of a rabid animal. Many viruses are spread by insects; for example, yellow fever and equine encephalitis virus. There is often a reservoir of virus infection in wild or domestic animals. Virus diseases are rarely spread by water, milk or food contaminated by virus.

Most viruses do not respond to drug and antibiotic treatment. Immune serum, from people who have had one attack of the virus disease, is often used to provide a passive IMMUNITY. This immunity is usually concentrated in the GAMMA GLOBULIN fraction of the blood.

Prevention of virus infection, or its damaging effects, is sometimes achieved by vaccines, killed or attenuated, made from the original infecting virus. Polio vaccine and yellow fever vaccine are notable examples. The control of insect vectors of virus diseases is also an important public health procedure.

Virus diseases. Among the most common virus diseases, discussed under their own names in this book, are: RABIES (hydrophobia), POLIO, the COMMON COLD, INFLUENZA, atypical virus PNEUMONIA, SMALLPOX, MEASLES, parrot fever (PSITTACOSIS), GERMAN MEASLES, CHICKEN POX, TRACHOMA and keratoconjunctivitis (EYE TROUBLE), HERPES (SHINGLES), MUMPS, insect-borne ENCEPHALITIS, and YELLOW FEVER.

Viscera—internal organs of the abdomen (for example, intestines) and chest (for example, lungs).

Visceroptosis—sagging of the intestines and other internal organs of the abdomen as the result, usually, of weakness in the ligaments that hold them in place and poor tone of the abdominal muscles. Wide belts and abdominal binders are sometimes required for correction.

Vision—see EYES; EYE TROUBLE.

Vis Mediatrix Naturae—a famous Latin phrase that means the *healing power of nature;* the tendency of the body to seek its own recovery from disease and accident. "I dress the wound; God heals it," said Ambroise Paré, the great military surgeon of the 16th century.

VITAMINS

Vitamins are organic chemical substances, widely distributed in natural foodstuffs, that are essential to normal metabolic functioning of human beings and lower animals. Only very small amounts are needed, but lack of the necessary amount, however small, results in a *vitamin-deficiency disease (avitaminosis)*. Among the classical examples of such diseases are rickets, scurvy, beriberi, and pellagra.

The word vitamin (then spelled *vitamine*) was invented in 1911 by a Polish chemist, Casimir Funk, who was trying to extract from rice hulls a chemical substance that would cure beriberi. He thought he had found an *amine* chemical *vital* to life. He hadn't, but his theory was correct: lack of certain chemical substances caused disease.

The chemical structure of many vitamins is known, and they can be manufactured literally by the ton. They are used to enrich foods, notably flour, from which natural vitamins are removed in the manufacture. Vitamins in the body enter into the complicated *enzyme* reactions by which food is digested, absorbed, and assimilated.

When different vitamins were first discovered, it was common practice to name them by letters of the alphabet. So many have now been found that it is more practical to give them chemical names. Thus vitamin B_1 is now called thiamine; vitamin C, ascorbic acid.

Vitamins are distinguished as fat-soluble—notably vitamins A, D, E, and K—and water-soluble—most of the others. Some are heat-labile, destroyed by cooking, notably vitamin C; most are heat-stable.

Are vitamin pills necessary? Generally, no. A good mixed *diet* of common foods, including the protective foods, supplies a human being with all the vitamins he needs (see DIET). Adding vitamin pills or concentrates to a good mixed diet will not increase pep and vigor or resistance to disease. For many people the ritual of taking vitamin pills is simply a sophisticated faith cure. Fortunately, moderate overdoses of vitamins do no harm.

Vitamin supplements are sometimes clearly necessary. They are needed whenever the dietary intake of vitamins is inadequate. This condition frequently occurs in the presence of serious, wasting illnesses, after surgical operations, on low-calorie reducing diets, and during pregnancy.

Vitamin needs differ with age and many other factors. Thus vitamin D is much more essential to infants and growing children than to adults. (See table of Recommended Daily Dietary Allowances under *diet.)*

Rarely is only a single vitamin missing from the diet. Most vitamin deficiencies are multiple; therefore vitamin pills and other vitamin preparations prescribed for preventing or treating disease contain a balanced supply of many vitamins.

Vitamins in the diet: Practically speaking, only a few of the many vitamins have to be seriously considered in formulating diets. Where these are found, the others are usually present also. These important vitamins are A, C, D, and three members of the vitamin B complex: thiamine, niacin, and riboflavin. The functions and sources of these vitamins are:

Vitamin A, once called the "anti-infective vitamin," helps to preserve the integrity of the skin and mucous membranes and other epithelial tissue, making them somewhat more resistant to infection. It aids growth and tooth formation. It is essential to the formation of "visual purple" rods and cones in the retina of the eye; its lack causes *night blindness.* Vitamin A is found in fish oils (e.g. cod-liver oil), liver, milk, egg yolk, and many green and yellow vegetables, where it exists as carotene.

Vitamin B complex includes a large number of water-soluble vitamins, including thiamine, riboflavin, niacin, pyridoxine, biotin, pantothenic acid, inositol, folic acid, and vitamin B_{12}.

Thiamine is essential for utilization of carbohydrates, normal appetite, and function of the digestive tract. Severe depletion of thiamine invites degeneration of the peripheral nerves (polyneuritis), a condition seen in BERIBERI and chronic ALCOHOLISM. Thiamine is not stored in the body as effectively as many other vitamins; hence it is the vitamin most apt to be lacking in the adult diet. Thiamine is often given to restore or improve appetite. Best sources of thiamine are pork and brewer's yeast; it is also found in whole grain, dried peas and beans, liver, and egg yolk.

Riboflavin is necessary for normal growth and for the integrity of skin tissue and mucous membrane. Lack of riboflavin may cause the lips to be sore and show slight fissures at the corners, the tongue to be red and sore, the eyes to itch and be extremely sensitive to light. Milk is the best source of riboflavin; other good sources are liver, kidneys, lean meat, peanuts.

Niacin, also called nicotinic acid, is the pellagra-preventive vitamin. Lack of niacin induces the symptoms of PELLAGRA (which see); namely, diarrhea, skin eruptions (dermatitis), and mental depression (dementia). Other symptoms are loss of appetite, loss of weight, and a sore tongue. Good sources of niacin are brewer's yeast, liver, kidney, salmon, lean meat, poultry, and eggs. Vegetarian diets are apt to be deficient in niacin.

Vitamin B₁₂, derived from liver, appears to increase the formation of red blood cells and has specific usefulness in treating pernicious ANEMIA.

Vitamin C, or ascorbic acid, is a delicate vitamin, not well stored in the body and easily destroyed by heat. It supplies a kind of cementing substance that binds cells together in the blood vessels, teeth, bones, and other tissues. Lack of it causes the capillary blood vessels to break rather easily (capillary fragility), producing such symptoms as spongy and bleeding gums, bleeding under the skin (petechiae), poor teeth, and tender joints. These are some of the symptoms of SCURVY, a disease both prevented and cured by administration of vitamin C. The best sources of vitamin C are citrus fruits—grapefruit, oranges, lemons, limes—and tomatoes.

Vitamin D, the "sunshine vitamin," is essential to the utilization of calcium and phosphorus, especially in proper bone and tooth formation. Infants and growing children particularly need this vitamin. Lack of it induces RICKETS and other bone disorders. Adults have little need of vitamin D supplements. When exposed to sunlight, the human body manufactures its own vitamin D. The ultraviolet rays of the sun turn sterols, fatty substances found in the human skin, into vitamin D. Exposure of milk to ultraviolet light (the Steenbock process) produces vitamin D milk. Cod-liver and other fish-liver oils are excellent sources of vitamin D; so are liver, butter, and egg yolk.

Vitamin E describes a group of oil-soluble alcohols (tocopherols). This vitamin is necessary to rats for reproduction and growth of their young. Its need or usefulness in human nutrition has not been established, though it is sometimes used therapeutically in treating habitual abortion and some degenerative muscular diseases. Best sources are wheat-germ oil, cotton-seed oil, egg yolks, and beef liver.

Vitamin K, or the coagulation vitamin, is needed by the human liver to produce prothrombin, essential to normal blood clotting. It is particularly necessary, and may have to be given, by injection, to newborn infants to prevent bleeding. Vitamin K is derived from alfalfa, fish meal, and hempseed oil.

Vitiligo—a SKIN disease, *piebald skin, leukoderma;* the presence of pale white patches on the skin (or hair) as a result of the loss of normal skin pigment formation underneath these spots. The cause is not known. The white areas become much more prominent as the rest of the skin is tanned. The condition sometimes occurs in Negroes, turning them white. There is no really effective treatment for vitiligo; but the white patches can be covered with skin-colored cosmetic creams or paints.

Vitreous—literally, glassy; the vitreous fluid, or humor, is the transparent liquid inside the eyeball proper, between the retina and the crystalline lens. *Aqueous fluid* is found in the front bulge of the eyeball, between the cornea and the lens. See EYES.

Vitro—IN VITRO means "in glass."

Vocal Cords—see THROAT.

Vomer—a thin plate of bone that divides the upper part of the NOSE into two nostrils.

Voicebox—larynx. See THROAT.

Volvulus—obstruction of the bowels due to knotting or twisting of a loop of bowel around itself. This is a surgical emergency.

Vomiting—retching; ejection by way of the mouth of stomach contents. It is an extremely common sign of disease, usually accompanied by nausea and some headache. In one sense it is a defense reaction of the body, which seeks to get rid of food that may disagree with it or which it is not ready to assimilate. Vomiting occurs when the "vomiting center" in the brain is touched off by any one of a number of possible stimuli; for example, stomach irritation, PREGNANCY, drugs (emetics) or poisons in the blood, disagreeable sights or smells, bacterial toxins, brain injury, hysteria, abdominal pain, abnormal motion (seasickness) or tickling of the throat.

Vulva—external SEX ORGANS, FEMALE.

Vulvectomy—surgical operation for removal of all or parts of the VULVA.

Vulvovaginitis—inflammation of the VULVA and VAGINA at the same time. See FEMALE TROUBLES.

W

Any word printed in SMALL CAPITALS *can be looked up under its own alphabetical listing for further information.*

Warts—growths on the SKIN. They can occur anywhere on the body, but usually appear on the hands, feet, and face. Warts exist in several different forms and seem to be caused by a VIRUS. However, there appears often to be some psychological or PSYCHOSOMATIC factor in their occurrence, because they are in fact often cured by suggestion. For other methods of removing warts, see treatment of plantar warts (on the soles of the feet) under the heading FOOT TROUBLE. Warts are almost never malignant. However, if a wart is enlarging, medical consultation should be obtained promptly.

Wassermann Test—a BLOOD TEST, which see, for SYPHILIS.

Water—H_2O; the precious fluid, essential to life, found in all body tissues; but sometimes, if contaminated with MICROBES, the vehicle of water-borne disease, such as TYPHOID and CHOLERA. Water can be made safe for consumption by boiling or by chlorination.

Water makes up 2/3 of the human body. The loss of 10% of body water is serious; 20%, through excessive bleeding or perspiration, usually fatal.

The adult body normally excretes about 2 quarts of water a day, principally in urine, but also by way of the skin (perspiration), lungs (breathing) and bowels (feces). The body tends to maintain a water balance, in which chemicals like sodium and potassium play an important part.

How much water should one drink a day? Enough to satisfy thirst, which is a keen index of water needs. Six to 8 glasses of water (or other liquid) a day are about enough to replace the normal daily water loss. In hot weather, water loss and water intake will normally increase.

It is perfectly safe and advisable to drink water with meals; but do not use the water to wash down chunks of unchewed food. The gulping of iced beverages or ice-water in large quantities is to be deplored because it distresses the stomach.

Wax—usually refers to the waxy substance, cerumen, secreted by the specialized cells of the outer ear. Wax may accumulate and plug up the ear, producing temporary deafness. Wax should be gently removed from the ear, preferably syringed or floated out with warm oil or water. See EAR TROUBLE.

Weeping—the seeping of fluid

from body surfaces, as in weeping ECZEMA.

Weight—see OBESITY, UNDERWEIGHT, DIET for information on body weight control. Sudden or rapid weight loss is always a signal for a medical check-up.

Wen—a small cyst involving the oil (sebaceous) glands of the SKIN. Unsightly wens may be removed by surgery or CAUTERY.

Wet Dream—the popular term for nocturnal emission of *semen*. This is a perfectly normal and harmless event, experienced by practically all males, beginning at puberty and continuing with declining frequency into adult life. The spontaneous discharge of semen during the night may or may not be accompanied by erotic dreams. More imaginative individuals may have more dreams. Wet dreams do not represent "lost manhood" in any sense of the word, and they require no treatment. They do not have to be prevented, and no sense of guilt should attach to them.

Wheal—a swollen, ITCHING area on the SKIN. See HIVES.

Wheeze—a common symptom of *bronchial asthma*. See ALLERGY.

"Whites"—discharge of whitish fluid from the vagina; leukorrhea. See FEMALE TROUBLES.

Whitlow—FELON; finger infection.

WHO—World Health Organization. It was organized at an International Health Conference in New York City, in June, 1946. Its charter was ratified by constituent government members and went into effect on April 7, 1948. WHO is the largest of the United Nations agencies. By 1958 WHO had a membership of more than 80 sovereign states—more members than the United Nations itself. Its headquarters are in Geneva, Switzerland, with regional offices in Washington, D.C., for the Americas; in Brazzaville, French Equatorial Africa, for Africa; in Alexandria, Egypt, for the eastern Mediterranean; in New Delhi, India, for Southeast Asia; in Manila, the Philippines, for the Western Pacific. The European office is intended for Copenhagen, Denmark.

WHO has about 1,300 staff members, and calls on experts freely throughout the world for technical assistance. In 1956 it was rendering technical assistance to 67 nations, through 600 diverse projects. For example, it has MALARIA-control projects going in many countries. WHO awards and administers 600 to 700 fellowships annually, collects and analyzes world-wide statistics, develops international standards of drugs (and other matters), and publishes a variety of bulletins, reports, and monographs of topflight authority.

WMA stands for the World Medical Association, whose constituent members are the national medical associations. Its relationship to WHO is the same as that of the American Medical Association to the U.S. Public Health Service. Organized in 1947, WMA had 52 national medical-society members in 1956. It has been concerned with medical ethics, education, and many other things.

Whooping Cough—*pertussis;* a serious childhood disease. The infecting microbe is a bacillus (H. pertussis). The source of infection is discharges from other infected children. The incubation period is commonly about one week, rarely longer than 10 days.

Unfortunately the disease often hangs on for a long time, usually from 1 to 2 months, during which the youngster is racked by paroxysms of cough ending with the characteristic whoop.

A child with whooping cough should always be under care of a physician. This is a serious disease!

Prevention of whooping cough can be accomplished by pertussis shots at an early age (3 to 6 months). These are usually given in combination with diphtheria and tetanus antigens (DPT).

Wind—flatus, passed from the anus. See FLATULENCE.

Windpipe—trachea; composed of hoops or rings of cartilage, lined with mucous membrane, it is about 4 inches long and extends from the voicebox in the throat down to the chest, where it divides into the two large bronchial tubes, one to each lung.

Witch Hazel—pleasant-smelling alcoholic solution that makes bruises feel cooler, and better. It is a solution of the witch-hazel leaf (*Hamamelis virginiana*) in alcohol; its medicinal activity is very feeble.

Womb—the uterus. See SEX ORGANS, FEMALE.

Wood Alcohol—methyl alcohol; a dangerous poison when ingested.

WORMS

Worms are parasites that sometimes take the human body for their host. Few, if any, are exclusive to man; they also infest animals, insects, fish, and other living creatures, for example, snails. Most of these parasites have a complicated life cycle, depending upon several hosts for the survival of their species. Worms obviously differ from MICROBES. They are much larger and can be seen with the naked eye; some commonly attain a length of 10 or 15 feet. (The eggs of worms, however, are microscopic in size.) Biologically, worms are well-developed, many-celled animals, usually with an overdeveloped reproductive system capable of pouring out thousands of eggs. Worms may or may not multiply in the body of the host; this is owing to their complicated life cycle. The eggs leave the body in the feces (bowel movements) and can be found in it. The diagnosis of worm infestation is usually made by finding and identifying the worm or its eggs in the feces. However, the diagnosis is sometimes made by finding the worm or pieces of it in other body wastes, or even in the tissues of the body.

Most of the worms that bother man are harbored, at least for some part of their life cycle, in the intestines and transmitted through contamination of soil, water, or food by human feces. The highly important matter of preventing infestation with these worms depends upon sanitation and hygiene—provision of pure water supplies, adequate sewage disposal, proper washing and preparation of food, and the like. Washing the hands before eating and after going to the toilet is one of the routine measures of personal hygiene that do prevent fecal-borne worm infestation. Not all worm infestations follow this pattern. Some worms, such as the filaria (threadworm) that causes FILARIASIS, are insect-borne. The trichinella, cause of TRICHINOSIS, is transmitted to man by eating infected meat, especially pork.

Worms lodged in the intestine rarely overwhelm their host. Very few deaths are ever reported. However, they usually weaken their victim by degrees. There are no absolutely typical symptoms produced by worms; indeed many people who are infested (and may be carriers of the worms to others) remain free of symptoms for a long time. The type and severity of symptoms depend both upon the species of worm involved and the number present.

Since the symptoms are so nonspecific, positive diagnosis must be made by a physician. Self-treatment for worms (or supposed worms) is especially to be avoided. Drugs used to expel worms are called vermifuges or anthelmintics, but they are not simple home remedies. The dosage and the conditions of use must be carefully prescribed. Among commonly used vermifuges are male fern, oil of chenopodium, and hexylresorcinol.

The intestinal worms most often found to bother human beings in North America are pinworms (*Enterobius vermicularis*), roundworms (*Ascaris lumbricoides*), hookworms (*Necator americanus*), and tapeworms (*Taenia*). Blood flukes, schistosomes causing SCHISTOSOMIASIS, are also extremely prevalent in tropical and oriental countries.

Pinworm (also called seatworm and threadworm) infestation

is exceedingly common in temperate climes. Pinworms are small white worms, about ⅛ to ½ inch long. They do not dig into tissue but simply inhabit the lower bowel. As many as 5,000 at a time may be present. They occasionally migrate to the appendix or the female sex organs. The female pinworm exits from the anus to lay her eggs—thousands at a time—in the tender skin at the anal orifice. Occasionally the worm cannot find its way back to the lower bowel and may be found on the bedclothing or underwear.

The chief symptom of pinworm is extreme itching around the anus. This leads to scratching and sometimes secondary infection. Other symptoms include mild intestinal disturbances, loss of appetite, and insomnia. Sometimes there are no symptoms.

If pinworm is positively diagnosed, all members of the household probably should be treated. The condition appears more frequently in children and in women than in men. A rigid hygienic regime must be enforced to prevent hands and fingers that touch the anus from conveying pinworm eggs and larvae back to the mouth. Antiseptic and soothing ointments are applied to the rectal area to reduce itching. Gentian violet or hexylresorcinol may be prescribed to be taken by mouth in carefully regulated doses.

Roundworms (Ascaris) are, next to pinworms, the parasitic worms that most frequently infest the intestinal tract. These nematodes are large white worms; the female may develop to 15 inches, the male to about half that size. Its normal habitat is the small intestine, where it holds itself by pushing against the opposite sides of the walls, in the manner of a curled spring. A few common roundworms may not produce any symptoms; a large number, 200 or more, may appear as a palpable tumor and cause serious intestinal obstruction. Sometimes these worms wander and may plug up the common bile duct, the appendix, and even the Eustachian tube from throat to ear.

The roundworm is exceedingly prolific; the female lays 200,000 eggs a day. These are excreted in bowel discharges and develop on the surface of the soil. They return to the intestine by ingestion. Here they develop still further into larvae, about 1/25 inch long. These make their way into the blood stream, thence into the lungs (where they may cause hemorrhagic pneumonia), from which they are coughed up into the throat and swallowed. Then they return to the small intestine, where they mature. This complicated process takes about 6 weeks.

A single properly prescribed treatment with hexylresorcinol or other appropriate drug will often get rid of all the roundworms. The drugs must be taken after at least 12 hours of fasting and are usually followed by a saline cathartic.

Roundworms are most common in children. Sometimes their presence produces symptoms mistaken for allergy.

Hookworm disease remains an important public-health problem in some southern states of the United States as well as in many other countries around the world. The situation has greatly improved, however, over what it was at the turn of the 20th century, when it was estimated that 5 million "poor whites" in the South were heavily infested with hookworm and that their "laziness" was really a symptom and result of this infestation. Hookworm itself is an ancient disease and there are a number of species of the worm that cause it around the world.

The hookworm is an internal bloodsucker, and this accounts for the many and serious symptoms it produces. The adult worm is about ¼ to ½ inch long, the females being somewhat larger than the males. The worms inhabit the small intestine, to which they attach themselves with something like teeth. They feed mainly on blood, each worm taking up to ½ cc. of human blood a day. The worms excrete a toxic substance which tends to make the tiny blood vessels to which they are attached swell up and burst and to keep the blood in them from coagulating.

Hookworms in the bowels, if present in any significant number, produce a continuing blood-loss ANEMIA. This is responsible for the commonly observed symptoms: apathy, lack of ambition, muscular weakness, dull skin, dry hair, and a constant feeling of being hungry. Hookworm itself is rarely fatal, but the persistent anemia, if uncorrected, causes the victim to run a downhill course and makes an invalid out of him.

The female hookworm in the bowel can lay up to 15,000 eggs a day. These are excreted in bowel movements, and their presence there makes a diagnosis of hookworm disease positive. When the eggs are deposited on soil, particularly sandy, moist, warm soil, they hatch into larvae within a day.

How, then, does hookworm infestation occur and reoccur? The larvae usually find their way back into the human body through intact skin. Going barefoot greatly favors the process; the retention of mud between the toes gives the larvae their great chance. Wearing shoes, therefore, is one important control measure against hookworm disease. When the larvae penetrate the skin, they set up an intense itching and inflammation, called "ground itch."

Sometimes, of course, the larvae are introduced into the body through contaminated food and water. Other important control measures against hookworm disease, therefore, include water purification and satisfactory disposal of human excrement. The deep, sanitary privy plays an important role.

When the larvae enter the skin, they make their way through the subcutaneous tissue into a blood vessel. Eventually they are carried into the lungs, where they manage to break out into the air sacs. At this point in their life cycle, they may produce in their victim a lung inflammation mistaken for pneumonia. Then the larvae travel up the bronchial tubes to the throat, often assisted by coughing. Swallowed, they get back to the small intestine, where they grow into adult hookworms fastened to the lining of the bowel. It takes about 6 weeks for the larvae that have entered the skin to become egg-laying adult hookworms.

The successful *treatment of hookworm disease* depends largely upon the constant application of the sanitary measures that prevent reinfestation with the worm. Even without treatment, the worms tend to disappear from the bowel if there is no reinfestation. About 90% will be eliminated in a year or two; but complete eradication may take up to 7 years. More active treatment is therefore desirable. Vermifuges, often tetrachloroethylene, are carefully prescribed. Iron compounds are given to correct the anemia, and an adequate diet is also essential.

Tapeworms are long, flat, thin worms whose primary residence is the human intestine. Although there are about 40 species of tapeworms, the ones that most commonly infest man are known as the beef, pork, dog, fish, rat, and dwarf tapeworms. The beef tapeworm is the largest, the dwarf tapeworm the smallest. The life cycle of most of these worms is perpetuated because cattle, pigs, fish, and other animals feed on something contaminated with human feces in which eggs or segments of the tapeworm are present.

Human beings are infested by consuming raw, rare, improperly cooked beef, pork, and fish or some food or water contaminated with dog, rat, and other animal droppings. The dwarf tapeworm, most common in children, is apparently passed from one person to another by food soiled with feces.

The adult tapeworm has a head (scolex) followed by a ribbon-like string of segments, usually capable of reproduction not only of additional segments but also of eggs. The segment farthest from the head is the oldest. The head has little hooks or sucking disks which it attaches to the bowel lining.

The symptoms produced in the human host by the presence of tapeworms vary with the type and number of worms present, and also the general health, tolerance, and resistance of the host. Some symptoms are highly specific; for example, the mass of millions of larvae (hydatid cyst) sometimes encountered with dog tapeworm. The common, but by no means specific, symptoms of tapeworm infestation include a ravenous appetite and false hunger pains in spite of loss of weight; diarrhea; secondary anemia; general weakness and nervousness. The diagnosis of tapeworm is confirmed by finding eggs or segments of the worm in the stool.

In the case of the *beef tapeworm*, as many as 2,000 segments or parts may be developed. Usually there is only one such worm present in the intestine of the host. However, such worms have been assumed to live as long as 20 years, producing 10 or more new segments a day, and to have attained a length of 40 feet.

The treatment of tapeworm often calls for fasting for 12 to 48 hours, one or more doses of saline cathartics, and appropriate doses of worm-killing drugs. The treatment is usually quite effective.

RINGWORM is not a worm; it is a FUNGUS infection.

Wound—a break in the continuity of the skin and other body tissues. The great risk in wounds is INFECTION.

Wrist—the link between the hand and the forearm, comparable to the ANKLE in the leg. See JOINTS.

Wryneck—a twisted neck; torticollis.

X

Any word printed in SMALL CAPITALS *can be looked up under its own alphabetical listing for further information.*

Xanthoma—a rare SKIN disease in which yellow plaques, composed of fatty substances, appear on the skin, especially on the eyelids.

Xanthosis—a yellowish discoloration of the skin, sometimes seen in DIABETES.

Xenophobia—fear of strangers.

Xeroderma—dry SKIN. The skin becomes rough as well as dry and often scales; this resembles *fish-skin disease*. There is an extreme and fatal form of this disease in which the skin also becomes brown-colored and ulcerates.

Xerophthalmia—a form of *conjunctivitis* in which the eyeball appears dry and without luster. It is associated with a lack of vitamin A and night blindness. See EYE TROUBLE.

Xiphoid—the sword-shaped lower end of the breast-bone.

X RAYS

Almost from the very day their discovery was first announced, X rays have proved of great and increasing value to the practice of medicine, and the preservation of human health. X rays are used both for diagnosis and treatment of disease and injuries.

X rays are also called *roentgen rays* in honor of their discoverer, the German physicist Wilhelm Konrad Roentgen (1845-1923). The science dealing with their use, particularly in medicine, is called *roentgenology*. It makes up a large share of the somewhat broader field of *radiology*, which deals with the use of radiant energy in all forms in the diagnosis and treatment of disease and hence includes the use of RADIUM and *radioactive isotopes*. The international unit of X-ray irradiation is also called a roentgen, abbreviated to *r*. An X-ray picture is a roentgenogram.

The discovery of X rays was more than a boon to medicine. It opened a new era in physics, which has also produced health benefits. Furthermore, X rays have contributed greatly to research in all fields of science and industrial technology.

Roentgen read his famous paper "on a new kind of rays," which he designated as X rays, at a meeting of the Würzburg (Germany) Physical and Medical Society on the evening of December 28, 1895. The paper began:

"If the discharge of a fairly large induction coil be made to pass through a Hittorf vacuum tube . . . or similar apparatus . . . there is observed at each discharge a bright illumination of a paper screen covered with barium platinocyanide placed in the vicinity of the induction coil. . . . The most striking feature of this phenomenon is the fact that an active agent here passes through a black cardboard envelope which is opaque to the visible and ultraviolet rays of the sun or of the electric arc; an agent, too, which has the power of producing active fluorescence. . . . Of special significance in many respects is the fact that photographic dry plates are sensitive to X rays. We are in a position, therefore, to determine many phenomena more definitely and so the more easily to avoid deception."

Later in the meeting Roentgen offered to demonstrate these astonishing rays that had the property of passing through solid matter. With them, he said, it was possible to visualize the bones of the hand. The chairman of the meeting offered himself as a subject and an X-ray picture of his hand was taken. The bones also showed up clearly on the fluorescent screen. The enthusiastic scientists present at the meeting immediately voted to call the new kind of rays roentgen rays.

What are X rays? They are electromagnetic radiations, or energy waves, of short wave length. This length is calculated in the neighborhood of 1/1,380,000,000 inch. On the broad scale of the electromagnetic spectrum, X rays come between ultraviolet rays and the gamma rays of radium. Radio waves (with wave lengths running up to 10,000 meters and more), infrared rays, the rays of visible light, and cosmic rays (shorter than gamma rays) are also part of the electromagnetic spectrum. All these waves travel at the speed of light, approximately 186,282 miles per second.

The wave lengths of X rays, which cover a considerable range, depend upon the voltage of electricity used to create them. The higher the voltage, the shorter the length. With the large atom smashers now available, X rays of hundreds of millions of volts' energy have been produced. But these are not usually practical. The so-called "soft" X rays sometimes used for treating skin diseases have a voltage of only 2,500 to 12,000 volts. Even the "hard" X rays employed for taking X-ray pictures rarely run above

100,000 volts. Extremely high voltage X rays (up to 2,000,000 volts) are sometimes used in treating CANCER.

Great technical improvements have been made in X-ray apparatus since Roentgen's first crude machine. Portable X-ray machines are available. Practically every hospital and a great many physicians' and dentists' offices include X-ray apparatus. The heart of the machine, however, remains a high-vacuum tube through which a high-voltage beam of electricity is discharged.

How are X rays used in medicine? There is no branch of medicine that does not have some use for X-ray diagnosis or treatment. The first use of X-ray pictures, and still a very important one, was in diagnosing FRACTURES and setting broken bones. Very properly, when there is even a suspicion that a bone may be broken, cracked, or chipped, the doctor insists on X-ray pictures. These pictures are taken from several angles so that no break will be overlooked and the relationship of the parts to one another can be exactly determined. Another early use of X rays was in the localization of foreign bodies—like bullets—in the human body.

The usefulness of the X-ray picture depends upon the fact that when X rays pass through a part of the body, the denser parts register heavier shadows on the photographic film or fluoroscopic screen. An X-ray photograph is really an unfocused shadowgraph. It is the *contrast* between the lighter and darker shadows on the film that enables the physician to determine what has happened inside the body. Great skill and experience is needed in making proper interpretations of the shadows on the X-ray films (or plates). A specialist in this field is called a radiologist or roentgenologist.

Chest X rays are of great value in the diagnosis of TUBERCULOSIS; affected areas in the lung show up as characteristic shadows on the X-ray film. Small "scout" films are used to make mass chest X-ray surveys of large populations. Chest X rays also reveal the size of the heart.

To get X-ray pictures of soft tissues in other parts of the body (including the skull), it is usually necessary to use some sort of contrast medium, opaque to the passage of X rays. Thus, for example, when the doctor wants X-ray pictures of the gastrointestinal tract (a so-called "g.i. series"), he has the patient first swallow a barium mixture. It is often given in chocolate milk. When X-ray pictures of the gall bladder, the kidneys, the urinary bladder, and certain other organs are needed, the doctor will administer beforehand a radiopaque dye which finds its way to the organ under consideration.

Treatment with X rays, and other forms of radiation, has its greatest usefulness in CANCER of many kinds. X-ray and radium therapy is often used in conjunction with surgery in these cases. The value of the treatment depends upon the fact that cancer cells are more sensitive to irradiation than normal cells. The degree of radiosensitivity varies among different kinds of cancer cells. High-power X rays, as noted, are used in treating cancer. "Softer" X rays are employed in the treatment of a variety of skin lesions. Under any circumstance, the normal tissue must be protected against undue exposure to the X-ray beam and scatter.

Are X rays dangerous? Potentially, yes; practically, no. There were a number of martyrs to X ray (and radium) among physicians in the early days of this discovery—before it was realized that cumulative small doses could be damaging and even fatal. Since then the application of safety factors (shielding with lead, for example) has been brought to a high pitch of efficiency and protection. X rays used in medical and dental practice are not dangerous to the patient. The amount of exposure when X-ray films are taken is minimal. However, the question has been raised as to how much radiation from all sources (including cosmic rays) a human being can take safely in the course of a lifetime. See ATOMIC ENERGY.

Y

Any word printed in SMALL CAPITALS *can be looked up under its own alphabetical listing for further information.*

Yaws—a tropical disease, caused by a spirochete *(Treponema pertenue)*, which has some resemblance to the causative agent of syphilis. It is not a venereal disease, however, and may possibly be INSECT-borne. The chief distinguishing marks are raspberry-red excrescences on the skin of the face, hands, feet and sex organs. These may run together into pustules and ulcers. The destruction of skin and bones, particularly the bones of the nose, may occur. Yaws yields to ANTIBIOTICS.

"Yellow Baby"—newborn infant with *jaundice,* suffering from ERYTHROBLASTOSIS FETALIS.

Yellow Fever—a virulent virus disease, eradicated from the United States. No case originating in this country has been reported since 1905. The disease is carried by the mosquito (Aedes aegypti), which has not been eradicated. A reservoir of the yellow-fever virus persists in jungle animals of Central and South America. An effective vaccine to protect against yellow fever is available.

Yoghurt—Bulgarian buttermilk; milk curdled by introduction of a MICROBE that produces lactic acid (lactobacillus). This drink is a stand-by of food faddists; fantastic claims of its value to human health have been set forth on the flimsiest evidence. See DIET.

Z

Any word printed in SMALL CAPITALS *can be looked up under its own alphabetical listing for further information.*

Zinc—a chemical element, a blue-white metal. It can poison, yielding symptoms like lead poisoning. However, many of its compounds (salts) have medicinal uses; notably *zinc oxide,* used in powder or ointment form for the relief of SKIN irritations.

Zona—SHINGLES; herpes zoster, which "girdles" the body.

Zonesthesia—the feeling of being held in by a tight girdle.

Zoonoses—animal diseases that can be transmitted to man. There are about 80 of them, including RABIES, UNDULANT FEVER, ANTHRAX.

Zoopsia—HALLUCINATION of seeing or being chased by animals.

Zoster—herpes zoster; SHINGLES.

Zygoma—the arch of bone formed by the junction of the temporal bone of the skull and the jawbone.

Zygote—the fertilized egg cell (see PREGNANCY).

Zymurgy—fermentation chemistry, by which PENICILLIN is produced; the art of brewing and winemaking.

APPENDIX

Medical Code Letters

SYMBOL	KEY
Abbreviations used in medical reports, hospital charts, and doctors' prescriptions	Meanings of abbreviations and symbols used by doctors
āā	equal parts of
a.c.	before meals
ad lib.	at pleasure
ADL	activities of daily living
AZ	Ascheim Zondek (pregnancy) test
b.i.d.	twice a day
BMR	basal metabolic rate
C.	centigrade (thermometer reading)
CA	carcinoma (cancer)
cc.	cubic centimeter
CNS	central nervous system
D&C	dilatation and curettage (of uterus)
dr.	dram or drams
EEG	electroencephalogram
EENT	eye, ear, nose and throat
EKG	electrocardiogram
extr.	extract
F.	Fahrenheit (thermometer reading)
GC	gonorrhea
GI	gastrointestinal
gm.	gram, grams
GOK	God only knows
gr.	grain, grains
gt.	drop
GU	genitourinary
GYN	gynecology

SYMBOL	KEY
IQ	intelligence quotient
mg.	milligram
min.	minim, a drop
mm.	millimeter
NAD	no appreciable disease
NPN	nonprotein nitrogen
NYD	not yet diagnosed
OB	obstetrics
O.D.	right eye
O.L.	left eye
OT	occupational therapy
p.a.	in equal parts
p.c.	after food (after meals)
PT	physical therapy
q.d.	every day
q.h.	every hour
q.i.d.	four times a day
q.s.	as much as is sufficient
℞	symbol for prescription
r.	roentgen (measure of radiation)
RBC	red blood count
S. *or* Sig.	give the following directions; label
TB	tuberculosis
t.i.d.	three times a day
TLC	tender loving care
tr.	tincture
Wass.	Wassermann reaction (for syphilis)
WBC	white blood count
♀	female
♂	male

Where to Get Help

A quick reference directory of professional associations—marked with a (P)—and health agencies from which specialized information about health questions and medical matters can be obtained by calling or writing. The agencies, of course, can and will be of help only in their own fields of interest.

AMERICAN ACADEMY OF GENERAL PRACTICE—Volker Blvd. at Brookside Blvd., Kansas City 12, Mo. (JE 1-0377) (P)

AMERICAN ASSOCIATION FOR HEALTH, PHYSICAL EDUCATION AND RECREATION, a department of the National Education Association of America—1201 16th St., N. W., Washington 6, D. C. (AD 4-4855) (P)

AMERICAN CANCER SOCIETY—521 West 57th St., New York 19, N. Y. (PL 7-2700)

AMERICAN DENTAL ASSOCIATION—222 East Superior St., Chicago 11, Ill. (WH 4-6730) (P)

AMERICAN DIABETES ASSOCIATION, INC.—1 East 45th St., New York 36, N. Y. (MU 7-3930)

AMERICAN FOUNDATION FOR THE BLIND, INC.—15 West 16th St., New York 11, N. Y. (WA 4-0420)

AMERICAN HEARING SOCIETY—1800 H St., N. W., Washington 6, D. C. (NA 8-2844)

AMERICAN HEART ASSOCIATION, INC.—44 East 23rd St., New York 10, N. Y. (GR 7-9170)

AMERICAN HOSPITAL ASSOCIATION—18 East Division St., Chicago 10, Ill. (WH 4-4350) (P)

AMERICAN MEDICAL ASSOCIATION—535 North Dearborn St., Chicago 10, Ill. (WH 4-1500) (P)

AMERICAN NATIONAL RED CROSS—17th and D Sts., N. W., Washington 13, D. C. (RE 7-8300)

AMERICAN NURSES ASSOCIATION—2 Park Ave., New York 16, N. Y. (OR 9-2040) (P)

AMERICAN OCCUPATIONAL THERAPY ASSOCIATION— 250 West 57th St., New York 19, N. Y. (CI 7-6717) (P)

AMERICAN PHYSICAL THERAPY ASSOCIATION—1790 Broadway, New York 19, N. Y. (CO 5-0430) (P)

AMERICAN PSYCHOLOGICAL ASSOCIATION—1333 16th St., N. W., Washington 6, D. C. (CO 5-0595) (P)

AMERICAN PUBLIC HEALTH ASSOCIATION—1790 Broadway, New York 19, N. Y. (CI 5-8000) (P)

AMERICAN SOCIAL HYGIENE ASSOCIATION—1790 Broadway, New York 19, N. Y. (CI 5-8000)

AMERICAN SPEECH AND HEARING ASSOCIATION—1001 Connecticut Ave., N. W., Washington 6, D. C. (ME 8-2363) (P)

ARTHRITIS AND RHEUMATISM FOUNDATION—10 Columbus Circle, New York 19, N. Y. (PL 7-7633)

ASSOCIATION FOR THE AID OF CRIPPLED CHILDREN— 345 East 46th St., New York 17, N. Y. (OX 7-3150)

BLIND (*See* American Foundation for the Blind; National Society for the Prevention of Blindness)

BLUE CROSS COMMISSION (of the American Hospital Association)—425 North Michigan Ave., Chicago 11, Ill. (MO 4-2457)

BLUE SHIELD MEDICAL-SURGICAL PLANS (The National Association of Blue Shield Plans)—425 North Michigan Ave., Chicago 11, Ill. (MO 4-7100)

BRAIN RESEARCH FOUNDATION—600 South Michigan Ave., Chicago 5, Ill. (HA 7-2684)

CANCER (*See* American Cancer Society)

CEREBRAL PALSY (*See* United Cerebral Palsy Associations)

CHILD STUDY ASSOCIATION OF AMERICA, INC.—132 East 74th St., New York 21, N. Y. (BU 8-6000)

CHILD WELFARE LEAGUE OF AMERICA—345 East 46th St., New York 17, N. Y. (OX 7-2960)

CHILDREN'S BUREAU (A division of the U. S. Department of Health, Education, and Welfare)

CRIPPLED CHILDREN (*See* Association for the Aid of Crippled Children; National Society of Crippled Children and Adults)

DEAFNESS (*See* American Hearing Society; Volta Bureau for the Deaf)

FAMILY SERVICE ASSOCIATION OF AMERICA—215 Fourth Avenue, New York 3, N. Y. (OR 4-6100) (P)

HEALTH INFORMATION FOUNDATION, INC.—420 Lexington Ave., New York 17, N. Y. (OR 9-4380)

HEART (*See* American Heart Association)

HOSPITALS (*See* American Hospital Association)

INFANTILE PARALYSIS (*See* National Foundation [for Infantile Paralysis])

MATERNITY CENTER ASSOCIATION—48 East 92nd St., New York 28, N. Y. (EN 9-7300)

MEDICAL LIBRARY ASSOCIATION—Secretary, c/o Yale Medical Library, 333 Cedar St., New Haven, Conn. (ST 7-3131) (P)

MENTAL HEALTH (*See* National Association for Mental Health)

MULTIPLE SCLEROSIS (*See* National Multiple Sclerosis Society)

MUSCULAR DYSTROPHY ASSOCIATIONS OF AMERICA, INC.—1790 Broadway, New York 19, N. Y. (JU 6-0808)

NATIONAL ASSOCIATION FOR MENTAL HEALTH—10 Columbus Circle, New York 19, N. Y. (PL 7-7800)

NATIONAL ASSOCIATION FOR RETARDED CHILDREN—99 University Place, New York 3, N. Y. (OR 4-0610)

NATIONAL ASSOCIATION OF SOCIAL WORKERS—95 Madison Ave., New York 16, N. Y. (MU 6-7128) (P)

NATIONAL COMMITTEE ON THE AGING (of the National Social Welfare Assembly)—345 East 46th St., New York 17, N. Y. (MU 7-8300)

NATIONAL COUNCIL ON ALCOHOLISM—2 East 103rd St., New York 29, N. Y. (SA 2-2767)

NATIONAL EPILEPSY LEAGUE—208 North Wells St., Chicago 6, Ill. (AN 3-6065)

NATIONAL FOUNDATION [FOR INFANTILE PARALYSIS], INC.—301 East 42nd St., New York 17, N. Y. (OX 7-7700)

NATIONAL HEALTH COUNCIL—1790 Broadway, New York 19, N. Y. (CI 5-8000)

NATIONAL LEAGUE FOR NURSING—2 Park Ave., New York 16, N. Y. (OR 9-2040) (P)

NATIONAL MULTIPLE SCLEROSIS SOCIETY—257 Fourth Ave., New York 10, N. Y. (OR 4-4100)

NATIONAL NEPHROSIS FOUNDATION, INC.—143 East 35th
St., New York 16, N. Y. (OR 9-6640)

NATIONAL REHABILITATION ASSOCIATION—1025 Vermont
Ave., N. W., Washington 5, D. C. (ST 3-3769)

NATIONAL SAFETY COUNCIL—425 North Michigan Ave.,
Chicago 11, Ill. (WH 4-4800)

NATIONAL SOCIETY FOR THE PREVENTION OF BLIND-
NESS—1790 Broadway, New York 19, N. Y. (CI 5-8000)

NATIONAL SOCIETY OF CRIPPLED CHILDREN AND
ADULTS—11 South La Salle St., Chicago 3, Ill. (FR 2-0390)

NATIONAL TUBERCULOSIS ASSOCIATION—1790 Broadway,
New York 19, N. Y. (CI 5-8000)

NEW YORK ACADEMY OF MEDICINE—2 East 103rd St., New
York 29, N. Y. (TR 6-8200) (P)

NURSING (*See* National League for Nursing)

POLIO (*See* National Foundation [for Infantile Paralysis])

PUBLIC HEALTH (*See* American Public Health Association;
National League for Nursing; National Health Council)

PUBLIC HEALTH SERVICE (A division of the U. S. Department of Health, Education, and Welfare)

RED CROSS (*See* American National Red Cross)

TUBERCULOSIS (*See* National Tuberculosis Association)

UNITED CEREBRAL PALSY ASSOCIATIONS, INC.—321 West
44th St., New York 36, N. Y. (JU 6-3411)

U. S. DEPARTMENT OF HEALTH, EDUCATION, AND WEL-
FARE—330 Independence Ave., S. W., Washington 25, D. C.
(EX 3-6300)

VOLTA BUREAU FOR THE DEAF—1537 35th St., N. W.,
Washington 7, D. C. (AD 2-0014)

Desirable Weights

FOR MEN AND WOMEN OF AGES 25 AND OVER

Weight in Pounds According to Frame (as Ordinarily Dressed)

HEIGHT (with shoes on) Feet	Inches	SMALL FRAME	MEDIUM FRAME	LARGE FRAME
		MEN		
5	2	116-125	124-133	131-142
5	3	119-128	127-136	133-144
5	4	122-132	130-140	137-149
5	5	126-136	134-144	141-153
5	6	129-139	137-147	145-157
5	7	133-143	141-151	149-162
5	8	136-147	145-156	153-166
5	9	140-151	149-160	157-170
5	10	144-155	153-164	161-175
5	11	148-159	157-168	165-180
6	0	152-164	161-173	169-185
6	1	157-169	166-178	174-190
6	2	163-175	171-184	179-196
6	3	168-180	176-189	184-202
		WOMEN		
4	11	104-111	110-118	117-127
5	0	105-113	112-120	119-129
5	1	107-115	114-122	121-131
5	2	110-118	117-125	124-135
5	3	113-121	120-128	127-138
5	4	116-125	124-132	131-142
5	5	119-128	127-135	133-145
5	6	123-132	130-140	138-150
5	7	126-136	134-144	142-154
5	8	129-139	137-147	145-158
5	9	133-143	141-151	149-162
5	10	136-147	145-155	152-166
5	11	139-150	148-158	155-169

Courtesy of the Metropolitan Life Insurance Company

Calorie Counter of Common Foods

FOOD	MEASURES°	CALORIES
Almonds 12-15 100
Apple butter ....1 tablespoon 40
Apples, baked ....1 large and 2 tablespoons sugar 200
fresh ....1 large 100
Applesauce, sweetened .....½ cup 100
Apricots
canned in sirup ....3 large halves
and 2 tablespoons juice 100
dried ....10 halves 100
Asparagus, fresh or
canned ....5 stalks 5 inches long 15
Avocado ....½ pear 4 inches long 265
Bacon ....2-3 long slices cooked 100
Bacon fat ....1 tablespoon 100
Banana ....1 medium 6 inches long 90
Beans
canned with pork ....½ cup 175
dried ....½ cup cooked 135
lima, fresh or canned ..½ cup 100
snap, fresh or canned ..½ cup 25
Beef (cooked)
corned ....1 slice 4 inches by 1½ by 1 100
dried ....2 ounces 100
hamburger ....1 patty (3 ounces) 300
round, lean ....1 medium slice (2 ounces) 125
sirloin, lean ....1 average slice (3 ounces) 250
tongue ....2 ounces 125
Beet greens ....½ cup cooked 30
Beets, fresh or canned ....2 beets 2 inches in diameter 50
Biscuit, baking powder ..2 inches in diameter 100
Blackberries, fresh ....1 cup 100
Blueberries, fresh ....1 cup 90
Bologna ....1 slice 2 inches by ½ thick 100
Breads
Boston brown ....1 slice 3 inches in diameter, ¾ thick 90
corn (1 egg) ....1 2-inch square 120
cracked wheat ....1 slice average 80
dark rye ....1 slice ½ inch thick 70
light rye ....1 slice ½ inch thick 75
white, enriched ....1 slice average 75
white, enriched ....1 slice thin 55
whole wheat, 60% ......1 slice average 70
whole wheat, 100% .....1 slice average 75
Broccoli ....3 stalks 5½ inches long 100
Brownies ....1 piece 2 inches by 2 by ¾ 140
Brussels sprouts ....6 sprouts 1½ inches in diameter 50
Butter ....1 tablespoon 95

°*1 cup equals 8 ounces. 3 teaspoons equal 1 tablespoon. 4 tablespoons equal ¼ cup.*

FOOD	MEASURES	CALORIES
Cabbage, cooked ....½ cup		40
raw ....1 cup		25
Cake		
angel ....1/10 of a large cake		155
chocolate or vanilla,		
no icing ....1 piece 2 inches by 2 by 2		200
chocolate or vanilla,		
with icing ....1 piece 2 inches by 1½ by 2		200
cup cake with		
chocolate icing ....1 medium		250
Cantaloupe ....½ of a 5½ inch melon		50
Carrots ....1 carrot 4 inches long		25
Cashew nuts 4-5		100
Cauliflower ....¼ of a head 4½ inches in diameter		25
Caviar ....1 tablespoon		25
Celery ....2 stalks		15
Cheese		
American cheddar ....1 cube 1⅛ inches square		
	or three tablespoons grated 110	
cottage ....5 tablespoons		100
cream ....2 tablespoons		100
Cherries, sweet ....15 large		75
Chicken		
broiled ....½ medium broiler		270
roast ....1 slice 4 inches by 2½ by ¼		100
Chinese cabbage ....1 cup raw		20
Chocolate		
fudge ....1 piece 1 inch square		
	by ¾ thick 100	
malted milk ....fountain size		460
milk, with almonds,		
sweetened ....1 ounce		150
milk, unsweetened ......1 ounce		140
mints ....1 mint 1½ inches in diameter		100
sirup ....¼ cup		200
unsweetened ....1 square		160
Cider, sweet ....1 cup		100
Clams ....6 round		100
Cocoa, half milk,		
half water ....1 cup		150
Coconut ....½ cup fresh		175
Cod liver oil ....1 tablespoon		100
Cod steak ....1 piece 3½ inches by 2 by 1		100
Cola soft drinks ....6-ounce bottle		75
Collards ....½ cup cooked		50
Cooking fats,		
vegetable ....1 tablespoon		100
Corn ....½ cup		70
Corn sirup ....1 tablespoon		75
Cornflakes ....1 cup		80
Cornmeal ....1 tablespoon uncooked		35
Cornstarch pudding ....½ cup		200
Crackers		
graham ....1 square		35

FOOD	MEASURES	CALORIES
Crackers *(cont.)*		
peanut butter-cheese sandwich	1 cracker	45
round snack-type	1 cracker 2 inches in diameter	15
rye wafers	1 wafer	25
saltines	1 cracker 2 inches square	15
Cranberry sauce	¼ cup	100
Cream		
heavy	2 tablespoons	120
light	2 tablespoons	65
whipped	3 tablespoons	100
Cream-puff shells	1 shell	85
Cucumber	½ medium	10
Custard, boiled or baked	½ cup	130
Dates	4	100
Egg	1 medium size	75
Eggplant	3 slices 4 inches in diameter ½-inch thick, raw	50
Endive	average serving	10
Escarole	average serving	10
Figs, dried	3 small	100
Flour, white or whole grain	1 tablespoon unsifted	35
Frankfurter	1 sausage	125
Gelatin, fruit flavored		
dry	3-ounce package	330
ready to serve	½ cup	85
Ginger ale	1 cup	85
Gingerbread, hot water	2 inches by 2 by 2	200
Grape juice	½ cup	80
Grape nuts	¼ cup	100
Grapefruit juice, unsweetened	1 cup	100
Grapes		
American or Tokay	1 bunch—22 average	75
seedless	1 bunch—30 average	75
Griddle cakes	1 cake 4 inches in diameter	75
Halibut	1 piece 3 inches by 1⅜ by 1	100
Ham, lean	1 slice 4¼ inches by 4 by ½	265
Hard sauce	1 tablespoon	100
Hickory nuts	12-15	100
Hominy grits	¾ cup cooked	100
Honey	1 tablespoon	100
Ice cream	½ cup	200
Ice cream soda	fountain size	325

FOOD	MEASURES	CALORIES
Jellies and jams	1 rounded tablespoon	100
Kale	½ cup cooked	50
Lamb, roast	1 slice 3½ inches by 4½ by ⅛	100
Lard	1 tablespoon	100
Lemon juice	1 tablespoon	5
Lettuce	2 large leaves	5
Liver	1 slice 3 inches by 3 by ½	100
Liverwurst	2 ounces	130
Lobster meat	1 cup	150
Macaroni	¾ cup cooked	100
Maple sirup	1 tablespoon	70
Margarine	1 tablespoon	100
Marshmallows	1	20
Milk		
buttermilk	1 cup	85
condensed	1½ tablespoons	100
evaporated	½ cup (1 cup diluted)	160
skim milk, dried	2½ tablespoons	100
skim milk, fresh	1 cup	85
whole milk	1 cup	170
yogurt, plain	1 cup	120-160
Mints, cream	½-inch cube	5
Molasses	1 tablespoon	70
Muffins		
bran	1 medium	90
1-egg	1 medium	130
Mushrooms	10 large	10
Mustard greens	½ cup cooked	30
Noodles	¾ cup cooked	75
Oatmeal	¾ cup cooked	110
Oil (corn, cottonseed, olive, and peanut)	1 tablespoon	100
Okra	10-15 pods	50
Olives		
green	6 medium	50
ripe	4-5 medium	50
Onions	3-4 medium	100
Orange	1 medium	80
juice	1 cup	125
Oysters	5 medium	100
Parsnips	1 parsnip 7 inches long	100
Peaches		
canned in sirup	2 large halves and 3 tablespoons juice	100
dried	4 medium halves	100
fresh	1 medium	50
Peanut butter	1 tablespoon	100
Peanuts	10	50

FOOD	MEASURES	CALORIES
Pears		
canned in sirup	3 halves and 3 tablespoons juice	100
fresh	1 medium	50
Peas		
canned	½ cup	65
fresh, shelled	¾ cup	100
Pecans	6	100
Pepper, green	1 medium	20
Pickles, cucumber		
sour and dill	10 slices 2 inches in diameter	10
sweet	1 small	10
Pies	(sectors from 9-inch pies)	
apple	3-inch sector	200
lemon meringue	3-inch sector	300
mincemeat	3-inch sector	300
pumpkin	3-inch sector	250
Pineapple		
canned,		
unsweetened	1 slice ½ inch thick and 1 tablespoon juice	50
fresh	1 slice ¾ inch thick	50
juice, unsweetened	1 cup	135
Plums		
canned	2 medium and 1 tablespoon juice	75
fresh	2 medium	50
Popcorn	1½ cups popped	100
Popovers	1 popover	100
Pork chop, lean	1 medium	200
Potato chips	8-10 large	100
Potato salad with		
mayonnaise	½ cup	200
Potatoes		
mashed	½ cup	100
sweet	½ medium	100
white	1 medium	100
Prune juice	½ cup	100
Prunes, dried	4 medium	100
Pumpkin	½ cup	50
Radishes	5	10
Raisins	¼ cup	90
Raspberries, fresh	1 cup	90
Rhubarb, stewed		
and sweetened	½ cup	100
Rice	¾ cup cooked	100
Roll, Parker House	1 medium	100
Rutabagas	½ cup	30
Salad dressing		
boiled	1 tablespoon	25
French	1 tablespoon	90
mayonnaise	1 tablespoon	100
Salmon, canned	½ cup	100

FOOD	MEASURES	CALORIES
Sardines, drained	5 fish 3 inches long	100
Sauerkraut	½ cup	15
Sherbet	½ cup	120
Soup, condensed	11-ounce can	
bouillon		25
mushroom		360
noodle		290
tomato		230
vegetable		200
Spaghetti	¾ cup cooked	100
Spinach	½ cup cooked	20
Squash		
summer	½ cup cooked	20
winter	½ cup cooked	50
Strawberries, fresh	1 cup	90
Sugar		
brown	1 tablespoon	50
granulated	1 tablespoon	50
powdered	1 tablespoon	40
Sweetbreads	1 pair medium-sized	200
Swiss chard	½ cup leaves and stems	30
Tangerines	1 medium	60
Tapioca, uncooked	1 tablespoon	50
Tomato juice	1 cup	60
Tomatoes, canned	½ cup	25
fresh	1 medium	30
Tuna fish, canned	¼ cup drained	100
Turkey, lean	1 slice 4 inches by 2½ by ¼	100
Turnip	1 turnip 1¾ inches in diameter	25
Turnip greens	½ cup cooked	30
Veal, roast	1 slice 3 inches by 3¾ by ½	120
Waffles	1 waffle 6 inches in diameter	250
Walnuts	8	100
Watermelon	1 slice 6 inches in diameter 1½ inches thick	190
Wheat		
flakes	¾ cup	100
germ	1 tablespoon	25
shredded	1 biscuit	100

Alcoholic Beverages

Beer	8 ounces	120
Gin	1½ ounces	120
Rum	1½ ounces	150
Whiskey	1½ ounces	150
Wines		
champagne	4 ounces	120
port	1 ounce	50
sherry	1 ounce	40
table, red or white	4 ounces	95

Courtesy of the Metropolitan Life Insurance Company